THE EARLY
SLAVS

THE EARLY SLAVS

SLAVS

*Culture and Society in Early
Medieval Eastern Europe*

P. M. Barford

Cornell University Press
Ithaca, New York

First published in the United States in 2001 by Cornell University Press.

First published in Great Britain in 2001 by
The British Museum Press
A division of The British Museum Company Ltd
46 Bloomsbury Street, London WC1B 3QQ

ISBN: 0-8014-3977-9 (cloth)

Library of Congress Cataloging-in-Publication Data
Barford, P. M. (Paul M.)
    The early Slavs : culture and society in early
    medieval Eastern Europe / P. M. Barford.
    p. cm.
    Includes bibliographical references.
    ISBN 0-8014-3977-9 (cloth)
    1. Slavs—History. 2. Europe, Eastern—
    Civilization.   I. Title.
    DJK27 .B365 2001
    947'.00491'8—dc21
    2001032591

Designed by James Shurmer

Jacket design by Slatter-Anderson

Maps by ML Design

Set in Sabon by Wyvern 21, Bristol

Printed in Great Britain by The Bath Press, Avon

Contents

List of Maps I–XII

The final series of twelve maps on pp. 394–405 have been produced to the same scale.

Preface

This book is conceived as an introduction to the early history and development of the cultures and societies of the Slavs as may be reconstructed from the archaeological, written and other sources.

In a book dealing with a subject perhaps exotic to some of its intended readers (or pedantically questioned by others), there are several concepts which should be explained at the outset. All dates quoted are AD unless otherwise noted. The term 'early medieval' is difficult to define in central and eastern Europe as – while most agree that the period begins some time in the fifth or (early) sixth century – scholars from individual countries date the end of the period differently. The tenth to eleventh century cut-off point of the main part of this book was for some countries the end of their early medieval period, while in other countries historians consider that it lasted a few more centuries. My use of the term 'Early Slavs' is a shorthand for the early medieval ancestors of the Slav-speaking peoples and does not imply that they formed a single ethnic group (see Chapter 1). The conventional division between South, East and West Slavs maintained here is a somewhat artificial one which is made mainly on linguistic grounds. In the case of East and West Slavs the division in the two language groups however occurred relatively late (probably ninth or tenth century) and it is thus somewhat inconsistent to talk of East Slavs in the seventh century; nevertheless there does seem to be a detectable difference in the material culture (and the way in which it is studied) running roughly along the line of the western border of the former Soviet Union throughout the period covered here.

Another concept which has been retained, despite its apparent romanticism and apparent political connotations (see Chapter 13), is the term 'Slavdom'. This is a term which came into more common use in the eighteenth century and is used here simply as shorthand for saying 'territory inhabited by people who we think in the main spoke a language belonging to the Slav language group'. There is however some historical justification for the term, which corresponds to the term 'Sclavinia', appearing in many early medieval written sources reflecting the knowledge of the time. The identity of the Slavs themselves is dealt with below in Chapter 1.

The 'eastern Europe' of the title is a shorthand term for 'central and eastern Europe'. One also has to be careful how one uses the term 'East Europe', which for the post-1945 generation of the English-speaking world has tended to be equated with the whole area (of so-called Communist countries) behind the so-called Iron Curtain. Many inhabitants of central Europe however (where Soviet hegemony was an unwelcome imposition) feel offended by the implied inference that they are part of the same unit as the former Soviet Union. In this book the term 'eastern' (with a small 'e') Europe is used to refer to precisely that, the geographically eastern part of the European continent (within which the area of the former Soviet Union is a distinct unit). The dividing line coincides roughly with a major linguistic boundary, in effect that between the Slav and related languages and the majority of the Germanic and Romance ones. The phrase 'east central Europe' which is used by some to refer to part of this area has been avoided here. Where necessary the term 'central Europe' has been used to refer to the area bounded by the Baltic, Elbe watershed, lower Danube and the former Soviet west border.

The research for and writing of this text was begun in a Europe which had a different shape from that in which the book was published. The historical events and archaeology covered here had for nearly half a century been considered within the boundaries of political organizations which in some cases no longer exist. Although attempts have been made here to transcend the limitations of the modern state boundaries (both pre-1989 as well as post-1989), the attempt to fit older archaeology into the framework of a new Europe shows how much still has to be done. When I use the term 'former Soviet Union' or 'former DDR' (or 'East Germany'), I do so not out of sentimental attachment to old political divisions, but because they fit the sense of the text. As we will see later in the book, Stalin used old ethnic boundaries to define the areas of his influence, and to some extent (for our purposes) he chose well. The ancient term Polabia (adjective Polabian) is used here to refer to the areas around the middle Elbe (in some Slav tongues 'Łaba'), but this is really another way of saying 'the former area of the DDR'. Other regional terms which may need explanation to some readers are Great Poland (Wielkopolska) and Little Poland (Małopolska): the former refers to the central area of western Poland around Poznań which was the core of the early Polish state, and the latter the area in the south-east around Cracow which later became the medieval capital. The term 'Bohemia' has been used instead of the use of the lone word 'Czech' as a noun. The term 'Pannonia' refers here to a general area occupied in turn by a succession of Roman provinces, which tended to shift, but the area concerned is a roughly rectangular area of lowland in the great bend of the middle Danube (bounded by the river between Vienna and Budapest on the north, and between Budapest and Vukovar on the east, the south boundary somewhere between Vukovar and Zagreb).

A particularly difficult question is the loose way in which the English language has used some of the terms concerning central and eastern Europe, to refer to a wide range of socio-political and ethnic phenomena. A case in point is the term 'Russia(n)', Soviet propaganda tried to claim the Kievan state as its predecessor. In fact the Soviet state derived from the Tsarist Russian Empire, which in turn had its origin in the Duchy of Moscow in the late medieval period. There is only the most tenuous of links between this and the Kievan state of the tenth century. In the following text the word 'Russia' is used rarely, and when it is it should be understood to refer to the Kievan state (or occasionally the modern country of that name). The term 'Rus' therefore refers to the situation before the division into Russians, Ukrainians and Belarussians.

Some of the archaeological groupings referred to here have names which are derived from the places where the importance, representativeness or general applicability of a particular phenomenon (usually a type of pottery) to the study of the subject was first understood. This inevitably creates terms which are difficult for the English reader to pronounce without help from a native speaker. Another problem is that, as archaeological interpretations alter, they are prone to change, to be amalgamated, superseded by others. In general, the terms most generally agreed and supported by current debates are those used here, with one important exception. The present writer does not accept that there is a 'Prague Culture' which occurs all over central and part of eastern Europe. There are historical reasons why this term began to be used, but its continuation has led to anomalies, and in my opinion it is time to redefine it (or rather return to the original meaning). The term derives from the identification by Ivan Borkovský in 1940 in the vicinity of the capital of Bohemia of a series of (ceramic) traits in material which could be identified as belonging to the earliest Slavs in Bohemia. Although it can now be seen that he included material of different dates and typological affinities in his group, it still seems legitimate to write of 'ceramics of Prague type' and 'assemblages of Prague type'. In recent decades however this material been linked by archaeologists with broadly similar material over a progressively wider area of Europe. Since the work of Irena Rusanova, many archaeologists have grouped the ceramic vessels from eastern Poland and western Ukraine into a single Prague-Korchak group (of which the Zhitomir type is a now obsolete sub-group). Within this zone however there is detectable geographical and chronological differentiation, and the material from the Prague area refers to a specific developed (and arguably later) form of the culture complex. I propose restricting the use of the term 'Prague Culture' to this material and using other local terms for the earlier and geographically more distant material from the Ukraine (returning to the original designation of the lone Korchak Culture) and the south of Poland (which will be referred to as the Mogiła group, a term first used by Michał Parczewski).

Another and potentially confusing terminological problem has arisen from the understandable tendency of the past decade or so for newly independent nations to change names of places from their former rendition to their locally more acceptable form. Nevertheless in writing here in English about these places I have decided to attempt to reduce multiplication of exoticisms by using the names (derivative of Russian or Serbo-Croat) familiar from the existing literature and maps; thus for example 'Kiev' appears as such (and not Kiyiv) and Chernigov is used instead of Chernihiv. Where however the place is less familiar, the local form has often been used. The writing of a book of this type has involved making a number of choices between many alternative spellings of not only place but also historical personal names. Where such exists, the version most commonly known in the English literature has been used where it is not too far from the original.

Where names and titles of works cited written in Cyrillic scripts are quoted, a phonetic transliteration has been adopted. There are several different options available and none seems of universal application: I have tried to use one which is internally consistent and best gives the pronunciation of the words represented. It is well to note that in certain eastern European languages the *j* is pronounced as *y* in yacht (and in some languages *ch* is read as in the Scottish word *loch*). Other eastern European languages have diacritical marks which affect how the word is pronounced: these tend to be ignored in some English versions of common names (probably because, as experience has shown, the more frequently used western word-processing software consistently fail to cope adequately with them), but their use here has been unavoidable.

In the text, several historical sources are frequently mentioned but have lengthy titles. These titles have thus been abbreviated here. The first is the set of chronicles compiled in Kiev in the twelfth century which are known (sometimes in variant forms) by many names (*The Kiev Chronicles, The Chronicle of Nestor, The* [Russian] *Primary Chronicle, The Tale of Bygone Years* etc.). These will be referred to here as the *PVL*, the abbreviation coming from the Russian for the last of these terms (*Povest Vremennykh let*). The other text is the book that the Byzantine emperor Constantine VII Porphyrogenitus wrote in the 950s for his son Romanus, called the *De administrando imperio* ('How to run the Empire'). The title of this extremely interesting document will be abbreviated here *DAI*.

The present book is one of the first general syntheses to make use of the newest chronologies of the archaeological data. The problems involved in dating the archaeological material are briefly summarized in the Introduction. When the study of early medieval archaeology was in its infancy in central Europe, a number of assumptions were made on which the typological dating schemes were based. Now that absolute dating methods (such as dendrochronology and radiocarbon) are being applied on a greater scale, it is being discovered that there were some fundamental errors in some of the old schemes. These are corrected here. This should always be borne in mind when consulting much of the supporting literature cited here.

Another problem is the citation of dates where they are derived from ancient written sources. The problems with rendering dates from the ancient written sources according to our calendar derive from the fact that they were originally computed according to a number of calendars. Some documents cite the year of reign of a monarch (which seems to have been the main option available to pre-Christian societies when they considered precise chronology of events at all), others use a linear calendar based on Christian notion of time. Even here there were differences, the Russian chronicles for example use the Creation as year 'o', while in the Western Church the starting point was the Incarnation. There are additional problems such as variations in definition when a year began and ended (so for example the Byzantine year began in September, while the Russian one began in March). These and several other factors conspire to create situations where – unless we know the month a particular event occurred – we can only say that in terms of our own calendar a single event happened in one of two years, and thus in the text the reader will meet compound dates (e.g., '899/900') for single events. In other cases even less precise compound dates are given where the written sources do not mention a date, but we can define the timespan within which the event must have occurred (for example the upper limit being defined by the year of death of one of the protagonists). There are also sometimes quite substantial differences in the chronological options offered for the same occurrences by different ancient authors (often writing long after the events and having themselves to arrive at the date by deduction); thus for example there are several different chronologies available for the early members of the Přemyslid dynasty to choose from (Chapter 12).

The structure of the book needs some explanation, as it has been attempted to merge historical with thematic sections. It begins with a long introductory section (this preface, the introduction and Chapter 1) explaining some basic concepts as required by a book presenting such material to a readership to whom some of it may be somewhat exotic. Much of this may be skipped by those familiar with the questions discussed. Chapters 2, 3 and 4 follow the history of Slav culture in the seventh to ninth centuries, a period of the crystallization of an identity for the Slavs and a period of increasing social and cultural change. Chapters 5 to 10 attempt to deal with several themes concerning these cultures in the period covered by this book – daily life, social structure, warfare, production and trade – and ending with the less material aspects such as belief systems and the change from pagan to Christian societies. The next two chapters (11 and 12) deal with state-formation among the Slavs treated in two main blocs, South and East mainly under the influence of Byzantium, and the West Slavs influenced by the Carolingians and Ottonians. The final chapter attempts to show the relevance of the Early Slavs to the modern world and the way that interpretations have been affected by political changes. The volume is completed by the notes, a bibliography, a summary time chart and an index. Since for a fuller understanding of the text it will be necessary to refer several times to some of the figures and most of the maps, it has been decided to include them all in a consecutive sequence at the end of the book rather than scatter them throughout the text.

The bibliography (pp. 320–4) is provided for those who wish to go deeper into the subject. In general much of the work done in eastern Europe since the 1960s has been of a high standard and worthy of wider appreciation. Where possible I have tried to find literature in western languages or which is more widely available. Most of the foreign-language articles cited here are well illustrated and even those in Slav languages have summaries in western languages, most often English, German or French. A selection of the latter is cited here, in the awareness that some of my readers of central European extraction may be able to use these texts. An additional factor is that one may expect that with increasing globalization, within the next few years considerable advances in the sophistication of computer translation programs will make these texts more generally available than they are at the moment. An exception to this rule is the omission of references to the excellent Polish reference book the *Słownik Starożytności Słowiańskich* (Wrocław) which appeared as a collective work in the period 1961–96. Many of the articles in the several thousand pages of these eight volumes are masterpieces of synthesis and cover virtually every aspect of the archaeology, history and culture of the Early Slavs (and much else besides) with full referencing and some choice illustrations. Each page of the present book would profit from several references to this work, but this would be of doubtful use to most of my readers, since the volumes are virtually unobtainable in western libraries.

The illustrations at the end of the volume (pp. 325–393) also require a few words of explanation. No book on ancient societies would be complete without a few pictures of the material culture being described, and this is especially true when, as here, it differs from that more familiar to the western reader. Selection of illustrations has been very difficult, and concentrates on showing the material which is used to differentiate cultures, and so, for the periods when our main sources are archaeological, this includes a number of pottery types. It will be noted that in accord with local conventions some of them have the section on the left according to western (British, German, American) archaeological custom, while archaeologists of certain eastern European countries (Poland, Ukraine, Russia) are adamant that it should go on the right. For several reasons, it was decided not to reverse here those drawings created to comply with a preferred convention. The number of other figures of archaeological finds could have been comfortably doubled or trebled without even coming close to being representative of the full range of cultural phenomena. I can only send the interested reader to the illustrations in the works mentioned in the Select Bibliography.

An integral part of this text is a series of maps showing the geographical and chronological interrelationships between the various cultural phenomena discussed. The series of twelve roman-numbered maps which follow the figures at the end of this book (pp. 394–405) have been specially drawn, taking into account much of the new work on the chronology and classification of the cultural groups discussed, and this is the first time some of this new information has been presented in this way. The apparent simplicity of the 'blobs' depicted therefore hides a considerable amount of work weighing up different possible versions and verifying the extent of each individual area with reference to the original published material. Nevertheless, as in the case of all historical maps, the reader should not be led astray by the apparent 'objectivity' of the graphical form of the presentation of these data: even here the drawing of each map involved a number of subjective decisions based on the best evidence available to me.

In general, after finishing the manuscript, I am inclined to agree with the pessimism of those colleagues specializing in some of the fields summarized here who predicted that this book would never be quite what I wanted it to be. I suspect that many of them will be disappointed by the way that I have dismissed some of their important detailed discussions in a few paragraphs or even words, but hope they will recognize that this is inevitable in a work of this nature. Nobody is more conscious of these problems than the author. In writing this text, I found that I have been forced to miss out more than I included, and have had to pass over aspects which passionately interest me but detailed descriptions of which have no place here. Although I have tried to cover (even if only in passing remarks) all aspects which seemed to me to be of importance for the general reader and western medievalist wanting an introduction to the history and archaeology of the area, and have tried to provide a useful selection of references to the rich literature, I am sure each and every specialist would have selected material differently, and (as is the nature of our discipline) placed perhaps differing interpretations on some of that which is included. I can only encourage them not just to express their criticism in eventual reviews but to produce a parallel text. I hope this book will nevertheless help to widen knowledge (and inspire curiosity) about those issues touched upon here and thus aid in some way the widening of the debates which surround them.

The research which led to this book was carried out during a lengthy period of stay in Poland. Even without such an admission, the observant reader would soon have discovered the research environment in which this book was written, including the concentration on Polish works in the notes and bibliography. There are several reasons for this (besides the contents of the libraries I use and the main eastern European language I read). Polish archaeologists have for a long time had an especial interest in most aspects of the Slav archaeology not only of their own country but also of neighbouring states. This book is the product of a specific period of the development of eastern European historiography. The period in which this research was done was arguably the best period to write such a work. The mass of work done in the 1960s and 1970s had been absorbed and discussed (at least as much as it was going to be) and there was a ready flow of information coming from other countries of the eastern bloc, within which there was a relatively uniform approach in archaeology (due to previous political circumstances). The collapse of the Soviet hegemony in 1989–90 led to a reassessment of some previously held views and paved the way for new interpretations. Now, a decade on, the initial controversies are giving way to a more settled consideration of new ideas and old data.

As mentioned above, the present work is the result of a lengthy stay in what was then the People's Republic of Poland, the government of which was extremely generous in supporting my research, which then enabled me to take up employment at the University of Warsaw to continue my work. Let this book be in a small way part of the repayment of my debt I owe to those who helped me in my research. The text presented here owes much to long sessions of discussion, sometimes argument, with a number of colleagues. I would like to thank particularly the following, who provided me information about their own work, some of which they may find printed herein. I should primarily like to thank my Professor and Promotor Jerzy Gąssowski and other colleagues at Warsaw University for many stimulating discussions. At the Polish Academy of Sciences, I should like to thank Dr Zbigniew Kobyliński, Professors Przemysław Urbańczyk, Andrzej Buko, Stanisław Tabaczyński, Helena Zoll-Adamikowa, Wojciech Szymański and Dr Marek Dulinicz. Other scholars to whom I owe a debt of gratitude include Professors Kazimierz Godłowski and Michał Parczewski (Cracow University), Olga Shcheglova (Hermitage, St Petersburg), Igor Gavritukhin and Elena Melnikova (Moscow), Martin Gojda and Nada Profantova (Prague), Peter Heather (London) and Wladyslaw Duczko (Uppsala). I have especially benefited from numerous and lengthy e-mail discussions on various topics concerning the revision of this text with Florin Curta (University of Florida) which have been extremely valuable. I would also like to thank Peter Heather and two other anonymous reviewers who read earlier drafts of the text, some of whose stringent comments prompted rewriting some sections. All of these people (and many more) have contributed to the thoughts I present here, but of course the author alone is responsible for the use which has been made of the material they provided.

Akademie-Verlag of Berlin gave their permission to reproduce Figures 39, 40, 45 and 55, and Izdatelistvo Naukova Dumka of Kiev gave permission to reproduce Figures 9, 60 and 67. I would like to thank them for their generosity. The publishers Wydawnictwa Artystyczne i Filmowe and Ossolineum in Poland and Litera in Prague and J. Sláma are also thanked for the reproduction of Figures 58, 46 and 35 respectively. The photographs in Figure 5 were supplied by Natalia Shishlina and taken by Michail Gonyany.

I would like to express my especial gratitude to British Museum Press for taking this daunting work into their publication programme and all those in that organization whose patience and help has aided its publication. In particular I would like to thank the production editor Nina Shandloff for her encouragement and especially forbearance throughout this project and copy editor John Banks for his care in picking up a number of infelicities of expression and inconsistencies of terminology which remained in my original text. Dorota Cyngot also checked part of the manuscript. I would like to thank Martin Lubikowski and his colleagues at ML Design for redrawing the maps for publication and James Shurmer for designing the book.

The original research for this book would not have been possible were it not for all of those in the Ministry of Education of the People's Republic of Poland (but especially Mr Edward Gontarz) for their interest in and funding of my initial research (much of the administrative work involved was dealt with by Dr Zbigniew Szafrański, to whom I am also grateful). A special debt of gratitude is also due to the librarians of The State Archaeological Museum and the Institute of Archaeology and Ethnography of the Polish Academy of Sciences, and Warsaw University's Institute of Archaeology for their hospitality, forbearance and generosity. My wife Anna and daughter Marta have also suffered the disorganization of daily life which the production of this text has created not only by my hours in the libraries and other trips, or engrossed by the computer screen or reams of barely legible notes, but also (relatively) silently endured the presence in our Warsaw flat of the shelves and numerous piles of books and papers, the scattered empty coffee mugs and other paraphernalia of research, for which I thank them.

Finally I would like to acknowledge my indebtedness to all the scholars who have devoted time and energy to work on the problems presented here. Without their hard work known to me from their published work, my own would have been quite impossible.

Chronological Summary

Dates	South Slavs	East Slavs	West Slavs
500–50 Map II	Sclavenes on Danube frontier	Korchak	Mogiła Group
550–600 Map III	Suceava-Şipot 560s: Avars settle on central Danube 580s: Slav settlement of Balkans begins Earliest fibulae	Korchak Penkovka Earliest fibulae	Sukow-Dziedzice Prague
600–50 Map IV	Suceava-Şipot Avar hegemony in middle Danube Settlements of Popina type	Penkovka Martynovka horizon	Sukow-Gołańcz Racibórz-Chodlik Devínská 620s–50s: Samo
650–700	c. 650: Slav settlement of Balkans slows Settlement of Croatia from 680s: Avars on middle Danube, Bulgars on lower Danube	Penkovka Luka Raikovetska	?650–70: 'reflux' Sukow-Gołańcz Racibórz-Chodlik Devínská
700–50 Map V	Bulgar consolidation and expansion	Luka Raikovetska Volyntsevo Borshevo	Sukow-Gołańcz Racibórz-Chodlik Devínská
750–800	 793–6: Avars destroyed	Luka Raikovetska ?Beginning of Slav expansion into northern forest zone	Sukow-Gołańcz Racibórz-Chodlik Devínská
800–50	Bulgar expansion Krum (803–14) Omurtag (814–31) Consolidation of Croats	Luka Raikovetska Volyntsevo Borshevo Slav expansion into northern forest zone Scandinavians in northern forests	Racibórz-Chodlik Devínská Feldberg Tornow 830s: Mojmir Rostislav (846–69) Menkendorf
850–900 Map VI	Slav settlement of Balkans Bulgar expansion Boris (852–89) Symeon (893–927) Golden Age of Bulgaria Consolidation of Serbs 894–6: Settlement of Magyars on middle Danube	East Slav tribal unions 880s: Consolidation of southern tribes under Kievan princes Oleg (879–912)	863–85: Cyril and Methodius Sviatopluk (869–94) Expansion of Moravian state 880s–90s: Bořivoj of Bohemia 890s–930s: Consolidation of Bohemian state (Spytihněv and Vaclav) Stronghold construction phase in Polabia and Poland
900–50	 Peter (927–67) DAI written	Igor (912–45)	906: Destruction of Moravia 928–48: German annexation of Polabia 935–72: Boleslav I of Bohemia 940s: Beginning of consolidation of Polish tribes
950– 1000 Map VII	950s–70s: Consolidation of Hungarian state 967–72: Destruction of Bulgaria	957: Olga in Constantinople Sviatoslav (964–73) Vladimir the Great (980–1015)	960s: Mieszko I 983: Polabian revolt 992–1025: Bolesław Chrobry of Poland

Introduction

A large area of Europe is today inhabited by people speaking Slav languages, and in central Europe the area colonized by them in the past was even greater than today. In total, well over half of Europe is, in terms of territorial extent (if not demographically), inhabited by communities speaking one of the many Slav languages and dialects. Despite this, their origin and early development are still poorly understood. In the period covered here the Slavs expanded from what seem to have been relatively small and obscure beginnings to cover a large area of the continent. Today about 268 million people in Europe speak a language belonging to the Slav language group (and one estimate puts the number of people of Slav extraction in the USA at 20 million).

This book will consider the developments accompanying the phase of expansion and the consolidative processes which led to state-formation. We will consider aspects of the development of Slav societies and their interactions with other peoples up to the period of the formation of nation states which form the framework of modern eastern Europe. In general therefore the book covers the period from the early fifth century AD to the end of the tenth century, from the period when the Slavs first appear as an entity in the historical records to the time when most of the area which they occupied was divided into stable states. The subject is a fascinating though complex one, made more difficult by the dearth of historical records and the relatively poor survival of the material culture used by the Slavs throughout most of the period covered here. Although this contrasts starkly with for example the written sources for other societies or the richer Merovingian and Carolingian material from grave assemblages and settlement finds, it is sufficient to create a vivid picture of daily life in early medieval eastern Europe.

The Slavs and their problems are little known in western (and in particular Anglophone) scholarship. They often seem to have been seen as 'too far away' for many western historians and archaeologists to consider in detail, and authors of general textbooks of European history (with a few notable exceptions) often satisfy themselves with a few generalizations on the subject. The Slavs have fallen victim it seems to a general tendency going back at least to the beginning of the nineteenth century to see Europe divided into two opposite halves, eastern and western, with the latter being seen as taking the leading role (a view fostered by the nineteenth-century development of colonialism). In this model the other half of Europe was seen as an appendage, a cultural backwater merely acting as a passive recipient of the benefits of western civilization.

Another contributory factor is of course at present the question of comprehension: most of the basic information on the early history of the Slavs is published in eastern European languages (though often with summaries in English, German, French and/or Russian). Although there are several texts in English on the early history of various countries in the area, and works and papers on specific aspects, there is a comparative dearth of recent books in English, both academic textbooks and works accessible to the general public, on the Slavs and the medieval archaeology of eastern and central Europe. As in the historical literature in general, much of what has been written in the past has been based on data which should now be reconsidered in the light of new sources and new interpretations. The most valuable overall survey in English is the book by Marija Gimbutas (1971) which is now seriously outdated in several respects; the same applies to the texts by Francis Dvornik (1949; 1956; 1959), which have a bias towards the written evidence. The excellent little book by Martin Gojda (1991) is based on a series of lectures: this has however restricted the scope of the subjects which could be covered. The text by Pavel Dolukhanov (1996) despite its promising title has serious limitations and in general cannot be recommended.[1] A recent book published in France by Michel Kazanski (1999) is a useful and well-illustrated survey of recent work. The literature in German concerning the Slavs is more copious (especially literature produced in the specific conditions of the former German Democratic Republic), and a number of recent works are listed in the general bibliography. Some of this work is summarized for the English reader in the translation of the book on German archaeology by Günter Fehring (1991). Several translations of eastern European authors have appeared in English, French or German, but are in general not very accessible in western libraries.

A number of Slav nations now seem set to join the European Union in the near future. This gives urgency to the task of attempting to understand the history of the cultures and societies of peoples which collectively occupy well over half of Europe, but who until now have been poorly served by western historiography. This is one of the reasons for the writing of this book. The author aimed to write a text which could be used as an introductory text for students of history, archaeology and European studies, while writing in such a way that it does not require specialist knowledge to understand. In the process of selection inevitable in writing a book like this, I have tried as far as I can to select examples from material which is (or ought to be) slightly better known in the west, and I have tried to resist the temptation to cite a lot of exotic-sounding place names which can mean nothing to the reader. Nevertheless there have been in recent years a number of startling new discoveries which should be mentioned. Where publications are cited, where possible I have restricted the list to items which should be more readily accessible and understandable in western Europe.

The sources

The study of the past is one of the most fascinating and frustrating of human endeavours. We can never know the answer to all the questions we may care to ask, and the nature of the questions is constantly changing; furthermore, if we think we have (and some are convinced they have) an answer, we can never be sure that the answer correctly reflects what actually happened. Later scholars, building on the foundations we lay, may place a completely different interpretation on the evidence we possess and for their purposes may require data which we at present habitually ignore or even destroy in our search for other types of evidence.

Everything we know about the past comes from what has chanced to survive. In the case of the Early Slavs, the scholar more familiar with the richer material from western Europe at this period may feel that this is not very much. We have a few written sources, and the material remains left by long-dead individuals and communities and the cultural traditions, folk tales or customs and social institutions may survive in an altered form for centuries and enable us to reach back to the past. Finally there is the evidence from the study of languages, which form the links between individual members of a community and which have been passed down through the ages. All of these types of evidence can be and are used to try to make sense of the past.

We should note that the period covered by this book bridges the gap between prehistory and history. The reader will note (and it is clearly visualized on the maps below) that at the beginning of the period we utilize the grouping of the material culture to define the object of our study. At various times throughout the area the written evidence takes over and gives us names and political organisms (and even the names of individual leaders) to replace the culture zones of earlier times. The bias in the quality and amount of information is visible in the case of areas for which written evidence is visible (for example the South Slavs) compared with those for which we are more reliant on the archaeological evidence. All sources have to be treated together, and the results obtained in one discipline must be critically checked in an informed manner against those obtained by the others, an ideal which is not always achieved (or perhaps achievable), although post-1945 central and eastern European archaeology has tended to be more multidisciplinary than some western traditions.

Over the past few decades there has been sharp disagreement in central Europe over the relationships between the various disciplines the common task of which is the interpretation of the human past. Archaeology has sometimes been described as a sub-discipline of history. This question cannot be discussed in detail here,[2] but in effect I think the roles should be reversed if we are to accept archaeology (*archeo-logos*) as the study of the past by use of the surviving sources. The written sources are equal, and not superior, to the unwritten ones and have to be studied in a similar manner. This in turn brings the problem of the relationship between the interpretation of the written and archaeological evidence. In some ways the archaeology of certain areas of Europe in the early medieval period may be characterized as 'text-driven', in that the existing texts dictate the programme and expectations of other disciplines studying the past. This is the case with societies for which there is a lot of written documentation, but equally in the case of societies with a paucity of written history. The effort to use and supplement the existing written sources can have an inordinate effect on the interpretation of the various types of evidence.

One relatively obvious feature of eastern and central European archaeology is the use by some (but by no means all) archaeologists and historians of methodology derived more or less from Marxism. The enormous influence of the work of the two nineteenth-century German philosophers Karl Marx and his friend and mentor Friedrich Engels on the way in which the past has been studied in eastern and central Europe in recent decades was due to a number of well-known historical circumstances. In the 1920s and 1930s in Stalin's Soviet Union a group of archaeologists and historians in Moscow and Leningrad constructed an interpretative framework for the Soviet historical sciences based on historical and dialectical materialism, derived from the writings of Engels and Marx (but also, and perhaps more specifically, Stalin). This 'Progressive' archaeology and historiography was encouraged by the Soviet state by various means to become the orthodox view, and when the sphere of Soviet influence expanded in central Europe after 1945 became implanted there. The effects were more visible in some countries than others, but in general these tendencies have left their influences on some aspects of interpretation of past societies in these regions, even though the ideological aspects were rejected some years ago. Only now is a younger generation of scholars attempting to step aside from the models of doing science adopted decades ago and applying new ones, giving rise to new visions of the past.

Historical sources

The beginning of the period considered here is on the threshold of history: we have a few written sources mentioning the names of particular social or ethnic groups (ethnonyms) and occasionally even concrete personalities. These are enough to whet, though not satisfy our appetite for more information. Most of the literary sources we have were compiled for the churches and courts of the Early Slav states; we have little secular literature. Many of the surviving documents thus reflect the interests of the elites (both secular and ecclesiastical) for whom they were written, but they are not always of much use in compiling our picture of the daily life of the Early Slavs. At the end of the period considered here the elite in various Slav states was becoming literate, and some older traditions may have been preserved in writing, although a desire to find a 'respectable' past to legitimize present conditions may also have resulted in the invention of a past, or the rewriting of history. As a result we have a few accounts of variable length and value, which sometimes go some way to filling the gap between what we want to know and what we are able to determine. The full story of the Early Slavs cannot be told from the written evidence alone; it must be supplemented by other forms of data.

There is a major difficulty with the written sources which is not always appreciated by the non-historian. We tend to place too much faith in the truth of the written word. If a chronicle says that a particular event occurred in a particular year or in a particular way, then nine times out of ten that 'historical' date or event is repeated uncritically in most of the subsequent historical syntheses. We tend to prefer to forget that the writers of the sources we use often had to arrive at their information and chronology by various indirect means, which can seriously undermine the reliability of the data they give us. These writers were intending to transmit information to their contemporaries or those who came after, and their accounts, like any report, can only reflect their own opinion and interpretation of the event from what they knew, and what they cared to tell us. Modern newspaper reports of the same event sometimes reflect the political bias of their writers for example; a historian functioning in the reign of a tyrant rarely tells us bluntly that his ruler is a bad one, in fact in the case of totalitarian regimes quite the opposite. In the same way during much of the period we are covering the Slavs themselves were illiterate, and the written sources about them were produced by their neighbours, who often had preconceptions of their own concerning the tribes about which they were writing.

Since parchment, papyrus and paper are perishable, most of the written material we have has survived because it was recopied in the past. Sometimes the document was edited (shortened or modernized) by the scribes copying it and the original lost. Sometimes they misunderstood the text and made mistakes in copying words or misplaced whole sentences. Thus source criticism is required to reconstruct a plausible version of the original text and the later alterations. Only then can the original text and these alterations be the subject of analysis. Another problem is that the written sources which we can now read represent a tiny proportion of the material that may have once been written down, and the interpretation of that which now survives is rendered difficult by the non-survival of material which might have been available to the original readers. The surviving texts in general were recopied only because they had some practical use to later societies, or for their literary value. Histories which reflected the glories of bygone ages and legitimated existing regimes and social conditions were kept; legally binding documents (such as laws and charters) survive for practical reasons. Lives of saints had value as documents of instruction, but also sometimes contain information about the period when they were composed and survive as part of the literature accumulated by the growing Church in the area.

The lesson is obvious: each piece of text needs to be approached individually and subjected to careful 'source criticism' to analyse what the writer was trying to say (and what he was careful not to say), from what sources he could have derived his information, and how the copy we have of the manuscript came to survive (and what later alterations and copying errors may have crept into the text in the process). Eastern European historians (for example Gerard Labuda and Henryk Łowmiański) have long been adept at this type of work, and can manage to squeeze a large amount of plausible though unverifiable information out of a very brief account. Sometimes the process can be taken too far, and, as with the interpretation of the archaeological record (see below), some of these interpretations can never be checked (as it is very unlikely that new written evidence will be discovered), and each age has its preferred interpretations of the basic sources. There are eight main groups of literary sources, briefly discussed below.

1. One of the texts which appears in almost all histories of the Early Slavs is the *De origine actibusque Getarum* ('*Getica*') compiled in Latin about 551 in Constantinople by an obscure writer by the name of Jordanes who had apparently served as the secretary of a military commander on the Danube (so we assume that he knew something about the Slavs in that region). His account is however (as the author himself proudly admits) little more than a paraphrase of the lost book under a similar title by the Ravennan courtier and scholar Cassiodorus. The original text was some ten times longer than that of Jordanes, who furthermore tells us that he made the paraphrase in three days' work! We must remember that what Cassiodorus and Jordanes wrote about the Goths and their neighbours was gathered from second- and third-hand sources and refers to areas deep inside Barbaricum several hundred kilometres to the north and east. These writers had a clear political purpose in the compilation of their histories and this may have affected their objectivity. If we had Cassiodorus's original text available, we would be better able to assess the information content of this book. Jordanes's text, used with caution, is however a useful source of information.

2. Early in the sixth century Slavs began to settle near and raid across the weakened northwestern frontiers of the East Roman Empire, and Roman and Greek writers of the period came into almost direct contact with various Slav groups. Their accounts are generalized (and unsurprisingly hostile) but also give some useful information.[3] One of the most important of these sources is Justinian the

Great's chronicler, Procopius of Caesarea, who in his three books *History of the Wars*, *The Buildings* and the *Secret History* tells of the Slav invasions of the 530s to 550s. Other historians such as Zosimus also tell us a little about these invasions. Another author whom we know as 'Pseudo-Maurice' (writing about 592/610) probably took part in the campaigns against the Slavs in the reign of Maurice Tiberius and was primarily concerned with the military abilities of the Slavs. We have the biographies of saints recounting how the Slavs were turned away by miracles connected with the saint's prayers, we have Papal letters to Dalmatian bishops concerning the Slav threats and so on.

3. The West Slavs were a potential military threat to the Merovingian and Carolingian Empires, and several Frankish and Carolingian chronicles mention political events in, and military missions into, Slav territory. One of these, Fredegar's *Chronicle* written in the seventh century, contains quite a lot about the Slavs and is the only information we have about the mysterious Samo and his kingdom existing between 623 and 633 (Chapter 3). The *Royal Frankish Annals* contain a lot of information about Carolingian attempts to deal with the Slavs. Another source, the so-called *Bavarian Geographer* (Fig. 1) written somewhere in the eastern part of the Carolingian empire about 840, is a list of tribes beyond the imperial frontiers with the numbers of defended centres each possessed. It is suspected that it was the result of some form of Carolingian intelligence-gathering for military or economic purposes. Other written sources concerning the western Slavs in the ninth to eleventh century come from the eastern expansion of the sphere of interest of the Germans under the Carolingians and Ottonians and attempts to convert the Slavs (Chapter 10). One of the most important later sources was the work of Thietmar of Merseberg (written *c.* 1020) in the imperial court and dealing with the time of Otto III. Several later accounts written by clerics contain information on the history and customs of the northwestern Slavs (Adam of Bremen, *c.* 1071, Helmold of Bosau, end of the twelfth century and Saxo Grammaticus at the end of the century). Herbord's account of the life of Bishop Otto of Bamburg includes an account of his mission to Pomerania *c.* 1120. Some of the information about Slav customs may be applicable to earlier times. We have a number of accounts of diplomatic missions and political affairs, which contain information about social conditions in this area, and also about the pagan religion. Later documents include charters concerning annexed territories.

4. For information about the East and South Slavs after the ninth century we turn to Byzantine documents. One of the most important of these sources was a book in which the Byzantine Emperor Constantine VII Porphyrogenitus (reigned 912–59) set out for the benefit of his son Romanus guidelines for running the Byzantine state and its diplomatic service. This *De administrando imperio* (*DAI*) was apparently compiled about 950 from reports of diplomatic missions:

it contains much information about the contemporary situation in the Balkans, and the Byzantine court had close connections with the Kievan Princess Olga.

5. Eastern Europe was also the scene of activity of a number of non-European travellers, including Arab traders mostly from Central Asia. These travellers have left interesting accounts of the lands they visited. These are all the more valuable (but more difficult to interpret) as they were made by people foreign to European cultural traditions. Some of them relate to ninth-century visits, but the majority come from the tenth century. Ibn Khurradadhbih was Director of Posts and Intelligence in Baghdad but knew quite a bit about movements of the Rus traders which he imparts in his *Book of the Ways and Realms* written in the 880s. Forty years later the merchant Ibn Fadlan took part in a diplomatic and trade mission sent by the Abbasid Caliph al-Muqtadir in 921–2 to the khanate of Bulgar on the Volga. His account of what he met on his journey has been preserved in extracts preserved in later manuscripts. Of the monumental works of the scholar al-Mas'udi only his *Golden Meadows* of *c.* 947 has survived: it too contains information on the Slavs. A source of considerable value is the account of a Jewish traveller from Muslim Spain, Ibrahim ibn Yaqub, who travelled to Slav countries in 965/6. This account is preserved in the work of the geographer al-Bekri. The Persian scholar Ibn Rusteh wrote his encyclopaedia (*Book of Precious Jewels*) about 903, but only the seventh chapter on geography has survived. Fortunately, it includes a description of the lands of the Slavs.[4]

6. Other records were compiled within the Kievan state under Byzantine influence. The important series of chronicles which I label here the *PVL Chronicles* was compiled in Kiev in the twelfth century. This chronicle preserves material from a number of sources, including Byzantine records and annals, ancient traditions and also (one suspects) invented material. The early part of the *PVL Chronicles* has been much edited, and conflates several earlier traditions which has led to some considerable confusion (see Chapter 11). Among the Byzantine documents transcribed are treaty (or rather trade) agreements, which do not survive elsewhere but were later for some unclear reason copied into the chronicles of the Kievan monasteries: they preserve an interesting series of names and other terms.[5] This document perhaps also draws on Byzantine records relating to the Balkans.

7. Slavdom is also mentioned in an idealized form in a number of the Viking sagas. Scandinavians settled among the Slavs on the south and east coasts of the Baltic; the Jomsborg of the Sagas is Wolin at the mouth of the Oder. The Vikings referred to the land of the East Slavs as Garðarike, the land of the strongholds. Many of the details have suffered distortion in the retelling.

8. Quite late in the history of certain West Slav states isolated individuals wrote histories. In 1025 Cosmas, a cleric of Prague Cathedral, finished writing his

Chronica Bohemorum, a lively account of the early history of the Czech state, and in 1112–16 an anonymous author, probably a French Benedictine monk from Hungary, known conventionally as Gallus Anonymous, gives us a version of the early story of the Polish state and its kings.

Archaeological evidence

The archaeologist studies the material remains and traces of the people living in the past, including their effects on their environment.[6] These traces can seldom be assigned to specific personalities, or related to closely datable events; the events studied are general and gradual processes made up of hundreds of individual actions which constitute the archaeological record. This is usually composed of material which over the centuries has been buried in the earth. Not all important human activities leave any direct archaeological traces, and these processes can only be indirectly inferred. Other activities leave an abundance of repetitive material, such as bones from butchery of domestic animals, and sherds of pottery from shattered cooking vessels. This material is left as rubbish littering a settlement area, and remains 'old rubbish' until an archaeologist attempts to interpret it. The animal bones can tell us about the animals kept and eaten, the size and health of the herds, the way the meat was butchered, cooked and eaten, the way that the waste was disposed of and many more aspects of life of the community. The pottery vessels can be used to discuss handicraft production and tell us about trade networks and artistic tastes, but the primary use of changing styles and manufacturing methods of pottery is for determining chronology.

The archaeologist studies the material traces of human activities in a number of ways. The distribution of certain types of artefacts and structures (such as brooches, house types, strongholds) can be used to gain significant information of several types. Of more importance however are the associations of artefacts, and their stratigraphical context within archaeological sites: this is more significant, telling us about the dating of the objects and about their cultural associations.

The archaeological sources however give a very imperfect picture of past life. With few exceptions (such as at Pompeii and in shipwrecks) the archaeologist finds a biased sample of the material culture of the people being studied. Even graves contain only those things the relatives wanted to put with the body; several forms of socially controlled selection were operating. In the case of settlement sites we usually find what was broken, discarded or lost on site, and not items which were prone to deposition, loss or damage outside the settlement (such as agricultural tools), nor were all materials useless after breakage. Broken glass could be (and was) collected and reused for making beads; copper alloy and iron could be reworked and were both relatively scarce raw materials. Of course, except in anaerobic waterlogged conditions, artefacts of organic materials (wood, leather, textile, fur, hair, straw, horn, wickerwork and so on) do not generally survive. We know from those waterlogged town sites which have been excavated that it was of precisely those materials that the Early Slavs made the majority of the items they used daily. The total evidence available to the archaeologist creates an unfavourable impression of cultural poverty and backwardness.[7] This would seem however to be an illusion, since the Early Slavs had a rich material culture largely of perishable organic materials. Thus they used a variety of wooden tools, vessels and basketry, it was from wood that they built their houses and made their idols, they wore clothes of wool, of linen and (after the tenth century) occasionally of imported silk. From a later period we have notes they wrote to each other on birch bark (from damp deposits in Novgorod in northern Russia). All these sorts of evidence are missing from the majority of Early Slav sites available for excavation.[8]

The question of buildings also must be mentioned here. In much of early medieval western Europe there is a tradition of sunken-floored buildings used alongside larger buildings with frameworks created by vertical posts set into postholes. In eastern Europe the large holes created by the sunken-floored huts can be detected (their filling differs from the undisturbed soil around them), but posthole structures are scarce after the end of the Roman period. Where a build-up of layers has allowed the evidence to survive later destruction it can be seen that ground-level buildings also occurred here, but built using the so-called 'blockhouse' technique (still surviving in nineteenth-century rural eastern and northern Europe and taken from there to the American Wild West where it is familiar from countless Western films). This consists of horizontal logs (or squared baulks of timber) laid horizontally one on top of each other to form walls (see Fig. 9). The gaps in between the timbers are packed with moss or clay to make it weather-tight. This building technique is and was extremely common across the whole area of central and eastern Europe – some of these structures were very substantial and well-appointed – and yet the archaeological evidence of such structures is very slight. The timbers at the bottom of the wall were laid directly on the original ground surface (or sometimes on stone 'pads' which are easily moved when the building is demolished). If there was minimal build-up of soil around the building during its life (as is the case on many sites, some towns excepted), once it has been demolished, there is very little trace left (even after a few months, let alone centuries) of the former existence of such a building. In these cases, lack of evidence does not mean that the missing buildings were primitive.

Since the archaeologist is concerned with exploring change through time, the most important and basic operation in archaeology is establishing a chronology. Certain types of utilitarian objects have changed little in form over millennia (for example, iron hammers, knives, blacksmiths' tongs and axes of unspecialized form). The best form for the required job was discovered long ago and even in the nuclear age we are using some tool forms which an Early Iron Age farmer would be quite at home with. Other artefact types changed form and decoration rapidly. Rather like cars and dress styles today, progressive stylistic changes took place in the cultural material of our ancestors and were transmitted across a group. Thus the style of female ornament (brooches, headdress ornaments, buckles) changed quite rapidly, both from region to region (see below) and chronologically. Some of these items can be dated fairly accurately (which in eastern European early medieval archaeological terms means give-or-take half a century). In the same way pottery styles also change spatially and chronologically, and indeed, owing to its ubiquitous occurrence, fragments of broken pottery are the most useful material for establishing the date of archaeological deposits. Early medieval Slav pottery however is very conservative when compared with the contemporary changes in western European material and can be used for dating only in broad terms.

Archaeological contexts which can be dated to particular years are relatively rare, especially in the absence of written sources, or closely datable artefacts such as coins with dates stamped on them. The results of radiocarbon dating are too imprecise (unless large numbers of dates are available) for our purposes. Far more promising and exact are methods of dating by dendrochronology. In many Slav sites inhabited over long periods of time, cool damp conditions reduce the rate of decay and result in the preservation of enormous quantities of water-logged wood. Dendrochronology relies on matching sequences of tree growth rings (their width affected by localized climatic fluctuations) of wood samples of different ages to build sequences which can be linked to the ring sequences of ancient but still growing trees. In this way a sample from an archaeological layer of unknown age can be matched against the master sequence, and the exact date of felling of the tree can be determined, or, if there is no bark represented, the age of the latest growth ring present can be determined.

Archaeology is not just about things, but about the people who once used the things we find and left the traces we interpret. It is not surprising that for a long time attempts have been made to identify 'whose ancestors' one was digging up. The ethnic identification of archaeological material is by no means as easy as was once assumed, and has been much discussed in recent years. Nevertheless there is evidence that dress styles may be ethnic indicators, and some dress styles have distinctive metal components, so, although the textiles and the bodies they adorned have long since decayed, ethnic indicators may still be detectable. A classic example are the 'temple-rings' and *zausznice* (behind-the-ear-rings) which are a feature typical of female Slav dress (Chapter 5). These were worn on linen or leather headbands, as a decorative and jingly element of the headdress. They occur only very occasionally outside Slavdom (in which case they may have come on a Slav bride or slaves). A typological study of these items has identified a number of types with localized distributions: thus thick tubular temple-rings are a feature found mainly in West Slav territory in Pomerania, and other types are characteristic of women's dress of various East Slav tribes (Fig. 36).

What is clear however is that in order to even attempt to study past ethnicities one has to take a number of factors into account, and study for example whole material assemblages and not single 'diagnostic' artefact types. These complexes of items may or may not be the identifiable traces of the material culture of specific groups of people. Archaeologists use the concept of 'archaeological culture' – referring to groups of phenomena, or rather their material traces, which occur in a specific definable zone in a specific timespan – as a basic taxonomic unit allowing the easy classification in chronological and geographical terms of divergent types of archaeological data. Ever since its formation, this concept has been one of the most widely used but also strongly debated of all archaeological concepts – this concerns especially the thorny question of the relationships between 'archaeological cultures' defined by modern scholars on the basis of their observations of the surviving material evidence to the past realities of ethnic groupings. Another problem concerns the precise way in which archaeological material is assigned to particular cultures, which accounts for some of the variation in their boundaries and extent on maps by different authors. We will return to this question in the next chapter.

The archaeological culture lies at the basis of the tradition of Continental archaeology. Archaeology in central Europe is predominantly practised in the mode labelled in his history of archaeological thought by Bruce Trigger 'culture-historical archaeology'.[9] The main aim of this mode of doing archaeology goes little further than classifying the archaeological material into cultures and then following the history of those taxonomic groups, their rise and demise, stylistic changes and replacement by others and so on, but without trying to ascertain the social processes which lie behind those changes. Since this book must to a large extent rely on the archaeological evidence gathered and interpreted by eastern European colleagues, the dearth of work using other approaches more characteristic of the schools of archaeology of other parts of Europe makes its presence felt in the present text. This is by no means a disadvantage when such basic information as date and precise taxonomic assignation of the investigated material is still under revision. To base a more sophisticated superstructure on the existing evidence would still perhaps be premature and is a matter for further work.

The archaeological record (in contrast to the quantity of written material) is at the moment undergoing a phase of rapidly expansive accumulation: new sites are constantly being examined, new finds constantly being made and interpreted. This in turn requires re-examination of old material and its interpretation. When a large proportion of this new material is published, it will create fresh opportunities for the better understanding of the past – and will suggest new questions which in turn only fresh examination of new or existing material can answer.

Ethnographic comparanda

Slav communities in some rural areas are even today surprisingly conservative, and these communities have until recently preserved the character of living ethnographic museums. Ways of life in the countryside of parts of the former Soviet bloc have hardly changed in many aspects since the late Middle Ages, despite several efforts of Communist governments to bring these rural communities into the twentieth century. Here were not only logistic and financial problems to be overcome, but also the innate resistance of many of these communities to attempts to alter their age-old traditional lifestyles. Thus agricultural regimes, tools and techniques, house styles, furnishing, dress styles and social attitudes could until quite recently be studied as functioning parts of a community, and may be used as interpretative tools in understanding the archaeological evidence. This evidence has long been utilized in central Europe in interpreting the archaeological material by such scholars such as Lubor Niederle, Stefan Czarnecki and Kazimierz Moszyński, followed by Boris Rybakov and Witold Hensel. In several central European states the advent of research techniques based on historical materalism on a Soviet model led to the formation of institutes for the study of the history of material culture, which attempted to unite the study of archaeology with ethnology.

The use of ethnographic material is not restricted to material culture. In one instance nineteenth-century travellers in far northern Russia were surprised to find that previously unknown folk traditions there preserved memories of early medieval rulers of the Kievan state far to the southwest who ruled in a mythical Golden Age. Other folk traditions seem to preserve details derived from the pre-Christian pagan traditions of the Slavs. Of course all this material must be used with caution, and subsequent layers of tradition of later centuries have to be identified and stripped away.

Linguistic evidence

The Slavic languages belong to the Indo-European group of languages, and it is in the context of the origin and spread of these languages that the development of the Early Slavs is seen. This is the context of Gimbutas's book for example. Volumes have been written on the original 'Proto-Slavic' language and where it originated and how it split as the Slav peoples began appearing over a wider area in the early medieval period. Here we will accept as a working model the probability that the Indo-European languages themselves dispersed and began to differentiate in the Early Neolithic period: this is the main thesis of the recent book by Colin Renfrew, to which the reader is referred for an interesting discussion of the relationship of linguistics to archaeology.[10] Notwithstanding this, the attempt to find Early Bronze Age Slavs in the archaeological material is, however, an abortive one. We may be relatively certain that there was indeed a Proto-Slavic language (it should be noted that, despite this, the language itself is a hypothetical one, no longer existing but reconstructed by linguistic effort), but, even if we feel that it is likely that the speakers of this language were present somewhere in eastern or central Europe by the end of the Neolithic, we have no way of knowing where they lived, in what numbers and in what relationship to speakers of languages of other groups. We cannot date any changes in these languages. Among the Indo-European languages the Slavic group is most closely related to the Baltic languages: both groups are strongly inflected and share similar constructions and vocabulary. This has led some to suggest the original existence of a 'Proto-Slavic/Baltic language' (or languages), from which the Slavic and Baltic groups (and perhaps others now vanished) later differentiated.[11]

Attempts have been made to identify the area of origin of the Proto-Slavic languages (and/or Proto-Slavic/Baltic) by studying the names of peoples (ethnonyms), old river names (hydronyms), place names (toponyms) and the names for various natural phenomena (the names of plants and animals of restricted range for example). By identifying where supposed 'primitive' river and place names of Slavic origin survive, it has been suggested that one can identify where these languages first developed. This type of approach has many drawbacks, not least identifying which names are Slavic rather than just general Indo-European, and which among them are more 'primitive' than others (and indeed identifying cases where names originally 'Slavic' were later replaced by others of a different linguistic origin). The boundary between river names of 'Slavic' type and 'Baltic' type is however relatively clear and forms at least one clear pointer to where it is unlikely that we should seek the homeland of the Proto-Slavic languages (Fig. 8). In the case of the names of plants and animals of restricted range, the argument was that the Proto-Slavic languages would not have names for plants and animals unfamiliar to them. All these arguments however assume that names do not change with time, and that there was no mechanism by which names were borrowed from other populations previously (or changed by those subsequently) inhabiting the area. One also has to be sure that the range of those animals and plants has not altered over time with environmental change. Some linguists place greater faith in toponyms, especially the names of topographical features such as rivers. Since they are relatively stable and passed between ethnic groups, these can be used to reconstruct the extent of Slav or Balt settlement. Unfortunately they cannot be used to date these settlement episodes.

Other scholars, most notably the Cracow linguist Witold Mańczak, have attempted to use the degree of lexical similarity between modern Slav languages and those assumed to be its neighbours in the past, and on the 'statistics' based on such assessments attempted to define the geographical nearness of the Slav homeland to the areas of origin of the latter. The method is however only as reliable as the underlying assumptions concerning the stability of language and mechanisms of change, which in this case seem mistaken.

The former existence of a 'Proto-Slavic language' (or languages) is easy to accept; what is less clear is where and when this language group arose, and under what circumstances. Few subjects have such exercised multidisciplinary scholarly ingenuity and raised so many tempers as this problem, which also has a modern political significance (see Chapter 13). Already by the nineteenth century linguists had proposed a number of areas where the Slavic language (and thus 'the Slavs') originated. One of the most popular concerned an origin in the unprepossessing wetlands and reedbeds of the great Pripet Marsh. To many Slavs, to have their origin in a swamp seemed almost as repugnant to common sense as to national pride, and for this reason subsequent scholars have made repeated attempts to claim a larger and more interesting territory for their ancestors. Most of these efforts have concentrated on various parts of the zone between the Danube delta and the Pripet and stretching from the Oder river in the west to the Dniestr in the east, and, although there are alternative theories, current thought seems to point to this general area as the nearest we can get for a 'homeland' of the Proto-Slavic languages.

Some writers have made attempts to identify the speakers of Slavic languages among the ethnonyms listed by the fifth-century BC Greek writer Herodotus (the Neuri being a favourite candidate) or Ptolemy and other classical sources. This relied on the 'Slav-sounding' etymology of the form of the name as it was transmitted at second or third hand in an alien tongue. Here I propose rejecting all of these surmises, interesting though they are.[12] Attempts have also been made to use early medieval tribal names to reconstruct processes of migration and creation of ethnic units. Thus there are two tribes which bear the name Croats, and some scholars have tried to derive the one from the other; not so understandable are other doubled tribal names such as the Polane which occur in Poland and the area of Kiev. We will see several other instances of this phenomenon, which may be due to convergence arising from similar rules for creation of ethnonyms.

The Slav group of languages at present is considered to contain thirteen languages (within which of course there are several dialects):

- East Slav: Ukrainian, Belarussian, Russian
- South Slav: Bulgarian, Serbian, Macedonian, and the southwestern group: Croatian, Slovenian (modern nationalist movements now claim that Bosnian and Montenegrin are also separate languages)
- West Slav: Polish, Kashubian, Sorbian (Sorbo-Lusatian), Czech, Slovak.

A fourteenth language is the Old Church Slav language, an archaic form of southern Slav used originally in the Moravian, Bulgarian and other areas, but now still used mainly in the ritual of the Orthodox Church. This is the language of some of the earliest texts written in a Slav language, and is a useful index to the form of the Slav languages in one region at a fixed point in time. These early texts are among the very few pieces of evidence which can be used to trace the break-up of the Slav linguistic unity

We must not forget the probable existence of other Slav languages which may have been lost by the end of the period covered by thus book. In the same way some of the languages such as Sorbian and Kashubian had almost died out by the beginning of the twentieth century. Sorbian dialects were still being spoken in the vicinity of Hamburg as late as in the eighteenth century. One region in which there was probably originally a greater variety of language was the dissected highlands of the Balkans. Many of these disappeared during later changes such as the South Slavic linguistic reforms of 1863.

What however is striking about the Slav languages is that speakers of Polish can make themselves roughly understood in their native tongue in for example a village in Croatia or Belarus or Ukraine: the similarities in structure, phonology and vocabulary between these languages is notable. Although the Romance languages have similar characteristics, those in the Germanic group for example do not. Since – owing to their wide geographical occurrence – the similarity of the Slav languages is unlikely to be due to convergence, this suggests that at an early stage of the development of each of these languages there was close contact between them, and from an original Proto-Slav arose the variety of Slav languages spoken today. The linguistic evidence suggests that these languages arose from dialects in a relatively restricted core area from which, already in the process of formation, they later spread. In addition, the relative similarity of these languages suggests that the time lapse between their original differentiation and dispersal may not have been as great as some authors assume, for a greater differentiation might be expected if these languages developed in total isolation for several millennia.

What is quite unclear is the way the Slav languages spread from the original core area where the Proto-Slav languages were spoken. It is clear that the traditional migrationary explanation cannot account for the diffusion of the language from a relatively compact area to cover half of Europe, whatever extended timescale in the early medieval period one wishes to adopt. Demographic expansion at this rate can be demonstrated to be biologically impossible. One possibility is that the Slav languages were already in use over a wide area of central Europe before the beginning of the early medieval period (Renfrew's Neolithic expansion model). The other is that they replaced existing tongues by a process of elite dominance (in which, by a variety of processes, people adopt the language of a social elite – thus Norman French partly replaced Anglo-Saxon in England, and the languages of Native Americans were in the process of dying out, being replaced by American English). A related model would see the Slav languages being a *lingua franca* within a community, such as within and outside the Avar khanate. None of these models is without its problems. It is difficult to see how the Slav languages maintained any coherence over millennia, while spoken by small isolated communities in other linguistic environments over a wide area, there was no real elite or social organization capable of creating a language shift in the sixth to ninth centuries and the influence of the Avars was limited with respect to the area in which we know Slav languages were spoken.

The similarities and the regularities in the differentiation of the various branches of the language group allow scholars to reconstruct the way in which the various linguistic changes occurred, and thus allow the reconstruction of the original root language, its vocabulary and its grammar.[13] One feature is shared by the Slavs of the Oder–Vistula area and the South Slavs (but not by the East Slavs), and it seems to have been one of the earliest changes to have taken place in the Proto-Slav language. This was the so-called 'metathesis of liquid consonants' (which some linguists suppose took place in the second half of the eighth century) (see Table 1).

Table 1

	Proto-Slav	Polish	Czech	Serbo-Croat	Russian
stronghold	*gardъ	gród	hrad	grâd	górod
edge	*bergъ	brzeg	břeh	brijèg	béreg
straw	*salma	słoma	sláma	sláma	solóma
milk	*melko	mleko	mléko	mlijèko	molokó

Note: The Proto-Slav language is a reconstruction, which is signified here by the use of the linguistic convention of an asterisk.

From these examples it can be seen that in Proto-Slav we have vowels before *r* and *l*, in the East Slav languages both before and after, while in the South Slav languages and Czech and Slovak the vowel follows *r* and *l*.

The Czech and Slovak languages have many features in common with the South Slav languages, from which it can be deduced that the Rudavy, Sudeten and Carpathian mountains initially formed an important linguistic barrier, and the dialects of these two languages should be considered as originally belonging to the South Slav grouping. The first Christian preachers in Moravia were Slav-(and Greek-) speaking missionaries from the Balkans who seem to have had no difficulty making themselves understood. It was in Moravia that the Old Church Slavonic language – with its strong links with South Slav languages – had its roots.

In another aspect however the Czech and Slovak languages (as well as the Sorbian/Lusatian languages) share a feature with the East Slav group, the replacement of the Proto-Slavic *g* with *h* (Table 2).

Table 2

	Proto-Slav	Polish	Czech, Slovak, Lusatian	Serbo-Croat	Russian, Ukrainian
foot	*noga	noga	noha	noga	nogá

Another characteristic feature is the distribution of the nasal vowels (such as *ą* and *ę* in Polish). In the south and east the nasal vowels are lost (Table 3).

Table 3

	Proto-Slav	Polish	Czech	Serbo-Croat	Russian
hand	*rǫka	ręka	ruka	rúka	ruká
heel	*pęta	pięta	pata	péta	pjatá

In the eighth century the consolidation of Germanic tribes in the area between Bohemia and the upper Drava (Drau) gave rise to the Bavarians, after the end of the ninth century the area between the middle Danube and Tisza was settled by Finno-Ugrian-speaking Magyars, and this, together with the existence of Romance-speaking Walacians, created a wedge of different ethnicities and languages between the South Slavs and their northern neighbours (Map VII). The Slav dialects originally existing in these areas died out. The division between South and West Slavs thus shifted three hundred kilometres to the south. From the eighth to tenth centuries therefore the Czech and Slovak dialects developed in contact with other West Slav languages. Modern Slovak for example has three main divisions: to the west the dialect is under strong Czech influence, in the middle the clear influence of Southern Slav (Serbian, Croatian) can still be detected, while in the east there is a strong influence of the Polish of the Cracow area.

We do not know what was the degree of linguistic differentiation within the areas of later early medieval states, or what local dialects and languages were replaced by the spread of Polish or Kievan dialects in the formation of the medieval Polish and Russian states. In the case of Poland for example the literature is invariably in Latin, and we have little evidence of the vernacular. A rare survival is a twelfth-century monastic document (the *Book of Henryków*) which preserves the first sentence in Polish where a man says to his wife, '*day ut ia pobrusa a ti poziwai*'; which in today's Polish would be rendered '*daj, ać ja pobruszę, a ty poczywaj*' (give it [quern] to me, I'll turn it and you rest). Rare

Old church Slavonic - ŽRŮNY = hand mill - Webster 1998

18

survivals of statements made in law courts written in the vernacular show that considerable regional differences in the spoken language existed in the fifteenth century (for example between Poznań and Cracow), and we may expect that similar differences existed at an earlier date.

The Russian languages divided into two main groups in the early medieval period (by the eleventh century); the northern languages were probably influenced by the Finnic and Baltic substrate and the dual political centres of the later Kievan state, Novgorod in the north and Kiev in the south. The northern languages are characterized by the retention of the consonant *g* and the unaccented *o*, while in the south *g* becomes *h* and the unaccented *o* becomes an *a*.[14] The further development of Ukrainian and Belarussian languages is due to Lithuanian and Polish expansion into these areas in the thirteenth to sixteenth centuries.

We cannot leave this subject without a brief comment on the effect of the theories of N. I. Marr (1864–1934) on the development not only of linguistics, but also the study of the ethnogenesis of peoples. Marr tried to apply Marxist theory to linguistics and argued that language is an ideology and thus a 'superstructure' with a class character which would change only with changing social formations. Marr's mistaken reasoning became obligatory in Lenin's Soviet Union. This led to a number of curious explanations of the origins of the peoples of the Soviet Union which had an effect on the interpretation of the historical and archaeological data (and in the period of the Stalinist purges political correctness was more a matter of necessity than nicety). In the 1930s few would criticise Marr: a rare exception was I. V. Got'e, the head of the history department at the University of Moscow who openly accused Marrist linguists of being incapable of tackling the problem of how the Slavs developed from the proto-Slavs. It was only in June 1950 that the most influential greatest theorist of Marxism of the period, Stalin himself ('at the request of a number of comrades') investigated the question and wrote a series of articles in *Pravda* (later published as a separate brochure, *On Linguistics*) which opened the way for the rejection of Marrism, to the initial relief of many Soviet historians and archaeologists.

We have seen that the sources for reconstructing the development of the Early Slavs are relatively abundant, but that their interpretation requires care and especially a scholarly and objective treatment of the sources. While intuition and even emotion may be inspirational in the proposition of hypotheses, they have no part to play in their testing and proving. Unfortunately Slav archaeology is one scientific discipline where this general rule has not always been observed. On the one hand this is due to the intractability of some of the data, on the other to the modern political conditions (Chapter 13). We are perhaps still a long way from understanding the processes outlined in this book, but this does not mean that we should not try to interpret and synthesize this evidence.

The geographical background

An understanding of the geographical background to the events discussed here is crucial to their understanding, and thus it may be worthwhile touching on a few of the salient points. A feature which is not often appreciated in western Europe is the vastness of eastern Europe, which may best be appreciated on a map if one ignores the long thin Italian peninsula – the contrast between the size of western and eastern Europe becomes greater. This huge area contains a great variety of types of terrain, soil types and climatic zones. The maps presented in this book should ideally each be compared with a large-scale physical map of eastern Europe, as we cannot show on the Figures in this book all the relevant features.

The most important feature on the map for our period is the chain of mountains dividing eastern Europe into a northern half and a southern one. North of the Carpathians and east Alps is an area of fairly flat plains (the North European Plain), to the south of which are smaller ranges of mountains and hills (Thuringian, Rudavy, Sudeten, Holy Cross mountains, Lublin Uplands, Podole). These in turn enclose three major basins (Czech, Moravia and Cracow-Sandomierz). The North European Plain is drained by several major rivers flowing north into the Baltic Sea (Elbe, Oder, Vistula, (Western) Bug, Niemen, Dvina, Volkhov) and those draining south into the Black Sea (Seret, Prut, Dniestr, Boh (Southern Bug), Dniepr, Don). The Dneipr system has tributaries Pripet, Goryń and Desna. The area around the Pripet is an extensive area of marshland with islands. Further east is the massive Volga system (with tributaries such as the Oka and Kama) draining into the Caspian Sea. To the south of this mountain chain is the more broken terrain south and west. These factors in turn affected the process of settlement and political unification and fragmentation of these two zones.

Running south of the Carpathians is the Danube, with tributaries Morava, Vag and Tisza on the north, and the Drava (Drau) and Sava on the south. Above Vienna the Danube flows between mountains. The middle Danube valley is a broad flatland with semi-steppe vegetation (the Carpathian basin) which has long attracted nomads from the east. These passed through the so-called Iron Gates from the broad plains of Walachia. South of the Danube are more mountain ranges, forming very broken country. The landscape of the Balkans is generally very broken with ranges of rocky mountains and hills with deep fertile valleys between them.

A consideration of the climax vegetation zones is important in the understanding of the processes involved in the expansion of the Slavs. These are shown in simplified form in Fig. 4. There is much evidence (especially from fossil pollen preserved in archaeological deposits) that the North European Plain was intensively afforested through most of later prehistory, where there were isolated clearances in the forest, separated by wide tracts of virgin forest. When the settlement structure of the German groups in this area began to collapse in the fifth century, many areas reverted to forest as clearances began to become overgrown. This was the sort of environment into which came the Early Slav settlers in most of central Europe. In the Balkans however there may have been extensive tracts of cleared land available for settlement – some of it recently abandoned owing to political factors. There are several types of forest which predominate in the lowlands of the northern part of central and eastern Europe (not forgetting the bands of wetland forest occurring in the bottoms of the main river valleys which were an important environment exploited by the Early Slavs). The proportion of deciduous and coniferous trees in the forest (as well as the precise species and varieties present) varies across this zone; in general though these forests were mixed coniferous and deciduous, with a predominance of pine, birch and oak, with beechwood in parts of the north. The lowland forests were dense, with thick undergrowth, and were difficult to penetrate. The valley sides may have contained clearings, owing to the grazing of wild herbivores and human activity concentrating near the water.

The nature of the vegetation affected the animals present in the forest. In general in most areas the same species were then present as today though in greater numbers, with the exception that wolf and bear had a wider distribution. In some areas elk, aurochs and (rarely) bison were to be found, and beavers were also relatively common. The Early Slavs clearly felt most at home in the vicinity of forest, which was an important resource for them. Apart from the wood for structural purposes and fuel, it held fodder for livestock, wild bees (for honey and wax) and fur-bearing animals (marten, squirrel, ermine and so on). Lakes and rivers had abundant fish and fowl, and their shores were favourite locations for settlement. In the upland areas there was a different vegetation, the nature of which also varies slightly with longitude and of course altitude. In general however the Slavs settled the valleys first, penetrating the uplands only at a much later date.

The landscape of the southern regions penetrated by the Slavs in the Balkans differed from that of the North European Plain. The earliest Slav settlements are found in the band of forest steppe down the west edge of and south of the Carpathians; they also settled on the Danube plain but later crossed the Danube into the Balkans. The natural vegetation of this area was the warm south European oak forests with beechwood in the highlands (pinewoods in Dalmatia). Along the coasts in Thessalonia the natural vegetation was of Mediterranean type with coniferous forests in the mountains.

To the southeast of the central European forests is the broad irregular band of the forest-steppe zone stretching along the northern edge of the steppes and merging into both vegetation zones at its edges. The drier climate of the forest steppe zone produce a characteristic open landscape on the relatively fertile soils with mixed deciduous forest (spruce with oak, alder and oak-hornbeam with maple lime and hazel). The forest was thickest in the valleys – though even here it contained clearings – and thinned out on the hilltops where grassland predominates (Fig. 5). This vegetation zone is very important, for it was probably somewhere here that Early Slav culture first crystallized, and it was along the forest steppe corridor that it spread west. The penetration of the central European forest zone was a phenomenon of a slightly later period.

To the south and southeast of the forest steppe are the broad flat pastures of the grass steppe. Here the environmental conditions favoured a nomadic existence, and during the whole early medieval period this vegetation zone was inhabited by a series of (non-Slav) nomadic pastoralist farmers. These broad flat grasslands coupled with the highly mobile lifestyle of the inhabitants of the area allowed for demographic and cultural movements from deepest Asia to penetrate the heart of Europe. This was the route taken by the Huns, the Avars and other Turkish-speaking groups, as well as the Mongols. Early medieval Slav settlement only rarely penetrated far south into this zone; the initiation of large-scale arable farming which has so changed the landscape of this area is a result of post-medieval colonization. Although the Slavs never extensively colonized the steppes, their culture was influenced through peaceful and hostile contacts by that of the steppe nomads.

The tundra and taiga areas in the far north of Russia were not settled by the Slavs until post-medieval times, though occasional hunting expeditions – for furs and other Arctic products – seem to have penetrated the area earlier.

Climatically eastern Europe in general has today what is termed a 'Continental' climate, with warm summers and cold winters. There is however substantial differentiation across this area, from north to south and east to west: thus the cold winters in the northeast that defeated Napoleon and Hitler contrast with the more Mediterranean climate of the Balkans. A similar temperature gradient occurs from east to west: in fact the line of the growing season of 210 days with temperature above +5°C which runs through Poland (Fig. 4) seems to mark a cultural boundary reflected in the density of known settlement. Where the season is shorter, Slav settlement seems to have been less dense and less well organized until a comparatively late period.

Of course we should not forget climatic change, which we know occurred in this time, but is a process which has been relatively poorly studied in eastern Europe. We know too little about the mechanisms of climatic change to know how far it is a valid exercise to project what we know of climatic change in western Europe and Scandinavia over eastern Europe.[15] As a working model we may assume that eastern Europe followed a broadly similar pattern to that in the west, that is the Migration period was cooler and wetter over much of western central Europe, while the ninth and tenth centuries represent some kind of climatic optimum. This model is probably valid for much of northwestern central

Europe, but perhaps less reliable for the areas to the south and further east. This is one of the pressing problems for future research.

Human activities too had a far-reaching effect on shaping the environment, and there has been much pioneer work done on this topic in eastern Europe in past decades. There is now very good evidence from the North European Plain that the cumulative effects of the deforestation of the slopes of river valleys, especially where the soil was poor, led to drastic changes in the micro-environment. Similar evidence has been noted in the early medieval Balkans. In the forest, the tree cover breaks the fall of raindrops, not all of which reach the forest floor. Additionally moisture is sucked out of the topsoil relatively soon after a rainstorm by the root systems of thousands of trees and transpired into the atmosphere again. When those trees were removed, part of the rainwater soaked deep into the ground, raising underground water levels and leaching nutrients from the topsoil, while the rest caused erosion of the ground surface and formed small streamlets. The net result of these processes was that stable forest soil systems that had taken tens of thousands of years to create were suddenly exposed to degradation and erosion. In a slow but unstoppable process the soil cover of the valley slopes was reduced in thickness and extent. This was only half of the catastrophe however, as this topsoil was washed into the main river valleys, which became choked with silt. This in turn caused a rise in water levels in the valley bottoms, which was at its greatest intensity on the North European Plain in the later twelfth and thirteenth centuries and resulted in floods and changes in the river course. Removal of tree cover was then a double human tragedy, because it was precisely in the river valley bottoms that many of the main settlements were sited. This process of forest destruction and soil degradation was not confined to the early medieval period – it had been going on since the Neolithic – but each phase of forest destruction was followed by a period of regeneration. However, the early medieval clearances were permanent; forest cut down in the period from the ninth century onwards in general rarely re-established itself, the human pressure on the landscape being too great.

The background to the expansion of the Slavs

A summary of the ethnic background is of importance to the understanding of the process of the Slav expansion of the sixth century. Two main zones need to be differentiated, the former area of the Roman Empire separated by the frontier (*limes*) from the area beyond. For the Romans, this political boundary separated civilization from the barbarian world and it is to the latter that the Slavs belong.

The province of Dacia had been given up in the third century. The new frontier was established on the Danube. A number of barbarians moved closer to the *limes*, and settled alongside the remaining indigenous but Romanized population, first Huns and various Germanic tribes. South of the frontier the population of the empire was of mixed ethnicity (Greeks and Macedonians, Thracians, Albanians, Geto-Dacians, and Illyrians and probably others); most of them – excepting those in inaccessible mountainous zones – by the end of Antiquity had become thoroughly Romanized. The population of the northern and western provinces (Noricum, Pannonia, Dalmatia and Moesia) to a large degree spoke Latin, but south of the Balkan mountains and especially on the coasts of the Black Sea and in many towns of Thrace and Macedonia there were strong influences of Greek culture (especially in the urban centres). The Danube frontier on the fringe of the foundering West Roman Empire was becoming progressively weakened, and various factors including attacks by barbarian raiding parties led to significant depopulation especially of the northern provinces along the Danube. These areas were therefore settled at the end of Antiquity by barbarian *foederati* of various ethnicity, which dominated the rural population; only the towns were still bastions of *romanitas*. These included the Ostrogoths settled in former Pannonia (but also for a time the Vandals and Heruli and later the Longobards). It was into this landscape that the Slavs arrived, first as barbarian raiders but, like those before them, later as settlers.

In the late Roman period much of the area of the North European Plain which was later occupied by the Slavs can be seen to have been occupied by a number of peoples. In the west were several groups of German tribes on the Elbe, to the east of these were zones occupied by the Przeworsk and Wielbark Cultures, and to the southeast on the steppe and forest steppe is a large area occupied by the Cherniakhovo Culture. To cut short a long scholarly argument on the relationship of archaeological cultures to ethnic groups, it seems fairly plausible to see these groupings of material culture as the archaeological reflection of among others the federations of Germanic groups known to the Romans as the Vandals (Przeworsk) and the Goths (Wielbark and Cherniakhovo). On the steppes and in the steppe and forest-steppe zone of the Carpathian basin were areas settled by nomadic and semi-nomadic Sarmatian peoples (such as the Alans).

The material culture of many of these Late Roman groups – especially those nearer the Roman frontiers – is well developed, with a wide range of products. The metalwork includes a wide range of personal ornaments, buckles, pendants, fibulae for fastening clothing. Hair was arranged with finely made bone combs. Settlements and graves often produce imported Roman goods such as pottery and glass vessels, and the range of local pottery is wide, ranging from cooking-pots and other kitchen vessels to fine flagons and cups, some of them clearly influenced by the imported wares. Much of this pottery was wheel-made and highly fired. Surface finish of some vessels is often elaborate, including highly polished surfaces with incised decoration. There is evidence for specialist craftsmen and extensive exchange of prestige goods (Fig. 6). The general impression that this material creates is that of a competitive materialistic consumer culture concerned with the acquisition of status and its exhibition through the use of showy prestige goods. The Germanic world and its imitators reflected the strong influence from the Roman Empire and were probably propagated by specific forms of social organization of the 'chiefdom' type.

In the forest zone to the north of these Germanic groups further from the imperial frontiers were other barbarians with considerably less developed material culture. Among these forest groups were the various cultural groups representing the Balts. In the vast forests to the north and east of these were various Finno-Ugrian groups (the Finno-Ugrian languages are not Indo-European). These relatively conservative forest societies were to play little part in the events of the Migration period; judging from the evidence, the pan-European historical processes of the period seems to have bypassed them for a while. Among the groups of this forest zone in the middle and upper Dniepr region is the Kievan Culture, which will be discussed in the next chapter.

Some time around the end of the fourth century the power structure of the whole area beyond the frontiers of the Roman Empire altered substantially. This process resulted from changes in the Empire itself which affected the whole power balance of the zone outside it. The frontiers became increasingly unstable and unable to resist the southern and westward movements of the Germanic tribes. The mirage of the good life to be found to the south was eventually to draw the barbarians – who included Germans and the Slavs – towards the crumbling frontiers of the Empire. The period also saw the movement of the nomad Turkic Huns into the area of the Black Sea steppe in the period between 375 and 400, and the consequent collapse of the Cherniakhovo Culture there (the Goths moved into the Empire in this period, while the related Gepids moved west into what had been the former province of Dacia). By about 420 the Huns had moved to the middle Danube, where they established a hegemony over the Germanic groups there, and in 433–53 under Attila the influence of the Hunnic Empire expanded further to the north and west. Under Hun rule on the steppes certain aspects of the Cherniakhovo culture survived in modified form amalgamated with Hun metalwork styles, which in and after the period of Attila had a tangible effect too on the elite metalwork styles in central Europe. It was in the changed situation after the collapse of the classic form of the Cherniakhovo culture that the Slavs become visible in the archaeological record.

Similar changes are visible in central Europe too. As the fifth century goes on, we begin to lose sight of the material culture typical of the Germanic groups not only in Ukraine but also in eastern and southern Poland, parts of eastern Germany and Slovakia. Pollen spectra from the peat bogs, such as for example at Biskupin in Poland and a number of sites in the Elbe region show that areas of cleared land were abandoned to forest at this time. At about the same time we hear from Roman written sources of the increasing Germanic presence within the Roman Empire. It is very tempting to see these two facts as linked and to see in this the evidence of barbarian population movement westward towards the warmer and economically developed Romanized areas of Europe. This process appears to have left large areas of eastern European forest with seriously depleted populations. Certainly whoever was now living in this zone was no longer using clearly identifiable mass material culture of recognizably Germanic type. As an example we may cite the collapse of Germanic settlement networks in central and southwestern Poland, represented by the sudden and widespread abandonment at the end of the fourth and beginning of the fifth century of all the larger cemeteries of the Przeworsk Culture which had been in use for several centuries.[16]

One or two items of late Germanic metalwork are found in this zone generally as loose finds. To the west were limited areas still inhabited by Late Germanic groups ('*Restgermanen*') in western Poland, Bohemia and the Elbe valley, as well as on the south coast of the Baltic (Map IV). To the south, other movements were taking place when the Longobards moved down from the upper Elbe and settled in the Carpathian basin, closer to the imperial frontiers after the collapse of Hun rule in 454.

I

The Formation of a Slav Identity

Who were the Early Slavs?

Before we begin to discuss the culture and history of the Early Slavs, we must first clarify the subject of this study. What do we mean when we talk of the Early Slavs? The Slavs today are a number of ethnic groups, most of them living today in various nation states in central and eastern Europe, and the main characteristic they have in common is that they all speak languages assignable to the Slav group of Indo-European languages. The term 'Slavs' is therefore primarily a linguistic one. When referring to the 'Early Slavs' here therefore, I intend to mean the people who we have good reason to believe speak spoke early versions of the Slav languages, and it should be stressed that I do not mean the term to refer to a single ethnic group. Nevertheless as we have seen, the linguistic evidence suggests that at some stage of the distant past the Slav language group may have had an origin among a relatively restricted population. This population spoke the same language, or dialects of it, and, to judge from similarities in the material culture of the Migration period, had similar lifestyles. To this extent the descendants of the 'Proto-Slavs' can be regarded as a series of related peoples. In earlier discussions of ethnicity the term 'race' tended to be very loosely used: certainly there is no question that the Early Slavs constituted a separate race of people. In physical terms the modern speakers of the Slav languages are members of the general Caucasian race, and show the variability typical of that group.[1]

In fact the term 'Early Slavs' could refer to at least four types of phenomena relating to our main types of sources:

- historical: the people referred to by early medieval (usually external) written sources as 'Slavs' (not all of course might have been, they may merely have inhabited the territory regarded by outsiders as belonging to the Slavs)
- archaeological: the people using the specific assemblages of material culture which the archaeologist associates with the Slavs
- ethnographic: the people whom historical and living tradition regards as the direct ancestors of the population now inhabiting Slav countries
- linguistic: the speakers of the early forms of the Slav languages.

These four phenomena have dimensions in different kinds of space and time, and do not always comfortably overlap.

To some extent therefore we have to consider that the concept of 'the Slavs' (and thus 'the Early Slavs') is an academic construct, but it is one with a long history. The similarity between the languages of a number of separate peoples of central and eastern Europe was already recognized in the medieval period: chronicles such as those of Kievan Rus and Poland clearly saw these states as part of a wider 'Slavdom'. The literary concept of a kinship between particular linguistic groups developed (possibly under Byzantine influence) and legendary origins of these states were presented for example in the form of the tale of the three brothers, Lech, Czech and Rus, who gave rise to the three peoples of Poland, Bohemia and Russia. For the medieval Christian chronicler, there was an additional reason to see the Slavs as being related, as they were all seen as descended from Japhet, one of the sons of Noah. Medieval scholars also found the works of ancient writers which showed that the area now inhabited by speakers of Slav languages had been previously occupied by peoples with other names (Goths, Sarmatians, Vandals and so on), and tried to make these into their ancestors. The literature of the sixteenth and seventeenth centuries continued these tendencies (for example the Polish nobility mistakenly saw themselves as descended from Sarmatians, setting them apart from the Slav ancestors of the commoner). The literature of the period also shows an awareness of the common origins and features of the various Slav peoples; this was to be developed in the pan-Slavism of the Romantic period.

The word 'Slav' appears only in the written sources of the medieval period and later. The sixth-century Greek (East Roman and Byzantine) authors write of *Sklavenoi, Sklabenoi* etc. to refer to the troublesome people who had made their presence felt on their northwest border (later Greek authors write of *Sklabinioi, Sklavenoi, Sklaboi, Sthlaboi, Sthlabenoi, Sthlabinoi, Sthlabenoi, Esklabinoi*). In early medieval and medieval Latin sources however – presumably writing mostly about the West Slavs – we hear of *Sklaveni, Sclavini, Sclavi, Schlavi, Sclavenia, Sclavinia* and *Sclavania*. The Arabs adopted one of these expressions but, because it would not harmonize with their phonetics, changed it into *as-Saqaliba*. These collective labels were employed by outsiders who however had inherited from earlier writers not only the descriptions of earlier literature but also the ideas of ancient geographers. Confronted by a confusing variety of ethnonyms, they fell back on earlier models and spoke of broad groupings, based on the perceived similarities in their language.

The name first appears to refer to a particular group of barbarians in the area north of the Danubian frontier in the early to middle sixth century. By extension the term was later used in the west to refer to other groups lying beyond their frontiers.[2] One of the earliest uses in the West was in Fredegar's *Chronicle* of about 660, where the term *Sclaveni* appears, and Boniface in one of his letters of 751 uses the name *Sclavi*. Early and late Carolingian sources (Einhard, *Annals of Fulda*) also use *Sclavi*. Einhard when listing the tribes conquered by the victorious Charlemagne adds that these tribes 'while speaking almost the same language differ greatly as regards custom and costume'. Other writers were less observant of local differences: Adam of Bremen (*Gesta Hammaburgensis*) notes that 'Sclavinia is ten times bigger than our Saxony, especially if one treats as part of it Bohemia or the Polan beyond the Oder, since they do not differ, either in customs or language'. It is clear from this that the main area he thought of as Sclavinia was Polabia.

Alongside 'Sclavi' and related terms, western sources also use another name for their eastern neighbours. Some medieval western scholars applied (variants of) the name 'Wends' (German *Wenden*) mainly for the Polabian Slavs. The concept had appeared by the time of Fredegar, who uses it (IV.68) in *c.* 660, and is also used by Boniface (in a letter of 746/7). It also appears in the *Annales Bertiniani* of the 860s and several other ninth-century sources.[3] This generic term derived from bookish traditions when writing in Latin. Antique sources (including Tacitus in his *Germania*) referred to the people living to the east of the Germans as the *Venedi*, and this term was obviously reused by monkish chroniclers to describe the peoples beyond the expanding frontiers of the Frankish kingdom.

The original term *Sclaveni* would seem to be a real tribal name (with a typical *-eni* plural ending). In all probability in the original tongue the name was closer to *Slavene*. Other closely similar tribal names appear at a later period (particularly where the Slavs came into contact with substantial populations of people from unrelated linguistic groups) and thus we have tribal names such as the Slovenes, Sloviane and so on. The individual Slavs groups themselves seem originally to have used the name to refer only to their own community and not all Slavs as a whole. (But the latter use also appeared by the twelfth century, probably as a result of the spread of the liturgy in Slavic which led to an awareness of its similarity to the vernacular of several groups, and the efforts of missionaries as well as the development of long-distance trade networks.)

Many suggestions have been advanced down through the ages as to what the root or roots of these terms might mean. Opinions have been divided whether the shorter or longer forms should be taken and whether the root word would have originally been written with an *o* or an *a*. From the thirteenth century the short form 'Slav' was taken as the original root (and derived from the word *Slava* – honour, glory or fame), but as early as the fourteenth century the longer form 'Slovenia' was used to propose the origin with the word *Slovo* (word, speech). It is interesting to compare this with the Slavs' term for their German neighbours, *Nemcy* (the dumb or mute). According to this model the Slavs would have called themselves the *Slovani* – that is the speaking ones (those who know the words) while they called some of their neighbours the dumb ones (those who do not know the words). In this way we can suggest that the Slavs saw themselves as a 'communication community' (see below, p. 31).[4]

Linguistic affinity alone is not enough however to create ethnic identity. In the period we are discussing, some Slavs for example spoke more than one language. We are reminded of Procopius's story (*Wars* XIII.24–XIV.36) of the impostor who was able to claim the false identity of a Roman general, Chilbudius, precisely because he spoke fluent Latin. Many people living in the Balkans probably spoke Slav and Greek (as we know from the Miracles of St Demetrius and the story of Cyril and Methodius). People living in frontier zones or multi-ethnic communities habitually speak two or more languages. We cannot talk of a Slav ethnicity, just because we are dealing with Slav-speakers: there have to be other elements linking the group together before we can refer to it as an ethnic group.

The question of the recognition of past ethnic groups is one of extreme complexity. The study of ancient social organizations and the way we 'label' peoples and place them as actors on the historic stage has always been a subject of interest among archaeologists and historians.[5] Ever since the *Siedlungsarchäologie* method of German archaeologists such as Gustaf Kossinna before the First World War which used specific types or assemblages of archaeological material to write ethnic history, the subject has raised high emotions. Interest in the study of past ethnicities and social organization has renewed in recent years and many types of evidence, including models derived from social anthropology and ethnology, have been drawn into the discussion, allowing consideration of the forms of social organization which might underlie the ethnonyms we read of in the written sources.

Ethnicity is one of the reflections of the ways in which communities differentiate themselves from the others ('us' from 'them'). A feature of human relationships is the constant need to establish identity with reference to a group, and that group defines its identity not only within itself but primarily with reference to another group or groups (many examples may be cited ranging from urban street gangs or English football supporters to various forms of national, religious or racial chauvinism). Such identities are thus prone to appear primarily in conditions of potential conflict between adjacent interest groups. On a larger scale, these differences are definable as 'ethnic': examples might be tribal identities in Africa or North America or modern nations. The key self-identifying factors leading to such a distinction are often more complex than the simple black-and-white manner in which they are usually expressed. There may also be several levels and types of 'us/them' relationships (the differences between interest groups and ethnic groups) and the nature of the frontier zones (rarely frontier lines) and the interactions between them.

Today the designations Pole and Russian, Slovak and Slovene are primarily ethnic but also national ones: they and other Slav peoples belong to nation states which formed after (in some cases well after) the tenth century. The very notion of a nation state is however relatively late, a product of nationalism which (although it existed previously) swept Continental Europe after the eighteenth century. We should resist all temptations to transpose modern ideas to early medieval situations.[6] We need therefore to apply a more general definition of ethnicity and ethnic groups, and in particular the relationship between language, culture and ethnic affinity.

One general concept which is proving useful is that of communication communities (*Verkehrsgemeinschaften*), a concept borrowed from linguistics, which was first applied to the interpretation of archaeological material in the 1960s to study the cultural groupings in Germanic and Scandinavian material. It has recently been applied to the study of the Early Slavs.[7] The term refers to a form of network of individuals connected by forms of communication, and, while this primarily concerns a language, recent studies of the theory of translation emphasize that this also implies a common ideology within which ideas can be exchanged. This in turn implies shared culture. Material culture is also a form of communication, and one of the messages it can be used to transmit is the 'belonging' to a certain group or having a certain status or attitude. Although language is one feature of a communication community and material culture another, this does not necessarily imply that the culture and language are equivalents, and this tells us nothing about ethnic identity.

Anthony Smith provides a convenient and useful definition of ethnicity in his consideration of the ethnic origins of nations; for him ethnicity is a matter of myths and symbols, memories and values, and is carried by forms and genres of artefacts and activities.[8] These create what he calls an 'ethnie' which is a human group, a concrete reality generated by the meaning conferred by the members of that group on certain cultural, spatial and temporal properties of their interaction and shared experiences. Ethnic groups and ethnicities are not inherent, they are created. Smith identifies six components of any ethnic group: a collective name, a common myth of descent, a shared history, a distinctive shared culture, an association with a specific territory, and a sense of solidarity. It is obvious that given such a definition we are at a disadvantage trying to study ethnicity in past societies.

In the period for which we have records there is less of a problem recognizing local socio-political groupings; chronicles talk of wars between tribes and states and raids of one people on another, we can sketch frontier zones, name leaders and identify what sort of social and political links unite those within an ethnic boundary zone or differentiate them from those the other side. We may have texts from which we can determine the vernacular language, and divine something of the traditions and culture of the people we are dealing with.

Before, however, the abundance of written records we are dealing with a 'people without a history' (or 'with a paucity of history') and from these we may have only a few scraps of written information and the anonymous archaeological evidence (though sometimes of specific type). The temptation to amalgamate them is strong; for totally human reasons we prefer to use ethnonyms in discussing the past rather than use abstract archaeological units such as 'cultures', but it is in precisely this field that many serious over-interpretations have been made in the study of the Early Slavs, and the efforts of scholars (especially Polish and Ukrainian ones) to identify proto-Slavs in the nuances of the archaeological evidence have sometimes relied more on wishful thinking than on scientific fact. The simple and hard fact is that from the finding of the sherds of a pot by excavation, there is absolutely no way that we can know in what language the user cursed as he or she dropped it. We cannot know what language was spoken by the user of a particular type of brooch any more than we can assume today that each wearer of Levi jeans speaks American English. Some types of material culture may be ethno-specific, but this cannot be assumed. Terms such as 'Early Slav pottery' and 'Longobard fibulae' used by archaeologists are shorthand terms for more complex and totally uncertain situations.

Nevertheless, the grounds for the belief that a certain complex of archaeological finds (known in the archaeological literature as Prague-type assemblages) in all probability represents the archaeological indicators of the Slavs needs to be set out here. These assemblages were first formally identified, as the name implies, in Bohemia in the 1940s, and there it was recognized that this was the culture of the people inhabiting the area in the early medieval period. Since the archaeological record did not show any breaks in continuity or development of these cultural phenomena before the rise of a written language (for it was in Moravia and Bohemia that Church Slavonic was written down in some of the earliest documents in the native language from the region), it seemed a fair conclusion that this was the material culture of the population ancestral to those Slav-speaking Moravians and Bohemians. Very similar material was to turn up in Bulgaria and the Ukraine, in situations supporting such an idea. It became recognized that there is a series of archaeologically visible phenomena which create recurring patterns, which gives reasonable grounds for accepting a cultural affinity between these groups. They form a horizon of assemblages of very similar character but involving a variety of cultural phenomena going right across eastern and central Europe, in regions where we know (or strongly suspect) that the Slav languages were established at that time. Although it is impossible to prove empirically, it would seem likely that the similarities of the material culture would reflect a similar convergence of ideology and probably (in this case a Slavic) language, the material culture being just part of a broadly homogeneous cultural package of which the archaeologist is capable of directly documenting only the more durable material elements. That is not to say that no Slav used any other kind of pot or lived in any other kind of house, nor that all who used these pots and lived in those huts were necessarily Slav-speakers. In the light of present knowledge (and in the absence of a better alternative) there seems no real reason to deny the likelihood of the current view of many scholars, which is to equate in general terms the users of this culture or group of cultures with the users of the Slav languages.[9]

The recognition that certain cultural phenomena could be the reflection of a particular group of people has led to attempts to try to find out how these people came into existence in the past.[10] Some scholars began to talk of the notion of studying the 'ethnogenesis' of individual groups. This is a field of study typical of some areas of central and eastern European historiography where attempts are made to combine the archaeological, historical and linguistic evidence to try to define when a 'people' came into existence. It is obvious that the difficulties of such an endeavour are great and the uncertainties many, which accounts for the many different opinions which have been voiced. This concept is difficult to apply in some cases (such as the 'ethnogenesis of the Slavs') since it is clear that there cannot be any question that the origin of a single ethnic group is meant.

The existence today of nation states in which one is assigned an ethnicity automatically at birth and by the way one is brought up (a process called socialization by anthropologists and sociologists) perhaps hinders an understanding of the potential fluidity of ethnicity, especially seen across a few generations. The early medieval 'tribe' or 'people' was apparently not a homogenous nor stable unit entry into which was determined solely by birth and genetics; the evidence suggests that individuals could often move between groups. Warriors with their families could apparently choose to belong to a group the leader of which was politically successful (which in the present context would primarily mean successful in war or raiding). Belonging to such a group would mean increased prestige for the individual or community. Being under the protection of such a leader would also give a sense of security. The core of such groups, whether large or small, was usually a dynasty of leaders which acted as a carrier and focus of traditions for the group self-identity.[11]

Thus for example the armies of 'Huns' who attacked the Goths in 375–420 probably comprised a few thousand 'real' Turkic-speaking Huns who had ridden their stocky steppe ponies all the way from the Mongolian steppe, probably accompanied by a few thousand more Iranian-speaking Sarmatians who had joined the group on its way across to the Black Sea steppes, where they were joined by the Alans, from another Iranian-speaking group from the foothills of the Caucasus. When they reached the Black Sea steppe undoubtedly many people who had previously considered themselves as belonging among the 'Goths' saw new opportunities in becoming part of the Hun horde in its move west. To judge from an account by one writer there were at least some people in that horde using words which sound suspiciously like Slav ones (Jordanes, section 258, informs us that the funeral feast of Attila was called a *strava* by some of its participants). It was this ethnically mixed multitude which the Roman writers and diplomats and modern compilers of historical atlases sum up in the one short word 'Huns'.[12] The Germanic 'tribes' which invaded the

Roman Empire probably had a similar mixed composition, as did the nomad Avars (see Chapter 2).

Belonging to a group may bring with it certain standards of behaviour and styles of dress. New members of a group in order to be accepted would often have adopted conformist approaches to the norms of the group. Other traits may have been symbols of prestige within the group. Thus the Avar elite wore a specific type of clothing which was fastened by a belt with ornate metal fittings. The wearing of this belt (which may like a knight's spurs have been symbolically given as a mark of a leader's esteem) was probably a status symbol, but it does not mean that each grave in which these fittings were found belonged to an Avar horseman who had come from Mongolia (the skeletons they are found with are rarely of mongoloid type); we shall see that some of these graves probably contained Slavs. Certain other types of ornament and dress acted (in the same way as modern so-called 'national costumes') to express and reinforce group identity.

One of the most important of links within a community of course concerns language. An outsider to a group will have to learn how to communicate in the *lingua franca* of the group. Socio-linguistic studies show how groups of different kinds use language and adapt them. Since the elite determine the mores and traditions of the group, it is they who will determine what language is spoken as a mode of communication within it. This is the model of elite dominance discussed by Renfrew.[13] It may take an individual two or three years to accumulate a sufficient knowledge of grammar and vocabulary to become assimilated into the group. Within a decade or so the group will have one main language, while individuals within it may use one or more languages at home amongst themselves. This will lead to each group of languages adopting 'loan words' from the other – often for concepts which are foreign to the original language. The group's language may therefore be derived from the pure use of an already existing model, or it may develop as a 'creole' or 'pidgin' language using elements derived from other languages. The early development of the Slav languages in a group made up of elements from different backgrounds is betrayed by the existence of loan words from a number of languages, including those from Germanic and Iranian. These overlie a substrate of elements derived from the Proto-(Balto-) Slavic language. Indeed it seems very likely that the Slav language was one of the main languages spoken as a *lingua franca* in at least part of the communication community that was the Avar khanate (which may go some way to explaining its spread especially south of the Carpathians).[14]

The crystallization of a Slav identity

We have a few ethnonyms in written sources previous to the beginning of the sixth century which some scholars, with varying degrees of credibility, have attempted to see as Slav in etymology. A number have been collected by Gimbutas in her book. If we accept that the Slavs and Balts (or Slavo-Balts) were already in the area of central and eastern Europe by the Early Neolithic, we may assume that part of the material culture of the entirity of prehistory was indeed used by people speaking Proto-Slavic (or Proto-Balto-Slavic) languages, and that the ethnonyms of these groups may well be accidentally preserved in a few written sources. To go beyond that to identify which part of the archaeological material represents Proto-Slavs and which not, to identify where the Proto-Slavs were living, alongside whom and in what relationship and numbers, is pure speculation. This book will therefore begin with the first identifiable and specific evidence for the presence of Slavs.

The first written evidence of the appearance of the Slavs comes from southern European sources from the East Roman-Ostrogothic culture circle. It refers to raids almost from the first years of the reign of Justinian (that is, from about 518), which is the period when (according to the *Secret History* of Procopius) the *Sclavenoi* started to become visible in the southwestern fringes of the forest steppe zone in the Danube frontier region.

One of the most important of these early records, a statement of Jordanes, has had a key role in studies of the origin of the Slavs and should be examined here. Jordanes is our main source of information on many aspects of central European history in the late Roman period. This is unfortunate, because it is here that he is clearly unreliable.[15] Jordanes begins his account with a description of Europe (sections 4–37) which it is quite clearly compiled from the works of earlier classical writers such as Strabo, Tacitus and Ptolemy and probably partly based on a lost work of Cassiodorus. In section 34 occurs a much-quoted passage referring to the mountains in Scythia which surround Dacia:

Along their left side, which turn to the north, beginning from the source of the river Vistula over a boundless area are settled the populous people of the Veneti [Venedi], which, although they took on different names from their clans and territories, in general are called Sclaveni and Antes. The Sclaveni occupy the area from the town of Noviedunum and the lake called Mursian to the river Danaster [Dniestr], and to the north up to the Vistula, where they have forest and swamp instead of towns. The Antes, who are the bravest of these people, dwell in the curve of the Pontian Sea spread from the Danaster to the Danaper.

This account has often been taken at face value and ever since the days of the nineteenth-century W. Surowiecki and P. Šafařík much discussed in the context of the discussions on the origin of the Slavs (and thus the search for the 'homeland' of the Slavs has become equated with the search for the ancient territory of the Venedi). If we examine Jordanes's account in context we can see that part of it is in fact a carbon-copy of a passage referring to the Venedi in Tacitus's first-century work *Germania* (section 46 of the standard text) which Cassiodorus was fond of quoting. This has been added to information from another source about the Sclavenes and Antes, and many scholars have made much of the position this implies for these two peoples (the Antes being placed by many Soviet scholars on the forest steppe); the geographical extent of these groups seems however to be a literary topos. Attempts at drawing a view of the described situation from the viewpoint of the classical geography which would have been known to Jordanes and his contemporaries produce a nonsense picture.[16] On balance it seems that this account has little value in discussions of the origin of the Slavs.

Procopius, writing about the same time in an excursus in his *Wars* (VII.14, 22–30) gives a lot of interesting and believable ethnographic detail about the Slavs pressing in on the East Roman frontiers. Among this is the information that the 'Sklavenes and Antes . . . speak one language, completely barbarian . . . they once had a single name, they were called Sporoi'. The etymology of this latter name has been debated. It seems most likely that it comes from the Proto-Slavic word for 'multitude'. Although these written sources are our earliest firm information about the existence of Slavs in central and eastern Europe, the Slavs (that is, communities speaking Slavic languages) however did not appear on the Danube frontier from nowhere, and they had an earlier origin elsewhere. This was a point well appreciated by Cassiodorus and Procopius – hence their desire to fill the vacuum utilizing earlier literary sources. We will however further examine the process of genesis of this people in the next chapter. The important feature of Jordanes's text and the parallel accounts of Procopius is that they give us the first descriptions of the Slavs and tell us what they called themselves. We will return to these accounts below.

What does seem demonstrated quite clearly by the written sources however is that before a certain period the East Roman Empire was totally oblivious to the existence of a barbarian people called the Slavs on their northern border.[17] The terms seem to be coined or adopted by East Roman writers as descriptions of a certain group of barbarians only in the 550s (though Procopius's assignation of the raids of some time in the 520s to the same people may have been hindsight).

The Slavs themselves preserved very few of their own traditions concerning their origin. One document, the *Bavarian Geographer*, reports that the Slavs originated in the territory of the *Zeriuani* (which may have been a report of a genuine Slav tradition rather than a bookish invention). Unfortunately, this tribe is totally impossible to locate on the map (attempts to link it with the later tribal union of the Severiane on the east bank of the Dniepr seem a false lead). The *PVL* reports that the Slavs originated in the south on the Danube. This Danubian origin was accepted by many medieval chroniclers such as Wincenty

Kadłubek (1206) and Jan Długosz (writing 1455–80) in Poland and a whole series of Czech chroniclers beginning with Cosmas of Prague in the twelfth century, and was maintained by later Russian writers. The South Slavs held the theory in high regard for the prestige it bestowed, but also supported the use of the Slav liturgy in their churches. In some discussions of the origin of the Slavs some credence is given to this tradition (for example in the work of the linguist O. N. Trubachev). It does not seem to be very well supported by the archaeological evidence however and we know that this account was originally offered as a consequence of deriving the early history of the Rus from Scripture.

From the beginning of the modern study of the history of the Slavs, it seemed that, of all the disciplines, linguistics was the one which held out the most hope in the search for the original location of the area where the Proto-Slavic language(s) were spoken. The primary data have been the linguistic and philological data, the use of river names (hydronyms), the analysis of place names, the appearance of supposed Slavic ethnonyms in old written sources, the terminology for climatic, topographical, floral and faunal phenomena, and on the basis of modern divisions between the Slav languages. Despite the considerable effort and countless hours of erudite thought and discussion and conflict expended on this problem, the linguistic search for a 'Slav homeland' seems so far to have proved abortive, inasmuch as a variety of mutually exclusive theories have been proposed, contested, modified and dropped (some to be revived again decades later). None of them has been able to withstand criticism. There seems to have been a lack of agreement on the methods to be used and what phenomena were or were not suitable for use as evidence in the investigations. These problems incline one to serious doubts about the viability of the methods used and indeed about the knowability of the location of the area where the Slav languages developed. A Warsaw linguist, Hanna Popowska-Taborska, has recently conducted a study of the various theories which have been presented and discussed over the past century or so. As the result of her survey, she found all of these suggestions wanting, and decided that we are not able to determine the origin of the Slav languages. She concluded her survey of the search for the location of this territory in which the Common Slavic language functioned in a very despairing tone:

after many decades of investigations and debate on the prehistory of the Slavs modern linguists have come almost at the same time to three extremely different theories which derive the ancestors of the Slavs:

- *from the region to the west of the middle Dniepr,*
- *from the area between the Oder and Vistula rivers,*
- *from the territory to the south of the Carpathians, in the Danube valley*

Can the matter of the study of ethnogenesis really be so hopeless?[18]

The matter is not completely hopeless: at least earlier suggestions based on the linguistic evidence, bringing the Slavs from the Near East or further afield, have now been abandoned. At least the area of search has been narrowed down to somewhere in the area where the Slavs are present today.

It might be suggested in the light of the concept mentioned earlier that some European languages may have reached their present location in the Neolithic, that the main period of spread of the Slav languages to cover the vast area between the Oder and the Dniepr may have taken place several thousand years ago. This would resolve the problem of explaining the expansion of the area inhabited by Slav-speaking groups in the early medieval period (but would make it a problem for prehistorians). There are however considerable problems in accepting this explanation. The primary one is the present close similarity of the Slav languages to each other, which, although we do not know much about the pace of linguistic change, is not what one would expect after several thousand years' development in communities scattered over such a wide area. Another feature falsifying this argument is that we know that within this wide area other languages came and went without having a perceptible localized effect on the Slav languages in the areas affected. These two factors suggest that the spread of the Slavic languages in their present form is a relatively recent phenomenon. If this is a process which occurred in the more recent past it may be suggested that we can find some trace in the archaeological and historical record of the process or processes to which these linguistic changes were related and which may explain how these languages may have spread from an original core area.

We have to start with the evidence from areas and times when we know that the Slavs were already in a territory. The search would start on the Danube at about the time when the written sources tell us that the *Sklavinoi* settled in this area and began to raid the East Roman Empire. Similar material culture was used by those Slavs which settled in the Balkans at a later date. We may also look in the area where the evidence suggests that Slav languages were spoken at an early date, such as Moravia, Bohemia, the Ukraine and other areas where we suspect that there was Early Slav settlement. By examining the archaeological material, we find that in these areas the Early Slavs are represented archaeologically by a limited range of very unpromising-looking material.

Most of the remains of their material culture found in excavations are utilitarian, small in quantity and very unprepossessing in character. Unlike the majority of earlier populations in this area, they used very few metal ornaments. Most of the material of this first phase of Slav culture consists of handmade and bonfire-fired gritty pottery of a restricted range of forms. This material, when compared with the fine fabrics of the pottery of the Przeworsk, Wielbark and Cherniakhovo cultures, has an extremely 'home-made' look. The dominant form found in the first phase of Early Slav culture comprises medium-sized cooking-pots with undifferentiated profile, the assemblages of so-called 'Prague type' (Fig. 11); these contrast very strongly with the various shapes and presumed functions of the much of pottery of the previous period. On the majority of the sites excavated, this pottery and animal bones are the main material found. It is unsurprising therefore that the study of the Early Slavs (like that of some other prehistoric peoples) has by default to be a study in pottery typology. We should not however forget that the pottery was primarily a functional item in a functioning household; thus its typology has significance in the context of the function and symbolism of the vessel form and decoration (or lack of either).

Slav settlement sites contain one other element which is characteristic: small square sunken-floored huts with internal ovens (Fig. 9). These are especially characteristic of the earliest phases of Slav culture and disappear as a characteristic building form in about the eighth or ninth century. These huts are sunken into the ground about half a metre to a metre (or sometimes more) and had wooden walls supporting a pitched roof. The stone-built ovens are especially characteristic and were situated in the corner furthest from the door – often this meant that they were on the north (cold) side of the hut. These huts probably did not have a long life; the building material was usually pine which has a relatively short life in the damp soil, and many of these huts were probably abandoned after about ten to fifteen years of use (few show signs of major repairs). The family may then have built another hut nearby, or moved to a new settlement site. Only a few people could live in any one hut, and probably extended families had several huts situated close to another. Settlements contain few other features.

Burials are rare: the ratio in the Ukraine in the sixth to eighth centuries would seem to be about six burial sites to every hundred known settlements; in Poland at the same time the figures are similar. They are usually simple urned cremations in small flat cemeteries or (rarely) under mounds, though in some areas (for example the west) other burial rites prevailed (see Chapter 9). None of the earliest Slav settlements is defended by an earthen rampart. Communally built earth and timber strongholds become increasingly common and characteristic among the Slavs only after the seventh century and are a prime source of information on settlement and social structure (see Chapter 5).

Where had these people and the material culture they used come from? Many of the types found in Early Slav assemblages have affinities with earlier material; thus the typical pottery may be degenerate continuation of a range of relatively formless handmade vessels found across central Europe and in the Ukraine (Przeworsk, Cherniakhovo and Kievan Cultures). The sunken-floored huts are also found in a more restricted area (mainly in the Cherniakhovo Culture zone). They take on a more specific character and occur consistently together only in the fifth century in a few restricted zones of eastern Europe.

There have been a great number of theories based on an amalgamation of the archaeological, historical and linguistic evidence accounting for the origins of the Slav languages and the peoples who spoke them. It is not the aim of this chapter to recount all of these theories, their archaeological and linguistic justification or the historical conditions under which some were created and some abandoned. The story is a fascinating and complex one, as various scholars have competed with each other to find the earliest Slav assemblages to prove that it was in a certain territory (often their own country) that one should seek the *Urheimat* of the Slavs. Unfortunately there is space here only for the introduction of a bare outline containing basic information about the most enduring of these theories (Fig. 8).

One of the earliest theories which has had an important effect on the way we see the origins of the Slavs was I. Borkovský's suggestion that certain features of the 'Prague-type' pottery he identified suggested that they had an origin among the native peoples of the Bohemian basin. This theory angered the Nazi authorities in the Protectorate of Bohemia and Moravia and his book was soon withdrawn from sale. The fact that his theory was seen as anti-German was one of the reasons why the Prague culture attained an early popularity.[19]

In the early years of Soviet archaeology, the Cherniakhovo Culture itself was seen as the archaeological reflection of the Proto-Slavs. This was the proposition of B. A. Rybakov, who published a short article in which he linked it to the series of metal finds known as 'Antiquities of the Antes' and attributed both to the Slavs,[20] arguing that the archaeological distribution of both coincided with Jordanes's description of the territory inhabited by the Antes. The association between the Slavs and the Cherniakhovo Culture was enthusiastically advocated after the war by the Russian archaeologists P. N. Tretiakov and M. I. Artamonov, and a number of Ukrainian archaeologists. This required the extension of the chronology of the culture to the seventh century AD.[21]

The theory of the origin of the Slavs in this area was revived by Irena Rusanova to give the Slavs a respectable fifth-century ethnogenesis in the Polesie region of the Ukrainian SSR. To serve that purpose she renamed Borkovský's Prague type (considered by her the 'Prague-Korchak' type) and used sites excavated in the Zhitomir area to establish an archaeological basis for a 'true' Early Slav culture.[22] The existence of early sites in the Polesie region is also supported by some Belarussian archaeologists on the evidence of the site at Ostrov near Pinsk, where handmade pottery of Korchak type (though with ceramic traits similar to northern sites such as a more biconical form and stabbed zones below the rim) has been found in square huts with corner hearths and Late Cherniakhovo fibulae and other metal objects.[23]

One of the other popular theories – proposed first by Tretiakov – identified the Kiev Culture of the middle and upper Dniepr region in the northern forest zone (in the former Belarussian SSR) as the archaeological manifestation of Slav-speaking populations in the period immediately before their expansion.[24] This derives from an older Soviet conception that the Iron Age Zarubinets Culture represented the Proto-Slavs. The Kiev Culture was recognized only at the end of the 1950s and beginning of the 1960s mainly by the work of V. N.

Danilenko. It seems to have been derived from the Zarubinets Culture of the Iron Age. Kiev assemblages are characterized by a series of handmade pottery vessels tending towards a baggy form, but with a predominance of vessels with a weak but sharp shoulder well below the rim. Flat round clay plates were presumably used to bake on. Metal objects include a variety representing influences from the Cherniakhovo Culture as well as the forest zone. The most interesting feature is however the use of square sunken-floored huts with internal hearths in the corner, reminiscent of those which appear in Early Slav settlements a century or so later. Graves consist of large pits in which pottery and burnt bones are mixed with ashes and earth.[25] The culture arose in the third century and lasted probably into the fifth. In the fifth century, in the place of the Kiev Culture, the Kolochin Culture develops: some scholars (for example Michał Parczewski), on the grounds of similarity of the archaeological material with Early Slav cultures, identify both as Proto-Slav. Although the Kiev Culture is situated in an area of old Baltic hydronyms, its possible role in the formation of the Slavs cannot be ruled out.

Another proposition saw the material culture of the Slavs as deriving in a wider zone, linking it with developments in the latest phase of the Przeworsk Culture (occupying roughly the area of modern Poland). This was the proposition of the Polish archaeologist Józef Kostrzewski, as much based on archaeological considerations as on patriotic (or rather anti-Nazi) ones, but it was also taken up by several Soviet scientists such as Valentin Sedov and Irena Rusanova.[26] This had the consequence of identifying the Bronze and Iron Age Lusatian Culture of the area between the Oder and Vistula rivers as the Proto-Slavs, a position vehemently defended by the great Polish archaeologists of the Poznań school, Kostrzewski, Konrad Jażdzewski and Witold Hensel. We will examine this idea further in the next chapter when discussing the so-called 'northern tradition'.

Another interesting idea was proposed in the 1950s, when Yugoslavian historians and linguists proposed a concept of a Slav homeland in Pannonia. They saw Prague-type pottery as developing there from 'Dacian' pottery. The Slovenian archaeologist Josip Korošec criticized the Soviet attempts to find a Slav homeland in the Soviet Union (and the inability in the 1950s to find there material of Slav type which could be dated as earlier than the Prague-type pottery).[27] This interpretation of course was closely related to the tenor of Soviet–Yugoslav relations of the late 1950s. There were other Yugoslav archaeologists however who could find nothing in the material culture of the area which should date earlier than the sixth century.

New ideas were introduced in the late 1970s and early 1980s in Ukraine, with Volodymyr D. Baran switching the emphasis from Polesie to the Carpathian foothills of the upper Dniestr and upper Prut region, where it has been claimed that the Early Slav material culture crystallized in the fifth century among people in contact with the users of ultimate Cherniakhovo Culture material.[28] This model of a Slav homeland has also been adopted by the Cracow scholars Kazimierz Godłowski and his disciple Michał Parczewski.[29] It was in this general area that in the Roman period a specific cultural zone had developed, characterized by a principal burial rite under earthen mounds, though these Carpathian Kurhans (mid third to mid/late fifth century) contain pottery and fibulae similar to those in use in the Cherniakhovo Culture (Map I). Excavations (for example at Kodyn and Rashkov)[30] started to produce evidence from the fills of typical square sunken-floored huts, suggesting that the earliest Slav pottery in this area was there contemporary with wheel-made pottery but also with the use of Late Cherniakhovo fibulae, making this pottery some of the earliest that could be reliably dated. The dating of these sites seems to be fifth century. Similar sites are found around the flank of the eastern Carpathians along the Dniestr, Prut, Seret and Southern Bug (Boh) with similar huts and early pottery of this type (Map II). The most characteristic element of these assemblages is a series of baggy vessels of undistinguished profile. The pottery assemblages of this group are rather monotonous, small and medium-sized vessels without decoration, handmade and bonfire-fired at relatively low temperatures. Alongside these vessels occasionally occur round ceramic plates, probably used for baking unleavened bread over hearths. Another characteristic trait of this group is the square sunken-floored huts with corner ovens of stone. The area of Ukraine immediately east of the sites on the Carpathian flanks has produced a second zone of fifth-century metalwork, some of it associated with Early Slav material. All these assemblages are in the forest-steppe zone in an area producing material of ultimate Cherniakhovo type but on the northern fringe of the former Cherniakhovo area and beyond that occupied by the Huns.

Material of similar early date has also been claimed from Moldavia (Moldava) further down the Prut and Dniestr. This has been named the Costişa-Botoşana pottery group, consisting of handmade wares which can be found with wheel-made pottery, and dated to the fifth or very beginning of the sixth century. At one of these sites at Hansca, near Kishinev in Moldova, a bronze mirror of the Chmi-Brigetio type found in Hunnic contexts and dated to the mid-400s was associated with similar pottery.[31]

Florin Curta has pointed out that further to the southeast there are a number of late fifth- and early sixth-century sites along the north bank of the Danube (in Walachia, Romania) which are chronologically comparable with and of a similar character to the material from the western Ukraine. These include a late fourth- to early fifth-century settlement at Ciresanu (Prahova district). A late fifth-century brooch with bent stem was found at Dragosloveni, in a sunken building. In both cases these artefacts were associated with handmade pottery resembling Korchak type. Some of the graves in the famous Sărata Monteoru cemetery have fibulae and belt buckles of late fourth- and early fifth-century types.[32] These sites appear just before 500 after a period of about a century when there is a total break in settlement pattern in the area.

The archaeological evidence from several of these areas seems to suggest a relationship between the rise of this type of material culture and changes which occurred in the Cherniakhovo Culture as a result of the Hun invasions of c. 375–400, the rise of Hun prestige and power, and then the collapse of Attila's hegemony in the 450s. These stormy events set the scene for the rise of a recognizable Slav material culture and the crystallization of an identifiable Slav cultural identity. It would seem that these changes also were responsible for initiating its spread, and likely that later westward expansion of the victorious Huns was accompanied by arrival of the first Slav-speaking settlers in the Danube region. This is primarily suggested by the spread of material culture of the types discussed (which is at a later date relatively firmly associated with the Slavs). We have seen that there is one slight piece of unexpected literary evidence in support of this hypothesis: some of the participants at Attila's funeral are reported to have used the word *strava* for the funeral feast, and this has been claimed as a Slavic term (as indeed it may well have been). The crystallization of a Slav identity is clearly a process occurring on the eastern and southeastern fringes of the Hun hegemony, and Slav warriors may have partaken of the fruits of Hun victories and taken opportunities created by their collapse. It may have been as part of Hun hordes that the methods of fighting of the Slavs underwent transformation; they may well have placed more emphasis on fighting on horseback than hitherto, making them a more mobile and faster-moving fighting force.[33] The influence of the nomadic hegemonies of eastern Europe in the formation of Slav speaking groups should perhaps not be underestimated.[34]

The apparently fairly sudden appearance of a relatively uniform material culture in the fifth century after the collapse of the classical Cherniakhovo Culture (together with its subsequent spread into areas of central Europe where we know from written sources that Slavs were penetrating) suggests that we can see here a material reflection of the appearance of Slav self-identification. The Slavs had presumably previously inhabited at least some of these areas alongside communities of other linguistic and ethnic affinities, and they were to fill the vacuum left by the collapse of the old order.

Two processes seem to have been involved in this initial phase of the crystallization of Slav identity and expansion of their culture. It is not clear to what extent the rapid spread of this culture across the area was due to migration; certainly there is little evidence of rapid depopulation in the areas suggested as Slav 'homelands'. Bearing in mind the demographic problems caused by a simplistic migrationist theory, a second mechanism would seem to have operated. This would be a process of accretion, the initial small groups of Slav-speakers being augmented for various reasons by newcomers from other local populations who then adopted the identities and mores of the new group (a 'created' rather than 'handed-down' ethnic identity). Whether or not at the moment of crystallization of the material culture these people were all Slav-speaking is debatable, but it seems that by the end of the period under consideration dialects of the Slav languages had been adopted by most of those professing these lifestyles.

The new cultural models were simpler than those of the fourth and early fifth century, less spectacular in contrast to those of many of the Late Roman period barbarian groups. The simplicity of the more spartan and egalitarian culture of the Prague and Korchak types however clearly had something attractive for great numbers of the population over considerable areas of central Europe. From the fifth century the *Restgermanen* and the users of the culture of the Early Slavs inhabited mutually exclusive zones. For most of the fifth to eighth centuries, there is little evidence of contact between these two completely different social systems, or indeed of outright hostility between for example Gepids and Slavs on the Danube.

2

Expansion and Assimilation: the Sixth Century

The first stages of the development of the Early Slavs in central and eastern Europe are among the most important in the process of the historical and cultural development of this area, and yet the written sources are unevenly spread both geographically and chronologically, while the archaeological evidence is even more difficult to interpret. In particular, the dating of the Early Slav settlements in this area is a most difficult problem, as there are few chronological 'fixed points'. Some previous attempts at producing a chronology have it seems involved a certain degree of assumption and wishful thinking. Recent changes in the way that the dating of the early material has been seen (particularly as a result of a more critical approach to the sources and a more widespread use of dendrochronology) allow us to attempt to examine the development of the situation following the crystallization of the Early Slavs in three main chronological stages. Two main types of evidence may be used here. The evidence from written sources gives us a lot of information on the events and phenomena affecting the area along the Danube (both inside and outside of the Roman and Byzantine frontier), a picture which the archaeological evidence neatly supports. Further from the frontier we are much more reliant on the archaeological evidence to construct a picture of the societies we are studying (and we should resist the temptation to extrapolate the data from the written sources beyond the area to which they are applicable).

We have seen that the linguistic evidence strongly suggests that the Slav languages and a Slav identity formed in a restricted area from where they seem to have spread over wide areas of Europe. The process of this expansion is still poorly understood. It is difficult to explain how it is possible that a relatively small number of Slav-speaking settlers from the east were able in a comparatively short time (two centuries) not only to take over a very large area of central Europe but also apparently effectively to wipe out most pre-existing cultural, linguistic and ethnic divisions in the area and overlay it with their own materially unimpressive pan-Slavic culture.

In the past, migration of populations was the preferred explanation of many changes in the archaeological material; now the scholar would be more inclined to demand an explanation of migration. The movement of families and all their goods, livestock, seed for the next year and food for the journey was not a decision which would have been taken lightly and we are ignorant of the reasons for, and mechanisms of, this process. This explanation of the spread of the Slav languages also involves considerable demographic problems. The rate of reproduction involved to fill the new territories with descendants of a small original population, no matter how the figures are calculated, is biologically impossible. It may also be stated that there is no evidence that there was wholescale depopulation of any of the territories claimed as the homeland of the Slavs in this period to reflect large-scale folk movements. The settlement of new lands by the Slavs should not perhaps be thought of as the result of a powerful wave of people which flooded into new territories. It was probably a long-term process taking place over many decades. The concept of mass migration should be supplemented by notions of small-scale movements of the 'wave of advance' model (or like the growth of the veins in blue cheese), the cumulative effect of which over a period of time – in the absence of restricting factors – leads to a general expansion of the area inhabited by the group as a whole.[1]

One possible solution is to hypothesize that there may have been a population over parts of this area which was especially prone to accepting or unable to resist Slav culture and was thus assimilated into the new groups. In some areas of central Europe, it may even have already been in part Slav-speaking.[2] The Slavs were clearly able to absorb individuals from other populations (this process is specifically noted in the East Roman written sources with respect to the Danubian Slavs). The analysis of Slav material culture (especially of the South Slavs), and results of some anthropological investigations, as well as (though to a lesser extent) the loan-words in philological studies, clearly demonstrates the significant biological and cultural contribution of the previous populations of these territories in the make-up of some of the Slav populations.

It is not clear precisely to what extent the archaeologically visible decline of identifiable material marking the collapse of the Germanic-type material culture in the fifth century in the northern areas of central Europe represents near-total depopulation. Perhaps there were people living in the central European forest zone who are extremely difficult to detect archaeologically? If so, who were they? It is possible that a certain degree of depopulation could lead to social and economic collapse which in turn disrupts social organization, and limits the production and acquisition of objects such as craftsman-made pottery, fine metalwork and the use of (for example) typical Germanic halls.[3] The disappearance of these traits need not mean the disappearance of the original population from this area, simply that the material culture had changed and was no longer being used to express 'German-ness'. It is equally possible that a Germanic elite left the area, and that, for one reason or another, the population left behind preferred not to use cultural markers of Germanic type. Perhaps we are seeing an expression of a changed world outlook on the collapse of the old social order, in which the Germanic-style zone with its extensive use of prestige goods and competitiveness was replaced by a styleless and more egalitarian material culture.[4]

Phase 1: *c.* 500–550

In western European archaeology the Migration period of the fifth and early sixth centuries is the time of the migration of barbarian tribes into the decaying Roman Empire. In the case of central Europe however it would be more appropriate to talk of two migration periods. The first lasts from the last decades of the fourth century and first half of the fifth, and is represented by a general thinning and disappearance of evidence for occupation of vast territories by Germanic tribes. In some areas there is a phase connected with the presence of the Huns.[5] The second migration period in central Europe is the appearance of material culture which seems to represent the Early Slavs. The precise chronological relationship between the two phenomena in different regions (and in particular the length of a hiatus between them) has not yet been established.

The first stage of the process of the lateral extension of Slav culture may be considered as shown by the extent of the earliest Korchak-type pottery and small square sunken-floored buildings. The extent of Slav settlement in the early sixth century is shown in Map II, from which it can be seen that the spread of this culture went in four directions:

- along the east flank of the Carpathians (through Moldavia and east Romania) towards the Danube plain and Balkans
- along the north flank of the western Carpathians (through southern Poland)
- along the south flank of the western Carpathians (west Slovakia and Moravia to Bohemia and through to Polabia), towards the middle Danube and Elbe
- eastwards into the Ukraine.

We shall consider each of these areas in turn below.

There are two alternative models of the appearance of the Slavs on the Danube plain opposite the northern frontiers (*limes*) of the Balkan provinces of the East Roman Empire. The first is that this is one of the primary areas of crystallization of the Slav cultural identity marked by the presence of late fifth- and early sixth-century settlements, suggesting that by the middle of the sixth century the Slavs were already settled in this area (Chapter 1).[6] The second alternative is to postulate that the appearance of Slavs in this area is due to some form of migration or penetration of this area at the very beginning of the sixth century perhaps in part to fill the gaps left by depopulation left by earlier movements of other groups which had moved into the Empire. The most likely direction for such a movement would be people moving south from the alleged core area in western Ukraine and Moldavia along the Prut river and narrow plains at the foot of the eastern arc of the Carpathians (through Moldavia and east Romania) before reaching the plains alongside the lower Danube and then extending along the north bank of the Danube.[7] These population movements would have followed the forest-steppe zone to occupy the Danubian Plain; a trace of such settlers may be the assemblages of Costişa-Botoşana type.

The ethnic situation in the area of the Danubian Plain at the beginning of the sixth century was extremely complex, with several strong groups of *Restgermanen* (Longobards, Gepids and Heruli among them) along the frontier.[8] Whatever the mechanism by which the Slavs arrived here, the reaction of the East Roman Empire may suggest that they perceived some kind of threat in unrest on the opposite bank of the Danube. The Slavs however did not yet attract the attention of writers in Constantinople by their warlike stance, from which one may infer that if any such folk movements of Slavs took place at this period we should envisage it perhaps more as a relatively peaceful expansion of migrating disorganized peasant communities towards the Roman frontiers. In general here the Early Slav material (found in Walachia, Moldavia and southeast Transylvania) appears outside the areas of concentrated Germanic settlement.

The written sources suggest that relative stability and peace lasted within the Slav territories (Danubian Sclavenia) outside the Roman and East Roman frontiers on the Danube through several decades of the sixth century. The apparently peaceful mode of the consolidation of Slav settlement encouraged close contact between the new peoples and the local population which hastened the processes of acculturation of the new arrivals, as well as the assimilation and Slavization of part of the indigenous population. The area seems to have been inhabited by a mixture of autochthonous populations mixing with foreign elements, among which (and probably its most dynamic element) were the Slavs. When the raids started later, the contribution of people brought from the East Roman Empire as slaves in the ethnic and cultural make-up of this area was also probably considerable. The archaeological evidence of the sixth and seventh centuries of the area to the north of the lower Danube, in Walachia and Moldavia, between the east Carpathians and the Prut, is thus of particular interest. This was the zone of direct contact between the South Slavs and the East Roman Empire. As befits such a situation, the material culture indicates a mixture of different elements: local archaeologists have identified elements which they associate with Slavs, Romanized indigenous populations (sometimes referred to as 'Dacians'), and the Greeks of the East Roman Empire.[9]

The Slavs are indicated in the archaeological record primarily by their pottery (including vessels reminiscent of Korchak type) and cremation burial rites, but also by typical buildings of a type previously known from the Ukraine (square sunken-floored buildings with corner ovens). It is interesting that in Walachia these structures are typically equipped not with stone ovens (as in Ukraine and Moldavia) but with a specific form of clay ovens (with clay trays and clay rolls for maintaining the heat in the hearth area).[10] The indigenous populations are probably represented by certain other building types (such as sunken-floored buildings with free-standing fireplaces).

Romanian archaeologists have provisionally identified a number of regional pottery groups, such as the Ipoteşti-Candeşti-Ciurel Culture.[11] The pottery groups of the area typically contain an intermixture regarded as representing Slav, 'Romanized indigenous' and East Roman elements.[12] The handmade pottery which represents these Early Slavs on the Danube plain differs from that in Moldavia and is somewhat more variable in style than the normal Korchak type of the Ukraine. The 'Romanized indigenous' elements are represented in these pottery assemblages by a continuation of some types of handmade ceramic vessels related to the former Romanized Dacian Culture. An especially interesting feature of these sixth-century pottery assemblages is the frequent occurrence alongside these handmade wares of wheel-made vessels, the form of which is thought to be related to provincial Roman ones. In the opinion of some scholars however this concept requires re-examination, since for example the dominant form on sixth-century military sites on the *limes* was a so-called 'grey gritty ware', which is very rare on sites north of the Danube. There are also morphological differences, such as the paucity of handled pots in the quantity of ceramic material excavated on Romanian sites.[13] East Roman influences are also visible in the form of some ornaments (fibulae, star-shaped earrings) and the presence of coins, and even amphorae.

This transdanubian zone is of extreme importance to our understanding of the Slav phenomenon as a whole. The area to the north of the lower Danube and the Danube delta was an area of crystallization of a Slav identity as much as the areas further to the northeast.[14] Here the adoption of a 'Slav' identity by groups of originally mixed ethnic origin in the face of an 'us/them' relationship in the frontier zone (with respect both to the 'Romans' on one side of the political frontier, and to other pre-existing and competing 'barbarians') was probably a key factor in the cultural unification of these groups.

Another reason for the importance of this area was that it was here that the Sclavenes first come to the notice of the East Roman and East Roman chroniclers (such as Procopius) which are our main source of evidence for their activities. At this period, the Slavs were hardly noticed by western authors, and thus the East Roman and Byzantine sources are our main written source. These accounts are affected however by the very specific concepts the Greek writers had about the barbarians with whom they were confronted. This has not always been appreciated by modern historians and archaeologists, who sometimes took the 'facts' presented by these accounts very much for granted. Recent analysis of these texts has concentrated more on exploring the East Roman and Byzantine thought world and the consequent limitations of the Greek accounts of the Slavs. It seems that as elsewhere the East Roman authors had used classical models to describe these 'others'. An example might be their use of the term 'democracy' in this context which is quoted approvingly by some historians, unaware that it was probably used in a pejorative sense to condemn the *ataxis* (disorder) of the barbarian world, in contrast to the rigid order (*taxis*) of the rigidly hierarchical civilized world (*oikoumene*).[15] Such a situation prompts caution in using these written sources, but does not negate their value totally. It would seem that, far from their having exclusively egalitarian societies, the various raids and incursions of the Slavs into East Roman territory must have been organized under some form of leadership (see below).

Notwithstanding these problems, we may find in these texts some information which seems useful and worth discussing. The written sources tell us for example of the presence by the middle of the sixth century of at least two groups, the Sclaveni and the Antes. Procopius writing in the early 550s (*Wars* I, V.27, 2) includes the information that 'the Sclavenoi and Antes . . . have their homelands on the River Istra not far from its northern bank'. Procopius's ideas of the geography of the area north of the frontier are however vague (he even thought that the Caucasus mountains extended round the Black Sea into Thrace: *Wars* VIII.3, 3). We have already seen that Jordanes, writing about the same time (*De Origine* V.34), informs us that the Sklaveni inhabited the territory from the town of Noviedunum and the Mursian lake to the Danaster (Dniestr) and northwards as far as the Vistula. The Antes occupied the area 'in the curve of the Pontian Sea spread from the Danaster to the Danaper[Dniepr], rivers that are many days' journey apart'. (We have discussed one aspect of this reference in the previous chapter.) Some scholars are inclined to go further in the location of these groups, but it should be noted that, despite their claims, neither the written or the archaeological materials allow us to define any boundaries to the areas occupied by these two named groups.

While the name of the Sclaveni persisted, probably owing to their role in the eventual colonization of the Balkans, that of the Antes disappears after being mentioned mostly as warriors in the company of the Avars in the works of a few East Roman writers.[16] These writers in their 'ethnographic' descriptions mostly treat the Antes as equals of the Sclaveni in almost all respects (as noted earlier, Procopius even tells us that they originally shared the name Spori); only in respect to their political history do they become separated in the writers' conciousness.[17]

From the beginning of the sixth century there were frequent raids by both Sclaveni and Antes across the Danube into Byzantium. Procopius in his *Secret History* as a criticism of Justinian says (XVIII.20) that 'the Huns, Sclavenes and Antes almost every year since Justinian came to power over the Romans' had been mounting their attacks. In his *Wars* (VIII.40, 5) however he says that the Antes attacked in the reign of Justin (518–27) when they were beaten back in a decisive and bloody victory by Germanus, a member of the imperial family and the commander of all the forces in Thrace. The Slav raids intensified in frequency and scale in the reign of Justinian from the 530s. Justinian's reign was characterized by extensive military expeditions to restore the frontiers of the former West Roman Empire, and it would seem that this inevitably left parts of the northern frontiers poorly manned. Hardly a year went by in this period without a major raid of the Slavs sometimes together with other peoples. These raids were to reach far into imperial territory. In 531 a new commander, Chilbudius, was appointed on the Thracian section of the frontier, and in his three-year term of office he not only halted the raids of the 'Huns, Sclavenes and Antes' but carried out attacks on their homelands. It was in one of these raids that he met a larger Sclavene army than expected and was killed. According to Procopius, this was the beginning of the failure to prevent massed raids of these peoples (*Wars* VII.14 1–36).[18] In 540 there was also a devastating raid of the Kutrigurs, a Hunnic tribe.

Procopius gives us (*Wars* VII.40, 1–8) an interesting account of the attacks of the Sclavenes in 550 when Justinian's cousin Germanus was setting off to fight the Ostrogoths. The Sclavenes crossed the Danube and were heading for Thessalonica, but when the Emperor heard this he called off the attack to use the troops to defend the threatened area. When the Sclavenes heard that Germanus (who was well known to them as the commander who had decimated the Antes three decades earlier) was at Serdika (Sophia), they decided to cross the Illyrian mountains to raid Dalmatia. Germanus therefore decided that these attacks were not such a great threat to Constantinople's interests in the Balkans and was about to recommence his march to Italy but died. These events however are of interest in that there is a strong suspicion that the Sclavene attack was prompted by Totila, king of the Ostrogoths, in order to delay the Roman attack. If so, this would be clear evidence of contact between a western leader and the Sclavenes, and this was the context of Jordanes's text, written on the eve of the Ostrogothic defeat by Justinian's general, Narses.

While East Roman writers paint the Sclavenes and Antes with one brush, they also tell us of inter-group conflicts. We hear of one of these events about 545/6 (Procopius, *Wars* VII.13, 24–XIV 36) when the Antes were at war with the Sclavenes. Soon after this we learn that Justinian offered the Antes the site of Turris, an abandoned fort which had been founded by Trajan on the left bank of the Danube, and the lands around it with the payment of a large sum if they would be imperial allies. The site concerned is perhaps today's town of Turnu-Măgurele at the confluence of the Olt and Danube. The Antes were to use this as a base to protect this portion of the frontier against 'Hun' attacks as *foederati*. It cannot be ruled out that the aim of Constantinople was to revive the quarrel between the Sclavenes and Antes which had just previously been resolved. This is the context of the 'phoney Chilbudius' story reported by Procopius: he was a man from the Antes whom they wished to have appointed as a Roman military commander to lead them and they tried to trick the Romans into believing that this was the real Chilbudius.[19] The Antes appear to have maintained their alliance with Constantinople for several decades until 602. Indeed soon after this treaty three hundred Antes were fighting the Ostrogoths in Lucania (*Wars* VII.22, 3).

The Balkans had already suffered several barbarian incursions: before the Slavs, the area had been visited by Visigoth and Ostrogoth hordes. By now the area was in a poor economic state. This is most visible in the impoverishment of Greece before 550. The area was not spared natural disasters: in 541 according to Procopius several urban areas were hit by a plague spreading from Constantinople – a mass grave found at Corinth would seem to be a trace of this or a similar event. Several violent earthquakes levelled Corinth and other adjacent towns. The archaeological evidence shows that in Athens and Corinth public buildings were abandoned and dismantled and houses and flour and olive mills were built in their ruins. Obviously the towns were becoming more 'ruralized': burial begins within their walls and monumental buildings cease to function. Only Thessalonica seems to have escaped these processes. Economic decline and troubled times are the joint factors explaining the depositions of an increasing number of hoards in the Balkans in the sixth and seventh centuries.[20]

As a result of the Slav threat, Justinian undertook the strengthening of the northern frontiers of the empire, restoring many of the Danubian forts and building new ones. This took place in the 530s to 550s. Very few forts on the Danubian *limes* do not exhibit traces of work done in Justinian's reign. A study of coin hoards demonstrates that the period around the 550s coincides with an economic 'closure' of the frontier, demonstrated by the complete disappearance of Roman coins reaching barbarians north of the Danube river in contrast to the previous decade or two (mainly during the reigns of Anastasius and Justin I) of renewed contacts between the two banks. This expensive defence system – described by Procopius in his *Buildings* – was however only partly successful in keeping the Slavs at bay, and the standing imperial army was relatively ineffective in dealing with the small mobile Slav fighting forces. Justinian's countermeasures however were only to have the effect of making the Slav raiding parties organize themselves more adequately to the task which now faced them.

Justinian also refortified existing and building new forts in the interior of the peninsula, for example near important passes through the Balkan mountains. There are remains of a large number of small to medium fortified sites all over the region, all of which seem to have been occupied for a brief period during the second half of the sixth and first two decades of the seventh century. Procopius tells us about peasants in Greece who had been turned into 'makeshift soldiers' (*Buildings* IV.2) and that Justinian had 'made the defences so continuous in the estates, that each farm either has been converted into a stronghold or lies adjacent to one which is fortified' (*Buildings* IV.1), though this probably refers more to the situation around Byzantium than deeper into the Balkans.

The second area where there was extensive expansion by the Slavs was along the north flank of the Carpathians. From the zone of earliest sites in Moldavia, the cluster of early sites of Early Slav material extends westwards along the north flank of the Carpathians, through southern Poland.[21] The earliest sites (the Mogiła group – or 'phase'), probably early sixth century, are situated in the southeast part of the country, in the region of Cracow. The sites include Cracow (Nowa Huta – Mogiła),[22] Bachorz and several others. At the moment there are relatively few sites of the Mogiła Group known. It is characterized by the familiar square sunken-floored huts with corner ovens, but, unlike the Korchak Culture further east, no certain cemeteries are known. The pottery vessels are tall and slim in shape, though in later phases tending towards a squatter form. This Mogiła group seems closely related to the Korchak Culture (and it is possible that in future it may be amalgamated with it). The date of the formation of the Mogiła group is unclear. It would seem to date to after the collapse of 'Germanic' cultures in southeast Poland (end of the fourth century or beginning of the fifth century),[23] but before the date of the metalwork hoard found in a pot in pit 45 at the Mogiła site: this is an important find because it also dates the beginning of the later phase of the Mogiła group (in which the vessels bear ornament) to the end of the sixth and beginning of the seventh century (Fig. 12).[24]

An important written source referring to this period reports the migration of the Heruli in 512 (Procopius, *Wars* VI.15, 1–4). This German tribe had been defeated in battle by the Longobards and split into two groups, one of which settled in Illyria, the second 'under the leadership of many men of royal blood passed through the territory of all of the Sclavenes', and after passing through a large area described as being completely deserted reached the territory of the Varnians (probably somewhere in the middle Elbe valley) before reaching Denmark *en route* to Thule (Scandinavia). This reference has been used to provide evidence of the rate of Slav expansion along the Oder route, and the empty area is thought to be Silesia.[25] This reference is however difficult to interpret, and it would seem unworthy of the reliance that some scholars have placed on it.[26]

A particularly interesting phenomenon occuring at this time in West Balt territory beyond the frontiers of Germanic and Slav settlement is the rise of the Olsztyn Culture (German *Mazurgermanische Kultur*). This is represented by a series of cemeteries in the Olsztyn region of northern Poland appearing in the second half of the fifth century but undergoing substantial changes just before the middle of the sixth century and lasting to the mid seventh century. These later graves contain metal objects with affinities in southern central Europe including types related to so-called Slav fibulae from the lower Danube delta (see below), and it has been suggested that they represent a group of mixed ethnicity but retaining close contacts with Germanic but also Slav cultures to the south. One site has produced pottery which its excavator feels is Slav.[27]

Another interesting phenomenon concerning north–south contacts is the flow of East Roman gold solidi to the southern coast of the Baltic, where they seem to have arrived by a mechanism involving movement among the *Restgermanen* of the area. This flow began in the late fourth century and increased in the period between 395 and 518, when it abruptly terminated.[28] Some investigators have linked this with the expansion into the intervening area by the Slavs cutting off the flow of coinage, but a particularly interesting fact is that these gold coins did not reach the Slavs themselves.[29] The archaeological evidence seems to suggest that the Early Slavs (at least on the North European Plain and forest zone) had little appreciation for or use for East Roman gold. It is interesting that the East Romans were able periodically to buy off the Avars with tribute (from the 560s to the 580s and 602–14) but this strategy was not really an option for them in their dealings with the Slavs. It would seem that Slavs measured their 'wealth' by other means than the accumulation of precious metals and its use in showy display as by the Avars.

The southwestern extent of the Mogiła group is unknown. It seems not unreasonable to link this with the cluster of sites south of the Carpathians in the Morava, Vah and Hron valleys (east Bohemia, west Slovakia). Some scholars (Z. Váňa, V. Baran) have seen this as resulting from a northwestward movement from the lower Danube plain, but the area west of the Iron Gates is relatively devoid of Slav settlement, and Avar–Slav settlement in the area after the 660s takes a different form. The earliest pottery of the Moravian sites consists of tall vessels similar to those of the Mogiła group and having analogies in the Korchak pottery of the Ukraine (but also including squat vessels characteristic of the later phases of the Mogiła group). In this area the pottery is also associated with the square sunken-floored buildings with corner ovens and flat cremation cemeteries with urned burials. Although some have claimed that these sites may date as early as the late fifth century, D. Jelínková dates the earliest pottery in Moravia to the sixth century, probably the middle to second half.[30] The earliest material from the Bohemian basin 100 km to the northwest (from which come the type-specimens of the Prague Culture) seems on the whole to be typologically later than the Moravian material.

We have at present relatively little information concerning the expansion eastwards and southeastwards in the Ukraine from the area where the Korchak material (named after a site on the Teterev near Zhitomir) first appears perhaps by the mid sixth century.[31] It seems that by the end of the sixth century the territory occupied by these groups extended over large areas of western Ukraine to the Dniepr in the east. The villages (Korchak and the somewhat later Ripniev)[32] were situated on the elongated terraces just above the floodplains of rivers, and were probably of short duration; they consist of shifting units of five to ten huts in contemporary occupation. The major building type was a small square sunken-floored hut with a stone-built oven in the corner. Small flat cremation cemeteries with urned and unurned burial are also the rule. The pottery forms are similar to those which we have seen elsewhere in central Europe at this period (though the Korchak type is of slightly different form from the material from further west, tending to be proportionally taller in respect to the greatest diameter, and the shoulders of the vessels are perhaps slightly better developed than in the western pots).

It is in this area (see p. 63) that some Soviet scholars would place the Antes ('the bravest of these people'), mainly on the strength of Jordanes's comments concerning their 'dwelling in the curve of the Pontian Sea spread from the Danaster to the Danaper, rivers that are many days' journey apart'. He is clearly referring here to the Dniestr and Dniepr, but what does 'dwelling in the curve of the Pontian Sea' imply? Do we imagine them as settled along the coast (on the steppes)? This information should be treated with some circumspection.

It is possible that in some parts of the Ukraine there was settlement from the northern forest zones by descendants of the Kiev Culture populations of the upper and middle Dniepr taking advantage of the changed social patterns and settlement networks arising from the political changes following the collapse of the Gothic state and Hun Empire. These people may have moved down the Dniepr to the south and southeast, and in interaction with other elements may have in some way been involved in the formation of the groups represented by the Korchak and the subsequent Penkovka Cultures (the problem of the Kolochin Culture is discussed below).

The precise length of this first phase of expansion of Slav culture is difficult to determine: the effects visible on Map II could have been the result of more than a century of expansion, or as little as fifty years. Although the effects may look modest, the areas of Slav settlement shown cover several thousand square kilometres and with a population density of several per square kilometre represent a considerable increase of population. We may suspect however that much of this was due in the first instance to the movement of Slav farmers seeking a better life (perhaps on the principle that 'the other man's grass is always greener') rather than military expansion. It would seem however that an equally important phenomenon was also the assimilation of populations met on the way. Such a process is hinted at by the written sources (see above, p. 58) telling us of the Slavs' eventual acceptance into their ranks of prisoners. One does wonder however whether some successful warrior bands formed in these areas may have not been gathering followers at this period.

Phase 2: c. 550–600

The expansion of the area of Slav settlement continued in the next half century, by the end of which we see signs of a consolidation of Slav settlement, and the stabilization of social organization. It is this second phase which sees the beginning of the process of the shaping of the full extent of Early Slav settlement. This now leaves in a decisive fashion its former concentration in the forest steppe zone, and starts to penetrate deeper into the forest zone of central and eastern Europe. Here, as in the earlier phase, the main source of information is the typology of the pottery, which over most of the area retained the broad characteristics of the Korchak-type material. Apart from this, the other material culture of the Early Slavs is remarkably consistent across the whole area from Polabia to Ukraine.

We observe in this period a further consolidation of Slav settlement in the Danube valley. The material north of the Danube has been interpreted by Maria Comşa as evidence of a so-called 'second wave' of Slav settlement formed by a population movement from central Ukraine (which some have linked with the Antes known from the written sources). In the mid sixth century the earlier Ipoteşti, Cindeşti, Ciurel and Costişa-Botoşana groups are replaced by material of the Suceava-Şipot type (initially identified on the basis of the excavation of a small cluster of houses in a salvage excavation for a pipeline). These assemblages consist of handmade pottery with extremely close affinities with the Penkovka material of the Ukraine found together with metalwork of ultimate Cherniakhovo type (including radiate fibulae, see below). Compared with the earlier groups, most of the material culture has a different character; most of its elements are linked to Slav material culture with fewer traces of intermixing with other populations, and these assemblages were initially taken to mean that at this period 'purely' Slavic settlements can be clearly distinguished from those of the native population.[33]

In the lower Morava and middle Danube valleys a discrete cluster of sites develops (in what is now southwest Slovakia and northeastern Austria) perhaps from about the middle of the sixth century after the area had been abandoned by the Germans in the fifth century.[34] This area was avoided by Longobards in the sixth century, but it was probably from here in about 545 that according to Procopius (Wars VII.35, 13–23) the exiled Longobard Prince Ildigis (Hildigis) together with a group of Slav and Gepid warriors moved southwards, crossing the Danube during the final phase of Justinian's Gothic Wars. After about 551 we hear very little of Slav raids: possibly this is due to the nature of the written record for this period, or maybe there was really a lull in large-scale Slav raids until the 570s.

The Slavs were still pressing in on Byzantium at the same time as Persian aggression to the east withdrew military attention and resources from the northern frontiers. The political and economic troubles of the East Roman Empire during the short reigns of Justinian's successors (565–78) were marked by raids of barbarians from beyond the Danubian frontiers deep into the Balkans.

The arrival of the Turkic-speaking Avar nomads in the lower Danubian area in the 560s further disrupted the situation.[35] The original Avars had been expelled from the destruction of a hegemony in the area of Mongolia, and after a spell on the Pontic steppes, with their numbers swollen with other peoples (including in all probability some Slavs), in 559–61 they settled on the north bank of the Danube, where they absorbed the Slavs already settled there. The East Romans attempted to enlist the aid of the nomad Avars to subdue the Slavs and other peoples north of the *limes* in return for payments from the East Romans to desist from raiding Byzantium. As a result, large quantities of imperial gold of the period were directed into the middle Danube valley and Carpathian basin as tribute (some of it being redistributed further to the north).[36] Avar attacks on their neighbours reached as far west as Thuringia (in 562–3) on the eastern edge of the Franks' lands. The Avars then became involved in a Longobard–Gepid conflict and destroyed the Gepids: they disappeared from history and the Avars occupied their lands. They then displaced the Longobards (who moved into the Roman Empire a few decades later (568) to take over Italy). The Avars themselves settled in the Carpathian basin (Justin II permitted them to settle in Pannonia by treaty in 570/1).[37] The struggles between the Slavs and the Avar newcomers over the strip of land along the lower Danubian frontier were bloody and were additionally fuelled by time-honoured East Roman policies of setting the one side against the other.

In 578 the Avars were asked by Justin II to attack the Slavs on the lower Danube frontier who were looting the East Roman territories. The Avars were allowed to pass through East Roman lands and were ferried across the Danube but it was in alleged furthering of these aims that the Avars also attacked East Roman territory and in 582 took Sirmium (Sremska Mitrovica, formerly in Gepid hands). This was the beginning of a series of Avar attacks which were to reach rich towns on the coasts of the Adriatic, Aegean and Black Seas. These attacks were especially serious in the 590s. It was in the wake of 'Avar' raids into the East Roman Empire throughout the later sixth and early seventh centuries that Slav raiders and later settlers penetrated these territories.

Soon after their settlement in Pannonia, and on the basis of their success in accumulating wealth and prestige in battle and as cash payments from the Empire, the Avars were soon able to establish a powerful hegemony in the Carpathian basin and on the middle Danube, dominating a large area of central Europe from the eastern Carpathians to the eastern Alps. As in the case of the Huns in a similar situation earlier, their warrior bands and settlements were peopled by men and women of diverse origins, including Slavs (and probably Bulgars). In the areas controlled by the Avars in the Danube area the Slav inhabitants were obliged to pay tribute and provide services for their overlords. In return, they were able to partake of the fruits of the political power of the Avars. In the early seventh century in a wide area south of the Carpathians (Moravia and Slovakia) the archaeological evidence demonstrates the emergence of a mixed Slav–Avar material culture, suggesting symbiotic coexistence. In particular it seems that elite fashions among the local inhabitants imitated the dress of the Avar aristocracy.[38] It has been suggested that the Slav language(s) served as a *lingua franca* in this ethnically mixed zone. This, coupled with a certain mobility within it and its wide extent, may prove to be one of the keys to understanding the spread of the Slav dialects south of the Carpathians. Certainly it is impossible to understand the southern Slavs at least without reference to the Avars.

The scale of Slav attacks on the Danubian frontiers and the Balkans was to increase again in the second half of the sixth century. It would seem that by the middle of the century the Slavs (particularly the Sclavenes) had become organized by some stronger form of military leadership capable of holding large warrior bands together, and the names of these leaders were to become well known by reputation to the inhabitants of the East Roman empire. We are told about some of the first of these larger-scale raids in great detail by Procopius, who informs us of large organized warrior bands up to three thousand strong (some of which split inside the East Roman Empire). In 547/8 (Procopius, *Wars* VII.29, 1–3) we hear of the raid of an army (*strateuma*) of Sclavenes which raided Illyria at will, and a fifteen-thousand-strong imperial army could not or would not engage with them. A little further on (*Wars* VII.38, 1–23) Procopius, describing the events of 549–50, gives a horrifying account of the Sclavene invasions of Illyria and Thrace. Attacking the fortified town of Topir on the Aegean coast near Byzantium, the Slavs first lured the garrison away from the walls where they perished in an ambush, and then took the town. Procopius states that these Slavs always slew the enemies they met. They reputedly murdered fifteen thousand civilians, men of all ages, and took only the women and children into slavery. The whole territory was covered in corpses which lay unburied on the roads. It is said that the men were not slain with swords or spears but by impaling on sharp stakes driven between the buttocks and erected vertically, or by beating about the head with sticks, or by being stretched out and tied between four posts driven into the ground. Others were burnt alive, shut into their huts with cattle and sheep which were too numerous to take back to the Slav homelands north of the Danube. While some of this may be literary topos, some of these observations probably had some grounding in fact. The Slav raids were accompanied not only by mass slaughter but also the capture of huge numbers of slaves, who were either resettled and put to work or ransomed. There are also accounts of the Slavs making off with huge herds of raided cattle. The written sources also mention that some prisoners taken from the Balkan areas after being freed stayed in the territories north of the Danube, were accepted into Slav society and did not return home (Pseudo-Maurice, *Strategikon* XI.4, 4–5).

In 550 Procopius tells us of a large group of Sclavenes who were preparing for an expedition to Thessalonica; with the news of the proximity of the imperial army led by Germanus they gave up this aim, and instead 'crossing all the mountains of Illyria, found themselves in Dalmatia' (Procopius, *Wars* VII.40, 7). The

Slavs were not always victorious: we also have letters from Pope Gregory I from 599 and 600 to the exarchate of Italy and the Dalmatian Bishop of Salona congratulating them on their victories over the Slavs (*Gregorii papae registrum epistolarum* IX.154, X.15).

In a couple of digressions in his book devoted to the Gothic Wars, Procopius gives us a lot of detail about the Slavs, those beyond the imperial frontiers as well as those inside. One passage in particular (*Wars* VII.14, 22–30) is frequently cited.[39] Here the author stresses that in contrast to the East Romans they had no centralized rule but were governed by 'democratic' decisions. In this 'ethnographic excursus' Procopius tells us that all the different groups spoke a single language. They worshipped pagan gods and spirits (see Chapter 9), they lived in scattered huts (*kalybai*, a word which expresses flimsiness) and often changed their place of abode. He describes their attire and weapons, and appearance: 'they are all tall and especially strong, their skin is not very white, and their hair is neither blond nor black, but all have reddish hair. They lead a primitive and rough way of life . . . and are always covered in dirt. They are neither dishonourable nor spiteful, but simple in their ways, like the Huns [Avars].' This account paints a picture of the Slavs' 'otherness' from the Byzantine world, and uses wording (such as the *kalybai*, which could also mean military tents) suggesting a military context for this information.

Another account written in 628–38 but referring to an earlier time has also been much used and abused in modern historiography. This is the mention by the author Theophilactus Simokattes (*Historia* VI.2, 10–16) of three men who were brought to the Emperor Maurice Tiberius in Heraclia (probably in 591/2). Theophilactus says:

> they were not equipped with any weapons or military equipment, their only burdens were citars [musical instruments] and they had nothing else with them . . . they said that they were from the tribe of the Sklavini, and they had their homes on the shores of the Western Ocean, and the [Avar] khan had sent embassies to them with rich gifts for their leaders in order to attract armed men to his army.

This reference would explain why Byzantine gold is found in the area north of the Avar territories. The three men claimed that they had been sent from the north to the Avar court with a refusal of help from their tribe(s), and the Avar khan had not allowed them to return home through his territory. They told the emperor that they carried musical instruments because they were not a warrior nation, and their land had no iron. This is indeed a tall story – one incidentally that the Emperor seems to have believed – and many modern scholars have followed him in his credulity, some even using it to prove the docility of their ancestors countering the rather bloody accounts of other East Roman sources. Theophilactus however seems to be reporting something which has been muddled with standardized idyllic images of barbarian life, and probably having no factual basis.[40] Quite apart from this, the account cannot be used – as some (such as the Polish historian H. Łowmiański) have attempted to use it – to prove that the Slavs had settled as far north as the Baltic coast. For one reason it may be noted that the Western Ocean was to the Greeks not the Baltic but the Atlantic. This much-quoted account cannot be relied on in any of its details.

It is about the middle of the sixth century that we observe clear signs of the strengthening of Slav settlement on the Danube. This is also the period when we observe the beginnings of the expansion of the Slavs to the south of the *limes*: their aim however was now not only to raid but also to settle in the richer lands of the East Roman Empire. Several types of evidence suggest very strongly that large areas of the countryside over most of the Balkans had already become seriously depopulated over the sixth century.[41] Very few examples of fifth- or sixth-century rural buildings have been excavated; the clay-bonded stone foundations of small rectangular buildings which have been found at Novgrad (Bulgaria) and Slava Rusa in Dobrudja (Romania) are exceptional. There are many reasons for this collapse of the rural infrastructure in the Balkan provinces.[42] The main one, apart from the obvious disastrous effects of repeated barbarian raids, seems to be that Justinian's legislation and fortification programme had seriously damaged what little was left of peasant life in the region. The whole political and economic system of the Balkans seems to break down, thus the monetary economy system collapses in Macedonia in the 560s and 570s (but in the Peloponnese in about the 650s; this is a reflection of the weakening Byzantine economy itself about the 650s).[43] Many of the towns of the area had gone into decline, and those that still survived as such were mainly on the coast where trade seems to have continued.

The process of settlement of Slavs in the Balkans increases in intensity at the end of the century (but ends about the middle of the seventh century, when considerable areas of the region were already relatively densely settled by the Slavs). The degree of Slav settlement in the area in the late sixth century is still debatable. In the past it was throught that the main area of settlement was in Lower Moesia along the Danube frontier zone in the area of Durosturum (now Silistra), and Bononia (now Vidin) where several rural sites have been found which were initially dated to this period, but now seem to be later, and the area behind the frontier thus less densley settled. It is notable that abandoned Roman forts were apparently not in general settled by Slavs in this period.

The end of the sixth century saw a serious weakening of East Roman hold over the Danube and the Balkans. Sirmium fell to the Avars and Slavs, and other bishoprics also fell, including Celeia, Emmona and Virunum. The movements of Slavs into the East Roman Empire (often accompanying Avar hordes) from the 570s and 580s are reported by Greek chroniclers such as Menander Protector (writing 582–4), who tells us of a Sclavene raid on Hellas in 578, and the *History* of Theophilactus Simokattes. In addition to describing the Slav raids within the empire, these writers also give us stories of events outside the *limes*, including the names of powerful leaders in such a way as we may believe they were well known by reputation to their readers. We have an almost contemporary account by John of Ephesus writing (about 585) of events in 581–4 in the reign of Maurice Tiberius when:

the accursed people the Slavs arose and passed through the whole of the Hellades, through Thessaly and Thrace, conquering many towns and forts, wasted and burnt, looted. They overcame the country and settled it freely and without fear as if it were their own, and strange to say to the present day inhabit it and sit secure in the lands of the [East] Romans without fear or cares, plundering, murdering, and burning, enriching themselves and robbing gold and silver, herds of horses and much weaponry, and they have learnt to conduct war better than the Romans.

Other sources (including the *Miracles* of St Demetrius, John of Biclar, and Evagrius) tell us that the Avars were invading the same areas about this time, and we may assume that there were many Slavs in these Avar hordes.

The written sources seem to indicate that in the 580s many Slav families had crossed into the Balkans, where they settled in large numbers on abandoned farmland in the interior. Many Slav tribes had settled in the region of Thessalonica, which became known as 'Macedonian Sclavinia'; after a great siege of Thessalonica about 586, part of the Slav tribes together with the Avars reached the Peloponnese, annexing fertile lands in the western part of the peninsula, and settled there on the lands they apparently obtained by displacing the local Greek-speaking populations. According to some later written sources, the Slav and Avar attacks had provoked the escape of the Greek populations of some regions to Sicily and other coastal islands. The so-called *Monemvasia Chronicle* is often cited here (though this ninth- or tenth-century source may be reporting merely hearsay).[44] The degree to which a Greek population had been replaced by Slavs and Albanians moving into deserted areas has been debated ever since Jakob Fallmerayer's (1830) demonstration of the number of Slav place names in the Peloponnese (reinforced in 1941 just before the eve of the Nazi occupation by the publication of a book by the German linguist Max Vasmer) arguing for an early and substantial Slav presence in Greece.[45]

In general however, the archaeological evidence for a Slav presence in Greece is still also extremely slight. While in some areas Slav material culture replaces other models, this is by no means the case in the south Balkans (in particular, modern Greece). Despite considerable evidence of early medieval Slav settlement, the characteristic material elements mentioned above are notoriously difficult to trace. The archaeological evidence recovered to date seems to suggest that Slavs settled in this area seem not as a rule to have built sunken-floored huts with corner ovens, seem not to have scattered quantities of 'Prague-type' pottery around their settlements and seem not to have practised the visible burial rites found further north. Archaeologically the Slavs are very difficult to identify in the south Balkans, even though the written and linguistic material proves beyond doubt that large Slav-speaking populations were present in the area by the seventh century. This cautions us from using the absence of archaeological evidence as evidence of absence.

There are only a few archaeological traces of this period on the Balkan peninsula, although a few sites in northern Bulgaria have been claimed to be of the sixth century. On these sites (for example that at Popina) there is handmade pottery with affinities with early Slav groups from the Ukraine with no traces of the other elements seen in the material from the north of the *limes*. In the material culture of Popina type there are few signs of contacts between the Slavs and the autochthonous populations. The main problem here has been that it would seem that these sites have been dated too early.[46]

Despite the Slav settlements there were still large areas of territory (at least nominally) in East Roman hands. The written sources show that this had included a number of the cities, but the archaeological evidence for this is sparse. We should also note the presence of certain groups of Slavs in the East Roman empire as mercenaries (Procopius writes for example of Slav soldiers who took part in the Italian campaigns).

The northwestern fringes of South Slav territory have had a complex ethnic and political history. The area (the former province of Dalmatia) had been the last surviving fragment of the West Roman Empire, and then been on the edge of Ostrogothic territory and by the middle of the sixth century coastal Dalmatia became part of the East Roman Empire (which it held longer than northern Italy, which was to fall to the Longobards between 568 and 572). A significant number of the original Romanized population also survived in Dalmatia, and the long-term process of symbiosis in this area had a considerable effect on the Slav culture (to a greater extent perhaps than in any other Slav territory). The Dalmatian area was being penetrated by the Slavs as early as 550 (Procopius, *Wars* VII.40, 7). It would seem that about the same time there was settlement of Slavs in Pannonia. The fall of Sirmium in 582 further weakened the western parts of the *limes*, allowing the barbarians further access to the western Balkans. Slav colonization penetrated this area from the east along the main river valleys (Sava and Drava) in tandem with the westward political expansion of the Avars in the period between the 570s and 590s causing the destruction of many pre-existing towns and settlements.[47] The looting expeditions of the Avars and Slavs even reached the shores of the Adriatic, and, although many Dalmatian towns were able to hold out as last bastions of the old order, many others fell victim to them. Dalmatia suffered especially in 612–14, when even the capital of the province (Salona) was attacked and the population moved inside the walls of Diocletian's palace at Split. Like the Balkans, this whole northwestern zone of South Slav territory had a mixed culture in which Slav, Avar, Carolingian East Roman and Roman features were evident, and this culture seems also to have had an important effect on the shaping of the cultures of other Slav groups, for example Moravian culture (Chapter 4). To some extent the area retained a certain autonomy from the Byzantines in the seventh century while Frankish western expansion was not yet reaching the Julian Alps.

In the Ukraine we may assume that the Penkovka Culture, which develops on the fringes of the Korchak zone, had accomplished much of its expansion in this second phase. The Penkovka material occurs in the Dniepr region southeast of the Korchak zone across a wide area from the edge of the Pripet marshes across the Dniepr into eastern Ukraine (middle part of Southern Bug (Boh), middle Dniepr and upper Donets around Kharkov).[48] The siting of the villages (such as the eponymous Lug I and II sites near the village of Penkovka, northeast of Kirovgrad) was similar to that of the Korchak group, on the elongated terraces just above the floodplains of rivers, and again they were probably short-lived, consisting of shifting units of five to ten small square sunken-floored huts with stone-built corner ovens occupied at one time. The Penkovka group on the left bank of the Dniepr is distinguished from that on the right bank in that there are no huts with corner ovens, but only free-standing hearths like those of the forest zone in the fifth century.[49] Possibly this area was settled by population movements from the regions of the upper Dniepr.[50] Small flat cremation cemeteries with urned and unurned burial are also the rule, but mainly concentrated in the Dniepr valley. In this Culture fortified settlements are unknown. The main feature distinguishing the Penkovka group from the Korchak material is the biconical form and in some cases slightly larger size of some of the pottery vessels. These vessels are of slightly more varied form than the Korchak type, often with out-turned rims. They are in general undecorated, except for a few cordons strengthening rims of the larger vessels; these are sometimes pinched to give a frilled effect. Round ceramic baking plates also occur. In contrast to the Korchak group, Penkovka settlements have produced a number of abandoned iron tools and items of decorative metalwork of Martynovka-horizon type (see below). Some Soviet archaeologists linked this material with the Antes known from the historical sources, though the grounds for such an interpretation are unclear.

In the area of Poland, most of the settlement of Korchak type was still in the southern regions, in the rich farmlands in the southeastern part of the country, though there was also some expansion and consolidation of settlement along the major river valleys. By the early part of the sixth century traces of the *Restgermanen* settlement had finally disappeared from the area of modern Poland[51] (though there was not a similar breakdown of the West Balts to the northeast). The material culture of the Early Slavs of the later sixth century differed little from that of the earlier phase, though M. Parczewski claims some changes in the form of the pottery vessels.[52]

To the south of the Carpathians we find a cluster of sites in southern Slovakia,

Moravia and Bohemia. The earliest material here appears however to date to the second half of the sixth century. The material culture is in many respects very similar to that of Poland, though whether this settlement developed as a result of movement south from Poland or west from the Ukraine or Moldavia through the Carpathians (via northern Transylvania) or by northern movement from Early Slav settlement in the Danube valley is as yet unclear. Since the early stages of development of the Czech and Slovak languages has much in common with those of the South Slavs (see p. 17), some scholars have felt that the latter option is the more likely. To the west in Bohemia is an area which produces a dense cluster of sites with Early Slav pottery (although in the early sixth century it still seems to have had some *Restgermanen* settlement). It was here that the Prague pottery was first differentiated and formally described, but it now seems that the earliest Prague-type pottery in this area appears to date to the second half of the sixth century.[53] In this area we find the other elements felt to be characteristic of the so-called Prague Culture, among them square sunken-floored structures with corner oven similar to those of the Ukraine (see Map VIII), and the concentration of small flat cremation cemeteries with Prague-type vessels used as urns contrasts with the situation in the areas around it. It is this together with the chronological relationships which provokes opposition to the extension of the term 'Prague Culture' to all baggy formless vessels of Early Slav type in a wide range of cultural contexts. Here we have a clearly defined zone which seems to demand a stricter approach to the terminology.[54]

The expansion to the west of the Early Slav cultural zone was reflected in the appearance of material of Prague type in the southern areas of Polabia. It would seem that well before this the tribal systems of the *Restgermanen* in this area had collapsed (a process perhaps related to disruptions caused by eastward expansion of the power of the Franks in the 530s into Thuringia). We observe that Early Slav settlements containing pottery of Prague type occur in precisely the same areas on the Elbe where there had been *Restgermanen* settlement.[55] It seems very likely that to a large extent this is because these were areas which had been cleared earlier and were easier to settle than the denser forest further away from the zones of Germanic settlement. Nevertheless in some of these settlement zones, pollen evidence showed that the forest had been regenerating before the Slavs moved in. The Prague-type assemblages spread along the upper Elbe and forked along the Saale and Havel but no further north than the Brandenburg region.[56] Probably this material developed under the influence of the Bohemian group to the southeast, and in part of the area urned cremations like those of Bohemia also occur. Among the material thought to be the earliest Prague-type material from the area, there is some dated now by dendrochronology to the 660s.[57] At the time of writing there is a lack of convincing evidence for early sixth-century dates for the Prague-type material or any other evidence of Slav settlement in the area.

The northern area of Polabia (north of a line from Brandenburg to Cottbus) about this time was occupied by groups using material culture of Sukow-Dziedzice type (see below). Archaeological evidence from parts of this area suggests a direct relationship between the abandonment of their settlements by the Germans and the arrival of the Slavs and the assimilation of the remaining indigenous inhabitants. The dating of the Slav settlement of the middle Elbe valley is however unclear. Recent datings by dendrochronology have shown that the dating of Early Slav material in some areas of the former DDR had been seriously wrong. Much of it was formerly dated from one to three hundred years too early, and former views about the Slav and Germanic settlement being nearly contemporary in the same region, or even on the same site, are shown to have been based on false premises.

For some years specialists have been talking of a 'northern tradition' occurring over most of what is now Poland (including Pomerania) and northern Polabia among the generally nondescript material culture of the Early Slavs. Only in the past few years has it been recognized that this cultural province forms a single unit.[58] This material is now known as the Sukow-Dziedzice Culture, named after two type-sites: Sukow – an undefended site under a later stronghold near Teterow in Mecklenburg in Polabia – and Dziedzice near Myśliborz in Pomerania.[59] It has recently been recognized that this zone contains material of slightly different nature from the Prague type and Korchak traditions. The Sukow-Dziedzice group is differentiated from the Korchak, Mogiła and Prague traditions primarily by the general lack of the square sunken-floored structures with corner ovens (there are one or two exceptions at Żukowice, and Jazów in lower Silesia: Map VIII). There was a different building tradition in the area, probably involving mainly ground-level buildings of 'blockhouse' type. So-called 'bath-shaped' features, shallow ovoid or sub-rectangular holes about 2–3 m long with flat or concave bases (Fig. 15), have been seen by some investigators as the remains of some form of undefined pit-houses with 'light tent-like constructions over them', though the evidence for this interpretation is unclear.[60] There exists the possibility that these features represent some kind of ritual activity accompanying the desertion of a homestead (see below).[61] The area is also characterized by an almost complete lack of cemeteries: whatever burial rite was practised, it left few traces. (The Alt-Käbelich type of cemetery, with deposits of a few bones, ashes and sherds within the fills of relatively large pits suspiciously like 'bath-shaped' features, is later – see Chapter 8.)

The Sukow-Dziedzice pottery consists of a category of handmade vessels which are mainly undecorated but occur in a greater variety of shapes than the cooking-pots of the Prague tradition, tending towards wider-mouthed and more 'open' forms. These assemblages include not only cooking vessels but also a range of plain medium-sized jars, globular bowls and jar-bowls (see Fig. 14 for range of forms). Sukow-type pottery occurs in Polabia between the Elbe and

Havel-Spree. It also occurs over most of northwest and western Poland.[62] The precise date of its introduction is as yet unclear, though a nominal starting date of (late?) sixth century should probably be assigned to it. In western Pomerania the beginning of the Sukow-Dziedzice type should be dated to the later sixth or early seventh century, while in Silesia it may have appeared in the course of the sixth century.

The origin of the Sukow-Dziedzice material is debatable. It is very similar in typology and range of form to the Korchak and Prague material, but it would be simplistic to see it as their northwestern variant, or even as derived from them. One recalls here the material which was used to support the hypothesis of the autochthonous origin of the Slavs in Poland: late Roman period and early Migration period vessels very similar in concept and style to the handmade vessels of Sukow-Dziedzice type. It certainly seems very probable that the Sukow-type material is a local development. This material seems also to represent Slav settlement but of a different cultural tradition. We seem to be observing here the traces of some process of assimilation and 'Slavization' of local populations across a wide area north of the Carpathians in reaction to some as yet poorly understood stimulus.[63] Unfortunately the precise rate of these changes is not yet known. Recent work has cast some doubt on the hypothesis (first proposed by Professor W. Szymański) that the 'northern tradition' was stimulated by influences from the northern forest zone of what is now Belarussia: the evidence for this now seems very tenuous. An interesting result of the conclusion that the Sukow-Dziedzice material is of local origin compared with the intrusive origin of the Mogiła group in the southeast area of Poland is that this may well have been responsible for the conflict which has developed (see p. 41) between the autochthonous school of Slav origins proposed by Poznań scholars (situated in the middle of the Sukow-Dziedzice zone) and the allochthonous model preferred by scholars from Cracow, sited in the territory of the Mogiła group.

If some of the Sukow-Dziedzice sites at the western extreme of the Early Slav material are of this date, it would seem that, in these first two phases, the westward extension of the Slavs was something in the region of 950 km from the nearest sites in Moldavia. There was also considerable expansion to the south, and an unknown amount to the east. The scattered settlement over this vast zone was to become consolidated in the next century, as we shall see in the following chapter.

3

Consolidation and Social Change: the Seventh Century

The third phase of the expansion of the Slavs falls in the period *c.* 600–700. The period following the last decades of the sixth century is one of relative stability, and one where new features start to appear in the Early Slav assemblages throughout central and eastern Europe. We also see the appearance of a few types of metalwork, and there are changes in the pottery assemblages. The period also sees the beginning of a phenomenon which was to become typical of the settlement pattern of the Slavs in the northern regions: the building of the first strongholds. The fifth and sixth centuries saw the Early Slavs rejecting the cultural traditions of other groups in favour of their egalitarian and simplistic cultural traditions, which spread rapidly as an interregional cultural foundation. The seventh century marks the beginning of the slow but eclectic acceptance of foreign cultural models, especially from the world of Byzantium and Longobard Italy as well as from and through the medium of the nomads (Avars). From the mid seventh century the whole of western Slavdom undergoes significant change, with the appearance of southern (Danubian) influences, including new pottery types and a new burial rite. Despite these changes, the other material culture of the Early Slavs is remarkably consistent across the whole area from Polabia to the Ukraine.

The changes in the material culture of the Early Slavs are manifested most noticeably in the pottery typology. Over most of the area in the first half of the seventh century however the preceding cultural divisions continue to persist. The Prague zone in the southwest continues to exist. To the northwest (Map IV) the Sukow-Dziedzice material enters a new phase, but without changing its basic character. To the east is a zone occupied by a series of assemblages which may be named the Szeligi-Zimno group, while the south is occupied by the Suceava-Şipot group and material of the Popina type. The seventh century sees however the general adoption of a new canon across western Slavdom. Vessels are not simple rough baggy shapes but an attempt is made to make their form more regular by use of some kind of turntable (but not the potter's wheel). The upper part of the vessel is thus smoothed-off and made more symmetrical. These vessels may be known as 'top-turned'. It is interesting that these changes appear at about the same time as the decline in the percentage of wheel-made pottery in Early Slav assemblages in the Danubian region, whence it may be suggested we may seek the inspiration of the technical improvements.

The starting place for our deliberations on these developments must for several reasons again be the Danubian frontier and Balkans. A peace treaty in 590 with the Persians (in return for Roman military aid to a usurper) allowed Maurice Tiberius (582–602) to transfer a large part of the Roman army from the east to the northern frontier and thus restore it, and then begin a war on the Slavs (both within and outside the Empire). For a decade the Romans and their allies the Antes with varying fortunes continued to be at war with the Avars and Sclavenes. In the 580s we hear of attacks by the Antes on Sclavene settlements. The wars culminated in a massive Roman invasion north of the Danube when they defeated the Avars, reputedly killing some thirty thousand of them (including the Khan's four sons) and obtaining great amounts of accumulated loot.

It is roughly to this period that another written source which is often quoted should be dated. This is the document known as the *Strategicon*, in effect a military manual supposedly written by the Emperor Maurice himself; its real author is known as Pseudo-Maurice. The text probably dates to some time between 592 and 610. He describes the Sclavenes and Antes 'in their own homelands', their character and way of life (including their hospitality), their agriculture and the womenfolk, who are noted as 'chaste beyond measure' to the degree that, after their husbands die, some willingly kill themselves, 'regarding widowhood as no life at all'. They live hidden away in forests and swamps, and raid and ambush their neighbours. Their armaments are described (see Chapter 7) and methods by which they may be overcome are suggested. Pseudo-Maurice says that they have no overall leader, but many petty chiefs and are constantly feuding among themselves. This interesting account contains many other interesting details, which there is no space here to give, but it is unclear how many are copied from earlier works and how many derive from observations made during the campaigns of the 590s.[1] It should be remembered though that this account can be applied only to Slavs living in the area north of the Danubian frontier.

Another writer of the period, Menander known as Protector (from his function in the imperial bodyguard), wrote about 582–4 an important history containing material known from eye-witness accounts. He tells us of the relations between the Slavs and Avars, mentioning the names of a few personages and the attacks of the Sclavenes and Avars on the Romans between 578 and 581, with many details. Some of the details contained in his work coupled with much other information formed the basis of the account of Theophilactus Simokattes written about 628–38. This contains a similar range of material and is one of our chief sources of information on the Avars in the period 585–602: from it we learn a little of their relationship with the Sclavenes and Antes.

After a military revolt in 602 caused by the hardships of the wars against the Avars however, Maurice was deposed and killed along with his whole family. His death was followed by a period of anarchy (struggles between city factions, political and religious disputes) which were for ever to change the face of the empire. They ceased only with the accession to the throne of Heraclius, son of the exarch of Africa, and the reorganizations which he undertook are acknowledged as marking the beginning of the Byzantine Empire. The disorder of 602 allowed the Avars to recover, and they attacked the Antes (Theophilactus Simokattes, VIII.5, 13) in revenge for their earlier attacks on the Sclavenes. This is the last mention of the Antes in the written sources, and some scholars believe that this attack was the cause of the end of that tribal union. The Avars then turned their attention to Thrace. The events in the reign of Maurice's successor Phocas (602–10) had weakened the frontiers, and both he and Heraclius (610–41) attempted to buy off the Avar attackers with high tributes, but this did not entirely stop their raids.[2]

The weakening and then opening of the frontiers allowed Slav and Avar raids to continue to trouble the Balkans, including the countryside and cities of Greece down to the Peloponnese during the course of the seventh century. In contrast to the previous century when it would seem many attacks were aimed at the southern tip and east of the Balkans (Greece and Thrace), the Avar raids of the first two decades of the seventh century were aimed mainly at the distant provinces of Dalmatia: in the years 612–14 the most important towns of the area (including Salona) were devastated. In 614–16 the Avars however attacked Thessalonica (with the aid of siege machines), and the chronicler Isidore of Seville says that in the fifth year of the rule of the Emperor Heraclius the 'Slavs took Greece from the Romans'.[3] The first half of the seventh century also saw the settlement of abandoned areas of the countryside of the Balkans by Slav families and communities.

We have seen that there is strong evidence that large areas of the countryside over most of the Balkans had become seriously depopulated during the sixth century. Despite Slav settlement of parts of the area, the seventh-century landscape of the region still seems to have been sparsely populated.[4] The Early Slav settlement seems to be contemporary with the thick layer of soil known as Younger Fill washed into many of the river valleys in Greece. This seems to have formed in the seventh century owing to extensive soil erosion, presumably as a result of a breakdown of traditional agricultural regimes.[5] Over most of the Balkans, occupation in towns had declined, and many sites were abandoned. Some towns on the coast survived, and trade seems to have continued. Economic problems of and economic change within the Byzantine Empire itself led to a collapse of the coin-using economy in the Peloponnese in about the 650s.[6]

It would seem that the maintenance of a standing army on the northern frontier had been placing an increasing strain on the imperial treasury. The evidence seems to suggest that in this period the troops supposedly defending the Danube *limes* relied heavily on *annona*-like distributions (that is, state-run distributions of food and supplies) presumably to a large degree supported financially by the rich eastern provinces rather than being supplied by a local agricultural hinter-land.[7] In the recognition that the frontier had been ineffective in keeping the barbarians out of the Balkans (large areas of which were by now settled by a considerable number of non-tributary barbarian groups), it was decided in the early years of the reign of Heraclius, apparently some time in the 620s, to under-take a reorganization of the system of defences of this part of the empire. It was decided to abandon a part of the northern frontier and to withdraw all imperial troops from the Balkans. There are relatively few forts or towns on the Danubian frontier which can be shown to have lasted through the first decades of the seventh century. The Balkans seem thus to have become a periphery but one almost directly adjacent to the core of the Byzantine state. Defence was con-centrated nearer the capital in the form of localized and mobile militia forces based in the towns. Some time in the seventh century in Asia Minor and Thrace soldiers seem to have been settled on small farms which they held on condition of military service, passing on the land and obligation to their eldest sons. This system later spread to other areas, leading to the militarization of the empire, and not only providing for the upkeep of the soldiery but also increasing the numbers of smallholders working the land.

In 626 the Avars joined a Persian attack against Constantinople in which the city was unsuccessfully besieged by land and sea. We learn from the sources of the period that there were a large number of Slavs present in the Avar forces, mainly in the capacity of infantry, but also manning the dug-out boats (*monoxyle*) which were used to ferry Persian troops across the Bosporus to the European side. The Byzantines sank the boats and many Slavs were killed; see-ing the military disaster it turned out to be, the rest left the battle. In the end the Avars withdrew. It seems that the fiasco in front of the walls of Byzantium seri-ously damaged Avar prestige; this was to lead to a decline in their influence in the Balkans in the period 626–50, and their supremacy was challenged else-where on the fringes of their hegemony (see below). The Avars became restricted in political significance to the central area of the Carpathian basin.

Early seventh-century Slav settlement in Macedonia and near Thessalonica was strengthened not only by new arrivals but also by a process of 'internal col-onization'. In addition new areas new regions of the Balkan peninsula were settled (for example Dalmatia and northern Thrace). By the end of the seventh century large areas of the Balkans were covered in areas of settlement of the Slavs. During the period of stabilization so caused, we see the appearance of a number of tribal names. The written data we have on the tribes themselves are very fragmentary, and allows only an uneven picture of the cultural pattern to be reconstructed (Fig. 16; Maps IV to VI). On the Danube in the area of former Lower Moesia, probably the area which had been colonized earliest, was an area sometimes known in Byzantine sources as 'Sclavenia'. This was inhabited by a number of tribes, including one known as the 'seven clans'; another was known as the Sieverzane (see below). A particularly large number of Slav tribal names are known from Macedonia – especially the region of Thessalonica (though the town itself remained Byzantine). This area too was known in Byzantine sources as 'Sclavenia', and the Slav languages were in daily use, as is witnessed by the ninth-century missionary brothers Constantine (Cyril) and Methodius, who were born near Thessalonica. Several of the tribal names here have apparent links with the East Slav tribal names (Smoleńcy, Druguvici). There are few Slav names known from the mountainous region of the interior: perhaps this was an area of very sparse Slav settlement.

The Slavs known from these written records are very difficult to locate archaeologically. The manifestations of Slav culture from the Balkan peninsula which can be linked with the early phases of colonization are still poorly known. One reason might be that in Greece and to some extent in other areas archaeologists have for several reasons tended to concentrate on the more spectacular traces of the ancient classical civilization of the region. The little evidence which exists is often poorly published and difficult to date. Rural sites of any kind are rare and in most cases these settlements are small, containing one or two houses, with very few large villages. Excavated sites include Popina, and Garvan near Silistra in Bulgaria. At Popina in northern Bulgaria a long-lived settlement was excavated which comprised over sixty sunken-floored buildings scattered over 3 hectares. A nearby urned cremation cemetery was explored. The houses were 3–4 m across and had a stone or clay oven in one corner. The associated pottery of the earlier settlement phase has similarities to the Luka Raikovetska pottery (see below) of the Ukraine. The site is dated from the seventh/eighth to eleventh centuries (though the excavator originally dated its beginning to the sixth century). At the site of Garvan, also in northern Bulgaria, similar features were found in another large settlement which began in the seventh century (containing pottery similar to Prague-type material) and lasted to the eleventh. Some 120 huts were excavated and two inhumation cemeteries.[8]

In the areas settled by the Slavs, town life seems to have virtually ceased, but it would seem that many towns had been in decline before the Slav settlement. At any rate the Slavs settled here had no need for enclosed settlements (the South Slavs, unlike those further north, did not build any strongholds). There is relatively little material from the ruins of Byzantine towns and forts (with rare exceptions such as Caričin Grad in Serbia). There is however a horizon of Byzantine coin and silverware hoard finds dating to the periods of the Slav raids, and several apparent destruction layers dated to the same period. There is also a scatter of radiate fibulae across the area, for example in Greece and Macedonia (for example Sparta and Nea Anchialos near Volos).[9] A find (hoard?) at Velestino in Thessaly contains animal-figure appliqués like those of the Martynovka hoard (see below). Excavations in advance of the construction of a new museum at Olympia in the western Peloponnese in 1959 found a dozen urned cremations in handmade pots. These vessels, and the objects they are associated with, have been given dates from the sixth to early eighth century.[10] Some male inhumation burials with weapons in stone or brick cists at Corinth, excavated by American archaeologists in the 1930s, were initially attributed to the Avars because they had belt fittings like some found in Hungary (similar burials have been found in Athens and Kruje in Albania, but also in association with the ruins of churches at Athens, Philippi and Tigani). The belt fittings suggest a date of about the mid seventh century; the association with churches and inhumation rites suggest that these burials are neither Slavs nor Avars. A similar buckle was found in recent excavations at Isthmia near Corinth in a settlement in the interior of a sixth-century fort.[11]

A particularly puzzling find is the massive hoard of silver belt fittings of Avar type and Byzantine silver from Vrap in Albania which probably dates to about 700.[12] The silver vessels had been for liturgical use (including one with an inscription showing it had originally come from Salamis on Cyprus – which the Byzantines had lost in the mid seventh century).

Despite the apparent intensity of Slav settlement in some areas, some coastal regions remained in Byzantine hands, and it is here that the Byzantine economy became focused. The towns of the Adriatic coast (Trogir, Zadar and Split and many Dalmatian islands) for example remained in Greek hands free of Slav settlement and maintained their contact with the Byzantine Empire. Some areas of the southeastern Balkans also remained under Byzantine control, and the Byzantine theme (administrative region) of Hellas was established by the end of the seventh century (it included Attica, Boetia and several islands, but not those areas of Greece which had been settled by Slavs). Athens remained a centre of culture, education and scholarship, and the organization of the Church continued in certain areas.[13] Much of the area of Thrace around Constantinople, and the shores of the Aegean around Thessalonica (and the town itself) also remained free of Slav settlers.

The late seventh century is also characterized by a rapid decline in the Byzantine economy. Study of Byzantine coastal hoards seems to pinpoint the beginning of economic changes and collapse which seems to have occurred about 650–70 in the reigns of Constans II (641–68) and Constantine IV (668–85). As a result of these problems the East Roman tribute to the Avars drops off relatively sharply in the 670s.[14]

After the beginning of the seventh century Byzantium seems to have done little to prevent Slav settlement in the Balkans. It is probable that the colonization by the new agriculturist populations of devastated and depopulated territories could have been turned to advantage by the eastern Emperors, if they could have made these new populations their tax-paying subjects. Moves were made by the later Heraclian emperors to change this state of affairs and to incorporate the Slav tribes of the eastern Balkans into the socio-economic system of the state.

They were subjugated by Constans II in 656/7. A little later Justinian II (688–95 and 705–11) extended this control. The institution of the Thracian theme in 680/7 represented the full restitution of imperial power over these territories. It was more difficult to subdue the Macedonian and Greek Slavs by force, and military expeditions were organized against them by Constans II in 656, and Justinian II in 686. Great numbers of Slavs taken prisoner in these expeditions were recruited into the army or resettled as smallholders to Bithynia in Asia Minor. More than once it was necessary to renew military action against mutinous Slav tribes. The tribes which came under Byzantine rule were obliged to pay tribute, supplying military aid and fulfilling other obligations. We hear for example (*Miracles of St Demetrius* II.3) of the Velegezites in Thessaly who in 677 were able to produce enough grain to relieve a besieged city. In other territories however the Slavs retained relative independence. The term 'Sclavenia' is often met in Byzantine sources, and seems to mean a Slav tribal territory independent of imperial rule. In the peripheral areas, far from the main centres of the empire, Byzantine power was more nominal, and not only were the tribes here able to retain their structure but we see the formation of new independent political organizations within the empire quite early. The Bulgar state is the prime example of this.

Considerable changes were taking place in the western regions of the Balkans in the seventh century. By this time Slavs had also settled on the eastern flanks of the Alps in the valleys of the upper Drava, Sava and Mura; the written accounts (such as Paul Diaconus, *History of the Lombards*) suggest that they had settled considerable areas of Dalmatia by about 641/2. It was at this time that Pope John IV sent Abbot Martin to pay ransoms for prisoners and relics captured by the Slavs. The process of the settlement of the Dalmatian coast and islands was to last for another century. As elsewhere in the Balkans, traces of the early settlers are difficult to find: there are very few archaeological sites producing Slav material which can be dated before the eighth and ninth centuries. Because of the mountainous terrain of the east Alpine area, Slav settlement here was neither dense nor even, and there was considerable survival of the autochthonous population, including the residue of a Germanic population. This finds expression in the character of the so-called Carinthinian Group dated to the seventh and eighth centuries, in the inventory of which can be found material with many connections to the material culture of late Antiquity and also analogies with contemporary Germanic culture.

Rather more problematic is the evidence for the settlement of the area of Dalmatia by the Serbs and Croats. The evidence is somewhat contradictory and its interpretation has become somewhat complicated as a result of its use in recent political struggles. The conventional view followed the mid-tenth-century account of Constantine Porphyrogenitus (*DAI* chapters 29–36), based in part on information obtained from Byzantine informants from one of the coastal towns of Dalmatia.[15] The text contains some duplication and interpolation, which complicates its interpretation. In particular it contains two different versions of the migration of the Croats. Constantine tells us that the Serbs and Croats arrived in the area during the reign of Emperor Heraclius, who encouraged them to free Dalmatia from the Avars and settle there themselves after conversion to Christianity. One of the accounts of the settlement of the Croats and that of the Serbs seem to be based on mythical accounts originating among those peoples: they have the typical features of an *origo gentis* legend (including in the case of Croats the tale of five brothers). The second version of the Croat narrative betrays a Byzantine source, and this seems to have a political motivation. It was presumably created to bolster Byzantine claims to suzerainty over them (especially with respect to the Bulgarians and Franks), since according to this account the Croats were settled at the will of, and with the permission of, the Byzantine emperor.

The picture from the written sources appears to be contradicted by the archaeological evidence. It would seem that the earliest Slav settlement in the interior of the western Balkans, whether 'Croat' or otherwise, cannot antedate the second half of the seventh century. A small settlement site excavated at Mušići near Sarajevo was formerly considered to be evidence of the 'first Slav settlement in Yugoslavia'.[16] A re-consideration of the pottery by Florin Curta shows that its specific, very peculiar, combed decoration cannot be earlier than *c*. 650. Further discussion about the beginnings of the so-called 'Old Croat culture', and its relationship with the Late Avar horizon in Hungary, is based primarily on the evidence of burial assemblages excavated in Kašić, Nin, Zdrijac and various other places.[17] Recent study of these cemeteries however has shown that the settlement of the Croats is unlikely to have taken place as early as Constantine Porphyrogenitus suggests. The earliest reliably datable phase of burials in these cemeteries should be assigned to about 700.[18]

Constantine's text (chapters 30 and 31) contains a mythical account of the alleged homeland of the Balkan Croats, a 'White Croatia' located somewhere in central Europe near Bavaria, beyond Hungary and next to the Frankish Empire, an area where the 'White Croats' still lived. It would seem likely that what Constantine had in mind is a large tribal group, the Chorvati on the northeast side of the Bohemian basin. This homeland however is problematic, since although other documents refer to it (Alfred the Great's translation of Orosius's *History of the World*, Ibn Rusteh, an Arab geographer in the tenth century, the *PVL*, and a charter of the Bishopric of Prague) none of them dates earlier than the ninth century, and there are no sources which refer to the presence of any group called the Croats in central Europe (or indeed the Balkans) before that date. The problem is compounded by other evidence which places a group of Croats (Chorvati) unknown to Constantine somewhere in the bounds of Kievan Rus (see pp. 99–100). Scholars debate whether to place them in the region between southern Poland and southwest Ukraine, or on the southeast fringes of the Rus state (the latter seems more likely).[19] Here we should also note a number of modern theories which, on the basis of the ethnonym and certain linguistic data, hold that the original name 'Croats' did not in fact refer to Slavs at all but was of Iranian Sarmatian origin and later adopted by their Slav subjects.[20]

The settlement of the Serbs is presented by Constantine in a very similar light. Some of the sentences of the Serbian account seem to be copied from the account concerning the Croats. Again a mythical homeland, 'White Serbia', is given, and placed in much the same area (with the additional information, 'in the country known by them as Boiki' – perhaps Bohemia). Unfortunately (unless Constantine had in mind the Sorbs of Polabia) there are no such people known in this area and 'White Serbia' may just be a literary fantasy. Again Constantine is at pains to show that these lands were settled by Byzantine permission after the Roman population of the area had been driven by the Avars to Dalmatia and Dyrrachium, and the Bulgars had no authority there. The extent of early Serb settlement is not known; the archaeological evidence is not yet sufficient either to date the first settlements or to show where they were. Neither is it clear when they settled the historic heartland of the later Serbian state in the upper Drina and its tributaries (Piva, Tara Lim and Uvac, the upper Morava, Raška and Ibar). By the time of Constantine there were a number of other tribes in the area related to the Serbs (including the coastal Zachlumianie, the name meaning 'in behind the hills'). The Belgrade scholar Djurdje Janković has claimed that the earliest finds from the area are the so-called *gromilas* (an archaic term meaning burial mounds) in Serbia, an idea which has become very controversial.[21]

Discussions are still continuing about the ability to identify the users of the Koman Culture, which occurs in the central Balkans (Macedonia and the Adriatic coast of Montenegro). The material includes handmade and wheel-turned pottery (including cooking-pots but also handled cups and flasks) and metal objects (including fibulae, star-shaped earrings, and objects of ultimately steppe patterns). Some have seen this as the material culture of the Albanians, while others (Josip Korošec, Bosko Babić) have linked it with the Slavs. Others still have seen it as linked with Romance-speaking populations (Vladislav Popović).[22]

The further fate of the South Slavs in the east Balkans was intimately linked with the story of another people, the Bulgars. They were initially a nomadic Turkic-speaking people,[23] originating on the steppes around the Sea of Azov at the beginning of the seventh century (probably from a union of Turkic, Utigur and Kutrigur Hunnic remnants, Avars and possibly Alans), leading to the formation of the so-called Khanate of Great Bulgaria on the Don and Caucasian steppe. This apparently split up in the period of rising Khazar power in the latter part of the seventh century. One part of the Bulgar coalition migrated to the middle Volga region (on the eastern edge of Khazar territories) and formed a powerful khanate from the ninth to twelfth centuries which was to play an important role in the relationships between the superpowers of Central Asia and the northern sea-routes (Chapter 11). The other significant development was however the numerous groups of Bulgar horsemen who began to take the traditional route of the steppe nomads westwards into 'Little Scythia' by the Danube delta. From here they started roaming the pastures on the north bank of the lower Danube on the eastern fringes of Avar-controlled territory, and there they established a hegemony over the Slavs settled in the Danube frontier region.

The Danubian Bulgars led by Khan Isperich (Asperuch) began to use their power base to attack the frontiers of Byzantium itself. They strengthened their hold on the Danube valley and then began to threaten Byzantine possessions in Thrace. By 680 they had become so powerful that they took over part of Lower Moesia in the north of Byzantine territory which was already settled by a large population of Slav communities, some of which had been established there several generations before. The written sources tell us that Isperich subdued the Slav groups known as the Seven Clans and the Sieverzane. In 680–1 the Byzantine emperor Constantine IV Pogonatus was forced to cede this territory and its inhabitants in return for a tribute to be paid to the Byzantines.

Other changes were taking place north of the Danubian frontier. In Moldavia the earlier cultures are replaced in the seventh century by the so-called Hlinca Culture, which seems to be a local variant of the Luka Raikovetska Culture of the Ukraine (see below). On the Danubian plain, the Suceava-Şipot material seems to disappear, though the date at which this occurs is uncertain (it is usually accepted that it ends at the time of the Bulgar invasion of c. 680, but there is no real archaeological basis for this). There is a large number of Early Slav sites now known in southeastern Transylvania.[24] Among them an interesting complex of sites has been investigated in the region of Dulceanca (Muntenia).[25] There was one other important enclave of sites in the region of Cluj (the Slav name for the Roman town of Napoca) forming a zone of Slav settlement in the upper reaches of the Mureş and its tributaries which apparently came into existence some time after the middle of the seventh century. These are mainly settlement sites and flat cremation cemeteries, some containing also inhumation burials. On the fringes of the area (and adjacent to the zone of Late Avar burials in the Someş valley) are the Someşeni and Nušfalau barrow cemeteries, which are unusual in that they seem to reflect eastern Slav traditions of construction.[26]

Further to the north there were important developments in the post-Prague phase in northern areas of central Europe. The typology of the relatively intractable post-Prague pottery of Polabia has been carefully studied.[27] The early post-Prague pottery traditions in the northwest of the area are a continuation of the Sukow tradition, now entering (from about the middle of the seventh century) a new phase of development, the Sukow-Gołańcz phase (the latter being a stronghold in Pomerania).[28] This is marked by the appearance of vessels finished on a slow wheel ('top-turned'), and vessel forms tend to change from weakly profiled vessels (some tending to a biconical form) of the Dziedzice phase to squatter open-mouthed vessels with rounded form. This pottery seems to last into the eighth century in much of the region.

Northeast of the Carpathians, most of Poland falls into three cultural groups (Map IV). In the northwest we see the eastward extension of the Sukow-Golancz zone, to the south of which is a group of material for which I propose the term Racibórz-Chodlik (after a cemetery near Katowice and an open site under a ninth-century stronghold at Chodlik near Lublin, both in southern Poland).[29] This material probably begins some time in the mid seventh century and lasts in much of the area through the ninth century (possibly even as late as the early tenth century). The pottery styles seem strongly influenced by styles from south of the Carpathians. The vessels are of a variety of forms and sizes: cooking-pots, jars and jar-bowls which have wide rounded shoulders and everted rims forming an S-profile. These vessels are frequently decorated with (wooden) combs with (usually) four to six teeth. These were used to form horizontal bands of grooving or wavy lines of various types (Fig. 18). Occasionally vessels were grooved horizontally over most of the profile. About 90 per cent of decorated pottery from this zone is decorated with these three motifs used in combination. As in the Sukow and Szeligi traditions the pottery was handmade, but some of it was made on a turntable or slow wheel: this is especially visible on the upper part of the vessel, which was often evened-up on a slow wheel. None of this pottery was wheel-thrown. It occurs across most of southeastern Poland and extends further north in the west. The settlements of this phase have the familiar square sunken-floored huts, but now the burial rite is characterized mainly by placing the cremated remains under earthen barrows in small (clan or family?) cemeteries. North of this between the Sukow-Gołańcz and Racibórz-Chodlik zones is a region with somewhat similar ceramics, but mixed with other poorly defined elements. This zone (for which I propose the term Central Polish group) is characterized by a lack of barrow-cemeteries, and its further definition would seem to be a task for future work.

At the beginning of the seventh century and possibly at the end of the sixth century towards the eastern side of modern Poland appears the cultural group represented by the strongholds at Zimno, Szeligi and Haćki in the zone between the Slavs and (broadly understood) the Baltic populations.[30] This cultural zone is represented not only by a specific pottery style (tall vessels of derivative Korchak type, but also squatter open baggy bowl forms) but also by a specific type of relatively weakly defended hilltop stronghold with internal layers. These may contain finds of rich ornamental metalwork of mixed cultural affinities (combining Byzantine-Lombard and steppe elements having a relationship to Avar and Martynovka-type finds). The date of the end of this group is as yet unknown.[31]

The situation is more complex to the south of these three zones. On the middle Danube and upper Elbe the Prague Culture seems to last into the late seventh century (and perhaps in some areas even to the first half of the eighth century). Within this broad zone on the west a distinct cultural group on the rivers Saale and Mulde seems to develop in this phase. It has a specific character which justifies differentiation, and I propose to call it the Saale group. In the seventh century this group is marked by a cluster of flat cemeteries containing assemblages of Prague type. The burial rite seems to continue into the next century when other areas have gone over to barrow burials. In this area some time in the late sixth century appears the pottery style known as the Rüssen type (named after the settlement site of Rüssen in southwest Polabia). This lasts in much of the area through to the ninth century (possibly even as late as the early tenth century). The pottery vessels are similar to Racibórz-Chodlik material, with a similar variety of forms and sizes: cooking-pots, jars and jar-bowls. These vessels, with their wide rounded shoulders and everted rims forming an S-profile, are also often decorated with bands of combed decoration like that of Racibórz-Chodlik vessels (this decorative scheme seems to have come among the influences from the Danubian zone). The pottery was made on a turntable or slow wheel, which was used to even-up the upper part of the vessel.[32]

Further to the southeast in Bohemia there seems to have been a continuation of the Prague Culture, and there is an apparent lack of distinctive material which may be regarded as characteristic of the period between the Prague Culture and the so-called pre-Moravian horizon.[33]

In the area south of the Carpathians and east of Bohemia we find a zone north of the Danube and extending across to the Tisza valley characterized by relatively primitive pottery vessels in post-Prague tradition. This cultural group appearing around the end of the seventh century and lasting through the eighth is known as the Devínská-Nová Ves type, after a cemetery on the Morava river near Bratislava where there were Avar and Slav graves together.[34] The cemetery began in the seventh century, but went on in use until the end of the next century. Most of the graves in this large cemetery (a thousand excavated graves) were inhumations, but among them were nearly thirty cremations. The artefacts in some graves were of Avar type, though the majority were of nondescript type, or typically Slav (such as S-shaped temple-rings). Most of the pottery at Devínská Nová Ves was of similar type: squat rounded vessels with out-turned rims and decorated with comb-squiggles and occasionally stamps. Some of this material was wheel-made. The Slavs settled here under the rule of the Avars reached a relatively high state of development, in part owing to the influence of nomad culture. Fighting by the side of the Avars they accepted a range of cultural traits, Byzantine, Frankish, Carolingian.

The typical Slavo-Avar material culture of the area occurs at a number of settlements and especially large inhumation cemeteries (Holiare, Želovce, Nové

Zámky, Alattyán, Kiskoros) in Slovakia and Hungary.[35] These large inhumation cemeteries suggest considerable settlement stability. The burials of men are sometimes accompanied by their horses, and the harness was put into the grave. From this we can see that the Avars clearly had a different style of riding from Slav warriors, and never used the Slav hooked spurs discussed below: they used stirrups, which do not occur in early Slav contexts. The belt and harness fittings in the male graves bear ornament of central Asian type which seems to be due to Avar influence. There are at least two horizons of these belt fittings: the earliest ones are tongue-shaped and have embossed and graven ornament, the later (Late Avar I c. 690–730 and Late Avar II c. 730–50) are cast with openwork decoration of griffins and plant-tendrils (Fig. 16). The question of the ethnic affinities of the men buried with this equipment has been a major source of academic disagreement between Hungarian and Slovak archaeologists over the past few decades. The Hungarians in general prefer to ascribe these graves to foreign nomads, the Slovaks see their furnishing as acculturation of Avar costume by indigenous Slavs. The matter has not been settled even by anthropological identification of foreign elements in the skeletal material.[36] The second phase of metalwork may have been brought to the area with a new wave of intruders, some of whom, according to Liptak's work, had mongoloid features. Women's graves of the end of the sixth and seventh century have temple-rings of star-shaped design and multicoloured glass beads. The material culture in these inhumation graves is relatively rich, even with glass vessels (which seem likely to have been Frankish imports).

It was somewhere on the western edge of this Avar–Slav cultural zone in 623 that a Frankish merchant named Samo who had been trading with the Slavs became leader of a Slav revolt against Avar overlords somewhere on the Frankish frontiers. Our main source for this event is book IV of the *Chronicle* of Fredegar, written in the 660s (where the Slavs are also referred to as 'Wends'). Samo became the ruler of a political organization usually referred to as a state, though mainly on the grounds that Fredegar used the term *rex* for what may have been simply a chief.[37] We know he allied himself with Derevan the '*dux*' of the Sorbs and accepted Slav customs (including twelve Slav wives). In 631 he was in conflict with the Frankish ruler Dagobert I who, after an angry diplomatic exchange, sent an army against him which was beaten at a place called Wogatisburg.[38] Samo died some time between 658 and 669 and his 'state' collapsed without trace. For generations historians have been arguing where Samo ruled and what was the extent of his territory. We are no nearer solving this mystery now than half a century ago: there are no archaeological traces of such a political organization, nor of the much-sought-after Wogatisburg. Very probably Samo was in fact a ruler of only local significance somewhere beyond the Bavarian border in the region of today's Vienna where the edge of Slav–Avar settlement projects up the Danube valley to the west. Here Dagobert's army

79

would have been stretched to its limits. Other scholars have suggested that Samo's kingdom was in the Morava valley or Slovenia, but these hypotheses seem to be wishful thinking inspired less by concrete evidence than by national pride on the part of the archaeologists who propose them, as both were well beyond the area of Avar control.

In the area to the east there is a lack of concrete information on the type of material which would represent the post-Korchak horizon in the western parts of the Ukraine, but in the centre of the Ukraine we may assume that the Penkovka Culture had already accomplished much of its expansion before the seventh century. It seems likely that the Penkovka Culture continues alongside the post-Korchak traditions further west. The precise nature of the boundary between these two traditions is unknown.

An important political factor in the area was the expansion of the Khazars. By 650 they had dominated the steppe from the Dagestan steppe north of the Caspian, much of Caucasia and the Black Sea Steppe between the Dniestr and Don; their influence extended far into the forest steppe zone to the north (up the Don, Volga and Kama rivers). On the steppes, their hegemony absorbed the Bulgars and Alans, and it was under Khazar influence that in the forest zone (in an area known by the legendary name Etelkoz) the Magyar (Hungarian) identity became crystallized. The Khazars developed wide networks of exchange and tribute collection, and, as we shall see in a later chapter, some of the southern tribes of the East Slavs were to come under their influence. By virtue of their geographical position and development of extensive trade networks the Khazars (who by the eighth century had ceased to be bands of armed raiders and achieved the status of a state) had close political and cultural contacts with Byzantium, Persia and the Arab world as well as with the barbarian tribes of the north.

The reflux

The period around the middle of the seventh century sees a number of changes taking place in the cultures of the Early Slavs: these seem to be suggestive of some south–north movement of ideas, if not people. This movement occurs across the Carpathian mountains, until now apparently separating the material to the north and south. Contact across the mountains may have of course occurred at an earlier date, but now we seem to see signs that these contacts were responsible for far-reaching cultural changes. We seem to detect some influences which flowed north from the Danubian area to the area along the north side of the Carpathians. The process is poorly understood and requires further research. It is visible in two main phenomena.

First, we see 'Danubian' influences appearing in the ceramics of the seventh century onwards in Poland and Polabia. This gives rise to a number of vessels with characteristic wavy line and horizontally rilled decoration over a wide area. These changes were discussed by Aleksander Gardawski in his consideration of the pottery from Chodlik, and, although much of this discussion is outdated, some of the general ideas he presented seem worthy of further deliberation.[39] The main reorientation of Gardawski's views may be to see these innovations as coming not so much from the Danubian frontier zone alone but from the wider area of the Avar khanate, which seems to have been the area of production and use of pottery similar to that which appears north and northeast of the Carpathian basin.[40] These changes are visible first in upper Silesia and western Małopolska, in the area formerly occupied by the Mogiła group assemblages. The same area is characterized by a number of imports of Middle and Late Avar metalwork, and some hoards of Byzantine coins. These seem to have come through the wide passage through the mountains known as the Moravian Gate from the scatter of Avar material to the north of the area of the Avar hegemony.[41]

The second phenomenon is an apparent change in burial rite (and thus perhaps ideology) which is evidenced by the (possibly sudden) adoption of the rite of barrow burials in the zone both sides of the Carpathians in the period around 650. Until then, most burials in the area were made either in flat cremation cemeteries or by a rite which leaves absolutely no recoverable remains. The earliest barrows appear in Moravia and Bohemia (Prochovské Skále, Nadslav, Gbely and Burovce),[42] that is south of the Carpathians (with perhaps some early outliers in the Dniestr valley). These barrows have a specific form (with horizontal wooden revetting at the base of the mound, enclosing a rectangular area) and with the cremated remains being deposited on top of the mound. The barrows of the late Avar period in northeastern Transylvania such as those at Someşeni near Cluj are chamber burials in barrows of a different type (as we have seen, the Avars themselves practised inhumation – sometimes with horses – in flat cemeteries). It is unclear why barrows should have been raised over this wide zone, but slight evidence seems to suggest that the impetus came from the south and only later penetrated the Carpathians. In one of the early barrows (at Izbicko near Opole) a gold earring of Middle Avar type was found.[43] The question of the initiation of the barrow burial rite needs further study.

Some have seen these changes as in some way connected with the changes occurring in the Avar khanate, especially in its northern fringes, but there is little real evidence for the strong influence of the Avars here, aside from a handful of items from this broad area. One of the possible causes may have been the systemic changes and collapse of the Byzantine economy of the period 650–70 and the sharp decline in the Avar tribute in the 670s. Perhaps this meant that groups of Slavs on the northern fringes of Avar territory were no longer focusing their attention on the wealth of the south: perhaps they looked further afield for opportunities for self-betterment.[44] The Slav and Bulgar invasions and settlement in the Balkans were perhaps as much a symptom of these problems as a direct cause. Throughout the Late Antique period and the Migration period the economic superiority of the classical civilizations had served as a magnet to the northern barbarians, drawing them south and west towards the frontier. Whether they were able to pass through the 'Iron Curtain' of the *limes* depended on a number of political, economic and military factors.[45] Now, even though the frontier was weak, the attraction was now also weaker. We now see cultural influences acting in the opposite direction towards the north. It is difficult to explain this phenomenon, detectable from the archaeological evidence (including the spread of Danubian and Byzantine styles), but it seems to be connected with changes in the economic potential of the south.

An end to austerity

Over the whole of Slavdom, the seventh century also sees the beginning of a new interest in ornamental metalwork. Apart from a few rare items, often of foreign inspiration, items of personal adornment and decorative metalwork generally are lacking in the earliest Slav assemblages. This general austerity is not however entirely dispersed by the new types which appear in the seventh century, since the metalwork types are relatively simple and restricted in range.

The most notable features of the period are a range of cast plate fibulae with headplates decorated with projecting 'fingers' which served to fasten clothing. These so-called 'Slav fibulae' are found across a wide area of southeastern Europe, though rarely north of the Carpathians or in West Slav territories.[46] The type developed from fibulae of the late Cherniakhovo group with wide flat plates, which often have semicircular 'radiate' heads and elongated rhomboidal footplates terminated with human or animal masks (they are broadly similar to 'Ostrogothic' fibulae of the Italian peninsula and Gepid finds from the Carpathian basin) but exhibiting a mixture of motifs and heavier, more massive ornament and form (Fig. 20). The variety of form and ornament probably had a symbolic significance, and may even have served to show affinity to a particular group. These fibulae are scattered across a wide area from the Mazurian lake district to the lower Danube and Crimea in the decades around 600 (though some examples may be as early as the first half or middle of the sixth century). There are regional variations: they occur in South Slav lands, but rarely in the West Slav territories, and are more common in Penkovka assemblages than those on the west bank of the Dniepr.

A second group of fibulae (the Dniepr group) dates to about the same period as the Martynovka horizon (indeed that hoard contained three of them) and the finds from the site at Pastyrskoe (Pastyr'ske). This is a more massive series of wide equal-armed fibulae derived from the prototypes. They have the bow nearer the centre of the object, with the head and footplate expanded laterally with anthropomorphic and zoomorphic decoration, or in the form of wide flat rounded or triangular plates. These appear in the first half of the seventh century. This group of fibulae develops further throughout the late seventh century (perhaps to the very beginning of the eighth). They are found also in the Caucasus and Crimea.

In the Balkans a series of simple fibulae with upturned foot and flattened (decorated) bow derived from Late Roman types was in use in several cultural contexts, including apparently Early Slav and Koman culture assemblages.

Another metalwork type which is characteristic of the period comprises armlets or bracelets of round-sectioned rod with expanded ends (Fig. 20). These were probably worn by men as well as women, and are an interregional type, found in Germanic contexts as well as across Slavdom.

A typical form of female ornament is the simple wire-loop temple-rings of bronze and occasionally silver, rings of wire 3–4 cm in diameter which appear sporadically in West Slav contexts (mostly towards the Baltic) perhaps by the seventh century, but more certainly in the eighth century. These were worn as a headband round the brow and temples. Some star-shaped silver temple-rings in the Danubian area may also begin in the seventh century, but examples are more certainly dated to the eighth century, when these ornaments were inspired by Byzantine jewellery fashions. Similar temple-rings are found in Ukrainian hoards, suggesting along with other phenomena close cultural links between the Danubian area and the Penkovka Culture. More frequently however the Martynovka-type hoards contain more showy jewellery of wire, larger rings some 6–9 cm in diameter and several types of spirals of bronze wire.

Another 'luxury' type connected with the toilet comprises the single-sided bone and antler combs with sub-triangular sideplates appearing on some West Slav sites (especially in the Cracow region) from about the middle of the sixth century and in use in the seventh and perhaps eighth centuries. Like the fibulae, these have prototypes in the Danube valley.[47]

Amber from the shores of the Baltic was a central European commodity which was widely traded through the ancient world. With the collapse of the Roman world we lose track of the amber trade through central Europe by the early sixth century, though Gepid graves still contain fairly large quantities. Little of this reached the Slavs however (exceptions are items from the Pastyrskoe assemblage and from Khatski, Ukraine, and an amulet from the Połupin stronghold in western Poland). In the seventh century however we have a few amber beads reaching settlements outside the West Balt territory. This exchange too was to increase in later centuries. An unpublished ornament from Połupin has an amethyst inlay.

Men were not averse to showy metalwork costume accessories. The main form these took was the fittings of leather belts of Avar type which are found in many male graves south of the Carpathians. A number of these items are found beyond the zone in the Carpathian basin dominated by the Avars. Belt-mounts of Avar type presumably served to enhance the status of their wearers and to emphasize their associations with the ruling elite, with whose agreement perhaps these objects may have been worn in the Avar realms.

A more specifically male metalwork type comprises the internally hooked spurs (Fig. 22) found in western Slavdom in a broad zone from the Elbe to the Bug and as far south as the Danube.[48] Originally their genesis was dated to the sixth century, but this early dating (based on a model of settlement continuity in the area of modern Poland) has now been questioned. The earliest examples date more probably to the mid seventh century. These spurs are of copper alloy or iron and have a short curved bow with a stout prick, and were fastened to a boot by straps through the hooked ends of the bow. The spurs are differentiated from contemporary Frankish spurs in that the hooks turn inwards. The earliest examples are found north of the Carpathians, in the area of central Poland, but typologically perhaps slightly later forms are found at Mikulčice in Moravia in the earliest (pre-Moravian) fortified settlement under the later princely strong-hold. This is currently datable to the very end of the seventh century. Only in the eighth century do these types occur more commonly in the area south of the Carpathians in pre-Moravian deposits. None is known from Moravian-period graves. These items were relatively rare: as in many early societies, it seems likely that the majority of these ornaments were prestige goods, enhancing or stating a social position. Thus it is notable that hooked spurs are found in several strongholds and the settlements associated closely with them, and rarely found on 'normal' open settlements.

A particularly problematic group of finds comprises a series of hoards of precious metal objects found over a wide area of the Ukraine. Many of these were accidental finds made in the nineteenth and early twentieth centuries, and being suitably showy antiquities for the ancestors of the Russian nation they were soon being hailed as the 'Treasures of the Antes'.[49] They are found in a cluster between Kanev and Cherkasy on the middle Dniepr, but also a number along the Desna and Seym, in the upper Donets and Oskol area, and in the upper reaches of the left-bank tributaries of the middle Dniepr (Sula, Psol, Vorskla). Beyond this are sporadic finds of fibulae and a few hoards which were presumably hoards of loot or tribute lost to neighbouring tribes.

About 1907 at Martynovka (Kanev district) near Penkovka a hoard of silver ornaments was found which was scattered among several collections. Part is now in Kiev and part in the British Museum, and the entire hoard (what remains of it) has recently been published.[50] These items have given their name to a series of hoards and loose finds of similar type which may be dated to the seventh century. Items of this type are sometimes found in assemblages of Penkovka settlements. The assemblage consists of wire spirals (ornaments), so-called *Sprossenfibeln*, equal-armed fibulae and zoomorphic or anthropomorphic plaquettes of sheet metal – depicting exotic beasts such as lions and hippopotami (Fig. 23). The Martynovka hoard also contained a number of harness and belt fittings of types which occur across a wide area from the Volga–Kama area and Crimea through the steppes to Byzantium and Longobard Italy. The source of the silver is hinted at by the East Roman and Byzantine silver vessels found in the hoards: those at Martynovka had control stamps of Justin II (565–78).

Another important hoard is the Gaponovo find, a hoard of 411 items from a Kolochin Culture (see p. 101) site near Kursk in the Desna valley. It included a series of women's headband ornaments, torques, various pendants, five fibulae and many glass, amber and coral beads. There are also belt and harness fittings, and other finds such as ingots. The finds have affinities in the Crimean and Balkan zone of provincial East Roman culture, the Volga area and the Azov/northern Caucasian cultural zone, but also Sassanian Iran. The hoard is dated to the second and third quarters of the seventh century. The Gaponovo find is exceptional for the analytical work in its excellent publication,[51] which allows us to see the finds in a much wider cultural and historical context.

There are in fact two groups of these hoards.[52] The first (typically containing mainly female ornament) dates to the second and third quarters of the seventh century. The authors of the Gaponovo report show that the burial of this first group coincides with the appearance of Byzantine prestige goods in the area, perhaps deriving from some kind of political alliance with the Slavs, but also coincides with the interruption of earlier traditions (end of the Penkovka and Kolochin Cultures and the creation of the Luka Raikovetska Culture). A second less numerous group contains later objects, from the end of the seventh and the eighth centuries, and coincides with the earlier phases of the Luka Raikovetska and Volyntsevo Cultures (see the next chapter). These hoards may be linked with the rise of Khazar power and consequent effects among the tribes living on the middle Dniepr river.[53]

Despite the attribution of these hoards by Soviet archaeologists to the early Slavs, especially to the Antes, they betray a mixture of cultural influences. Many of these items have closer affinities with the type of animal art and geometric appliqués which for centuries had been worn on the showy dress of nomad tribes of the steppes, and their appearance in the Penkovka territory may be a result of cultural contacts between the southern groups of eastern Slavs and nomads such as the Alans or Avars on the north Pontic steppe.[54] In particular, one may point to the expansion of the exchange systems and political interests of the Khazar hegemony, which was increasing at precisely this time: this may have provided the primary impetus for the distribution and imitation of this kind of metalwork as well as for the adoption of foreign elements.

The first strongholds

At about the same time, a series of strongholds appears over a relatively wide zone of western Slavdom. These sites will be discussed further in a later chapter, but a few aspects of the earliest examples need to be mentioned here. There has been a tendency in the past for archaeologists to date the earliest strongholds rather too early, for revision of the dating has shown that there are very few of these sites anywhere in Slavdom for which a date before the seventh century can be proved.

This type of enclosed settlement is known in most Slav languages by a word derived from a common root (*gardъ) which seems to have meant 'enclosed', thus in modern Polish gród, in Slovak hrad, in Russian goród etc. At a later date (see Chapter 8) the semi-urbanization of these sites led to this term acquiring the meaning of 'town' in addition to its primary meaning. The interesting fact is however that it was only in the seventh century (at the earliest) that this settlement type developed, and the fact that this word preserves a similar form in most of the Slav languages suggests that their differentiation did not occur until after this date. These sites were not built in the Migration period; they begin only with the new social conditions formed during the process of consolidation.

The distribution of early medieval strongholds is uneven across the area, and the same differentiation is seen in the distribution of the earliest examples. There are at least two main zones: an eastern one with very few strongholds, and a western area where there are perhaps rather more. It is however difficult at this stage to produce an accurate map, owing to the problems of chronology caused by recent redating.[55]

The form of these sites is somewhat variable. On the whole they consist of an area of land which is in a relatively 'defensible' or commanding position (in the middle of a bog, peninsula on a lakeside, high peninsula overlooking a valley, and so on), which has been made more defensible by adding an earthen or earthen and timber rampart or ramparts. Their function was not however entirely defensible, as some have open sides which could not withstand a concerted attack. This is not to say that they are not an indicator of intertribal warfare, or that they had no military function. Their relative weakness suggests however that any armed conflict between groups was more like the raids of weakly organized societies and not the attacks of a large disciplined army of a centralized state. We must also bear in mind that the construction of the rampart and digging of the ditch involves a substantial effort of a group of people, presumably working under some form of overall control. It seems that the ramparts enhanced the prestige of these sites, a suggestion which is supported by the probable elite metalwork found associated with some of them. It has been suggested by some scholars, on the analogy of superficially similar sites from the forest zone of Belarussia and Russia, that some of these sites may have had a cultic function. This may be the explanation of the richer finds from some sites, which may be some kind of votive or ritually deposited material scattered in the enclosure.

There is also a group of sites which has a relatively consistent character of material culture. These sites include Szeligi and Haćki in Poland and Zimno in the upper Bug valley. They are on steep hilltops and have relatively simple defences. Szeligi is a settlement complex of the beginning of the seventh century (though originally dated to the mid to late sixth century), investigated in 1959–68 by Professor Wojciech Szymański and fully published. The promontory stronghold here produced much pottery and some metalwork. Although the metalwork is datable, carbon 14 dating of charcoal from burnt timbers produced calibrated results at the beginning of the sixth century; presumably this dates the trees used in the constructions as much as the site itself.[56] The case of Haćki near Białystok in Poland is interesting: the assemblage contains many scattered cremated human bones, but also a large quantity of metalworking waste, so it could equally be a production site associated with the elite. Several items of metalwork from the site have affinities with seventh-century material from the Danubian area (the attempt to date this site too by radiocarbon has produced problems). The stronghold at Zimno is also overdue for reconsideration: among the rich assemblage of finds we note metalworking waste and a bronze coin of Justinian or Justin I (518–65) together with metalwork belonging to the same general horizon as the material from Haćki and Martynovka. Further to the east is the stronghold at Pastyrskoe near Cherkasy in the middle Dniepr valley. This is a circular enclosure 60 m in diameter with a series of internal subdivisions. The site was excavated by Vladimir Chvoika in 1898–1901 by trenching (but also by deep-ploughing to bring buried objects to the surface) and the site was re-excavated in 1949. It produced an ornament hoard and also scattered metalwork of Martynovka-horizon type. It is possible however that the stronghold is an ancient one – it resembles Scythian ones and the relationship between the metalwork and ramparts is unclear. The unparalleled quantities and type of metalwork from this site suggest that it was of great importance in the settlement network of the middle Dniepr region in the latter half of the seventh century.[57] Equally unclear is the dating of the defences around the hilltop at Kiev. Some investigators (such as Rybakov) have claimed a date of the sixth century for their construction on the evidence of early pottery and a Justinian coin found here, but the evidence for such an early date is far from clear.

It has been suggested that the earliest strongholds have an origin in the strongholds of the northern forest zone, especially the Tushemla-Bancherovska group.[58] This is seen as the prime evidence for an eastern origin for the 'northern tradition' of Poland and Polabia which we discussed on pp. 65–6. As can be seen from Fig. 24, these sites actually cluster in the west of the area, which would suggest that their origin is not explicable by this simplistic migrationist model.

4

Decisive Decades:
the Eighth and Ninth Centuries

In the previous two chapters we have explored the tentative emergence of a series of new cultural traditions and followed their spread across much of central and eastern Europe. We have seen that, for most of the period we have been considering, Slav culture was relatively consistent over wide areas. The ninth and early tenth centuries saw the splitting of the previously relatively culturally uniform area inhabited by Slavs into a series of more discrete zones. The most obvious are the developing differences between the three main blocks, the South, West and East Slavs. Within these major blocks there were smaller broad cultural units, some of which had influence on the later historical development of central and eastern Europe, influencing its present form and character.

In this chapter these two crucial centuries will be discussed at some length. The framework presented here is rather new: fresh thoughts on the dating of the archaeological material have had a massive effect on our conceptions of the rate of change. In the Ukraine for example the Volyntsevo material (see pp. 96–7) is now dated later than formerly, but it is in Polabia and Poland that new thinking (together with the application of absolute dating techniques such as dendrochronology) has led to a completely new picture. We have already discussed changes in the dating of the hooked spurs which has shifted the dating of some pottery assemblages and sites forward almost two centuries. In the same way Tornow and Feldberg pottery in the DDR was formerly dated two or three centuries too early. Now changes which in previous syntheses were spread over several centuries have as a result of this revision been telescoped into a completely new and dynamic picture.

The eighth and ninth centuries were a period apparently marked in many areas by an increase in growth of the Slav populations. These processes are difficult to measure and there is a lack of evidence from some regions of Europe. Thus we have few sources of information for the sizeable territories inhabited by the South Slavs, except for rough and incidental estimates by Byzantine writers of the numbers of people forming tribes; since we have difficulty locating their settlements in the field and the evidence from cemeteries is poor, the archaeological evidence cannot be brought into the discussion. The situation is equally bad for the territories of the East Slavs (but here at least we see a denser scatter of archaeological sites dated to this period than to earlier ones, hinting at a denser occupation of the landscape). In the territories of the West Slavs we have better data. Here we experience the same problems in the interpretation of the written evidence (the mid-ninth-century *Bavarian Geographer* for example includes information on the number of *civitates* of each of the peoples mentioned, but the significance of this information is unknown). The area has however been well covered by archaeological surveys which give a very clear indication of the number, distribution and dating of archaeological sites. This is particularly true of Poland, where a project of government-sponsored systematic and detailed fieldwalking of the entire country and inventorying the discovered sites has been carried out since 1978. The database this project has produced is a very valuable research tool. One of the features which can be studied on the basis of numbers and dimensions of sites is the population increase in the early medieval period. In western Wielkopolska it can be estimated that at the beginning of the sixth century population densities were lower than one person per square kilometre, at the end of the ninth century the figure was at least three times greater, population growth increased in the tenth century, and by 1200 there were population densities of seven per square kilometre (today the population figures for the same area are between twenty and fifty).[1] Although these figures are only approximations, they give an idea of the scale of population growth, but also the degree of settlement of the landscape. With population growth came a necessity and possibility of a series of cultural and organizational changes not encouraged by lesser population densities.

The eighth and ninth centuries were also a period when Slav culture became strongly influenced by more 'advanced' neighbouring cultures, leading to cultural change. These processes of cultural transmission and assimilation were obviously complex, and many factors affected which features of neighbouring cultures were rejected and which were accepted by Slav communities. In many cases though we have clear examples of interactions between core and periphery where the cultural patterns of a more 'advanced' society were adopted by (or forced on) a neighbouring society being in some measure less developed. Not all of these changes were to the ultimate benefit of the new host (and they led to some degree to a loss or reorientation of local cultural identity). Neither should it be assumed that these processes of cultural change due to external influence were necessarily unidirectional.

The South Slavs (Bulgars, Serbs and initially the Croats) came early on under the strong influence of Byzantine culture. The Slavs had settled in the agrarian landscape and social system created by the East Roman Empire and were affected by the territorial ambitions of Constantinople. These factors were to affect the way in which these societies were to develop in subsequent centuries. The culture of the East Slavs absorbed elements deriving from several central Asian and steppe cultures (Khazars, Pechenegs and the Islamic states of central Asia): this is especially visible in the art styles, particularly of the metalwork. By the ninth century several tribes had fallen into the orbit of the interests of the Khazar state. The influence of ninth-century Scandinavians on the formation of the Kievan state is the subject of recent discussion, and in the tenth century Kiev came under the strong influence of Byzantium.[2] The West Slavs were too far away from the Byzantine frontiers to have been directly influenced by them, but were not totally isolated from their political influence, and many scholars have seen in Byzantine fashions the origins of the silver ornaments worn by the women. The strongest influence on the West Slavs was however also from a successor state to the Roman world, due to the eastward expansion of the Carolingian and Ottonian empires.

The South Slavs and Byzantium

Realignment of Slav culture first took place in the territories south of the Danube, and it was here that they had the strongest effects. As we have seen, various Slav groups had penetrated the Balkans down to the south of Greece in the sixth and seventh centuries, and settled there. Their settlements are as hard to find as those of the contemporary 'Byzantine' populations, and it would seem that both groups had a 'Dark Age' material culture which was equally archaeologically imperceptible. We have seen that settlements of the Popina type in the northern areas of the Balkans should now be dated to the later seventh and eighth centuries (rather than the earlier dating formerly assigned them). These are villages consisting of a few scattered sunken-floored buildings which were periodically replaced.[3] The fact that the same site was used for several centuries suggests that the settlement network was becoming stabilized in these areas. A further symptom of this stabilization is the formation of tribes, which are known from the written sources. These emerged as the main form of socio-political organization among the South Slavs during the period of settlement stabilization of the seventh century. Relatively quickly however the specific conditions of the area led to the formation of larger socio-political units, including tribal unions, such as the Seven Tribes (or Seven Clans) of the south bank of the lower Danube. In the eighth century the Peloponnese was known in Greek sources as 'Sclavonia terra', a name perhaps representing the organization of tribes there into a form able to resist Byzantine pressure. Only at the end of the eighth and beginning of the ninth century did the Byzantines attempt to regain control over some of these lands (which was fully achieved only in the mid tenth century).[4] At the end of the seventh century however the Byzantine state was forced to give way to the rising power of the Bulgars and officially recognize the first independent state in the Balkan peninsula. This was the beginning of the formation of a new socio-political and cultural unit in the Balkans, one with considerable influence on Byzantium itself.

The settlement of the Bulgars in Little Scythia and then inside the Byzantine Empire at the end of the seventh century (Chapter 3) was to have serious effects on the political balance of the area. During the reigns of the Amorian and Macedonian emperors of Byzantium the Bulgar khans expanded their territory, at the expense first of Slavs south of the Danube and then of the Empire itself to create a powerful khanate which was to last nearly three centuries. The distinctive Bulgarian ethnicity was to emerge from a symbiosis of Slav and Bulgar elements (and possibly other elements such as remnants of earlier Romanized Thracian populations) over a period of several centuries. The precise mechanisms of this complex process of cultural assimilation have been a much-discussed theme in Bulgarian historiography for several decades. It would seem that, despite being politically dominated by a Turkic elite, the Slavs were able to retain their ethnic identity, language and own tribal leaders. Indeed it is the survival of the language and the gradual acquisition of elements of the Slav culture by the Turkic ruling elite which is one of the most interesting features of this relationship. Here the 'elite dominance' factor seems to have been overridden by the usefulness of the *lingua franca* of the Slav dialects of the area as a communication medium within a much more numerous substrate within the emergent state.[5]

The Bulgarians made political gains from becoming involved in the power struggles which split the reign of Justinian II (695–705). The political problems following the fall of the house of Heraclius did not at first allow Byzantium to resist the Bulgars, but in 756 under the Isaurian emperor Constantine V Copronymous (741–75) the Byzantines concentrated their forces on trying to smash the Bulgars. After several dozen years of bloody battles they failed. The Bulgars emerged from the conflict with the boundaries of their territory relatively intact. Bulgarian forces were involved in the Carolingian attack on the power of the Avars (793–6), and for a brief period the Bulgars seem to have gained control of extensive areas of Transylvania and part of the Carpathian basin in the power vacuum created by the collapse of the Avar khanate (the Carolingians presumably being unable to extend their frontiers further to the east than the great bend of the Danube). This period was marked by increasing political centralization under Khan Krum (803–14), who began a series of wars against what was left of the ninth-century Byzantine Empire. This began in 807 with an attack on Thrace and northern Macedonia, occupied to a large extent by Slavs. The Byzantine emperor Nicephorus fell fighting against the Bulgarians (811) and Michael I was also defeated by them (813).

The gains of Krum were continued by Khan Omurtag (814–31). He divided the enormous territory into eleven areas, each governed by an official appointed by the state accompanied by a retinue. By these means the original compact group of Bulgars settled in a restricted area of the Lower Danube scattered in various enclaves all over the country. Similar resettlement of the Slav subjects broke down existing tribal boundaries, and enhanced the process of the creation of a new ethnic identity. The khanate soon lost its nomadic character. It became modelled on the structure of the Byzantine Empire, from which it accepted many cultural patterns. The remaining elements which were still barbarian were however firmly Slav in character, with very little owing to central Asian cultural influence. The process of the 'Slavization' of the Turkic ruling dynasty was completed in the ninth century, with the establishment of a Slav tongue (Old Bulgarian) as the state language (and today the Bulgarian language contains only a few thousand Turkic words).

The first centre of power of the Bulgar khanate was the delta and lower reaches of the Danube, and there is some archaeological evidence that several abandoned Roman forts on the *limes* may have been reoccupied in the early ninth century, probably in the reigns of Krum and Omurtag. The centre of the state was soon shifted (probably by the reign of Omurtag) to Pliska, an enormous urban site modelled on Byzantine cities and surrounded by an earthen rampart in the centre of which was a large walled compound containing the palace and sacral buildings. The area around was divided by paved streets, and was served by waterpipes and a sewerage system.

In the second half of the ninth century the Bulgar realms expanded southwards into the Balkans and at the end of the ninth century the Bulgar khanate was at its maximum extent, covering large areas of the Balkans and Carpathian basin (Fig. 25; Map V).

One stumbling block to unity in the Bulgar state was the religious plurality. The Slavs had their own polytheistic pantheon (Chapter 9), there were probably Christian inhabitants in the state, but the Bulgar elite apparently believed in Tangra, the God-Heaven. It would seem from some accounts of western writers that Christian missionaries had made some converts among the noble families in the ninth century, and Jewish and Muslim missionaries were apparently also conducting religious propaganda in the area. These religious differences created problems for a ruler trying to create a centralized state: not only did they encourage dissent, they also meant that different religious communities had different moral values and laws. The accession of Khan Boris (852–89) was followed by an alliance with Charles the Bald of Francia, and his forces took part in an attack on the East Frankish kingdom and the Croats. In 862 Boris was able to wage war on Moravia and the Byzantines again in alliance with the East Fankish kingdom. These contacts with Christian powers no doubt convinced him of the need to do something about the religious disunity of his own state. It was in this context that we should see the acceptance of Christianity, first accepting the Greek liturgy from the hands of Byzantine missionaries, but then switching to the Roman Church in pursuit of political gains, before switching back to the Byzantine rite (but in the Slav language not Greek). The Slav Church in Bulgaria was strengthened by the acceptance of clergy who left Moravia in

885 (see below). Boris enforced the conversion of his pagan subjects (carried out with a certain amount of bloodshed), and some two decades later Bulgaria was a Christian state. Boris resigned the throne and retired to a monastery, but, when his son made some moves favourable to paganism, Boris deposed and blinded him and installed his younger son Symeon on the throne.

Symeon (893–927) had been destined to be the head of the Bulgarian Church and to this aim had been sent to the Magnaura school in Constantinople, where he had become acclimatized to Byzantine culture. Unfortunately just a few days after coming to power he already came into conflict with the emperor Leo VI over foreign trade, and this was to be the beginning of a series of conflicts between Bulgaria and Byzantium.

In 893 the capital was again moved, from Pliska to the smaller site at Preslav: this had stone walls and the central palace complex was larger and had additional trading functions. As at Pliska, the outer enclosure had urban characteristics with many impressive churches. The Byzantine-style architecture was embellished with decorative glazed brickwork and architectural stonework. It was from here that Symeon ruled most of the Balkan peninsula and was crowned tsar of the Bulgars. This was the golden age of Bulgar culture when art, literature and architecture flourished.

After a few years, Symeon declared war on Byzantium and invaded Thrace; the wars were to last until the end of his reign. The Byzantines encouraged the Magyars to invade the Bulgarian coastal regions, and Symeon's army was fighting on two fronts. After defeating the Magyars, Symeon's troops invaded the Byzantine Empire and took the western regions of the Balkans, forcing the Byzantines to sign a treaty in 904 acknowledging all his territorial gains. Symeon seems then to have developed the ambition to create a united Slavo-Byzantine empire with him as the ruler. After having failed to achieve this by marriage, he again invaded Byzantium in 917.

Further south in Greece the Byzantines had reconquered their lost lands from the Slavs. In 782/3 Constantine VI had sent an army into Thessalonia and the Hellas, where the Slavs were vanquished and forced to pay a tribute to the emperor. He then moved his attention to the Peloponnese and took many captives. The Slavs revolted against Byzantine administration in 805/6 but were defeated, only to rise again in 840–2. Some time afterwards a new theme was created on the Peloponnese, and building was begun in the cities, including Athens (church of St John the Baptist, 871). Despite this activity, some Slavs retained their autonomy and culture, even until the time of the Fourth Crusade (1204).

To the west of the Bulgar khanate, the northwest areas of the Balkans were from the end of the eighth century the scenes of a struggle for power between the Franks and Byzantines. The area entered the sphere of influence of Bavaria and the Frankish and Carolingian empire, at times forming an eastern 'march' (allied and subordinate territories ruled semi-autonomously by indigenous leaders and subject to German colonization). At other times Carinthia in the upper valleys of the Drava (Drau) and Mur rivers and centred on Krnski Grod (Karburg near Klagenfurt) retained its independence. The area came under Frankish rule in the early ninth century. The name *Slovenes* is recorded only quite late (sixteenth century); earlier Latin documents used the terms *Sclavi, Sclavani, Sclaveni* (but also *Vinades, Vinadi* and *Vinedi*).

The coastal towns of Dalmatia, though surrounded by settlements of the Croats, were still Byzantine in culture and political affinities, and these had an enormous effect on the culture of the Slavs. Croatia became drawn into the culture of the West, though the survival of the Byzantine liturgy, which arrived here from Pannonia in the ninth century, is a curiosity. The Croats became a state only in the first decades of the tenth century under Tomislav (910–28). The Serbs to the north and east acknowledged Byzantine supremacy in the ninth century, but at the turn of the ninth and tenth centuries, as a result of dynastic conflicts, the area passed into the hands of the Bulgarians under Symeon; they freed themselves in the early tenth century only to come shortly afterwards under Byzantine rule.

Mention should also be made here of the Albanians surrounded by these other groups. These were apparently the remnants of pre-Roman Illyrian inhabitants of the peninsula (belonging to their own linguistic group), scattered by and surviving successive annexations, though rarely achieving autonomy. In the early modern period their distribution was quite wide in the Balkan peninsula (in part though owing to later resettlement under the Ottomans).[6]

The area to the north of the Sava was of mixed ethnicity. With the final destruction of the Avars in the 790s, we see groups of Slavs settled or settling in lower Pannonia in the great bend of the Danube (among them the Pannonian Croats and Abodriti). While Upper Pannonia (the area around Vienna) became a march of the Frankish Empire, the Slavs of Lower Pannonia had by the second half of the century been organized into some kind of independent political entity by Prince Pribina.[7] From the initial core of his estates in the area on the River Zara which he had received as a *beneficium* from Louis the German (with his main centre at Zalavár), by encouraging the growth of the economy and in particular by colonization of the forested and swampy areas of his territory, he was with the agreement of Louis able to increase his power and develop the Church in his kingdom (subservient to the Salzburg diocese). Pribina was killed in 860 in fights with the Moravians (see below). His son Kocelj continued his father's work, but under the influence of Constantine and Methodius in the 860s accepted the Slav rite. In 869 he had the Sirmium bishopric formed for Methodius, but later Pannonia was linked to the Moravian diocese.[8] In the 890s however the area was devastated by the Magyars and the area later became the core of the Hungarian state.

The East Slavs

One of the divisions in Slavdom which has tended to be emphasized by archaeologists of central Europe is that between East and West Slav. This feature, one
of the most frequently and strongly drawn lines on the cultural map of early
medieval central Europe, is perhaps to some extent a back-projection into the
past of the present situation, as the divide tends to be drawn on the frontier
between Poland and the former Soviet Union (see Chapter 13). It is thus of considerable interest to examine the origin and nature of this cultural division.[9] By
the end of the ninth century the material culture is relatively uniform on both
sides of this line, and it is only with the expansion of Kievan power after the last
decades of the ninth century that we see the establishment of differing cultural
patterns along this line. At this time, the area of the later Kievan state could be
split into at least three zones (Fig. 29; Map v). The area of the forest steppe in
the west was the region in which the Slav identity seems to have crystallized a
few centuries earlier. Over the other side of the Dniepr also in the forest steppe
zone is the Volyntsevo cultural area with a different settlement pattern. To the
north in the forest zone was an area penetrated by the Slavs, but even well after
the ninth century Slavs were probably in the ethnic minority over much of this
area, but with concentrations of settlement (for instance in the upper Niemen,
Dvina and Volkhov). These concentrations increased with the resettlements
which seem to have taken place in the period of operation of the Kievan state.

In the Ukraine in the eighth and ninth centuries we are still reliant on the
archaeological evidence for our studies of cultural processes. New cultural elements appear in place of the Penkovka Culture, and several features disappear,
such as metalwork of Martynovka type. The developments in western Ukraine in
this period led to the creation of the so-called Luka Raikovetska culture (Fig. 26)
developing from the earlier 'post-Prague' elements. The precise date of the beginning of this material is uncertain but it seems to have begun in some parts of the
Ukraine by the eighth century (or perhaps as early as the third quarter of the
seventh century) and continued into the ninth and tenth centuries.[10] This culture
shares many features with its predecessors, such as village and house form, and
burial rite, but again archaeologists have concentrated their attention on the
pottery. The general form of these vessels is similar in that they have relatively
weak rounded shoulders relatively high up on the vessel. The vessels of the Luka
Raikovetska culture after the end of the eighth century can be wheel-made,
although handmade pottery continues in use. The pottery is ornamented by wavy
comb-lines or horizontal bands of combing (though combed decoration had
sporadically occurred on vessels of Korchak type). Some vessels have pinched
rims or a row of holes made on the neck of the vessel. The vessel adopts a more
S-shaped profile with an out-turned rim. This ceramic tradition seems another
case of influence from the Danubian region. The difference between this and the

Racibórz-Chodlik material to the west is difficult to discern; Soviet and Polish archaeologists tend to think of these two groups of pottery as distinct and mutually exclusive in their distribution. The dividing line between them was agreed to be the Bug – which was no coincidence as this is the line of the modern frontier between the two states. The lack of precise criteria to differentiate these groups of pottery, and the fact that material of clear Luka Raikovetska affinities has been found west of the Bug in Biała Podlaska and the Liw valley in eastern Poland,[11] rather cast doubt on the clearness of the division. In recent years the wide Luka Raikovetska zone has been seen as having subdivisions. To the west of the Dniepr are assemblages of the classic Luka Raikovetska Culture which develops here from pre-existing traditions (as on the site of Makarov Ostrov near Penkovka), while to the northeast an earlier Sakhanovka-Luka Raikovetska group has been recently defined. Sakhanovka-type material is found on a number of sites on the right bank of the Dniepr, as well as in the Desna and adjacent valleys including the sites of Penkovka and Volyntsevo.[12]

The type-site at Luka Raikovetska itself is an open settlement under a much later stronghold, but this period sees the increase from the eighth century in numbers of strongholds being constructed. In the Ukraine at least twenty-five have been identified, interestingly enough mainly from the fringes of the area, along the Pripet (Khotomel, Babka), a cluster of eight sites in the Kiev area, probably including the first enclosure at Kiev itself since the pottery found there in associated deposits is dated to the eighth and ninth centuries,[13] and along the edges of the Carpathians.[14] The settlements of this culture are notable for the increased number of iron objects found in them – presumably increased production meant that this was no longer an especially rare material. Some iron however occurs in hoards, such as the material from Makarov Ostrov.

To the east on the left bank of the Dniepr between the upper Oka and Don in the eastern Ukraine is the Volyntsevo group.[15] This represents a later development of the eastern periphery of the Penkovka zone (the relationship of this pottery style zone to the Luka Raikovetska material has yet to be established). This group, previously assigned a slightly earlier dating, is now seen as having developed in the eighth century.[16] The type-site is an open settlement and cemetery near Putivl' (Sumy district) in the Seym valley, situated in a valley and surrounded by bogs. The open villages contained sunken-floored huts of typical form, though some were quite large. Burial was by cremation and urned or unurned remains, often covered by barrows, though some cemeteries contained only flat graves. Some of these cemeteries were large, and contain relatively rich grave goods such as glass beads and metal ornaments and iron objects. A particular feature of the material culture of the Volyntsevo Culture is the amount of Islamic silver which is found, either occasionally as loose finds or more often as hoards. Settlements and graves in the area also produce silver jewellery (rings, bracelets) more frequently than other areas of the East Slav lands at this time.

These coins flowed into the area from Khazaria or from the lands of the Bulgars on the Volga and Kama (see Chapter 8). The Volyntsevo Culture is now linked with the 'Romny' type of sites.[17] These are a series of eighth- to tenth-century settlements situated on steep promontories or in boggy places and surrounded by earthen ramparts and ditches and found along the Desna, Seym, Psol, Sula and Vorskla rivers. The type-site is the 'Monastyrishche' stronghold near the town of Romny in the Sula valley, which was excavated in 1901 (but published only in 1925). Although in the south of the region of their occurrence these sites fall in the area dominated by the Penkovka Culture (which had very few, if any, strongholds), the northern part of the zone of Volyntsevo-Romny sites develops in a region where there had been sites containing Kolochin material (see below). The material culture (which seems to represent a clean break with the patterns of the past) seems to suggest some form of Slavization of indigenous groups leading to the formation of new social arrangements and material culture.

The Borshevo group is formed by a compact cluster of sites to the east of the Volyntsevo-Romny group on the upper Don around Voronezh and Lipetsk in Russia and also in the upper Oka. The main type of settlements known are eighth- to tenth-century strongholds very similar to the Romny sites, and some scholars link them into a single group. They are named after the stronghold and cemetery at Bolshoe Borshevo.[18] This site contained rectangular sunken-floored structures with corner ovens. The ramparts were built of limestone. The Borshevo group of sites develops on the edges of the Moshchino Culture (see below) but extends into the Finno-Ugrian area to the northeast (Fig. 29). The involvement of the Slavs in the process leading to the formation of this cultural group is less clear.

The strongholds in the forest-steppe zone on the left bank of the Dniepr are densely built-up settlements having the appearance of fortified villages composed of sunken-floored huts with ovens in the corner. Unlike those in the earlier Penkovka houses, these ovens are of a different construction: they are built of clay. The pottery is mainly handmade, and some of these sites also produce Islamic dirhems. One of the strongholds is a hilltop site at Novotroitskoe near Lebiedin in the Psol valley (Ukraine), where the steep sides of the hill form a natural defence.[19] The site contained about fifty sunken-floored huts from the eighth and ninth centuries and produced many agricultural, craft and other tools. There was also a hoard containing silver items, including Islamic dirhems. The site was apparently destroyed by a raid, possibly of the nomad Pechenegs. The occupation layers of the Borshevo sites produce finds suggesting that the inhabitants were farmers (growing millet among other crops), and quern fragments were quite common. The main types of livestock were herded, but they also supplemented their diet with hunting and fishing. Since many of the animals hunted were also fur-bearing species, the pelts were presumably used for exchange.

To the southeast of the Volyntsevo-Romny sites and south of the Borshevo sites is an extensive zone in the middle Don and upper Donets valleys stretching across to the lower Volga. This is characterized from the middle of the eighth century by the occurrence of assemblages of the Saltovo-Maiatskii Culture, which is the archaeological reflection of the hegemony dominated by the Khazars.[20] These assemblages contain wheel-made pottery and high-quality metalwork, including types of weapons and harness ornament which are specifically nomadic. The burial rituals include inhumations in underground 'catacombs'. The area contains a variety of settlement sites, ranging from the ephemeral traces of encampments of yurts to large stone-walled 'urban' sites. At the edge of the Khazar land at the interface with the Slav groups discussed above is a line of so-called 'white-stone fortresses' built in the late eighth or early ninth century (Maiatskoe is one of these, while Saltovo is a nearby settlement and cemetery).

It would seem that the origin of the Volyntsevo-Romny and Borshevo sites can be linked in some way to the consolidation of Khazar power on the adjacent Don steppe. The flow of Islamic silver coins into the area would mostly have come through Khazar hands. The construction of strongholds may reflect the need for defence against either nomad raiders or would-be tribute collectors, or may reflect some form of display of prestige generated by increased wealth. These sites have been equated by Soviet archaeologists with two cultural areas which the later written sources name. From the *PVL* (which incorporates information on the ethnic makeup of the area of the later state) we learn of a tribe which moved into the area (reputedly from the Danube) and 'settled on the banks of the Desna, Seym and Sula and were called the Severiane'. The tribal territory of the Severiane given by the *PVL* seems to match quite closely the distribution of the archaeological assemblages of the Volyntsevo Culture. The name means 'the northern people', which suggests that (whichever individual local groups coalesced into this larger tribal union) they had at some time established an identity by opposing themselves with some group in the south. This raises the question whether the name reflects a real or invented migration from some southern region, or whether it referred to the Khazar-dominated zone to the south. The *PVL* tells us that the Severiane and Viatichi paid a tribute to the Khazars in 'silver coin and squirrel furs', and we have already noted the strong influence of the Khazars on the forest steppe zone from the late seventh and through the eighth century.

The tribal identification of the Borshevo sites has been the subject of some discussion, but a new possibility has arisen from the study of the written sources of the eleventh century. One of the puzzles has been the location of the tribe of the Chorvati (Croats) who appear several times in the *PVL* (s.a. 907, 992 and in the *PVL*'s list of peoples of Rus). These are not the same as the 'White Croats' mentioned in the *DAI* (see pp. 74–5), but seem to be a separate group which disappears from the records after an attack by the Kievan prince Vladimir in 992, and was presumably amalgamated into the Rus state. Several historians have tried to locate them on the basis of the scant sources. Two locations are possible: the first somewhere between the Vorskla and the upper Don, the second on the upper Dniestr somewhere in the region of the present Polish border. A close study of the evidence has suggested that we may discard the western variant and locate the (Eastern) Croats somewhere on the southeastern fringe of the early Russian state near the upper Don.[21] Perhaps it is to this group that we should assign the Don strongholds. The relationship between these Chorvati and those of southern and western Slavdom remains unclear.

The archaeological evidence suggests that the tribe or tribes in this area had achieved some form of wealth and perhaps organization by the end of the ninth century, presumably involving some means of generating wealth and prestige by controlling some form of long-distance exchange through their territory. The relative importance of this area was presumably based on its proximity to the Khazar state and was only to be eclipsed by Kiev in the last decades of the ninth century. It is worth noting however that there were no traditions that the rise of the Kievan state was accompanied by the taking of some overall centre in this region (at least there is no mention of this in the *PVL*, which seems to have incorporated at least some oral traditions).[22]

The territory which was later to become the domain of the Poliane with the central stronghold of Kiev seems to have had only limited importance in the ninth century, despite the large enclosure on the hills above the Dniepr and the efforts of the *PVL* chronicler to give the prehistory of the area some substance. He evokes the mythical Kiy, a ferryman, and the legendary rulers Askold and Dir whom in his day tradition linked with the rise of the tribe. We have seen however that there were a number of strongholds in the area, and a limited flow of Islamic silver into it from the Khazars. Some Khazar influence here seems suggested by the evidence of the written sources.[23] The two-hectare stronghold on Starokievskaya Hill was probably built some time in the eighth or first half of the ninth century. Another enclosure was built on the adjacent Zamkovaya Hill in the later eighth century.[24] Franklin and Shepard have suggested that this enclosure might have been 'raised to provide a secure compound for semi-nomadic collectors of tribute on behalf of the Khazars and storage of their takings'.[25] The huge town-like enclosure (Podol) below the strongholds was added at the end of the ninth century. There was a cemetery on Starokievskaya Hill which contains coin-dated graves and other finds dating from the turn of the ninth and tenth centuries.

Other sites in what was later to become the territory of the Poliane include the stronghold at Chernigov on the Desna/Seym which arose in the middle of the ninth century in an area already containing other strongholds. Some 10 kilometres down-river is the Shestovitsy cemetery which closely parallels the Kiev

Starokievskaya cemetery in both date and richness (including some burials in wooden chambers in both cemeteries).[26] Obviously these two places were centres of elite power and the graves represent the retinues attached to them.

The early stages of the formation of two other probable similar cultural units, the areas later inhabited by the Dregovichi and Radimichi tribes (either side of the middle Dniepr), are still poorly known. There are slight indications that parts of the area were to some extent penetrated by the Luka Raikovetska culture.

The northeastern fringes

The area to the north and east of the sites we have just been discussing, in modern Belarussia and southwestern parts of the modern Russian Republic, was occupied by a series of archaeological groups which do not (by virtue of their position) occur in any early written sources. Their ethnic identification is hotly debated by eastern European archaeologists. The groups concerned are the Kolochin Culture and the northern groups, the Tushemla-Bancherovska and Moshchino Cultures.[27] Many archaeologists (such as V. V. Sedov) feel that these groups should be considered as Slavs. Although this was apparently an area of expansion of the Kievan state in the late ninth and tenth centuries, such claims need to be treated with some circumspection.[28] These cultures are well within the area of Baltic hydronyms, and it seems more likely that this area was not originally inhabited by Slavs. We have seen that there is considerable evidence for some form of overlap between the cultures of the Proto-Slavs and Proto-(East-) Balts in the period preceding the Slav migrations, and this in some way may be sufficient to account for the similarities in the material culture of the second half of the first millennium AD which have prompted some to claim these northern forest tribes as Slavs.

The Kolochin pottery tradition of the forest zone develops from the Kiev Culture which itself is derived from the Zarubinets Culture (at one time thought by Soviet scholars to represent the Slavs in the Iron Age). The earliest assemblages have handmade vessels similar in idea and form to the Prague and Penkovka types. The pottery is tall and slim, with the shoulder either rounded or fairly sharp at about half the height or two-thirds up the vessel. Rims are simple in profile and only slightly everted (Fig. 28). The assemblages contain small ceramic plates used for baking, like Korchak assemblages. Kolochin assemblages contain a number of grotesque metal objects somewhat related in style to the Martynovka-type material. The houses are small square sunken-floored huts with central clay hearths (but there are no square huts with ovens of the type typical of the Korchak and Prague Cultures). Unlike Zarubinets and the forest cultures to the north, the Kolochin Culture has few defended sites or strongholds (except the eponymous site itself). Burials are flat urned cremations, though some pit-graves with bones scattered in the fill are known. The Kolochin

Culture occurs on the southern edge of the forest zone, and a few sites occur in the middle Dniepr just above Kiev, but most of the sites are in the forest zone along the Desna and Seym rivers and their tributaries.

Deeper into the forest zone further to the north are two other zones of forest cultures, the Tushemla-Bancherovska and Moshchino Cultures. The pottery of these cultures is however very different in style to the Korchak type, and includes a much wider variety of vessel form. Apart from open settlements, the main settlement form is a series of refugial strongholds which seem to have had a cultic significance, such as Tushemla itself. The square huts do not occur in these sites, but they have simple irregular shallow dug-out pits which may have been the underfloor cavities of ground-level structures. Finds assemblages include a number of massive and grotesque metal forms, some of them with enamelled decoration.[29]

Some archaeologists have gone further and detected Slav elements in the Long Barrows Culture and Sopki Culture even further north. These cultures – existing from the sixth or seventh century – are however in areas of Finno-Ugrian hydronymy and their identification as Proto-Slavs is highly unconvincing.[30]

The ends of the Kolochin and Tushemla-Bancherovska Cultures have been variously dated: some Belarussian archaeologists place them as early as the end of the seventh century, others see them both as lasting throughout the eighth century. Since however the Romny zone overlaps the Kolochin Culture and the Borshevo group, the Moshchino Culture, it would seem that their formation marks the end of these two groups in these areas at least. The nature of the archaeological material occurring in the area between the end of these cultures and the rise of the Russian state is not yet determined.

What is clear is that by the ninth century there was already some form of Slav penetration into these areas. The mechanisms and precise timing of this process are still completely unclear.[31] It seems possible that Slav expansion at some stage before the ninth century had led to the establishment of Slav enclaves in the upper reaches of the Dniepr and its tributaries the Berezyna and Soz, from where it branches out into the upper Niemen, the upper Dvina, the upper Velikaja and the Lovat. Another route would run up the Desna to the Oka. The first areas to be Slavicized were those north of the Pripet and Desna, parts of the territory of the Dregovichi, the Radimichi and further to the east the Viatichi (partly formed on a substrate of the Borshevo Culture). Eventually the Slavs took over the zone of the former Long Barrows Culture and this became the territory of a tribe later known as the Pskov Krivichi, centred on the stronghold at Pskov (dating perhaps from the mid ninth century). The northernmost group, finding themselves in the areas of Finno-Ugrian and Baltic peoples (in the area of the Sopki mounds), called themselves the Slovienie (date uncertain).

The existence in the north of some kind of polity ruled by Varangian adventurers, known to the local tribesmen as the 'Rus' and in fact of Scandinavian origin, has recently been discussed by Franklin and Shepard and this need not be repeated in detail here.[32] These 'silver seekers from the north' settled in the northern zone alongside Balts, Finns and other populations (apparently including Slavs) in such settlements as Staraia Ladoga (from the mid eighth century) and Gorodishche near Novgorod (from the mid ninth century). They were primarily interested in the high-quality furs to be had from local tribesmen and their value in tapping into the flow of silver from the Islamic world (in which the Khazars and Bulgars played the role of entrepreneurs). Gorodishche is thought to be the Holmgard of the sagas where a Varangian leader established himself as the nominal ruler of a vast territory and adopted (from the Khazars) the title *khaganus*. It was from here that trading expeditions set out to the south and east, notably to the region of the upper Volga (just to the north of the later position of Moscow) deep into Merian territory. It was the establishment of long-distance trade networks which was responsible for the founding of trade outposts at the edges of the areas of activity of these adventurers in the area of the upper Volga and the upper Dniepr near an important portage at Smolensk (the Gniozdovo site founded in the late ninth and early tenth centuries). It was from Holmgard that in 860 a huge crowd of Vikings and no doubt Slavs and other adventurers launched an attack on Constantinople. Soon after this, Photius tells us that a Christian mission with a bishop had been sent to these people, but this seems to have come to nothing.[33]

Between the East, South and West Slavs

Before we pass to a discussion of the West Slavs, we should pause to consider the border area between the East, South and West Slavs, for it is here that several tribal groups seem to have existed which have been almost 'written out' of history by later victors.[34] We should be aware that the *PVL* story may well have had good reason to obscure the earlier history of this region, before the expansion of Kievan power here well after the beginning of the tenth century; similarly these border territories do not attract the attention of Polish chroniclers and their western predecessors. We know very little about these groups, but their existence warns us about the dangers of oversimplification (of the type 'East' or 'West' Slav) and also reminds us that we know from the written sources only of those tribes or groupings that the written sources care to tell us about. Only accident may inform us about certain of the linguistic, cultural and ethnic groups which may have been wiped from the pages of history by an expanding state at the threshold of literacy.

The first group which should be mentioned is the Du[d]lebi, who appear only in the *PVL*, where in the list of the peoples of Rus it is stated that 'the Dulebi lived on the Bug, where now the Volynians . . .'. And the tribe is accordingly added to the list of tribes under the year 907. In another place the *PVL* reports a legend concerning the domination of a tribe called the Dulebi by the Avars (Obri – 'giants'). This is a strange record, and is more likely to refer to another tribe, perhaps the Balkan tribe of that name. By the middle of the ninth century this tribe (if it ever really existed) seems to have broken up and is replaced by other groups which had territorial names (such as the Bużane, mentioned by the *Bavarian Geographer*). These in turn seem to have been subsumed into the Volynians (mentioned in the middle of the tenth century by al-Mas'udi as the 'Valinyana').

Adjacent to these people were the 'Lachs', a term which appears in later written sources such as the *PVL*. Another name for what appears to be the same group is rendered Lędziane (*DAI*: Lendzanenoi or Lendzeninoi) or Lendizi (*Bavarian Geographer*). This refers to a group of Slavs who in the ninth century lived in the zone beyond the later edge of Derevlane territory somewhere in the region of the upper Bug valley. In the *DAI* they appear as tributaries of Rus, but by the end of the tenth century have disappeared with Polish expansion into the area.[35] The Lachs seem to have developed a specific cultural identity which is only now being realized (for example they may have been among the builders of the large circular multivallate lowland strongholds of the Chodlik type).[36]

The West Slavs

In some respects cultural development among the West Slavs was in the eighth and ninth centuries a continuation of previous traits. There were however a number of new features, some of which were of a more general nature. Here, as in the Ukraine, for some unknown reason, stone ovens were replaced by clay ones (or huts without ovens) over most of the area probably by the eighth or ninth century. Over most of the area (Poland, eastern Germany, Bohemia and Slovakia), the eighth and ninth centuries see an intensification of the construction of strongholds (see below), which seems to be connected with increasing social organization, but also social unrest. In the ninth century there is a growth in material wealth apparent in an increase in numbers of artefact types, and in the development of trading centres on the Baltic coast. Changes are of course also visible in the pottery, and – traditionally – we will begin with this.

In Polabia[37] and in central Poland is a zone of sites with biconical thin-walled pottery vessels (Fig. 30) decorated on the shoulder by horizontal incised lines or cordons. This so-called Tornow type (named after a type-site on the Spree) is now dated by dendrochronology to the ninth century, more probably to the first half of the century though it may have eighth-century prototypes and probably continued in use until the tenth century.[38] This pottery is associated with a series of open settlements in the southern part of Polabia, and a series of compact circular strongholds (also said to be of Tornow type) which began to be built in the last decades of the ninth and early decades of the tenth century. These also occur in Great Poland (Map V). In central and western Poland (in Wielkopolska), within the Sukow-Gołańcz zone there is an area also with ninth-century sites featuring biconical vessels, forming a eastern extension of the Tornow group (the so-called Tornow-Klenica group, Klenica being a Polish stronghold).[39]

In the same way another pottery type associated with a specific form of settlement has been redated. The pottery occurring in northern Polabia and in western Pomerania is known as Feldberg type (Fig. 30). The vessels are squat and rounded in form, and characteristically decorated in horizontal zones with incised lines, cordons and stamps on the upper body. This material is now dated to the period from the mid eighth century to the mid ninth.[40]

Of somewhat uncertain date too are the biconical vessels with combed latticing or panels on the upper part of the vessel occasionally interspersed with stamp impressions. This Menkendorf pottery (Fig. 31) occurs on the Baltic coast in the northwestern periphery of Slav settlement in the territory later occupied by the Obodrite tribe, but also further south in the Spree valley and in Wielkopolska across to eastern Pomerania. It seems to date to the ninth and tenth centuries. Menkendorf-type pottery also occurs further west, for example in the lowest layers at Międzyrzecz and Poznań (ninth century), and also on some sites in western Silesia. Similar pottery occurs in Szczecin and Gdańsk in Pomerania where it may have lasted to the beginning of the tenth century.

This angularity and decorative schemes of the Tornow, Feldberg and Menkendorf pottery is thought very probably to have been influenced by the form and decoration of contemporary Frankish and Carolingian pottery.

To the south of this pottery zone is the Rüssen pottery zone, which is a continuation of earlier patterns. This material is now known as the Leipzig group. This area is notable for cemeteries containing inhumation burials, some of them with silver ornaments of uncertain date. Heinrich Rempel dates these graves as early as the eighth century, but this has been questioned and there is no reason to date this material so early. These cemeteries are mostly probably tenth century.[41]

To the east, the Racibórz-Chodlik and Central Poland pottery zones last in much of the area through the ninth century (possibly even as late as the early tenth century). In the eighth and ninth centuries the quality of this ceramic steadily improves, and more of it is made on a slow wheel. The general rounded forms of these vessels contrasts with the angular form of the Tornow and Menkendorf pottery further west. As yet there are no clear indicators as to how this material should be split chronologically or geographically; almost certainly regional differences will become clear with increasing knowledge.

South of the Carpathians the general forms are also rounded, and are a continuation of the Danubian ceramics of Devínská-Nová Ves type. The vessels are perhaps taller than Racibórz-Chodlik vessels, with a tendency for the rims to be more vertical. This southern tradition merges westwards into Bohemian ceramics and eastwards into the Luka Raikovetska tradition. This whole wide zone is characterized by a seemingly monotonous series of vessels of S-profile and egg-shaped bodies decorated mainly with combed wavy lines and horizontal rilling. Similar forms occur also in the Balkans in this period. This typological unity suggests that some form of contact still existed between widely scattered Slav communities.

An area of special interest is the coastal strip of Pomerania, where there are changes in the form and structure of the strongholds and the patterns of deposition of silver hoards: these suggest some form of centralization of power which (to judge from changes in the patterns of the flow of silver bullion in the area) seems to have arisen here in the 830s.[42] Before this period the area was divided into a number of smaller regions which differed markedly, for example in the settlement pattern. Some areas were dominated by large strongholds (perhaps defended villages), while other regions had no strongholds at all. At the end of the ninth century and continuing into the tenth century, the part of Pomerania now in Poland became covered by a series of small regular circular strongholds, and the regional differences within the area are levelled out. Further to the west in northern Polabia, however, strongholds of a different form began to be built: these were large densely occupied multi-enclosure hilltop sites. These sites, associated with Feldberg-type pottery, have become known as the 'Feldberg type' of stronghold (once envisaged as refuges or fortified villages), though this has recently been challenged.[43] This ninth-century transition is reflected also by increasing density of settlement across Pomerania, by the settlement of new areas and by changes in the spatial patterning of settlement. These changes seem to relate to the formation of some form of centralized socio-political structure, which was well on the way to state formation. The period is also marked by the accumulation of silver bullion in the form of Islamic, and later western, silver coins. Although some relatively strong tribal unions were to form in the area, this did not result in the formation of a state. Wulfstan, a ninth-century visitor to the area, refers only to it as the 'country of the Slavs' divided from Witland (the Elbląg uplands where Truso lay) by the mouth of the Vistula.[44]

In the later ninth century on the Baltic coast there were several large densely built-up trade and production centres, sometimes surrounded by ramparts, which took part in long-distance exchange. There are several early ninth-century hoards of Islamic silver around the Vistula mouth around the site at Truso which was in Prussian territory near the frontier with the Slavs on the Vistula. The prosperity of this area continued throughout the ninth and tenth centuries. Other early emporia (such as Reric and Ralswiek) were founded on the south coast of the Baltic at this time. Later in the ninth century economic growth definitively shifted to the west to the sites around the Oder mouth;

dendrochronological results indicate that Wolin's port for example was built 880–90.

Further south in central and southern Poland we see a ninth-century rise in the frequency of new strongholds being constructed. These were of a variety of forms, but many were relatively compact ringworks or related types. One site, at Gostyń near Legnica, was burnt down probably in the late ninth or early tenth century and produced many finds, including weaponry (spears, arrows, a battle axe) and domestic items (knives, shears, a firesteel and pot-hook).[45]

The ninth century saw centralization of power developing in the areas occupied by the West Slavs and under especially strong influence from their western neighbours, the Carolingian Empire. The sixth-century eastward expansion of the Merovingians had barely affected the Slavs then just penetrating the area of the Elbe and upper Danube. The only readily visible effect of Frankish influence in this period is the acceptance of certain styles of weapons (such as the sword found in the Oder near Friedrichsthal kr. Angermünde) and perhaps the hooked spurs mentioned above. It was only with the involvement of Slavs in the Saxon Wars of Charlemagne (772–804) that there was increasing Frankish interest in the Slavs who were allied either to the Saxons or to the Carolingians.[46] The *Royal Frankish Annals* of these years after 780 contain a considerable amount of information: the Nordliudi, Sorbs, Wilzi, Smeldingi, Linones and especially the Obodrites are of continued interest for the annalists. In 789 Charlemagne led a major expedition against the Wilzi (Weltabi), crossing the Elbe on fortified wooden bridges and attacking the stronghold of their leader Dragawit and laying waste to vast areas of territory. The *Royal Frankish Annals* are full of details about how Charlemagne formed alliances with certain Slav leaders and set them against others. This was linked with the conversion of some of these groups to Christianity, though other events presented by the annalists suggest that these conversions were somewhat insincere. Carolingian interest in the Slavs did not decrease after the death of Charlemagne in 814. During the reign of one of his successors (probably Louis the Pious or Louis the German), somewhere in the eastern part of the Carolingian empire in about 840, someone compiled a document (Fig. 1) known as the *Bavarian Geographer* entitled *Descriptio civitatum et regionum ad septentrionalem plagam Danubiae* (Description of the 'towns' and regions to the north of the Danube). It accompanies the list of tribes beyond the imperial frontiers with the numbers of defended centres (*civitates*) each possessed. It is suspected that it was the result of some form of Carolingian intelligence-gathering for military or economical purposes. This list is of considerable interest for the historian, though the reliability of the number of strongholds given is clearly not great; neither is it easy to locate unequivocally many of these tribes on modern maps of early medieval settlement.

Recent dendrochronological work, especially by Joachim Henning, shows that stronghold construction in this area has two main phases: (1) last quarter of the ninth century and first half of the tenth century, and (2) middle and third quarter of the tenth century.[47] If one looks at a map of early medieval settlement in the Elbe lands however, one can see that in the period between the late eighth and early tenth centuries there are concentrations of large strongholds in several zones along the frontier with the Carolingians. There is a group of large sites in the north, between Starigard and Lübeck, and a small cluster near Menkendorf (Lochnitz valley); but the largest cluster is in the Havel valley near Brenna. The largest strongholds however are those in the Peen and Tollensee valleys in the centre of the Feldberg zone.[48] This picture strongly suggests that proximity to the imperial frontiers was able to promote local leaders to some importance and allow them to consolidate their power. They probably did this either by diplomatic relations or by gathering loot from raids on Carolingian territory. The latter strategy was a somewhat risky one in the times of strong rulers such as Charlemagne, but in the period of relative weakness from the Treaty of Verdun (843) to the accession of Henry the Fowler (918) attacks on the eastern marches of Saxony and Thuringia may have been a viable option.

The end of the eighth century and the ninth century also see however considerable Carolingian influence in metalwork and pottery styles. We have discussed Tornow and Feldberg pottery above, and Frankish swords, harness fittings and spurs also infiltrated eastwards into central Europe.[49] Charlemagne even issued an edict forbidding the supply of Frankish swords to the Slavs (see Chapter 8), but a number of archaeological finds of such items show that this was ineffective.

Moravia and Bohemia

Despite the progressive strengthening of the power of Slav leaders shown by the archaeological evidence, it was only in the early part of the ninth century that the first West Slav state, that of Moravia, was established. (For the question of the definition of a state and discussions on the more general aspects of processes of state-formation see Chapter 6.)

The tribal divisions in the Morava valley of the ninth century seem to be represented by detectable regional differences in the pottery assemblages.[50] Along the Morava valley there seem to have been settlement complexes in the Olomouc region, the central areas of the valley, and in the lower regions of the valley at its junction with the Danube (the Bratislava region). To the west were concentrations of settlement in the Brno region and the valley of the Dyje.

In the ninth century we see the centralization of power in major strongholds in these regions along the Morava valley along a major river route linking north and southern Europe through the Moravian Gate in the Carpathian mountain chain. Moravia was north of the Danubian zone of Avaro-Slav settlement, though it was strongly influenced by its southern neighbours, but it was also ready to accept influences from the west. After the destruction of Avar power by Charlemagne together with the Bulgars in 793–6 new impetus was given to the development in Moravia of the rich culture which had been forming in the area since the end of the seventh century.[51] This is evidenced among other things by the emergence of a new style of metalwork appearing here under late Avar and Carolingian influences, the so-called Blatnica (-Mikulčice) horizon (Blatnica is a rich barrow containing a Carolingian sword and its fittings excavated in the nineteenth century). The area became of considerable importance and legates from the Moravian leaders were met by the Carolingian emperors at Aachen (811), Paderborn (815) and Frankfurt (822). The transition from the pre-Moravian phase to the Moravian state is marked by new developments in the material culture, for example a development of ferrous metallurgy (Chapter 8). A more telling aspect is however the centralization of power in large fortified centres such as those in which hooked spurs of eighth-century type occur (Mikulčice, Pobedim, Brno-Lisen (Staré Zámky), in the valley of the Morava) while several north Slovakian strongholds appear in the eighth century (Vyšca, Spišká Tomášovce). At the beginning of the ninth century we see the construction of many other tribal hillforts. Each of the tribal zones noted above had a series of strong tribal fortifications, such as in the central areas of the valley (sites at Stare Mesto, Mikulčice, Pohansko), and in the lower regions of the valley at its junction with the Danube (Devin, Bratyslava), in the Brno region (Blučina, Staré Zámky, Rajhrad), the valley of the Dyje (Znojmo). In the north Olomouc was probably founded in or before the early ninth century, on a hill overlooking the Morava valley. It was to become the capital of the area in the tenth century.

The strongholds of the area have a distinctive rampart structure and form. The ramparts have an outer drystone wall with an internal timber structure filled with earth (Fig. 34).[52] In plan these sites – usually situated on a high steep-sided hill – tend to be several hundred metres across and formed of several contiguous enclosures surrounding a central area which often contains elite structures. The external enclosures were inhabited and exhibit evidence of craft activity.

In the 830s, under Prince Mojmir, the Marharii (as they appear in the *Bavarian Geographer*) were expanding eastwards into the Slovakian mountains (Prince Pribina was expelled from Nitra). After Mojmir's death about 846 Prince Rostislav continued the policy of expansion. This was the beginnings of the process of the creation of a state which was known to Constantine VII writing his *DAI* a century later as 'Great' Moravia. One of the conditions of being accepted into the European Community of the times was to be seen to be a Christian leader of a Christian nation. Anxious, however, to prevent being manipulated by the Franks, Rostislav sent to the more distant imperial rivals in Byzantium. In 863 Cyril and his brother Methodius (Slavs from Thessalonica) came to Moravia to found a Slav church. Cyril had studied in Constantinople and went as a missionary to the Khazars. He seems also to have contemplated a mission to Bulgaria, which is probably why he devised the precursor of an alphabet which still bears his name to translate the Gospels into a Slav language. The Moravian Church was bitterly opposed by German churchmen. While Rostislav lived, Methodius (who after Cyril's death in 869 had taken over the archbishopric) could count on the ruler's support, but in 869 Rostislav fell into the hands of Louis the German, who promptly blinded and deposed him. Rostislav's nephew Sviatopluk (869–94) continued the policy of extending the Moravian realm to the east and west, but appeased the clergy of the German emperor and after the death of Methodius in 885 (previous to which he had spent three years in a Bavarian prison before being reinstated by the Pope), the Slav liturgy was banned from the Moravian Church, and the Slav clergy fled the country to Bulgaria and Dalmatia.

The Moravian state underwent considerable expansion, especially in the 870s under Sviatopluk (Fig. 33). In the 870s or 880s the Moravians made a bid to extend their power northwards across the Carpathians to the broad fertile lands in Silesia and Małopolska. The *Life of Methodius* (XI.1–3) tells us of the fulfilment of a prophecy uttered by the bishop: 'there was a very powerful pagan prince on the Vistula [53] who persecuted many Christian folk and did them great harm. The Bishop sent a messenger to warn him "it would be good for you, my son to be baptized in your own lands by your own will otherwise you will be baptized in slavery in a foreign land", and this came to pass.' There is little clear archaeological or written evidence however of a permanent extension of Moravian centralization of power in Małopolska or to the west in Silesia, or – as has been claimed by some historians – into Pannonia. Indeed modern historiography has tended to question the former claims of huge neighbouring territories permanently annexed by the Moravian state. The Moravians however were able to annex Bohemia and unite the area to Moravia in the 880s. The possible implications of the so-called *Prague Document* are dealt with below (see Chapter 12).

The brief period of the flourishing of the Moravian state is represented in the archaeological record by a remarkable assemblage of material traces. There is a change in the fortified centres: they are now sited in lower-lying positions on river crossings (such as Mikulčice) and several take the form of clusters of non-contiguous enclosures. These massive strongholds take on the form of urban centres, with stone churches – usually rotundas or of basilican form (Fig. 63) – and other traces of Christian religion (pectoral crosses) and inhumation cemeteries adjacent to churches. Another noticeable feature is the rich material culture – the standard of the pottery increases markedly. Production of iron probably increased, as shown by the quantities discarded or deposited as hoards. Most impressive however is the range of fine silver jewellery: various forms of female headdress ornament, crescent-shaped pendants (lunulae), ear-rings, and hollow globular silver buttons for elaborate finery (Fig. 35). Much of this is decorated with fine filigree. The designs seem to be influenced by south-ern models, especially Byzantine fashions. The independent dating of the incep-tion of this jewellery is difficult to establish, because this type of material is seldom found in coin hoards, for the simple reason that south of a line well to the north of the Carpathians, for some reason which is not quite clear, no silver coin hoards occur in the whole of the ninth century.[54] Most scholars assume that the appearance of these ornaments accompanied a general increase in wealth (at least in some sections of society) with the rise of the state.[55]

In the final decade of the ninth century and the beginning of the tenth, signif-icant political and ethnic changes were taking place in the Carpathian basin (in the area of modern Hungary and western Romania). The area was gradually infiltrated (894–6) by the Magyar horsemen who were already familiar with central Europe – they had been used for example by Rostislav of the Moravians in 862 in his wars against the Franks.[56] As a result of these raids some Magyar clans (including that led by a leader called Arpad) had gained considerable influ-ence. In the face of expansion of the Pecheneg Turks into their steppe homeland, Arpad led a large number of Magyars west and they finally settled in Pannonia.[57] The arrival of this new entity was utilized to political advantage by its neighbours. In 894 the Magyars aided Sviatopluk of Moravia against the Bulgars and Franks. The Magyar presence was also advantageous (at first) to the eastward ambitions of the German rulers who set them against both the Bulgars and the Moravians. The opportunities for this were created by the death of Sviatopluk in 894, and by the quarrels between his three sons which rent the state. These differences were encouraged by Arnulf, the king of the East Franks, who was interested in bringing about the fall of a dangerous and insubordinate power on his eastern border. At Arnulf's instigation the Magyars turned their attention to the Moravian state and together they succeeded in destroying it by 906. The archaeological evidence for the destruction and abandonment (lasting for a century or so in many cases) of the Moravian strongholds at this time is eloquent. From Pannonia, however, the Magyars attracted attention to them-selves by launching a series of destructive raids into central Europe.[58]

The story of the Moravian state has tended to overshadow that of the rise of the Bohemian (Czech) state. By the early ninth century in this area there were a number of strong but independent tribes (Czechs, Lučane, Lemuzi, Zličanie, Croats, Dulebi) concentrated especially in the Moldau valley in the centre of the Bohemian basin on another important transcontinental route. We see here also the rise of large tribal strongholds (for example Stará Kouřim, Budeč and Dolanski) ranging in size from about 20 to 40 ha; the outer enclosures were inhabited and the inhabitants engaged in craft activities. Rulers of these tribes appear in the written sources, such as Lecho (or Becho) who in 805 was fighting

Charlemagne. In the second half of the ninth century however we see the beginning of the unification of these tribes under the leadership of chiefs of the Přemyslid dynasty (at first under the patronage of Sviatopluk of the Moravians who had annexed the territory in the late 880s).[59] This Moravian influence is visible in the culture of Bohemia at this time, for example at the stronghold at Stará Kouřim.[60] The subsequent history of the Bohemian state is considered further below (pp. 251–6).

5
Daily Life

Despite what some (including certain archaeologists) may think, archaeology is not just the study of things – nor history just the study of political events: both study people. For the people who have been the subject of our discussion in previous chapters, their life had nothing in common with modern academic issues concerning pottery typology, socio-economic structures or even ethnic issues. These are modern constructs which we use to attempt to understand past social complexities. What we are really interested in is the people we are studying, what they were like, what they thought, how they experienced their daily lives.

Unfortunately the written sources say very little about life in Slav villages or about daily life of their inhabitants, which can be best reconstructed from the archaeological evidence. We can find and excavate their houses and deduce how the space was used, we can study their cooking pots and sift through their rubbish-dumps and – ultimately – examine the remains of the people themselves by excavating their graveyards. This chapter aims to present a generalized overview of this evidence: there is no space here to detail thoroughly regional and chronological differences. In the case of the Early Slavs however the material culture is surprisingly similar over a wide area.[1]

The people

Unfortunately for the archaeologist and physical anthropologist, the rite of burial by cremation was in use over most of Slavdom from the sixth to ninth centuries (and lasted much longer in many areas, especially in East Slav territory). This rite with the accompanying distortion and fragmentation of the skeletal remains has robbed us of much useful anthropological material for most of the area and period covered in this book. Although one or two diagnostic fragments may tell us about the age or sex of the individual (at least to a certain degree of likelihood), since not all bones found their way into the burial, such evidence is scant. The fact that over most of Slavdom the cremation rite was practised is bad enough, but also (as discussed in Chapter 9) in many areas there is a singular lack of burials: clearly some rite was in use which leaves absolutely no archaeological traces.

Inhumation burials provide more information, and in addition often contain items of dress and ornament (and sometimes other objects) which can tell us about the wealth and perhaps social position of the individual. The inhumation burial rite is characteristic of the later period (becoming more common in the ninth and tenth centuries in most areas), although inhumation graves occur south of the Carpathians at an earlier date. The anthropological characteristics of the remains from the inhumation cemeteries in the West Slav zone have been better studied, and we will have to use this evidence as characteristic of the whole area and period in the absence of any alternative.[2]

The average height of adults can be determined from longbone measurements: in one Polish cemetery men were 167 cm on average tall (156–73 cm), and women 151 cm. (150–4 cm). Many medieval skulls from West Slav cemeteries tend to be rather broad-faced and short (that is, round and not long heads), though preliminary research seems to show that this is a feature developing more markedly after the twelfth century. Limbs tend to be strong and muscular. We have little reliable data on other aspects of the appearance of Early Slavs from the archaeological or historical data. In modern populations blond, brown and black hair are present, the darker colours perhaps predominating in some areas. Darker skin coloration is also relatively common compared to recent northwestern European populations.

Physical anthropologists can by examining the bones (by a variety of methods) determine the age of death of the individuals found in the excavated graves. We do not have full information on infant mortality, as graves of one-year-old and newborn babies are seldom found (in part this may be due to the dissolution of their bones in shallow graves, or perhaps they were not buried in the community cemetery before a certain age). Nevertheless it seems that in those cemeteries where this aspect has been carefully studied, for example in Bohemia and Moravia, around 30 per cent of the graves were of children who died before they were six, and up to 12 per cent of children aged six to twelve. The statistical average of ages of death of the populations represented in many cemeteries is about twenty-seven years, but the average age of adult death however was about forty years for men and thirty-three for women. About 40 per cent of men died before they were 40, and 60 per cent of women. Very few men (fewer than 4 per cent) lived to be more than sixty. The difference in ages of death of men and women is to a certain extent a result of frequent deaths of young women during and just after childbirth. It seems likely that most families had numerous children, but information on childbirth frequencies (determinable from examination of the female pelvis) has yet to be collated. In many Slav cemeteries where it can be determined, we find for some reason more bodies of men than women.

Unfortunately, we cannot determine the precise causes of death of most of the individuals we find the remains of. It seems likely however that many deaths were from diseases which today are controllable. Skeletal remains can also tell us about certain diseases and injuries, from which we can tell that the Early Slavs suffered from the same diseases that we have, including arthritis and cancers. Some bones have hideous injuries, clearly caused in warfare. Some of them had healed some time before the individuals died. Fractures of longbones are relatively common, and in the majority of instances had healed in correct axial position without dislocation, so medical care was at a relatively high level. There is little evidence from Slav skeletal remains for poor nutrition. In general, Early Slavs apparently had much better teeth than today: a third of adult skeletons examined from Moravian cemeteries had no caries and had lost no teeth. The health of the teeth varies with age, but even 15–20 per cent of the older individuals had perfectly healthy teeth. In most cases women had worse caries than men, probably owing to decalcification in pregnancies.

Dress and hygiene

Most of the information about Slav dress comes from the cemeteries and iconographic sources. The latter however show mostly religious themes where there is a noticeable influence of Late Antique dress styles, and we may also expect that areas in close contact with Byzantium would accept cultural models from that source. Thus we find Byzantine fashions being copied among the south Slavs and in the Kievan court: thus need not reflect the everyday dress of their subjects. We have also written accounts such as those of Jewish or Arabian travellers, whose reports are more valuable because (unlike their Slav contemporaries) they treated the different dress styles as a curiosity compared to that of their own people, and thus sometimes recorded more details. Dress was however often one of the more visible attributes of 'otherness' and it is possible that some details have been exaggerated in the written accounts created by outsiders.

The typical dress which can be reconstructed from these sources is summarized below. Unfortunately the details do not allow as full a reconstruction as we would like: we have no information about underwear for example. We should also remember that we should expect some chronological and regional variation across this wide area in the half millennium studied here. It is obvious that there were also seasonal differences in clothing, and also social differences. Poorer peasants for example may have worn leather boots only on special occasions: we have some ethnographic evidence that for everyday use some wore wickerwork shoes and presumably in summer went barefoot. There is some evidence that increasing differentiation in quality and style of dress of the elite appears with the rise of more complex social organizations. Again most of the evidence comes from the end of our period, with the appearance of towns and the accompanying increase of organically rich waterlogged deposits in which material such as textiles and leather survives.

In general, men wore long-sleeved tunics of linen or wool which extended to just above the knee. The lower part may have been pleated. The tunic was fastened at the waist by a leather belt (metal buckles and belt-ends of which are found in some graves). Under this tunic were some form of tight breeches, extending down to the ankles. Procopius describes the dress of Slav warriors in the Danubian region and tells us that 'some of them . . . wear only a kind of breeches [*anaksyrides*] pulled up to the groin'.[3] Shoes, half-boots or calf-boots would be worn on the feet. The lower legs were sometimes cross-gartered. Over the tunic may be worn coloured woollen cloaks (sometimes with a lining of material or fur), fastened at the right shoulder, leaving the right arm free (this is clear from the iconographic sources, but the nature of the fastening leaves no traces in the graves in Slav cemeteries). Sometimes it seems the cloaks could have been made of leather. Hats were also worn, as were mittens in winter. Some of the overclothes and hats were trimmed with fur. Leather shoes and boots for both men and women (or rather their fragments) are found in waterlogged deposits in some towns, where they seem to be cobblers' waste.

It appears that women's dress was more variable. Probably these differences were due to geographical and chronological differences of the sources, but the dress may also have varied according to season. Ethnographic parallels suggest that other differences may be due to the marital status of the woman. Some women wore long patterned linen tunics, while the legs were covered by one or two full wrap-around aprons tied around the waist. Other iconographic representations show long single-piece dresses of linen or wool which extended from the neck to the ankles. The sleeves of these dresses were usually long, but could be loose or tight-fitting. The skirt could be full and pleated or relatively tight. Some iconographic sources show knee-length dresses, occasionally off-the-shoulder. Some dress styles required the woman to wear an apron over the dress, tied at the waist. In wet weather they wore a squarish shawl thrown over both shoulders. Later in the period it seems that cloaks became more fashionable, worn in the same manner as men wore them, but fastened in some regions more often with a fibula. Fastening at the front on the breast was rarer. In cold weather both sexes probably wore fur cloaks or maybe coats.

The most distinctive item of Slav women's dress was however the headdress. Young girls wore their hair loose, or in plaits, with a linen headdress. Ethnographic evidence suggests that young girls had one type of head covering (or went without one) until the day of the wedding, when a different type of head-covering was substituted.[4] The Arab writer al-Qazvin says of the East Slavs that 'their unmarried daughters go out with uncovered heads, so that everybody can see them. If anyone fancies any of them, he throws over their head a piece of material.'[5] This would appear to be a distorted reference to the ceremonial donning of this item of clothing which was part of the wedding service (the *oczepiny*). Married women wore their hair gathered up under a covering (very occasionally traces of hair are found in graves; for example at Radim in Bohemia a plait of hair was found wound round the forehead of a skull). These headdresses thus varied not only with social position but also with the age and marital status of the wearer. They were apparently held on by a leather brow-strap, and these from at least the ninth century were ornamented by metal rings and plates – often of silver. These were presumably an expression of status, and were perhaps not an element of everyday dress, but maybe worn on special occasions (and to the grave). The headdress rings worn on a band of leather or textile over the temples are characteristic of Slav female dress, while the ornaments worn on the flaps of other types (so-called *zausznice*) are more characteristic of the East Slavs. There was clearly an elaborate code attached to the wearing of the various types of headdress, which we are as yet not able to read. There is however a regional difference in types: tubular rings are more common in Pomerania, while at a slightly later date in East Slav lands (Fig. 36) certain types are specific for particular areas (tribes). The corrosion products of the metal ornaments of the headbands sometimes preserve small areas of skin and hair in female graves (Fig. 37).

Women's dress also included various types of ornament, such as in the case of wealthier families silver earrings, hollow silver beads, solid or twisted wire bracelets and occasionally neckrings. These objects are also found in the silver hoards (Chapter 8) and it seems that, aside from their decorative value, these items were treasured for their intrinsic worth. Probably these items were in part wedding gifts to the bride from the bridegroom's family. Other items include multicoloured glass beads, and in the East Slav territory glass bangles (mainly at the end of our period). Also a relatively late phenomenon over most of Slavdom are rare beads of amber and of imported crystal, carnelian, fluorite, bloodstone and chalcedony further afield.

On the belt was often hung a knife, which served for cutting and eating food and was carried by men, women and children. Sometimes a small perforated whetstone was worn alongside the knife for keeping it sharp. Pouches at the waist sometimes contained firesteels and flint, and presumably tinder. Women sometimes carried keys to the home or to chests.

The Slavs were especially prone to assimilating styles of their neighbours. Thus in the East Slav areas we find traces of influence of the nomad dress styles in clothing and ornament. In the northern forests Scandinavian fashions were sometimes copied by Slavs, and in the Kievan state the elite costumes were also affected by Byzantine and Khazar stylistic influences. The costume of Slavs living around the Carpathian basin was strongly influenced by the dress of the Avars (the men adopting the Avar belts for example); at a later date contacts with the Magyars had the same effect. Large hollow globular decorated buttons modelled perhaps on Byzantine originals were worn by Moravian and South Slav nobles to fasten thick coats. In West Slav territory, Frankish styles were assimilated and on the north coast Scandinavian brooches and pins occur in some graves, presumably of Slavs. Probably some of these items had their origins in cross-ethnic marriage unions resulting in cultural mixing in individual households.

Clothing was also sometimes used to differentiate ethnicity. We have discussed female ornament and dress styles, but it seems that male clothing could be used to express group identity. Gallus Anonymous (1.6) describes the meeting of Bolesław the Bold of Poland and Emperor Otto III of Germany (1000): 'next the king had his men stand like choirs on a wide plateau, and in the separate ranks distinguished the various colours of their dress', suggesting that the different patterns of stripes had a regional significance as well as perhaps signifying social rank.

Personal hygiene of the Early Slavs cannot be measured by modern standards, neither was it comparable to the level of for example the contemporary Byzantines and Islam. Thus we find negative opinions of the dirtiness of the Slav groups raiding the Empire. This was another facet of the 'otherness' that was being stressed. Nevertheless the written and archaeological sources demonstrate that the East Slavs took saunas, how regularly we do not know (though the *PVL* suggests that in Kiev the inhabitants took a sauna every day, this is perhaps an exaggeration). The sauna seems to have been a custom adopted from the tribes of the northern fringes of the Rus state and took the form of a shallow pit inside a wooden structure in which a fire was built, on which large boulders were heated. Then water was poured on to the stones making vapour in which dirt was sweated out of the pores. The process was aided by beating with twigs and pouring cold water on the body. The sauna was an important part of the ritual of greeting a guest and also ceremonial cleansing before certain rituals.

Toilet facilities were however primitive by modern standards (but this was common among almost all medieval cultures of Europe). In some later households toilet seats (consisting of a stout plank with a hole about 25 cm in diameter) were erected over pits and were enclosed in wooden sheds (such as one found recently in Wrocław).[6] Such structures are not very often recognized archaeologically, but are mentioned in the written sources, such as when in 1034 the Czech Prince Jaromir is found murdered while sitting on the toilet. In most cases in rural areas in the absence of archaeological evidence for sanitary facilities it seems however that these needs were met by going into the fields or forest. One may imagine that this facilitated the spread of disease.

Clothes were washed by wells, lakes and streams, using wooden paddles to beat the dirt out. The Slavs also knew of the making of soap by at least the eleventh century (and probably earlier). Combs of antler and bone, often finely decorated, are relatively common (Fig. 37) and seem to have been frequently used. Most of them were produced in local ateliers, but items produced in workshops on the Baltic coast were traded far (and are useful as chronological indicators, as well as for demonstrating trade networks). Locally made wooden combs of similar form are found also in waterlogged deposits. In tenth-century Novgorod, combs made of Caucasian palm were imported from the north Caucasus. Ivory combs were also imported occasionally.

Many Slavs shown in the iconographic sources have beards, though in the later period (when we have more such sources) more clean-shaven faces appear. Recognizable razors are rare before the late ninth century, when folding razors occur in Bohemia and Moravia, Croatia and the Kievan state in association with high-status artefacts. Before this however sharp knives could have been used – or perhaps Slav men did not shave. Tweezers were used for plucking out surplus hair and thorns, shears were used for cutting hair. Possibly women used simple forms of cosmetics, but the evidence for this is slight.

The family home

We may assume that the basic social unit was the family. There has been much literature on this topic, generated by Friedrich Engels's famous little book *The Origin of the Family, Private Property and the State* (1884). In early Slavdom, the written sources suggest that the basic unit was the patriarchal extended family, which carried with it the linking of several of these into clans. The concept of the extended family or *zadruga* in the form often discussed in this context on the basis of ethnographic evidence is applicable mainly to the southern Slav regions, principally the mountain zones.[7] Recent studies suggest that this highly politicized notion was an invention of the nineteenth century projected back on to early Slav society.[8] It would be incorrect to use this model as more than a rough guide to possible settlement structures among other Slav groups in different environments.

Marriage rites included the symbolic exchange of goods in return for the bride: this suggests monogamous marriage in most circumstances. Polygamy was practised however by the elite in some societies; thus we hear of the twelve wives of King Samo, while Mieszko of the Polane had before his baptism seven wives ('according to custom'). The *PVL* tells us that men of the Radimichi, Viatichi and Severiane had two or three wives. Pagan Polabian Slav leaders were also polygamous according to the Christian sources. We have little direct information about pagan courtship and marriage rituals, but the ninth-century Arab author of the *Anonymous Relation* notes the sexual freedom of the East Slav girl before marriage. Some written sources however, such as Pseudo-Maurice, note the chastity of Slav women after marriage.

There are a number of references in a few ninth- and tenth-century Arab written sources to the practice in East Slav lands that, when a man died, his wife and slaves were placed on the funeral pyre with his body. The wives were said to go to their death voluntarily, regarding their own lives as over when their husbands died. How widespread this practice was we cannot say: it is evidenced only in a few written sources referring to the eastern areas of the Kievan realms and may apply mainly to the non-Slav element of Rus society. These accounts include the famous and frequently quoted reference by Ibn Rusteh, describing human sacrifice (a young female slave) in a Rus funeral on the Volga.[9] There is evidence from the study of cremated bone from West Slav territory however that graves can contain more than one individual, hinting that this practice may have been more widespread (though perhaps only in certain social strata).[10] The references to this rite tell us something also about the status of slaves in Slav society. Although there is little evidence for them archaeologically, they are evidenced in the written sources (see Chapter 8).

The status of women is difficult to determine from these sources. It would seem that although societies may well have been patriarchal (as in many agricultural communities) the woman in the role of mother and keeper of the domestic hearth had considerable authority in the home. We have only a little evidence on how children were treated in these societies and on the rites of passage accompanying their becoming adults. An interesting reference is the story reported by Gallus Anonymous (I.2) of the ritual known as *postrzyżyny*, practised in central Poland, where a boy's hair was cut for the first time and he received a name. From the context of the story, this may have happened on his seventh birthday.[11]

Family homesteads often consisted of clusters of several buildings, presumably of differentiated function. The main building type found consists of sunken-floored huts, often with stone or clay ovens in the corner. Some of the sunken-floored buildings were living accommodation; others lack ovens and may have been storerooms. Some of the settlements are well enough preserved to demonstrate that the sunken-floored structures were accompanied by ground-level buildings (which do not always however leave archaeological traces).[12] These, like the walls of many of the sunken-floored buildings, were constructed of 'log-cabin' ('blockhouse') construction: horizontal logs jointed at the corners and packed with clay or moss to form a windproof wall (Fig. 9). Life within such structures was probably rather cramped, and indeed we suspect that many of the daily activities were carried on outside the buildings. Probably these huts were used primarily for sleeping in and storing one's few possessions. The superstructure of these huts is rarely possible to reconstruct. Some archaeologists envisage them as primitive windowless and smoky structures with pitched roofs resting on the ground surface, while others see the sunken floor as only a small portion of a much more complex and sometimes multistorey structure rather like a modern two-up-two-down.[13] There is often little archaeological evidence to allow us to choose between these alternatives in particular instances.

We know little about the internal fittings of such huts: there are few traces of bedding or storage chests, despite careful study of the carbonized remains of several of these huts which had been burnt down. The internal ovens built of stone or clay which are found in most of these huts probably served as a source of heat, and also to dry the contents of the hut sunken into the damp earth. They were presumably also used for cooking. Cooking was done in pottery vessels (few metal vessels are known). The Slav kitchen probably included also a number of storage vessels of pottery and wood. Some Slav pottery assemblages contain flat clay disks about a centimetre thick and 30 cm diameter: these probably served for baking flatcakes over a hearth. In other areas (except South Slav territory) badly made fired clay rectangular trays with upturned edges (in Polish *prażnice*) were probably used for parching grain. We know little about eating utensils: probably most adults carried a knife which served for eating, together with wooden spoons of a variety of shapes which are relatively common finds. Pottery assemblages lack bowls or cups; presumably such vessels were made of other materials. The Slavs have been referred to as having had a material culture of wood, and indeed in many waterlogged layers of towns a wide variety of turned, carved and stave-built vessels are known.[14]

The *Life* of St Otto of Bamburg written about 1160 by the Benedictine Herbord tells us a little about daily life in western Pomerania at the time of Otto's mission there in 1124–8. He tells us (II.41) that 'each householder had a house to himself, clean and comfortable' and that the walls were whitewashed and herbs were used on floors to keep insects at bay and sweeten the air. He further notes (II.41) that 'the table is always full of everything to drink and eat, and after finishing one thing, another is laid. Mice are kept away, not by mousetraps, but by placing a clean white cloth over the food so that it awaits the feast.' Herbord, like other early medieval writers, notes the hospitality of the Slavs towards guests, a tradition which the various Slav nations preserve today. (It is also the main motif of the story of Piast, the founder of the Polish royal dynasty, in which Gallus Anonymous tells us how he attained power after he had offered hospitality to two mysterious wanderers who had been turned away by the prince, whose dynasty was eventually replaced by Piast's sons.)

We know regrettably little about Early Slav cuisine. One suspects that many of the vegetables and fruits known from the waterlogged levels in later towns were known also to the Early Slavs (including onion, pea, broad bean, lentils, cucumber, parsnip, parsley, walnut, peach, plum, cherries, apple, pear, hops). The end of our period was a climatic optimum, and so even grapes may have been grown north of the Carpathians in the ninth and tenth centuries. Slav farmers cultivated many types of grain: millet was especially popular, as were wheat (various types), rye and barley. This was used not only as flour for baking but in the form of groats as a vegetable. Beer was brewed and drunk, and in some areas wine may have been consumed. Meat from domestic and hunted animals was much appreciated. In many central European bone assemblages domestic cattle bones are most frequent: this was clearly the major meat source, with pig a close second. There are of course regional and chronological differences in precise percentages (Fig. 38).[15] Sheep was never popular as a meat dish: many bone assemblages contain less than 10 per cent, though in the mountainous regions of Slovakia sheep and goat bones form a much higher percentage. Of the hunted animals (which form a few per cent of many excavated bone assemblages) deer of various types and boar were clearly enjoyed. Bird bones are less commonly found; among them the most common are domestic chickens and wild duck and goose. Fish bones are found on some sites, though shellfish seem not to have been eaten. We may assume that milk products were consumed, and they still form an important part of the rural diet in some Slav countries. What we cannot tell is the proportion of meat to vegetables in the diet, nor can we do more than guess how meals were cooked. The utensils for which we have evidence (most of them pottery) suggest that food was cooked by boiling, simmering and baking. There is an apparent lack of utensils for frying.

Food was grown in fields near the home, beyond which there was pasture for the livestock. Beyond this was the forest: the zone nearer the homestead was heavily exploited, for wood and forest products for the home, but beyond this was a zone which was probably more rarely visited (Fig. 39). The size and arrangement of the fields are unknown. We do not know whether land was farmed by each family separately or to what extent (if at all) there were common fields. Similarly, we do not know anything about the spatial division of the settlement area. There are generally no fence lines found; perhaps the area was divided by hedges, or perhaps it was completely undivided.

The rural settlement of the period was generally undefended and usually lay close to water, such as a lake or stream, presumably to meet domestic needs (wells were dug only occasionally in such settlements) and those of livestock. The plan of most such settlements (where the size of excavation allows it to be interpreted) consists of one or more discrete homesteads, often rebuilt over several generations (Fig. 40). When a building fell into disrepair, it was not rebuilt in the same place, but a new one was built nearby; thus the settlement as a whole spread laterally and its nucleus shifted with time. Each homestead consisted of a cluster of buildings of differing function (some of these may have been for animals – though no clear evidence has come from Slavdom of internal accommodation of livestock on rural sites). Typical examples are Dessau-Mosigau in East Germany, Březno in Bohemia, Żukowice in Silesia and Korchak or Penkovka in the Ukraine.[16] Sometimes the number of homesteads is greater and creates the impression of a village, sometimes up to several hectares in extent. Where there is evidence of relatively small communities (as for example phase I at Tornow, which perhaps contained about three hundred people), it is possible to think in terms of communities of several related extended families. It is more difficult to accept that this is the case in communities of larger size (such as Feldberg, which perhaps held six hundred to twelve hundred people).

These settlements were usually relatively short-lived. This seems to have been due to limitations on the size of the settlement: it would seem that when this limit was reached and there was still demographic growth, part of the community would leave the settlement and found a new one some distance away. After a time the whole settlement was abandoned in favour of a number of satellite settlements. This pattern of shifting short-term settlement is of course partly responsible for the phenomenon of the expansion of the Slavs themselves. In some cases one may suspect that the movement was slight (a few hundred metres in the same micro-region); in others it may have been more of the order of a few kilometres into adjacent areas. The factors limiting the size of the settlements can only be guessed. It has been suggested that the limit is due to limited soil fertility arising from a slash-and-burn economy. Others see it as a natural consequence of concentrating cultivated lands as close to the house as possible. With the expansion of the settlement new plots would thus have to be created on the most suitable (and easily cleared) land at greater and greater distances from the dwelling. When a certain limit was reached and the new plots were too far from the nucleus of the settlement, it would seem that it was felt more economical to move the homestead nearer the fields.

The picture presented above, based on the archaeological evidence, of the tendency to live together where possible, but also of the movement of (young) families away from the family homestead into virgin forest to literally carve out from it a new life for themselves, implies one additional element. It is probable that the scattered settlements created by this mechanism felt some form of community with each other, and it is this which creates the clan. A clan in this context is a series of extended families which are thought by their members to be in some way linked with one another, for example by belonging to the same descent lineage, that is, having the same ancestors. (Matters concerning ideology are discussed in Chapter 9.) The cult of the ancestors was probably of considerable importance. It had a unifying role in the society of the living, linking it to the land, legitimizing group territory and linking the clan with the seasonal cycle of life and death.

6

The Order of Things:
Social Structure

The complex processes initiated by the Slav expansion and subsequent demographic and ethnic consolidation culminated in the formation of tribal groups,[1] which later coalesced to create states which form the framework of the ethnic make-up of modern Eastern Europe. The long process of internal political and ethnic development which preceded this is therefore of fundamental importance for understanding the origin of the peoples making up at least half of the European continent today.

The available evidence suggests a slow process of consolidation of social groups between the seventh and ninth centuries. There is much evidence that social structure of the Early Slavs was based around clans, linked by blood relationships of its members. In the period before the seventh century these were relatively egalitarian, while from the seventh century we see increasing evidence of differentiations of status within these organizations, leading eventually to class divisions and the development of centralized socio-political organizations and states. This process gradually becomes more visible in the archaeological and written sources (although the beginning of the process is as difficult to discern in the archaeological record as it probably would have been to a contemporary observer). We have seen in a previous chapter the beginning of these changes within the structure of Early Slav society hinted at for example by the appearance of prestige goods and the first strongholds. Other changes occur also in the material culture of these groups, and these are related to the effect of 'new social conditions' as one writer expresses it.[2] It is clear however that some changes were occurring, apparently accelerating as time went on.

The evidence for these social organization of past societies is difficult to come by, and even more difficult to interpret. The written sources of course occasionally mention something which can be used in such an investigation, but only with the appearance of social structures large enough to interest literate neighbours. The interpretation of these sources is difficult. The use of terms such as '*dux*', '*princeps*', '*primores*' or even '*rex*' in Latin documents created outside Slavdom by strangers does not necessarily imply that these institutions existed there in the same form as in the area where the documents were compiled, simply that these were the words which most closely approached the writer's conception of what he observed or heard of. We may learn of a few tribal names, but only rarely are we told where those tribes lay, still more rarely are we in a position to say where a given tribe's territory began and ended. Terms such as 'large area' and 'a populous nation' appearing in these documents hardly help us in this respect. We cannot know either how many tribes existed of which our authors are ignorant or do not wish to inform us.

The organization of ancient societies has been studied for several decades in eastern and central European historiography.[3] In the decades since the 1920s, much of this work in the area was prompted and coloured by Marxist agendas and concepts. This has tended to focus attention on such issues as class-divisions and class-conflict, but also been prone to simplistic evolutionist interpretations about 'feudal' relations developing from pre-existing formations and developing into 'capitalism' along the lines suggested by Marxist dogma.[4] The study of social organization also became popular among a young generation of American archaeologists who developed evolutionary theories of social development based on the work of social anthropologists which has focused on such questions as power. Discussion around these themes has raised a number of important questions concerning social organization in the past. While we may attempt to steer clear of overtly evolutionist schemes, we may utilize some of the concepts arising from this discussion here.[5] One may look at the problem of social organization either from the top looking down, and start with a discussion of power, or from the base looking at the way in which the settlement pattern reveals social relationships of a different kind.

Big men and chiefs

In social anthropology several categories of power have been recognized. These may include military force, control over the economy and control over ideology. Societies may be classified on the basis of the way that these various kinds of power operate within it. This classification may take the form of a hierarchy. At the lowest level is the egalitarian society where no individual has any permanent power or influence over his or her fellows. Only in times of military conflict do individuals or group of individuals become leaders of raids or defence, but their powers are restricted to this realm. The archaeological evidence seems to suggest that Early Slav society fitted best this model in the Migration period.

Other societies are based around communities which have so-called 'big men'. A 'big man' is a dominant personage in a society with weakly developed social stratification, and is distinguished by virtue of prestige, but has little authority. This person may maintain his position by means of manipulation of wealth: the most frequent manifestation of this is to host communal gatherings which usually take the form of feasts at which wealth is not only displayed but also conspicuously consumed.[6] Several members of the same community may compete with each other in this field. Wealth and agricultural surplus are redistributed throughout society by these means, the gathering of the community around the 'big men' acting as channels for the redistribution network.

At a higher degree of social stratification, the society tends to take on the characteristics of what is called a 'chiefdom'. In contrast to 'big men' the chief has considerable authority and is able to maintain it permanently; his position is ascribed, often hereditary. In order to produce the resources to maintain the system a chief generally exercises power over a larger-scale society (a population counted in thousands rather than hundreds). A chiefdom is characterized by a system of central accumulation of surplus (rendered to the leader as a regular tribute) and its redistribution to his followers or in any other way allowing him to attain certain economic, social and political aims. This type of 'tribute economy' is the basis of the functioning of the economy of a chiefdom.[7] The increase in social and socio-political complexity of 'chiefdoms' compared with the clan structure of simpler tribal societies involves institutional changes in the structure of the polity, including the formation of inherited inequality in personal status and centralization of power. A chiefdom may support a certain degree of craft specialization and is often characterized by the construction of large-scale monuments.

An important element of the chief is the ability to back up his authority by force. The landscape of chiefdoms thus often contain a number of fortified centres from which that force is exercised, and the power structure is maintained by the existence of a retinue (which in the central and eastern European literature is often called a *druzhina*). This is a group of high-status warriors who owe their allegiance and social position to the person of the chief. The members of the retinue exercised power in the name of the leader; one of their principal functions was the collection of tribute and presumably the punishment of those who attempted to oppose his will. The retinue was often composed of warriors drawn not only from the region controlled by the chief but also sometimes from other areas. The written sources tell us for example that the retinues of tenth-century Kievan princes contained many Scandinavians, and the archaeological evidence from Russia and Poland suggests that besides Scandinavians there were steppe elements in the so-called 'retainer culture' which developed.[8] The logic in employing foreigners was not only the expertise in different military techniques they brought with them, but also their greater loyalty due to a lesser tendency to get involved in local squabbles. The rich graves of the retinue (for example in the Kievan state) not only allow us to see the wealth and social position which could be attained by belonging to a retinue, but also allow us to identify the positions of the main centres of power. In most areas of Slavdom they occur near major fortified centres or other strategic locations.[9]

The written sources make it clear that the leader was responsible for the upkeep of his retinue, and thus we hear of Igor of Rus being prompted to take a greater tribute to distribute to his men. Ibrahim ibn Yaqub tells us that in Poland in 965:

The taxes Mesko collects in metal coin [? text unclear here] are used to pay the allowances of his warriors, every month each one receives an allotted amount of these. He has three thousand armed men in divisions, and a hundred of them are worth ten hundred of other [warriors]. He gives his men clothing, horses, weapons and everything they need. And when a child is born to one of them he pays it a wage from the moment of birth, whether it is a boy or girl. And when it grows up, if it is a man, he finds him [?] a wife and pays the bride-price to the bride's father, if it is a girl, he pays the dowry to the girl's father.

Although this text refers to the situation in the tenth century, it gives some idea of the type of relationship possible between a leader and the men of his retinue.

The organization of the polity would be affected by the size of the area which might be effectively administered and defended from a centre. This would usually be an area about 1500 square kilometres (i.e. a circular area about 44 km radius), and has a central place which is nowhere more than 40–100 km from the boundary of the territory (a distance of 25 km representing a typical day's journey on horseback at normal pace). In order to deal with the increased size and geographical range of their polity, chiefdoms (and states) are thus forced to create a hierarchy of subsidiary centres (thus ranked below the chiefly elite may be a hierarchy of leaders of smaller and simpler types of organization). There is a range of chiefdoms from the small-scale local chief to, at the upper end of the continuum, 'developed chiefdoms' which merge into states. It is difficult to draw a line between the 'princes' who ruled the latter and the powerful chiefs of tribal unions (one of the principal differentiating features of chiefs in the Middle Ages was the way in which their authority was recognized by the leaders of adjacent more powerful states – such as the German and Byzantine emperors – or by the Pope).

Although there is some evidence that the change from an egalitarian type of community to chiefdoms may well explain the rise of social and territorial organizations north of the Carpathians, this model is not the only one which may be applied to the Early Slavs. A somewhat different situation is what anthropologists might call 'pantribal sodalities'. These are links between communities created by factors unconnected with kinship and where such an association is advantageous. They tend to occur in areas where two cultures are in regular contact and especially where there is conflict between them. The creation of alliances within such sodalities makes possible the escalation of conflict involving larger numbers. A good example of such a situation is the creation and development of pantribal sodalities among the Plains Indians of North America in the eighteenth and nineteenth centuries. This was made possible by the introduction of the horse, the change from foraging to bison hunting and other changes. In particular the period is notable for the number of tribes which adopted horse-riding and moved to the Plains to take part in this new lifestyle. The competition between these tribes for a share in the resources of the area and the conflict between indigenous populations and the white settlers led to the need to form militaristic pantribal warrior associations. It was from the ranks of these that a strong leadership emerged to lead raids and the summer bison hunt, though this leader was not autonomous and was reliant on the approval of the gathered warriors. The rapid spread of the Ghost Dance religion was an important means of creating and intensifying tribal spirit, and common participation in these fervent rituals became an important forger of new tribal (ethnic) identities.[10]

It would seem that there are several similarities between this kind of situation and that of the Early Slavs, particularly in the Danubian area, where they came in contact with the Romans. It is here that we see the assimilation of different elements in the creation of an expanding group of people with a similar and new material culture. It is here that we observe the emergence of some kind of ethnic self-identification (including the adoption of the name Sclavenes), and it is here that we meet the names of the first chieftains, the leaders of warrior bands and (just as in the case of Geronimo – which was not his Indian name) well-known by name to the readers of the Greek accounts. We are told by Menander of Dauritas (Daurentius), who defied Avar threats in the 560s. We hear from Theophilactus Simokattes of other Slav leaders in the 580s and 590s, such as Ardagastus, Peiragastus and Mousokios. We know little about the other functions of these leaders in tribal society; we hear of them only in a military context. Procopius tells us in his 'ethnographic excursus' (*Wars* VII.14, 22–30) that in contrast to the East Romans the Slavs had no centralized rule but the decisions of the chiefs were tempered by 'democratic' decisions.[11] The Romans well knew of the potential of external military threat or other pressures to create leaders. Pseudo-Maurice (*Strategikon* XI.4, 30) warns about not pressing the Slavs too hard, for this could 'lead to unity among them and the establishment of a single leader'. It would seem that not only the large organized forces of Slavs which the East Roman and Byzantine writers tell us crossed the *limes* but also their unification as an ethnic group were primarily a result of the interaction of the Slavs with the Roman world. Once however the warrior bands gave way to settlers, the creation of smaller tribes based on more local hierarchies began to develop.

The creation of pantribal warrior associations is closely related to another phenomenon which has appeared in some previous accounts of the social structure of Early Slav society, and that is the concept of 'military democracy'.[12] This concept (wherein social organization was based on the executive power of all weapon-bearing men with an elected leader) derives from Engels, who in turn derived it from Morgan's observation of the Iroquois and ahistorically added information from Tacitus and other classical writers. The application of this model to the (Danubian) Slavs was aided by the East Roman writers who described their 'democracy' (lack of central power). This term however is an academic construct firmly set in the framework of an evolutionist dogma describing the process each society would pass through in its passage from a 'primitive' society to a 'slave-owning' or 'feudal' one. As such it has limited analytical value.

Settlement patterns and social organization

One of the most visible archaeological correlates of social organization is the spatial relationship of settlements in the landscape. These patterns have been well studied in certain areas of Slavdom, especially in the west (Polabia, Poland, Bohemia, Moravia and to a lesser extent Ukraine). Settlement in eastern Europe in the early medieval period was much less dense than in some areas of western Europe (and indeed this is still true today). The pattern of sites in well-studied areas does not form a continuous spread of equally spaced settlement of equal density in each period, but rather forms clusters resembling a leopard's spots. The rural settlements are grouped into a series of settlement cells a few kilometres across, often situated along river or stream valleys. These are separated by areas where the settlement density falls off (Fig. 43). The settlement cells developed as a result of natural expansion from single centres and probably form communities linked by family or clan relationships; to walk from one side of the settlement cell to the other was a matter of a few hours. They seem to have formed the basis of the simplest form of territorial organization outside the community, and we have some information about them from written sources. In Poland they were known as *opole*, and in the South Slav zone as *zupa*. Constantine Porphyrogenitus (*DAI* chapter 29) notes that these were governed by 'elders' and that this was the case in other Slav countries. The *PVL* notes that the men of the Poliane 'lived each with his own clan in his own place', indicating the two most important factors in determining communal affinity: genetic links and communality of inhabited and exploited territory.

An important question which should be addressed is that of land ownership, since this is fundamental to the question of whether a society was 'feudal' or not (see below). In the absence of the legal tracts and charters and other such documentary proof of land ownership in western Europe (especially from the Merovingian and Carolingian realms as well as from the later Anglo-Saxon kingdoms) the relationships of land ownership in early medieval central Europe are however impossible to demonstrate before the twelfth century.[13] We know little about the size of individual land holdings or indeed anything about how land use was organized (for example whether in some communities land was farmed in common). It is uncertain whether Slav strongholds served as the centres of private estates. One key matter is to determine whether the tribute paid to leaders was payment for the rights to use a particular area of land (as in the feudal system) or whether it had some other function. The available evidence seems to suggest that it served as some form of acknowledgement of belonging to a particular group under the protection of a particular leader rather than a right to inhabit a particular patch of land.

The settlement cells tend to cluster into larger groups which are relatively discrete, and are separated from each other by areas containing few settlements. It seems fairly reasonable to link these groups of sites with the territories of clans and with what may conveniently be referred to as tribes made up of several clans. These units start to crystallize with increasing population density by the eighth century in many areas (though in some the process had begun in the seventh century or even in the case of certain South Slav groups in the late sixth century). These tribes form the basic territorial division of Slavdom, and some (but by no means not all) appear in the later written sources. The existence of these tribes was based on biological factors – such as intermarriage between clans and real or imagined descent from common ancestors – and exploitation of a common territory. It follows that bonds within these groups were strengthened by other common features of public life and tradition and, although we lack more concrete data, probably of religious cult and world-view. Typically petty tribal territories in West Slavdom in about the ninth century occupied between 250 sq km and 2500 sq km. Good examples can be traced by correlation of the written and archaeological sources in Bohemia, Silesia and Wielkopolska (Fig. 44).[14] At a slightly later date, tribes united into even larger tribal unions which may have controlled territories of about 7000 to 20,000 sq km, and were often the core from which early states developed.[15] The hierarchical arrangement of society is visible in the settlement structure. There is often a visibly differentiated 'central place' surrounded by a hierarchy of subsidiary centres.

The tribes and tribal unions had distinctive names. They usually end in the plural -ie or -ane. The root of many of these names is territorial (as with the Bużane inhabiting the area around the River Bug, the Wislane on the upper Vistula (Wisła), Ślężane under the mountain Ślęża). Other names seem to differentiate their bearers from a clearly defined 'other' group: we have mentioned the Slovenes, the Slovienie (which may be related to the root *slovo – the 'ones knowing the words') and Severiane ('the northern folk'). The origins of other names are less easy to understand, such as the Polane, Poliane (from pola, field), Derevlane (from drevo, tree) and so on. Others are even more difficult to understand: some sources suggest that there was a Silesian tribe called [G]łupiegłowy ('stupid [in the] heads') which is hard to accept as a name a people would choose for themselves.

The role of the strongholds

The progress of this process of increasing centralization can be detected not only in the written records but also in the archaeological evidence, in the traces this has left in the landscape. In West Slav areas and most of the East Slav territories, many of the settlement cells have at their centre (more rarely at their periphery) a major settlement unit distinguished by being enclosed by an earth and timber rampart (more properly a vertical wall made of an unhewn timber framework filled with earth or rarely rubble) with an external ditch. These sites, still visible in the landscape today (and some still functioning as major population centres), were surrounded by a number of open settlements, and thus often form the focus of the local settlement pattern. These strongholds are thus important for understanding many aspects of Slav archaeology, especially social structure, and this explains why they have been accorded so much attention in the literature and research programmes.[16] At a later period many of the major sites appear in the written records as the chiefly seats (estate centres?) of the tribal 'princes'. It seems that this network of sites and the settlement hierarchy of which they formed a part had an important role to play in the process of state formation among the Slavs. It seems reasonable to see the strongholds as a reflection of the existence of some form of social stratification. They probably represent the seats of persons of some importance locally able to command the help of others to raise such labour-intensive earthworks.

As in the case of the rural settlements around them, the strongholds are seldom situated far away from water, often by lakes or small rivers, or on high scarps on the edge of major river valleys, sometimes in swamps, but rarely on hilltops which are remote from water. They vary in size from 30 m in diameter to several hectares, though most sites of the pre-state period are about 0.5–1.0 ha in area. There is some considerable variation in density and also the layout of internal occupation. Some have no sign of permanent occupation, and may be regional meeting-places or refuges. Some contain single homesteads in the centre, many contain ranges of buildings round the interior of the rampart, while others, especially in the north and west (for example Feldberg in northeast Germany) and among the Volyntsevo group of sites, resemble fortified villages with scattered buildings (which may be roughly arranged in rows). In many cases there is external occupation in the close vicinity, often outside the gate (e.g. Tornow, Polabia; Klučov in Bohemia, Fig. 45). Construction of these sites began only with the new social conditions formed during the process of social consolidation, a process which began in many areas by the end of the seventh century, with an increasing frequency in the ninth to tenth century. They are characteristic of the Early Middle Ages of East and West Slavs, and similar sites were being constructed by Slavs until the twelfth or thirteenth centuries. Strongholds like this were not constructed by Slavs south of the Danube, though in Bulgar territory small forts were constructed at strategic points – these were modelled more on Byzantine patterns.

Strongholds clearly required communal labour to raise them, In most cases, at least in the case of smaller strongholds, the number of people needed to construct such a structure would be greater than the number that could live within it (though they may all have been able to take refuge in its defences in time of danger). It is most reasonable to see this labour as having been drawn from the adjacent settlements.[17] This implies either that people were coerced into building the earthwork (perhaps by some form of social obligation to the people whose home it was to be) or that they did so willingly because they felt a need for one (for example as a symbol of prestige for the community, rather like a nineteenth-century town hall). The evidence does not allow us to choose between these two alternatives; perhaps the answer lies between the two extremes. In the western zone of early sites there are a number of relatively large enclosures (in Polabia, Bohemia and southwest Poland) with little sign of permanent dense occupation. These have been interpreted as corrals and 'refuges' where people and livestock could be gathered in times of danger of attack by neighbouring groups. Perhaps they served also as regional meeting places.

Occasionally, as in the case of the ninth-century stronghold at Pohansko near Břeclav in Bohemia, the dwelling of the lord can be recognized. The house and its outbuildings were surrounded by palisades and fences which produce the impression that the complex was modelled on the courts of Frankish nobles. The compound also produced the remains of an early ninth-century masonry church decorated with frescos and surrounded by a cemetery of richly furnished graves.[18]

From the eighth and ninth century there is a change in the pattern of construction and an increase in the number of strongholds being constructed.[19] Now fewer of them are differentiated by finds richer in quality (though they do still tend to produce more finds than open sites), and the evidence suggests that they were permanently occupied by one or more family units. In much of western Slavdom, the sites of this phase (end of eighth and ninth centuries) tend to take the form of a small and medium ringwork some 30–100 m across. In the west of the area they tend to be associated with Tornow-type pottery and, since they are similar in form to the type-site, they are known as strongholds of the Tornow type. Similar sites occur in Pomerania. The distribution of these later strongholds forms a similar pattern to that seen earlier, with the densest scatter in the western Poland, Pomerania and Polabia. In central and eastern Poland and Belarussia and much of the Ukraine such sites are less thickly distributed.

As we saw in Chapter 4, on the eastern fringes of the East Slav territories (left bank of the Dniepr to the upper Oka and Don) most of the known settlements are almost solely of settlements of enclosed, or defensible, type. These are often high up on scarps overlooking river valleys or in swamps (for example

Monastyire, Bolshoe Borshevo and Novotroitskoe), often enclosed by ramparts. These sites are densely built up inside and are one of the main characteristics of the Romny-Borshevo group of the eighth to tenth centuries.[20]

Strongholds are a settlement type appearing over most of Slavdom by the ninth century. Although there are many traits in the external form which are similar, we should be wary of assigning one overall interpretation to them. They do seem however to be the reflection of a co-ordinating force which led to their construction. The rampart differentiates the settlement inside and immediately outside it from other unenclosed settlements in the vicinity. Some of these sites seem to have acted as some form of central place in a settlement hierarchy, a place where certain activities and social forms had their focus.

Some areas of Slavdom however do not possess enclosed settlements of this type. Most notably, they do not occur (at this date) in most of the territory inhabited by the South Slavs. Here the Slav settlement structure is based on unenclosed rural settlements and sparse occupation of walled towns and forts of Graeco-Roman origin. The Slavs in this area seem to have been partially absorbed into pre-existing social and agricultural systems and perhaps to some extent had not been able to (or felt no need to) express their communal affinity in this way as much as in the Slav colonization of the northern forest zones. They instead adopted the social models of the Romanized population they lived alongside.[21]

States and nations

As mentioned above, the end product of the process of social development was the state, and we have suggested that the period covered by this book sees the emergence of many of the states and nations inhabiting central and eastern Europe today. We have already discussed the brief *floruit* and disappearance of the Moravian state and also the creation of the Bulgar state. In these discussions though we have so far tended to avoid the basic question: what is a state and what is a nation? There is a multitude of definitions, many revolving around the same themes. The dictionary definition of 'a self-governing political community occupying its own territory' would not satisfy many anthropologists or sociologists. Robert Carniero defines the state as 'an autonomous political unit encompassing many communities within its territory, having a centralised government with the power to collect taxes, draft men for work or war and to decree and enforce laws'. Some modern sociologists defines the state as 'an institution in which autonomous power over a geographical area is concentrated . . . [with] . . . a monopoly over the legitimate use of force within a given territory'. Vander Zander is blunter: 'The state is a social organization that exercises within a given territory an effective monopoly in the use of physical coercion. In the final analysis the state rests on force, power whose basis is the threat or application of punishment.'[22]

The concept of a nation is however a more complex question. In general in its modern form the concept developed relatively late, at the end of the eighteenth century and the beginning of the nineteenth. A nation is a 'permanent community of people regarding themselves as having a common history, culture, language, territory, political and economic institutions, which finds expression as national awareness among its members'. The term (deriving from the Latin) also includes a notion of common descent; the Slav term *naród* has a similar root: it now means 'nation', but had a primary meaning of 'people, crowd'. The differentiation of an ethnie (see p. 31) and a nation is thus primarily one of scale.

We may define two types of state: a nation state, which forms from the political organization of a people who consider themselves to be related in some way, and a power state, which incorporates peoples of different ethnic affinities under a common banner and authority. Most postwar European states are nation states (though in Stalin's eastern Europe the creation of these states was aided by massive ethnic deportations, and in the modern world improved means of communication and the media have been breaking down barriers between regional cultures within and between different states). Before the First World War the major states (such as those of the Habsburgs or the tsars) were multi-ethnic, and multicultural, which in the end was to lead to their demise. It seems that in the early medieval period most of the states which are referred to in the written sources were power states, formed by the subsuming of various local and regional groupings. Most early medieval rulers however seemed to have recognized (as did almost all later ones) the importance of imposing some form of unity and promoting a 'national feeling' among the people of their realms in order to discourage moves towards decentralization. In other words, like a giant roller the state was to level out any local irregularities. These developments may have been imposed by force, encouraged by imposing a common ideology of some form (and propaganda), or may have developed naturally. These factors may have involved a common religion, linguistic unity, the invention of shared ideals and traditions, a common enemy or the establishment of a unified material culture. Many examples of similar phenomena can be found in ancient and modern history.

The boundary between the early state and a tribal organization is very fluid: many early states are organized in a manner reminiscent of that of chiefdoms (the differentiating factor being that of scale), and the state in its formative period incorporates many elements of pre-existing (tribal) structures. For this reason, some anthropologists prefer to define a distinct stage, 'the Early State'. The disappearance of the elements of tribal structures and the stabilization of social differentiation by a slow cumulation of political and socio-economic changes mark the transition from an early state to a mature one.

Unlike tribal societies, states bring non-related peoples together under some form of linking structure and oblige them all to pledge allegiance to a government. The populace pays a tax to support the bureaucracy necessary to run the state (some anthropologists regard taxation and the existence of a professional bureaucracy as the main characteristics determining whether a given polity is a state or not). Many of the redistributive systems developed to support these essential services were very complex. The bureaucracy is based in central places, one of the principal functions of which is to collect revenue (taxes and tolls) and distribute it to the government, the army and all in the employment of the state and ruler. These central places are characterized by public buildings (often on a large scale), which include religious structures and workplaces for the administrative bureaucracy.

States are characterized by a more diversified economy with greater productivity, and increased specialization in many spheres of life. State societies are generally stratified into different social classes (peasant farmers or serfs and poorer urban populations forming the lower ranks, with specialist craftsmen, merchants and priests and ruling classes above them), though in early states the boundaries between social groups ('emergent classes') are relatively poorly defined. Power was usually based on kinship links which open the way to holding positions of power (the place of individuals in the elite was often determined by their relationship with the ruling family and other privileged lineages). The elite is however not stable and is ultimately reliant on the goodwill of the ruler: it lives mainly off tribute from dependants and from loot from raids on neighbours. States have a large populations with a higher population density than tribal societies and territorial boundaries are clearly defined, though there is potential for territorial expansion, with a reduction in internal strife.

Although it is not proposed to discuss this problem in detail here, since in the eastern European literature the word 'state' is often linked with the word 'feudal' (or 'early feudal') we must deal briefly with the thorny question of feudalism in early medieval central Europe. I have my doubts regarding the universal usefulness of this 'mental pigeonhole' concept (gaining currency of course in central European archaeology from the writings of Engels and also Stalin).[23] The term is often used in central European archaeology without attempts to define it properly, and yet in many works it forms the basis of the interpretation. The authoritative dictionary of the Polish language for example defines *feudalizm* as a 'socio-political system widespread in Medieval Europe in which the basis of the relations of production was land which was owned by the feudal lords and the obligation of subjects (peasants) to render services due to personal obligations and in return for allowing the tilling of land assigned to them by their lord'. Feudalism in western Europe is a term referring to a quite specific legal situation and is strongly connected with land ownership, that is, private property (a theme about which of course Engels was especially concerned). Since we have little evidence of land ownership (see above) we have no clear evidence that what is termed 'feudalism' by central European archaeologists would be understood as such by western European historians dealing with the well-documented evidence from Carolingia for example. The term is perhaps better avoided in any discussions of social relations in Slavdom as a whole, though it may be applicable in certain areas of the West Slav territories after the twelfth century where however feudalism developed under strong influence from the German Empire.

There have been many models of the formation of states. Some workers have attempted to follow a model of relatively slow socio-economic growth, seeing the transition from the egalitarian to hierarchical structure as a slow 'natural process of change' within a society.[24] In order for the early state to be stable there has to be a continuous supply of economic surplus to support the system: one important factor might be the control of the resources of high-productivity environments (such as agriculturally rich areas).The mere existence of surplus does not however automatically cause the creation of a state, but creates such a possibility. In other cases competition for a scarce but desirable resource may be the cause of greater social complexity. In other cases historians have been prone to see the formation of a state as due to the charisma and qualities of a single exceptional person as founder.[25] An oft-quoted example is the rise of the kingdom of Chaka Zulu in historical times, but the rise of such a polity does not occur in a vacuum: it is also the result of certain pre-existing conditions.

In the period of colonial expansion before the World Wars, the role of military force was seen by many writers as an important factor in the creation of more complex social structures. The state was seen as an instrument of oppression, designed to confirm social inequality.[26] F. Oppenheimer saw these inequalities arising from the conquest and subjection of one people by another. This had as a purpose the economic exploitation of the defeated; conquest thus lay at the root of the formation of the state. Similar theories have been proposed by other writers in more recent years. There seems no doubt that the historical development of some areas and peoples was strongly affected by conquest of one socio-political organism by another, and the general accumulation of territorial gains and the subjugation of conquered regions by various means (see Chapter 7). As a general mechanism for state-formation, it is however rather an unsatisfactory model when isolated from other socio-economic processes. Conquest of one tribe by another did not always lead to state-formation, and clearly the conquering and conquered peoples in these models must themselves already have had some form of political organization (and stratification). Territorial conquest can be achieved only if the conquerors have a ready-made political and military power-system which can be introduced to follow up the initial victory.

In studying the process of state formation, we should consider the difference between a state which forms on the basis of its own internal growth and consolidation, and those ('secondary states') which form as a result of stimulation by the existence of an adjacent 'primary' state to which the area concerned is a periphery.[27] In the period and area we are discussing, it is the latter form which seems to have been more common (in other cases, however, state and other political forms existed alongside each other for generations, but the latter did not develop into states). In the case of the South Slavs, we seem to have secondary states which arose as a direct result of influence from neighbouring primary states, and accepted cultural models from them. In other cases (such as Poland) we observe a development which is more spontaneous, but still involves outside influence (Chapters 11–12 below).

Secondary states may arise as a result of influence from a primary one by two main mechanisms acting together or separately. The first involves direct interference from a neighbouring group (conquest). The second acts in a more indirect manner. A local leader gaining a monopoly over contact with economic resources – especially prestige goods – coming from a more advanced social organization will have gained a means for exercising power over his subordinates, but the adjacent state has also gained a method of exercising power among the outsiders beyond its borders. By cutting off the supply of material goods and goodwill essential for the functioning of a system, or switching attentions to a political rival, it can threaten the power base of adjacent rulers and affect internal politics. We know from the written sources that the Carolingians and Byzantines for example were adept at such manipulations.

The formation of states may leave archaeological traces. In many cases the formation of a centralized state came about by the destruction of previously existing power structures; local centres were often more or less violently destroyed and replaced with new power bases. The introduction of new land ownership systems may lead to visible changes in rural settlement patterns too. Recent work in Poland has drawn attention to horizons of destruction of strongholds, especially visible across Wielkopolska. These are sometimes accompanied by new strongholds constructed nearby. Similar evidence is seen in Bohemia.[28] This is interpreted as evidence of the process of destruction of the old tribal centres and replacement by strongholds forming part of the repressive and administrative system of the new state (the relocation of the sites showing a desire to maintain control over an area but at the same time to emphasize the permanence of the break with the past tribal system). In other cases, changes in pottery typology seem to represent the (perhaps forced) resettlement of entire populations as a result of conquest, or the movement of populations to take advantage of new opportunities provided by new lands opened up for settlement by military annexation. Recently in Poland, Andrzej Buko has shown that in the late tenth century vessels of biconical form similar to those of Wielkopolska appear in pottery assemblages (such as in the major stronghold at Sandomierz) of rounded egg-form southern type. He interprets this as a possible trace of the penetration of this area by populations from Great Poland as this region was joined to the Polish state.[29] Similar effects are visible in Moravia, where Mazovian and Wielkopolskan pottery appears at the time of the Polish conquest at the beginning of the eleventh century.[30]

7

Warfare

The written evidence suggests that life in the early medieval period all over Europe was often punctuated by episodes of violence, and it seems that warfare of one type or another was endemic to almost all early medieval societies. In this context the term 'warfare' covers a wide range of hostilities from small-scale raiding by neighbouring groups (raiding for loot, revenge attacks as part of a blood-feud, or the sort of ritual warfare where boasting and insults predominate over blood-letting) to wars of domination or conquest, attempts to take over new territories or annex new resources (large-scale military operations by armies of more centralized political organizations).

The written sources contain quite a lot of information on ancient warfare. Most textbooks contain information concerning Slav attacks on Byzantium in the Danube frontier area and the Balkans (chiefly derived from Procopius and Pseudo-Maurice). Here we read about their use of techniques of guerrilla warfare and the size of bands of raiders, though here we should bear in mind that what is reported may in part be mentioned to highlight the methods used by the Slavs which contrast with the tactics of the Byzantine army. We should bear in mind that these sources are also trying to explain away the recent successes of the Slavs. The information in the *PVL* about techniques used in Rus attacks on Byzantium would seem largely to be interpolation which is late in date and also reflects rather the techniques of Varangian raiders and less those of the Slavs themselves (and the extent of techniques adopted from steppe nomads is not clear). These techniques were also affected by Byzantine warfare. The other main sources of information are the Frankish and Carolingian chronicles. In general however, in comparison to the Byzantine literature, the Frankish and Carolingian records do not tell us much about Slav fighting methods: they mainly tell of Carolingian penetration into Slav territory.

Certain types of archaeological evidence may also give us information. Among these the evidence of fortifications (the strongholds) is the most obvious. Physical traces of acts of warfare may be noted, such as destruction levels on excavated sites (burning, deliberate destruction of buildings and stronghold ramparts) which have been found in some areas but are easy to misinterpret. There is not much evidence of wounds and fractures in the bone evidence, or burials with spearheads or arrowheads embedded in them, but this is due most often to the prevalence of the cremation burial rite over much of the area in the pre-state period. When battles were fought away from the settlement, we may assume that the dead may not always have been buried in their 'home' cemetery but in graves on the battlefield. Weapons are not often present in Early Slav finds assemblages (swords, spears, spurs, axes of Moravian type and so on); they were rarely subject to casual loss, and were infrequently placed in graves in the pre-state period. Weapons however need not reflect actual warfare but may be prestige display items.[1]

Inter-group skirmishes

We learn from Byzantine sources of inter-tribal skirmishes, such as between the Sclavenes and Antes on the Danube. The presence of strongholds in northern Slavdom from the seventh century onwards and the general improvements in the effectiveness of the weaponry of the period seem to hint at similar inter-group rivalry throughout the period considered here over most of this area. At a time when social organization was relatively poorly developed, the scale and scope of warfare was limited: for most of the period considered in this book, the most that many Slav groups could attain was small-scale raids.

Since most of the tribal groupings considered here were relatively small, until the rise of states the number of invaders was limited. A typical barbarian warrior band of the early medieval period may have contained only two hundred warriors. Since smaller armies cannot carry much excess baggage in the form of supplies, the invaders were usually able to survive only from what they could obtain on foreign territory. Penetration of enemy territory would be limited in time and distance (a small army cannot afford to be cut off from its homeland). The invading group cannot however afford to stay in one area of enemy territory too long, as this might allow time for the natives to raise larger forces against it.

Motives for war may vary: raids may be intended to acquire loot to be shared out among followers of a particular leader, to avenge a wrong, to subdue a neighbouring leader; or they may be conducted so that the young warriors can gain prestige and win their way into the ranks of warriors. Warriors might go off in relatively small groups on raids for a few days to prove their manhood and to gain booty. The motivation for many of these actions would have been prestige, which, measured in non-material terms, has always been an important factor in social structure in many societies. Battle-honours and material generosity were common status-enhancers, and warfare may have been something more like a somewhat dangerous community prestige game rather than a fight to annihilation. In primitive warfare, the function of leadership is very weak. Social pressure from the community and loss of personal prestige are the only pressures on the warrior to fight. He fights for himself or to protect his family and village. If however a leader can link warriors to him personally, by an oath – and if he reinforces these links by honouring that group with wealth (goods) and prestige – warriors will fight first and foremost for him. This as we have seen is an important feature in promoting socio-political development.

The formation of warrior bands was also an important element in the binding of communities: we have seen how men may have joined successful groups – presumably bringing their families with them – in their advance across the political maps of Europe. This mixing was described in Walter Pohl's excellent essay concerning the Avars and Bulgars.[2] An interesting illustration of this process is the grave at Mellingen near Weimar in Germany, where a skeleton of a man with a horse (and thus a burial of conventional Avar type) was associated with two spurs of a type found only in West Slav contexts.[3] Both burial type and spur were outside the normal range of distribution of these types of finds, and it is easy to imagine this as the burial of a wide-ranging 'Avaro-Slav' warrior.

The equipment and tactics of the Danubian Slavs are mentioned in a number of Byzantine written sources. Procopius in several passages of his *Wars* described Slav armaments. For example from the 'ethnographic' fragment concerning the Sclavenes and Antes in their homeland inserted in the Chilbudius story (*Wars* VII.14, 25) we learn that the Slavs 'fight on foot, advancing on the enemy, in their hands they carry small shields and spears, but they never wear body armour. Some of them do not have either a tunic [*chiton*] or cloak but wear only a kind of breeches [*anaksyrides*] pulled up to the groin.'[4] Although this passage says the Slavs and Antes north of the Danube fought on foot, elsewhere Procopius uses wording which suggests that his description might refer to horse-borne warriors. While we have a considerable number of spearheads, we have little archaeological evidence of the shields mentioned by Procopius, which were probably circular wooden constructions covered with leather without a metal umbo. There is no evidence of the Slavs using helmets until quite a late period. The sword is rarely mentioned in Byzantine sources and it would seem was used mainly by the elite. Other written sources describe the equipment of Sclavene raiders: thus we have a mention of their use of the bow, sling and axes in the life of St Demetrius. John of Ephesus informs us that the Slavs and Avars learnt how to use siege machines from the Byzantine army (the use of 'wolf-pit' traps around their settlements mentioned in some Byzantine written sources should perhaps also be counted as the influence of Byzantine tactics).

As we have seen, one of the best-known literary sources referring to the early Slavs is the *Strategikon* of Pseudo-Maurice, written about AD 600 and describing how best to attack the Slavs in their Danubian homelands. This document was probably compiled by someone who had actually taken part in the raids on Sclavene territory in Maurice's reign. In the relevant passage (XI.4, 1–45) we are told that in their homelands north of the Danube they lived in 'forests, by rivers, swamps and wetlands difficult of access; because of the frequent dangers threatening them, they build several entrances to their settlements' . Nothing however is said about the construction of strongholds by the Slavs. We are told that they hide away their produce, leaving nothing in a visible place. According to the Byzantine writer, 'They lead a piratical way of life, attacking their enemies in forested terrain, or in confined or steep places. They usually use ambushes, sudden attacks and tricks, either in the day or night.' They tended not to fight in an organized fashion, nor did they like to fight in the open. Later it is mentioned how they lay in wait for a retreating invader to attack in ambush in the forest to retrieve the loot (and Pseudo-Maurice advises the invading army to fell the forest on the intended route home), and also how the Slavs lay ambushes around fortified camps, and drew soldiers away from the defences and attacked them from the flanks. The dense settlement structure in river valleys allowed easy communication of an attack, and the inhabitants of settlements further away were able to prepare ambushes for the invading army. The writer also has something to say of Slav arms: 'They are armed with short spears, each man carries two, some of them with a large shield, though one difficult to use. They also use wooden bows and small poisoned arrows.' We are also told that there were infantry and cavalry (XI.4, 35–6). In the section on how to organize attacks on the Slavs (XII.8, 20) leaders are advised not to take wagons or too much heavy equipment with them, as it will slow them down in the terrain where the Slavs are likely to attack.

These sources of course reflect the specific situation in the Danubian region and we are not able to know whether these references may be applied to the evidence from other areas of Slavdom.

Organized force

The Slav invaders of the East Roman and Byzantine Empire in the sixth and seventh centuries formed relatively well organized armies of some considerable size under a stronger leadership creating a substantial threat to the northern provinces of the weakened empire. In part the degree of organization of the Slavs was a response to the nature of the forces they were up against (especially after Justinian's improvements of frontier defences in the 530s–50s). Procopius mentions attacks by a 'throng' (*omilos*) of Slavs and sometimes gives estimates of their numbers in thousands. Sometimes we also have the names of the chiefs who led these huge war bands on their raids.

We have seen above (Chapter 6) that the need to compete with 'outsiders' is one factor which can lead to the formation of pantribal warrior associations (or sodalities) which can in some cases lead to the creation of an ethnic identity around this group of fighting men. The case of the rise of new tribes of North American Plains Indians has been cited as a recent example of this. It would seem very likely that the rise of the large organized forces of Slavs which the East

Roman and Byzantine writers tell us crossed the *limes* (especially after the 570s) would be best explained by a similar mechanism. It would seem that the creation of this fighting force in opposition to the Roman world was the main factor in the growth of an ethnic identification of the Slavs on the Danube.

With the centralization of power in chiefdoms and states (together with the imposition of an authority which was difficult for the individual to resist) and the increase in the size of polities, we see the increase in size of organized warrior bands which could be mobilized. This allowed the conducting of warfare for the purpose of conquest of new territory and holding it, which had the effect of supplying revenue for the tribute economy. The ability to organize force on this scale was the principal requirement for state-formation.

One problem which remains to be completely resolved is the degree to which the horse was used by Early Slav warriors. Theophilactus Simokattes (VI.7, 2) tells us that in the Danubian region the elite and their retainers were often mounted. Most invading warrior bands would of course have also been accompanied by draught animals to carry supplies and the resultant loot, and Theophilactus Simokattes (VII.2, 4) describes the Slavs as making a circle of their wagons during a battle. The nomad horsemen archers usually coming from the eastern steppes were able to subdue large areas, a pattern which is repeated throughout the early medieval period (the Huns, Avars, Bulgars and Magyars). It would be surprising if the surrounding populations were slow to learn a lesson from this fact. At first probably an elite prerogative, increased use of the horse will have increased the mobility of the troops. One may suspect that the speed of movement of the Slav hordes invading the East Roman Empire may have been due to the use of horses; indeed Procopius uses for the Slav attacks of 548 (*Wars* VII.29.2) a term *strateuma* which he elsewhere employs for troops on horseback. The account of John of Ephesus writing of events in 581–4 tells us specifically that the Slavs busied themselves 'robbing . . ., herds of horses and much weaponry, and they have learnt to conduct war better than the Romans'. Indeed in 536–7 Procopius tells us (*Wars* V.27, 1–3) that there were Slav and 'Hun' horsemen as mercenaries in the imperial army.

By the end of the sixth century therefore the horse seems to have been in relatively wide use among the Slavs. Theophilactus Simokattes (VII.4, 11) tells us about how in the course of a raid the Slavs 'dismounted from their horses in order to cool themselves and give their mounts a rest'. There is a little archaeological evidence in the form of bridle parts (bits) from a few Romanian sites. In general though remains of horses, kept in herds in the fields and pastures outside the settlement, would not be expected to occur in settlement debris. One is reminded of the story (*PVL* s.a. [912]) of Oleg's horse which died; the prince had to ride out to look at its remains which had been left to fall apart on the surface.

The Avar raids on East Roman and Byzantine territory in which the Slavs took part were presumably carried out from horseback. The Avars seem to have later brought the stirrup to Europe: this was an important element of the harness, for it enabled the horseman to sit more firmly in his seat and allowed a spear to be used as a lance. It is possible that this pattern was adopted by the Slavs in the seventh century, for the hooked spurs which appear over central Europe (though only to the north of Avar territory) may be linked with the use of heavy cavalry in a charge.[5] The horse was also probably important to the armies of the Bulgars penetrating the Danubian frontier from the steppe (Fig. 47).

The horse was in use among the Slavs at a later period too. Constantine Porphyrogenitus was probably exaggerating when he informs us of the sixty thousand horsemen of the Croatian King Tomislav, but this gives an indication of the probable importance of cavalry in the Slav warfare of the period.[6] In the pre-state period these were steppe horses, but the bone evidence from Poland suggests that large strong warhorses were being bred there on princely and nobles' estates probably by the end of the tenth century. We are informed by Ibrahim ibn Yaqub staying in Prague in 965–6 that in the kingdom of Mesko (Mieszko) to the north the prince's retinue was a horseborne troop, and that Prague was notable for the production of 'saddles, bridles and the flimsy shields which are used in those countries'. It may be that the ramparts of strongholds were developed as much against cavalry charges as for any other reason.

With the formation of regular armies by the developed chiefdoms and early states, the power and scope of warfare increased markedly.[7] The most common disputes will have been of a political nature, though raids seeking loot or to disable a potential enemy may have been carried out too. The main aim of the attacks will now be to subordinate the attacked communities to the will of the leader of the army (that is, the invading state) and to extend the area of territory under permanent and direct control of a leader intending to extend his power. The territorial extent and intensity of the attack is considerably increased in the case of a large and well-organized army. A larger army can carry many of its own supplies; the invaders can be supported by well-organized supply-lines and are not reliant for supplies only on what they can obtain on foreign territory (a 'scorched earth' policy by the retreating natives could endanger a large army). Also if the attack is carried out for territorial gain, as soon as an area is subdued, a new state apparatus is set up, a primary aim of which will be to keep the supply-lines to the front open.

Military role of strongholds

The strongholds which appear over most of northern Slavdom from the seventh century are usually seen as structures of primarily military function. It should be noted that undefended settlements are much more common in most areas of Slavdom, and settlements are not always situated in more defensible positions (such as hilltops). The strongholds are therefore sites with some kind of 'specialist' function. It is perhaps simplistic to see them exclusively as military sites, but we may examine their possible manner of functioning as such.

An obvious function of strongholds is as 'refuge strongholds' (*Fluchtbergen*). The archaeological evidence for these sites is that they are large defended areas from which there is little evidence of permanent buildings. They are thus interpreted as fortified areas built to protect a community which would gather there to shelter in times of external threat, presumably together with their livestock.

Another function is as a military base. We have few references to the forces from these sites sallying out to meet the enemy in the field, but there are a number of accounts of sieges. The success of an invader's attack would depend not only on its military strength, but also on its ability to move faster than the messengers and warriors of the attacked community before they could raise a force to counter-attack. The potential military role of strongholds in this scenario in theory is clear: they would have contained and protected a military force whose function was either to destroy an invading force or to keep the invader occupied while reinforcements could come from other areas. The invader would have to destroy the stronghold and its contained force in order to advance further, otherwise the stronghold would act as a focus for forces which would be ready to pursue or ambush the invader on the way home.

Many of the earliest strongholds have relatively weak defences, and we may imagine that in the early part of the early medieval period they were not a major feature in the tactics of warfare. Their ramparts may have defended against sudden raids by relatively weak forces. On the whole however the defences seem to have the value of demarcating an elite settlement from the outside world, and endowing it with prestige. One may also infer that they were not meant to withstand a siege, but that any fighting was done outside the stronghold.

By the eighth and particularly the ninth centuries in the northern parts of Slavdom, a number of rather better-defended strongholds were being constructed, and it is with these sites that one can see that they were beginning to be used in a tactical sense. Some of them seem to form networks of territorial defence. Some consist of several conjoined enclosures: the inner one was the stronghold proper, while the outlying ones were probably for the horses of the fighting force and used to protect the local people in times of threat.

The defence of a stronghold has two main aspects: the first is resisting the invader, and the second is physically surviving a siege. Probably with the appearance of larger armies, strongholds could have been besieged for relatively long periods. The Russian chronicles (*PVL* 6454) mention that the army of Princess Olga besieged Iskorosten the whole summer, after which its inhabitants were starving. Much of the resistance of the defenders must have been passive, and restricted to guarding the wallwalk and firing on the attackers. Here bowmen and slingmen will have been on constant service on the battlements. There would have been hand-to-hand fighting if scaling ladders were used, or if the wall was breached, and surprise sallies on the enemy camped outside the wall, or to attack small groups who succeeded in getting close to the wall. Ideally, inside the stronghold will have been everything necessary for surviving the siege. This includes a large quantity of food, a source of fresh water and materials for repairs to structures and equipment.

It would obviously be of advantage to site open settlements near to strongholds, in order to have the opportunity to make use of its protection should the need arise. Very often we find one or more open settlements directly outside the ramparts of a stronghold, often mainly agricultural, but also the focus for craft production servicing the inhabitants of the stronghold. The proximity of such a settlement was additionally advantageous for those inside the stronghold who on hearing of an impending attack would be able to rapidly gather additional supplies from the adjacent settlement. Those settlements closer to the stronghold could however expect to suffer at the hands of besieging forces.

We have seen that Early Slav settlements tend to form clusters, and we find that the areas between settlement complexes often have the form of empty buffer-zones of virgin forest. This may suggest some form of inter-group hostility: there is some evidence that these empty zones were deliberately left free of settlement not only to form clear boundary zones but primarily to make their penetration difficult. Since there was little hope of gaining supplies from communities met on the way, the conducting of raids across such territories by an enemy would require the consumption of substantial supplies.

An example may be the Silesian *Przesieka* (*schlesische Grenzwald*) which is known from the early medieval written records as an extent of thick forest which formed an impenetrable barrier on the frontier of a given territory and which the local inhabitants were forbidden to weaken in any way.

Another feature which seems to have appeared at about the same time is linear earthworks. These early medieval ramparts, from a few hundred metres to a few kilometres in length, tend now to be poorly preserved and difficult to trace, and seem to have run between natural obstacles such as forest and marsh. There are three main groups. In Ukraine just to the south of Kiev are the so-called *Zmievy Valy* (dragon walls) defending that town against attack from the south. The Silesian ramparts (*niederschlesischen Dreigräben*) were probably constructed in the eighth or ninth century (at the latest the middle of the tenth) to block movements from the west. A similar defence is seen in Kujavia between the Warta and Vistula rivers, again probably built between the ninth and eleventh century to prevent Pomeranian incursions in the south. To the west there is a whole series of similar ramparts in Saxony and Thuringia.[8]

Imposition of will

With the increase of warfare waged for territorial gain, mechanisms had to be developed to maintain control over the newly acquired lands. This process was most effective in situations where there had already been some form of centralized control. A simple *coup d'état*, a switching of leaders, was all that was required. A people already paying tribute to a central power would, in the interest of leading a peaceful life, presumably be relatively easily 'persuaded' to transfer its demonstration of subservience to a new leader able to back up his demands by the threat of force. Two options were open to the victorious invader. The old tribal aristocracy could be retained and by a variety of subtle or more brutal methods made subservient to the needs of a new master. The other option was to destroy them utterly, and take over the leaderless people, using loyal men (usually from the retinue or the new leader's own family) appointed as overseers. The early part of the *PVL* contains an instructive range of anecdotes reflecting these various approaches. According to this source (s.a. 6370 and 6390), Rurik reputedly settled 'his men' in the strongholds of northern Russia, as did his kinsman Oleg. The chronicler notes that in the 880s Oleg took over the tribute which had been paid by several tribes to the Khazars (s.a. 6391-3). It would seem that the first option was chosen: the local leaders retained their positions and directed tributes and allegiance to the new ruler. We later read that in 914 Igor extorted a higher tribute from the native Derevlane nobility which had been subjugated three decades earlier. In 945 however in another attempt (at his retinue's request) to raise the tribute Igor was captured and killed. He was buried outside the chief stronghold of the Derevlane at Iskorosten. Prince Mal of the Derevlane was obviously making a bid for the Kievan throne (as is shown by his proposal of marriage to Olga, Igor's widow). He wished to replace the Kievan line with his own native dynasty. The siting of Igor's grave outside his personal stronghold was presumably intended to legitimate his taking of power (by conquest). Olga took terrible revenge for the treachery of the Derevlane, her husband's death and the attempt to create a new ruling dynasty. She besieged and then burnt the stronghold at Iskorosten, and captured the Derevlane elite; the rest of the inhabitants of the stronghold were either killed or given as slaves to her men. We are not told what happened to Mal: to judge by what had happened to his emissaries, his fate would not have been a pleasant one. After that Olga went through the land of the Derevlane establishing a new tribute.

In Bohemia and Wielkopolska it seems from the archaeological evidence that a different option was chosen. The rise of the first states in these areas is represented in the archaeological record by the slighting (demolition) of the tribal strongholds and their replacement on the same site or nearby with totally new constructions. This presents a picture of a more brutal manner of operation. It seems that the tribal power was totally obliterated and replaced by new men, and no attempt whatsoever was made to pretend a continuity of power.[9]

Prisoners of war

The fate of prisoners of war was either to become slaves or to be resettled far from home: slaves were a valuable (and mobile) source of revenue for the victorious army. Byzantine written sources tell us that prisoners captured by Slav invaders of the Balkans were treated variously. Pseudo-Maurice (*Strategikon* XI.4.1–45), states that the Slavs are a hospitable people and do not keep prisoners indefinitely, 'but lay down a certain period after which they can decide for themselves if they want to return to their former homelands after paying a ransom, or to stay among the Slavs as free men and friends'. Procopius (*Wars* VII.14.7–22) hints at a similar process, at least in the case of slaves from other Slav tribes. Elsewhere however in the same book (*Wars* VII.38, 1–23) Procopius describes an earlier invasion in 549–50 of Thracia and Illyria. He states that these Slavs always slew the enemies they met. On capturing Topir, they reputedly murdered fifteen thousand civilians, men of all ages, and took only the women and children into slavery. Some of the men were shut into their huts with cattle and sheep which were too numerous to take back to the Slav homelands north of the Danube and the houses set on fire. In 550 however the Slavs for the first time took large numbers of prisoners and drove them north of the Danube. In 551 they repeated the action in Illyria, killing and destroying everything that they could not take and taking prisoners. The taking only of women and children seems to have been dictated by the difficulties of preventing possible escape and rebellion by male prisoners. Children would be particularly defenceless removed from their homes, and would be reliant on their captors for survival; growing up in a barbarian environment they would be prone to assimilation in their foster communities. Women with children in their care would be less likely to escape or fight their captors. They could not only work for but also be sexually exploited by their male captors.

In a later period there is considerable evidence for the large-scale forcible resettlement of defeated populations. This process seems likely to have began with the rise of the state, but was particularly prevalent in the Kievan state in the eleventh and twelfth centuries. The resettlement of entire populations had four main functions:

- to break down old social ties based on kinship and territorial bonds, thus preventing effective opposition to new social conditions (this was the logic of Stalin's ethnic mixing in the Soviet Union)

- to settle potentially rich but underdeveloped lands in one's own territory to increase revenue. The use of enforced settlement from outside was a way of rapidly increasing production. Recent archaeological evidence from Wielkopolska shows this process in operation in the tenth century.

- the controlled depopulation of areas in selected areas of a new state. This could have for example a significance in the organization of defence, creating wide zones of unpopulated no man's lands between one's own territory and neighbours.

- the settling by new populations which were loyal to a new leader of conquered areas which had previously been weakened by ethnic deportation. The colonization of the northern lands of Kievan Rus by groups drawn from the south (such as Volynians) was a means not only of weakening resistance in troublesome areas but also of creating new ethnic identities in the resettled areas. The substrate of what is now Belarussia was originally Balt (or Balto-Slav), but resettlement by the tenth century created ethnic mixing and reformation. Although the Balt hydronyms remain, the area is now ethnically Slav.[10] Recently evidence from ceramics at Sandomierz in Poland has been interpreted as a possible trace of the penetration of this area by populations from Wielkopolska when Małopolska was joined to the Polish state (see pp. 137–8).

8

Production, Consumption and Exchange

The study of production was a 'politically correct' research topic under Communist regimes. According to the tenets of historical materialism, the material goods created by the labour of the working man were linked with the socio-economic forces which created them; in the former Soviet bloc therefore some considerable attention was paid to early technologies and production in general.[1] Regardless of ideology, it is clear that the scale and organization of production tells us something about society itself. We may attempt to determine to what extent a society was composed of self-sufficient communities with small-scale local economies, and to what extent there was production, storage and exchange of an agricultural surplus and the ways in which this was used. Agricultural surplus may be directed for example towards elites and used by them in various means to uphold their prestige, or to support a standing army or to patronize expert craftsmen. Small-scale local economies have only limited possibilities in these areas. One of the most noticeable archaeological indicators of these relationships is thus the phenomenon of craft specialization. In a small-scale economy there are few specialized roles: each hand is needed at the plough, to feed the pigs, at the harvest and in many other domestic chores. The manufacture of material goods (leather, textile, pottery) is therefore by necessity a small-scale 'cottage industry' conducted by members of the community when other tasks allow. This means that levels of production are low, usually only related to immediate needs of the community; the time spent on the manufacture of individual items is limited, and there is little opportunity for developing sophisticated craft skills. This is visible in for example the poor quality and sometimes even primitiveness of some of the items which the archaeologist finds. This reflects relatively poorly developed craft specialization. By the seventh century we see the beginning of the appearance of more and more specialist craftsmen creating objects of a superior quality. These people were clearly freed from some of the agricultural obligations of their neighbours and were supported in some way from surplus production.

It has been suggested that these craftsmen were patronized by elites, who received surplus agricultural produce as some form of tribute, and redistributed it to those whom they saw fit. Craftsmen – particularly metalworkers – who wandered from community to community, from the household of one elite to another, are relatively well attested in the archaeological and historical material from the whole of early medieval Europe, and the interregional styles of Slav metalwork suggest that styles may here have been transmitted by similar mechanisms. We have seen (Chapter 6) that many of the metalwork items could have served as prestige goods, worn by the elites, and distributed to supporters – who by displaying their access to such goods emphasized their social status. These were the beginnings of a consumer society in the former relatively egalitarian social structure.

With increasing centralization of power, we see a 'tribute economy' developing, where the elite drew a tribute in the form of agricultural 'surplus' and other products (for example furs, wax, honey). The elite then disposed of this resource within a restricted social context. The goods obtained and redistributed by leaders as tribute would be used to support retainers and others not directly engaged in agricultural production. In addition to necessary supplies, prestige goods, or perhaps scarce raw materials or bullion, may have been involved. Another sphere where the chief could use his revenue was in lateral exchange or gift-giving with the leaders of other polities. There were probably a variety of systems by which such tribute was collected, stored and used. This tribute was perhaps not payment for land-holding rights as in the feudal system but rather an expression of loyalty to a particular polity and paid for the protection of a particular leader (or perhaps in more pragmatic terms to avoid being classed as an 'other' liable to attack by that leader). In the same way the payment of 'protection money' by the East Roman and Byzantine Empires to barbarians to prevent their attacks was seen not as an expression of political dominance but rather simply as an element in foreign policy, and for the barbarian leaders as an essential element of the tribal economy.

This brings us to the question of the medium of exchange. It is difficult for us today to imagine a society which functioned without the use of money, but for most of the period studied in this book there were few coins in circulation. Silver and gold coins were imported from neighbouring states with monetary economies (Byzantium, western Europe and most surprisingly from the Islamic Near East and central Asia), but these coins often served as bullion and special-purpose money (it seems that from the ninth century silver was to some extent used in large transactions). In several cases, it would seem that these coins were produced with the specific aim of using them to trade with the Slavs. The coins are discussed in more detail below (pp. 175–83). Silver bullion (jewellery, scrap and ingots) were also used as a medium of exchange. The fact that silver objects which reached the area functioned primarily as bullion is shown by the brutal way many very fine pieces of jewellery, coins and other items have been cut up into smaller pieces (so-called hacksilver) for purposes of exchange: its value was expressed by weight and not artistic quality. Scales and their weights are found at a number of sites on trade routes.[2] It is not clear to what extent coinage was used by Slavs inhabiting the Byzantine Empire in the Balkans; it seems however from the decline in the number of finds that they had little use of Byzantine copper coinage, and probably used money mainly as a means to pay taxes to the emperor where appropriate or in large transactions.

For everyday needs the Early Slavs seem to have practised a natural economy, that is self-sufficiency supported by exchange of material goods by barter or gift-exchange in a manner observable in the recent past by ethnographers in numerous native societies. We can only imagine how this process operated in early medieval Europe, and how exchange was regulated and controlled. One household may have had for example an excess of pots (fewer may have been lost in accidents in firing), but the chickens were off laying; a neighbour with more eggs than expected but accident-prone in the kitchen might be grateful for a few more cooking-pots but had little time to make them. Another household would receive surplus from a neighbour and would remember to repay the social debt at a later date for example by helping in the gathering of the harvest. The possibilities are endless. Probably material gifts between neighbours in an egalitarian society were the basis of a complex network of shifting social obligations, all based on common goodwill and memory of past good deeds, supported by tacit or declared public disapproval of greed or miserliness. The concentration of goods in the hands of a smaller group of people would endow such a mechanism of exchange with overtones of patronage, a beginning of social differentiation.

In certain cases it would seem that high value special-purpose money was issued by certain chiefs as part of the tribute redistribution economy. This was presumably a status-enhancing policy in imitation of the monetary economies of neighbouring polities. Only much later in most regions does it seem that an extensive 'regional' economy developed, one in which exchange took place in a variety of social contexts within a more or less wide region. For this type of exchange the use of a commonly accepted medium of exchange is required. In most cases this implies a large-volume 'small change' coinage.

The development of the economy was often closely linked with military aggression. An effective means of gaining access to desired resources was to take them by force from neighbouring groups. Loot from raids and resulting tribute payments were used to finance individual and group ambitions, while attacks were carried out by temporary raiding parties (the maintenance of which was relatively cheap since they would have provided their own weapons and lived off the land in the invaded territory and then disbanded when the action was over). With the appearance of larger standing armies, the conducting of warfare became a greater burden on the economy of the elites who headed them. One of the methods of gaining more supplies for these troops and other purposes was to invade a neighbouring territory and impose a tribute on a subject community.

Long-distance trade can be followed from the written and archaeological evidence (recognition of imports, and numismatic material).[3] While so-called 'down-the-line gift exchange' (and other types known from ethnographic studies) may have been a mechanism for the movement of goods across large territories, there is also evidence for the movements of merchants. This is considered below. The establishment of long-distance trade networks in a period of political fragmentation and transport difficulties is one of the more notable features of the period. Scholars note the close connection between long-distance trade and the creation of states, but it would seem that the establishment of trade is not the factor that precipitates the formation of a state; rather that control over such trade is one of the features characterizing centralized rule.

Agricultural production

The basis of the economies of the Early Slavs was clearly agricultural production. Pseudo-Maurice (XI.4, 5) for example, writing of the Danubian Slavs, tells his readers that even they were far from being just a band of marauders, they were also effective farmers and they had 'an abundance of all kinds of animals and agricultural produce'; the missionaries among the Polabian Slavs at a later period tell us a similar story. The archaeological evidence adds to this picture.[4] The farming of the Slavs, even allowing for some regional differences, seems in general to follow much the same pattern over most of the area which they settled and may be discussed here as a whole.[5] In many areas there seems to have been a development of farming techniques in the period between the initial expansion and the tenth century, and we see a gradual improvement in (and new types of) agricultural tools. To some extent the improvement of crop yields which these changes brought allowed the accumulation of surplus, which is one of the preconditions of the rise of more complex social organizations. The importance of agricultural production is demonstrated by the number of iron hoards buried in the Carpathian basin and in Bohemia and Moravia, a third of the contents of which are often composed of agricultural ironwork.[6]

It is therefore somewhat unfortunate that we do not know more about the way in which agriculture was organized. We know little about the size of fields, and the size of individual holdings (or whether in some communities land was farmed in common). The three-field fallow system seems not to have been in use by the Early Slavs (coming into general use only in the thirteenth and fourteenth centuries), and the most typical regime would seem to be the 'alternating-fallow' method. This involved the exploitation of a piece of land as arable, until the soil showed signs of exhaustion; then it would be left fallow and the adjacent plot would be cultivated. The fallow land was used as pasture, and then after a time when its soil had recovered (a period of a few to a dozen or so years depending on the location and soil conditions) it was returned to arable, and the former ploughlands turned over to pasture. The process would be repeated until the soil became almost completely exhausted, and (as we saw in Chapter 5) the settlement would then shift to a new location and the fields would become overgrown with forest. The sparse population, and the ease of gaining new farmlands did not encourage the development of more intensive farming methods. Pollen analysis (of which there are many examples from Polabia and increasingly from Poland) has shown the cycle of temporary clearances, as well as demonstrating the importance of cereal cultivation and the weeds which affected them, but also the changes in the forest around due to human activity. We can only guess about the levels of production, and the balance between plant and animal products in the farming regime.[7]

The move to new lands involved the clearance of the forest, and the easiest way to achieve this was to burn down part of the forest. (This was easier in the case of a coniferous forest, deciduous forest would need slash-and-burn techniques to be applied.) This would remove many of the trees and kill off the undergrowth, but would still leave stumps and roots to be removed. The ash from burning would act as a fertilizer for the newly cleared land. It is thought that manuring with midden material (where practised at all) was carried out only in the plots nearer the settlement (this is detectable mainly in the scatter of artefacts from the settlement which got into the midden material spread on the fields). Beyond the infield area would be a series of pastures in clearings or on valley slopes in which the livestock were kept.

From the location of their settlements, we can see that the Slav farmers preferred more fertile soils. They often chose to settle on fertile valley bottom soils (well-watered and enriched by earlier soil erosion from valley slopes and upriver caused by over-exploitation by previous farmers from the Neolithic), and they chose areas near water for their livestock herds. They moved to poorer soils only under pressure from growing populations. In some areas north of the Carpathians, pollen analysis has shown that the areas the Slavs were moving into were heavily forested; the same presumably applies in the northern zone of East Slav lands. In other areas however the landscape had been abandoned only some years or decades previously, and it would seem that clearance was less arduous. An example may be many areas of the Balkans, where the Slavs seem to have settled former agricultural land.

The Slavs had a light plough, which in its simplest form could be a wooden ard, though numerous finds of iron ploughshares and coulters show that from the sixth century onwards more sophisticated ploughs were in use too. These tools cut into and broke up the earth; the mouldboard plough was not to be introduced in many regions until after the twelfth century. Several types of ploughs and their components have been recognized, the greatest number coming from the ironwork hoards of the Carpathian basin region (see below). The form of the other agricultural tools employed by the early Slavs did not differ much from those earlier in use in the Roman world.[8] Various types of iron hoes were also in use, and a wooden spade was fitted with an iron edge to its blade to increase its efficiency.

Other tools connected with agriculture were of wood. We have thus very few finds of the harrows which we know were used to break up the lumps of the soil. These were of wood; indeed ethnographic parallels suggest that a segment of coniferous tree trunk with projecting stumps of branches dragged across the field served the purpose very well.

When ripe the corn was cut with sickles, of which several different types and sizes are known. In the Carpathian basin the sickles of the early period tend to be only slightly curved (type A), with the blade at right angles to the hafting. Later – by the beginning of the ninth century – a new type (B) appears which has a backward curve from the handle before the blade sharply curves round in the other direction (like the modern gardener's 'hook' for cutting weeds). This tool was much better balanced and served for cutting the crop lower down, allowing the straw to be used. Threshing was done with a wooden flail.

The principal cereal crops grown were millet, barley and several varieties of wheat: these are mostly hardy varieties which thrive even in poor soil conditions. The quantities of grain found on site (having become carbonized during the processing) show that variable proportions of grain were brought into the settlements for processing from the neighbouring fields. Although this tells us something of the crops, it does not tell us about the proportions of different types of cereals being cultivated. At Mikulčice wheat was dominant in excavated assemblages (96%), and next rye 2.5% and barley 1%. At Pobedim in Slovakia however barley accounted for 69%, rye 18%, wheat 12% and oats 12%. Ibrahim ibn Yaqub tells us of two sowings of crops a year (the sowing of a winter cereal). At Tornow, near Calau in Polabia, evidence was found suggesting that rye and barley were sown in the autumn and wheat and millet in the spring. Millet was grown in the northern regions among the West Slavs.

To judge from the excavated remains (mostly preserved seeds), vegetables raised, probably in spade-dug garden plots, included onion, carrot, radish, turnip, parsnip, cucumber, pumpkins and cabbage. Pea, broad bean, lentils and vetch (vicia sativa) were also cultivated. Herbs included parsley and garlic. Hops were grown, probably for making beer. Fruit trees cultivated in orchards include cherry, apple, pear, several varieties of plums, and peaches. Vines were also grown in the southern regions, but in the conditions of the climatic optimum by the tenth century they were apparently also being grown (or at least grapes consumed) in the West Slav lands. Walnuts were also appreciated. Oil-producing plants include flax and hemp: flax was used also for producing textiles, and hemp could be used to produce oil and rope. Oil would be made in wooden presses, of which parts have been found on some sites.

In order to use cereals the grains had to be milled, and some sites produce fragments of stone querns. These were apparently used at first in an oscillating motion, back and forth, but by the ninth to tenth century fully rotary querns were in use. These stones were often imported from specialist quarries (such as the ones on the slopes of Ślęża mountain in Silesia) and were probably valuable and well looked after: these substantial and robust objects were rarely abandoned as settlement rubbish. This cannot be the whole explanation of the rarity of broken fragments, and one is forced to conclude that in many settlements flour and groats were made by other means (for example in a wooden mortar as was used for crushing other plant matter).[9]

Agricultural surplus was valuable only if it could be kept in usable condition over a period of time. Grain could be kept fresh in dry conditions free of vermin, such as sacks in lofts or specially erected granaries. There is little evidence of storage in pits. The storage of vegetable products created greater problems. Some foods, such as mushrooms and certain fruits, could be dried.

We have seen that rearing of livestock was practised in many homesteads alongside the arable farming. The animals not only produced meat but in the 'alternating-fallow' system they had an important role in the fertilization of exhausted soil. Some animals produced milk from which a number of different products were made, and were a source of skins for leather. Others were used for draught, pulling the plough or wagons. On most Early Slav sites, the dominant domestic animals are pig and cattle. The Slavs reared several types of cattle, and these could serve as draught animals, and be a good source of meat; females could supply milk. Pigs were prized for their flesh, but also relatively easy to rear (and in many cultures were traditionally left to forage in forests around medieval settlements, and could be fed on domestic scraps). An Islamic source (the *Anonymous Relation*) of the tenth century says that the Slavs are 'a people which drives pigs out to pasture like sheep'. Sheep and goat rarely account for more than 10–15 per cent of any bone assemblage, though in some mountain districts (such as Moravia and Slovakia) these proportions may be higher. The situation is different of course in the regions towards the steppes and in certain regions of the Hungarian steppe (the Alfold) where large herds of cattle and sheep belonging to a nomad aristocracy (Avar, Bulgar or Magyar) probably dominated. Horse was rarely eaten, to judge from the bone remains found in settlements; its primary use was as a mount (it was also used as a draught animal and for light work on the farm, though it could not pull heavy loads owing to the lack of a proper harness). Besides these animals, the Slavs reared a number of domestic fowl. The remains of chickens are relatively common on many sites, while those of ducks and geese are also found, though in this case it is less easy to distinguish domestic species from hunted fowl.[10] We know from the written sources (among other things mentioned as a tribute) that the Slavs obtained honey and wax from bees, but it is difficult to tell whether these were wild or farmed; archaeological finds regarding medieval apiary are rare.

Selective breeding especially in recent times has led to considerable changes in the appearance, proportions and size (especially meat yield) of domestic animals. The several breeds of cattle reared by the West Slavs were usually small, 1.2 to 1.3 m high at the shoulder. Pigs were also relatively small (about 0.7 m at the shoulder), with long legs and large heads in proportion to the body (as in wild breeds). They were variable in size and appearance (in some cases we may suspect cross-breeding with wild or feral populations). There were several breeds of sheep (averaging some 0.6 m height) with different fleece qualities and other characteristics. The horses were in general similar in size to the recent Przewalski horse (1.35–1.40 m at the shoulder), though from the tenth century we see an increase in height owing to the introduction of new breeds (probably from the west).

The quantitative proportions of post-consumption domestic animal remains found in settlement debris has been studied in the case of many individual sites (Table 1).[11] The synthesized results show that the pattern varied with region, type of settlement and time.[12] Thus rural settlements may contain a different bone debris pattern from an elite site (stronghold) in the same area: this seems to be due to the consumption of different kinds of meat by the inhabitants (and, in the case of elite sites, the structure of tribute rather than overall production). On some sites we see different consumption patterns represented by assemblages

Table 1: Main species represented in a selection of Early Slav bone assemblages from different regions and periods, percentages (by fragment number)

Site	Century	Cattle	Pig	Sheep/goat	Horse
Ripniev (Ukr.)	VI–VII	63	22	7	8
Khanska (Mol.)	VI–VII	41	25	14	19
Szeligi (Pol.)	VI(?), VII	48	36	15	2
Popina (Bul.)	VIII	50	23	20	6
Popina (Bul.)	IX	41	22	31	6
Styrmen (Bul.)	VIII/IX	50	21	29	4
Dridu (Rom.)	IX–X	44	19	26	6
Dessau (Polabia)	VII(?)	56	33	10	2
Pohansko (Boh.)	VIII–X	44	36	15	3
Staré Mesto (Boh.)	VIII–X	16	48	25	5
Nitransky Hradok (Slov.)	VIII–X	51	28	9	6
Devinsky Jazer (Slov.)	VIII–X	46	22	24	6
Tornow B (Polabia)	IX	45	42	11	3
Podebłocie 3 (Pol.)	VII–IX	41	28	23	7
Żukowice 9 (Pol.)	VII	47	46	7	–
Bonikowo (Pol.)	VII–X	33	54	11	–

Sources: Z. Kurnatowska 1977, *Słowiańszczyzna południowa*; K. Polek 1994, *Podstawy gospodarcze państwa wiekomorawskiego*; J. Herrmann (ed.) 1985, *Die Slawen in Deutschland*; A. Gręzak and B. Kurach 1996, *Konsumpcja mięsa w średniowieczu*; adapted by the author

from different areas of the complex (for example pig bones may be more prevalent in a stronghold than a settlement immediately outside its rampart where cattle bones might be found). On some sites we see temporal variation: thus on some Polabian sites discussed by Herrmann (Tornow for example), we see a rise in cattle bones with respect to pig with time, while on others, such as Dessau-Mosigkau we see a reverse situation. It has also been noted that in Poland, for example, the composition of animal bone assemblages is very different from that of the same region in the Roman period.

There are also regional differences: in the pre-state period in Poland, for example, bone assemblages in Pomerania seem on present evidence to be dominated by pig remains while contemporary sites in the east of the area are dominated by cattle remains. A similar situation is seen in Polabia, where pig-dominated assemblages cluster in the north. This if it is not due to site status (as in the case of the proportion of hunted animals in post-consumption remains) is probably an index of the degree of afforestation of a particular territory.

The herds seem mainly to have been kept in the open: there is little evidence of special housing for them, though large ditched compounds attached to some strongholds (particularly in southern Poland, Bohemia, Moravia and Slovakia extending into the western Ukraine), would seem to have served as kraals for periodically containing livestock (or horses). The age structure of many bone assemblages shows that the herds were managed by selective culling, probably at the onset of winter. Some iron hoards contain the blades of scythes 30–5 cm in length which were used for cutting grass to make winter fodder for livestock The grass was probably collected from natural riverside meadows, where the summer growth was lush. It would be cut and left to dry in the sun, periodically turned and then gathered with wooden rakes. Special whetstones were used for sharpening the scythes (and sickles). The hay was then gathered into stacks and used in the winter.

The storage of animal products presented problems. Meat could be smoked or salted. Salt was an important commodity in the early medieval period; apart from its culinary use, it was a potential preservative for foodstuffs, such as salted pork and fish. It was obtained in early medieval Europe from two main sources: the evaporation of seawater, and the evaporation of brine from salt-springs. Climatic conditions for solar evaporation existed on the south coast of the Baltic (in the early medieval climatic optimum at least) and the Mediterranean coast; the use of saline springs in south-eastern Poland and Transylvania[13] is attested by the archaeological and documentary evidence though mostly in the period after the mid ninth century. Although direct evidence is lacking, one may assume that salt manufactured at both types of sites was probably widely traded by the Slavs in relatively large quantities. Indeed documents suggest that in an attempt to curb Moravia's power Arnulf requested the Bulgar khan to prevent salt coming down on the Mureş river to Pannonia (thus blocking Moravian access to this economically important resource).

The animals from the forest also provided food, and bones of hunted wild mammals are generally found in post-consumption remains on Early Slav sites, though usually in low percentages. In pre-state Poland the quantity of wild mammal bones usually forms some 4–5 per cent of bone assemblages, rarely more than 10 per cent. In the period after the rise of the state this percentage falls on rural sites, though it remains constant and even rises on stronghold sites, perhaps reflecting a status difference in the practice of hunting. In parts of Polabia in Havel–Spree land, the proportion of wild animal bones was much higher than elsewhere.[14] In most assemblages of wild mammal bones excavated from settlements, boar usually dominates, but we also find red and fallow deer remains, hare and occasionally aurochs and (where the habitat was suitable) elk, and occasionally bear, though it is not clear whether the latter was eaten. Beavers were hunted for their fur, as were a number of smaller animals (martens, fox and so on), the bones of which are occasionally found in settlements. We should not forget the importance of fishing, even though small fish bones seldom survive on archaeological sites.

Craft products

The process of the development of craft specialization is clearly visible in the material studied by the archaeologist.[15] In particular, these trends are visible in the pottery. We have already seen that the typology of pottery has been one of the key factors in the archaeological study of Early Slav culture, of the chronology of the settlement of various territories and of regional differences between them. Technological studies and ethno-archaeological work were pioneered by Polish archaeologists in the 1940s and have been used to reveal details about the organization of production.[16] Changes in the organization of pottery manufacture have been linked with changes in social structure and organization of craft production.

In terms of the organization of production, it is clear that pottery vessels of the Prague tradition and related types were produced by craftsmen (or women), possibly even in domestic workshops. The clay was mixed with gritty material to improve its working qualities. In some cases this 'temper' was sand; more often it was made by crushing burnt stones or sherds and sifting the resulting grits. Occasionally other material such as vegetable matter might be added. The vessels were hand-built, by coils or strips joined with wet clay; the surfaces were roughly smoothed, or even wiped with some material such as grass. After drying, the pots were fired at relatively low temperatures (about 800–1000°C) in bonfire-type kilns. The colours of the finished vessels were pleasingly variable, from black to brown and orange-brown patches. It would seem that at this period the production of pots was something which could be done by almost anyone. Some of the earliest Prague-type vessels are of execrably bad quality, which shows that the manufacturer was not very practised, and probably did not make pots for a living.

Wheel-made pots, presumably specialist products, occur in some early Slav assemblages of the Migration period on the Danubian frontier and in the western Ukrainian assemblages of early date (such as at Kodyn). There is some discussion whether this material is residual rubbish from earlier occupation, or whether wheel-turned pottery was used (and made) by the Slavs in these areas. Contact with indigenous populations and proximity to the products of the East Roman empire may suggest that the latter is not as impossible as some scholars would have seem to have assumed. The traditions of wheel-thrown pottery continued in the Avar khanate.

Some time after this in Poland and Polabia, probably by the end of the seventh century, pottery vessels began to be made on a slow wheel, which was used to form the top part of the pot and give it a more regular shape. The speed of rotation of the wheel was not sufficient to 'throw' the pot. The surface of these vessels is more finely finished than earlier types or those produced by hand in domestic workshops, and may have a horizontal zone of decoration. This consisted either of horizontal bands of incised lines, or of wavy lines made either with a stick or with a four- or five-tooth comb (Fig. 18). Firing was still in relatively simple bonfire kilns though now at higher temperatures, and the colour produced by firing was more carefully controlled. Now relatively dark colours predominated. Variations on these themes gave rise to most of the types of pottery which we have been discussing in this book. The quality of these vessels is suggestive of the beginning of some form of craft organization and the establishment of workshops.

The same types of change take place in the Ukraine somewhat later. The earliest wheel-made pottery of the Luka Raikovetska horizon seems to date to the end of the eighth century, for example at Monastyrek, where an assemblage of handmade and wheel-made pottery is associated with a dirhem of 761/2.[17]

In the ninth and tenth century we see a dramatic change in the quality of pottery production over a wide area of Slavdom. In southern Polabia and the middle Oder valley the Tornow-tradition pottery appears. Further north we see the appearance of Feldberg pottery. These carefully made biconical and rounded decorated vessel forms seem to be imitating pottery of the Carolingian Empire, although very little of the latter actually seems to have made its way eastwards.

It is in the tenth century in Wielkopolska that we see the development of thin-walled pottery made on the fast potter's wheel (Fig 30). These vessels with their sharp shoulders and decoration on the upper part of the body are a continuation of the Tornow tradition. Similar changes take place elsewhere in Slav pottery assemblages about the same time. The vessels are fired in closed kilns, which allowed a higher firing temperature (over 1000°C) and closer control of the colour of firing. Again dark colours were preferred, but also tending towards a medium-dark grey for cooking-pots. The higher speed of the wheel allowed a more regular and closer-spaced horizontal line decoration, and more imaginative zoned decorative schemes. There is little doubt that these vessels were made by skilled and specialized craftsmen. It is possible that these craftsmen were to some extent itinerant, until the development of fixed markets allowed them to settle in one place.

Although as we have seen, pottery could have been produced in a domestic setting, other products were not so simple in their technology and probably imply some level of knowledge and skill. These crafts could thus be practised only by people with specialist knowledge and skills. Among the most important of these was the production of iron, and its smithing to produce tools. Iron was needed by all communities, but seems to have been manufactured in the early medieval period by (possibly itinerant) specialists who worked using local ores and fuel sources. Much literature on the subject of iron production and utilization was written in the former Soviet bloc countries. One may suggest that a special interest in this topic was engendered in part by the economic programmes of quick industrialization of these countries promoted by the new elites.[18]

In the Roman period iron was produced in central Europe in a number of very large industrial-scale plants in the forest. The technology of these ironworks was however lost, and Migration-period iron production was at a much lower scale of organization. The source of the metal was bog ore (natural iron oxides recovered from the edges of swampy areas). This had to be roasted in an open charcoal fire before it could be used. It was then loaded into a surface-built shaft furnace of clay with charcoal. After it had been reduced at a temperature of over 1100°C the metal was separated from the waste material (slag and ash). The spongy metal then had to be heated again and hammered to drive out the rest of the slag. It was then shaped into bars ready for transport away from the production site and ready for smithing. Some of these bars were heated in charcoal fires to make steel, some of which was of a high quality.

Ironsmiths made a vast range of objects, ranging from simple knives (not all of which when examined metalographically turn out to have been so simple in structure) to tools and decorative items. Weapons required similar technology and need not always have been made by separate craftsmen.

Although iron ores were relatively common over much of the area, regional and chronological differences are visible in the scale of production. Iron is a rare material in Migration-period contexts; although in common use, it seems to have been valued as a raw material. When a tool wore out or broke, it was not thrown away but re-forged into something else. Iron tools were rarely discarded or lost on settlements, especially in small rural communities (except in Bulgar territory where such losses were apparently more common than elsewhere).[19] Outside Avar territory, metal objects were only occasionally put in graves. Iron was too expensive for common use in woodwork; except for specialist joinery, nails were uncommon over most of Slavdom until the eleventh century.[20] In the Ukraine at the beginning of the Luka Raikovetska period, and also in Moravia in the ninth and possibly tenth centuries, collections of iron tools and scrap are found which demonstrate the range of tools produced. These hoards form a horizon right across central and eastern Europe,[21] though their interpretation is controversial. Some have seen them as the scrap stock-in-trade of itinerant specialist craftsmen (buried for safety and never recovered), while others have seen them as communal wealth hidden in a time of attack. Florin Curta has recently suggested that such burials might represent some ritualized destruction of wealth. The interpretation of individual cases is however difficult and should be linked with the frequency of broken objects and whether the metal parts were buried with or without their wooden handles and so on. What seems to be the oldest of these hoards at Moravský Ján in Moravia (now Slovakia) is dated by the inclusion of a set of Late Avar bronze harness mounts of the eighth century and illustrates the range of items likely to be met in these hoards.[22] This hoard was buried in an iron cauldron, covered by fragments of a second one and included fragments of a pot-chain for suspending the cauldron, a ploughshare, a hoe, three vinyer's knives (evidence of the cultivation of vines), two iron 'spuds' (for cleaning the ploughshare during ploughing), axes, two spade shoes, an auger, two anvils, two stirrups (not a pair), a lance head, three harness bits and a key. The fact that all of these items were fitted in a single iron vessel suggests that in this case just the metal parts of composite objects had been committed to the ground.

The production of items from non-ferrous metal was also relatively advanced. Copper alloy and silver fibulae and items of the Martynovka type, hooked spurs and fibulae were cast. Some were finished by filing or other forms of cold working, and by the use of many decorative techniques such as gilding and engraving. We have already discussed the belt fittings found in Avar-controlled territory. These appear in the late sixth century, and the earliest examples are of relatively simple form, made of sheet metal with punched and engraved decoration. Later examples after the mid seventh century were cast openwork fittings with complex ornament of scrolled vegetable and zoomorphic motifs (Fig. 20). Objects of copper alloy were probably very costly: there is no clear evidence of the exploitation of copper ores in the Carpathians and Sudeten mountains at this period, though some production may have taken place in southern Europe. In the northern and eastern parts of Slavdom, very probably scrap metal was the main raw material used. The mixed compositions of some of these items suggest that this was the case.[23] Copper alloy may have been derived from the melting and continued circulation and recirculation of broken objects (such as the small collection of broken objects from Nowa Huta near Cracow: Fig. 12).

Gold was only rarely employed by the Early Slavs, and silver probably derived from Byzantine coinage, small amounts of which trickled through the Carpathian basin in the sixth to eighth centuries. Byzantine silver plate seems to have been exchanged within Slav territory, as shown by several hoards from the area north of the Danube, such as the hoard of Byzantine silver vessels, four massive bracelets and other jewellery, eighteen coins of Constans II (641–68) and Constantine IV (668–85), two silver ingots and other objects from Zemiansky Vrbovok in Slovakia dating to the end of the seventh century.[24] Byzantine silver vessels are also present in the Ukrainian hoards of the Martynovka horizon of the second and third quarters of the seventh century. After the end of the eighth century, silver became available to some parts of society at least in the form of Islamic dirhems from central Asian mints (see below). This gave rise to an explosion of silver jewellery – mainly headdress ornaments. These finds date from the ninth but especially the tenth century among the West Slavs, though some items from Moravia have been dated earlier. The styles of these ornaments are markedly interregional, but probably strongly influenced by Byzantine fashions, though some central Asian influences cannot be ruled out. Similar items have been found in the hoards of Kievan Rus.[25] It is difficult to determine to what extent similar metalwork in Scandinavia is imported and how much was made in Scandinavia.[26] The production of such elaborate and delicate ornaments required a high degree of craft specialization and skill.

Alongside the metalwork produced locally, there was also exchange of metalwork within Slavdom: thus Avar metalwork is found as imports north of the Carpathians. The metalwork of the Blatnica horizon formed in Moravia in the period 790–830 following the collapse of the Avars is also found there. Other types of metalwork were also imports into West Slav territories from the Carolingian Empire.[27]

What little evidence we have suggests that the Slavs had a material culture which made extensive use of wood.[28] Unfortunately, apart from finds of a few rare iron carpentry tools, we have little evidence of woodworking techniques before the appearance of towns with deep waterlogged deposits. Wood was used not only for building houses and their internal fittings but also for many other everyday items. Wooden vessels seem to have been in common use: stave-built buckets of different sizes are evidenced by iron hoops and fittings, and carved and turned bowls and vessels were also probably used in most households. Wooden dippers had a particularly elegant shape (Fig. 48). There are traces of Early Slav structural carpentry in the form of house walls which survive in waterlogged deposits or which had been burnt. Wells often have well-preserved wooden linings which show elaborate joining techniques. Despite the elaborateness and decorativeness of Slav carpentry and woodworking skills, such items are not as permanent in the archaeological record as pottery or metalwork, which presents the archaeologist with a biased picture of the 'poverty' of Slav material culture.

Leather and textiles likewise do not survive well before the appearance of towns. Leather was produced by tanning hides, using a series of techniques probably known only to specialist craftsmen. It was used in the production of shoes, and other items of clothing and horse harness. Closely related to leather are furs, which were collected from forest animals (fox, beaver, lynx, sable, ermine, marten, weasel and squirrel), and after tanning served as a useful medium of exchange. The fur trade was of considerable importance for the economy of some northern peoples able to trade them with southern European communities.[29] The *PVL* records that certain tribes paid tribute first to the Khazars and then to the Poliane in squirrel furs from each family. The control of the fur trade was obviously of some importance; indeed it would seem that it was the value in the southern markets of fur produced in northern forests which was largely responsible for the considerable quantities of Islamic silver which at times flooded into the area around the Baltic Sea.

Both linen and woollen textiles were used by the Slavs. Spindlewhorls are common finds, which suggest that thread production was carried out at home. There are few loomweights (this is probably due to the fact that the beam looms in use were of types not requiring weights). It is thus not possible to know to what extent textile production was a home craft too. Some of the weaves found in archaeological materials are however complex, which suggests that they were the product of specialist craftsmen. Occasional finds of silk come from imported fabrics which arrived in Slav territories along the Silk Routes or from Syria via Byzantium. Silk itself has been found in early ninth-century contexts at Wolin: one piece was a silk ribbon of 'samitum' weave and thought to be of Syrian origin. Ninth-century layers at Wolin also produced fragments of fluffy woollen textiles. These were probably used as warm blankets or overcoats. Similar textiles occur in Birka and Lund in tenth-century layers and seem to be influenced by the technique of knotting oriental carpets. Tenth-century levels from Wolin produced three fragments of knotted pile rugs. These were probably local products using techniques derived from eastern carpet-making. Similar knotted rugs were found at Opole (tenth century) and at a cemetery at Schirmenitz near Oschatz. This suggests that such carpets were imported to Pomerania, at least by the tenth century.[30]

Another natural raw material which was used relatively extensively was bone (and antler). This was used for a variety of simple tools which were probably produced in the home. One type of object of these materials however, combs, required considerable skill: they were probably the products of craftsmen working in specialized workshops. These combs were made of thin plates of antler sandwiched between side plates of bone or antler and held with metal rivets; the antler was usually collected in the forest after it had been shed by the male red deer in the autumn. The first combs used in West Slav territory were probably imports from the south in the sixth to eighth centuries.[31] At a later period, production of these items tended to concentrate in the craft and trade centres on the shores of the Baltic in the ninth and especially tenth centuries.[32] It would seem that the craft was organized as an activity of a small number of itinerant craftsmen who frequented major trading places and regional centres. At the beginning of the ninth century there were extensive changes taking place in the organization of the comb workshops of the Baltic region: the considerable formal variation visible in the eighth century is gradually replaced by only very few standardized types. Comb manufacture changes its character, becomes much more standardized and soon embarks on a regular mass-production which is characteristic of the Viking period. Most of the forms which were produced in the ninth century are not found earlier, but one form of comb made from the seventh century (Fig. 37) has a simpler form and is similar to contemporary combs in Frankish contexts.

In the same coastal craft centres, items were also made of amber, which was probably collected on the shores of the Baltic after winter storms and brought to the craft centres and exchanged for other goods. The evidence of amber production in the sixth and seventh centuries is less certain than formerly thought (see p. 83), but at the site of Truso amber objects were being made in the ninth century. In this century there is evidence that some of this production shifted to the west, into coastal ports such as Wolin. Here the primary products were beads.

Glass bead types across north Europe are very similar: they seem to have been a common item of exchange The production of glass beads was also carried out in the ninth century at the coastal trade centres all around the Baltic.[33] This was a highly specialized and relatively conservative craft practised by a small number of individuals, at first operating from migratory workshops operated by semi-specialist craftsmen, associated with places of exchange along the coasts of the Baltic. Before the ninth century, the activity occurred at a number of small sites, and was associated with the practice of other crafts. In the last quarter of the ninth century (or perhaps a little earlier) this picture changes with the emergence of a new mode of production with a large output, concentrated in fewer but larger workshops accompanied by a marked difference in style, technique and raw materials. The raw material was imported glass scrap from western (Carolingian) Europe. Before the ninth century, imported glass is very rare indeed in Early Slav contexts north of the Danube. At the beginning of the ninth century however there is a rapid inflow of imported beads to Scandinavia and the Baltic region; the beads include millefiori examples probably of eastern origin (similar beads were reaching both eastern and western Europe at this time). This massive importation of beads had a disastrous effect on the local production. Only very few types of local northern European beads occur by the middle of the ninth century. The influx of foreign products reduced local production and forced it into a mode of further standardization and re-organization of the production.

In both East and West Slavdom after the ninth century appear a number of obviously imported beads of chalcedony, rock crystal and other semi-precious stones. These are most likely imports from the Near East or Byzantium. The precise date of the appearance of the first of these beads is not yet known; while cabochons (and even late antique cameos) of semi-precious stones are found in Moravian metalwork, semi-precious stone beads are rare in Moravian graves. It seems likely that the date of the introduction of these beads in the lands of the West Slavs should be dated to the tenth century (though Callmer would see their import as contemporary with the wave of imported glass beads at the beginning of the ninth century).[34]

The slave trade

In our earlier discussion of the social structure of the Early Slavs we have mentioned the existence of slaves. In the period of the invasion of the Balkans, Byzantine sources tell us that the Slavs captured local people in huge numbers and took them north of the Danube where they were put to work or ransomed for economic advantage. We find slaves mentioned in the later written sources concerning the Slavs. This phenomenon is thus of considerable importance in any discussion of the economy of the Early Slavs.[35]

The phenomenon of slavery is for a number of reasons somewhat difficult for us to comprehend. In particular it is too easy to confuse early medieval slavery with the types of chattel slavery practised in the recent past. Recent studies suggest that this is an inadequate analogy. We have seen that the Sclavenes welcomed their former slaves into their society, we have seen in the case of Malushka that a slave could be the mother of a great ruler. Slavery was at times an important element of the economic structure of several social systems (though its importance was overstressed by some scholars in Communist countries, as a result of the famous scheme of Morgan and Engels – the latter also made this problem difficult to discuss in objective terms in certain scholarly environments).

Slaves were captured as a result of military action. In a world without maps or social services, no special force was probably needed to keep a person in slavery once he or she was several hundred kilometres from home. Once ties with the home community were severed, and the captive had little possibility of finding his or her way home, he or she was probably totally dependent on captor and later owner for survival.

The existence of slaves is difficult to detect in the archaeological material[36] and it is thus hard to assess the scale of the phenomenon in different periods in different territories, but mentions of (East) Slav slaves for example are relatively frequent in the Islamic written sources. Some sectors of the Muslim economy relied on the use of slave-labour, and the maintaining of the numbers of slaves at work was a fundamental problem. Since Muslim law prohibited the enslavement of any free Muslim, or any free non-Muslim who was a law-abiding tax payer of the Islamic Empire, after the end of Muslim expansion at the beginning of the eighth century the main source of slave-labour was therefore their acquisition from lands outside of Islam by tribute, by capture or simply by purchase. This gave rise to a massive development of the slave trade in countries bordering on Islam. The slave trade with the Muslim world was obviously of extreme importance to the eastern European economy by the tenth century, and probably was well developed in previous centuries (it was probably a major source of income for the Khazar state for example). The slaves from northern Europe were called by the Arabs *al-Saqlabi* (Slavs), and from about the beginning of the ninth century the word 'slave' and 'Slav' also became almost synonymous in the Latin of the Carolingian empire.[37] Slavs were used as the praetorian guards of the Umayyad caliphs of Cordoba (probably these had initially been captured by the Carolingians in northern Europe). Venice, on the edge of Slav lands and in maritime contact through the Mediterranean with the Muslim and Byzantine states, became a flourishing centre of this trade (apparently as early as the eighth century).

Within Slavdom itself it seems that slaves were also kept in some households: there are a few mentions of this in the literary sources (chiefly referring to the East Slavs). The scale and significance of this phenomenon is difficult to assess.

Trading places and production centres

In the eighth and ninth centuries a specific settlement type appears, to which archaeologists have given the name emporium, or port-of-trade: this is specifically (though not necessarily exclusively) associated with production and exchange. These settlements probably had a function of controlling the passage of goods across boundaries and serving as a means to levy tolls and market dues on them. They were often sited near major territorial boundaries, and often in inlets or estuaries, seldom on the open shores (suggesting that they were prone to pirate attacks). The development of this type of settlement seems to be a function of the rise of some form of more centralized social structure (of the chiefdom type). Some investigators have been prone to see these sites as early towns, or perhaps 'proto-towns'. While they certainly seem to have been trade and production centres, there is less evidence that they served some form of centralized administrative function, and little evidence that they had an ideological (religious) significance. They were perhaps meant only to generate revenue for the leader's coffers, and to attract the prestige goods on which the system thrived.

Emporia began to appear also in the eighth and ninth centuries on the south shore of the Baltic (and continue in the tenth century when new settlements such as Gdańsk and Kamien Pomorski are founded). That the rise of these sites was related to the establishment of long-distance trade networks is suggested by the Islamic silver (see below) which reached the Pomeranian Slavs at the beginning of the ninth century (which was not much later than its initial arrival in eastern Europe). It is not clear however to what extent the arrival of Islamic silver in the areas is a cause and to what extent an effect of this process. The distribution of sites connected with this first wave of silver (Fig. 54) shows that western Pomerania has the densest concentration of silver hoards in Europe in the period. The socio-economic situation in these areas seems to have caused them to be especially 'receptive' to Islamic silver in the eighth and ninth centuries.[38] It is here that there have been a number of finds of Islamic coins in the occupation layers of settlements (strongholds at Bardy, Kędrzyno, and Lubieszewo all near Kołobrzeg in Poland) and graves (Świelubie in the same area).

All the evidence points to these sites being multi-ethnic contact zones. The emporia were probably inhabited by visiting merchants, resident craftsmen, resident services of various types, and by agents of the ruling authority. The visiting merchants came in groups, without their families, bringing merchandise. Storage facilities for their goods, animals and slaves would have to be provided, as well as accommodation for the merchants. Resident craftsmen probably lived with their families, as did those providing services. From all three groups the ruling authority could extract some form of 'payment' (possibly 'in kind') for the use of the facilities the emporium afforded, which would be extracted by his agents who would also (with a team of armed supporters) be responsible for law and order in the settlement. Some of these sites had planned street layouts, others were more randomly built up. Some have defences or are situated near defended enclosures.

The importance of these trading centres to the ambitions of leaders is illustrated by the fate of the Slav emporium of Reric, a trading centre in the territory of the Obodrites (probably somewhere near Lübeck). In 808 as the *Frankish Annals* inform us, the Danish king attacked and destroyed it and deported the craftsmen and merchants to his own kingdom where he built a new trading centre at Hedeby near Schleswig for them. The tributes paid by those using the new centre were to strengthen the royal treasury.

The site at Truso (now Janów Pomorski, near Elbląg in northeast Poland) actually lies on the West Balt side of the frontier zone between Slav and West Balt territory on Lake Drużno (now dried up). It was visited at the end of the ninth century by the traveller Wulfstan, whose account of his seven-day sea journey from Hedeby to Truso is copied into a translation of Orosius's *Historia adversus paganos* done by King Alfred of England. This site was long sought for and was at last located in 1982 and a portion excavated by Marek Jagodzinski.[39] The excavations produced both Balt and Slav but also imported Carolingian pottery and glass of the ninth century, Islamic coins (the last dating to 820), a Hedeby bracteate of *c.* 825, evidence of amber-working and the remains of several large timber buildings and a number of ships. There are also nearby Scandinavian burials on the Neustatterfeld site at Elblạg.[40] The area contains a number of early dirhem hoards which contain coins up to the 830s and then stop.

Wolin (Fig. 69) is a particularly interesting example of an emporium. Here a series of settlements appears along the shores of the mouth of the Dzwina river as it flows into the Baltic. Part of the settlement was enclosed with a rampart, while timber revetting on the shore formed a harbour, which dendrochronological results indicate was built between 880 and 890. The settlement levels of the site are rich in finds of various types, both manufacturing waste and finished goods, all contained in layers typical of early Slav 'proto-towns' consisting of wood waste and masses of animal manure.[41] On the hills around the site were a number of cemeteries: some of the graves were marked by barrows, others were flat cremation and inhumation graves. The grave goods found with some of the burials are of Scandinavian type. Wolin is known as Jomsborg in the Icelandic sagas and famed for being the setting for some of the events depicted.[42]

Another typical example of a Pomeranian emporium is Menzlin, where alongside the Slavs lived Scandinavians (perhaps merchants) who buried their dead in adjacent cemeteries in typical 'ship-settings' of standing stones.[43] In the second half of the eighth century a similar settlement functioned at Ralswiek on Rugia, where there were there were various craftsmen and merchants, among them Scandinavians. In Pomerania in the vicinity of Kołobrzeg at the end of the eighth century and beginning of the ninth several local centres of trade and production arose, which preceded the formation of the settlement complex at the mouth of the Parsęta river in the second half of the ninth century. The fact that fragments of Islamic coins appear here in settlement layers of strongholds suggests that these coins played some part in monetary exchange at these centres. It is notable that so far such coin finds are absent from the occupation layers of the cluster of sites around the mouth of the Oder (Wolin, Szczecin etc.). The barrow cemetery at Świelubie near the Kołobrzeg site contained Scandinavian grave goods.

The ship-settings at Menzlin and the ports of Wolin and Ralswiek are not the only traces of seagoing vessels. We have their actual remains as wrecks recovered from a number of sites on the shoreline of the Baltic, such as Ralswiek where a ninth-century sailing boat 14 m long was found sunken in the harbour: it had places for ten oars. A similar vessel of similar date was found at Szczecin, under the deposits of the later town which had encroached on the shoreline. Dendrochronological work showed that the ship contained timbers of 834–41, but that repairs were made in 896 and 903.[44]

The Islamic silver of central Asian origin which was flowing into the Baltic in large quantities came through northern Russia via the Khazars and Volga Bulgars. In northern Russia there are a series of settlements which have been identified as involved in this trade, probably as collecting points for the goods which were to be taken south. On the River Volkhov just by its mouth into Lake Ladoga with access to the sea is the famous site at Staraia Ladoga (near St Petersburg). The oldest layers here date to the 750s or 760s, together with the first wave of Islamic silver in this area.[45] Although there has been much debate on the topic, it seems from the house types that among the first settlers there were mostly Scandinavians and Slavs (and not just Finns as has formerly been claimed). The site, covering an area of about 10–12 ha (which in its first phase was undefended), has produced a rich array of finds, glass beads, antler comb fragments and Islamic coins. At Staraia Ladoga are barrow cemeteries containing Scandinavian-type finds among others; the site thus shares many of the characteristics of the emporia of the Pomeranian coast.

Inland in Russia there were also a number of 'craft and trade places' which formed at the end of the eighth century and beginning of the ninth century in the northern areas of East Slav territories, especially in the tribal territory of the Slovienie tribe[46] such as Novyh Dubovik, Knayazha Gora on the Pola river and Zolotoe Koleno on the Msta, both on the watershed of Lake Ilmen. Finds of dirhems in occupation layers hint at other likely sites (for example an early ninth-century one from the stronghold at Kamno near Pskov). It is not unreasonable to see these as nodes in the long-distance trade routes connecting the Baltic with the Black and Caspian Seas.[47]

Similar settlements in the Finno-Ugrian and Baltic territories in the upper Volga can also be dated to about the beginning of the ninth century.[48] These sites seem to suggest a relatively well-developed coin-using economy in the northern forest zone by the early ninth century. Probably the setting-up of trading posts was in some way instrumental in inducing cultural change among the natives.

These northern emporia seem to have been trade centres in which there was a certain amount of production (as in those centres on the Baltic coast). There is little evidence that they fulfilled any administrative function, they are rather reminiscent of the outposts of the Hudson's Bay Company: multi-ethnic communities occupied by traders, entrepreneurs and warriors who were to guard the wealth of the settlers against hostile parties. It is unlikely that these Russian sites can be classed as towns (see below).

Trade routes

Sea routes across the Baltic or Mediterranean waters were exploited throughout the early medieval period, as is shown by the continued Byzantine hold on the Balkan coast and the evidence of connections between the northwest and southeast coasts of the Baltic. All that was needed were seagoing boats which could be beached on a suitable shore.

Inland it was a different matter. One may imagine that the organization of a trading expedition across hundreds of kilometres of uncharted and sparsely inhabited territory was a risky business. A traveller was exposed to many dangers, unsure of the reception of the peoples whose lands he passed through, and he presumably met with many linguistic problems along the way. The elites at various nodal points along these routes profited by the taking of tolls and protection money as a condition of passage through their territory.

Road systems as such were probably largely non-existent; each road network served only local needs and travellers made their way forward only by picking their way from one settlement to another.[49] This would still leave expanses of trackless forests and wastes to be crossed. We imagine that rivers were the main routes used because of ease of navigation (and we note that the names of rivers are among the few geographical facts that are known to and reported by outsiders concerning the lands of the Slavs). The search for a crossing or circumventing of each major tributary watercourse would have made this a laborious process. The establishment of fords and bridges would have stabilized the routes and funnelled traffic through particular areas, and it is at such places that we may expect strongholds (to defend the route or to enforce payment of tolls for using it) and other settlements to be placed.

In other cases, such as the Dniepr route, river transport was used. Constantine Porphyrogenitus in chapter 9 of *DAI* tells us of how the Rus princes would journey round their lands with their retinue, collecting tribute from their Slav subjects (the *pogost'*).[50] In April the goods would be loaded into boats made out of hollowed-out tree trunks (*monoxyla*) which had been made in the winter and as soon as the ice had melted floated down the Dniepr to Kiev, where the boats were sold to the Rus, who equipped them with oars. In June the flotilla set off down the Dniepr. Constantine describes the difficulties of the route, and gives the names of the seven Dniepr rapids (the sites since 1927–32 submerged in one of Stalin's grand hydroelectric schemes) in both Slav and Rus (that is, Scandinavian) languages. The first three rapids were negotiated with the help of shallow-draught boats, lightened by putting most of the passengers ashore. The fourth rapid however was not attempted by boat. The boats were unloaded and carried overland. At this stage the expedition was threatened by the nomad Pechenegs, who would take advantage of the vulnerability of the merchants on this stage of the journey and plunder them. The remaining three rapids were negotiated by boat again. Four days later they left the river and sailed along the Black Sea coast in the same boats fitted with masts and sails to Constantinople. The journey lasted about six weeks.

The overland routes can be hypothetically defined by plotting the distribution of imported goods which travelled along them which were presumably used on the journey to obtain supplies or goodwill. A good example is the distribution of Islamic dirhems in East Slav territory: in some areas they form linear clusters separated by areas where such finds are scarce. Further pointers are important sites set up at what seem to have been nodal points of these routes: these seldom shifted their location, and indeed in some areas of Poland, for example, parts of the road system running between these centres (now towns) are probably on the line of the routes used in the early medieval period. In a few cases considerable hollow-ways have been eroded where these age-old tracks cross the brows of valley slopes.

The merchants

Merchants would be people who were able to cross ethnic, political and cultural barriers. They not only had to negotiate the journey itself, but had the added problem of transporting a bulky or valuable cargo, and also supplies necessary for the journey. For this reason it seems likely that they travelled in groups. It is not certain how frequently a merchant would travel from one end of the trade route to the other and then back; perhaps the traded goods passed through the hands of many middlemen on the way across the continent rather than being carried by one trading party. Merchants would probably travel in groups and need guides and perhaps translators. They themselves were probably armed – or were accompanied by armed men to protect them from ambush. We recall here the military prowess of the Frankish merchant Samo which won him an influential position among the Slavs (pp. 79–80).

One other group of enterprising commercial travellers, and one which is recognizable to some extent in the archaeological record, is the group known variously in the written sources as Varangians or Rus, who penetrated the south and east coasts of the Baltic, founding trade posts there, and opening up routes along the great eastern European rivers 'from the Varangians to the Greeks'.[51] The term 'Rus' (the origin of the adjective Russian) has aroused great controversy. It appears in the written sources applied to several groups of people coming from the forest zone, some evidently Scandinavian, others apparently Slavs. Sometimes they are merchants and sometimes warriors and sometimes the elite of the Rus state. This is the crux of the so-called Varangian problem (see Chapter 11). It would seem that some enterprising Vikings of the early ninth century, prompted by the flow of Islamic silver into the Baltic area, were among those who shifted their operations nearer the source, in order to partake of the flow of this bullion through the northern forests by managing the fur trade with the Khazars and Bulgars (the intermediate source of this silver) or directly with the central Asian states.[52] Rus merchants were relatively well known in the steppe zone and central Asia. According to the Persian writer Ibn Khurradadhbih in his treatise *The Book of Ways and Realms*,

the Rus merchants are a sort of Slavs, they take beaver skins and the pelts of polar foxes and swords from the most distant parts of the Slav country to the Rumnian [Black] Sea, and the tithe is levied on them by the king of Byzantium. If they wish they go along the Tanais [?or Tin = Don], the river of the Slavs, and go through the straits of the capital of the Khazars, their ruler levies the tithe.[53]

Ibn Fadlan on his journey to the Bulgar khan in 921–2 came across a trade post of the Rus which may have contained both Scandinavians and Slavs. He tells us:

Never have I seen a people of such perfect physique. They are as tall as date-palms and reddish in colour. They wear neither coat nor kaftan, but each man carries a cape which covers one half of his body, leaving one hand free. No one is ever parted from his axe, sword and knife... They are the filthiest of God's creatures ... as lousy as donkeys. They arrive from their distant lands and lay their ships alongside the banks of the Volga ... and there they build big houses on its shore. On beaching their vessels each man goes ashore carrying bread, meat, onions, milk and nabid [beer?] and takes these to a large post with a face like that of a man, surrounded by smaller figures and behind them are tall poles set in the ground. Each man prostrates himself before the large post and recites 'O Lord, I have come from distant parts with so many girls, so many sable furs' (and whatever other commodities he carries). 'I now bring you this offering ... Please send me a merchant who has many dinars and dirhems and who will trade favourably with me.'

Ibn Fadlan also gives details of other Rus customs.

Movements need not have been one-way. It seems that some Islamic merchants and craftsmen penetrated the north in the early medieval period. In this context it is interesting to note metalworkers' tools from Kiev with Arabic inscriptions and a bone stylus from the Pomeranian emporium of Ralswiek also inscribed with Arabic or Aramaic characters. Franklin and Shepard mention sites in the forest steppe which have produced camel bones, obviously from a caravan which wandered far to the north of the Central Asian steppes.[54]

In the *PVL* we have examples of the few surviving early medieval trade treaties (s.a. 907, 912 and 945) which stipulate the conditions under which (in return for meeting certain conditions) Rus merchants were to be received in Constantinople:

as much grain as they shall require ... supplies for six months, including bread, wine, meat, fish and fruit, baths shall be prepared for them in any volume they require. When the Rus return homeward they shall receive from your Emperor food, anchors, cordage and sails and whatever else is needed for the journey.

The sale of silk and slaves was regulated, as were punishments for infringements of the laws of both parties by the other. The Russian merchants have to carry some document issued by their prince confirming their status. It is not clear, however, whether this text may be treated as typical of the sort of arrangements which governed the movements and stay of merchants in foreign territories.

In the west there is a little documentary evidence concerning the movement of merchants from the Carolingian empire into Polabian territory. This penetration was limited by the Carolingians themselves. The Capitulary of Diedenhofen (805) issued by Charlemagne[55] sets this down very clearly. The document does not set down the frontier, but the limit of penetration:

> As for how far merchants heading for the Slavs and Avars may procede with their goods. Namely in Saxony as far as Bardovik where Hredi is in charge, and to Schezla [near Celle] where Madagaudas is in charge, and to Magdeburg [where] Aito is in charge, and to Erfurt [where] Madagaudas is in charge; to Hallstadt [unknown – near Bamburg?] [where] Madagaudas is also in charge, to Forcheim and to Breemburg [probably Pfreimt] and to Regensberg where Audulf is in charge, and to Lorch where Warnar is in charge. Let them not take arms or armour for sale. If any of them are found carrying these, let all their property be taken from them, and let half of this go to the palace treasury, and let the second half be divided between the mentioned leaders and the finders.

It looks as if these merchants were to go to these places and seek out the named officials, who would make arrangements for the further transit of the goods.

Media of exchange

The degree to which a monetary economy flourished in the northern parts of Barbaricum in the Roman period is debatable, but what is certain is that from the Migration period the economy of most areas of central and eastern Europe was a natural one based on barter. Outside the Byzantine economic zone, there were apparently no fixed monetary measures of value in central and eastern Europe until the development of long-distance trade in the ninth century. Value was probably measured in terms of items such as cows, slaves or products of various kinds; as in the case of more local exchange, this system probably also functioned through a complex series of mutual social obligations.

There is also some evidence that there were a number of items which functioned as 'non-monetary units of exchange' The first are the so-called grzywny, spatulate bars of iron about 20 cm long of a flat axe-like shape with a loop at one end (Fig. 51). These begin in the ninth century and have a distribution south of the Carpathians, though they are found in Małopolska – including a massive hoard in a wooden chest found in Cracow. The chest contained 4212 grzywny of total weight 3630 kg. Similar currency bars were in use in contemporary Sweden. The other items are the so-called Silesian bowls, flat slightly concave disks of thick sheet iron 15 cm in diameter. These have a distribution north of the Carpathians in Silesia and middle Polabia, appearing there in the eighth century (Fig. 51). The precise manner in which they functioned and the signifi-cance of the shape is not fully understood.[56]

Ibrahim ibn Yaqub tells us that in Prague the Slavs used small pieces of cloth as a means of payment: 'light handkerchiefs of very fine cloth in the form of netting which have no use whatsoever'. The best possible explanation of this reference is suggested by several Polish silver hoards (admittedly of the eleventh century) in which the small fragments of hacksilver were contained in pieces of knotted linen cloth in groups of fragments of identical weight.[57] It seems likely that this was the means of circulation of the extremely small pieces of silver found in some of the early hacksilver hoards.

We also know from the East Slav sources that skins were used as a means of payment of tribute and so on. This is understandable in the light of the value placed on northern furs by societies further south.

In addition to this type of material, the Slavs used coins coming from states with a monetary economy. This either was used as bullion or sometimes changed hands as complete coins. There is a pattern to the way in which these coins appear in the archaeological record.

Silver hoards

The main source of information about the economics of long-distance trade is the silver coins and other objects contained in a large series of silver hoards which are a notable feature of the archaeology of East and West Slav lands from the late ninth to the late eleventh or early twelfth century (and continuing in Russia until the mid thirteenth century). These hoards clearly represent the accumulation of great wealth but their interpretation causes some problems. Are these merchants' hoards, or did they belong to the ruling classes of the state? What is the relationship between hoarding and circulation?[58]

The character of these hoards changes with time, and their distribution is uneven. The coins in the hoards of the ninth and early decades of the tenth century are almost exclusively from central Asia and usually found whole (though fragments may occur – presumably broken to provide 'small change'). The ninth-century hoards (unlike those of the tenth and later centuries) seldom contain other objects of silver or of any other type. They were usually buried in perishable containers; very few were hidden in pots.

The hoards containing Islamic coins and single finds are found across a wide area of northern Europe (Figs. 54 and 56). From the whole of north and eastern Europe an estimated two hundred thousand coins are known to have come from 1400 finds. (Vast numbers of coins were probably found in the past which were not noted in the archaeological literature from the eighteenth century onwards, and probably some hoards still remain to be found.) These hoards are found all around the Baltic; the same types of finds do not appear however west of the Elbe, or south of the Carpathians, and are rare in southern Poland (and most date from after the beginning of the tenth century).[59] It is notable that the flow of Islamic silver into eastern and central Europe is concentrated around the Baltic and the river routes between the Baltic and Islamic world. The occurrence of objects made of this metal shows that Moravia was clearly supplied with silver from somewhere (perhaps Byzantium or Bavaria), but it did not (at least as far as the surviving evidence shows) take part in the circulation (or at least hoarding) of Islamic silver.

Tenth-century hoards still consist mainly of coins from Central Asia, but with variable amounts of hacksilver. The latter consists of whole and cut coins, whole and broken ornaments and ingots (both of bar form and flat 'spills' of molten metal). Attention is drawn especially by the manner in which masterpieces of the silversmith's art (silver ornaments) are treated as hacksilver. These hacksilver hoards are commonest in northwest Poland and Polabia but scarcer in other Baltic countries.[60] Ornaments in hoards date from the tenth century onwards (about 250 hoards from West Slav lands). These hoards demonstrate quite clearly that, in comparison with western Europe, in the tenth century the exchange systems of eastern Europe were still at a relatively primitive level.

The frequency of hoards rises in the tenth and first half of the eleventh centuries. After about 950 the hoards take on a different structure: they contain increasing quantities of coins of western European origin. During the early eleventh century the amount of hacksilver decreases and we find more whole coins of western European origin. In the second half of the eleventh century the number of hoards drops sharply over the entire area. In central Europe the appearance of ornaments in hoards ends about the end of the eleventh century, but they continue in Scandinavia longer. Throughout most of the period, there was little difference between northern and southern Russian hoards. The flow of western coins into Russia (especially in the south) was slighter than to West Slav lands. North Russian hoards have more in common with those of the rest of the Baltic zone until the late tenth century. After the eleventh century, south Russian hoards contain few or no coins but mainly silver ornaments (together with ingots and a few bronze and gold objects), and the deposition of ornament hoards continues here to the mid thirteenth century, long after they disappear elsewhere in Slavdom, that is, in the twelfth century.

Byzantine coins

In the late fifth century central Europe became part of a large system of circulation of Byzantine gold solidi. These coins passed through the Carpathian basin (gained as tribute by the Huns and Germanic tribes settled there), and gravitated towards the Baltic Sea.[61] The precise mechanism of the flow of coins and the reason for their deposition in hoards around the Vistula mouth and the western part of Polish Pomerania are not clear; it seems that this flow is in some way connected with the movements of Germanic groups in the area, and cultural influences from Scandinavia on the Pomeranian coast in the fifth century. What is especially difficult to conceive is how these coins passed through the apparently empty terrain of the Vistula valley in the early part of the period. The flow of these coins shifted to the east about 518–20: this has been interpreted by Kazimierz Godłowski as being due to the movements of the Slavs into the eastern parts of Poland cutting off the routes of travel of these coins. The flow of these coins into northern Europe was reduced after this, but lasted until about 565, when it seems to have been terminated by the movement of the Avars into the Carpathian basin.[62]

In the area south of the Danube, Byzantine coins continued to function for a while after the Slav invasions, for example several hoards from Athens and Corinth of the 580s. In Macedonia the youngest coins found are those of Justin II (565–78), while in Greece there is a hiatus: the youngest coins in the Peloponnese are from the reign of Constans II (641–68). This would seem to mark the end of the coin economy in the area. In Serbia and Croatia there is a decrease in coin hoarding in the seventh century which reflects lessening economic contacts with the Byzantine-held Dalmatian coast. Byzantine coinage reappears on a large scale in the Balkans only with the conquest under Nicephorus I (802–11).

After the 560s, Byzantine coins continued to flow north of the Danube, probably in part to pay tributes to the Avars and Bulgars. They were probably consumed in these areas, but a relatively small number reached the areas north of the Carpathians. Most of these were silver siliquae and miliarense. Byzantine gold coins of the seventh century are found infrequently across wide areas of central and eastern Europe, but after the eighth century are relatively rare (they are found only occasionally in eighth- and ninth-century hoards and as single finds in settlements and graves; they rarely penetrated the north of the Russian plain). Hoards are mainly grouped along the Dniepr and its tributaries. Byzantine milarensia of the ninth century are also rare in eastern Europe and occur only very occasionally in Russia and the Baltic zone alongside Islamic and western European coins. There seems to have been little exchange involving coinage between Byzantium and the Kievan state between the ninth and twelfth centuries (though this is apparently in conflict with the trade treaties preserved in the *PVL*). Byzantine copper and silver coinage flows into the area only in the tenth century, when there is an increase in the number of Byzantine coins in hoards in the Kievan state. Byzantine silver coins appear in the north Russian and Polish hoards of the late tenth and early eleventh centuries alongside Islamic and western coins.

Islamic silver coinage

One of the striking features of the archaeological evidence of the Early Slav economy is the huge number of extremely exotic coins which flowed into the area of northern Europe at this period. In the eighth and ninth centuries this material comes almost exclusively from the Islamic empire. It was in the closing years of the eighth century that the first silver coins of Islamic origin started to flow into Slav territory in large quantity. In the first wave of coinage we find mostly examples struck in the central parts of the Umayyad caliphate (this wave contains coins from Baghdad, Basra, Kufa, Wasit, Isfahan and al-Muhammadiya in Iran and Iraq). Coins from North African and Spanish mints are extremely rare in eastern Europe. From the end of the ninth century, central Asian mints also joined in (present-day Turkistan, Kazakhstan and northern Iran), and coins minted in the Samanid states. It is coinage of the central Asian Samanid states which is commonest in the hoards of the early tenth century.[63] These coins were produced from the output of the largest silver mines in this part of the world, servicing the mints at Samarkand, Bukhara and al-Sas (Tashkent).

The study of this material raises a number of complex issues, which can only be touched upon here.[64] Although in Islam there were a number of denominations in circulation of three main metals, copper, gold and silver, it is only the latter (known as dirhems) which are at all common in the north. They bear legends of ideological character in Kufic script, and also contain the information about the ruler and place of minting and the date, which give the possibility of analysis of the chronology and direction of flow of these objects. One of the gateways to Europe from the caliphate was Chorezm, and merchants from here penetrated to the north, to the Volga Bulgars and to the south, into the caliphate. It seems likely that the Khazars on the Don were the middlemen through whose hands these coins passed on their way to the north.

The frequency of Islamic coins in the hoards shows that the flow of silver from the eastern caliphate varied considerably from decade to decade and must have had an effect on (or have been an effect of) the socio-economic system of those peoples importing the silver. A number of periods of increased or decreased flow of Islamic coins travelling northwards can be identified from the analysis of the repeating patterns of dirhems deposited in the ninth- and tenth-century hoards from eastern and central Europe (similar patterns can also be found in Scandinavia):

- The earliest group of hoards in the area have been dated to the period 800–25, though some scholars see its beginning in the 780s (or even 770s). This *first wave* lasts up to 830–3 (the end of the reign of the Abbasid caliph Abd Allah al-Ma'mun) when new coins were occurring regularly in some numbers in the hoards.

- In the mid 830s until the 840s or 850s virtually no newly minted coins were concealed in hoards; apparently only pre-830s dirhems were in circulation among the Slavs.

- The dating of the *second wave* of coinage has been much discussed: estimates range from 840–50 to 870–9 (though some place its end at the end of the ninth century and beginning of the tenth). During this time a small number of newly minted coins were deposited with larger quantities of late eighth- and early ninth-century dirhems.

- There follows a period beginning perhaps 870–9 to the 890s when again very few coins seem to be passing northwards.

- In the *third wave* of the 890s a new flood of freshly minted dirhems entered the area; tenth- and eleventh-century hoards contain mostly coins of the period 890–950.

- After an early tenth-century peak, the flow of Islamic coinage into the area in the tenth century was irregular, and there were regional fluctuations in the supply. Most tenth-century hoards contain few ninth-century coins, as the wave of the early decades of the century drowned out earlier issues. After about 930–50 however the number of new coins flowing into eastern Europe declines. By the end of the second decade of the eleventh century the flow had almost ceased.

In an extremely important and careful study of these coins, the Poznań scholar Władysław Łosiński adduces evidence that in many cases that the capacity of the northern market was so great that only ten and twenty years elapsed between the date of minting and their deposition in hoards. If this is correct, then coins of this period in fresh condition may be considered in this area as relatively good chronological indicators. Łosiński proposes that the evidence of the differential flow of coins suggests that it is controlled by economic forces and adduces from this that the Islamic silver coins functioned as coinage within most of the societies between which they passed. In support of his thesis that they were used in East Slav territories as a medium of exchange he cites the occurrence of these objects in the occupation layers of settlements of the late eighth and early ninth centuries, especially along the Volkhov river and at Staraia Ladoga in the lowest levels.

The hoards formed in the eighth or at the turn of the eighth and ninth centuries occur in northwest Slav territory (from the south shore of the Baltic to middle Silesia and Małopolska) in north Russia and neighbouring Baltic countries, Jutland, southeast Finland, Bornholm, Gotland, Oland and Aland islands. There are forty hoards dated to this period. Most of the oldest hoards are concentrated on the south coast of the Baltic in Pomerania and around the Vistula mouth (around Truso?). They are rarer north of the Baltic (excepting on Gotland). There is an interesting correlation between the distribution of hoards and the presumed areas of penetration of Slav settlers by the early ninth century in the northern forest zone. There is a consistent cluster in the tribal areas of the Viatichi, Krivichi and Slovienie (but also in the tribal areas of the Radimichi and Severiane). They also appear in the Finno-Ugrian areas, a few in the territories of the Balts, though mostly again in areas which seem to have been penetrated by Slav colonization. Relatively few are found along the Volga and in Khazaria. The structure of the hoards suggests that contacts between the East Slavs and Khazaria were begun in the 780s, broken off in about 810 and renewed about 820.

The second wave of Islamic silver into Europe is represented in forty-two hoards deposited after *c.* 840 and lasting until after 879 which have a quite different distribution to that of the first-wave material. There is an expansion north of the Baltic, and a clearer concentration in East Slav lands (Fig. 56). On the south coast of the Baltic there is a clear movement towards the west away from the former concentration around Truso. One of these hoards is that from Ralswiek (buried after 842) which is one of the largest from the area (2.75 kg); unfortunately it has yet to be fully published. Once again Gotland is well represented. In eastern Europe the concentration of hoards in the territory of the Viatichi in the Oka basin (thirteen hoards) is notable. The majority of the rest come from the territory of the Slovienie and Krivichi. Hoards of this period are however rare in the southern parts of Russia and the Ukraine, for example around Kiev. We see at this period increased evidence of interest in routes to the Baltic other than through Ladoga. This seems to be suggested by the concentrations of hoards along the Dvina suggesting the rise in importance of Polotsk and Vitebsk down to the Dniepr where in the tenth century arose the settlement complex at Gniozdovo. There seems little doubt that the silver was used in the East Slav territories as a medium of exchange by the time of the second wave. Again a certain number of these coins have been found in occupation layers.

These hoards show that after the failure of silver flow at the end of the first wave there was slight contact throughout the following period, followed by renewed contact on a grand scale, when coins of the 860s and 870s flowed into the area in relatively large quantities, together with earlier issues still in circulation in the source area. Whatever the explanation of the structure of these hoards, the flow of silver into the area stops abruptly with issues of the late 870s, and it is also to this period that the majority of eastern European hoards date (perhaps another sign of social and or economic crisis). There was another breakdown in contacts between the East Slavs and the Khazar khanate and indirectly with the caliphate. With the first appearance of the first signs of economic crisis at the end of the first decade of the ninth century the centres of northern Russia reduced the flow of silver outwards to Scandinavia, affecting the quantity of silver reaching the northern shores of the Baltic. Can we in some way link this fall in silver with the processes leading to the rise of the early

Kievan state which the *PVL* dates to precisely this period? Was the silver crisis the cause of social tensions which were resolved by the increase of inter-tribal warfare and conquest of new territories and tribute? Was it perhaps the result of rediversion to princely hands of tribute which was formerly distributed by tribal leaders to the Khazars?

Islamic issues of the 880s and 890s seem to have reached eastern Europe only in the third wave of the flow of silver at the end of that century. The hoards of this third wave contain, alongside these older dirhems, coins representing the expansion of the flow of Samanid coins beginning in the last years of the ninth century and the beginning of the tenth. The products of the Samanid mints dominate tenth-century assemblages.

The exchange of Islamic silver finished in the last years of the tenth century when the Samanids were beaten by the Seljuks: this coincides with the exhaustion of the Transoxanian silver mines. The flow dries up on the peripheries first, on the Baltic, in Russia 980–90, but in the caliphate itself later still.

Western European silver coinage

A few ninth-century Carolingian coins are found in West Slav contexts, reflecting trade with the Carolingian empire. An 'obol' minted in Troyes between 842 and 875 under Charles the Bald was found at Kamien Pomorski in western Pomerania and seems to be one of the earliest coins in the region. Other Carolingian coins of early date, or even earlier, have been found in hoards of the tenth and eleventh centuries. Bracteates minted in Dorestad of the end of the ninth century and tenth century, bearing the legend 'Carolvs' (imitations of Carolingian types) are known, but again from later hoards, as are Hedeby bracteates – minted *c.* 830 to 970–80. Hedeby bracteates have been found at Truso, but also at Gniozdovo.[65] The regular flow of western European coins into Russia begins however only about the 960s and 970s.

By the second half of the tenth century over most of Slavdom, Islamic coins are totally replaced as a source of bullion and medium of exchange in central and eastern Europe by western European coins. These were now flowing into the Baltic zone in large numbers, some of them as tributes from western monarchs paid to ward off Viking attacks – such as the Danegeld paid until 1030 by the English (hence many hoards in Polabia and Poland contain large numbers of coins of Ethelred II, 978–1016, and Canute, 1016–35). It was only with the discovery and exploitation of the silver of the Harz mountains about 950 that the mintage of silver coins in huge numbers was able to take place in Saxony. In the late tenth and eleventh centuries the majority of coins in use in central Europe were Bavarian (mostly flowing through Bohemia) and Saxon issues, especially of the Otto-Adeleide types depicting a church or crown with a cross on the reverse.[66]

In the late tenth to the end of the eleventh century another series of small silver coins (*Sachsenpfennige*) were struck in Saxony from silver from the Harz mountains for use in trade with the east. Many thousands of them (about seventy thousand of an original issue of perhaps some five million) appear in Polabian and Polish hoards, but they were apparently not in circulation in the place of issue. These relatively plain small uninscribed coins are not easy to date; there are several main types, most of them having an equal-armed cross on the reverse. The main characteristic of these coins however is that the edge of the flan was beaten to thicken it, giving the coin a 'rim' around the image (*Randpfennige*) which had the effect of making the coin appear more substantial but also protecting the design from wear. After about 1090 these coins appear only in Silesia and Polabia, and in the next decades their distribution is restricted to Polabia.

Local currencies

It was in the middle of the tenth century however that the mintage of coinage began in the emergent Slav states. These were usually silver denars (pennies) struck to the same module as western coins and often modelled on their design. The coins of the early rulers had a specific function: they were struck in relatively small numbers for the main purpose of enhancing the status of the ruler rather than as a regular currency. Hoards of this period sometimes contain a few of these local issues alongside many more foreign (western European) issues.

In the Moravian state there was no coinage issued, but in Bohemia the Přemyslid rulers of the Czech state (and later their rivals the Slavnikovice) began mintage, probably some time (973?) in the reign of Boleslav II. There were a rich variety of types and legends, mostly modelled on western (mostly Bavarian) coins, but also some types related to Byzantine designs. There were two mints in early Bohemia, that of the Přemyslids at Malin (near Kutna Hora) and the Slavnikovice at Libice. In Hungary it was Stephen I (997–1038) who began minting silver coinage modelled on Bavarian issues. In Poland mintage seems to begin in the reign of Bolesław the Brave (992–1025), and his coins again were modelled on western issues. There is a series of denars related to the Otto-Adeleide types with the legends MESCO, but these probably date to the reign of Mieszko II (1025–34).[67] There is a break under subsequent rulers in the middle of the eleventh century, but issues began again about 1070 under Bolesław the Bold. All these coins of course had legends in Latin, and religious symbolism prevailed. The exception is a rare issue of Bolesław I of Poland which bears a legend in Cyrillic, and seems to date to the short period after his capture of Kiev (1018).

In Russia however a completely different pattern was established. The coins emphasize the significance of the person of the ruler – unusual in Europe at this period – and the coins have Cyrillic legends in Russian. Another unusual feature was the use of gold coinage alongside the silver. These coins were modelled on types of Byzantine, and to a lesser extent other oriental issues. The first coins were struck by Vladimir I (978–1015) but ceased after the death of Jaroslav the Wise (1019–54), and were not renewed until the fourteenth century.

These states without their own sources of silver all began to mint coins of their own at about the same time, and the break in the issue of local coinage occurs in Poland, Russia, Sweden and Norway at similar stages of economic development. One has the impression that the issue of the first coinage had a role to fulfil in the strengthening of the state, but few economic advantages resulted.

The Bulgars did not as a rule mint their own coinage but were content to utilize Byzantine coins. The first coins to be issued by the Bulgars appeared in the early thirteenth century when curious large-diameter concave copper bracteates (one-sided coins) were issued.[68]

At various times in Slavdom we see the growth of a monetary economy, the use of coinage for local exchange. Rulers were quick to see the economic advantages of the issue of their own coins in the changed economic situation of the later part of the early Middle Ages, and the granting of minting privileges (mainly to bishops and noblemen) was later to be a source of income. This change to a local market economy seems to have taken place in Poland in the 1070s, at about the same time as it occurs for example in Scandinavia.

The origin of towns

The Slavs on the whole settled in areas which had no previous tradition of the construction of towns. In the former Roman province of Dacia – now Romania – most of the towns had fallen into ruin in the fourth century and were abandoned by the time the Slavs got there. In the Balkans, the Slavs initially found towns which were still functioning; they had little use for them however and settled the hinterlands. The archaeological evidence suggests a decline of the towns in much of the area. By the third quarter of the seventh century there was virtually no town life over much of the Balkan peninsula. Only in the areas controlled by Byzantium – especially on the coasts – did (some aspects of) urban life continue.

In the process of the creation of the Bulgar Empire, some of the old fortified centres (such as Plovdiv) were resettled, and architectural elements from them were often reused in the new buildings. Several new urban complexes such as Pliska and Preslav were also built: they were modelled on Byzantine towns with their planned layout and their types of structures. The nature of other sites (for example, ninth-century Pernik near Sophia) is less easy to determine, they may have been small walled towns or masonry strongholds. The Bulgar expansion north of the Danube in the ninth century however does not seem to have been accompanied by the establishment of towns in the area.

The question of the origin of towns among the West Slavs has attracted a vast literature. Before the Second World War the main model applied in central Europe was that proposed by historians who supposed that towns in the area were defined only by their 'location', that is the issuing of a charter, which meant that towns as such arrived in West Slav territories only with the German settlers after the thirteenth century (an interpretation which seemed to support German claims of their innate superiority over their eastern neighbours). Archaeological discoveries after the War by Slav archaeologists, particularly in Poland and Bohemia, were used to question this model. This work showed that the strongholds of the area were large and densely built-up areas (some of them with a planned layout) which had some kind of elite and administrative functions; some had structures connected with cult. Debris from craft activities showed that many of these sites functioned as production centres, and finds of scales and weights and various imported items suggested they functioned in long-distance (and perhaps local) trade. This matched the bundle of criteria usually used to identify urban settlements, and it was therefore assumed that these were towns.[69] Recent more detailed examination of the problem has shown great variety in these settlement complexes, and it seems clear that the development of urbanism in Slavdom was a complex process with several stages, and with very clear regional differences. One of the principal problems has remained the definition of a town, and the cultural-relative nature of such definitions.

In Polabia and Poland, many previous considerations of the topic of the origin of towns have concentrated on the coastal emporia (see above), which tended to be large undefended areas to which merchants seem to have come, though some were permanently settled there. It is difficult for us to decide whether these sites were indeed 'towns' in the narrow sense of the definition, or were perhaps 'proto-towns' (whatever we understand by that term).

Such sites are however absent inland in West Slav territories. Over most of Poland, Polabia and Bohemia were strongholds which have produced evidence of imports and craft production, sometimes from the enclosed areas themselves, and sometimes from the dense extramural settlement which often accompanied them. Some of these strongholds were undoubtedly command posts of the early state manned by the retinue of the ruler and thus had an elite, military and administrative function (even if only to collect tribute). The long-distance trade, accumulation of surplus and craft production were mainly geared towards satisfying the internal needs of the inhabitants of the stronghold complex itself (the restricted economy of the 'retainer culture'). These sites have some characteristics of towns, but were these strongholds with their clear military, administrative and elite functions necessarily towns just because there is evidence of production and exchange in and around them? For these ambiguous sites it seems more appropriate to use the term 'stronghold-town'.

Changes seem to occur with the rise of a regional economy, which seems to be marked in Poland for example by the appearance of the new coinage of the 1070s. With this came changes in the stronghold-towns (and especially in their extramural settlements) which seem to have led to the creation of something more recognizable as urban sites functioning as market centres in the expanding early state economic system. It seems likely that these changes started in the core of the state and affected the peripheries of Silesia and Mazovia only a few decades later. In the course of this process some of the old strongholds developed into towns (Poznań, Gniezno, Wrocław, Opole, Cracow, Lublin), while other formerly large and important centres were reduced in status or abandoned. In the areas of southern Polabia which were left in the German Empire after the 983 revolt, urban development was similar to that further west (that is, in Saxony and Thuringia), while in the areas independent of German rule the development of urban centres was considerably retarded, and many sites had to be (re)founded in the twelfth century.

The status of the central places of the Moravian state is also uncertain. The very extensive strongholds of the period have a superficial urban appearance, but again a closer examination of the evidence from sites such as Stare Město and Mikulčice suggests that they consisted of a central princely enclosures surrounded by enclosed and unenclosed suburbia with nobles' dwellings and churches and craftsmen's quarters. Again it seems that these are stronghold-towns, elite settlements reflecting a restricted economy, and after the collapse of Moravia many of these sites were abandoned.

Bohemia on the other hand seems to have supported a flourishing regional economy already by the 970s. Here there are several tenth-century sites which seem to be urban (Levý Hradec, Prague, Libice, Pilzno). With the expansion of Czech power north of the Carpathians, several new towns came within the Czech orbit, including Wrocław and Cracow (see the account of Ibn Yaqub cited above).

The development of urbanism among the East Slavs has recently been considered by several scholars.[70] In southern (inner) Russia the rise of stronghold-towns as tribal political and administrative centres was a result of the consolidation of settlement, and the development of production and exchange; they developed in the centres of densely settled areas. These sites seem to have developed around administrative centres in the middle of settlement concentrations. A prime example is Kiev, which originated as a stronghold complex on a series of defensible hills on the high scarp of the Dniepr. Excavations have shown rich early settlements on Zamkaya Hill and on Starokievskaya Hill; the latter was at some stage surrounded by a rampart. The interior was densely built up and contained a religious sanctuary and evidence of production (pottery, metalwork). The expansion of the town to adjacent areas and the creation of the Podol suburb took place at the end of the ninth century. Excavations in Vyshogrod, Chernigov, Pereiaslavl, Liubech, Belgorod and other Ukrainian towns show the same pattern. These towns were permanent agglomerations usually of comparatively large area surrounded by wooden and earthen defences which divided the area into two or more enclosures. The smaller 'inner' one (*detinets*) contained the more impressive buildings, a magnate's dwelling, a masonry church and so on. The outer enclosures usually were in part agrarian centres (presumably with a considerable agricultural hinterland) but also carried out the secondary processing and redistribution of products. The finds from these sites belong almost exclusively to what has been termed 'Old Russian culture' together with a number of items which are obviously imports. Most of these towns were in existence by the early eleventh century and show economic growth in the twelfth century. In a later period the Russian towns were founded by the local boyars but their functioning depended on merchants and craftsmen; they acted as nodes for long-distance trade. These stronghold-towns emerged as local centres of political and military power or as regional administrative centres.[71]

In northern (outer) Russia the pattern is different. Here stronghold-towns were founded in areas without dense settlement and without a hinterland. Settlement and economic growth seem to have been initiated only by the construction of the strongholds. In several places however the large sprawling (and undefended) pre-existing trade emporia are replaced by stronghold-towns, often sited in a different place. This suggests that the control of the trade routes was one of the principal functions of the latter, but also the resiting may have been a reflection of a change in organization of this trade. We thus see the replacement of Gniozdovo by the stronghold town of Smolensk, of Ryurikovo Gorodishche by Novgorod, of the Sarskoe Gorodishche by Rostov, the replacement of the emporia at Timerevo (and adjacent sites at Mikhailovskoe and Petrovskoe) by Jaroslavl and so on. Northern stronghold-towns were situated primarily on important river crossings and often on the peripheries of territorial zones, where it was possible to control the trade routes into and out of these zones and collect and distribute tribute. These towns were, E. N. Nosov claims, 'military-administrative, trade and craft centres which were not connected directly with tribal structures': he notes that the finds assemblages from these centres are 'more polyethnic' than those from southern Russia. We see also a surprising amount of evidence for agricultural activity connected with these stronghold-towns. There are thick layers of animal dung around the buildings, some of which seem to be housing for animals, there are finds of agricultural tools, and later written sources tell us of the cattle and field plots of town dwellers.

The most extensively excavated of these sites is Novgorod. Here the ninth- and early tenth-century site at 'Rurik's stronghold' (Ryurikovo Gorodishche)[72] was replaced by Novgorod ('New Town') in about the middle of the tenth century (the earliest dendrochronological dates from the site come from the 950s, but it is not clear how much earlier the site had been in existence). This large site with its fifteen thousand inhabitants became one of the main centres of the northern parts of the Russian state, and excavations in several areas of the town have produced much evidence of the life of its inhabitants.[73] The cold and damp conditions of the build-up of layers which formed in the town had produced anaerobic conditions in which perishable materials had survived. Here were found the remains of wooden buildings of 'blockhouse' technique resting on horizontal sill-beams laid directly on the ground surface. It was also found that the streets had been paved with thousands of transverse wooden beams side-by-side, and these had been periodically replaced as the ground level rose owing to continual dumping of waste. In the build-up of layers were found organic finds such as textiles, wooden objects and even documents written on birch bark. Excavations on a smaller scale in other towns in north Russia (such as Grodno and Polotsk) have produced similar evidence.

9

Pagan Ideologies

It is especially difficult to discover anything about the spiritual life of an ancient population. Nevertheless attempts at reconstruction of Early Slav religious beliefs are an important aspect of our efforts to bring the past lives of these people closer to us.[1]

For most of the area of Slavdom we have very little written information, and the existing material is rather enigmatic. We have a little evidence from East Roman writers (as in the famous 'ethnographic excursus' of Procopius). We have other information from a series of eleventh- and twelfth-century sources concerning missionary work among the Polabians.[2] There is also a certain amount of information in the *PVL* and the Arab authors. Most of this material however comes from a relatively late period and need not necessarily reflect practices of the earlier period. The 'pagan' belief systems of the people in whom we are interested differed from that which was acceptable to the rest of the contemporary literate world, since most of the written sources were compiled by Christians (and in the east, Muslims) who exhibit a clear distaste for writing about paganism (as a work or invention of Satan). Indeed, many of those who were in the position to observe pagan practices at close hand were those missionaries who were determined to sweep all traces of the old beliefs away. This partisanship of the sources has meant that the existing descriptions of events and opinions are presented almost entirely from the Christian point of view. The illiterate other side (living entirely in the sphere of oral culture) was unable to express itself in writing and thus unable to inform us of its own point of view and its version of events. Some of its traditions were forgotten or suppressed, although some isolated facts still found their way into the later Christian literature.

The other main source of evidence is provided by archaeology, but, while the archaeologist is able to recover many of the material aspects of daily life, to discover anything about the spiritual life of an illiterate people is especially difficult. Our most easily accessible evidence for ideologies of the Slavs comes from the excavation of burials; the manner of disposal of the dead is often a good indicator of the beliefs of the spiritual world. The other archaeological evidence is rather scarce, and, as always when dealing with ritual and cult, very difficult to interpret.

Another important source is however ethnographic material. In rural areas even into relatively recent times the villagers still kept some old customs –

despite the opposition of the Church. On the basis of the interpretation of the recorded rural folk beliefs, together with philological research and also comparison with other Indo-European beliefs, several attempts have been made to reconstruct ancient Slav religion. The ethnographic material collected in rural districts in the nineteenth century is difficult to interpret however, since we do not know how many of these customs derive from practices arising after the introduction of Christianity.

The evidence we have is enough to demonstrate that the religious beliefs and practices of the Early Slavs had much in common with the religious beliefs of other Indo-European peoples, and on this basis some of our fragmentary evidence can be tentatively fitted into a reconstructed model. The picture is however still incomplete and full of doubtful points.[3] There is no reason to think that there was one consistent religion across the whole area of Slavdom, or that it remained unchanged through the centuries; indeed one would expect the ideology to be remodelled to suit changing social contexts. There was almost certainly regional and temporal differentiation, and there seems to have been especially marked change at the period preceding the introduction of Christianity and/or state-formation. We should be aware also that 'old' (pagan) traditions are not fossils but probably continued to develop even after the introduction of Christianity.

Demons and the spirit world

Like any religion, that of the Early Slav peoples developed in part from the traditions of an earlier period. As in many early religions, a belief in spirits and demons of various types seems to have played a large role in Early Slav religion (and it is this facet of Early Slav spiritual beliefs which has best survived in the folk traditions of later centuries). Some of them came from the spirits of dead people; others were entities which had an independent existence. Apparently demons were everywhere, in the home and in nature – in rivers, springs and trees. Certain types of inanimate objects such as holy springs, trees, copses and stones were particularly prone to being inhabited by demons and were thus worshipped, though these cults were aimed not at the object itself but at the supernatural power which inhabited them. Various bad spirits lived on the edges of bogs and waters as well as in forests. It is not however clear to what extent these demons were individualized and named. Two terms, Czart and Bies, are old Proto-Slav names (later applied to Satan himself), but most of the demonic names known from later sources are etymologically later constructions. Demons and spirits had influence on human lives, but were also to some extent dependent for their continued existence on the offerings people made to them.

An important role seems also to have been fulfilled by the cult of the ancestors, and spirits of the dead which could exert some form of influence on the living. Indeed it was from the world of the dead that various familiar spirits of the home and hearth were derived. These friendly spirits helped with tasks around the homestead. Other spirits of the dead were less friendly, and it was necessary to apply magical practices to prevent them from returning to disturb the living. These malevolent spirits were envisaged in later folk tradition as in many other rural communities as small, naked, hairy, dark-coloured (or red-skinned), with the ability to burn or spark, often with extra fingers or toes, a limp, with a large head with thick eyebrows, odd teeth, thick lips, long nipples and a lack of sex organs; they could also make themselves invisible. They could cause all sorts of trouble, from scaring with strange cries and shrieks to causing death and illness.

The vampire, a male blood-sucking demon (*stryg*) deriving from the unquiet dead and connected in popular consciousness with eastern Europe, seems to have been of Balkan origin (probably ultimately deriving from Roman traditions), but is later found in West and East Slav contexts. In Russia however offerings were made to vampires as for other spirits. Vampires were cruel demons which fed from the blood and souls of people, usually from the vampire's own family. In folk tradition, they were drawn from drowning victims, suicides, victims of hanging, women who died in labour, couples who died on the day of their wedding and in Christian times children dying unbaptized (interestingly enough 'normal' violent deaths seemingly did not lead to these problems). A series of unexplained deaths in the same family or village would give rise to fears that a vampire was at loose in the community.

Water had a significance in terms of its properties in purification, as well as in fertility. In mythology it also divided the land of the living from that of the dead, and it was from the world of the dead that many of the water spirits which we know of were thought to derive. The flow of water in streams led to thoughts about strong water demons who had to be placated. In Russia there were thought to be demons, themselves the victims of drownings, who waited for the opportunity to drag down other victims into some waters. In Bohemia and Slovakia these *vodniki* took the form of youths who appeared by the shore in the light of the moon. The placation of such spirits might involve rituals of 'feeding the waters', offerings of salt, bread or animals such as fowls in periods of drought, or during journeys by water, or in building causeways or bridges.

In Ukraine and Belarus the spirits of young girls who had died unnaturally become *rusałki*: pretty, naked girls with loose hair dressed with wreaths and garlands of flowers. These were water spirits in winter and forest and meadow spirits from the spring. They danced on the meadows by the new moon, according to some versions, tempting passers-by to join them and setting them riddles, and tickling people until they laughed themselves to death (an interesting addition to Indo-European demonology!). They were apparently especially dangerous in May (the week around Whit Sunday). They were related to a group of similar female demons known from the South Slavs (Croats, Serbs, Bulgarians, Slovaks). These *vila* were very strong beautiful naked girls, armed with bows and arrows, who lived in springs, in caves, under trees and stones. There were two varieties, mountain spirits and water spirits. Men left offerings for them even as late as the thirteenth century. They could transform into swans, or snakes, horses, falcons, wolves and whirlwinds. When these battle-maidens (like the Germanic Valkyries) were dancing on the mountain-tops or meadows they would shoot at anyone who came close, or draw them into their ring and dance them to death. There are some accounts however of *vila* who married mortal men.

The forest spirits in general did not derive from the world of the dead. In Slav folklore the secrets of the forest world seem to have come to existence by themselves, deriving from the opposition between the home and the wilderness, that which was familiar and inhabited opposed to that which was empty and strange. The forest remained the preserve of untamed powers of nature. Even today to be alone in a dark forest can be felt by some to be an unnerving experience, suggesting that these primeval instincts may not have been killed off by modern civilization; for the Early Slavs the powers hidden in the shadows were real enough. The forest was the home of the demon of the forest (*lešij*), ruler of the animals, with many personifications (such as wolf-shepherd). In general hostile to humans, he took on the form of a wolf, owl or whirlwind. He is accompanied by Baba Yaga, mistress of the forest (mountain-mother). The written sources frequently mention holy copses or woods, inhabited by forest spirits of various kinds. As late as 1156 (after a pagan revival), the monk Helmold visiting the area of Lübeck in the northwestern fringes of Obodrite territory found a cult-place of Proven (perhaps Perun) within which was a sacred oak fenced with stakes, but with no idol. In the nineteenth century in the Voronezh province on the way to the wedding a young couple would walk round a certain oak tree three times and place an offering by it. Other trees such as lime and birch could also be holy according to recent folklore.

Demons of vegetation were especially venerated, and the year's main holy festivals seem to have been associated with major changes in vegetation. These festivals were celebrated by singing and dancing, often with the consumption of much alcoholic drink. The spirit world was involved in a number of rituals which were repeated each year. The rites involved have a dualistic nature: some have clear connections with a cult of water and its purifying role, while others have an element of fire symbolism. The two however interconnect in several ways to suggest that they may originally have formed part of a more elaborate system. Some of these survived the conversion to Christianity in relict form into recent folk tradition. Some pagan festivals were taken into the Christian calendar and given new meanings; many of these have connections with some aspect of fertility cults. Other rites which survived in folk practice, often against the express wishes of the Church, are more insidious relics of folk beliefs from some part of the pagan religion. It is easy today, faced with their relict form, to underestimate the power of these rituals, which have been repeated cyclically over at least a millennium. In the beginning they were connected in the eyes of the people as being a necessary condition of the continued existence of the world and society.

A spring custom found in several Slav countries involves a straw mannekin, dressed in women's clothing, which is carried through the village and thrown into a river or pond. In Poland this occurs on the first day of spring, and the effigy is called Marzanna (other versions: Marianna, Morenie or Dziewanna, or Dudula-Dodola). It is possible that the straw effigy is in some way a substitute for a sacrifice to the water spirits, or perhaps it is a symbol of the overcoming of death at the end of winter. The latter is suggested by the existence of a similar rite in Russia, where the effigy is male and called Kostroma. A more sinister element is hinted at by the clearly aged nature of the effigies once drawn by ox-cart through certain villages in former Yugoslavia before being 'drowned', which suggests the sort of rites discussed in the famous work by Frazer.[4] In a symbolized form the rite was practised at the beginning of the new (farming) year and at midsummer. The burning or drowning of effigies, branches, straw, decorated with garlands of flowers, and ribbons, would symbolize their passing into another world. The spring equinox was probably marked by some form of purification ceremony, involving ritual bathing, of which a relict is a popular folk ritual of possible similar origin: the throwing of water over young girls by village boys in Poland on Easter Monday. The Whitsun fixed in the Christian calendar on the fiftieth day after Easter Sunday usually falls in May and was another important festival in rural Poland hijacked by the Christian calendar. Its celebration in southern Poland had some features in common with the mid-summer festival.

This festival which was especially difficult for both the eastern and western Church to eradicate was that of what was thought to be the shortest night in the calendar, St John's Night (24 June), the festival known as Kupale in parts of Russia. Huge fires were lit on hilltops, around which young people gathered and danced and sang 'and gave honour and prayers to the Devil. The young women will not allow this pagan custom to die out in Poland', as one Polish writer wrote in 1562. The seventeenth-century *Hustyn Chronicle* describes the scene thus:

in the evening the simple folk of both sexes gather together and plait wreaths of poisonous plants or roots, and girding themselves with flowers, they kindle a fire. Elsewhere they erect a green branch and joining hands dance round it singing their songs . . . then they jump through the fire, in this manner offering themselves in sacrifice to the demon [bies].

In Ukraine, Belarus and Russia the ritual involved the burning of a straw effigy (*Mar[a]* – death?) which sometimes had a head in the form of that of a horse or ox. In other places a blazing wheel (solar symbol) was pushed down the slope. The events of the night often ended in orgiastic behaviour among the young participants, of which excesses the Church disapproved especially.

At harvest various rituals involved the last stook of corn, the last ear of corn. Often garlands were made of corn; sometimes these were anthropomorphic with names such as 'Grandpa', 'Old Woman' or simply 'Old'. At the winter equinox, in several countries, the Slavs still celebrate All Souls' Day as an occasion to visit the graves of their ancestors, clean them, light candles and sometimes share a meal by the graveside.

The Soviet researcher Natalia Vielecka detects in the complex series of rituals summarized above relics of an archaic belief. [5] She believes that they represent a dialectic between life and death, which would be represented by Slav concepts of moving from one world to another (rather like a shaman's spirit-journey). The relationship of the one world to the other is understood as the relationship between the living and the ancestors and the influence of the spirits of the dead on the world of the living. The ancestor cult was an agrarian cult, to which was due the ensuring of the normal growth of vegetation. The dead – especially the important dead – took their place after death in the world of the gods who controlled such matters. Various rites, not only funerals, had the important function of sending people to the other world to maintain the proper course of events on earth. She sees the various rites involving effigies and fire-jumping as symbolic signs, substitutes for human sacrifices.

The gods

It seems that the concept of god was relatively weakly developed among the early Slavs; much of the evidence points to a much-wider-spread belief in demons. There is a short mention in the 'ethnographic excursus' of Procopius, which is our main source for the early period. He said (*Wars* VII.14, 22–30) that the Sclavenes and Antes

believe that one of the gods, creator of the lightning, is the one ruler over everything, and sacrifice to him cattle and other sacrificial animals. They do not accept predestination, but . . . when they are threatened by death – in illness or war – swear, if they are spared, to sacrifice to the god in return for their lives . . . They worship rivers, nymphs, and all kinds of gods, and to all of these they make sacrifices and at the same time as they sacrifice they predict the future.

It is difficult to know how reliable this information might be. [6]

The main evidence we have for the existence of a pantheon of gods comes from the end of our period. It is possible that the concept of gods developed only at a relatively late date. There is a little evidence to show however that some demons may already have been promoted to the status of gods at the time of the crystallization of Slav identity and the migrations. Probably because of this, what seems to be the older horizon of gods (Perun, Svarog, Volos) is found widely scattered. In general ancient Slav religion, like many others, seems to have been concerned with nature, and especially fertility. It seems to have been aniconic, without representations of the deities for most of the pre-Christian period. There are few finds of cult sculptures or temples until the end of the period; there are also no words to refer to these phenomena in the Proto-Slav language.

One point of interest is the syncretism of Early Slav religion. Some features which can be reconstructed have aspects in common with those recorded in the Icelandic sagas – themselves reflecting earlier (Germanic) tradition. It is possible that some of these traits may have been introduced to the area of the crystallization of Slav identity during the period when the forest steppes were occupied by the Cherniakhovo culture. Other influence from the steppes is reflected in traces of Iranian (that is, Sarmatian) etymology such as the names of some gods mentioned in East Slav sources (Svarog, Stribóg, Khors) and the Slav word for god (*bog*). In East Slav lands there may have been some indirect influence on Slav religion from the belief systems of Scandinavian settlers (possibly the same applies to regions of Pomerania). Some writers have suggested that the Slavs were aware of classical mythology and, by a curious inversion of the *interpretatio romana*, adopted elements of it for their own use, adding new gods where needed.

The sources do not permit us to say much about Slav concepts of theogenesis, cosmogenesis or anthropogenesis. Helmold tells us that the Slavs thought that all gods came from one and that the degree of blood relationship with the main god determined the relative importance of each. We also have information in the *PVL* that Dazhbóg was seen as the son of Svarog.

Two main gods, Perun and Svarog, seem to have had especial importance. The cult of Perun is the most widely represented in the written evidence. It would appear that it is Perun who is mentioned in the account of Procopius cited above. He is similar in name and attributes to the Lithuanian Perkunas (and possibly the Nordic Fjorgyn). Perun was a weather god connected with lightning (*piorun* in Polish), storms and rain, and thus fertility. Thunderbolts (in reality, fossils, Neolithic polished axeheads and fused glass from thunder strikes) were important and powerful amulets. Trees struck by lightning were regarded as holy: Perun was especially associated with oak trees. As guardian of fertility and rain, Perun was probably the main god in the Slav pantheon. He was the dynastic god of the Kievan princes; he is mentioned in the *PVL* in 945 and 971 when oaths were sworn in his name. In 980 a large statue of this god was erected among others by the royal court in Kiev, and a few years later we hear of the toppling of the statue (and a similar one at Novgorod) into the river when the Russian prince was converted to Christianity. The description of the statue in the *PVL* ('a silver head with a mouth of gold') is coloured by biblical overtones and need not be accepted as authentic. The idea of erection of a statue seems to be a late innovation, under foreign influence: the Perun cult was probably originally aniconic and celebrated in open-air cult centres, among them mountain tops. It is not clear how the cult of Perun was celebrated, but it presumably involved fire, and some writers even suggest that the occasional making of human sacrifices cannot be ruled out. Perun was later equated with the old white-bearded St Elias who travelled the heavens in his fiery chariot.

The sun was very important to the Early Slavs, and folk customs from southern Poland, Belarussia and Ukraine preserve prayers to the rising and setting sun. The god Svarog is evidenced in sources from Russia and Pomerania (Thietmar, Adam of Bremen), which suggests that he was worshipped over a wide area of Slavdom. He was a sun god, a god of fire, probably the domestic hearth. His cult was linked with features connected with the agricultural activities of the Slavs: the sun was needed for ripening crops, and fire was an important element in clearing land, making the home and disposing of the dead. The family hearth was ideally kept burning permanently, except when ritually extinguished for rekindling on the summer solstice (when a bride moved into a new house in some areas she took embers from her mother's hearth to kindle a fire in her new home). There was a major temple of Svarog at Radogoszcz in Polabia in the twelfth century, which contained a statue of the god, wearing a helmet and cuirass. It is said to have been covered in gold and had purple hangings around it. In several late sources he is linked with another god – his son (also a god of the sun and fire), whose name in some sources is Dazhbóg but with several other names derived from that of his father.

Another powerful god known mainly from the Russian sources is Volos (Veles, Vłas), god of the herds. A Czech demon also bears the same name which may suggest that his cult was initially widespread. According to some authors he may be linked in some way (or as well) with wealth. The Slav name of the Pomeranian seaport Wolin may come from the god's name. Apart from this we know very little about the external form of his cult. Some writers however, on the basis of the importance attached to him in the Russian sources, think that he may not have been initially simply a god of cattle-herders but may have played a more important role in the Early Slav pantheon. Bruckner links the original significance of Volos with the cult of the dead ancestors, with the underworld (seen perhaps as across the sea). Volos thus seems to have linked some form of element concerning nature (the bull-cult) with those concerning the structure of society (ancestor-cult). After the conversion to Christianity he was linked with the Byzantine St Blasius (Vlas or Vlah in the Slavic liturgy) who was also the guardian of cattle.

Other Russian gods known from the later sources (Khors, Stribóg, Simargl, Mokosh, Siem, Rgiel, Jarilo) are simply names about which we know little. The third name however is that of an Iranian desert demon with a dog's head and bird's body, which seems to have been accepted into the pantheon some time before the twelfth century. Mokosh was perhaps, like Simargl, more a demon than a god. She was a water spirit, also associated with female tasks in the home such as spinning and weaving as well as the laundry and childbirth. Jarilo too may have been a demon, who was honoured by a festival lasting several days after Whitsuntide criticized by St Tikhon Zadonskij in the eighteenth century.

As we have noted, the cult of these gods was generally aniconic, but there were exceptions. One particularly interesting find is the stone statue found in the River Zbrucz near Liczkowiec in southwestern Ukraine in 1848 and now in Cracow Museum (Fig. 58). This square-sectioned limestone post 2.7 m high has four faces and is divided into three zones.[7] According to the Soviet scholar B. A. Rybakov, these possibly represent a scheme of the world. The lower zone represents a kneeling three-headed chthonic god (perhaps Volos) holding up the earth, the middle zone the world of men and women, who are represented with joined hands as if dancing around the statue. This contains two male and two female figures. Above them in the upper zone, representing the heavens and gods, are four divine figures, each having a long tunic and similar hand position. That on the front of the post is a female who holds a horn in her left hand (fertility goddess? – female counterpart of Perun?); on the left side a similar figure holds a ring. The male figure on the right side of the post has a horse and a sword with asymmetric grip and represents a warrior figure – possibly Perun himself. The figure on the back of the post has no attributes. All four heads have a common conical hat which gives the whole post a phallic form, linking it with fertility cults. The statue was probably made at the end of the ninth century, perhaps under mixed Slav and nomad influence. In 1984 excavations in a stronghold just above the findspot of this the most famous Early Slav idol revealed what was interpreted as the socket from which this statue was toppled in the tenth-century conversion of the country.[8]

In Kievan Rus we have no evidence of the construction of roofed temples, but there have been several cult places excavated.[9] The *PVL* tells us of open-air cult places in the tenth century on high river banks which contained large statues of the gods to whom oaths were sworn. A hilltop cult place called in modern times Peryn overlooking a loop in the River Volkhov near Novgorod was excavated in 1948–52. It was a ring ditch formed from eight scoops surrounding a central mound. There were postholes in the ditch bottom, possibly from wooden cult statues which had stood there. In each scoop there was a hearth built of stones on which ritual fires had been kindled (Fig. 59). The site was damaged by later huts (twelfth to fourteenth centuries) and had been (perhaps deliberately) ploughed flat.[10] A number of similar ring ditches with central post-settings have been found in northern and eastern Russia (at Pskov and Khodosoviche near Rokachev). Other northern cult sites in the Smolensk region and Belarussia were banked or ditched enclosures, low-lying circular enclosures with low banks about 30–40 m in diameter. Others in southern regions were simply exposed elevated places used as cult places, with or without cult statues or offering places.

In Poland there are a few small statues, but no temples. There are however a series of cult places on high steep-sided hills, such as Łysa Góra near Kielce and Ślęża mountain near Wrocław. These too seem likely to have been built at the end of our period (although the dating evidence is insecure). The choice of these high places may have been connected with some kind of sun worship, or perhaps was due to high places being those which the lightning god seeks for his coming. The three peaks of the mountain at Ślęża are surrounded by drystone walls and there are also several large stone cult statues around it. The mountain impressed German troops invading the area in the early tenth century (Thietmar VII.59): 'this stronghold lies in the country of Silesia, which was once named after a large and very high mountain . . . that mountain was greatly respected by the inhabitants because of its enormity and because of its function, as the cursed pagan rituals were held there'. The past tense is used because the sanctuary had been destroyed by the Polish kings a few decades earlier. At Łysa Góra within the stone rampart a Benedictine monastery was founded in the twelfth century; some stone statues were destroyed in the eighteenth century and folk festivals held here at Whitsun were banned in 1468.[11] Another Polish holy hill was Wawel rock adjacent to Cracow, which was not built up until the tenth century, when the rock was covered by a complex of churches and the cathedral. Here there were legends of a dragon which inhabited a cave at its base and was slain by the legendary (pre-Piast-dynasty) ruler Krak. There is a similar mountain in Bohemia associated with foundation legends of the Přemyslid state at Řip northwest of Prague: it too has an early medieval church on its summit. There are few traces of cult structures from central and northern Poland, though possible cult ring ditches similar to the East Slav examples have been claimed from Trzebiatów in Pomerania.

As we have seen, it is from Pomerania and Polabia that we have the most written evidence of the worship of gods, but there is no justification for back-projecting the situation depicted in the written sources into the past of those areas or into other areas of Slavdom. The situation described by Christian writers here developed as a result of specific historical conditions. The northwestern fringes were conquered by Charlemagne as a result of his Saxon Wars, but the rest of the area was conquered in a push to the east begun by Henry I in 929 and continued by Otto I after 948. This was accompanied by an attempt to convert compulsorarily to Christiantity the Slavs between the Elbe–Saale and Oder. After a pagan revolt in the weak reign of Otto II in 982–3 much of the northern part of the area was able to develop as an independant pagan Slav state on the fringe of the Ottonian Empire until it was again annexed in the period after 1127. In the course of these events Christian writers had good cause to take notice of the collapse and renewal of the Polabian sanctuaries. There is evidence to suggest that, in the century and a half of independence, the reorganization and strengthening of the Polabian local cults (utilizing patterns derived from the Christian Church) played an important part in the establishment of a strong tribal power structure in opposition to the Ottonians.

Among the Pomeranians a key place – apart from Svarog (Svarozhyts) – was held by Świętovit (Svantevit), a god of fertility as well as war. The latter element may however have been a later addition to the attributes of this deity – understandable at a time of the fight of the Pomeranians to retain their independence. Świętovit was imagined as riding by night on a dark horse against the enemies of his believers, and the horse seems to have been a cult animal. On etymological grounds it has been suggested that the names of other Pomeranian gods (Jarowit, Rugewit and Trigłów – the three-headed) are possibly later creations to replace older names which probably taboo prevented being said. Their attributes suggest that they too had some connection with nature and especially fertility. Several other names are distorted in the transmission and we know little about their cults (Prove, Porewit, Turupit, Pripegala, Podaga). By the time we come to learn of the Pomeranian religion it was relatively elaborate with a developed priesthood, temples and cult statues. Possibly these features were adopted quite late under influence of Christianity and in conditions of stress from pressure from the west. A specific feature of some of these gods is their polycephalism: several of them have three or four faces on one head. This is an especially characteristic feature of the Polabian idols described in the written sources and some of which still survive, like the double-headed wooden figure from Fischerinsel in the Tollensee, or a miniature figure found in Wolin.

We possess a relatively large amount of evidence for temples and the organization of cult from the period after the pagan revolt in Polabia.[12] Several temples with well-developed priesthoods are mentioned in the written sources, such as that at the end of the peninsula inside a stronghold at Arkona on Rugia described in 1208 by Saxo Grammaticus (*Gesta Danorum* XIV.39) as destroyed by the Danish King Waldemar in 1168 as one of the last reserves of West Slav paganism in a Christian Europe. This site was excavated in 1921 by Carl Schuchardt, who found a number of postholes probably belonging to the temple. Saxo tells us that the building contained many ornaments and animal horns, and was hung with purple hangings and the wooden walls painted vith various designs. In the centre was a huge wooden statue of Svantevit with a drinking horn in his right hand, into which wine was poured at harvest festivals and the level of liquid in its bowl used to predict next year's crops. A nearby temple of similar form destroyed by the Danes was dedicated to Rugewit, who had seven heads and carried eight swords. Porewit and Porenut also had temples in the area. Thietmar tells us of the destruction of 'Riedagost' (Rethra), where the god's statue was surrounded by others dressed in 'terrible helmets and cuirasses' and surrounded by war booty. Bishop Otto of Bamberg visited Szczecin twice, in the 1120s: here there were several temples, the most important of which was a hilltop site dedicated to Triglav (Trigłów), which was richly sculpted and painted inside and out, and had deposits of war booty inside. At Wolin he found a temple with a sacred spear which was completely rusted and said to be that of Julius Caesar (Herbord III.26). Another outdoor cult place became the site of the church of St Adalbert.

Burial rites

Although the evidence for the gods is somewhat sparse, the archaeological evidence of death is in some areas relatively profuse. Death faces the living with the question of the proper disposal of the corpse, and the manner chosen to do this is a way of expressing more than just the loss of a loved one. The archaeo-logical examination of burials can provide useful information on a number of aspects of Slav culture. This is derived not only from the manner or treatment of the corpse and form of the grave, but also from the objects which were some-times placed in the grave. The cult of the dead apparently had an importance for the community, providing a continuity between past and present members of particular groups, a means of determining identity. The funeral was thus accompanied by ceremonies involving speeches, prayers and offerings, in fun-eral wakes of various types. At intervals after the death the grave (if there was one, see below) would be visited. (In some areas it would appear that feasts were often also held forty days after, or on the anniversary of the death, or on a special day of the dead.) Graves may be reused by several members of the group, further strengthening the link between individual members in life as in death.

Despite the important role fulfilled by the cult of the ancestors, it seems that the picture of life beyond the grave was rather foggy. In later Russia the land of the dead was known as the *nevedomaja strana* (the unknown side [direction/ way]). The presence of grave goods in some burials (including weapons and food) may suggest that it was imagined that life continued after death and it was conceived as similar to life on earth. It seems to have been believed however that the dead who had left the world by natural means were still present in some form among the living. At recent rural Belarussian funerals for example a place was left at the table for the shades of the ancestors, who were summoned at the beginning of the feast. It was from among the shades of dead clan members that the friendly demons were drawn which aided the clan, multiplying the family's fortunes, helping with spinning, caring for horses. Some of these home spirits gained personal names.

In the fifth to ninth centuries, most groups of Early Slavs practised cremation, and this burial rite dominated until the beginning of Christianity. We have seen evidence of a solar and heavenly cult: the pyre was probably seen as a correlate of the light and heat of the sun, and it was combined with a purifying process. It seems that the funeral pyre was – among other things – a means of freeing the soul from the body in a rapid, visible and public manner, allowing participants in the funeral to take part in the process and, by turning the mortal remains into ash, enforcing the soul's passage into the underworld. As a Rus merchant told Ibn Fadlan in the early tenth century, 'you Arabs are really stupid . . ., you take a man you love and respect and throw him into the earth for the worms to eat, we on the other hand burn him and in a twinkling of an eye he is in paradise'. Whoever this merchant actually was, the sentiments he expressed would probably have been common to all those cremating societies in which he moved.[13] The burning may have been accompanied by various other rituals, such as feasting, self-mutilation of some of the mourners and also some form of games (*tryzna*), which are mentioned in the written sources from Russia and Bohemia. It seems that these practices were still current there as late as the eleventh century. According to Cosmas (III.1), when Břetyslav came to the Czech throne in the 1090s he still found

funerals, which took place in the forests and fields, and dances, which were conducted according to pagan customs, and setting-up shelters at the junction between two or three roads as if for the comfort of the spirits. Thus they practised godless games which they practised above their dead, dancing with masks on their faces and calling up the spirits of the dead.

The small houses which were set up at crossroads were for the benefit of the spirits who were passing from their place of rest to the abodes of the living. (Even today in many rural areas in eastern Europe wayside crosses and shrines are set up at crossroads.)[14]

The community of living and dead was divided also by a zone of spirits which were hostile to humans, various types of ghouls, witches and in particular vampires. These spirits seem to have been conceived above all as having belonged to people in whose death there had been something unnatural or where the corpse had not been found and given proper burial, and it was sometimes necessary apply magical practices to prevent the souls of the unnatural dead returning to disturb the living. It thus seems that the destruction of the corpse by burning was an important part of the burial rite and if this was denied (by the body being buried unburnt, such as the victims of violence, or lost, as in the case of drowning) the spirit was destined not to reach the spirit world and thus had to stay on earth.[15] There are few traces of special rites known for protection against vampires in the cremation graves; the main problem seems to have arisen with the introduction of the inhumation burial rite. Clearly in the pagan rites the emphasis would have been more on the spiritual side of the matter of death, whereas the Christian rite – while recognizing the spiritual aspect of death – also laid emphasis on the corporal aspects. Early Christianity also emphasized the integrity of the material remains after death and the importance of their proper disposal in accordance with the dictates of the Church (in so far as these could be enforced – see below).

The change to inhumation burial was thus an especially significant change in the attitude towards the dead. The practice was not unfamiliar to the Slavs (it had been practised by several cultures in the Roman period, and was the dominant burial rite of the Avars on the middle Danube), but, apart from a few isolated early examples which have been found in Moravia and a few doubtful examples from southern Poland, in general seems not to have been acceptable to the Slavs before the arrival of Christianity. The Christian insistence on the laying of intact bodies into the ground was a shocking innovation which was seen as likely to upset the balance of the spirit world. When cremation was replaced by inhumation, western Slavdom seems to have experienced a vampire panic. The collective disquiet led to magical acts involving the freshly dead intended as protection against the spreading of vampirism. These included placing rocks over the burial, putting flour in the coffin, defacing the corpse, and occasionally beating a wooden peg or nail through the head or chest. It is possible that the placing of offerings in inhumation graves may have been an anti-vampire measure.[16]

Cremation was carried out on a pyre of wood built somewhere outside the settlement. The body was placed on it fully dressed, and possibly accompanied by selected objects. In the few cases where we can examine the layout of the body from the fragments remaining in situ on pyre sites (because for some reason they were not fully collected), it seems that the head of the corpse was orientated towards the western side of the pyre (so that the raised head would face the rising sun). The burnt remains were then collected and disposed of in several forms of graves.

The most common form of 'grave' over most of the area seems however to have been a method of disposing of the mortal remains (which one assumes had been cremated first) by a method which is difficult to detect archaeologically. This absence of graves is not due to our poor knowledge of this area and is one of the enduring mysteries of Slav archaeology. Whatever was done with them, in many cases these remains are lost to archaeological sight. The ashes may have been scattered in water, or on the land, perhaps in some special holy place (such as a holy grove);[17] they may have been put in some above-ground wooden structures (perhaps 'houses of the dead') and naturally scattered when this collapsed. What seems certain is that this disposal took place at some distance from the settlement, as few scattered pieces of cremated bone are ever found in the fills of features. This question needs further research to resolve.

In some cases however the bones were buried in various forms of earth-dug graves (returned to 'mother earth'?). In the Korchak, Penkovka but especially the Prague Culture graves from Moravia to Polabia the remains were gathered and put into holes in the ground, sometimes in a container, most often a pot. Sometimes apart from the ashes, buckles, occasionally fibulae and other objects are found in the cinerary urn with the bones. We do not know whether these graves were marked by posts: we may assume that this was often the case. Most of these cemeteries are relatively small, containing from a few to a few dozen graves. These are probably family or clan burial grounds.

A somewhat exceptional site for its size and richness is the large cemetery north of the Danube at Sărata Monteoru in the Buzau region of southeastern Romania (excavated since before the Second World War by teams from Bucharest led by Ion Nestor and latterly by Ligia Barzu). Apart from a number of interim reports,[18] the medieval cemetery (which overlies a rich Bronze Age cemetery) has not yet been properly published. The cremation burials are either in urns (of the 'Prague-Korchak type' but with wheel-made pottery) or pit-graves without urns. The site has produced mainly graves of the sixth and/or seventh century, but also a few artefacts which point to a date in the second half of the fifth century, much earlier than that traditionally accepted for Sărata Monteoru and the arrival of the Slavs in this area.

Another variant of this idea is the so-called Alt-Käbelich type of grave found in the Sukow zone (named after a site at Alt-Käbelich in the Neubrandenburg region). Here the bones were scattered in the upper fills of large oval pits (reminiscent of the 'bath-shaped' domestic features of the Sukow-Dziedzice zone).[19] These are relatively large but shallow pits containing fragments of cremated bone and charcoal and broken pottery in the earth fill. Their interpretation is more difficult. The low quantity of ash and charcoal with respect to the amount of earth in these features would suggest that these were not simple holes dug beside the pyre into which the latter was shovelled. Possibly the hole was filled only after a lapse of time (a year?), after which the remains of the pyre had become overgrown with grass, hindering its collection. The creation of an earthen grave by the burial of the pyre remains would have here the character of a symbolic action. This emphasizes that the cremation and the creation of a grave were seen as two separate actions.

Above-ground burials also took place. The *PVL* tells us that the Viatichi, Severiane Radimichi and Krivichi put cremated remains in urns which were then placed on the top of posts set in the ground by roads (recalling what Cosmas wrote – see above). The chronicler hints that this form of burial was still being practised among the Viatichi in his own day.

Another common type of grave was the barrow burial, usually relatively low and about 3–4 m in diameter. These were often grouped into small cemeteries, presumably belonging to one family, clan or community. They occur across the central zone of West Slav territory and much of the area inhabited by the East Slavs. Although sporadic barrow cemeteries are known from both sides of the Carpathians, they became common in the West Slav area north of the Carpathians only about the middle of the seventh century. The mound was probably intended to represent a sacral hill (the so-called cosmic mountain), and this seems likely to be a reflection of the significance of the peak sanctuaries in Early Slav culture which we have discussed above. The barrow was perhaps a peak sanctuary in miniature, though some barrows (such as two large mounds near Cracow and several in Kievan Rus, for example at Gniozdovo and Chernigov) reached considerable sizes. The barrows were heaped from earth from quarry scoops from around the outside of the mound, and were probably built by the whole community gathered for the funeral. They often had wooden or stone constructions inside. There are several types of these barrows.

The evidence available suggests that most frequent type of disposal of the human remains was not under the mound but in a container (such as a pot or box) holding the ashes placed on the top of the mound, perhaps in some form of wooden shrine or house of the dead. As the mound settled, the pot and bone tumbled down the sides of the mound into the quarry scoop around it. This explains why earlier excavators searching for a central burial under the mound (in the expectation that these mounds were like prehistoric burial mounds) interpreted many of them as cenotaphs. This type of mound burial occurs over much of West Slav territory (southern Poland, southeast Polabia, Bohemia and Slovakia, although to the north and east there were zones free of barrows). Chambers are rare in West Slav areas, but these barrows sometimes have a revetment consisting of a square wooden framework 3–7 m square made of horizontal (corner-notched) beams resting on the ground surface and support-ing the body of the mound. Sometimes this covers the remains of the (or a) pyre. These horizontal constructions are most common between the Elbe and the Bug, but also occur further east in the upper Dniepr and even in the upper Oka area – which would make any attempt to see them as 'typically West Slav' pre-mature.

The rite of burial involving barrows was more varied in East Slav lands. In the eighth to tenth centuries in the Desna and Seym valleys, and the Oka, the only type of burial was the barrow, but in the territory of the Severiane the remains were generally placed on the top of the mound, while in the mounds of the Viatichi burials were made in wooden chambers under the mound.[20] The wooden constructions within barrows also exhibit variation across the area. In several areas there are internal constructions (chambers) which contained the remains and an external revetment or fence. Chambers are found in the barrows of the upper Don and upper Oka where they seem to be related to the Borshevo group and the Viatichi. In the latter cases they are rectangular chambers set near the edge of the round mounds which are revetted by a ring 6–12 m in diameter (of vertical posts) and open on the outer side. They contain the bones of several individuals. Chambers are also a characteristic feature of the retainer graves of Kievan Rus. An interesting enclave of sites occurs also in northern Romania: isolated examples of barrows with chambers containing collective burials in mounds revetted by rings of vertical posts.

The changing patterns of burial rite can be followed in maps of the northern half of Slavdom.[21] In the first phase (to the mid seventh century) there are only very few cemeteries known from the whole area of Slavdom (Map IX). Across the northwest side of the map in the Sukow-Dziedzice area there is a broad zone (zone A) where there are very few burials known: clearly the rite of disposal of the human remains is not easily archaeologically detectable and deposition in the ground was the exception rather than the rule. The dashed zone running across eastern Poland on Map IX represents a mysterious 'buffer zone' where there are several cemeteries (Siemonia, Jozefów) where pots reminiscent of Sukow-Dziedzice forms occur in cemeteries reminiscent of those further south and east.

Across a large area where Early Slav pottery occurs, burials were made in small cemeteries, where the cremated remains were placed in pits in the ground, often in handmade pots of Korchak or Prague type. There were seldom any other objects placed in the grave.[22] There are several zones where such cemeteries are relatively common. These include the Saale area, Bohemia, Moravia (all three areas with Prague-type pottery) and in the Penkovka zone, and two areas on the right bank in the middle Dniepr valley near Dnepropetrovsk. In eastern Slavdom there are very few burials of the period from the fifth to seventh centuries, though there is relatively dense Korchak and Penkovka settlement in regions where there are no cemeteries known. Only a few percent of the known Penkovka sites are cemeteries.[23] Some burials in the Korchak zone in the region of Zhitomir (zone C) were however made in or on mounds. On both sides of the Carpathians in southeast Poland, Bohemia and Moravia and in the upper Dniestr valley we see the appearance of several early barrow cemeteries.

South of the Carpathians is a zone where there were early Avar inhumation burials with horse harnesses and sometimes with the horses themselves (for example at Alattyán in Hungary).[24] These traditions seem to have had little effect on Slav burial customs in the area. In the zone occupied by the Avars, and especially on its fringes in Moravia and Slovakia (Dolní Dunajovice, Holiare), there are however cremation graves known, sometimes occurring in the same cemeteries with inhumations. Some writers have seen these as the graves of Slavs living under Avar rule, but not giving up their traditional beliefs. The best known of these cemeteries is Devínská-Nová Ves (near Bratislava).[25] There are very few early graves known from the lower Danubian plain and the Balkans (Map IX, zone A/B₂). The available evidence suggests that in the Balkans cremation was also the rule in the sixth and seventh centuries, but one has to accept that Slavs assimilated into post-classical communities in the Balkan area will have also been buried in inhumation cemeteries.[26]

The picture changes dramatically in the period from the mid seventh century to the mid ninth century (Map X): there is considerably more burial evidence, and the patterns become more complex. Along the north part of western Slav lands there is still a zone (zone A) with very few detectable cremation burials. Part of the explanation of this may lie in a specific rite (reflected in the less easily detectable graves of Alt-Käbelich type) which seems to have been practised from the eighth century until the tenth in western Pomerania and northern Polabia (at least).

In the region of the mouth of the Oder perhaps about the middle of the ninth century appears a zone (H) with a few large cremation cemeteries, containing many graves, some of which contain atypically rich burial goods including Scandinavian imports. Some of these burials were probably of Scandinavians.[27] These large cemeteries probably reflect the rise of large stable social structures in the Oder mouth at this period. In Pomerania there are also several barrows with burials taking the form of a cremation layer under the mound.

In several areas where the flat urn cemeteries of Prague type had been common before the seventh century, it seems that they continued into at least the eighth century. This seems to be the case in the Saale area, along the left tributaries of the middle Elbe, the area around Prague itself, on the right bank of the Morava and southwest Slovakia and southeastern Bohemia along the Danube valley above Bratislava (Map X b zone B_{1-3}). Here flat cemeteries continue the older tradition, while in the same general area are new barrow cemeteries alongside the older rite.

In the Ukraine the flat cemeteries of the Dniepr region seem to have been replaced by cremation burial rites involving the construction of a burial mound. In a wide zone extending from the Ukraine to Polabia there is a zone of barrow cemeteries (zone C). The earlier barrows of the Ukraine (zone C_4) have an uncertain extent to the north, and the relationship with those between the Bug, Narew and Niemen is unclear. Most of the Ukrainian and Belarussian sites were excavated long ago, and the rite is unknown, but many of the sites in Podlasie were barrows constructed over a cremation layer.

To the west is another area of barrow burial (zone C_1) in southern Poland but also (and more densely) south of the Carpathians (zones C_2 and C_3). These sites are characterized by having the burials placed on the outside and not under the mound (though a group in Moravia and Slovakia has inhumations in barrows). The extent of barrow burial in central Poland (zone A/B/C) is not yet clear since many of the barrows were destroyed by post-medieval agricultural activity, a process continuing in the early twentieth century. Even in areas where the original distribution of these sites is reasonably well known, it would seem that the original number of barrows is too small to account for the entire population and it seems that they contained the remains of only part of the community, the rest still presumably being buried using a rite which has left fewer traces. We have seen that the spread of barrows north of the Carpathians in the mid seventh century is accompanied by new pottery styles and seems to relate to some kind of increased contact between communities from both sides of the Carpathians. Whether or not the general acceptance of barrows themselves originated south or north of the Carpathians can be resolved only by further work. In Moravia this zone initially overlaps with a zone of mixed inhumation cemeteries with a few cremations (a northern outlier of the Avar cemeteries to the south). In the mountains of Transylvania is a discrete group of sites having mixed traditions of West Slav pottery but East Slav types of barrow construction (including the rich barrow at Someşeni-Cluj with Late Avar type metalwork with pottery of Slav type).

Within the arc of the Carpathians there is the zone of Avar inhumation cemeteries noted above. Around its fringes we see a few flat cremation cemeteries and also inhumation cemeteries which contain cremations (such as Devínská-Nová Ves). To the south of the zone of barrows and the Avar cemeteries is a broad area (zone E) extending into the Balkans where there is very little evidence of graves, suggesting that, alongside other practices, a type of burial rite not leaving archaeological traces may have been in use here. In the lower Danube valley is a spread of inhumation sites also containing cremations probably in some way connected with Avar settlement in this region, and to the southeast a zone of flat cremation cemeteries.

In the eighth and especially ninth centuries in the East Slav territory, we see an eastwards and northwards spread of the zone of burial mounds from the central area of the Ukraine. These become relatively dense in the period of the functioning of the Luka Raikovetska Culture. Most of these cemeteries are small groups of barrows, scattered all over the area of western Ukraine, from the headwaters of the Pripet and its tributaries to the middle Dniepr and Dniestr. There are also a number of graves not covered by barrows. In the Volyntsevo area are a number of barrows with the burials generally contained under the barrows (either as layers under the mound or in wooden chambers). The relative frequency of this rite seems to have distinguished the Volyntsevo burials from other East Slav areas. The known distribution of these barrows does not however correspond to that of the culture itself. They are restricted to the lower Desna and Seym river valleys, while apparently being absent from the Sula, Khorol, Psol and Vorskla valleys.[28]

In the period following the mid ninth century (c. 850–950/1000) the pattern becomes somewhat more simple. By now the custom of burial in flat cremation cemeteries had disappeared from most regions, still perhaps surviving in Pomerania. The zone of large cemeteries at the Oder mouth (zone H) continues to develop (with the addition of boat-shaped stone-settings in some cemeteries).

In the tenth century the number of burials in this zone exhibiting Scandinavian tendencies increases. The burial-free zone A north of the Carpathians spread in extent even further, while in the west across the centre of the area the quantity of barrow cemeteries thinned out somewhat. Relicts remained in the Neisse river area north of the Carpathians, with a few scattered sites in the upper Elbe valley in Bohemia and in Moravia. The main feature of the period is the appearance of the first inhumation cemeteries in Moravia and on the middle Danube plain between Budapest and Vienna, and also in Bohemia near Prague.

In the eastern parts of Slavdom, the burial rite under barrows established its hold over a wide area where it became the dominant type. With increasing density, the cemeteries can now be seen to form clusters which to some extent seem to relate to the tribes recorded in the *PVL*.[29] The construction of these barrows has not yet been as well studied as in the case of the West Slav mounds, but it seems that both the rites of burial, on the top of the mound as well as within it (as layers under the mound or in wooden chambers), were practised. (In the territory of the Viatichi, burials were made in wooden chambers under the mound, but to the south in the mounds of the Severiane the remains were generally placed on the top of the mound.)

It is to this period that the main written sources relate. We have many tales from ninth- and tenth-century Islamic traders who came into contact with Rus merchants along the routes from the Varangians to the Greeks. These accounts by foreign and biased observers of various ethnicity moving through multicultural zones should be used cautiously. The Arabs were particularly interested in the burial rites of the people they met in the lands of the Slavs, which they likened to the Hindu ritual which was known to them. Ibn Rusteh has this to say of a Rus funeral: 'when one of them dies they burn him up in fire, while when they die their women cut themselves on the hands and face with knives. When the body is burnt, they go to the place the next day and take ash from that place, put it in an urn and put it on a mound.' This sounds more like a Slav rite than any of those assigned to the Varangian Rus. Several Arab sources also tell us that, when a man in this community died, his wife also accompanied him to the grave, but how widespread this custom was is not known. It is interesting to note that it also appears in one Byzantine source. Pseudo-Maurice writes of the Slavs that 'their women are very honourable, even to the extent that to the death of their husband they add their own, willingly suffocating [?] themselves, since they do not regard widowhood as life'. The account of a Rus funeral on the Volga includes the death of a slave girl who accompanies her master.

A particular category of burial found in the East Slav territories comprises the burials made in wooden chambers, usually under an earthen mound. These 'chamber burials' or 'retainer burials' are characterized by rich grave goods containing objects from a variety of different areas and traditions. These graves are interpreted as the burials of Scandinavians (or those wanting to be buried like the Varangians) who would seem to be powerful members of a princely retinue. They are found at a number of burial sites (Timerevo, Staraia Ladoga, Pskov, Gniozdovo, Chernigov, Shestovitsy and Kiev, but similar graves have also been found at Birka in Sweden). These wooden chambers were 1.5 m or more across and built of planks or beams: the dead man could be accompanied by horses, a female (perhaps either wife or slave), and a large number of other items. The weaponry, bridle fittings and the ornaments of the woman bespeak the wealth of the buried man. Many of these items are not of specifically Scandinavian type. A typical example is the mid-tenth-century Chernaya Mogila in Chernigov, an important centre of the early state on the northern periphery of Poliane territory (150 km up the Desna from Kiev). This huge mound was excavated by D. J. Samokvasov in 1872–4.[30] The mound is 11 m tall and 40 m in diameter (raised in two stages) and contained the remains of a wooden funeral house containing the burnt bodies of an adult man, a woman and a young warrior. On top of the first phase of the mound (and thus covered with the second) were placed burnt remains from the funeral pyre with two sets of arms (swords, helmets, scale armour), a saddle, seven spears and many arrowheads, five knives, remains of a shield, and many other items, including drinking horns with mounts decorated with mythical ornament (probably deriving from a steppe – perhaps Khazar – milieu), a set of glass gaming pieces, an iron cauldron with a burnt ram and birds' bones and a horned ram's head. The grave also contained a bronze idol (of a sitting god holding his beard – most probably Thor). The rich furnishings of this burial recall the luxury goods coveted by the princely retinues (such as Igor's *druzhina*, which prompted him to increase the tribute demanded of the Derevlane).

Concepts of time

One feature of interest is to try to reconstruct how the Early Slavs saw time, in particular their place between past and future. We have seen that the seasonal cyclical festivals and the ancestor cult suggest that they saw themselves as part of a continuum of which the living and the ancestors were part, but there is little evidence that they had a wholly linear concept of time and that the past was any more for the Early Slavs than a misty anachronous entity. In illiterate and early literate societies there is usually a period which may be counted living memory (and so events going back some eighty years) separated from the so-called distant past, which tends to be a mythical account.[31] That such a distant past did in fact exist for the Slavs is indicated by local traditions such as the attachment to some sites such as barrows and strongholds of the names of famous personages of the mythical past (and the stories of characters such as Askold and Dir in the *PVL*). Our appreciation of how the Early Slavs saw their past is hindered by the fact that much of the pagan ancestor lore seems not to have been regarded as worth recalling by those first Christian writers, which is why we have few pre-Christian legends recorded (in contrast for example to the hero literature and kinglists of the Germanic tribes). It would seem that at the period of the conversion to Christianity local dynasties sought other means for their legitimization. At the beginning of the twelfth century, the chronicler of early Poland, Gallus Anonymous, ending his brief sketch of the story of the country before the conversion, wrote 'But let us not dwell on the history of a people whose recollections are lost in the forgetfulness of the centuries and whom mistaken idolatry has condemned, and pass briefly over it to the recording of matters which faithful memory has preserved'.[32] The pagan past had been forgotten and was not worthy of dwelling on. For the chronicler, history began only with the conversion. It seems that the hostility of the Christian scholar in tandem with the levelling tendencies of the early state had caused the loss of the early traditions over much of this area. When in the fullness of time the early chroniclers of Slavdom wished to extend the scope of their works into the prehistory preceding the conversion, they had to make do with stringing a few vague traditions together with a lot of invented material.

Procopius in the 'ethnographic excursus' quoted earlier tells us that the Sclavenes and Antes 'do not accept predestination, but . . . when they are threatened by death – in illness or war – swear if they are spared, to sacrifice to the god in return for their lives . . . at the same time as they sacrifice they predict the future'. This may be a literary topos referring to pagan religions in general, but several written sources tell us of the Slavs' belief that the future could be foretold. Mentions of the role of priests in predicting the future by a variety of means (in particular the quantity of harvests) in Polabia are also known. The *PVL* contains an excursus on soothsayers (attached to the story of how Oleg's death caused by his horse had been predicted). It seemed that this was due not so much to a belief in predestination as to communication with the gods to whom all decisions belonged. It was also believed that the gods' decisions could be influenced from earth; the worshipper had the hope of obtaining the favours of the god by sacrifices, prayers and magic acts.

10

Towards a Christian Europe

Slav paganism collapsed as a result of an onslaught from both the eastern and western Churches mostly in the ninth and tenth centuries.[1] Modern historiography treats this event with hindsight as of great significance: for many scholars the conversion of the Slavs marks their entry into the 'medieval community of Europe' with a united ideology and cultural norms. This process not only represents the destruction of the ideological basis of the existence of many of the pagan societies existing at this time, but it represents also a decisive phase in the growth of the influence of the Church in Europe.[2]

By the time of the conversion of the Slavs, large areas of the rest of Europe had been Christian for more than half a millennium and with a few exceptions, up to the end of the sixth century, Christianity had been restricted to the area of the former Roman Empire. As a result, the Christian states of Europe (in effect the Germanic kingdoms of western Europe and the Byzantine Empire) were economically well-developed and often organized into strong and militarily effective political entities well aware of their unity and power. In the seventh and eighth centuries the evangelical call *'docete omnes gentes'* was again heeded, and the process was begun of extending Christendom first to areas which had reverted to pagandom (such as England) and then beyond the former Roman *limes*. At the end of the eighth century Christianity began to reach Slavic peoples, initially the South Slavs. The conquest of the Polabian Slavs in the 920s to 960s led to the forced conversion of the Slavs here and the creation of new bishoprics. This was followed by the next and decisive phase of the later tenth century, and its result was the Christianization of nearly the whole of Slavdom (with Poland and Russia), Hungary and Scandinavia. About the year 1000, substantial areas of the European continent were already Christian (and much of the rest would be converted in the next and final phase beginning in the twelfth century).

The period was however not one of uninterrupted growth of the Church. The rise in status of the Patriarchate of Constantinople (following loss of those of Jerusalem, Antioch and Alexandria to the Muslims) and that of Rome (owing to its involvement in secular politics) had led to rivalry, both claiming to be the legitimate continuers of the imperial traditions of the Church of Rome. This rivalry, fuelled by the increasing liturgical differences between these two Churches, gave rise to a series of disputes and splits (one of the most important was the Photian schism of 867–9 in which some of the newly converted Slavs were also involved). These disagreements eventually crystallized in the formal recognition in 1054 of the separateness of the Byzantine (Eastern Orthodox) Church and the western (Roman Catholic) Churches. The process of separation though had been well under way before that, and this was reflected in the organization and form of the areas under their influence. The struggle to raise the prestige and power of the Churches was reflected in their efforts to increase the area of their influence by the conversion of the pagan peoples beyond the pale of contemporary civilization.

The conversion of the Slavs was not only the result of ecclesiastical policy, but was also encouraged by secular rulers. The more advanced Christian nations, apart from their conception of duty to bring enlightenment to their brethren, had very real political aims in attempting the alteration of the ideologies of their pagan neighbours. Cultural imperialism of this sort was to be an important factor in establishing closer control, exploitation and domination (and even annexation) of adjacent territories. The sponsoring of missionary work can thus hardly be separated from politics. In general, since the politically fragmented societies of the pagan world were often at an ineffective pre-state or early state stage of development, this ideological confrontation took place in situations where the Christian side had the advantage.

Very often, conversion was achieved by the baptism of a native ruler who then encouraged his subjects to follow, since the ruler had a decisive influence on the political form of society and controlled the ideological sphere within which it functioned. In many of these polities religious and cultural life crystallized around the courts of rulers and their nobles. The sacral was a very important area of community life; and religion was not determined by individual conscience alone.

The routes to Christianity in different states were various, but in few cases does it seem that the transition was a smooth linear one. Modern historiography, looking at these processes with hindsight as progress, has rarely considered the conversion of pagan early medieval societies to Christianity as a process involving ideological and ethical conflict. One should not ignore however the fact that the introduction of Christianity attacked the very ideological roots of tribal societies, usually characterized by stubbornly looking back towards their ancestral past. The Christian missionaries were dealing not with 'secular' peoples but with peoples with clearly defined religious and ideological structures: paganism was a necessary element of the integration of whole communities and the determination of group identity. In the decades following the conversions the pagan religion had enough force to return when various conditions encouraged large-scale apostasy. These pagan revivals took on the guise of open political opposition to the ruling elite, which suggests that the antagonism of the population to the new ideology was in many cases more than short-term.

Bearing in mind the extreme internal social conflict such moves could provoke, why did native rulers allow and even encourage these important ideological changes to take place? It is clear that there must have been important long-term gains to be made by doing so. It is clear that in the specific political situation with which we are concerned, Christianity 'ennobled' the state and its ruler and allowed them access to the advanced civilizations of the community of Christian states and peoples. The imposition of a new unifying ideology was a useful counter to political fragmentation of a new centralized polity. Another extremely desirable consequence of Christianization for royal power was the sacral enhancement of the person of the ruler. The Christian ruler, whether a prince or a king, was also and above all the assignee of the power of God.

This process of conversion to Christianity thus marks a vital stage in the consolidation of a common ideology shared with other more advanced European states. Throughout the Middle Ages the Christian states in general tended to despise their pagan neighbours, and only in certain situations did they find themselves able to enter alliances with them. In the seventh century for example when Samo, leader of the Slavs, proposed an alliance to the ambassador of the Frankish King Dagobert I the latter is said to have replied haughtily that it was not possible for 'Christians and servants of God to enter an alliance with dogs' (*Chronicle of Fredegar* IV.48), a remark which was to cost the Franks dearly. Accepting the Christian ideology opened for the emerging state the way to acceptance into the civilized world, and also facilitated the cementing of inter-dynastic marriages (an important factor in the power politics of the period).

It is significant that the change to a new religion appears in most areas at the same period as the transition from tribal organizations to centralized state. The two processes seem to have been intimately connected in many cases. The ideological transition in central and eastern Europe from a system incorporating various types of paganism to one based on the Christian religion seems to have been deliberately stimulated: it appears to have been found that existing religious systems retarded development of the sort of social relations which the ruling elite regarded as desirable. The process of uniting previously separate tribes and scattered communities each with its own communal ideology under a centralized rule was an extremely difficult process, often attained by conflict and shedding of blood. Even when this subjugation was accomplished, the degree of coherence of the freshly united state was still not great: it was rather a conglomerate of extremely varied territories and peoples, often connected with each other only by the autocratic will of the ruler opposing any resistance and by force removing any irregularities in the social fabric of the new polity he was aiming to create. Paganism, with its characteristic particularism, was absolutely impossible to use as a means of unifying the scattered elements of these societies in this way (although as we have seen attempts were made), but time and time again it was found that the imported and monotheistic Christianity was a useful tool in promoting social unity and aiding the authorities of the early state in their struggles with decentralizing tendencies in a way that no pagan religion could have done. In this way the Christian religion as practised in early medieval Europe was a strong and effective supporter of a centralized political system, and thus was an advantageous ally for a leader wishing to concentrate power in his hands. It is in this context that these new changes should primarily be seen.[3]

Of some importance too was the fact that the Church could supply the ruler with educated people, able to read and express themselves in writing, to serve as envoys and prepare documents. This was necessary to create a centralized bureaucracy on which the existence of the state was to rely.

Missionaries and bishops

The process of the creation of Christian communities of the various Slav peoples involved two phases: a missionary phase and then the slow process of consolidation of the Church (which we will see was often in itself connected with continued missionary action in rural areas). There were five main types of mechanisms by which the various pagan Slav peoples were converted to Christianity. These acted in various combinations in various situations.

First, they could have absorbed a new idea through daily contact with Christian populations. The Goths of the Black Sea area, together with the Gepids and Longobards as well as the remnants of the Romanized Dacian population along the Danube *limes*, had been converted (though probably only nominally) to Christianity in the fourth century – and thus the early Slavs may have come into contact with this belief even before their invasions of the Balkans. The incursions of pagan Slavs into the Balkans led to some extent to the breakdown of the episcopal system in the former Roman provinces in the Danubian region and much of the Balkans, but this does not mean that earlier traditions including those deriving from Christianity (or rather ideas deriving from it) totally disappeared from these areas; some Slavs may have became converted to Byzantine Christianity in their settlement of the area as a result of settling alongside Christian communities.

Second, in some cases missionaries chose (or were sent) to work in foreign territory where the local leaders were not inclined to support, or at best not interested in (and at worst hostile to) Christianity. In the absence of authority from a secular power directly supporting the missionaries, argument and persuasion were the only means available, and in such situations adherents of both the old and new belief systems were in an equal or similar position. In general however attempted Christianization carried out in such conditions was repeatedly shown to be futile.

Third, conversion may have been achieved by missionary activity sponsored by external polities. Missionary activity was undertaken by the Franks, and in the seventh and eighth centuries some isolated Slav groups on the easternmost fringes of the Frankish Empire west of the Elbe were converted to Christianity. In the middle of the seventh century, Pope Martin I seems to have initiated missionary activity among the Slav groups settled in Dalmatia and in the seventh and eighth centuries there was Bavarian missionary activity in Slovenia, where Princes Gorazd and Chotimir were baptized about 700. In the eighth century Prince Pribina was settled in the Balaton area after conversion to Christianity. Throughout the next two centuries the Byzantines were to continue these missionary activities among the Bulgars and the Rus, and the western Church concentrated its activities on the Slavs nearest to them. The ecclesiastic organization established by these missionary activities often reflected their political role, with huge territories subservient to external bishoprics in the neighbouring core state.

Fourth, the imposition of Christianity could be a result of military action from outside, as in the case of the Polabian Slavs after the Ottonian conquests. Christianity was seen by the majority of the people as something foreign and hostile, as an agent of a foreign power. This often created resistance and this encouraged passivity concerning the new ideology, expressed in a superficial and illusory conversion. In the event of the temporary or permanent removal of the external pressure, the new religion was rejected as a foreign imposition, priests were expelled or murdered, churches were destroyed, and the old cult was resumed in a pagan reaction.

Fifth, in cases where Slav states apparently came to Christianity 'independently' (which by no means excludes organizational help and the employment of personnel from the outside), the new ideology was imposed (by example, persuasion, or force) as a result of a deliberate decision by the native ruling elite. This also created social conflict, but active opposition to the new ideology was the equivalent to opposition to the ruler. In these societies various factors encouraged the rest of the community to adopt the god of the ruler and it is clear that among those who belonged or aspired to belong to the new social elite of the new order there were probably many who for various reasons quickly came to terms with the new ideology. In all probability (like Marxism in postwar central Europe) this new ideology was adopted to mark 'belonging' to certain social groups, which could have aspired to considerably greater status and greater opportunities. As with Marxism, the evidence currently available from Poland shows that Christianity was probably a movement particularly popular in new social conditions amongst the young. This is suggested by the fact that the earliest cemeteries which can be relatively reliably dated were founded not at the date of conversion but several decades later. It would seem from this that many of those converted still had before them several decades of life before their deaths created the first phase of graves in the new cemeteries. The older generation whose social position and chances for advancement may have been independent of their beliefs may have been more resistant to the new influences.

Even if supported by the local rulers, the initial missionaries came up against a number of difficulties in their task. The first was of course the linguistic problems encountered in preaching to a people of a totally different language group. Some missionaries had the required linguistic abilities, others had to rely on translators. In addition to this was the completely different conceptual apparatus of Christianity, which was incompatible with that of the pagan beliefs and made accurate communication of the new creed more difficult.

Rural societies were understandably wary of strangers who arrived and started denigrating the gods which they and their ancestors had revered for generations and the worship of which was at the same time at the centre of their own self-identity. Although pagan pantheons were recognized to be less exclusive than the Christian one, fear of the revenge of the old gods, angered by the appearance of Christian missionaries, was a fairly general phenomenon.[4] Missionaries often made an especial point of provocatively belittling the pagan gods, depicting their images as the completely useless products of human hands which were not in any position either to harm or help. (This is the context of the considerable zeal with which these missionaries carried out the destruction or defiling of the idols and desecration of holy places; such actions provided an easier and quicker way to convince the pagans of the efficacy and the power of the new religion together with an immediate demonstration of the impotency of the old gods.) The 'mission of action' paved the way for the teaching of the catechism. Although however the pagan images and sanctuaries themselves were regarded as the lifeless and useless products of human handicraft, pagan cult was regarded by the missionaries as the work of the Devil himself. Since there was no possibility of discussion with the work of Satan, it had to be rooted out and suppressed, and with all available means. The arrival of Christianity in many areas was to create a complete break with not only the beliefs but also the customs and traditions of the past.

An effect of the missions among the Slavs (among whom, unlike some of the population of the barbarian kingdoms of the west, knowledge of Latin or Greek was likely to be extremely meagre) was the establishment of a need to translate the gospels and liturgy into Slav languages, and for the first time in Moravia and Bulgaria (ninth century) and in Kievan Rus (from the late tenth century) the Bible was read in a non-classical language, which caused some opposition in the more conservative western Church. The establishment of a literary language with its own scripts (Glagolitic, Cyrillic) was an important step, potentially allowing the new beliefs to reach all members of the congregation, and not just those versed in the classical languages. It is also one which provides us with important evidence of the early form of some dialects of the Slav languages. Where the liturgy was in Latin or Greek, most of the congregation in rural districts especially could probably get very little idea of what was being said in the ritual; the introduction of a Slav liturgy in Moravia was an important break-through, and shows that the Byzantine mission had as its aim not just the sum-mary conversion of an educated elite but the evangelization of the people. It seems that the Roman bishops in Moravia, in opposing the use of the Slav liturgy, were more interested in the political role of a more elitist Christianity.[5]

A by-product of the introduction of writing was the establishment of a nation-al literary language (which, where this was not Latin or Greek but the native one, would in turn lead to imposition of certain central linguistic models over outlying areas). The use of existing texts would lead to the acceptance of Graeco-Roman and Byzantine literary models. At first the texts which were written were mainly liturgical in nature, but the lives of local saints and eventually dynastic histories and chronicles began to be produced. These mark a change to a new approach to time, and a new notion of history. However before this happened, Slav paganism had had no chance to establish a literature, and by the time interest was expressed in the distant past the old oral traditions had been forgotten by a society to whom they were no longer relevant. What is most interesting and uncharacteristic was that it seems that in most cases this applies even to the pagan 'origin' legends (and dynastic genealogies) which most ancient communities treasured; these had later to be re-invented by scholars.

In addition to the introduction of literacy, the Church also gave new impetus to the development of art, and entry into the orbit of pan-European art styles. Much of this ecclesiastical art drew its inspiration from western and Byzantine circles. Besides this, the Church introduced new architectural styles. The churches built as a result of the conversion of the Slavs were the first masonry structures in many of these areas (though in the case of the South Slavs it seems that the technology had not been forgotten). The earliest churches were founded exclusively in central places, towns and strongholds, which may have contained both impressive episcopal basilicas and smaller private chapels (*Eigenkirchen*). These private churches founded by and for the use of single families or clans were especially numerous in towns: about a hundred of them existed in Pliska, and in the eleventh and twelfth centuries there were several hundred private churches. The Moravian stronghold at Mikulčice contained twelve churches.

These churches are the most spectacular traces of the new ideology. In the west the style of buildings was based on that of Ottonian realms and perhaps Italy and is known as 'pre-Romanesque' architecture.[6] Many of these buildings were of two forms. The first is the typical western European early medieval church form, small rectangular stone structures with apses or rectangular presbyteries. Some of these are of basilican form. Simple basilican churches were widespread among the West Slavs and the western areas of the territory of the South Slavs. The second type was the 'rotunda', a small circular building with a diameter of about

6–10 m and eastern apses. These rotundas seem to have developed in Dalmatia (for example the church of St Donat in Zadar), recalling the Church of the Holy Sepulchre in Jerusalem (but perhaps influenced by other architectural forms such as San Vitale in Ravenna or Charlemagne's palace chapel at Aachen). From here the form was spread to Moravia and further afield. The rotunda was to become a particularly popular form of church in central Europe from the ninth to the eleventh (or twelfth) century, being built in many of the main centres of Bohemia (especially), but also Poland and Hungary. It is among the South Slavs of the Balkans and the East Slavs that we see the construction of multi-cellular structures with multiple domes on the Byzantine model. The distribution of this type of church (*cerkov*) is coincident with that of the eastern Church. The model for this kind of church was Hagia Sophia and the Church of Sts Sergius and Bacchus in Constantinople built in the 530s, but developed in subsequent centuries to give the typical form of the Eastern Orthodox church.[7]

Once the missionary phase was over, the organization of the nascent Church was established, and the bishops were to play key political roles in the new states. As part of the establishment of the Church, it was granted a relatively large number of estates from which it drew revenue. The matter of whether or not a new diocese was established for the newly converted territory was of key importance: the establishment of a diocese within the territory ruled by a newly converted leader (usually based in his chief stronghold) was an affirmation of his independence. It is significant that by no means did all the newly converted territories have their own Church organization from the beginning; some were run from external archbishoprics, this being the case particularly among the West Slavs converted in the Ottonian period. The Polabians, the Obodrites and the northern Veleti came under Hamburg-Bremen, while the Sorbs and central districts were administered from Magdeburg, the see founded in 958 by Otto I for the purpose of governing the Church of the Slavs (giving it equal rank with Cologne, Salzburg, Mainz and Trier and chosen for his burial place). The first archbishop (Adalbert, d. 981) was made Metropolitan of the Slavs and established the dioceses of Naumberg, Meissen, Merseburg, Brandenburg, Havelburg and Poznań. The church in Bohemia was long part of the Regensburg see (until the founding of the Prague diocese in 973), and Salzburg was the main centre for the Church in the south. In the early period of conversion, many of the priests active in an emergent state were of foreign origin; thus Bavarian missionaries were active in Moravia and Hungary. This had important cultural and political consequences, but was often resented by the newly converted elite's subjects. The establishment of a diocese with subordinate bishoprics and native priests within an emergent state was therefore an important political event. The Moravian state had its own bishopric, as did Poland at Poznań (966). Kiev was for a long time the only bishopric (988) in the vast territories of Kievan Rus. The growth of the Church is shown by the establishment of supplementary dioceses in Poland (Gniezno, Wrocław, Kołobrzeg and Cracow) in the year 1000 and in the Kievan state in the eleventh and twelfth centuries (Pereiaslavl, Polotsk, Smolensk, Novgorod, Belgorod and Bryansk, the extensive northeastern territories receiving dioceses only much later). The boundaries of the early dioceses are often known from written sources (such as that for Prague discussed in Chapter 12) and are usually thought to correspond to the boundaries of political control of the state at the time of defining these frontiers.

From pagan leaders to Christian princes

We have seen that the person and attitude of the ruler was a key feature in the success of the Christian missions. It was these few individuals who took decisions which were to affect fundamentally the socio-political and cultural development of whole societies, not just in their own times but down through the centuries. Some of the reasons why these decisions may have been made have already been touched on above.

We have seen a number of high motives for these actions: the need to react to external pressure, a need for a unifying ideology for a new polity. We should not forget however more personal motivations. In some cases we hear of the marriage between a (usually powerful) pagan ruler and a Christian princess from a neighbouring state (such as Mieszko I of Poland and the Czech Princess Dobrava). Usually the Christian party imposed, as a condition for allowing such a marriage to take place, if not the prior conversion of the ruler (as in the Polish case) at least the assurance of the freedom of worship of the wife in the husband's court (for whom it was necessary to organize a centre of the Christian cult in the residence of the ruler as a Christian enclave in the very heart of a pagan country).[8] In such cases the conversion of the husband under the influence of a pious wife and those around her was expected (and sometimes these hopes were rewarded, sometimes not).

In many other cases though, rulers succumbed to external pressure. Throughout the ninth century there were many attempts by the Carolingians to convert their pagan eastern neighbours. The *Frankish Annals* report several episodes when Slav leaders came to Frankish towns to receive baptism, as in 845 when Louis the German was attending to his eastern frontiers, and forced fourteen Bohemian princes to undergo baptism at Regensburg in 845 and thus become his allies. The Obodrites who were allies of Charlemagne also accepted Christianity in the early ninth century, as a result of centralizing tendencies. Another Slav leader converted to Christianity was Pribina, who was a prince of Nitra driven out of his homeland in 833 by Mojmir, prince of the Moravians; he fled to the East Frankish kingdom, where he was baptized. In 840 he was settled with land in Pannonia in the east and with the approval of the German ruler was able to increase his power and develop the Church in his kingdom (though it remained subservient to the Salzburg diocese).

The Moravian Prince Mojmir was baptised in 831, and Moravia thus initially came under the influence of the German Church, as part of the diocese of Passau. In 852, at a synod at Mainz, Moravian Christianity is described as primitive with many pagan elements. In 846 Prince Rostislav became ruler of the Moravians, achieved independence of the German Empire and expelled the German missionaries. Louis the German was angered by this behaviour and attempted an invasion in 855, but this failed. Rostislav realized that his internal and external power in the state depended on an independent Church organization closely linked with the state and upholding its political and cultural interests. Pope Nicholas I (858–67) however refused to send a bishop who would oppose German interests in the region. In 862 Rostislav therefore sent an emissary to Byzantium, and on the advice of the Patriarch Photius the Emperor Michael III entrusted a philosopher-monk called Constantine and his brother Abbot Methodius who had just returned from a brief mission among the Khazars to establish a mission (863).[9] Constantine, a Slav-speaking native of Thessalonia, prepared himself by inventing the Glagolitic alphabet based on Greek uncial letters for writing selected parts of the Scriptures in the Slavic dialect of Thessalonica, and introduced the Slav rite into Moravia (though it is possible that it had been created with a mission to the Bulgars in mind).[10] This was a new departure, for the Church had until then held that the only proper languages of the liturgy were the three written above the Cross (Hebrew, Greek and Latin). The introduction of a Slav liturgy further threatened German attempts at cultural imperialism as a means of domination; the Germans again attacked Moravia in 864, and Rostislav had to allow German missionaries into his state. This led to tension between the German clergy and those using the Slav rite. The brothers sought support in Rome, where Constantine died in 869 (after entering a monastery under the name of Cyril).[11] In the meantime in Pannonia to the south, Pribina's son Kocelj accepted the Slav rite under the influence of Constantine and Methodius. He had the new Pope (re-)erect the Sirmium bishopric for Methodius, but the bishop was soon abducted and imprisoned in Bavaria. In 873 the Moravian bishopric was recreated by Pope John VIII (872–82) and Methodius was appointed archbishop (with a see at Staré Město), though he was often in conflict with the ruler Sviatopluk. After the death of Methodius (885) however the Slav rite was forbidden in Moravia by Pope Stephen VI (885–91) and at the instigation of the German bishops Sviatopluk expelled the monks trained in the Slav rite, who sought safety in Slovenia and Bulgaria where they continued their activity.

The conversion of Bohemia was a complex process. The forced conversion of the fourteen Czech princes at Regensburg had had no lasting effect. In 883–4 the Czech Prince Bořivoj I was baptized, apparently in the Slav rite by the Moravian archbishop and not the German one; this was part of the Prince's politics of creating an independent Czech state. His successor Spitygniev rejected in the words of a German source 'the curse of idolatry' and was baptized into the Latin Church (probably before or in 895). One of his successors, Wenceslas (Vaclav I, 921–35), was remembered in later legend as especially pious (though this may have been in part prompted as a reaction to his fratricidal murder).[12] It was he who had churches built in all the strongholds scattered throughout the lands of the Přemyslids. At this time Bohemia was part of the Regensburg diocese; the bishop was represented by the archpresbyter of Prague. The diocese of Prague was founded only in 973.

The conversion of the Western Slavs to Christianity was not of course a continuous success story. After early successes, there was a lull in its progress which seems to be related to the lack of internal cohesion and prestige of the post-Carolingian period. In Polabia, the frontier between Christianity and paganism had been driven eastwards, especially under Henry I, but in 983 there was a massive uprising against German rule in the Elbe area during a period of weakness of the Ottonian state. One of the ways in which this manifested itself was in a pagan reaction: the churches were destroyed and the clergy chased out of the territory. The Polabian pagan revolt of 983 had a wider effect as it cut off other parts of west Slavdom from direct Christian influence.

In 966 Mieszko, prince of the Polane (who were beginning their expansion which was to lead to the formation of the state of Poland), was baptized in order to marry a Christian, the Czech Princess Dobrava. The conversion was thus due more to direct influence from southern neighbours, the Bohemians, from whom they accepted the Latin rite. The first bishops at Poznań were subject to Magdeburg, but the creation of the archdiocese in Gniezno (1000) asserted the increasing role of Poland. Poland was itself then the moving force in the conversion of the Pomeranians together with their political domination (tenth and eleventh centuries) and attempts to convert the Baltic Prussians (symbolized among other things by the ill-fated mission of Adalbert/Wojciech in 997).

One of the main Frankish successes was the conversion in 972 by German missionaries sent by Otto I of Prince Géza of the ferocious Magyars, whose raids had been a scourge of central Europe.[13] Géza's conversion was however not an entire success, for he still continued to sacrifice to the pagan idols (and countered reprimands from the Christian priests: 'why not, I am rich enough to do it . . .'). Hungary's conversion completed a chain of Christian states to the east of the Frankish realms.

Despite these efforts, paganism survived in a large zone between the gains of the East and West Churches. The pagan religion survived in independent Slav states in Polabia (until the baptism of Gotschalk of the Obodrites in 1045, and in 1124 of Warcisław, prince of western Pomerania), but only finally extinguished by the capture of the pagan temple at Arkona on Rugia by the Danes in

1168.[14] The eastern extent of the influence of the Polish bishops and the western extent of Kievan Christianity are not clear, but there would seem to have been a huge territory only weakly influenced by either through the latter half of the tenth century and being incorporated into first one and then the other state only in the early decades of the eleventh century. In Poland a breakdown in centralized power in the 1030s also led to a short-lived pagan revival. Christianity was slow to take root in Russia. The same applies to Pomerania; the Prussians were converted only later in the medieval period with the activities of the Teutonic Knights (after 1225), and Lithuania only in the 1380s.

The Byzantine Church was also active in the missionary field. It took advantage, as we have seen, of the situation in Moravia in the 860s, installing the Byzantine rite in Slav form. It was no less successful nearer home, in Bulgaria. Khan Boris (852–89) was promised missionaries by Louis the German which would have brought him under the sway of the Roman Church, but the prospect of a powerful state allied to Rome just by the Byzantine frontiers was not a welcome one for the emperor Michael III the Drunkard (842/3–67), who promptly declared war on Bulgaria. The chronicles record 863 as one of the worst droughts in living memory and the land had been visited by forty days of earthquakes. Feeling unable to conduct war with Byzantium, Boris sent envoys to the Byzantines promising to observe the eastern rite. Boris was baptized (taking the Christian name Michael). The enforced conversion of pagan subjects was begun, a number of nobles who would not submit were killed, and Boris's own son was one of the casualties. People objected not so much to the religion as to the fact that it was brought by foreign priests and was the instrument of an external foreign policy. Boris was faced with an uprising of some of the nobles in the peripheral areas, anxious to preserve the status quo.

In 866 we find Pope Nicholas I writing to Boris with the responses to 106 questions which he and his advisers had sent him to check against what the Byzantine clergy had said. This document is a most interesting source of information not only on Bulgar concerns and thus life at the court, but also on the attitudes of the ninth-century Church.[15] The Bulgarians asked about religious matters (baptism, prayer, fasting) and daily life (for example whether sex is permitted on Sundays, how many times a week one may bathe) as well as local customs (whether it is permitted to wear trousers, and whether the traditional battle standard of a pony's tail was to be used). An analysis of this text offers a means to assess the process of conversion and the preservation or absorption of pagan elements in a particular set of circumstances.[16]

Very soon after this Boris subordinated the Bulgarian Church to the Roman Pope (at that time not backed up by any genuine military power). This seemed to allow the Bulgarians the possibility of the independence of the ecclesiastical organization from outside authority and closer control by the state. The western clergy (among them the future Pope Formosus) gradually drove off the

Greek priests and attempted to take over the organization of the Church. This was the occasion of the issuing of an encyclical by Photius the patriarch of Constantinople denouncing the presence of the Latin missionaries in Bulgaria and the use of the '*filioque*' clause in the Creed. Finding that the Roman Church would not allow the degree of autonomy required by the ruler (that is, the granting of an archbishopric), Boris again subordinated his Church (*c.* 870) to the more amenable Byzantine Church, and once and for all determined the future political and cultural destiny of the state. A massive basilica and twenty other churches were added to the area around the palace at Pliska. The Greek language became once again used for public worship and secular business, which would have endangered the local culture, had it not been for the next decisive move, which came two decades later (885/6) when the Bulgarian Church offered sanctuary for the followers of Cyril and Methodius expelled from Moravia. The introduction of the use of the Slav language and script (and works created for the Moravian church) to replace the Greek of the Byzantine rite here was important in deciding the cultural orientations of the Bulgarian nation over the next centuries and was of no little importance for the development of Slav literature and culture. The rejection of the current trilingual dogma (according to which Christianity could be preached only in Greek, Latin and Hebrew) was a daring break with Byzantium, as was a decade later the banning of the use of Greek in the religious service. In 893 at an ecumenical council in Preslav it was decided to adopt a script valid for state and Church based on the spoken vernacular of the majority of the state's population, the language of the Bulgarian Slavs (Old Bulgarian). In the period of the *floruit* of Bulgar culture under Tsars Symeon and Peter, a Bulgarian (largely ecclesiastical) literature was created and an academy founded by the disciple of Methodius, Clement of Ochrid (subsequently metropolitan of Bulgaria), which made Greek theology available to the young Slav Church. The clergy was initially mostly of Greek (Byzantine) origin.

Byzantium sent a bishop and clergy to the far north to the Rus, who had returned there after a raid on Constantinople in 860. This mission seems to have come to nothing.[17] The Byzantine missionary activity in Russia had another false start in the 950s when Olga was baptized in Constantinople, but also accepted a mission from the western empire. Her son and successor, Sviatoslav, was however a confirmed pagan. It was some thirty years later, in (about) 988, that her grandson Vladimir the Great of Russia became a Christian after taking Kiev from his brother. At first Vladimir unsuccessfully tried to raise Perun, one of his pagan gods, to the role of the highest god (the 'uniting-god') of the lands of the Rus. When this failed, the great prince began to look around for other religions, and accepted Christianity from among the leading world religions of the time (Judaism, Islam and the two branches of Christianity).[18] He found eastern Christianity most acceptable to his purpose and thus chose the Byzantine rite for his people. Again a woman seems to have played a key role in this process. Vladimir had helped Basil II of Byzantium to quell a revolt and in *c*. 987 married Anna, the emperor's sister. The *PVL* records that he threw down the pagan idols he himself had not so long before erected and proclaimed in Kiev that the people should assemble by the river on an appointed day for baptism. He added, 'Whoever does not turn up at the river tomorrow, be he rich, poor lowly or slave, he shall be my enemy!'[19] The new religion was imposed by force.

Christianity and the people

The Church aimed to make its influence universal, not only throughout society (and thus affecting all individuals of every status) but also as the institution which was present at and even controlled all stages of the development of the each individual (birth, choosing a mate, death and a whole host of other rites marking the passage of time). The Church was by these means to make itself indispensable to the social order of medieval European society.

We have seen however that, in the early decades of the conversion, Christianity was mainly restricted to the social elites, and we should be aware that the decisions and preferences of the socio-political elite were not automatically transmitted to the bulk of the population. The degree of acceptance of Christianity by all the subjects of a state was dependent on a number of factors, not least the methods used to transmit the outward forms and inner content of the new ideology throughout society. We are not very well informed about the reaction to missionary activity in rural districts, away from the centres of elite power. It would seem however that the new ideology made slow headway in these agricultural communities in conditions of relative mutual isolation and characterized by their conservativism, with the rhythm of their lives so closely intertwined (especially in the sphere of belief) with the natural rhythm of nature. In the framework of the existing concepts of such communities the acceptance of Christianity would have automatically implied a break of the all important links with the customs and ways of the ancestors which were at the very basis of the group identity. In central and eastern Europe the archaeological evidence (especially from cemeteries) and ethnographic evidence show that pagan customs long survived the formal baptism of the leaders: for several decades after the formal conversion, only a relatively small number of members of society had accepted the new religion, while many still clung to pagan practices and symbols.

That the pagan beliefs had not lost their hold on the populace is further illustrated by the mass apostasy which is relatively frequently mentioned with horror in the written sources. This resulted when certain situations provoked a conflict of loyalty and orientation. Among these were natural disasters and military failures affecting the people and the ruler who had decided to accept the new belief and raising questions about the wisdom of rejecting the old gods, who, it could be argued, were now seen to be taking their revenge. These situations created ideal conditions for the activation of forces aiming to restore the old and still familiar pagan order of things.

Even when the process of the gradual increase of Christian influence was more advanced, it seems that some pagan customs were absorbed by the Churches of central and eastern Europe. From the point of the pagan religions, this syncretism was acceptable because these belief systems often had no pretension to exclusiveness with reference to other religious systems, and had the ability to absorb other gods into the pantheon in a manner incomprehensible to the Christian clergy. In the process of conversion, there must have been many situations of conflict which could not be resolved according to the wishes of one of the sides, and situations requiring radical and unconventional resolutions, especially from the point of view of Christian orthodoxy. As a result many people were christened, married and buried according to rites which incorporated greater or lesser degrees of pagan folk customs alongside Christian rites. The Church in East Slav regions retained an especially large number of pagan customs and syncretic beliefs, and in Russia the characteristic fusion of Christian and pagan features was known as *dwojevierje* (double belief).[20] The decision (or negligence) of the Church prelates in allowing such practices reflects the fluidity of the Church itself in the period of these conversions.[21]

This syncretism affects folk customs more than actual religious beliefs. The initial activities of the Christian missionaries were aimed at destroying the cults of the major gods, and this seems to have taken place in many cases relatively rapidly, perhaps suggesting that belief in these gods (as opposed to demons) was in fact relatively weakly rooted among the common folk. The place of these major gods was taken by either the Christian God or saints (Elias, Nicholas, Blasius). As we have seen in the previous chapter, ancient pagan festivals, gods and heroes were accepted into the Christian pantheon. Despite this, belief in the demons and in the efficacity of various magical practices continued for many centuries. The clergy itself did not doubt the existence of the demons, but tried to forbid their cults. We have many examples of sermons preserved in which magical and pagan cultic practices are condemned: these are a major source of information. The clergy accepted however some pagan practices into the Christian liturgy, such as the sanctification of water, fire, food and seed corn, and also the practice of leading a procession around the fields.

One of the most telling ways of following the progress of Christianity is to follow changes in the burial rite. Over most of Slavdom, inhumation burials seem relatively quickly to have replaced cremations and became the general rule: the rite seems in most regions to have spread together with Christianity.[22] A high proportion of rural inhumation cemeteries (or many of those on the fringes of dense centres of population) have no stone or even timber churches in them. Burials in so-called grave-field cemeteries were often arranged in family groups; indeed the whole cemetery was probably used by a clan or community (Fig. 64).[23]

In other cases the inhumation cemeteries of churchyard type were organized around the early churches (even those within strongholds); some of them are still in use today. Only with the establishment of rural parishes were rural cemeteries exclusively of churchyard type (in Poland the latter becomes the rule in most areas by the middle of the twelfth century).[24] This process reflects another important change; in contrast to grave-field cemeteries, churchyards collected burials from the whole parish, which often contained several different communities. Here the Church was cutting across former social structures in a manner which meant that society was being organized in a new way.

In these cemeteries the graves were in rough rows or sometimes groups (perhaps by families). Burials were made in shallow graves, sometimes lined with planks or stones. The body was laid on its back with head to either east or west, and generally clothed. In some cases (in contrast with cremations, where grave goods seldom occurred) in the first inhumations in some areas the bodies were accompanied by objects such as pots containing food, ornaments and weapons placed in the graves. This custom of placing grave goods lasted until at least the twelfth century in northeastern Poland (Mazovia and Podlasie). It is not clear why this should appear in the period of Christian influence. The provision of grave goods in inhumation burials occurs even in churchyard burials in Moravia, and it is difficult to escape the conclusion that this fact must have been known to the clergy conducting the funeral service. The eastern Church was even more tolerant of (or powerless against) the survival of pagan customs. In the Kievan state, burials were still made under barrows into the twelfth century, though often the bodies were accompanied by crosses, the only concession made to the new religion in the burial rite.

In both these cases we can see how difficult it was for the Church to combat deeply rooted pagan beliefs and folk customs which (especially in rural centres at a distance from the elite centres) survived long under the veneer of Christianity. In the thirteenth century the Church (and in particular the begging orders) had enormous difficulties stamping out paganism even in the towns of central Europe, which was a symptom of much more widespread problems in rural areas. It took a long time for the Churches of these states to provide a comprehensive ministry to the entire population.[25] Even in the eleventh and twelfth centuries, old cult centres such as Łysa Góra in southern Poland were still frequented; as late as the nineteenth century the local priest still had to fight the lighting of fires in Whitsun on the peak of this mountain. In some Slav countries to this day there is a custom of visiting the cemetery and decorating family graves on All Souls' Day (the Polish *Zaduszki*), sometimes partaking of a meal in the process, which seems to be a survival of pagan customs accepted by the early Church.

The eastern Church was equally tolerant towards (or powerless against) other pagan rites such as dances and festivals. The Roman Catholic Church had slightly more success in fighting these practices (though the process was nearly completed only in the nineteenth century by progressive industrialization, and dispossession of the peasantry caused the breakdown of village communities which effectively ended many of these local customs).

In some cases the early laws of rulers forbade these practices. The decrees of the Bohemian Prince Břetyslav I issued between 1035 and 1055 (and preserved in the relation of Cosmas) are an example of the oldest Slav laws, in this case based on Canon Law. There are eight articles, forbidding polygamy, introducing exile for those breaking their marriage vows or leading an immoral life (or inciting abortion), introducing punishments for murder, forbidding trading and working on holy days and finally forbidding the burial of the dead outside of (official) cemeteries. Bolesław I of Poland also enforced Christianity using rather drastic measures; for example the German Bishop Thietmar (VIII.2) reports that, in his state, the punishment for adultery was to put the woman to death, but to take the man, nail his genitals to a wooden beam of a bridge and leave him there with only a sharp knife to free himself with. For breaking the Lenten fast, a transgressor had his teeth knocked out. The fact that it was necessary to introduce such measures indicates that, despite official sanction, Christianity was making little headway against established social mores such as those concerning polygamy and burial rites.

A different form of nonconformance to the mores of the Church is expressed in the adoption of heretical belief systems. One of the most influential to appear in the period and area discussed here was Bogomilism, which was based on a Manichaean philosophy. It arose – perhaps as a result of social conflict – in the period of the decline of the Bulgarian state by the middle of the tenth century, and was relatively widely accepted, especially by the peasantry. This system proposed (among other things) a world view in which that which was material and visible was the creation of evil, while that which was spiritual was created by God. These two were seen as in active opposition, in which Good would triumph. The main problem was that the Bogomils regarded the organized Church and the state as creations of the negative forces.[26]

11

State-formation: the South and East Slavs

The ninth and tenth centuries saw the beginnings of the final stages of the process of the formation of the early states which created the basis for the nations which still appear on the map of modern central Europe. Although there have been many events in the intervening thousand years which have dramatically altered this picture (some of which are summarized in Chapter 13), the ethnic units established in the tenth century proved surprisingly enduring. In this respect, this period is for much of the area a formative period of modern Europe, and this seems a fitting place to close the account of the development of early societies of central and eastern Europe. It will be noticed that with the rise of states (and the appearance of writing which accompanied this event) we are able to give a much more detailed account of the societies we are writing about than was the case when we often had little more to build on than the ceramic evidence. Our discussion moves from a concentration on the material culture to a discussion of political events: we have more information on concrete personalities (usually belonging only to the elite) and information about ideological change and other features poorly visible through the material remains with which the archaeologist deals.

The Bulgar khanate and its neighbours

The formation of the Bulgarian state is a relatively straightforward case of the indirect influence of a primary state (Byzantium) on a newly arisen social organization and subsequent direct acceptation of foreign cultural models in an ambitious social and political policy of the elite. By a process of assimilation of existing populations and social institutions the Bulgars gave rise in the seventh century to a new society (we discussed this process in Chapter 4).[1] The Byzantine influences on the organization and material culture of the Bulgar state become very clear in the ninth and tenth centuries. We saw that Symeon, educated in Constantinople, even apparently had grandiose ambitions to take the imperial throne in Constantinople. Although he did not achieve this, after his defeat of the Byzantine forces at Anchialos in 917 he did style himself 'emperor and autocrat of all the Bulgarians and Greeks'. The new capital at Preslav abounded in palaces and churches, filled with paintings, marble, gold and silver. The khan on his throne, robed in pearl-embroidered purple, was surrounded by a dazzling suite of boyars. John the Exarch wrote: 'If a stranger returning from Preslav were asked what he had seen there he could only reply that he knew not how to describe it all, and only seeing it with one's own eyes could give an idea of such splendour.' An academy was created in which translations were made of Greek classics into the Bulgarian language. It is notable however that the main works copied were ecclesiastical histories, rhetoric and legal works. This was a literature of translations and not the setting for the creation of a Bulgarian national literature, still less history.

Symeon's eldest son Peter began his reign (927–67) with a major invasion of the Byzantine administrative district of Macedonia, probably as a show of strength to gain support for his rule. The raid was soon over and the Bulgar troops were in retreat. This was followed by the conclusion of peace with Byzantium (and Peter married Maria Lecapena, granddaughter of the Emperor Romanus I Lecapenus). In 945 the Byzantine emperor recognized the right of Peter to use the title 'Emperor' and granted the Bulgarian church the status of a patriarchate (Clement of Ochrid was appointed metropolitan).

In the older literature, Peter's comparatively long reign is usually represented as a period marked by the dramatic decline of Bulgaria, when it lost power, reputedly becoming a 'harmless Byzantine protectorate' in the throes of economic exhaustion caused by the ambitions of Symeon. Certainly there are signs of decline. At the beginning of his reign (933), Peter lost the territory of the Serbs. The Bulgars lost the chance of creating a South Slav empire and turned their attention once more towards Byzantium. Invasions of the northern territories by Magyars led to other territorial losses, such as Transylvania. Again the Danube formed the northern frontier of the state, and Pecheneg raids troubled this area too. There were also internal problems in the Bulgar state. Bulgarian historians have noted the appearance of deepening social rifts (caused, some have suggested, by the fact that Bulgar culture had been undermined by the Greek influences affecting the elite), and also increasing unrest among the boyars (some of whom supported the alliance with Byzantium, while others were against it). Two plots were organized by Peter's own brothers. Internal dissent was encouraged by the pressure of deepening class divisions and hardships for the peasants. This is used to explain why so many embraced the Bogomil heresy, since Bogomilism repudiated the state and the Church (believing them to be a creation of Satan). It is now recognized that some of these factors may have been overemphasized by scholars in the past to explain the demise of Bulgaria, which had seemed so powerful only decades before.

Although a comparison of Symeon's and Peter's reigns from the point of view of military achievement (especially from the viewpoint of Byzantine narrative sources) may be unfavourable to the latter, if we examine the material evidence the picture is entirely different, suggesting a period of political consolidation and economic expansion.[2] Intellectual and cultural life seems to have been a continuation of the trends set in the golden age of Symeon. This was possible in a period when the state enjoyed good relations with Constantinople (which clearly still considered the Bulgarians a potential political and military threat).

These crises coincided with a period when Byzantium was gaining strength. By the end of Peter's reign, Bulgarian–Byzantine relations were on the verge of collapse, and the Tsar's two sons, Boris and Roman, were taken hostages in Constantinople. The Emperor Nicephorus Phocas incited Sviatoslav of Kiev to attack Bulgaria. The Bulgarian army suffered a defeat in 967, eighty fortresses fell and Dobrudja came under the rule of the Rus. Sviatoslav in alliance with Byzantium had extended his rule over the western steppes and down the Black Sea coast to the Danube mouth. He took the important centre at Preslaviets on the lower Danube (an important trading centre the location of which has not yet been conclusively identified – but perhaps Prislava (Nufarul) on a branch of the Danube or possibly Kudakioj near Tutrakan 50 km southeast of Bucharest). It was here that, according to the *PVL*: 'goods gather from all parts: gold, clothes, wine, fruits from the Greeks [Byzantines], silver and horses from the Czechs, and Hungarians, furs, wax, honey from the Slavs and slaves from the Rus'. Sviatoslav apparently intended to create a joint Russian–Bulgar state centred on Preslaviets and allied with the Magyars and Bulgars. (Unfortunately for him he failed to subdue the Pechenegs on the steppes between the Seret and Dniestr rivers, who split his new conquests from the core of the Russian state.) After Peter's death in 967, his son Boris II ruled as Bulgar khan for a short while, but under the Byzantine John I Tzimisces (who replaced Nicephorus in 969) the Bulgarian state continued to suffer military setbacks. In 971 John dethroned Boris and made him captive in Constantinople and made a treaty with Sviatoslav. The Byzantines took over most of the southwest territories of the Bulgar state, and as a result of this Byzantine expansion the First Bulgar Khanate was destroyed (972), leaving only remnants in the Macedonian mountains. (In the same year however Sviatoslav was killed by the Pechenegs and the Danube delta no longer formed part of the Kievan state.)

The Macedonian area remained independent of Byzantium under the sons of the Boyar Nikolaos, one of whom, Samuel (976–1014), was acclaimed tsar (980) of the multi-ethnic so-called West Bulgarian Empire. Under his rule there was a brief revival of Bulgar fortunes: he was able to regain Serbia and take back from Byzantine hands large territories. The success was temporary: the Bulgars were again crushed (1018) by the Byzantines under Basil II the Bulgar-slayer (who at the end of a cruel war resorted to blinding fifteen thousand Bulgarian prisoners leaving only one in each hundred men with one eye to lead the others home – Samuel died of a heart attack on seeing this sight). Four years later the dynasty was extinct, and between 1018 and 1185 all former Bulgar territories were subject to Byzantine rule. The Bulgarians vanish from the political map until the thirteenth century.

The early ninth century saw the consolidation of the Serbs, who seem archaeologically represented by a number of ninth- to eleventh-century cemeteries (Cecan near Vučitrn, Maticane, Badovac and Gračanica near Priština). The Serbs had been incorporated into the Bulgar empire at the turn of the ninth and tenth centuries under Symeon, but after his death the Serbian leader (*Zupan*) Čestav united the Serbian tribes against his successor Peter, and managed to achieve a short-lived independence (933). But the collapse of Bulgar power and the victory of Basil II brought their territory under Byzantine rule. This brought the Serbs under the influence of Byzantine culture and the eastern Church (reflected among other things in their use of the Cyrillic alphabet). The state achieved autonomy only in the twelfth century under the Nemayich dynasty.

The coastal territory known as Zeta (roughly today's Montenegro) was the central area of the state of Duklianie, which formed at the turn of the tenth and eleventh centuries and also included much of south Bosnia and Hercegovina. This had developed from the unification of the tribal territories of the Dukliane tribe (which settled around the abandoned Roman town of Dioclea) and the Travunianie to the west. The area was conquered by Čestav and brought into the Serb kingdom; it regained independence in the second half of the tenth century, but came under Byzantine rule. It passed under Bulgar rule again in the period of the Western Bulgar Empire, but passed to Byzantium in 1018 (gaining independence under Stefan Dobroslav (1031–51) when an expansion further to the west into the territory of the Zachlumianie followed in the eleventh century).

Croatia further to the west became absorbed into the western, Latin cultural circle and Church. In the eighth century it had been organized in seven provinces. The area bordered with the Ostmark and was threatened by Charlemagne, but managed to remain independent. In 876–9 several of these provinces united to form Croatia on the Adriatic coast with an adjacent province of Slavonia inland (Pannonia). About 910–14 Tomislav became the ruler of Croatia and united it with Slavonia. He was crowned by a papal legate as the first king in 924/5. The state owed its allegiance to the Roman Church from the beginning. It initially celebrated the Mass in the local language, but, after a period of use of the Glagolitic alphabet, began to use the Latin alphabet. After the death of Tomislav there was civil unrest and central authority was weakened and peripheral provinces (such as Bosnia) fell away. Native rule lasted until the area was conquered by Hungary in 1102.

In the ninth and tenth centuries the Carinthians are represented by the development in Austria and Slovenia of the Köttlach Culture, named after a site in Austria and typified by its rich enamelled jewellery. The area of western Carinthia had been overrun by the Franks in the late eighth century during Charlemagne's reign and with Pannonia became part of the Ostmark. A revolt under Duke Ljudovit was put down in 818–22 and the Duke fled from his city of Sisak to the Serbs. Otto I incorporated those lands into the Duchy of Carinthia in 952 (and this was later split into the Duchies of Carinthia, Carniola and Styria).

The final decade of the ninth century and the beginning of the tenth century saw the settlement of the Carpathian basin by the Magyars who, having established their suzerainty over the Slavs already settled in the area (and allied to the Germans and Byzantines), attacked both the Bulgars and the Moravians. The consolidation of Magyar settlement in the Carpathian basin brought a new foreign element into the complex ethnic situation of the area. In the tenth century in the area north of the Sava we see the rise of the cultural (or rather style) group known (after a site in Croatia) as Bialobrdo, a mixture of Slav–Avar, Magyar, 'Old Croat', Köttlach and Moravian influences. This type of material culture (with its characteristic jewellery of plaited wire, two-piece sheetwork pendants, snake-head bracelets and S-shaped temple-rings) extends through the area occupied by the Magyars in Hungary, Slovakia, and part of Transylvania (where elements survived into the late Middle Ages and even form a motif in recent folk costume).

The encouragement of the aggressiveness of the Magyars for short-term aims by neighbouring states was to prove dangerous. After the destruction of the Moravian state in 906 and the occupation of Pannonia, by the mounting of a series of destructive raids into western Europe the Magyars became a potential threat to the west itself.[3] At the battle on the Lech near Augsburg in 955 the Germans defeated the main force of Magyars, and raids on Germany, Italy, Burgundy and France ceased. The Hungarian state was created under the rule of the Arpad dynasty, and in 972 Prince Géza was converted to Christianity. It was in his reign that the state took on from its western neighbours some of the trappings of civilized life, with elaborate public buildings and other features. His son, Stephen (1000–38), received his crown from the Pope and united the country under his sole rule – abolishing the older pagan rights of dynastic succession. It was in this period that the linking structures of the new state not only abolished existing tribal divisions among the Magyars but also effectively eliminated the ethnic differences between the Magyars and indigenous populations of Slavs and others, thus producing the Hungarian people (in contrast to the Bulgars however the Slav element was largely subsumed by the Magyar, a feature which is immediately detectable in the language spoken there in the Middle Ages). Another important result of Stephen's reign was that in taking Transylvania, together with Byzantine expansion northwards, he drove a wedge between the South and East Slavs which was to become an established feature of the geography of central Europe.

Another central European people which has not so far been discussed is the Romance-speaking populations of the Balkans, which are the last remnants of the fringes of the Latin-speaking zone. Many of the enclaves of Romance language (Istrian and Meglano-Romanian, the Macedonian groups, the Vlach communities south of the Danube) were disappearing by the eighteenth century. Of these peoples only the Vlachs south of the Danube (appearing in the historical records from the tenth century) became a major force in the region when the Asen brothers led a revolt against the Byzantines in 1186 which led to the formation of the so-called Second Bulgarian Empire (crushed by the Ottomans in the fourteenth century). The main remnant of these Romance-speakers in the area today are the Romanians and Moldavians, formed from the later medieval kingdom of the Walachians.[4]

The Kievan state and its neighbours

The ninth and tenth centuries saw the formation of the East Slav state, that of Kievan Rus. The Kievan state was, in its eleventh century form, a political organization of massive proportions, covering some 990,000 sq km. The written and archaeological evidence clearly suggests that this had been formed over a period of time from the subjugation of a number of separate tribal groupings (which had themselves formed earlier by centralizing tendencies). This centralization was probably achieved by military might, forcing the attacked tribe to submit to the rule of the central leader and to render him tribute and other services (such as participation in military levies) in return for being allowed to continue to inhabit their former territory unmolested and even protected by the powerful state. Despite this, such a large state remained a confederation of regional arenas of power and, when central power weakened, strong separatist tendencies became visible.

It would seem that the cultural and linguistic amalgamation of the various communities was encouraged by the consolidation of administrative and ideological power. Centralized rule by a social elite contributed greatly to the spread of common cultural and aesthetic values as well as to the creation of a common Old Russian speech; these levelling influences first operated in the higher ranks of the society but gradually filtered down. A key part in the process of bringing elite values to the ordinary person may have been played by organized religion, especially the Christian Church. A side-effect of these processes was the loss of individual regional histories, and, when the story of Kievan Rus came to be written down, much of the history was subjugated and manipulated to the traditions of the Kievan elite and to serve its interests. The *PVL*, despite being one of the most important sources for the history of the Russian state, has only limited value. It was compiled in several stages between the 1070s and 1118 (but no surviving manuscript is earlier than the early fourteenth century). The chronicle uses oral tradition; some documents and certain pieces of information are emphasized, others missed out and others still interpolated or made up by the chronicler. This was of course a common manner of writing 'history' in the early Middle Ages. One of the main problems is that, even in cases where one suspects that a Byzantine source should have lain behind the record (for example an attack on Constantinople), the dates, where they can be cross-checked, are wrong by several years. In other cases we simply do not know how dates were assigned to events.[5] Another key for Kievan history is a whole chapter in *DAI*, written down in the 950s, which contains information on the organization of Slav trade on the Dniepr.

The origin of the Russian state is one of the most discussed problems of modern historiography of eastern Europe, and reveals the interesting relationship between the written record and other sources, but also the social context modelling historical interpretations (see Chapter 13).[6] According to the traditional account, presented in the *PVL*, a 'Rus' (Scandinavian) leader named Rurik was called in by four tribal unions of the north (Slovienie, Krivichi, Vesh and Meria) and the two marginal ones (Chuds and Muromia) to rule over them, and this rule was later extended over the rest of the Kievan state by his kinsmen Oleg and Igor. Kiev was supposedly taken by Oleg only in 882 and joined to the emerging state. Scholars have pointed out that the *PVL* was written when Rus was being split into minor princedoms and beset by permanent feudal wars. The annalist was attempting to create the history of a unified state with a single dynasty of rulers ruling in an unbroken father-to-son line of descent with no other claimants, in other words the ideal paradigm of a state. This story was meant as an appeal to the princes as descendants of a single forefather to unite and prevent the ruin of Rus.

The Scandinavians and the Kievan state

The issue of the nature of the role of the Scandinavians – the so-called Varangians – from central Sweden in the formation of the Kievan state was a contentious one in the nationalism of the Stalinist period, and was condemned by the majority of Soviet historians, not only in the 1950s but until the 1970s. In the 1980s however a number of Leningrad scholars began to question these views, propounded mainly by the Moscow school.[7] The nature of this Scandinavian influence has since been hotly debated, since both the archaeological and the written sources can support various interpretations.

The so-called 'Varangian problem' derives primarily from the foundation legends of the Kievan state recorded in the *PVL* (s.a. 859) and the capture of Kiev by Varangian forces to found the dynasty (s.a. 882), and the way which some investigators accept these tales to various degrees at face value and others reject them. An additional element is the account of the *Bertinian Annals*, which tell of emissaries from the 'Rhos' who arrived at the court of Emperor Louis the

Pious in Ingelheim in 839 from Byzantium: Louis found that they were in fact Swedes. A third element comprises the treaties of 912 and 944 drawn up between the 'Rus' and Byzantium which are preserved in the *PVL* (presumably copied in the 1090s from the Byzantine archives): these give us the names of many of the main warriors who had sailed down from 'the land of the Rus' to Byzantium in those years, and it can be seen that the majority of these names given in these documents are Scandinavian. The fourth element in this pattern is the archaeological evidence for the presence of Scandinavians in several parts of East Slav territory.

The name 'Rus' has aroused much emotion. Some scholars see the term as applying only to Scandinavians, others to people from the 'land of the Rus' (whatever that means). Both in the *Bertinian Annals* and in the treaties contained in the *PVL* the 'land of the Rus' (or Rhos) could be interpreted as the Kiev region, where the tribal territory of the Poliane incorporates in the south the valley of the River Ros (55 km south of Kiev). Some Soviet scholars attempted to derive the name 'Rus' from this, but this explanation is etymologically difficult to accept. Recent work by Melnikova and Petrukhin has shown fairly conclusively that (as many have suspected all along) there is little doubt that the term 'Rus', known to the Arabs as 'ar-Rus' and the Finns as 'Ruotsi', was applied to Scandinavians.[8] The term could have been applied by extension to a wider range of people but there is little doubt that its intended meaning was to refer to Scandinavians (and indeed people from the area of Sweden) settled in the north of what later became the Kievan state. These Varangians probably formed only a relatively small minority; despite the evidence of Scandinavian settlement, there are very few place names of Scandinavian origin in Russia, and there is very little influence of Scandinavian languages on the language of the East Slavs. The Scandinavians fulfilled several roles in the East Slav territories: some were clearly adventurers living in the wilderness of eastern Europe or traders plying along 'the route from the Varangians to the Greeks' (Byzantium), and at a later date some were warriors who entered the service of certain chiefs as part of their retinue.

A relatively large number of sites in the area of the Kievan state have produced finds of Scandinavian type; this material comes from settlements, strongholds, trading sites and cemeteries.[9] Usually individual sites produce considerable quantities of this material, suggesting that Scandinavians settled in communities. Of course the mere presence of an object made in Scandinavia or of a style used in Scandinavia does not mean that the last person who used it before it was deposited in the ground was a Scandinavian. Graves are an important pointer: a number of these objects are found in graves which have other objects (or the burial was made by a rite) of non-Scandinavian character. Obviously these imports were prestige goods for several local communities. A number of graves however match Scandinavian assemblages so closely that there is little doubt that they represent burials made in accordance with the customs of an immigrant people. According to A. Stalsberg, Scandinavian objects have come from 140 sites (413 assemblages), but in only 88 cases out of 303 burials could they be classified as specifically Scandinavian.[10] Even at Ladoga out of seven hundred excavated mounds (excepting the Plakun cemetery), only thirty can be considered purely Scandinavian.

Scandinavian settlement on the southeast shores of Lake Ladoga is evidenced in particular by the extensive barrow cemeteries perhaps of the ninth to eleventh centuries on the plains around Tikhvin (some 100 km east of St Petersburg).[11] This initial core area of Scandinavian settlement was concentrated in the river valleys between the Syas and Ort rivers on the fringe of the territory of the Slovienie tribal area among the Finno-Ugrian Vesh (an area of about 170 by 100 km). These settlements and cemeteries (including the famous cemetery of Scandinavian burials, some of them in boats, at Plakun) were created by colonists who mostly probably came from middle Sweden. It is probably here, if anywhere, that we should seek the origin of the Rurik myth, and indeed his name is associated with an early stronghold (Ryurikovo Gorodishche) built according to dendrochronology about 889–948 on the site of an earlier (eighth- to ninth-century) trading settlement 200 km south of the emporium of Ladoga. Other early Scandinavian finds come from the Krutnik settlement on the shores of Lake Beloozero, and from the Sarskii fort and Timerevo (on the Kotorosl near later Rostov). These latter sites seem to be exchange centres on the trade routes which were to continue to function into the tenth and later centuries. No unequivocally ninth-century artefacts have been found along the Dniepr (the creation of the emporium at Gniozdovo should be dated at the earliest to the turn of the ninth and tenth centuries).

It seems likely from the archaeological evidence that there was indeed extensive Scandinavian penetration of parts of the forest zone in the northern part of the Kievan state, and on this basis it is probable that some credence may be given to the tale of the *PVL* that some form of Scandinavian control may even have been established in the northern lands (*PVL* s.a. 859, 862). The Scandinavians, apart perhaps from seeking *Lebensraum*, were intent on tapping into the flow of trade between the Baltic and the forest interior of the country, an exchange in which, as we have seen, Islamic silver played an important role. We have also seen (p. 103) that a Varangian leader began styling himself as 'khagan' of the Rus, an imitation of the title of the Khazar ruler with whose subjects they came into contact several hundred kilometres to the southeast. There seems no doubt that Scandinavians played a major role in the economic life (and later the military actions) of the Kievan rulers; whether they actually played the role in the ninth century as the *PVL* suggests is far more debatable.

Most of the Scandinavian grave finds from East Slav territory are tenth- (from the 930s) and eleventh-century in date, and form several specific clusters.

From about the middle of the tenth century we find an expansion of this type of material into four regions of Russia. The densest spread is in the Ladoga region, with outliers at Novgorod and Pskov. The next densest scatter is a series of cemeteries in the region of the upper Volga (in the area where Jaroslavl was later founded in 1015), in a southeastern extension of the territory of the Slovienie (on the frontier with the territory of the Meria and Vesh), and extending up the tributary valley to Rostov. This was an area previously sparsely inhabited. The third region of Scandinavian settlement finds is in a similar eastern expansion of the territory of the Krivichi in the Kliazma valley in the region of Suzdal (the stronghold here perhaps dates to the ninth century, but the first historical reference comes from 1024). A number of mound burials here on the Kliazma have tenth-century Scandinavian ornaments. A fourth region where rich cemeteries with Scandinavian artefacts and burials occur is on the upper Dniepr in the Gniozdovo–Smolensk region.[12] We know from archaeological evidence that, in the huge cemetery of barrows at Gniozdovo which predates the foundation of the stronghold at Smolensk, the earliest graves of Scandinavian type date to the mid tenth century, and it is not improbable that these graves are those of settlers who came here in the 940s. There are also a number of finds in the Chernigov and Kiev areas.

All of these were important centres in the Kievan state, and it seems very likely that these Scandinavians were settled here with their families (many of the graves are of women with Scandinavian brooches which were worn as part of a specific costume) as part of the prince's retinue. It should be noted that most of these finds occur in frontier areas of the Kievan state, just where one would expect task forces of mercenaries.

The origins of the Kievan state

It seems that the core of the early medieval Russian state was the tribal union known as the Poliane in the centre of the forest steppe zone in the Dniepr valley and having its seat of power in the massive stronghold at Kiev.[13] Although there is earlier settlement on the hilltops here, and despite earlier dates proposed for it, the earthen rampart seems to date to the eighth or ninth century. The *PVL* tells us of two legendary rulers of Kiev who were killed by the founder of the dynasty. In the chronicler's day the sites of the graves of both of these rulers were known, though in both cases churches had been built over them. Dir's grave was under the church of St Irena near St Sophia's in the centre of the old town (Dir's name also appears in an Arab source). Askold is known only from the *PVL* and he is said to be buried on the 'Hungarian' Hill. It is difficult to disentangle the origin of these traditions. In the *PVL* Askold and Dir function alongside the mythical founder of the town, Kiy (typically one of three brothers), in creating a native pedigree for the town and people of Kiev before the events reported under the year 882. Askold and Dir are linked by the chronicler with the attack on Constantinople of 860 (which the *PVL* misdates).

The Kievan state developed in a zone of contact between various other political organizations and ethnic groups. The tribal territory of the Poliane was a crossroads between different cultures. The earliest contacts seem to have been with the Turkic Khazars settled on the steppe between the Don and Dniepr. By the end of the eighth century their influence stretched from the Caucasus to the middle Volga and Don valley, where they established a multi-ethnic federation across major transcontinental trade routes.[14] They seem to have been an important obstacle in the process of centralization of power by the Kievan princes. We have a lot of information about contacts with Byzantium from the end of the ninth century. Apart from finds such as coins, the written sources depict the Kievan rulers as raiders (though eager to establish regular trade contacts). Further to the east on the middle Volga was a second state, that of the Volga Bulgars, which also played a similar role to the Khazars, but emerged however as a significant entity only in the first half of the ninth century. We have already seen that there were also attempts by the Kievan rulers to establish in the 960s some form of control over the Danube Bulgars.

It is of note that the major tenth-century stronghold-towns of the central core of the later state are very close together. One of them, Vyshogrod, only a few dozen kilometres from Kiev, was a royal centre (the *PVL* tells us that it was Olga's stronghold). Several others – Chernigov, Liubech, Pereiaslavl – were also very important.[15] Is it possible that these were the centres of the smaller individual tribes which amalgamated to form the Poliane tribal union? It is unclear when the other tribal unions which lay behind the formation of the Kievan state were formed. Various pieces of evidence seem to coalesce however to suggest the increasing centralization of power in the populations inhabiting the territory in the vicinity of the Dniepr valley by the late ninth century. The lack of evidence of these tribal unions in the *Bavarian Geographer* despite its mention of the Khazars might (though one cannot place too much reliance on this negative evidence) give us a *terminus post quem* of the middle of the ninth century for the formation of these tribal unions. The names reported as chosen by these tribal unions is interesting: we have already noted the Severiane, and the names of the Poliane and Derevlane translate respectively as 'people of the clearing/field' and 'people of the forest'.

The next stage in strengthening that position would be the extension and consolidation of that power by one of these rulers over a wider territory. The results of these conquests seem not at this stage to have been the total annihilation of the previously existing tribe, but its subordination to the victorious leader: this seems to have mainly consisted of supplying tribute for the ruler's upkeep (and that of his retinue) and also the supply of warriors for military expeditions against neighbouring polities.

The *PVL* is unusual in that it does not present the history of the Kievan state as a continuum from its legendary founders but introduces a new dynasty of 'rightful' rulers descended from Rurik. As the legend goes, Rurik was invited in by the peoples of the north (in the same way as the people of Israel requested someone to rule over and judge them as reported in the Book of Samuel). It is Oleg, whom the chronicler makes a kinsman of Rurik, who arrives in 882 and with the aid of warriors from the north (apparently Varangians, Chuds, Slovienie, Meria, Vesh, but also Krivichi) by means of stealth (disguising themselves as merchants) they take the town and kill Askold and Dir. This tale contains traditional elements and is part of a cycle of tales associated with Oleg inserted into the *PVL* between 879 and 912 with a lot of inserted 'padding' and containing much material of similar nature, though it is not ruled out that this oral tradition might contain a kernel of reality.[16] One has no way of knowing how the *PVL* chronicler assigned these events a date; the tales themselves contain no clues and one has the impression that the chronicler had trouble filling the space in this part of the text, which accounts for a number of extraneous tales.[17]

One of the details the chronicler offers is the motif of a tribute imposed by the Khazars on some of the East Slav tribes before their conquest by Oleg, which suggests that the memory of the Khazar domination of the area was still fresh in the chronicler's time. According to the *PVL* the Khazars extracted tribute from several of the East Slav tribes; in 859 they are said to have taken one silver coin and a squirrel skin from each hearth from the Poliane, Severiane and Viatichi.

The Oleg tales in the *PVL* also contain the story of how the Kievan state was formed around the core-tribe of the Poliane as a series of annexations by military force. Beginning in Kiev ('the mother of Russian stronghold-towns'), adjacent territories were annexed by the Poliane under Oleg.

Year 6390 [882] . . . [this is the account of Oleg taking control of the Poliane centre at Kiev]

Year 6391 [883] Oleg began to fight the Derevlane and, defeating them, took from them the tribute of a black marten.

Year 6392 [884] Oleg went forth against the Severiane and defeated them, and applied a light tribute on them, and did not allow them to pay the Khazars tribute, saying: 'I am against them, and there is no need for you to pay.'

Year 6393 [885] Oleg sent an envoy to the Radimichi and asked, 'Who do you pay tribute to?' They replied: 'To the Khazars'. Oleg told them, 'Do not pay the Khazars but pay me'. And they gave Oleg a silver coin[18] [from each hearth] as they had given the Khazars. And Oleg ruled the Poliane and Derevlane, and Severiane and Radimichi, and with the Uliche and Tyvercy he made war.

We are not told anything about the Viatichi. This triple arrangement with its repetition looks very much like an oral account: again the dates are of uncertain origin.[19] Whatever the truth behind the Oleg tales as reported, they suggest that some time before the end of the ninth century in the forest-steppe zone the East

Slav tribes were already organized into large tribal unions. These socio-political organizations were in addition already relatively centralized, as the account suggests that they were conquered in a relatively short time. We have here in a nutshell the essence of the mechanisms creating an early state: military defeat of a neighbouring group which had already become centralized and characterized by an economy which could be exploited, the imposition of a tribute and the promise of protection against rival claimants. Oleg's conquest redirected the Khazar tribute. We also note the implication that the Poliane tribute was lighter for the Severiane than the Khazar one.

That the events of this period were geared towards concentrating economic power in the hands of a small group is suggested by two Byzantine documents incorporated in the *PVL* narrative concerning Oleg. These are treaties, or rather trade agreements, purportedly for the years 907 and 912. The status of the first document is disputed: the attack which reputedly preceded it looks like a fable (and is not reported in Byzantine sources); it would have been drawn up in the reign of Leo I the Wise. The second includes the name of Constantine VII. We have already noted the number of Scandinavian names in the Rus who are named in these documents.[20]

The Uliche mentioned in the fragment of the *PVL* quoted above are noted as the Unlizi, a '*populus multus*', in the *Bavarian Geographer*. Their state of warfare with the Kievan state was maintained in the next few decades: their main stronghold Peresechenia fell to the boyar Svenald about 940 only after a three-year siege. The location of this tribe and their main stronghold has been much debated. Some would place them on the margins of the forest-steppe somewhere to the south of the Poliane on the west bank of the Dniepr and on the Boh. They were tributary to Rus in the 940s and 950s, but later seem to have moved to the Boh and Dniestr next to the Tyvercy (which is where they are said to be in the *PVL* list of the peoples of Rus).

The Tyvercy were a tribe settled somewhere on the Dniestr and Prut (the ancient name for the Dniestr was Tyras). Oleg seems to have defeated them in the 880s, and they are stated by the *PVL* to be allies of the Kievan state in 907. They are said to have taken part in the 944 raid on Constantinople with the Rus. After the middle of the tenth century the Tyvercy and Uliche disappear from history. They may have been amalgamated into the Kievan state, or may have retained independence.

The evidence seems to suggest that the core area of the early Russian state (inner Russia) was in its essentials a zone of radius about 350–400 km around Kiev on the three sides in the forest zone. This had an area of some 328,000 sq km, an area as large as most other early medieval polities. It was this area which was the state proper, within which the cultural influences from the south were more strongly felt. To the east the Viatichi tribe were at first beyond this zone (and we will see that several rulers of the tenth century had troubles keeping control over this tribe). To the west the Dregovichi are not mentioned as being part of the state in this first stage of its development. The area of steppe to the south was for most of the period outside the state, and maintaining the status quo would have depended on alliances with the nomads there.

Oleg died, according to the *PVL*, in 912: 'and there was great grief, and they took him and buried him on the hill, which today is known as Shchekovica. His tomb can be seen there today, called Oleg's tomb. And the years of his reign were thirty and three.' We are not told anything of Oleg's wife: was she Scandinavian or Slav?

The northeastern fringes

An important feature of the early Russian state, and one which was to last into later centuries, was the division into two main parts. To the south was inner Russia, the area around Kiev, but to the north and east were the northern territories of what would later be known as outer Russia (*Zalesskaya zemlya*) beyond the forests to the north of the river crossings of Smolensk and Polotsk by the Okovsky forest and to the east beyond the Desna and Seym. The population of these areas had originally been non-Slav (mainly Finno-Ugrian and Balt), but they had been gradually settled by Slavs from the ninth century.[21] These periph-eral territories retained their tribal divisions longer than the rest of the state, and remained cultural backwoods in which the Russian princes had a complacent 'colonial' attitude in many senses until at least the twelfth century. Much of the land was not governed as such, but mainly served as a catchment area for tribute – for which the establishment of a rigid state ideological structure in these thinly populated and poorly developed territories was not necessary. It was here that the pagan religion survived in rural districts longest. Within this area were how-ever a number of central places (stronghold towns) within which cultural life reflected that of the core state to a greater extent than their hinterlands.

The nature of Kievan influence in the northern lands in the late ninth century is unclear.[22] The area to the north of the area of the early Kievan state was the hinterland of the most important centre in the area, Gorodischche near the shores of Lake Ilmen. Despite the interpolations and comments of the *PVL*, it would seem that the main contribution of the northern tribes from this area in the history of the Kievan state was to take part as vassals or adventurers in the Varangian raids on Constantinople which from time to time passed down the Dniepr. It seems likely that this zone formed a single and separate territorial unit which was only much later joined to the Kievan state.

This northern hinterland was also limited in size. The territories of the Balt-speaking tribes along the east shore of the Baltic Sea (approximately the present areas of the Kaliningrad Oblast of Russia, Lithuania, Latvia) and the Finno-Ugrian tribes (the area of modern Estonia), despite their desirability from the point of view of long-distance trade, were never part of the northern hegemony nor of the later Kievan state.[23] This would seem to be because they were too distant from the core of the territory to be held. In the northern territories, the boundary is about 200 km from Novgorod, and here at the margins we find several major centres (Pskov, Ladoga). This 200-km radius contains the western half of the later Novgorod land and Pskov territory. The territory however trails 300 km into the backwoods to the east towards the Volga trade route, where the centres at Rostov, Suzdal, Jaroslavl and Vladimir were later founded (again on the edges of the territory). To the south were several major early centres such as Smolensk, Vitebsk, Polotsk and Briansk, some of which were founded as towns at a later date. They lie roughly on the junction between the later inner and outer Russia.

The shape and position of the territory of four of the later Slav tribal units of the area (Fig. 66) seem to support the picture that they resulted from some form of expansion from the south. In the centre, just outside the zone of Luka Raikovetska Culture (but in the Kiev Culture zone) were the Radimichi on the upper Dniepr and Soz. To the west were the Dregovichi, looking like a result of expansion along the north side of the Pripet and its left-bank tributaries. To north of both these groups was a huge area occupied by several groups which in a later period were collectively known as the Krivichi (Pskov Krivichi, Smolensk Krivichi etc.), mostly in the valley of the Western Dvina. Further to the east in the valley of the upper Oka were the Viatichi. It is not yet clear from any archaeological evidence whether the fifth unit, the Slovienie around Novgorod (who the *PVL* tells us 'called themselves by their own name', perhaps meaning the common name of all Slavs) were also settled here before the ninth century.[24] The distribution of Islamic silver of the first wave (770–833) suggests that there was relatively extensive contact between the area of the Volyntsevo culture and the areas to the northwest, towards the Baltic Sea between the Dvina and Volkhov, and it was probably partly along these routes that the Slavs themselves were expanding. The formation of these groups is still a process which is not clearly understood. Archaeological evidence suggests that Slav settlement was scattered in the dense northern forests where the soils and agricultural conditions were unfavourable. Present evidence suggests that the settlement structure focused around strongholds (often in lowland and marshy positions). The material culture from the settlements is extremely poor, which is an even greater contrast with the finds of hoards and single finds of Islamic coinage from the area (see Chapter 8). The stronghold at Pskov, on the edge of Krivichi territory, is an especial puzzle. There is a settlement under the stronghold which contains pottery looking suspiciously like Korchak material, and the rich finds assemblage contains pottery apparently of Tushemla type as well as local forms. The stronghold itself was apparently built in the eighth or ninth century. It seems difficult to explain this assemblage in the light of present knowledge.[25]

At the time of the writing of the *PVL* several traditions were current about the origin of these northern tribes and their characteristics before the advent of the Kievan state. The *PVL* makes a distinction between two groups of East Slavs – the Poliane and Derevlane – and the other group, the 'Radimichi and Viatichi, who come from the Lachs'. It goes on to tell the story of two brothers who with their people settle in specific areas. Later on in the same passage, the chronicler paints a not too flattering picture of the neighbours of the Poliane before they were annexed by the Kievan (Polianian) state, and treats the Radimichi, Viatichi and Severiane as one group of similar customs.[26] Although it is unwise to build too much on the writing down in eleventh-century Kiev of what may or may not be older oral traditions (in addition one involving a clear element of local chauvinism), they might be a distorted reflection of real but distant events. Whether or not the Radimici and Viatichi really were resettled Lachs (see below) is uncertain. Sedov suggests that there is linguistic evidence and evidence from building types that the Pskov and Novgorod Slavs came from the upper Vistula region, though this evidence is not particularly convincing.[27]

We have seen that, apart from Slav settlers, Scandinavians – mostly from central Sweden – were initially particularly active in the economic exploitation of the northern forest zone.

The consolidation of the Kievan state

The Kievan state was consolidated under the rule of Oleg's successor Igor 'the Old' (912–45). The change of ruler may not have been a smooth one.[28] We are told that at the beginning of Igor's reign the Derevlane dropped out of the tribal federation. Igor defeated them and imposed a greater tribute.

It was apparently in Igor's reign that the so-called 'retainer culture' was formed, with its eclectic (especially Scandinavian) cultural influences. This is represented by male burials with weapons of Scandinavian and sometimes nomad type, many of them rich chamber burials. These graves would represent a core of foreigners who were settled on the fringes of regions of Slav settlement (such as in the upper Volga valley) or at important nodal points on trade routes (such as Gniozdovo),[29] and these would seem to represent members of the princely retinue (*druzhina*) and their families. The power some of these men amassed is also implied by the large size of some of the mounds that were thrown up over their tombs (for example some of the big mounds at Gniozdovo) and the investment of wealth that the grave goods represent. These burial assemblages (including the Chernigov Grave discussed in Chapter 9), with their mix of different elements and their deliberate rejection of specific ethnic traditions, were being used to express social status, above and outside the former tribal system, and reflect the differences between the new social strata and the old tribal aristocracy. This 'retainer culture' would seem to have been formed some time in the 930s,[30] and would mark the establishment of a group of men from outside existing tribal arrangements to whom could be entrusted the various tasks involved in the controlling of such a wide area.

In this early period, the retinue was to have considerable power. The treaties with the Byzantines include mentions of a number of nobles and princes, each of whom we may presume had his own retinue of warriors. One of these was the boyar with a Scandinavian name Svenald whose retinue rivalled in splendour that of Prince Igor himself. It was Svenald who was to lead the reprisals against the Derevlane and also attacked the Uliche in 946 (and later fulfilled an important role in the reign of Olga and her son).

It seems likely to have been under Igor's rule that the northern territories were added to the area controlled from the Kievan core. Probably in 903[31], in a dynastic marriage, Igor married Olga, a princess from Pskov, chief stronghold of a semi-independant Slav tribe to the north (the Pskov Krivichi). Pskov was an important (late?) ninth-century centre on the Velikaja river at its mouth into a large lake on the boundary between the Slavs and Prussian tribes, and as such it controlled one of the major trade routes into the Baltic. It was also in the 940s or 950s that the dendrochronological dates from Novgorod show that this town was founded to replace the old Gorodishche. It is tempting to see this as a move by Igor or his son to consolidate his power in the north (Constantine Porphyrogenitus in his *DAI* tells us that Nogorod was the stronghold-town of Sviatoslav, son of Igor). The break with the old tradition was not however complete: we see in the *PVL* that there was a story that the founder of Novgorod might have claimed direct descent from Rurik, whom the northern Slav tribes had explicitly asked to rule them. This may have been the context for the creation of the Rurik legend in something like the form in which it has come down to us.

Igor unsuccessfully attacked Byzantium in 941 with a massive army, and in 943 he received tribute from both Byzantium and the Danubian Bulgars. In 944 he again attacked the Pechenegs and then Byzantium (with an army which the *PVL* asserts was of 'Varangians, Rus, Poliane, Slovienie, Krivichi and Tyvercy'). The resultant treaty (apparently preserved in Byzantine court archives) contains the names of the main warriors in his retinue: among them fifty are clearly Scandinavian and only three Slavic. The treaty (somewhat less advantageous for the Rus than Oleg's of 911) was ratified by the Byzantines in the Hagia Sophia cathedral in Constantinople and Igor swore an oath by the idol of Perun on a hill outside Kiev.[32]

In the following year, the *PVL* (s.a. 945) has the story that the retinue of Prince Igor compared their dress and wealth with that of the retinue of Svenald (see above) and they urged Igor to go to the Derevlane to collect additional tribute. In the course of this (as the tale goes) Igor was captured and killed. The death of Igor left his kingdom in the hands of his wife, the Duchess Olga, acting as regent (945–64) for his young son Sviatoslav, a circumstance leading to the formulation of several legends in later historiography about this colourful princess. The dramatic story of Olga's violent and cruel revenge against the Derevlane for the killing of her husband looks like another piece of oral lore containing traditional motifs. Mal, the victorious leader of the Derevlane, had offered to marry the widowed Olga (thus intending to replace the Varangian dynasty with a local one), but Olga first had the envoys killed, then the elite who came to accompany her to the Derevlane capital, and then those who gathered to take part in Igor's funeral. She then engaged on a campaign against all the Derevlane strongholds (in which Svenald played a major role), culminating in the reduction of the tribal centre at Iskorosten and putting the tribal nobility to the sword or enslaving them. Iskorosten was burnt to the ground, and only then were the Derevlane subsumed into the Kievan state and a new, one presumes higher, tribute was established. Although this story probably contains elements of fable, it demonstrates the cruelty with which the achievement of political unity was often accomplished.

In 957 (or perhaps 955) Olga journeyed to Constantinople as guest of the Emperor Constantine VII Porphyrogenitus. The story goes that Constantine wanted to marry her, but she agreed to be baptized (taking the Christian name Helena) with Constantine as her godfather, after which she argued she was not able to marry him as one could not marry one's father. Relationships with Byzantium became rather strained, and by 959 Olga had sent an envoy to Otto I with a request for bishops, Adalbert, a monk from Trier, set out in 961 as a missionary bishop for Russia, but the following year he was driven back to Germany (he later became bishop of the new see of Magdeburg, where he died in 981).

The effective administration of a state with an area considerably greater than any other contemporary polity was clearly a major problem. This was achieved by the settling of trusted men in strongholds scattered across the country, each of them in charge of a territory and owing absolute allegiance to the ruler. It was probably in the reign of Igor (and Olga) that the system of *pogosty* was institutionalized. The term refers in this period to a group of villages arranged around a central place occupied by a state official who was responsible for collection of tribute or taxes (later this term is applied to a unit of political and fiscal administration, especially in the northern territories around Novgorod). The existence of the *polyudye* (the tribute-gathering rounds of the Kievan prince and his entourage) is of particular importance. The concept, typical of the early medieval period, is that of a wandering monarch who went periodically round his realm with his retinue and followers, setting up court at various central places on the way. These central places gathered tribute or taxes and administered his state. The earliest written evidence for the existence of the *polyudye* is from the mid tenth century, and that of 948 was described by Constantine

Porphyrogenitus: it lasted from November to April. The route apparently ran through the fringes of tribal territories, and not through their centres to reduce the travelling time. The route passes through major strongholds on the way from Kiev (Vyshogrod, Liubech, Smolensk and Chernigov). These were strong-hold-towns where the tribute was collected and stored, and then in spring, when the rivers were clear of ice, the goods were floated down to Kiev in boats.

Olga had died in 969 but Sviatoslav had begun his brief lone rule in 964. He was a pagan, rejecting his mother's Christianity, and he spent most of his hectic reign in glorious military exploits. He completed the conquest of the wild country of the Viatichi hitherto under Khazar suzerainty and forced them to pay him tribute (*PVL* s.a. 964 and 966). In the mid 960s he destroyed the Khazar khanate and even fought in the Caucasus. As a result of Sviatoslav's activities, Russia briefly controlled the whole steppe from the Don to the Dniestr. A Byzantine description of the Prince's appearance and dress[33] shows that he had adopted the styles of the nomads in whose territory he had been fighting and been victorious. His rule over the steppes suggests that his armies probably adopted the nomadic methods of fighting from horseback and the appropriate types of weapons. In 967–71 Sviatoslav extended his rule down the Black Sea coast to the Danube mouth. In alliance with Byzantium he attacked the Danubian Bulgars and took the town of Preslaviets (see above). It appears that Sviatoslav had intended to create a joint Russian–Bulgar state, but had failed to subdue fully the Pechenegs on the steppes between the Seret and Dniestr rivers which split his new conquests from the core of the Russian state. He was forced to return to Kiev in the face of renewed attacks by the Pechenegs (968), but in 971 he returned with Svenald and some ten thousand men (or so the *PVL* tells us) to the Danube to attack Byzantium together with the Magyars and Bulgars. After initial successes in 971 he had to agree to a treaty with Byzantium, swearing that 'he who broke the oath would be cursed by Perun and Volos the god of flocks, and he should become as yellow as the gold of his ornaments and destroyed by his own weapons'. On his return to Kiev however in 972 he was besieged over the winter in a stronghold-town on the way (Bialoberezh) and then in 973 he was ambushed by the Dniepr rapids by the Pechenegs (who made a drinking-cup from his skull). His southern conquests did not long survive him.

It is in this period (950s to 970s) that the flow of Islamic silver from Central Asia dwindles. After 980–90 it ceases to flow into the northern forests and Baltic. Possibly this was due to economic difficulties in the caliphate itself, and this may have been a contributory effect to the destruction of the Khazars. In East Slav lands, the missing silver was only slightly compensated for by a slight trickle of Byzantine silver north. There seems to have been a shift in the routes by which the Islamic silver reached the area before this, through the territory of the Volga Bulgars.

It would seem that throughout the later part of the tenth century there was increased Slav settlement in the northern territories. The typical sunken-floored structures have been found at a number of sites, though mainly still in the vicinity of the major trade routes. To judge by the combinations of grave goods and burial rituals at cemeteries such as Gniozdovo and those of the north, there was much intermingling and intermarriage between the three main populations of the area, between Balts, Slavs and Scandinavians. It is very probable that the *lingua franca* used for much of the exchange in this zone was Slavic. By the mid tenth century, Rus on the middle Dniepr were using Slavic terms and members of the ruling family were known by Slav names.

Despite the decrease in foreign bullion flowing into the area, the period of Kievan greatness was reached in the reign of Vladimir the Great. Vladimir, whose reign is glorified in the chronicles and certain of the *byliny* (folk tales), ruled from 980 to 1015. He was the youngest (and illegitimate) son of Sviatoslav by one of Olga's servants and had been installed in Novgorod (*c.* 970) but gained the Kievan throne after the death of his father and the civil war in which Sviatoslav's rightful successor (his son and Vladimir's half-brother Jaropelk) was slain. Like his father, Vladimir spent much time on military exploits. He consolidated and enlarged the state further, resisting breakaway attempts by the Radimichi and Viatichi. He undertook further military expeditions against the Volga Bulgars, and also in Crimea, which for several decades had been the scene of conflict between Rus and Byzantium (in the treaty of 944 Rus had given up Vladimir's claim to Crimea, but in 988 he took Cherson). In 988 Vladimir strengthened the southern frontier of his territory against the Pechenegs, constructing a network of strongholds according to the *PVL*, 'along the Desna, Oster rivers, along the Trubezh and along the Sula and the Stugna. And they chose the best warriors from among the Slovienie, the Krivichi, the Chud and the Viatichi. The warriors from these lands made up the garrisons of the newly built strongholds.' These garrisons were thus made up by resettling men drawn from all over Russia in the manner described in Chapter 7.

The strongholds which Vladimir constructed were of two types. There were smallish forts, similar to those of an earlier period, but also at about this time in the Russian lands appears a new type of stronghold. These were large, sometimes several hundred metres across, and tending to an overall rectangular form. The interior of these strongholds was divided into two or more enclosures, often of a more irregular form. The inner enclosure sometimes contains stone structures, usually one or more churches. Typical examples of the tenth century are Halicz, Vladimir Volynski, Turov, Smolensk, Staraia Riazan, Belgorod, Vyshogrod, Pereiaslavl, Liubech. The ramparts of these 'Riazan-Belgorod type' forts have varied internal construction, often with a timber box-frame at the base (the rampart at Pereiaslavl had unfired clay block construction in the timber framework).[34] A typical feature of tenth- and eleventh-century Russian strongholds is their open-backed construction of the upper wooden elements (Fig. 67). This type of wooden wall appears in Russian wooden forts built in Siberia in early modern times.

The 'dragon walls' (*zmievy valy*) on the middle Dniepr south of Kiev (see p. 146) were enlarged in the tenth century. Radiocarbon dates from one of the inner walls are around the 960s for the timbers used in the construction of one of its segments (perhaps related to Sviatoslav's defences against the Pechenegs). It was probably in the tenth century that a second major alignment, 145 km long, was added to the system 50 km outside the earlier ramparts on the right bank of the Dniepr, running in part along the north bank of the Ros river. This is related to a series of strongholds of the tenth and eleventh centuries arranged in a line and spaced fairly regularly (between 11 and 15 km apart).[35] It has been suggested that this defence system was constructed by Vladimir and Jaroslav the Wise.

One of the results of Vladimir's campaign was a drive west. In 981 Vladimir took Przemyśl, 'and other strongholds' from the 'Lach' people in the Bug valley (see p. 262), establishing a new and lasting boundary of East Slav territory and commanding an important node of trans-European trade routes. The Russian state seems however to have been little interested in this area before Mieszko of Poland took it in the 970s. Vladimir also attacked the Jatviagians (a Prussian tribe) There is also a dense cluster of strongholds in the upper Niemen valley to the northwest of the Dregovichi dated broadly to the tenth and early eleventh centuries: these seem likely to have been a result of the drive of Vladimir to the northwest (perhaps to tap into another trade route to the Baltic).[36] The finds from these sites seem to be a mixture of Dregovichi and Volhynian type, and it seems likely that we see here another example of ethnic mixing by internal colonization. The consolidation of these two new areas of settlement in the eleventh century allowed the Kievan state to extend its frontiers to the west by 50–100 km with the establishment of several new centres such as Vladimir Volynski, Drohiczyn and Sutiejsk.

It is clear that, even by the 980s, the state which Vladimir ruled consisted of a collection of peoples who, while owing allegiance and tribute to him, to some extent retained their tribal identity and customs (indeed we see that, even at the time of the writing of the *PVL*, memory of tribal identities, laws and customs was still intact). In the 980s, in his attempt to unite the Russian tribes, Vladimir attempted to establish a central pagan cult to replace regional traditions. In 980 he had an idol of Perun erected on a hill outside Novgorod (where the temple was excavated in 1951). In Kiev he set up idols on a hill outside the palace court, 'wooden figures of Perun (with a head of silver and his mouth of gold), Khors and Dazhbóg, Stribóg and Simargl, Mokosh, and he and his people made sacrifice to these idols'. Later on Vladimir rethought his policy concerning a state religion, and after consultation with several missionaries of different religions (and rejecting Islam) he made Christianity the state religion, marrying in 988/9

Anna, a Byzantine princess of the Macedonian dynasty. Kiev became a close ally of Byzantium and a major Christian state. The *PVL* tells us of the despair of the people of Kiev when their idol was thrown into the river (we recall here the finding of the Zbrucz idol in the river below the hilltop sanctuary).

The baptism of Vladimir in 988 is usually seen as one of the turning-points in the development of Old Russian culture – Russia was flooded with missionaries, clergymen, craftsmen and artists who transmitted, at first to the elite, Byzantine ideologies and artistic values which were to have an effect on the cultural development of the nation as a whole in subsequent centuries. It was under Vladimir that the state developed several of the external forms and internal structures which would determine the course of its further development. Monasteries were founded which were to become the centres of culture and literacy. It was here the first chronicles were to be compiled. With the help of Byzantine architects, Vladimir built in stone the Tithe church in Kiev (a copy of the Pharos church of St Mary in the imperial palace in Constantinople).

Vladimir rebuilt the walled circuit of Kiev and also founded a number of stronghold-towns in Russia (Belgorod in 991, Pereiaslavl in 992). Despite the existence of these and other sites, Kievan Rus was an essentially rural society with a relatively low level of urbanization. Although functioning as administrative and trading places and centres of production, they took on more and more the role of local marketplaces. It was in the reign of Vladimir that the first coins were struck in silver and gold. They usually bear the image of the prince on his throne (or the head of Christ or saints), and on the reverse the trident mark of the Rurik dynasty.[37] These coins were partly modelled on Byzantine issues, but with inscriptions in Cyrillic. The weight of these coins indicates that these were high-value prestige issues, but they were of ephemeral nature.

After Vladimir's reign, the throne was disputed between his sons, leading again to civil war (1015–19). The Russian state was divided into three territories: Kiev, Novgorod and Polotsk together with Chernigov. Poland took advantage of this strife to invade Russia, getting as far as Kiev (1018). When Jaroslav defeated his brother Sviatopelk he reunited the state, wrote the first version of its laws and strengthened its economy. The walled circuit of the town of Kiev was enlarged once more. The town was by now extensive, covering an area of some 70 ha. It was a centre of trade and production (including jewellery and other metalwork, glasswork, ivory carving and religious paintings), and a major centre of artistic excellence and culture. The complex included the fortified core (*detinets*) with the princely court and several churches.

Jaroslav the Wise (1019–54) was a patron of Byzantine-style culture (the gigantic Sofia *sobor* in Kiev, later to become the principal church of Old Russia, was founded in 1037).[38] The Russian Church was directly subject to the patriarchate of Constantinople and for two centuries nearly all the metropolitans and bishops were Greeks. Jaroslav also cultivated links with western European monarchies, including English and Norwegian princes; he married the daughter of King Olaf of Sweden. Jaroslav minted ephemeral special-purpose coins like those of his father, but probably only in the early part of his reign. After about 1020, minting of Russian coins ceases (and begins again only in the second half of the fourteenth century). For a while foreign coins seem to circulate in Russia, but about the end of the eleventh century coin finds almost cease. Russia seems to have entered a phase of virtually no use of coinage, although in the northern zone hacksilver circulated about as long as in other parts of the Baltic zone.

In Jaroslav's reign we see the final development of the process known as feudal fragmentation, a process which many eastern and central European states underwent in the eleventh and twelfth centuries. The sprawling areas of the early states, linked by some overall coercive force, split into more compact self-reliant units ruled by a strong local leader. New forces had led to the crystallization of power on a more local level: these new units changed from a loose confederation of regions to rival territories with strong separatist tendencies. Possibly the decline of a central monopoly over the luxury markets and the development of local markets may be a contributory factor in this process. The history of these states becomes a confusing kaleidoscope of changing rulers and interregional conflicts leading to fusions and fissions of these statelets under personal rule (a pattern familiar from later medieval history). Despite these changes it seems that an overall feeling of ethnic unity was maintained, and the *PVL* expresses this and reminisces of the advantages of a united state.

In summary we see that the process of formation of the Russian state had at least a triple genesis. The first was the annexation of already centralized adjacent territories by a centralizing power and the establishment of mechanisms for exploiting, controlling and consolidating the new territories. The second stage involved the imposition of a common cultural idiom, at first local but later the acceptance of cultural influences from a neighbouring primary state. The third stage consisted of the growth of a local economy with the changes in the economic infrastructure this involves. The many and different influences which gave rise to the Russian state and culture (East Slav, Byzantine, steppe nomad, Scandinavian, Khazar) made the Kievan state a phenomenon unique in contemporary Europe. Although the early medieval state itself was shattered in the thirteenth and fourteenth centuries by Tatar and Mongol invasions, its culture has left a lasting legacy in modern Europe.

12

State-formation: the West Slavs

The process of formation of states in the territories occupied by the West Slavs was in many ways due to similar phenomena as that of the early Russian state, but in this case the prime movers, were the Carolingian and Ottonian states, which led to them being drawn into the Latin (Catholic) sphere. Here though the influence of more advanced primary states was much more marked. The story of the political organization of the West Slavs is mainly connected with the expansion of Carolingian influence to the east. This expansion was not only necessary for the keeping of peace on the eastern frontier, but was also dictated by economic reasons (it was one of the main means of expanding the economy). After the conquest of the Saxons and Bavaria in the 770s and 780s, Charlemagne organized 'Marks' along the east frontier of his realms. From these regions expansionist and punitive invasions of the territories further east were launched, such as that which destroyed the Avars in 791–803. The necessity of providing a strong buffer between the Franks and the barbarian Slavs (Obodrites), Wilzi, Sorbs) caused the Frankish officials stationed on the border (Counts of the Marks, *Markgrafen*) to become persons of especial importance. They were entrusted with large standing armies, and the prospect of almost continuous military action drew to their service all the restless fighting men who looked to warfare as a means of advancing themselves. Since it was advisable for the safety of the borders to retain there men with experience and vested interests in the areas, this was the occasion of the creation of a series of powerful families which produced the new nobility of these regions.

There are many incidents recorded in Frankish annals which illustrate that the Franks were interested in controlling the neighbouring peoples by means of military action and diplomacy. At Frankfurt in 822, for example, Charlemagne received embassies and presents from all the Slavs on his eastern borders, the 'Obodrites, Sorbs, Wilzi, Bohemians, Moravians and Praedenecenti, and also from the Avars living in Pannonia'. A year later he was judging dynastic quarrels among the Wilzi and reprimanding a leader of the Obodrites at the same palace.

The Carolingian Marks were extended in later years. Henry I (919–36), himself from one of those powerful eastern families, invaded the Polabian territories and created the Meissen Mark. Otto I (936–73) created further Marks in the region east of the Elbe and Saale and restored the southeastern frontier regions damaged by Magyar raids. While German bishoprics in the south competed to control the territories beyond the frontier, in the northeast new bishoprics were erected in the new Marks. German colonization of the eastern fringes of the Empire began in the early tenth century.[1] In Bohemia Otto III (983–1002) continued the policy of trying to effect a domination of the east. Blocked by the apostate and independent Polabian Slavs, he applied diplomacy and other pressures to bring 'Sclavinia' under his influence as part of the renovated West Empire along with Rome, Gaul and Germany (Fig. 71).

The Bohemian (Czech) state

Although in the rest of Slavdom the period after the middle of the ninth century was to see the rise of new states, in the area south of the Carpathians it saw first the collapse of the polities which had formed here earlier. As has been discussed above (p. 111), after a period of several decades of growth but weakened by internal divisions, the Moravian state had been dismembered by 906 by the interference of Arnulf, king of the Eastern Franks, in league with other outside powers (the Magyars).

The origin of the Bohemian state has tended to be overshadowed by the story of Great Moravia.[2] To some extent however the Bohemian state owes its existence to several other factors, and not just its proximity to the Moravian hegemony. Bohemia as a territorial unit has rather good natural borders. It is formed by a river basin around the tributaries of the upper Elbe (including the Moldau), and is surrounded by mountains, on the north the Erzgebirge and Sudeten which divide it from Polabia and Silesia respectively, the Czech (Bohemian–Moravian) uplands which form a less well-defined boundary between Bohemia and the Moravian valley to the east, beyond which to the southeast is the Hungarian plain. On the southwest and west are the mountain ranges of the Bohemian forest (Böhmerwald, Bayerischer Wald and Oberpfälzer Wald), beyond which were Bavaria and East Frankia.[3] The whole area of the fertile Bohemian basin was by the early ninth century densely occupied by several large tribes. There were the Lučane and Lemuzi in the northwest, in the middle there were the Czechs in the area where Prague was to be founded on the Moldau, in the northeast were a group called the Chorvati (Croats) on the Dubrava (this is probably the group mentioned as the 'White Croats' in the *DAI*), and the Pšovians had a territory on the Elbe around modern Melnik between the Czechs and Chorvati. To the south on the upper Moldau basin were the Dulebi (Doudlebi). Other tribes in the area included the Litomierzycy, Zličanie and Siedličanie.

Because this was a fertile and well-defined geographical region, it is not surprising that there were centralizing tendencies visible. In the former and now somewhat obsolete archaeological terminology for Bohemia, the 'Old Hillfort period' (originally dated 650–800) was envisaged as succeeded by the 'Middle

Hillfort period' (dated 800–950), since the first half of the ninth century sees a dramatic increase in the number of hillforts being built (such as those at Budeč, Levý Hradec, Stará Kouřim, Pohansko and Dolanski). These were large tribal strongholds, massive multi-enclosure earthworks, ranging in size from about 20 to 40 ha.[4]

The wealth of the area also prompted bids to take it over by the more powerful states. Throughout most of the ninth century, the tribes of Bohemia had as their neighbour the strong state of Moravia. Another threat came from the west, from the eastern parts of the Carolingian and German empires. Pushes to the east are evidenced in the *Royal Frankish Annals* under the year 805 when Karl, Charlemagne's son (d. 811), led an expedition into the area and 'ravaged the land from one end to the other and killed their chief Lecho'. In 806 in another invasion 'troops from Bavaria, Alemannia and Burgundy were sent into the country of Bohemia . . . after laying waste much of the land, the army returned without serious losses'. With the strengthening of the position of Louis the German after the Treaty of Verdun (843), the Bohemians understood that they were threatened by external circumstances. As a reaction (and perhaps under the influence of Sviatopluk of Moravia), fourteen nobles and local rulers accepted Christianity from east German bishops at Regensburg in 845, though they abandoned the faith a year later when they found that it offered them no protection against German aggression. Throughout the 840s and 850s there was a series of German raids on Bohemia and Moravia (but this was also a period which saw the rise of Moravian power).

The unification of the tribes of the Moldau basin was achieved probably under the patronage of Sviatopluk of the Moravians in the second half of the ninth century by Bořivoj I (d. about 889/90) of the strongest tribal dynasty of the period, the Přemyslid rulers of the Czech tribal group. The Přemyslids were able by conquest to extend their rule over the territories of neighbouring weaker tribes. The core of Přemyslid territory was a zone of fertile farmlands about 60 km in diameter in the confluence of the Moldau, Elbe, Ohře, Berounka and Sázava rivers; from this centre was to begin the territorial expansion leading to the formation of the Czech state under this dynasty.[5] The central position of this territory at a major crossroads of trans-European trade routes and the productivity of the land itself must have been important factors in this increasing power. Bořivoj married Ludmila, a princess of the Polabian Sorbs (later a martyr and saint): he and his wife were baptized by Methodius in about 884 at the Moravian court. They took a priest back home and built a rotunda (St Clement's) at their principal seat at Levý Hradec. The acceptance of Christianity by the ruling family prompted a pagan revolt soon afterwards, and Bořivoj fled to Moravia. The revolt was put down with Moravian help (leading to an increase in Moravian influence in the area, for example as at the stronghold at Stará Kouřim). On his return to Bohemia, Bořivoj moved his capital from Levý

Hradec to Prague (where he built the church of St Mary on the promontory where Prague castle now stands above the loop in the Moldau). This phase of Bohemian history is evidenced by many items of Moravian provenence found in the settlements and cemeteries of this period. Under Moravian hegemony, Bořivoj was able to continue the uniting of the tribes in the Bohemian basin. The death of Sviatopluk in 894 and subsequent internal strife allowed Bohemia to shake off the Moravian yoke, but in 895 all the Bohemian princes appeared in Regensburg to renew their alliance with East Frankia. One result of this was that Prague became part of the Regensburg diocese (Bohemia had formerly belonged to Passau).

In the period of the Magyar invasions, Bohemia was relatively safe behind a wall of mountains. The destruction of the Moravian state however at the beginning of the tenth century and the consequent power vacuum led to new opportunities. Under Spytihněv (895–915), son of Bořivoj, the Czech state was internally consolidated.[6] It was Spytihněv who built the first defences around Prague castle, and it was he who commanded the construction of an ingenious system of strongholds allowing complete control over the whole area of Přemyslid territory. These strongholds (including Mělnik, Stará Boleslav, Libušín, Tetín, Lštení) built in the first half of the tenth century together with pre-existing forts at Budeč and Levý Hradec formed a circle around Prague at a radius of about 26–34 km, forming what historians call 'stronghold organization' which was the basic form of socio-political organization of early states not only in Bohemia but also throughout western Slavdom. Prague became the centre of the religious life of the state, the bishop of Regensburg was represented by an arch-presbyter based in Prague, and most of the priests were Bavarian (though Slav priests who had fled from Moravia practising the Slav rite were also tolerated).

In the tenth century, Bohemia was (alongside Bavaria and Saxony) one of the most highly developed areas of central Europe, but it was an area which was particularly strongly influenced by Bavaria. This is visible in the cultural and political development of the new state. The primacy of the Přemyslids was acknowledged by the other Bohemian chiefs, but outside the relatively compact Přemyslid realms other areas of Bohemia were still pagan and had a less well organized socio-political system.

After the death of Spytihněv and the short rule of his brother Vratislav (915–21), there was conflict in the Přemyslid family reflecting the two factions, pagan and Christian. The drama was to be played out in 921 between two powerful women: the pagan Drahomir (from the Polabian Veleti people), wife of the dead Vratislav, and Ludmila, his mother. Ludmila was guardian of Vratislav's son Vaclav. Legend asserts that Drahomir, jealous of her influence, had Ludmila murdered by suffocation (later legends made a martyr of her). In the end however the Christian party succeeded and Vaclav became acknowledged leader (921–35).

It was Vaclav I (Wenceslas) who was to begin the next stage in the uniting of the tribes living in the Czech basin. He also tried unsuccessfully to make Bohemia independent of German rule under Henry I, but this led only to increased pressure (the Germans invaded Bohemia in 922 and in 929 and took the capital Prague). The inability of Vaclav to break with the Christianity based on the Bavarian mission increased opposition against his rule as the Old Slav rite went into disuse. The opposition instigated by Drahomir was led by his younger brother Boleslav I, who was ruler of the region of the Pšovian tribal territory. In 935 Boleslav usurped the throne after having his brother murdered by being hacked to pieces. (Wenceslas was canonized in the eleventh century and, as a result of his strengthening the Přemyslid dynasty, was the main patron of Bohemia and subject of several legends, of which the most famous concerns St Vaclav and Ludmila.)

Boleslav I (935–72) considerably strengthened and extended the early Czech state after taking it over from his brother. Despite his opposition to Bavarian overlordship, he was forced in 950 to submit as tributary to Germany under Otto I, and subsequently (955) came to the aid of the Germans in their struggles with the Polabians (one element in the power politics of the area was German support for the Slavnik family, rival to the Přemyslids). It seems that at some time prior to this (perhaps in 936) Boleslav had sent his armies into north Moravia and taken Olomouc, and thence through the Moravian Gate north of the Carpathians, into Małopolska where he took Cracow and then the territories of the Lędziane, including the Przemyśl and Czerwień strongholds. From here he seems to have exerted his influence far to the east (according to the *Prague document* 'as far as the Styr'). Many of the tenth-century strongholds of southern Poland (the so-called Great Strongholds, *wielkie grody*, of southeastern Poland and some in Silesia) are of similar form to those being built in Bohemian territory at this date.[7] In 965 Boleslav was named by Ibrahim ibn Yaqub 'king of Prague, Bohemia and Cracow'. Boleslav also sent his armies into Silesia, and here Wrocław was founded (its name suggesting it was the town of a Czech leader Vratislav): the dendrochronological dates from its rampart suggest that this took place in the 940s–60s. When the Prague diocese was founded in 973 (see below) it seems to have contained an extensive tract of land north of the Carpathians which would seem to be the result of these conquests: according to the *Prague document* setting out its boundaries these lands stretched from the Milzi tribe in the west to the regions of the upper Bug in the east. In taking these lands, Boleslav's aim seems not only to have been conquest (gaining land, booty, tribute and slaves) but also the ability to control the important trade routes leading through these areas. These lands were to remain in Czech hands until the area of Silesia and Małopolska were annexed by Poland in 988–90.

The marketplace of Prague, the Bohemian capital, was visited by many foreign merchants, and produce of many countries was on sale there, including many slaves. In about 965 the Jewish traveller Ibrahim ibn Yaqub gives a description of Bohemia which is worth quoting in full:

Bohemia: this is the land of King Boyslavits, the distance from the city of Prague to that of Cracow is three weeks' journey and its frontier is lengthwise with that of the Turks [Magyars are meant]. The city of Prague is built of stone and chalk and is the richest in trade of all these lands. The Russians and the Slavs bring goods there from Cracow; Muslims, Jews and Turks from the lands of the Turks also bring goods and market weights [coins]; and they carry away slaves, tin, and various kinds of fur. Their country is the best of all those of the northern peoples and the richest in provender. For one small coin, enough flour is sold there to suffice a man for a month, and for the same sum enough barley to fodder a riding animal for forty nights; ten hens are sold there for one penny. In the city of Prague they make saddles, bridles and the flimsy leather bucklers that are used in those parts, and in the land of Bohemia they make light fine kerchiefs like nets, embroidered with crescents which are of no use for anything. Their price there at all times is ten kerchiefs for a penny. With these they trade and deal with one another and they possess jars of them. They regard them as money and the most costly things are bought with them, wheat slaves, horses, gold, silver and all things. It is remarkable that the people of Bohemia are dark and black-haired, blonds are rare among them.

In 963 and 965 Boleslav allied himself with the rising power of Mieszko I, the prince of the Polane of Wielkopolska, and one effect of this was that he gave his daughter Dobrava in marriage to the Polish prince, on the condition that the Polane would accept Christianity.

Bohemian territorial expansion continued after Boleslav's death under his son Boleslav II (972–99). In his reign the Prague diocese was founded, including extensive tracts of land to the north of the Carpathians. In 980 the alliance between Poland and Bohemia was broken, followed by the Polish annexation of Silesia along the whole length of the middle and upper Oder in 988–90. Possibly at the same time the Poles took Małopolska – the region of Cracow – which was perhaps taken and ruled by Mieszko's son Bolesław I Chrobry ('the Brave').

The Bohemian state, like many others in this period in this part of the world, was torn apart by internal struggles between the nobles (who in this case seem to have come from the original tribal nobility). Despite their strength, the Přemyslids had a rival in the Bohemian basin; 60 km to the east of Prague is the stronghold of Libice, which in the second half of the tenth century was the seat of the Slavnikovice family controlling, presumably under the Přemyslid hegemony, a large part of the eastern part of the area. This rivalry was begun in the reign of Boleslav I by Slavnik (d. 981) and continued by his sons. One of these, Wojciech, pupil of Adalbert of Magdeburg mentioned above (pp. 217 and 244), became the second bishop of Prague in 992 when he took the name Adalbert.[8] In 995, taking advantage of Adalbert being in Rome with his brother Gaudenty, the Přemyslid Prince Boleslav II took Libice and killed nearly all the remaining members of the Slavnikovice family. Soon after this Adalbert, who was unpopular because of his attempts to reform the clergy of his diocese, left Prague and went first to preach in Hungary. In 996 he was invited to Poland by Bolesław Chrobry, whence he set out to evangelize the Prussians, at whose hands he met a martyr's death in 997 (see below).

It was in the tenth and eleventh centuries that many of the old tribal centres in Bohemia were destroyed and replaced by others nearby (paired strongholds).[9] The interpretation of this would seem to be that the old tribal nobility was destroyed and their seats slighted and they were replaced in the settlement hierarchy by new sites which served as the central places in the new state organization (Fig. 68). A good example is Stará Kouřim, east of Prague: the original tribal centre of the ninth and tenth centuries was replaced by a second stronghold (St Jiří) in the eleventh century, and then in the thirteenth century a town was founded nearby.

The area of Moravia in the east remained independent of Bohemian rule for a while. In the 940s al-Mas'udi mentioned a separate people, the *Marabin* (Moravians) under the rule of a leader called Ratbir. With the organization of the Church in 973 under Boleslav II there seems to have been a separate Moravian diocese, centred on Olomouc – which is also mentioned as a separate territory in the document known as *Dagome Iudex* of *c*. 990 (see below).

The rising power of Poland in the late tenth and early eleventh century and political struggles within Bohemia at the end of the reign of Boleslav III (999–1003) allowed Bolesław I the Brave of Poland to take large territories to the south of the Carpathians. He took Moravia (ostensibly in order to gain free access to the route to Rome), and part of today's Slovakia, but found it largely empty. The presence of pottery very similar to that in Wielkopolska and the use of a type of rampart construction also characteristic of that area suggests that he had to bring his own artisans with him. In 1003–4 Bolesław also took much of Bohemia, replacing his deposed cousin Boleslav III on the throne, before deposing him himself, blinding and imprisoning him. After Polish rule over Bohemia collapsed, there were two more weak rulers (Jaromir and Oldrich), and Moravia was reclaimed from Poland only in 1019. After the murder of Jaromir, Bohemia was temporarily reunited under Prince Břetyslav I (1034–55) and in the first year of his reign after the death of Mieszko II he attacked Poland and carried off much loot (including the body of St Wojciech/Adalbert). After his death however under his sons the country split into feudal fragments which were reunited by the Přemyslids only in the thirteenth century.

Polabia and Pomerania

The Polabian Slavs occupying the flat lands of the North European Plain around the middle Elbe and its tributaries between the Sudeten mountains and the Baltic coast seem to have taken a surprisingly long time to break out of the clan-tribe type of system to form anything approaching a state, particularly when one considers their proximity to the Carolingians and Ottonians.[10] The settlement pattern of the area shows very clearly the distribution of tribes known from the written sources: there is especially dense settlement in the north or the region nearer the Baltic coast, south of which is a less densely settled area. In the valley of the Havel is the territory of the Stodoranie (Havelanie) around their main centre at Brenna. Further up the Spree were the Sprevanen, the Veleti or Lutize (with the neighbouring group Lebuser near Lebus). In the upper Spree were the Milzi, occupying a dense zone around their centre at Budziszyn surrounded by a clear settlement vacuum. In the west of the region, south of the Elbe in the valleys of the Saale, Weisse Elster and Mulde, is the very dense settlement of the Sorbs (Fig. 32). All of these tribes are mentioned in the *Bavarian Geographer* and they played a key role in the processes of state formation.

Some scholars have suggested that the tribes of the upper Elbe may have been influenced by Moravia in the 880s, but it seems more likely that at a later date the Bohemians interacted in some way with the Sorbs and Milzi.[11] The main influence in the area came, however, from the west, from the Carolingian and Ottonian realms. Apart from the evidence of this in the written sources (mainly of the ninth century onwards – of which of course the compilation of the *Bavarian Geographer* would be a prime example), there is some material evidence of the effects of contacts with the Germans. While trade goods seem rare, we have seen that some ceramic styles were copied. If one looks at the evidence supplied by the distribution of strongholds, one may observe areas near the frontier where there are several settlement enclaves characterized by denser settlement and larger strongholds.[12] Possibly these were built by leaders who had considerably more power than their neighbours to the east, and a possible source of this power (if it was not loot) could be diplomatic payments to friendly rulers by the Germans.

Pomerania, the strip of land along the south coast of the Baltic, is a region which has often been overlooked in general histories of the Slavs, primarily because authors have been concerned to show the area as being an integral part of the history of the Polish or Polabian Slavs, and yet this obscures the fact that for a large part of the early medieval period they had a separate development. To the south of the coast on the eastern (now Polish) part the coast is backed by high morrainic hills of clay to the south of which is the swampy Notec valley which cuts the area off from the centre of the later state in Wielkopolska. In the west (former DDR) the area is cut off from the central area of Polabia by dense forest in which there were few settlements.[13] The Pomeranian coast was there-fore isolated from the territories to the south, and there was much less difference between these two parts of Pomerania in the early medieval period than the later and the present political situation would suggest.

We have seen that in the ninth century Pomerania was already becoming politically organized and benefiting from long-distance trade. This is especially hinted at by the emporia which were being established here by the final decades of the ninth century: Reric, Menzlin, Ralswiek on Rugia, Szczecin and Wolin in the Oder mouth, Bardy in the Parsęta valley near Kołobrzeg. These were engaged in long-distance exchange with German, Scandinavian, Balt and north-ern Russian centres around the Baltic, were regularly and densely built up and had a distinctly 'proto-urban' character. The prosperity of this area in the later ninth and tenth century is demonstrated by a concentration of silver hoards in the area (Chapter 8), and the political consolidation which allowed these northern Polabian tribes to challenge even the German Empire.

The northwestern fringes of Polabia (the hinterland of Hamburg) were conquered by Charlemagne as a result of his Saxon wars of 772–804: here he constructed the so-called *limes Saxoniae* – a line running through uninhabited no-man's land between the Saxons settled north of the lower Elbe and the Slavs. The *limes* was established a few kilometres east of Hamburg. Somewhere within this line was the emporium at Reric which was attacked by Godfred the king of Denmark in 808. The establishment of a Frankish port on the south coast of the Baltic to tap into the flow of trade (especially Islamic silver?) was probably one of the aims of the Carolingian campaigns here. Beyond this frontier were the Obodrites, a union of several groups (Vagrovie, Polabiane, Gliniane and Varniovie), who were allied with Charlemagne for most of his reign. Because of Carolingian support, a strong political organization came to exist in the territory of the Obodrites.

Despite conflicts with the Germans, many of which are mentioned in the *Frankish Annals*, tribes such as the Obodrites continued to flourish in the ninth and tenth centuries. The beginning of the tenth century saw the inception of what has been christened the *Drang nach Osten* ('Drive to the east') which – with the consequent clash of cultures – would dominate the history of northeast Germany until the end of the twelfth century. The most notable feature of the process in Polabia was its violence (unlike the history of the German expansion into Austria, Bohemia and Hungary). Each bloody military action left its trail of atrocities and the subsequent revenge raids. Whole tribes were nearly exterminated. The process began in 928 when Henry I of the Saxon dynasty annexed the Obodrite lands. The rest of the area between the Elbe and Saale and the Oder was conquered in a push to the east begun in 929 and continued by Otto I after 948. As a result of these campaigns, the frontiers of the German Empire were relatively rapidly pushed 120–200 km to the east, and German civil and ecclesiastical administration was established east of the Saale and Elbe. The eastern frontier of the new Mark was established on the middle and lower Oder, and then ran southwards between the Neisse and Bobr rivers near the present Polish frontier. The territorial organization (*burgward*) of the new Marks (Meissen in the south, Lusatian in the east, and Merseberg and Żytyce in the west) was based on the territories of the previously existing tribal stronghold system. The conquest was accompanied by an attempt to convert the Slavs between the Elbe–Saale and Oder to Christianity compulsorily. New bishoprics were founded to serve these new lands, at Havelburg and Brenna (Brandenburg), centres of the Brzezane and Stodorane, in 948, at Magdeburg, Oldenburg, Merseburg, Zeitz near the line of the old frontier and Meissen (the centre of the Milzi tribal union) in 968. A new system of strongholds was constructed in the tenth century in the southern part of the newly conquered territory, especially along the Elster river. Germans settled in and around these strongholds, but there was little effective colonization of outlying areas.

There was an uprising of the Obodrites in 955 when their Prince Nakon together with his brother Stojgniev fought and lost a battle with Otto I at Reknice (despite this he is mentioned in 965 by Ibrahim ibn Yaqub as having equal importance as the Polish Mieszko I and Boleslav I of Bohemia).The next uprising of the Polabian Slavs in the reign of the weak Otto II in 982–3 again mainly affected the tribes in the north, in the hinterland of the Baltic coast. This time the Germans suffered a decisive reversal of fortunes, and the tribes of the northeast of the Polabian region formed a tribal confederation called the Lutize (a name which appears towards the end of the tenth century for a tribal union formerly known as the Veleti). This rose up against German rule, destroyed a number of strongholds and drove the German ruling elite out of its territory. There is no doubt from the written sources that the main instigators of this uprising were the pagan priesthood (the main centre was the cult-centre at Radgoszcz somewhere in the territory of the Redari). The rebellion was joined in 990 by the Obodrites in an uprising also instigated by a pagan revival. The diocese of Oldenburg and the Christian mission among the Obodrites was terminated and the German ruling elite withdrew from the territory, which – despite attempts by Conrad II (1024–39) to reconquer it – developed into an independent Slav state on the edge of the Empire. The Lutize and Obodrites were joined by the Stodorane and the Brzezan tribes, centred on Brenna and Havelburg respectively, who also gained independence.[14]

The pagan uprising gave rise to political organizations which retained (though probably in somewhat modified form) the old pagan tribal structures and customs, a very interesting survival into a period where there is an abundance of written sources.

The coastal towns of western Pomerania retained their tribal character until the twelfth and thirteenth centuries, when written sources such as Otto of Bamberg allow us to see some of the institutions. They were inhabited by members of the elite, supported by the priesthood, and they engaged in trade and piracy. There were also merchants, free craftsmen, fishermen (who also had smallholdings in the area and fought when needed). These centres also attracted foreigners, such as the Scandinavian settlers in Wolin (Jomsborg) who are mentioned in the Viking sagas.

The tribes south of the watershed between the Havel and middle Elbe (Meissen Mark and part of Lusatian Mark) had been unable to break out of the Ottonian Empire. The Germans however seemed unable to drive further north and west in the tenth century and concentrated mainly on strengthening their hold in the south. South of the frontier the Sorbs in the German Empire were absorbed into the social and political system of that political organism. Unfortunately until recently the political atmosphere in the former DDR did not encourage the close study of the processes of the transformation of Slav tribes into part of the German nation.

To the northeast in the third quarter of the tenth century, the Polish state was trying to gain control of Pomerania in order to take part in long-distance trade networks through the Baltic. Mieszko I invaded the areas of Pomerania around the mouth of the Oder and to the east in the late 960s, attacking the Veluanzane (Wolinians) and the Veleti, who were helping them resist Polish pressure. Since the territory of the Veleti had been annexed by the Germans in the period 929–39, this expansion required the tacit assent of the German emperor. In 972 however the German Margrave Hodon invaded territory east of the frontiers established by Henry I, but was beaten back at the battle of Cedynia on the Oder. Further east, the Polane were also attempting to take control of the area around the Vistula mouth, and it would seem that the port of Gdańsk was founded about this time (though it is not clear whether in the period of Pomeranian independence or as a result of the conquest).[15]

The Polish ruler Bolesław I the Brave took advantage of the crisis of the 980s and invaded the newly independent territories of the Lutize and Lubus land. This Polish expansion towards the west took the frontier between Polish territory and the German Empire some 30 km west of the lower Oder (almost to modern Berlin). In 1002 however Wolin and Szczecin Pomerania broke away from the Polish state, followed in 1038 by the eastern regions around Gdańsk.[16]

In the 1040s Prince Gotschalk of the Obodrites (1010–66), who was allied to the Saxons and Danes, was able to unite the territory and attempt to convert his people to Christianity and introduce bishops at Stargard, Menzlin and Raciborz. He was killed in a pagan reaction in 1066. In the course of these events Christian writers had good cause to take notice of the collapse and renewal of the Polabian sanctuaries. There is evidence to suggest that, in the period of independence, the reorganization and strengthening of the Polabian local cults (utilizing patterns derived from the Christian Church) had played an important part in the establishment of a strong tribal power structure in opposition to the Ottonians.

The end of the Lutize union came with the weakening effects of internal struggles in the 1050s, followed by a German invasion in 1068–9, when the temple at Radgoszcz was looted. Nevertheless it seems that even after German conquest, these people retained a certain amount of independence until the twelfth century. The territory around Brenna and Havelburg was retaken only in the mid twelfth century by the Germans after years of fighting. Only then did German colonization of these territories begin.

Poland

The development of the early state of Poland in the valleys of the Oder and Vistula in the centre of the North European Plain between the Carpathian mountains and Baltic coast represents a classic example of the formation of an early state.[17] The historical and archaeological evidence combine to create a picture of the expansion of an original core tribe (the Polane of Wielkopolska). The soils of the area are fertile and summer climate is good; possibly the inhabitants of the area were able to produce and mobilize a surplus. By the period of state-formation, palaeodemographic evidence seems to show that there had been a threefold population increase in four centuries, and population growth was still on the increase (discussed in Chapter 4). The Polane established long-distance trade links with Pomerania, and as a result, in the 940s or thereabouts, organizational changes were taking place in Wielkopolska: the hoards show that relatively large quantities of silver were flowing south from the Baltic coast. At about the same time a few other northern products start to move into the area and adjacent regions (antler combs, occasional amber beads).

At this time, it seems that for one reason or another the Wielkopolskan Polane had begun to form themselves into what seems to be a polity or polities with some characteristics of a chiefdom. In the settlement pattern this is clearly visible in the reorganization of the system of strongholds. Before the mid tenth century there were relatively few strongholds in this area, but now a dense network of new sites was constructed. These were both small well-defended sites and major central places. The dating of the beginning of this phase is fixed by the increased wealth now becoming available in the form of hoarded silver from Pomerania, and it is very tempting to connect this with the new dendrochronological dates (940) from the rampart at Gniezno and other strongholds of the area.[18]

About 960 Prince Mieszko of the Piast dynasty of the Polane began his reign. Mieszko, clearly a capable warrior and a skilful politician, was very active in expanding his realms. This is evident from the written sources, but also can be detected in the archaeological record, which show the process of territorial aggrandizement and institutionalization of power leading to the formation of a state. This was centred at first on the old tribal centres of Gniezno and Poznań in Wielkopolska. In many areas of Poland, former tribal centres seem to have been destroyed and replaced by new ones (a further example of 'paired strongholds'). It seems that the rise of the Piast state in the 960s was a notable factor on the international scene for several adjacent rulers. We have seen that Boleslav I of Bohemia soon made him his ally, and Ibrahim ibn Yaqub during his stay in Prague learnt much about this new 'king of the north'. He writes: 'As for the country of Mesko it is one of the most extensive of their [Slav] countries. It is plentiful in provisions, meat, honey, and fish [?]. To the king belong all tributes collected in his country. The taxes Mesko collects in metal coin [? text unclear here][19] are used to pay the allowances of his warriors.' The rest of this passage, concerning the number and inner organization of Mieszko's retinue (quoted above in Chapter 6), suggests that someone in Prague with whom Ibrahim conversed was indeed very interested in the rising might of this prince: this was something which did not escape the attention of the German emperor Otto I either.

In 960–7 Mieszko was fighting the Pomeranians and Wolinians for control of Pomerania, and also Lubus land. He was thus concerned to create a strong western border on the central and lower Oder. This brought him into conflict with the Veleti and Woliniane (and, because of their links with a German Count Wichmann, brought him to the attention of the Ottonian elite). The alliance with the southern neighbour, Boleslav of Bohemia, and a dynastic marriage were to secure the southern border during these struggles. Mieszko was accompanied by the Bohemian army on his expedition against the Woliniane, which was crowned with success in 967. It seems that peace was made with the German emperor, whose Northern Mark bordered on the lands of the Woliniane. This was achieved by Mieszko agreeing to pay tribute for the land 'between the Oder mouth and the Warta river'. As a result of the alliance with Bohemia, Mieszko had been baptized: he probably saw the Church as a political tool for linking his state with civilized European states, and giving support for centralizing tendencies, but also perhaps as a way of securing himself from possible future German intervention under the guise of missionary activity. A (missionary) bishopric was established in Poznań (968).

Comparatively little attention seems to have been paid by Mieszko to the question of the eastern frontier; the exact extent of Mieszko's state to the east (that is in Mazovia and Małopolska) is not known. It seems that a large area of Małopolska was initially outside the state. In the 960s it seems that these areas were relatively sparsely inhabited forest zones with a poorly developed economy. It is possible however that in the 970s there was some expansion into these areas with the founding in Małopolska of sites such as Sandomierz, Przemyśl and the Czerwień strongholds, which were constructed as a buffer zone. In Mazovia at the same time there seems to have been expansion up the Narew and Biebrz rivers. The Kievan state under Sviatoslav and Vladimir I was more interested at this time in expanding its influence to the south (Bulgaria and Byzantium) than in what was happening beyond the forests and mountains to the north and west. When however the new ruler Vladimir noticed the Polish expansion, he seems to have taken a fresh interest in the area and started to expand into the same areas (see p. 247). Despite this, as we have seen, there was still a broad zone of no-man's land between the two states.

Wars with Germany after about 972 (about which we know little) resulted from a change of the German emperor's eastern policies, but ended in the alliance with the Empire of 979. When the Polabian revolt broke out after 983 and German control of these areas collapsed, Mieszko expanded into the areas of the former Marks, and, in alliance with the Saxons, he attacked the Obodrites and Lutize, extending his lands further to the west. Dobrava, after having borne a son (Bolesław, named after her Czech father) and a daughter, Świętosława, died about 979. Soon afterwards, in 980 Mieszko married Ode, the daughter of Dietrich the margrave of the Northern Mark, thus straining Polish–Bohemian relations. By his second wife Mieszko had other children (which would have given rise to dynastic conflict had Bolesław I of Poland not dealt swiftly with them on his father's death).[20]

Mieszko utilized the new situation after the Polabian revolt to advantage to add (988–90) Silesia and perhaps (about 990) Małopolska to his kingdom to try to bring within his rule territory based on the natural borders of the mountains to the south but also to gain control over the routes running along the Oder valley and through the Moravian Gate (thus controlling the route from western Europe, through Prague and Cracow, to Kiev and Byzantium). This expansion however brought him into conflict with his former allies in Bohemia.

In order to safeguard his conquests at the end of his life about 990, Mieszko employed diplomacy. In a document which is known as *Dagome Iudex* (after the first two words of a twelfth-century copy in the Vatican archives) he entrusted his lands to the Pope. The document is important for the definition of the boundaries of his realm (called *Schi-gnesne*, presumably a reference to the Polan capital at Gniezno). These were defined as 'beginning from the side along the sea, then the frontier of Prussia to the place which is called Rus, and the Russian frontier as far as Cracow, and from Cracow to the Oder straight to the place called Alemure, and from there to the lands of Milsko, and from the frontiers of Milsko along the Oder to the town of Schinesche'. There are many mysterious features about this document which cannot be fully discussed here. It seems though that it delimits boundaries which are relatively close to those of today's state. In the 990s therefore Mieszko's realms reached the sea, and bordered on the lands of the Baltic Prussians in the northeast, and the Rus state in the east. They reached the frontiers of the territory of Cracow (and thus Małopolska was not then part of his state) and Olomouc in Moravia and the Milzi to the southwest. The final place name mentioned is interpreted as Szczecin, though whether the town was part of Mieszko's realm or excluded is not known.

Mieszko died in 992 leaving the kingdom to his one son from his second marriage, who was soon expelled by his half-brother Bolesław the Brave, son of Dobrava, who strengthened royal control over the area. Bolesław began his reign (992–1025) by uniting Cracow (later to be the medieval capital) to Poland; he strengthened holdings in the north and south (Pomerania and Silesia) and attempted to expand west and east. It also seems that in his reign the eastern frontier in Mazovia and Małopolska was stabilized. He also attempted to gain some control over the neighbouring (non-Slav) tribes to the north. The former bishop of Prague, Wojciech/Adalbert – who had been driven out of Bohemia by interdynastic fighting – was sent as a missionary to the Prussians, where he met a martyr's death. Bolesław bought the body back and placed it in a church in the princely capital at Gniezno. Wojciech/Adalbert was canonized in 999.

In the year 1000 Bolesław hosted a summit meeting at Gniezno with the young German Emperor Otto III, who had come with a papal legate to visit the tomb of St Wojciech. Bolesław went out of his way to impress Otto by the wealth of his kingdom, an aim which he seems to have achieved. At the summit, several new bishoprics – Gniezno (now established as the Polish archdiocese), Cracow, Wrocław and Kołobrzeg – were established in order to strengthen ecclesiastical organization in the kingdom, which was henceforth to be independent of that of the German Empire. It would seem that at the same time Otto had 'crowned' Bolesław with his own diadem, and called him 'brother and partner of the empire' and 'friend and ally of the Roman people'. The meaning of these gestures has been debated. Thietmar notes drily: 'may God forgive the Emperor, that making him a tributary, he raised him so high'. German historiography has tended to emphasize the first aspect, Poland as tributary, while Polish historiography has preferred to see these events as marking a true coronation and recognition of Poland's equal status with respect to the Empire. Whatever Otto's intentions, as a sign of his authority[21] Bolesław was awarded a replica of the 'Holy Lance', part of the Imperial Regalia (the original containing a fragment of nail from the Holy Cross).[22] In return, Bolesław gave the Emperor the arm of St Wojciech, golden vessels, and three hundred of his armed men. Otto was clearly anxious to use this new alliance as the instrument of German control over wide areas of Slav territory. With (at first) the support of the German emperor, Bolesław extended the frontiers of Poland, to the west (in 1002 Lusatia, Lubus, Milze) at the expense of the Polabian Slavs, but then later turning his attention to the south (into Moravia with an attack on Prague in 1003).[23] A few years later he further expanded to the east, into southern Podlasia and

Volynia – together with an attack on Kiev at a moment of weakness of the Russian state in 1018 after Vladimir's death and a feud between his sons. The culmination of these ambitions was the coronation of Bolesław in 1025, this time with a crown sent by the Pope. The recognition of the Polish state by Otto did not however prevent increasing conflict with the German Empire in the reign of Henry II (1002–24) and frequent invasions from the west (creating a permanent gulf between east and west in this area and ultimately leading to the loss of parts of the western territories, especially Silesia and western Pomerania, which became part of Poland again only in 1945).

Under Mieszko and Bolesław the state underwent a number of important socio-economic transitions which are typical of the changes taking place in other areas of Slavdom at the state-formation stage. The most striking feature was the dynamic growth of the new social system and similar progress in the diversification of material culture. In the archaeological evidence we can observe at this period indications of marked social stratification, and a further demographic increase (it is estimated that about 1.25 million people inhabited late tenth-century Poland, in an area of 250,000 sq km). Archaeological evidence shows the increase of craft specialization and consequent technical improvement from the mid tenth century in a number of crafts (pottery, shoe-making and leatherwork, bone and antler-work, and fine metalworking). There is a visible rise in living standards among at least part of the population.

The social structure of the early Polish state broadly resembled that of Carolingian feudalism. The ruler moved between several royal centres (*sedes reges principales*) with his court and personal troops (*druzhina*), while a count palatine handled administrative matters. Local administration was based on the strongholds with power in the hands of an elite hierarchy answerable to the holders of the most important regional centres (which were later known as 'castellanies'). These were entrusted with wide military, administrative, judicial and fiscal powers over the people residing in the neighbourhood. In densely settled areas the radius of influence of the centre did not exceed 14 km, though territories were larger on the fringes of the state. It seems that through the armed men attached to the five hundred or so strongholds in early Piast Poland the state exercised a monopoly of armed force. They were also the centres where tribute was exacted. The strongholds of the centralized state were inhabited by large groups of lords and strong military garrisons: this led to a growing demand for consumer goods, demands which were satisfied by the extensive luxury trade and also stimulated local production.

The process of urbanization had its beginnings in the settlements of craftsmen in and near the strongholds, presumably even before state-formation. As elite centres these sites also functioned as political and administrative centres as well as nodal points in exchange networks.[24] The settlements adjacent to the strongholds became the focus for the economic development of the late eleventh century; some of them had been surrounded by earthen and timber ramparts like the strongholds themselves, though the settlements and strongholds each performed a different function. These settlements were relatively small built-up areas (which may sometimes have had a regular plan and wooden-paved streets) and housed a motley population: members of the elite, members of the military garrison, merchants, innkeepers, artisans and servants, as well as peasants. Although we know little about the social conditions of life and work of these people, it seems likely that they were settled by the will of the lords of the strongholds, or settled there of their own accord; part of their output was presumably rendered to the lords of the strongholds. Written sources mention markets adjacent to many strongholds. It was not however until the formation of local exchange networks that these centres took on most of the characteristics of medieval towns.[25]

The state tried to control trade routes: Gdańsk was founded in the last decades of the tenth century to try to capture some of the Baltic trade from other centres on the Baltic coast. It is in this context that we should see the first attempts at minting a coinage by Polish rulers (at first mainly for prestige) at about the time that the flow of Arab silver into the Baltic dries up. These coins were modelled on the issues of Bavaria and Saxony. Material from about 350 coin hoards and over 150 single finds of coins from settlements and graves serves as evidence of the two pecuniary functions of silver money (for thesaurization hoarding, and as currency) and as reliable evidence of the changing structure of monetary circulation. Silver hoards of the period after 950 contain many western European coins (English, Danish and German – including some especially minted for trade with the Slavs) as well as fragmented silver jewellery, which was clearly used as a medium of payment (by weight). Silver hoards become much rarer from the second half of the eleventh century, and from this period we have more numerous mentions in the written sources of markets, both rural and attached to strongholds.

Bolesław I's son, Mieszko II (1025–34), was a weak ruler. He repulsed a German invasion in 1029, and in 1030 attacked (Old) Saxony, but in 1031 lost the throne in civil wars with his younger brothers supported by the nobles (and a combined German and Russian attack). He regained power at the cost of handing his father's conquests of Lusatia, Slovakia and Moravia over to the Germans (1034). After his death Poland was devastated by a Czech attack by Břetyslav I, who, among vast quantities of loot, took St Wojciech's body back to Prague. The prestige of the country was returned under Kazimierz the Restorer (1034–58), though at the expense of further compromises with the German emperor. It was under his son Bolesław II the Bold (1058–79) that we see fundamental changes taking place in the economy of the state.

The extent to which the subject peoples felt themselves to be ethnically related to the Polane however may be judged by the frequency with which the early state split up. Pomerania was held only briefly a number of times before the fifteenth century; Mazovia split from the Polish state under Duke Miecław in 1039–47. Even the central part of the state dissolved into feudal statelets ruled by minor princes of the Piast dynasty between 1138 and 1333. This allowed Silesia to be separated from Poland, though parts of it were still ruled by princes of the Piast dynasty until the sixteenth century. This suggests that the populations in these areas felt a kind of separateness from the central power of the state. We do not even know to what extent the populations of Pomerania or Silesia spoke a form of the Polish language.[26] In the period of weakness of the state certain nobles gained power, such as the Count Palatine Sieciech, who several time rebelled against the crown until he was exiled in 1099.

13
The Early Slavs and the Modern World

By way of a conclusion to this book, it seems worth considering the relevance of the Early Slavs to the modern shape of Europe. The ethnic situation created by the end of the tenth century was a persistent, but at the same time peculiarly unstable, situation, both features having considerable effect on the development of modern Europe. The cultural boundaries established at this period have affected the shape of European culture as a whole, shaping identities and defining the values which people live (and sometimes have died) for. It is debatable to precisely what degree the average Russian, Pole, Serb or Croat is like he or she is as a result of decisions taken by leaders and political events in the ninth and tenth centuries, but it is undeniable that each one of us absorbs from society a mental template, a world-outlook which is characteristic of the community into which we were born, and that the world out look of a community owes much to shared traditions, and a common conception of the past. The past is important to all of us, it is on this that we collectively and individually build our self-identity, and the majority of us have a strong desire to find out how our ancestors really lived, thought and reacted ('what they were like'). That is why historians write books like this and the general public read them.

As we discussed in the introduction, no matter how 'objective' he or she is trying to be, the historian is capable only of presenting an interpretation of events. It is inherent in our nature that, in general, we believe mainly that which confirms our vision of the world around us. Even a scholar – that is a person professionally engaged in shaping society's world outlook – can only with extreme difficulty escape this trap. The way a historian or archaeologist sees the past is basically conditioned by the way he or she sees the present, and the conditioning is so deep that rarely is this easily detectable to contemporaries. With hindsight and the delayed identification of a *Zeitgeist* is it possible to see the way in which former interpretations of the past were led in certain directions by various social and political trends. We should bear this in mind when we try to reconstruct history in a period when Europe itself and European society are undergoing enormous transformations, as they are at present.

In the year 1000, the German Emperor Otto III held his crown over the head of Bolesław I, ruler of neighbouring Poland, apparently signifying his approval of the proposal of that ruler to be crowned king. Polish historians treat this as a symbol of the might of Poland at this time (arguing that Otto would not have agreed to such a gesture otherwise) and Poland's 'entry into Europe'. German historians have regarded it as being symptomatic of the subordinate role of Poland as an eastern march of the Empire, Bolesław's position being approved by the emperor.[1] In the *Evangelia* of Otto III written in 1000 for the Benedictine monastery of Reichenau on Bodensee (Fig. 71), the Emperor is shown as sitting in majesty between representatives of the lay and sacral powers, while four ladies with strange headdresses representing, as the legend informs us, 'Scauinia, Germania, Gallia and Roma' are represented as bearing him tribute. This represents the universalist tendencies of Otto, to create an united Europe under his authority. This seems to be the aim behind a series of raids from the Ottonian Empire into Polabia and Poland throughout the tenth century. These were the successors of a series of events of military and political intervention to the east and the formation of friendly client kingdoms which had begun under the Carolingians, the creation of Marks and ultimately their absorption into the German state. In this manner Bavaria and Carinthia became part of the German state by the ninth century. Ottonian and later German rulers were only continuing the policy of their forerunners. It is notable that at the time of Otto there was still a notion of Sclavinia (Slavdom), the concept that all the Slav nations in the sphere of influence of the Ottonians could be treated alike.

The German drive towards the east continued throughout the next centuries. Apart from their military activity, the Germans were politically – and economically – active in the east. We have seen that they probably were the motors behind the formation of complex socio-political organizations in the areas bordering on their territories (Polabia and Pomerania). They were instrumental in the forming of the Bohemian state in the first decades of the tenth century. The creation of the Magyar state in the tenth century (again prompted by the Germans) also led to an eastern expansion of German influence which continued throughout the twelfth and especially the thirteenth century (including German colonization of parts of Transylvania in this period). Similar colonization was taking place in Polabia and Silesia, Pomerania and Prussia). A high point in this process was the eastern expansion of the German Empire by the end of the fourteenth century deep into what had originally formed part of the Piast state of Poland; Silesia was to be under German and Habsburg rule for almost six hundred years until 1945. At the same time many of the Slav states were adopting cultural forms and institutions which were to bring them fully into the orbit of western European culture, and a place of their own in the growing international economy. This is especially true of Poland under Casimir the Great (1333–70), and of the reigns of Louis the Great of Hungary (1342–82) and Charles the Great of Bohemia (1333–78).

In the south the Serbs became for a while the dominant power in the Balkans under the Nemanyich rulers culminating in the considerable territorial expansion of the reign of Stefan Dushan (1331–55). The Second Bulgarian

Empire (1185–1396) was also a major force in the Middle Ages. Both these states maintained to some extent their Byzantine heritage, whereas Byzantium itself had fallen to the Fourth Crusade, which was followed by the creation of a patchwork of Latin states.

In the later Middle Ages in other parts of Slavdom the Slavs were being absorbed into other states. The various peoples (including Slavs) inhabiting the Balkans were absorbed into the Ottoman state in the fourteenth and fifteenth centuries. The short-lived Serbian empire was annexed by Seljuk Turks, who after the battles of Kosovo-Polje (1389) and Varna (1444) expanded across the Bosporus and into the Balkans. The Serbian principalities and Bosnia came under Ottoman rule while Croatia and Dalmatia came under Hungarian and Venetian rule. These events were to establish the ethnic and religious make-up of the areas, which was to endure for several centuries.[2]

In the east, the Kievan state split into a number of semi-independent principalities in the course of the eleventh century (a process occurring in several other of the larger European states – such as Poland – at the same period). In the 1240s, the Mongols expanded into the steppes and invaded the southern Russian principalities, establishing the khanate of the Golden Horde. Only the northern Russian principalities remained relatively independent of Mongol overlordship (though adopting certain cultural features from the steppe hordes). In the course of the fourteenth century the Mongol power waned, and supremacy was gained by the principality of Moscow, from which the Russian state was reborn under Ivan III (1462–1505). The state expanded southwards again into the forest-steppe and steppe zone in the sixteenth century.[3] In the west of Russia however the expansion of the Lithuanian state into the Dniepr watershed in the late thirteenth and early fourteenth centuries had annexed the core areas of the Kievan state, and it was in this area under Lithuanian and Lithuanian–Polish rule in the thirteenth to sixteenth centuries that the Belarussian and Ukrainian languages and ethnic identities were established.

There was considerable competition for the Baltic coast. In the tenth century the area of the present Baltic states was occupied in the south by a series of tribes speaking the Balt languages (Prussians, Jatvings, Lithuanians, Kuronians, Livonians and Letgalians), while the northern parts were occupied by Finno-Ugrian-speaking Estonian tribes: these peoples had all successfully resisted Kievan expansion. In the first two decades of the thirteenth century much of their territories were annexed by the Teutonic Knights, a crusading order composed mostly of German knights, which established a state here which lasted until the fifteenth century. They added much of Pomerania to their annexations by the thirteenth century (by which time eastern Pomerania had separated itself from Polish rule). The German state of East Prussia which arose from the western part of this territory was to last until the end of the Second World War. Pomerania was annexed by the Polish and German states (and also at the end of the twelfth century Denmark was a contender), but managed brief periods of independence. In the mid seventeenth century the area was occupied for several decades by Sweden.

In this manner Slavdom was nibbled away from all sides, and areas at the fringes became parts of non-Slav political organisms. As a result of the various political events of the late Middle Ages and post-medieval periods the ethnic and political layout of early medieval Europe was thus to a large extent rearranged. By the beginning of the nineteenth century, much of Europe was partitioned between the Prussians and Austrians in the west and the Ottoman and Russian Empires in the south and east (Fig. 72).

The neat coloured areas of historical atlases however hide a more complex situation. The concept of states consisting of a single nation is a relatively modern notion: most states on the map of fourteenth- to nineteenth-century central and eastern Europe were multi-ethnic, multi-linguistic, multi-religious (and thus multicultural) political units. Thus the Polish and Lithuanian Republic before the partitions consisted of a western zone which was mainly Polish-speaking, but there were large numbers of Germans and Jews in the towns and to a lesser extent in the country; there were Dutch and German settlers in the northwest rural districts and in some areas in the south. The eastern zone was Ukranian- and Belarussian-speaking, with some Lithuanian and Polish settlement – primarily of the petty nobles. Jews were less prominent, but their place was taken by other minorities, such as Armenians. There were also Tatars and Cossacks in the southeast. The northwestern parts were purely Lithuanian. As far as one can tell, there seem to have been very few decentralizing movements until the nineteenth century, and, despite inevitable social tensions, in many of these areas the evidence seems to suggest that these various ethnic groups and cultures co-existed relatively peacefully. We have seen that some of the early medieval political units may have had similar multicultural structures, and that a single language used for official purposes did not exclude the existence of other ethnic and linguistic divisions within society.

In most of the post-medieval political units there seems to have been little or no cultural pressure on the Slavs to change their way of life and culture. Such a process is seen however in the west, where the Lusatian languages were extinguished by the German dialects. The process was a lengthy one, and lasted long after the German conquest of the area in the ninth and tenth centuries: the last remnants of Slav languages in the region of Hamburg disappeared in the eighteenth century, and a few isolated traces of other dialects existed in rural areas of Lusatia until the middle of the twentieth. In the eighteenth and nineteenth centuries the Prussian authorities attempted to stamp out Slav culture – and almost succeeded. Slav languages existed as national languages in some states (such as Poland before the partitions) or as a series of dialects spoken amongst communities of other nationalities (such as in Silesia and Lusatia which had long been parts of German and Habsburg states, and Slovakia, long linked to Hungary and Austria). The Czech, Russian and Polish languages have a long literary tradition, but others became literary languages only in the nineteenth (Slovak, Serbian and Croatian) and even twentieth century (Macedonian). The nineteenth century was to see the beginning of a close study of these languages: a pioneer was the Czech scholar Jozef Dobrovský (1753–1829), who wrote (in German) a study on the Old Slavic language, but also a history of the Czech language and literature. In some of these areas the national language and cultural tradition was largely restricted mainly to the rural populations. Romanticism encouraged the study of these disappearing cultural traits in local folklore and ethnography. Some Slav patriots were greatly influenced by the ideas of the German philosopher Johann Gottfried von Herder (1744–1803), who not only wrote an influential work on the origin of language (1772) but also supported the inalienable rights of each nation and emphasized the importance of a national language, traditions and folk culture. Herder's work achieved popularity in central Europe for he also emphasized the role of the Slavs in European history. Another German philosopher, Georg Wilhelm Friedrich Hegel (1770–1831), had a differing view of the role of the Slavs. He wrote of the 'east of Europe' being the house of the 'great Sclavonic nation', a body of peoples which 'has not appeared as an independent element in the series of phases that Reason has assumed in the world' – in other words quite separate from the development of western Europe.

The latter view was to prevail around the beginning of the nineteenth century which saw the emergence of a perceived east–west division of Europe. Western European historians, inhabitants of countries which were for the most part engaged in the colonization of undeveloped countries, saw their part of Europe as in some way special and predestined to take a leading role in the world. This attitude is reflected in many texts written at the time in which eastern Europe, and in particular the Slavs, are marginalized. This is a tendency which continued well into the twentieth century. According to many textbooks and curricula produced in the West and the United States even today, the history of Europe in the Middle Ages concentrates on the story of the Franks and Carolingians, their successors and western allies.[4] The Slavs and all eastern peoples are excluded from playing any significant role in the history of Europe and are reduced merely to the role of passive spectators. It was thus in central Europe that a conflict developed between a self-centred western historiography, which portrayed the Teutonic and Latin West as the defenders of the post-classical heritage against the threat of the barbarian Slav world of the east, and the national histories of the Czech and Polish peoples, who were forced in their national versions of history to denounce the German *Drang nach Osten*. The situation was more complex in the Balkans, where other issues were also involved in the discussion of the perception of the past of individual nations.

The Enlightenment and rise of movements for the restoration of the small European states (the National Revival) of the second half of the eighteenth and beginning of the nineteenth century began to affect most of central and eastern Europe. It concerned the nations then forming parts of the superpowers of the time – the united Habsburg monarchy and Hungarian state, the Russian Empire – and incorporated in the Prussian state. There was a revival of interest in national identities, and this was reflected in a rise of interest in national histories and antiquarianism.[5] This was initially due to western influence and was especially strongly felt in Bohemia and Poland, where the loss of political sovereignty also turned attention to the cultural heritage of the past.[6]

Russia experienced something similar at the beginning of the nineteenth century under the influence of Romanticism; a tendency developed to turn from the study of the classical heritage to that of the Russian Slavs. This was to develop into pan-Slavism (a political movement aiming to unite all the Slav peoples under Russian hegemony). The Russian historian Nikolaj Karamzin was an initiator of this movement. The Poles however in the nineteenth century fought the ideals of pan-Slavism, perceiving it as an ideological weapon in the attempt to 'Russify' Polish lands which had been taken in the partitions of the end of the previous century. The Czechs, Lusatians, Bulgars, Serbs, Croats and Slovenians however welcomed it as a weapon in their fight against German, Habsburg and Turkish political and cultural domination.

The Balkans, in the struggle against the effects of centuries of Ottoman domination, were particularly prone to such processes. One of the most notorious cases involves the theories of the German journalist Jakob Fallmerayer, whose *History of the Morean Peninsula*[7] was published as a response to Russia's involvement in the struggle for Greek independence against the Ottomans (Germany's allies) and the philhellenism and popular support in Europe and America which accompanied it. Fallmerayer used the written sources and the place names to suggest that the ancient Greeks had been annihilated in the early Middle Ages and the ancestors of the modern inhabitants of Greece were in fact Slavs and Albanians who had settled there in the Middle Ages and adopted the Greek language from the Byzantines. He claimed that the modern Greeks were an inferior, mongrel people undeserving of their ancient past. As may be expected, this view of the ethnogenesis of the Greeks enraged (and still enrages) Greek nationalists and is probably one of the factors which contributes to our poor understanding of the archaeological evidence for the settlement of the Slavs in this key area.

Perceptions of early Russian history were also to be affected by a similar challenge to their national identity in the 'Normanist' controversy which was prompted by the legend of the 'Calling-in of the Varangians' in the *PVL*. This legend was treated as a literal report of history by nineteenth-century German and Scandinavian historians: the Germanic northmen were seen as having brought civilization to the 'backward' East Slavs. This view was countered by Russian historians and philologists, to whom such a suggestion was above all an insult to their national prestige. These anti-Normanist views were especially strongly voiced in the mid 1930s in Stalin's isolationist Soviet Union. The *PVL* version of the rise of the Russian state was not only unacceptable to national pride, but at variance with Marxist theory (which saw the rise of the state as being a result of inner forces and not of outside influences). Several Soviet scholars (Boris A. Rybakov, Boris D. Grekov) were to try very hard to disprove the Normanist theories. To counter this arose a neo-Normanist school in the west (Holgar Arbman, A. Stender-Petersen).

Another version of the same idea, the predominant civilizing role of the Germanic peoples, was to develop from another national chauvinism, and was to have a more widespread effect. In 1895 the young philologist Gustaf Kossinna presented a paper, 'Über die vorgeschichtliche Ausbreitung der Germanen in Deutschland', at a congress of the German Anthropological Society at Kassel.[8] In this paper he first put forward his views, which were later to have considerable influence, on the role of the Germanic peoples in prehistory, and in particular the view that ethnic groups could be identified by the definition of specific groups in material culture. These views were not totally original, but it was the way that they were expounded by Kossinna and his followers which had a key importance for the direction of development of much of central European archaeology throughout the whole of the twentieth century. In particular Kossinna and his followers believed that throughout history the 'Aryan' Germans had brought civilization to other culturally less well-prepared peoples and nations. It is obvious that this school of prehistory was offensive to scholars of the nations the Germans claimed to have civilized.

It was in this period that we see the first steps taken in the construction of a modern knowledge of the ancient cultures of the Slavs. An extremely significant event was the publication (1902–24) of the eleven volumes of the study *Slovanské starožitnosti* (*Antiquities of the Slavs*) by the Czech scholar Lubor Niederle (1865–1944), with its amalgamation of the historical, archaeological and ethnographic evidence.

The outbreak of the First World War was precipitated by ethnic quarrels in the Balkans, which were caused by breakaway tendencies of the Balkan states in the Austro-Hungarian Empire and rivalries arising after the break-up of the Ottoman Empire. Russia once again perceived interests in the Balkans and entered the War on the side of Serbia, and Germany declared war on Russia. The 1917 Bolshevik Revolution (caused by the German advance deep into western parts of the Russian Empire in 1915 and 1916) and the regime this created was to be one of the key features on the map of Europe, affecting geo-politics throughout most of the rest of the twentieth century. At the Versailles congress of 1919, several new nations reappeared on the political map: peoples who had maintained their cultural identity now emerged from the larger units, in particular the dismantled Austro-Hungarian empire. The German empire lost not only its Kaiser, prestige and army, but also eastern areas to Poland. Soviet Russia gave up areas of the western fringes of the former tsarist empire (this included parts of Poland, Ukraine and Belarus, as well as the Baltic states). In the new nations the past was again invoked to aid the rebuilding of a new feeling of nationhood. In many of the central European states emerging from the First World War there was an intense development of historiography and archaeology. The search for a national past to provide an identity in the new world order was perhaps not a priority, but was certainly pursued with vigour.

The peace established by the League of Nations was short-lived. In 1933 Adolf Hitler came to power and the German people found a voice and recovered the strength to oppose what they felt were the wrongs of Versailles (which Hitler had in a rambling manner described in *Mein Kampf*, setting out his view that some races were superior to others; the Slavs were seen as an 'inferior' people). Less than twenty years after the end of the First World War, German eastward expansion into Bohemia and Poland (which Germans saw as their former 'homelands' in the east) was to begin the Second World War and the Germans were set to resolve the Slav problem in former 'Ostgermania'. In the Nazi period, the historical and archaeological evidence and Kossinna's model were used in an uncritical and politically biased manner to support policies of eastern expansion. The original territorial demands against Bohemia were based on the argument of the existence there of a German cultural minority; similar arguments were advanced in the case of the Polish corridor. The presence of material culture of Germanic type was used to suggest that certain areas of central Europe were 'ancient German homelands', thus justifying their 'reconquest' by Panzer divisions, and the displacement and destruction of 'inferior' peoples (Jews, Slavs, Gypsies and so on) inhabiting those lands, who were claimed to be later intruders.

There was a reaction by Polish and Bohemian archaeologists, who showed by reference to the archaeological data that there had been Slavs in those territories before any Germans had set foot in them. The Poznań school of the ethnogenesis of the Slavs associated with the person of Józef Kostrzewski has its origin in these polemics. This was one of the theses of Borkovský's 1940 study of the Prague type (and the reason why it was withdrawn from the bookshops by the Nazi authorities).

Hitler aimed to succeed where Charlemagne and the Ottonians had failed; he wanted to reshape Europe, to unite it under a German rule in order to fulfil the alleged historical mission of that nation. A romanticized and biased archaeology and cultural history were to add ideological support to the New Europe formed by the *Blitzkrieg*, concentration camps and the SS firing squads. The local culture was to be stamped out in the conquered territories and replaced by a

German world view. It was Hitler who said that a nation does not live longer than its culture, and this policy was expressed with most violence in the case of Poland. Polish archaeologists such as Kostrzewski spent the War in hiding from the Gestapo. Rudolf Jamka, the prewar excavator of Krak's mound near Cracow, had been twice interrogated by the German authorities to make quite sure that he had not hidden evidence of a Viking burial which the Germans expected that the mound covered (and would 'prove' the role of the Germans in the founding of the Polish state).

Like Hitler in the Sudeten, Stalin too had policies of ethnic unification. On the basis of a secret protocol to the Molotov–Ribbentrop treaty of 1939, the Soviet Union regained 'Ukrainian' and 'Belarussian' lands in the west which had been lost to Poland in 1920, and also annexed again the Baltic states. Germany however made the mistake of invading the Soviet Union in 1941 (and again late Roman-period Gothic occupation of the Ukraine proved a useful political tool).

The end of the War, with victory going to Allied forces and Stalin's Red Army, was to create a somewhat more enduring New Europe than the agreements closing the First World War. At the Tehran, Yalta and Potsdam conferences of 1944 and 1945 new boundaries were drawn which were a logical conclusion to the rather half-hearted compromise measures of Versailles. To some extent, it seems that the fact that the present state of European national boundaries is a mirror of the early medieval situation is due to at least two of the participants in the Yalta Conference in 1944, Churchill and Stalin, planning it that way – the first perhaps for reasons of the logic of history, the second because he needed the past to justify the present. It seems that Stalin's advisers were guided by pan-Slavist ideals when drawing the new frontiers. The new frontiers of Poland were drawn close to their tenth-century lines, and the boundaries of the Comecon countries (the Iron Curtain) match quite closely the furthest extent of Early Slav settlement (for example the western frontier of the Democratic Republic of Germany). It seems that this was deliberate. Milovan Djilas writes[9] of Stalin's disbelief and disappointment when he learnt from him that the Albanians (included in the Soviet bloc) were not a Slavic people and of the role that pan-Slavism played in the early discussions in the Kremlin with the leaders of the new members of the Soviet hegemony.

Stalin learnt well the lessons of previous rulers who resettled populations to enhance the unity of a state and dilute ethnic populations. Ethnic mixing in the Soviet Union was a state policy, intended to create a single 'nation of the Soviet nations'. The cultural heritage of these groups was also to be a common one, and thus the regime demanded that the history books and archaeology textbooks should emphasize the links between these peoples. In the lands claimed from Germany and Poland the German populations were loaded on trains and sent to defeated Germany, Poles were resettled from the former Polish territories of what was now 'Western Ukraine' and 'Western Belarus' and sent to the areas (Silesia, Pomerania etc.) taken from Germany. These moves were justified by ethnic and historical arguments which were ranged alongside modern contingiencies.[10] In Poland it was stressed for several decades that at Yalta and Potsdam the country had regained her historical frontiers. The territories in the north and west annexed from the German Reich were often officially referred to as the 'Recovered Territories' (*Ziemie Odzyskane*). Another feature of the period was the attempted imposition of Russian as the new *lingua franca* of the Soviet hegemony, enabling scholars of different countries to communicate their work. The fact that it was imposed sometimes meant that central European scholars were unwilling to make as much use of this opportunity as they might have done.

In the Soviet bloc, archaeology was to play a significant ideological role linked with pan-Slavist attitudes and thus legitimating the new order (and redrawn frontiers). In the late 1940s in almost all member states of Comecon, there was encouragement for archaeologists to undertake a new kind of research project. One of the favoured topics of study was the rise of the early medieval states which gave rise to the nations now under Soviet hegemony. Historical materialism was to be the paradigm which was to govern the way in which that past was to be investigated. Another factor was the inevitable portrayal of Fascist Germany as simply a continuation of the permanently hostile attitude to the Slav nations reflecting the *Ostpolitik* adopted by the Ottonians and their successors.

In Poland preparations for the thousandth anniversary in 1963–6 of the first appearance of the nation in history, in association with which the majority of the central places of the Piast state were excavated, were begun with state support by 1948. In Czechoslovakia study of the Moravian state was begun also in 1948 (excavations at Staré Město and Mikulčice in 1954). In the late 1940s and 1950s East German archaeologists also began a study of the early medieval Slavic past of their territory which clearly differentiated it from the western occupied zone (excavations at Tornow). Bulgaria began to study the rise of the Bulgarian state also in 1948 (excavations at Pliska and Preslav). Russian archaeologists had long been studying the origins of the Kievan state and linking its expansion with the later Muscovite state, but also made considerable advances in the study of the Early Slavs in the same period (1945–50). Now their experience and methods of work using historical materialism were used as examples by a generation of young central European archaeologists eager to work with the new opportunities that these studies (and the new paradigms) created. In 1965 the first congress of the International Union of Slav Archaeologists was held in Warsaw; the second (1970) was held in (East) Berlin, and subsequent meetings were held in other central European capitals such as Bratislava. The political nature of these research projects was emphasized by the low-key study of the early medieval origins of non-Slavic peoples (such as in the Baltic states), and the attention which was paid to disproving the myths and conclusions of German – especially Nazi – science.

In Poland, for example, excavations were carried out to show that Silesian towns now inhabited by Poles had Slav and not German beginnings, that 'early Polish' culture was highly developed and (in opposition to what had been written in the Nazi propaganda literature) developed independently of German or Scandinavian influence.[11] In Czechoslovakia the glories of Moravian culture of the ninth century were exposed and extolled; a similar pattern was established in the DDR, where the long political independence from the German Empire in the tenth and eleventh centuries and the development of an indigenous Slav culture were emphasized. For a long time in all three areas this was achieved at the cost of playing down the clear Ottonian influences in the material culture. In the DDR this was carried to the extent of the Ottonian conquest and reconquest being extremely neglected in archaeology and history textbooks; inclusion in research programmes of the study of these phenomena seems even to have been actively discouraged. In Polish textbooks of the Communist period, the early medieval Germans are presented in an almost totally negative light, as interested only in brutal conquest and interfering in internal affairs of the Polish state. In contrast archaeological works stressed the 'peaceful coexistence' of the inhabitants of the Polish and Kievan states in the area of contact in Podlasie for example.[12] There is some evidence however that not many Polish or Soviet archaeologists were particularly interested in examining the real nature of events on this troublesome frontier.

Much greater problems were to be caused by another facet of this phenomenon. In the years between the World Wars Polish archaeologists – especially those from Poznań, led by Kostrzewski – began to express the hypothesis that the area between the Oder and Vistula rivers was the original homeland of the Slavs. There were several grounds for this view, but the most important was perhaps not scientific: it was an emotional issue in a state which had recently gained independence, but felt threatened by powerful neighbours. German scholars had insisted that the area had been inhabited first by Germans at least by the Roman period, and that the Slavs had moved into the Oder–Vistula area from the east only later when the Germans migrated into the Roman Empire. Kostrzewski's views gained the tacit approval of the Soviet-sponsored ruling elite of the post-1945 state and more importantly of the Polish public for whom it gave a 'comfortable' past. After the War, Kostrzewski and his former students – among whom Witold Hensel and Konrad Jażdżewski took an early lead – began to propagate their autocthonous model of Slav origins in Polish territory. All sorts of ingenious arguments were used to prove cultural continuity between the third millennium BC and the present, and any attempts to discuss the opposite view were for a time treated as revisionism of the worst kind, and a challenge to the authority of the doyen of Polish archaeology and his pupils. Polish archaeology was dominated by this autochthonous model until Kostrzewski's death in 1969 (though some of the effects of this model are still being felt). In 1979 a Cracow professor, K. Godłowski, published his 'little yellow book'[13] which began to spell the end for the simplistic views of a Slav ethnogenesis between the Oder and Vistula. At the same time however some scholars outside Poland were beginning to turn away from the interpretations of German science to the Polish autochthonous views, paradoxically at a time when some of the Poles themselves were abandoning it. As we have seen, the ethnogenesis of the Slavs is a complex problem, and matters have not been helped by the tangling of the problem in modern social and political needs.

One aspect of this problem needs further consideration: whether the Polish autochthonous model was preferred by some scholars – perhaps only subconsciously – paradoxically as an antidote to Soviet pan-Slavism. Poles could hold their heads high among all the Slav nations as inhabitants of the true homeland of the Slavs. Thus, far from being a tool of the Soviet ideology, the autochthonous model perhaps also fuelled more local ambitions.[14]

If we accept a greater participation of local indigenous populations in the formation of the Sukow-Dziedzice assemblages than in the case of the Mogiła group, this sheds a somewhat different light on the autochthonous or allochthonous arguments on the origin of the Slavs in Polish archaeology. Rather than being a purely political struggle, it was a contrast between two different schools of archaeology, centred on Poznań (J. Kostrzewski, W. Hensel, K. Jażdżewski) and Cracow (K. Godłowski, M. Parczewski) in two ancient cultural zones. If our interpretation of these cultural phenomena is correct, it is not surprising that the observed evidence led to the construction of opposing models. The mistake was made when it was attempted to apply the same model to the whole of modern Poland (this subconscious model may itself derive from an awareness that Poland had supposedly returned to its historical borders) without allowing the possibility of different processes in operation in different areas.[15]

Another interesting and telling case is the role of the Moravian state in the formation of a Czechoslovak national identity. The ancient Moravian state lay in the middle of the long state which was defined after the end of the First World War in order to be the common homeland of the Czech and Slovak peoples. These two ethnic groups had been for most of the period (at least from the seventeenth century) relatively strongly culturally differentiated. It was in the Moravian state (most often – following Constantine Porphyrogenitus – referred to in the literature as 'Great Moravia') straddling the area of cultural division that the origin of the modern people was sought.[16] This however was done to the detriment of a balanced picture of the development of the Bohemian state, the origins of which tended to be overshadowed in the textbooks by the Moravian state (Chapter 12).

It is interesting to note that the specific types of overall model accepted in the study of early medieval central Europe have affected the way that the detail is interpreted. The principal surprise for central European archaeologists studying this period in the past few years has been a complete revision of the chronology. The hooked spurs discussed in Chapter 4 were for a long time dated as beginning in the fifth or sixth century, since – it was argued – they must have been derived from the spurs of the Przeworsk culture of the Roman period. This was a consequence of the Polish autochthonous model of Slav origins, and totally ignored the existence of much more similar hooked spurs (though with the hooks turning outwards) in the Frankish kingdom in the seventh century. The problems did not stop there: the spurs were one of the few 'datable' objects found in Early Slav contexts, and pottery was dated by association with these spurs, the early strongholds too. In effect as a result of this, many sites and events of the early phase of Slav settlement were for some thirty years (1950s to 1980s) dated a century or two too early. By a series of related but also tenuous arguments concerning the relationship between early medieval and Roman period populations, pottery of the Tornow and Feldberg types was also dated two centuries too early by East German scholars; this meant that pottery of Prague and Sukow types was fitted into a much shorter timespan than it had really occupied. This in turn gave a false picture of the density of settlement in Polabia in the first phases of Slav settlement. Again, the redating of Tornow and Feldberg pottery has allowed them to be seen as an expression of another form of influence from the areas beyond the Elbe; the development of several phenomena in Polabia can now be seen as due to Carolingian influence.

Here a few words need to be said on the topic of the use of Marxism in the study of the past in central Europe. In general in the period of Communist hegemony (after about 1948) there were four main reactions to the use of Marxism visible in the published literature. Some scholars did not use historical materialism at all in their works, and produced texts which were just catalogues of material or simple presentations of events and phenomena. There was a second group who attempted to utilize fully (or appear to use) the paradigms of Marxism in their historical research and considered the social and economic interpretation of the phenomena described – the material conditions of existence, internal social relationships; their works may or may not contain an extensive range of quotes from the Marxist classics. A third group of workers produced works predominantly of the first type, but made them more politically proper by the addition of a sprinkling of carefully selected quotes from the Marxist classics. A fourth group unconsciously used Marxist concepts in their works because they unthinkingly repeated modes of reasoning and working taught them at university without being totally aware of their Marxist roots and being in ignorance of alternative models. A variety of socio-political and individual factors were responsible for the complex picture which emerged.

There were regional, institutional and chronological differences in the use of Marxism. In general in the Soviet Union, DDR and Czechoslovakia, many of the more important writers fell into the second group. In Poland there were a substantial number of Marxist works written between 1948 and 1956, after which the number dropped off sharply.[17]

A reaction can now be seen in the years following the collapse of the Communist hegemony. In general (and somewhat simplifying a more complex situation), one may observe just two types of archaeology. The first applies philosophical concepts to the interpretation of the raw data. These may or may not include Marxist-prompted models, or they may derive from western European traditions (which were somewhat ignored, perhaps as too 'cosmopolitan', in most central European countries in the Communist period). The effect is to produce an archaeological interpretation which investigates and tries to explain processes acting on ancient societies. The other school studiously ignores such work, and is firmly rooted in the Continental 'culture-history' school, intent only on typological classification of 'finds' (artefacts) and ordering them into groups, the succession of which is then merely described. Disappointingly, instead of building on the interpretative models of the former generation in a more sophisticated manner, much of the archaeology of the former Soviet Union (Belarus and Ukraine particularly) seems to have fallen into this latter mode.[18]

The situation in former Yugoslavia was slightly different. The break between Tito and Moscow in 1948 meant that this state was not subject to the same forces as most of the others. In fact, in a state formed out of six provinces, many of which could claim some kind of role in the early history of the Balkans, and some of them with some form of past ethnic identity, close investigation of the early medieval past could have led to problems and seems not to have been overly encouraged in the Tito era (the Roman past was a much more comfortable subject of study). It is characteristic that in the years preceding and following the break-up of the Yugoslavian state, medieval archaeology and the reinterpretation of the historical records have had a renaissance. The need to create a new ethnic history from the past here as elsewhere has not however always led to balanced scholarship. This is especially true of the immediate aftermath of the recent Kosovo conflict.

Another interesting case is the situation in Romania, where Transylvania in particular has been a contested territory (forming as it did for a long period part of the Hungarian state). Under the Ceauşescu regime Romanian nationalism increasingly stressed the autochthonous origin of the Romanian people, and the presence of other peoples in this area has tended to be played down. Cemeteries with pottery of clear Slav affinities have been claimed to be of a native 'Dacian' origin and so on. Many important sites remain to be published. Unfortunately this policy has hindered a full appreciation of the nature of Slav settlement in this key area.[19]

Many modern states have thus invested considerable effort into the construction of their medieval past, but what is clear here is that we are dealing here not with medieval history but with modern identity politics built on narratives of the past. The origin of states, and evidence of unbroken continuity of existence despite all adverse factors has been sought. Medieval history here acts rather as the scene for actions which are perceived, not only as creating a distinct origin for a modern community, but also as definitive – once done they should not be undone. Of course such 'significant' events are to be chosen with care and their significance upheld with much scholarly argument. Since one of the features creating an ethnic (national) identity is an 'us/them' situation, it is not surprising that many of these histories have portrayed a nation surviving various external and internal threats. The notion of conflict is therefore given prominence, for example Bulgaria in conflict with Byzantium, Serbia with the Turks, Bohemia and Poland with the Germans. It is not surprising that the medieval battlefields of Kosovo and Grunwald/Tannenburg are still frequently visited sites.

The processes of collapse of the Soviet hegemony in 1989 and 1990 has led to new socio-political conditions which in turn have given rise to different ways of seeing the past. In particular we see a number of publications treating as separate subjects the history of specific regions which were formerly treated as part of a larger whole. Thus we see a 'new' archaeology of the Ukraine and Belarussia appearing to replace the thick volumes of *Arkheologia Soyuza Sovietskikh Socialisticheskikh Republik* which treated vast areas as homogeneous wholes. The production of particulate texts demonstrates the gaps in our knowledge which this concealed.[20] The fact though that many of these new accounts are written in a national language rather than a congress language (i.e. Russian) in which they would have been written in the Soviet era makes them more difficult to use by outside scholars.

If in the Cold War years after the Second World War in many countries there was a tendency towards pan-Slavism and to claim vehemently that all civilizational advances had been made by the Slavs independently of western influence, the pendulum has swung back the other way. The desire of several central European states to join the European Union has been matched by the voices of historians who have tried to show a 'European unity' at various periods of the past. What was formerly (but informally) a taboo question is now openly discussed. In the new situation, Polish and Czech scholars are now happy to admit the positive influences which their neighbours the Germans played in a number of socio-political and economic processes.[21] In Poland, the slow, painful and inefficient centrally planned economic growth of the post war years was matched by a model of early medieval state-formation which emphasized the slow cumulation from generation to generation of various factors which as the historical processes unfolded gradually gave rise to a Polish state. After 1989 – in a period of rapid expansion of the post-Communist economy – new views were put forward by young scholars, who saw the formation of the Polish state as being an almost overnight event caused by the careful political wheeling-and-dealing of a dynamic, enterprising but ruthless and strong leader. This most un-Marxist model may be seen as a fresh interpretation of the past for the 'Yuppies' of the new Poland. In a period of increased political and economic co-operation around the Baltic, and new investment of foreign capital in the post-Soviet economy, the Normanist models of the beginning of the Kievan state are at last finding new favour among Russian scholars.

These scholars apparently feel that any changes bringing eastern Europe closer to western post-Roman Europe are simply natural evolution towards civilization. The precise mechanisms and motives of both sides involved in the process are seldom considered, neither is the destruction of pre-existing cultural models. Models of cultural imperialism or even core and periphery are seldom being explicitly applied in the study of these processes by central European scholars in their headlong rush to join a 'Europe' which they feel the Iron Curtain has so long divided.

Another area in which there has been a backswing from the old imposed ideologies is in the visibly altered attitude of scholarly writings to the Church. This is especially the case in Poland, where the Catholic Church under the Polish Pope John Paul II has experienced a new era of post-Solidarity political ascendancy. These ideologies do not always allow an objective appreciation of the nature of Slav ideology (which is largely seen only in opposition to Christianity).[22] There is also a tendency to present a very one-sided picture of the role of the (Catholic) Church in the formation of the Slav states, which is seen almost entirely as a civilizing and beneficial advance from the darkness of paganism.

One wonders however if these new visions of the past are not so much based on a balanced and objective consideration of the evidence as due to the ambitions of a number of young central European scholars who seem particularly determined to produce an antithesis of the Marxist interpretation of history and who in their desire at all costs to overturn the ('Marxist') interpretations of the senior generation find themselves entrapped in an interpretative model which ignores the possibility of a 'third way'.

The chronological revolution of the past few years in the study of early medieval central Europe is showing a completely different picture to that which became established by the late 1950s and which was current even five years before this book was written. This is due to the process of abandonment of older models and the slow recognition of the effects they had on forming other types of interpretation. It is an odd reflection that in the anaerobic deposits of many deeply stratified sites in central and eastern Europe masses of preserved wood were thrown away in past excavations. Now dendrochronology is being widely applied and showing that former assumptions on chronology were wrong. It is difficult to see why the technique was not more widely applied in the past. Now, such dating is becoming more commonplace, but the task of accumulating the new data has only just begun. In particular we need a series of dendrochronological dates for the construction of strongholds (especially in Kievan Russia), and to fix the dates of ceramic types. The picture which is now emerging as a result of the new chronologies is not yet complete, but certainly will differ markedly from that which has appeared in most of the textbooks. Some of the new datings appear here in English for the first time; and this is only one of the first of a series of rewritings of the early history of the Slavs which must appear in the next few years.

In a period when European identities are being rethought, we are also becoming more aware of the existence of a spectrum of cultural phenomena rather than the black-and-white picture of ethnicity that was formerly accepted. We can now accept more easily the existence of multicultural areas, populations of different 'ethnicities' living alongside each other to a greater or lesser degree. Regions such as Pomerania and Silesia may well always have been areas of this type well before the German presence in the area from the thirteenth century increased the effect. Another obvious example is the Bug valley and Podlasie between the East and West Slavs. These cultural differences and affinities only later became subordinated to political factors tending towards cultural unity with the rise of strong state organizations.

The moves towards the potential creation of a united Europe in the near future are having an effect on how we perceive cultural identity and diversity. Perhaps a globalization of culture and new technologies will be able to remove the communicational, ideological and relational difficulties which have so often prevent cultural understanding between peoples. Part of this must be the ability to understand other and diverse foreign cultures, to see them as part of a common European historical heritage which is an essential part of breaking down barriers between them. Perhaps a closer understanding of other cultures together with the abolition of frontiers and greater mobility will lead to a closer relationship between the different peoples which will one day make up the new federation of Europe. At the time these words were written, though, an uncomprehending world watched on as the roads of Kosovo filled with refugees driven from their homes by former fellow inhabitants of a multi-ethnic society and foreign planes were bombing targets which until recently had been barely noticed names on maps of far-off lands. During this conflict both the Serbs and Albanians employed not only arguments on human rights but also historical arguments of the type 'we were here first' and 'this is our historical homeland', claims which not a few scholars and other authors endorsed or attacked. It is clear that even not even at the end of the twentieth century could the significance of such arguments be dismissed and ethnic conflicts which they supported (or created) be easily diffused.

The contrasts between the interpretative models for the past established in the countries of central and eastern Europe in the Communist period and those which were proposed in the years immediately following 1989 are an interesting illustration of the way in which modern social conditions affect the way we see or want to see our past. At the time of writing the contrast is too great for us to have confidence that any one view of the past is the one which will unconditionally be adopted in future. I hope that some of the views presented in this book will be seen as at least a step in the right direction.

Notes

Introduction

1 See the review by Peter Bogucki (1997) in *The Slavic Review* 56 (3), 551–2.

2 See L. Klejn 1993, 'To separate a centaur: on the relationship between archaeology and history in Soviet tradition', *Antiquity* 67 (255), 339–48; J. Topolski 1976, *Methodology of History* (Warsaw/Dordrecht/Boston).

3 For the problems of the interpretation of the Byzantine written sources, see G. Majeska 1997–8, 'The Byzantines on the Slavs: on the problem of ethnic stereotyping', *Acta Byzantina Fennica* 9, 70–86.

4 T. Lewicki 1956 and 1977, *Źródła arabskie do dziejów słowiańszczyzny*, vols I and II (Wrocław); T. Kowalski 1946, *Relacja Ibrahima ibn Jakuba z podróży do krajów słowiańskich w przekazie al-Bekriego* (Cracow); D. Mishin 1996, 'Ibrahim ibn Ya'qub at-Tartushi's account of the Slavs from the middle of the tenth century', pp. 184–99 in M. B. L. Davis and M. Sebök (eds), *Annual of Medieval Studies at the CEU 1994–1995* (Central European University, Budapest); P. Charvát and J. Prosecký (eds) 1996, *Ibrahim ibn Ya'qub at-Tartusi – Christianity, Islam and Judaism Meet in East-Central Europe, c. 800–1300 AD* (Prague). See also B. Lewis 1982, *The Moslem Discovery of Europe* (London).

5 *The Russian Primary Chronicle: Laurentian Text*, edited and translated by S. H. Cross and O. F. Sherbowitz-Wetzor 1953 (Cambridge, Mass.).

6 For the methods of the archaeologist see K. Greene 1996, *Introduction to Archaeology* (London) (or one of the earlier editions). See also C. Renfrew and P. Bahn 1991, *Archaeology: Theories, Methods and Practice* (London). Some specific cases from central European archaeology are dealt with by G. Fehring 1991, *The Archaeology of Medieval Germany: An Introduction* (London).

7 Gustaf Kossinna is reported to have begun his Berlin lectures on the Slavs with the provocative statement 'und jetzt möchte ich über die Kultur oder eher über die Unkultur der Slawen sprechen' ('and now I would like to speak of the culture, or rather the un-culture, of the Slavs'). Such an attitude could be based on a comparison between the surviving remains and those of the contemporary Frankish cemeteries, but only reflects the boundaries of our perception through archaeology.

8 Ethnographic collections in many European museums are replete with items made of organic materials from various native cultures collected before these cultures disappeared. These give a totally different picture of those cultures from the scraps of pottery and fragments of tools etc. which are the materials most likely to reach the archaeologist from the same cultures; these taken alone might present the archaeologist with a biased and false picture of cultural poverty. This is worth bearing in mind in our discussions of Slav material culture.

9 B. Trigger 1989, *A History of Archaeological Thought* (Cambridge), pp. 148–206.

10 C. Renfrew 1987, *Archaeology and Language: The Puzzle of Indo-European Origins* (London). The theses contained in the book have been much criticized and a number of modifications may be suggested, but nevertheless they do seem to explain some of the features of central European archaeology better than any other model.

11 For the distribution of Balt hydronyms see V. N. Toporov and O. N. Trubachev 1962, *Lingvisticheski analiz gidronimov Verkhnego Podneprovia* (Moscow).

12 Owing to a widespread misunderstanding, the Veneti (or Venedi) of several of these first-century sources were assumed to have been Slavs on the dubious authority of Jordanes, a sixth-century author. It can be demonstrated that, in keeping with Late Antique literary and scholarly traditions (and as in other parts of

his account), Jordanes projected the situation of the sixth century on to his literary knowledge of the geography of the classical world.

13 Not being a linguist by training, I have based this section on the work of several better qualified authors, in particular Jerzy Nalepa 1988, 'Charakterystyka językowa dawnej Słowiańszczyzny' in L. Leciejwicz (ed.), *Mały słownik kultury dawnych Słowian* (Warsaw), pp. 445–57, from which my examples are drawn.

14 An important source of evidence is the documents written on birchbark from Novgorod. The earliest (perhaps eleventh century) have archaic features including words similar to the Proto-Slav language, but these features disappear by the mid thirteenth century: see work by A. Zalizniak, quoted by V. V. Sedov 1987, 'Origine de la branche du nord des Slaves Orientaux', p. 167, fn 7, in G. Labuda and S. Tabaczyński (eds) 1987, *Studia nad etnogenezą Słowian i kulturą Europy wczesnośredniowiecznej*, vol. 1 (Wrocław).

15 For Scandinavia and some of the western European literature see K. Randsborg 1980, *The Viking Age in Denmark* (London), pp. 45–51.

16 K. Godłowski 1985, *Przemiany kulturowe i osadnicze w południowej i środkowej Polsce w młodszym okresie przedrzymskim i w okresie rzymskim* (Cracow), p. 124.

Chapter 1

1 The modern traveller may notice a slight difference in morphology which is characteristic of central and eastern Europe. Darker hair and skin colours do tend to be slightly more common than further northwest; limbs and bones are more robust, faces tend to be rounder.

2 It would seem that the term was transmitted by the Avar khaganate, the Longobards and the Bavarians, all of whom were in contact with both South and West Slavs.

3 The use by Fredegar of the terms 'Slav' and 'Wend' has been examined by F. Curta 1997, 'Slavs in Fredegar and Paul the Deacon: Medieval "gens" or "Scourge of God"?' *Early Medieval Europe* 6, 141–67.

4 This view does tend to overstress the dichotomy between 'Slav' and 'German', and it is relatively certain that the speaker of a language of the Slav group one side of a local frontier would feel little affinity with a Slav on the other side merely on the grounds that linguistically their two languages or dialects were closer to each other than to Germanic languages unknown to them across other frontiers several hundred kilometres to the west. One may suspect that most Early Slavs probably lived in almost total ignorance of more than their own local community and its immediate links.

5 The extensive literature on ethnicity includes a seminal study by the Norwegian anthropologist Frederick Barth 1969, *Ethnic Groups and Boundaries: The Social Organisation of Cultural Differences* (Oslo); see also E. E. Roosens 1989, *Creating Ethnicity: The Process of Ethnogenesis* (Berkeley/Los Angeles); A. D. Smith 1981, 'War and ethnicity: the role of warfare in the formation, self-images and cohesion of ethnic communities', *Ethnic and Racial Studies* 4, 375–95; A. D. Smith 1986, *The Ethnic Origins of the Nations* (Oxford/Cambridge); and also A. Bacal 1991, *Ethnicity in the Social Sciences: A View and a Review of the Literature on Ethnicity* (Coventry).

6 For the archaeological aspects of the problem see S. J. Shennan (ed.) 1989, *Archaeological Approaches to Cultural Identity* (London); the article by Walter Pohl 1991, 'Conceptions of ethnicity in early medieval studies', *Archaeologia Polona* 29, 39–49, is especially useful. See also S. Brather 2000, 'Ethnische Identitäten als Konstrukte der frühgeschichtlichen Archäologie', *Germania* 78, 139–77.

7 M. Parczewski 2000, 'Kultury archeologiczne a teoria wspólnot komunikatywnych' in S. Tabaczyński (ed.), *Kultury archeologiczne a rzeczywistość dziejowa*, pp. 207–213 (Warsaw).

8 Smith 1986, *Ethnic Origins*, pp. 22–31. I am grateful to Florin Curta for drawing my attention to this work and discussion of some of its contents with me.

9 In addition, we should note that only by making such an assumption about the association of some kind of archaeological assemblages with the Slavs will we be able to extend their history further back than the first written records. To deny that language could be linked with cultural packages would deny us the possibility of even attempting to resolve the problems of the early history of these peoples by archaeological means.

10 The modern study of the origin of the Slavs had its beginnings with the small book *Śledzenie początku narodów słowiańskich* [Seeking the origin of the Slav nations] of Wawrzyniec Surowiecki (1769–1827), read at a meeting of the Warsaw Society of the Friends of Science in 1824. His ideas were given greater currency by the Slovak scholar Pavel Jozef Šafařík (1795–1861), the author of the influential *Slovanské starožitnosti* [Antiquities of the Slavs] (1837). The further history of the study of the origin of the Slavs is briefly touched on in Chapter 12 below.

11 This type of arrangement is discussed by R. Wenskus in his seminal work of 1961, *Stammesbildung und Verfassung* (Cologne/Graz), which, although it primarily refers to Germanic groups, can to some extent be applied to many other groups. Another useful article is the text by Walter Pohl cited above.

12 The non-specific manner in which this term was used is revealed by the way that Byzantine and later Frankish writers refer to the Avars as 'Huns'. The term 'Scythians' was also similarly frequently misused in the past.

13 C. Renfrew 1987, *Archaeology and Language: The Puzzle of Indo-European Origins* (London).

14 H. G. Lunt 1985, 'Slavs, Common Slavic, and Old Church Slavonic' in *Litterae Slavicae Medii Aevi: Francisco Venceslao Mares Sexagenario Oblatae*, edited by Johannes Reinhart (Munich), pp. 185–204 (esp. 203), or H. Birnbaum 1992, 'Von ethnolinguistischer Einheit zur Vielfalt: die Slaven im Zuge der Landnahme der Balkan-halbinsel', *Südost-Forschungen* 51, 1–19 (esp. 7), or H. Birnbaum 1993, 'On the ethnogenesis and protohome of the Slavs: the linguistic evidence', *Journal of Slavic Linguistics* 1, 352–74 (esp. 359). See also J. Nichols 1998, 'The Eurasian spread zone and the Indo-European dispersal' in R. Blench and M. Spriggs, *Archaeology and Language II: Correlating Archaeological and Linguistic Hypotheses* (London/New York), pp. 220–66, esp. 241: 'the Slavic [linguistic] spread seems to have been the spread of Slavic speech and ethnic identity combined with Avar political and ideological institutions'. I am indebted to Florin Curta for these references.

15 See P. Heather 1989, 'Cassiodorus and the rise of the Amals: genealogy and the Goths under Hun domination', *Journal of Roman Studies* 79, 103–28. Jordanes's text on the Venethi has been discussed at some length by F. Curta 1999, 'Hiding behind a piece of tapestry': Jordanes and the Slavic Venethi', *Jahrbücher für Geschichte Osteuropas* 47, 321–40.

16 The town of Noviedunum (a Celtic name) was probably situated near the Danube estuary, in Little Scythia; the location of the 'Mursian Lake' in this context has been debated. From other sources we know that it was the reputed source of the Danube on the boundary between 'Scythia' and 'Germania'. The Vistula itself was seen as marking the boundary between these two geographical areas.

17 To some extent this applies also to the Antes, although a group of that name appears in the much earlier writings of Pomponius Melus and Pliny as a tribe in the Caucasus area. This would in turn suggest that this early Roman-period ethnonym referred to a group which should perhaps be counted rather as Sarmatian.

18 H. Popowska-Taborska 1993, *Wczesne dzieje Słowian w świetle ich języka* (Warsaw), my quotation comes from page 144. For an English summary see H. Popowska-Taborska 1997, 'The Slavs in the Early Middle Ages from the viewpoint of modern linguistics', pp. 91–6 in P. Urbańczyk (ed.), *Origins of Central Europe* (Warsaw).

19 I. Borkovsky 1940, *Staroslovanská keramika ve střední Evropě: studia k počátkům slovanské kultury* (Prague).

20 B. A. Rybakov 1943, 'Ranniaia kultura vostochnykh slavian', *Istoricheski Zhurnal* 11–12, 73–80.

21 The Ukrainian archaeologists initially upheld this view, even after Artamonov revised his previous views and argued, in 1955, that the Cherniakhovo culture represented a coalition of ethnic groups under the leadership of the Goths.

22 Among them the eponymous site at Korchak: I. P. Rusanova 1963, 'Poselenie u s. Korchaka na r. Tetereve', *Materialy i Issledovania po Arkheologii SSSR* 108, 39–50.

23 A. Egoreichenko 1991, 'Poselenie u d. Ostrov Pinskogo r-na Brestskoi oblasti', *Archaeoslavica* 1, 61–82.

24 M. Shchukin 1986–90, 'The Balto-Slavic forest direction in the archaeological study of the ethnogenesis of the Slavs', *Wiadomości Archeologiczne* 51 (i), 3–30. For the Kiev culture see M. Kazanski 1999, *Les Slaves: les origines (Ier–VIIe siècles après J.-C.)* (Paris),

pp. 21–30; see also I. P. Rusanova and
E. A. Symonovich (eds) 1993, *Slaviane i ikh
sosedi v kontse I tysiacheletia do n.e. – pervoi
polovine I tysiachletia n.e.* (Moscow);
R. V. Terpilovski and N. S. Arashina 1992,
Pamiatniki kievskoi kultury (Kiev).

25 V. Danilenko 1976, 'Piznozarubinetski
pamiatki kyivskogo typu', *Arkheologia* 19,
65–95; R. V. Terpilovski 1984, *Rannie slaviane
Podesenia III–V vv* (Kiev); *Arkheologia
Ukrainskoi SSR* 1986, II, 100–13.

26 J. Kostrzewski 1965, *Zur Frage der
Siedlungsstetigkeit in der Urgeschichte Polens
von der Mitte des II. Jahrtausends v.u.Z. bis
zum frühen Mittelalter* (Wrocław); see also
the work of the Polish linguist Tadeusz
Lehr-Spławiński 1946, *O pochodzeniu i
praojczyźnie Słowian* (Poznań). For Soviet
archaeology: V. V. Sedov 1979,
Proiskhozhdenie i ranniaia istoria Slavian
(Moscow); V. V. Sedov 1994, *Slaviane v
drevnosti* (Moscow); I. P. Rusanova 1976,
*Slavianskie drevnosti VI–VII vv: kultura
prazhskogo tipa* (Moscow); Rusanova and
Symonovich (eds), *Slaviane i ikh sosedi v
kontse I tysiacheletia do n.e. – pervoi polovine
I tysiacheletia n.e.*

27 J. Korošec 1958, 'Istrazhivania slovenskie
keramike ranogo sredniego veka v Jugoslaviji,
Rad Vojvodanskih Muzeja 7, 5–12; J. Korošec
1967, 'K problematiki slovanske keramike v
Jugoslaviji', *Arheološki Vestnik* 18, 349–55.

28 The main problem is that these artefacts could
be redeposited and not in real association. Also
some of the 'early' assemblages contain material
which could be of a later date, such as some of
the rims with finger-tip decoration.

29 K. Godłowski 1979, *Z badań nad zagadnieniem rozprzestrzenienia się Słowian w V–VII w.
n.e.* (Cracow); K. Godłowski 1983, 'Zur Frage
der Slawensitze vor der grossen Slawenwanderung im 6. Jahrhundert', pp. 257–84 in
*Settimane di Studio del Centro Italiano di Studi
sull'Alto Medioevo* 30 (Spoleto); M. Parczewski
1991, 'Origins of Early Slav culture in Poland',
Antiquity 65 (248), 676–83.

30 Kodyn: I. P. Rusanova and B. A. Timoshchuk
1984, *Kodyn – slavianskie poselenia V–VIII vv.
na r. Prut* (Moscow). Rashkov: V. D. Baran
1988, *Prazhskaia kultura Podnestrovia (po
materialam poselenii u s. Rashkov)* (Kiev).

31 Teodor, though, saw this material as earlier
than the assumed date of the Slav 'migrations'
and as evidence of a continuity of the native

(Romanized) population east of the Carpathian
mountains during the fifth to seventh centuries.
Dan Gh. Teodor 1983, 'Conceptul de cultură
Costişa-Botoşana: Consideraţii privind
continuitatea populaţiei autohtone la est de
Carpati în sec. V–VII', *Studia Antiqua et
Archaeologica* 1, 215–27. Hansca: I. A.
Rafalovich 1972, *Slaviane VI–IX vekov v
Moldavii* (Kishinev), p. 33 fig. 3/8.

32 The late fifth-century horizon in Romania is
discussed by F. Curta (forthcoming), *The
Making of the Slavs: History and Archaeology
of the Lower Danube Region ca. 500–700*
(Cambridge); see also R. Harhoiu 1990,
'Chronologische Fragen der Völker-
wanderungszeit in Rumänien', *Dacia* 34,
169–208. The Cireşanu site is published by
V. Teodorescu 1984, *Anuarul Muzeului de
Istorie şi Arheologie Prahova* 1, 51–100.
Dragosloveni: M. Comşa 1972, 'Directions et
étapes de la pénétration des Slaves vers la
Péninsule Balkanique aux VIe –VIIe siècles avec
un regard spécial sur le territoire de la
Roumanie', *Balcanoslavica* 1, fig. 4/2. For the
Sărata Monteoru finds see U. Fiedler 1992,
*Studien zu Gräberfelder des 6. bis 9.
Jahrhunderts an der Unteren Donau* (Bonn),
pp. 82; 84; 83 fig. 11/5, 7; and 85 fig. 12/3. I am
indebted to Florin Curta for information about
these sites.

33 This suggestion remains pure hypothesis but
would go some way towards explaining the
later successes of the Slavs in the Balkans, and
also how a previously comparatively obscure
group begins to exercise such 'authority' in the
area as to attract to it new people, as seems to
have happened.

34 We will see below that the establishment of the
Avar hegemony in the same areas seems to have
paved the way for the formation of new cultural
elements and also the expansion of Slav settlement even into the crumbling East Roman
Empire itself.

Chapter 2

1 For the wave of advance model see
A. J. Ammerman and L. L. Cavali-Sforza
1984, *The Neolithic Transition and the
Genetics of Populations in Europe* (Princeton),
p. 67; see also A. J. Ammerman and
L. L. Cavali-Sforza 1972, 'Measuring the rate
of spread of early farming in Europe', *Man* 9,
674–88.

2 P. M. Barford 1994, 'Germans, Slavs and Balts in Neolithic Central Europe? East European challenges to new Indo-European theories', *Barbaricum* III, 63–71.

3 Z. Kobyliński 1989, 'An ethnic change or a socio-economic one? The 5th and 6th centuries AD in the Polish lands', pp. 303–12 in S. Shennan (ed.), *Archaeological Approaches to Cultural Identity* (London).

4 This is reminiscent of what Gandhi tried to achieve at the end of colonial rule of India. One might even suggest that perhaps we are seeing here the expansion of some ancient non-materialistic counterpart to the modern 'Green movement'.

5 J. Werner 1956, *Beiträge zur Archäologie des Attila-Reiches* (Munich); E. A. Thompson 1948, *A History of Attila and his Huns* (Oxford).

6 F. Curta (forthcoming), *The Making of the Slavs: History and Archaeology of the Lower Danube Region ca. 500–700* (Cambridge). See also H. Wolfram and F. Daim (eds) 1980, *Die Völker an der mittleren und unteren Donau im fünften und sechsten Jahrhundert* (Vienna).

7 Z. Kurnatowska 1977, *Słowiańszczyzna południowa* (Wrocław), p. 21. This book (in Polish with no summary) is a useful synthesis which has greatly aided the formulation of parts of this chapter.

8 To the east in the eastern arc of the Carpathians there were also groups speaking Romance languages, remnants of the original population of the deserted Dacian province: these people contributed to the Romance-speaking Wallachians and eventually the Romanians.

9 Though for a criticism of some of these concepts see F. Curta 1994, 'The changing image of the Early Slavs in the Rumanian historiography and archaeological literature: a critical survey', *Südost-Forschungen* 53, 225–310.

10 For these Walachian clay ovens see Suzana Dolinescu-Ferche's (1995) paper on clay ovens inside sixth-century houses from Dulceanca, 'Cuptoare din interiorul locuinţelor din secolul al. VI-lea e.n. de la Dulceanca', *Studii şi Cercetări de Istorie Veche şi Arheologie* 46, 161–92.

11 S. Dolinescu-Ferche 1984 'La culture "Ipoteşti-Ciurel-Cîndeşti" (Ve–VIIe siècles): la situation en Valachie', *Dacia* 28, 117–47.

12 It is worth bearing in mind that these taxonomic divisions were created in the archaeological material in the assumption that they would demonstrate the gradual assimilation of the Slavs into native communities (and not vice versa).

13 I owe this and much else in this subsection to information from and discussion with Florin Curta.

14 Curta, *The Making of the Slavs*.

15 For a concise introduction to some of these problems see G. Majeska 1997–8, 'The Byzantines on the Slavs: on the problems of ethnic stereotyping', *Acta Byzantina Fennica* 9, 76–86. See also R. Benedicty 1965, 'Prokopios' Berichte über die slavische Vorzeit: Beiträge zur historiographischen Methode Prokopios von Kaisareia', *Jahrbuch der Österreichischen Byzantinischen Gesellschaft* 11, 51–78; A. Kollautz 1979–80, 'Die Idealisierung der Slawen bei Theophylakt als Beispiel seiner ethnographischen Darstellungsweise', *Rapports du IIIe Congrès International d'Archéologie Slave* (Bratislava), vol. 2, 189–204.

16 Most of these references come from the works of Procopius of Cesarea in connection with events in the reign of Justinian (527–65) but most of the other references (Menander, Theophanes, Pseudo-Maurice) refer however to events in the reign of Maurice (582–602). After the beginning of the seventh century however the Antes no longer appear in East Roman written sources.

17 Although Procopius informs us in a famous passage (the 'ethnographic excursus' of *Wars*, VII.14, 22) that Slavs and Antes lived in 'democracy', Jordanes (*History of the Goths*, 247) tells us that the Antes had a King Boz who was crucified along with his sons and seventy elders by the Amal Goths under Vinithar, son of Ermanric. This story is however almost certainly an invention of Cassiodorus or another of Jordanes's sources to glorify the Amals. The generally reliable Ammianus Marcellanus tells us that Ermanric's son Vithimar attacked the Alans and not the Antes.

18 The story has an interesting ending which Procopius relates at length. A barbarian was taken for the dead commander and an attempt was made to get a ransom for this 'phoney Chilbudius'. This event seems to have been modelled by Procopius to resemble Greek comedy.

19 The point is that Procopius was aware that they had at this time no strong overall leadership: this is what he stresses in his 'ethnographic excursus' discussed elsewhere in this chapter.

20 On the significance of these hoards and their changing character and distribution see F. Curta 1996, 'Invasion or inflation? Sixth-to seventh-century Byzantine coin hoards in eastern and southeastern Europe', *Annali dell' Istituto Italiano di Numismatica* 43, 65–224.

21 This material has been studied by Michał Parczewski, who in his work (M. Parczewski 1988, *Najstarsza faza kultury wczesnosłowiańskiej w Polsce* (Cracow), p. 114) proposed naming this the Mogiła phase of the Prague Culture – named after the Mogiła site examined during extensive rescue excavations preceding the construction of the Lenin ironworks at Nowa Huta near Cracow. Personally, as explained above, I would prefer to link it not with the (later) Prague material but with the Korchak material. See also M. Parczewski 1991, 'The origins of Early Slav culture in Poland', *Antiquity* 65 (248), 676–83.

22 R. Hachulska-Ledwos 1971, 'Wczesnośred-niowieczna osada w Nowej Hucie–Mogile', *Materiały Archeologiczne Nowej Huty* 3, 7–210 (Cracow).

23 K. Godłowski 1985, *Przemiany kulturowe i osadnicze w południowej i środkowej Polsce w młodszym okresie przedrzymskim i w okresie rzymskim* (Wrocław).

24 E. Dąbrowska, 1984, 'Skarb ozdób brązowych z VI–VII w. na stanowisku 62A w Nowej Hucie-Mogile', *Archeologia Polski* 29, 351–69. See also Parczewski, *Najstarsza faza kultury wczesnośredniowiecznej*, p. 51.

25 It is in such a context that the reference is usually quoted, but Procopius can only have received information from Thule, which the rest of the chapter makes clear is Scandinavia, at second hand. This is an interesting parallel to the story of the Scandinavian origin of the Amal Goths which Jordanes reported about the same time as Procopius was writing. For an interesting suggestion concerning the relationship of these two accounts see W. Goffart 1988, *The Narrators of Barbarian History (A.D. 550–800): Jordanes, Gregory of Tours, Bede and Paul the Deacon* (Princeton), pp. 93–101.

26 If we were to treat this reference literally it would mean that the Heruli inexplicably moved first east, around the Carpathians (through modern Moldavia) before turning west and reaching the Warnian territory through southern Poland. Unfortunately, the reference is probably incorrect in referring to extensive settlement of the Sclavenes at such an early period, and it is possible that, in writing 'through all the tribes of the Sclavenes' like Jordanes, Procopius imagined the latter as a people whose territory extended back from the Danube northwards to the source of the Vistula: this would then make much more sense. One also notes that the theme of an uninhabited wasteland north of the Danube appears elsewhere in Procopius (*Secret History* XVIII.18). These two factors somewhat reduce the believability in the literal truth of the information of the Heruli story in Procopius.

27 This culture lacks a recent summary. Many of the references to previous work can be found in J. Kowalski 1991, 'Z badań nad chrono-logią okresu wędrówek ludów na ziemiach zachodniobałtyjskich (faza E)', pp. 67–85 in [J. Okulicz] (ed.), *Archeologia bałtyjska* (Olsztyn). The 'Slav' pottery is published and its implications discussed by J. Okulicz 1988, 'Problem ceramiki typu praskiego w grupie olsztyńskiej kultury zachodniobałtyjskiej', *Pomerania Antiqua* 13, 103–33.

28 The potential significance of this phenomenon for dating the movement of the Slavs was noted by K. Godłowski 1979, *Z badań nad zagadnieniem rozprzestrzenienia się Słowian w V–VII w. n.e.* (Cracow), pp. 40–1 ryc. 1 and 2.

29 A few Justinian coins reached the Ukraine, including at Kiev and Zimno (in the latter case a silvered copper coin).

30 On this material see D. Jelínková 1990, 'K chronologii sídlištních nálezů s keramikou pražského typu na Moravě', pp. 251–81 in *Pravěk a slovanské osidleni Moravi* (Brno). The earlier dating is preferred by M. Gojda 1991, *The Ancient Slavs* (Edinburgh), p. 12. See also J. Zeman 1976, 'Nejstarší slovanské osídleni Čech', *Památky Archeologické* 67, 115–235.

31 As pointed out in the Preface, the Korchak Culture develops into the Prague Culture only in certain of its areas of occurrence and becomes the Prague Culture at a later stage of the migration. For this reason it seems inconsistent to talk of the Korchak material as the Prague-Korchak Culture as some have done. For the Korchak Culture see Y. V. Kukharenko

1961, *Srednevekovye pamiatniki Polesia* (Moscow); V. P. Petrov 1963, 'Pamiatniki korchakskogo tipa', *Materialy i Issledovania po Arkheologii SSSR* 108, 16–38; V. V. Sedov 1982, *Vostochnye slaviane v VI–XIII vv.* (Moscow, *Arkheologia SSSR* 14), pp. 10–19; I. P. Rusanova 1976, *Slavianskie drevnosti VI–VII vv.* (Moscow), pp. 12–55; *Arkheologia Ukrainskoi SSR* (1986) II, 135–53.

32 I. P. Rusanova 1963, 'Poselenie u s. Korchaka na r. Tetereve', *Materialy i Issledovania po Arkheologii SSSR* 108, 39–50; V. D. Baran 1963, 'Ranneslavianskoe poselenie u s. Ripneva (Ripnev II) na Zapadnom Buge', *Materialy i Issledovania po Arkheologii SSSR* 108, pp. 351–65.

33 For Suceava-Şipot see M. D. Matei 1962, 'Die slawische Siedlungen von Suceava (Nordmoldau, Rumänien)', *Slovenská Archeológia* 10, 149–74. For the interpretation see D. Gh. Teodor, 'La pénétration des Slaves dans les régions du sud-est de l'Europe d'après les données archéologiques des régions orientales de la Roumanie', *Balcanoslavica* 1 (1972), 29–42.

34 H. Friesinger 1978, *Die Slawen in Niederösterreich* (Vienna).

35 O. Pritsak 1983, 'The Slavs and the Avars', pp. 353–432 in *Settimane di Studio del Centro Italiano di Studi sull'Alto Medioevo* (Spoleto); W. Pohl 1988, *Die Awaren: ein Steppenvolk in Mitteleuropa 567–822 n.Chr.* (Munich).

36 The Byzantine gold solidi reaching the southeastern zone of the Baltic shores however abruptly decline in quantity after issues of 518 but were still reaching the western areas after this. This seems to be evidence of the date of the final collapse of the *Restgermanen* settlement in Poland (Godłowski, *Z badań*, p. 45).

37 Around 576 the Turks also extended into the Caucasus, and the easternmost people, the Khazars, were soon to establish a hegemony there over the Alans, Hunnic remnants and southern Finno-Ugrian tribes living there. This was to have important consequences for later development of eastern Europe.

38 This is the context of the interesting remarks of Walter Pohl 1991, 'Conceptions of ethnicity in early medieval studies', *Archaeologia Polona* 29, 39–49.

39 This passage is inserted in the middle of the narrative concerning Chilbudius (*Wars* VII.14, 1–36) at a point where mention is made of the popular assembly and has all the characteristics of a fragment concerning the 'ethnography' of the area north of the Danube copied from a (lost) earlier work which has been inserted here and has no real connection with Procopius's narrative. The source of this information and its date are unknown and thus should obviously be used with great caution. This is unfortunate, as it is one of the most oft-cited fragments of Procopius's work concerning the Slavs. Perhaps it is a fragment of a lost work connected with the activities of the real Chilbudius about 530.

40 Kollautz, 'Die Idealisierung der Slawen'.

41 This process had begun much earlier: the network of Roman *villae rusticae* had already broken down after the middle of the fifth century and none of their sites shows any clear sign of reoccupation after being abandoned. For the countryside see J. Henning 1987, *Südosteuropa zwischen Antike und Mittelalter: archäologische Beiträge zur Landwirtschaft des 1. Jahrtausends u. Z.* (Berlin).

42 Despite a considerable increase in numbers of sites datable to between the late seventh and late ninth century, the countryside was still relatively poorly populated even when Byzantine power was restored in the late tenth and eleventh centuries along the lower Danube. There is a renewed growth in the countryside in the Balkans only in the twelfth and thirteenth centuries.

43 See R. Hodges and D. Whitehouse 1983, *Mohammed, Charlemagne and the Origins of Europe: Archaeology and the Pirenne Hypothesis* (London), pp. 54–76. The regular flow of coinage in the area begins again only with the early ninth-century Byzantine reconquest.

44 P. Charanis 1950, 'The chronicle of Monemvasia and the question of Slavonic settlement in Greece', *Dunbarton Oaks Papers* 5, 141–66.

45 J. Ph. Fellmerayer, 1830, *Geschichte der Halbinsel Morea während des Mittelalters* (Stuttgart); M. Vasmar 1941, *Die Slawen in Griechenland* (Berlin); M. W. Weithmann 1878, *Die Slawische Bevölkerung auf der griechischen Halbinsel: ein Beitrag zur historischen Ethnographie Südosteuropas* (Wiesbaden/Munich); Ph. Malingoudis 1983, 'Toponymy and history, observations concerning the Slavic toponyms', *Cyrillomethodianum* 7, 99–111.

46 The date(s) assigned to the Bulgarian sites by Zhivka Vazharova are currently under revision. See, for example, R. Koleva 1992, 'Za datiraneto na slavianskata grupa "Popina-Garvan" v severoiztochna Balgariia i severna Dobrudzha', *Godishnik na Sofiiskiia Universitet 'Kliment Ohridski'. Istoricheski Fakultet* 84–5, 163–82; R. Koleva 1993, 'Slavic settlement on the territory of Bulgaria', pp. 17–19 in J. Pavuj (ed.), *Actes du XII-e Congrès international des sciences préhistoriques et protohistoriques, Bratislava, 1–7 septembre 1991*, vol. 4 (Bratislava).

47 The process is considered by Z. Kurnatowska 1977, *Słowiańszczyzna południowa* (Wrocław), pp. 33ff.

48 For Penkovka see D. T. Berezovets 1963, 'Poselenia Ulichei na reke Tiasmine', *Materialy i Issledovania po Arkheologii SSSR* 108, 145–208; Rusanova, *Slavianskie drevnosti VI–VII vv.*, pp. 85–112; Sedov, *Vostochnye slaviane v VI–XIII vv.*, pp. 19–28; *Arkheologia Ukrainskoi SSR* II (1986), 153–67; M. Kazanski 1999, *Les Slaves: les origines (Ier–VIIe siècles après J.-C.)* (Paris), pp. 96–120.

49 The settlement of this area is detailed by E. A. Goriunov 1981, *Rannie etapy istorii slavian Dneprovskogo Levoberezhya* (Leningrad).

50 It is symptomatic that (perhaps as a reflection of a desire to perceive some cultural unity of this broad area now forming modern Ukraine) this zone has not – as logic would demand – been differentiated as a separate archaeological culture, only into right and left bank Penkovka.

51 K. Godłowski 1985, *Przemiany kulturowe i osadnicze w południowej i środkowej Polsce w młodszym okresie przedrzymskim i w okresie rzymskim* (Wrocław).

52 M. Parczewski 1988, *Początki kultury wczesnosłowiańskiej w Polsce: Krytyka i datowanie źródeł archeologicznych* (Cracow); Parczewski, *Najstarsza faza kultury wczesnosłowiańskiej w Polsce*, p. 114; M. Parczewski 1993, *Die Anfänge der frühslawischen Kultur in Polen* (Vienna); the latter is basically a translation of the first-mentioned text.

53 I. Borkovský 1940, *Staroslovanská keramika ve střední Evrope: studia k počátkum slovanské kultury* (Prague); Zeman, 'Nejstarši slovanské osídlení Čech', 115–224; Jelínková,

'K chronologii sídlištních nálezů s keramikou pražkého typu na Moravé'.

54 See also J. Zeman 1979, 'K problematice časně slovanské kultury ve střední Evropě', *Památky Archeologické* 70, 113–30.

55 J. Herrmann 1979, 'Probleme der Herausbildung der archäologischen Kulturen slawischer Stämme des 6.–9. Jh.', pp. 49–75 in *Rapports du IIIe Congrès International d'Archéologie Slave* (Bratislava); also J. Herrmann 1968, *Siedlung, Wirtschaft und gesellschaftliche Verhältnisse der slawischen Stämme zwischen Oder/Neisse und Elbe* (Berlin), Abb. 6 and 11. See also J. Henning 1991, 'Germanen – Slawen – Deutsche: neue Untersuchungen zum frühgeschichtlichen Siedlungswesung östlich der Elbe', *Praehistorische Zeitschrift* 66, 119–33; also P. Donat and R. E. Fischer 1994, 'Die Anfänge slawischer Siedlung westlich der Oder', *Jahrbuch für Brandenburgische Landesgeschichte* 45, 7–30.

56 Herrmann, *Siedlung, Wirtschaft und gesellschaftliche Verhältnisse*; J. Herrmann (ed.) 1985, *Die Slawen in Deutschland: ein Handbuch. Geschichte und Kultur der slawischen Stämme westlich von Oder und Neisse vom 6. bis 12. Jahrhundert. Neubearbeitung* (Berlin), pp. 21–32.

57 J. Henning and K.-U. Heussner 1992, 'Zur Burgengeschichte im 10. Jahrhundert – neue archäologische und dendrochronologische Daten zu Anlagen vom Typ Tornow', *Ausgrabungen und Funde* 37 (6), 314–24; J. Herrmann and K.-U. Heussner 1991, 'Dendrochronologie, Archäologie und Frühgeschichte vom 6. bis 12. Jh. in den Gebieten zwischen Saale, Elbe und Oder', *Ausgrabungen und Funde* 36 (6), 255–90. This redating has been discussed by M. Dulinicz, 'Datowania absolutne i względne wybranych stanowisk wczesnośredniowiecznych Słowiańszczyzny zachodniej', *Światowit* 39, 14–31. On the possible shakiness of the previous chronology see J. Gąssowski 1984, 'O pewnych sprzecznościach w badaniach archeologicznych wczesnego średniowiecza', *Folia Praehistorica Posnaniensia* 1, 191–9.

58 Zeman, 'K problematice časně slovanské kultury'; Parczewski, *Najstarsza faza kultury wczesnosłowiańskiej w Polsce*, p. 114; K. Wachowski 1997, *Śląsk w dobie przedpiastowskiej* (Wrocław).

59 Sukow: E. Schuldt 1963, 'Vorbericht über die Ausgrabungen im Gebiet der Alten Burg von Sukow, Kr. Teterow', *Ausgrabungen und Funde* 8, 200–5; E. Schuldt 1963, 'Die Ausgrabungen im Gebiet der "Alten Burg" von Sukow, Kr. Teterow', pp. 217–38 in *Bodendenkmalpflege in Mecklenburg* (Schwerin); E. Schuldt 1963, 'Die Slawische Keramik von Sukow und das Problem der Feldberger Gruppe', pp. 239–61 in *Bodendenkmalpflege in Mecklenburg* (Schwerin). Dziedzice: A. Porzeziński 1975, 'Zasiedlenie Pomorza Zachodniego w VI–VII wieku n.e. w świetle dotychczasowych wyników badań archeologicznych', *Slavia Antiqua* 22, 29–67.

60 This was for example one of the main types of feature discovered at Żukowice, a large rescue excavation carried out in southwestern Poland before the construction of a copper mine, though square sunken-floored huts were also found here. See M. Parczewski 1989, *Żukowice pod Głogowem w zaraniu średniowiecza* (Głogów).

61 Similar arguments have been advanced by John Chapman concerning the destruction of certain prehistoric houses in central Europe which may provide some form of analogy for these mysterious features. John Chapman 1998, 'Deliberate house burning in the prehistory of Central and Eastern Europe', pp. 113–26 in A. Gustafsson and H. Karlsson (eds), *Glyfer och arkeologiska rum – en vadbok till Jarl Nordbladh* (Gothenburg).

62 Between the Sukow-Dziedzice and Mogiła groups in Poland is a zone of sites of uncertain cultural affinities. Most characteristic are small flat cremation cemeteries – Siemonia, Międzybórz, Nieporęt, and Jozefów and settlements (Wyszembork) with pottery having affinities with the later phases of the Mogiła material.

63 One may even risk a tentative and somewhat heretical question: to what do we owe the assumption that this material represents a Slav-speaking population? The answer to this question is that, if it were not, there would be little to explain the appearance of the Polish language since the centre of the early medieval state (where Polish was certainly spoken) is right in the middle of the Sukow zone.

Chapter 3

1   B. Zástěrová 1971, *Les Avares et les Slaves dans la Tactique de Maurice* (Prague).

2   For the numismatic evidence of these tribute payments see M. Kozub 1997, 'The chronology of the inflow of Byzantine coins into the Avar khaganate', pp. 241–6 in P. Urbańczyk (ed.), *Origins of Central Europe* (Warsaw).

3   Isidore of Seville, *Chronicon* (*Patrologia Latina* 83), col. 1065.

4   J. Henning 1987, *Südosteuropa zwischen Antike und Mittelalter: Archäologische Beiträge zur Landwirtschaft des 1. Jahrtausends u. Z.* (Berlin).

5   C. Vita-Finzi 1969, *The Mediterranean Valleys* (Cambridge); see also J. M. Wagstaffe 1981, 'Buried assumptions: some problems in the interpretation of the "Younger Fill" raised by recent data from Greece', *Journal of Archaeological Science* 8, 247–64. The mudslides in Italy of May 1998 which occurred as this chapter was being written seem a modern parallel to the formation of these deposits.

6   See R. Hodges and D. Whitehouse 1983, *Mohammed, Charlemagne and the Origins of Europe: Archaeology and the Pirenne Hypothesis* (London), pp. 54–76. The regular flow of coinage in the area begins again only with the early ninth-century Byzantine reconquest.

7   F. Curta (forthcoming), *The Making of the Slavs: History and Archaeology of the Lower Danube Region ca. 500–700* (Cambridge).

8   Popin-type material: Zh. Vazharova 1965, *Slavianske i slavianobulgarski selishche v bulgarskite zemi ot kraja na VI–XI vek* (Sofia). Garvan: Zh. Vazharova 1986, *Srednievekovnogo selishche s. Garvan, Silistrenski okrig VI–XI v.* (Sofia).

9   For these fibulae in general see J. Werner 1960, 'Neues zur Frage der slawischen Bügelfibeln aus südosteuropäischen Länder', *Germania* 38, 11–120.

10 Observed by Tivadar Vida and Thomas Volling (information from F. Curta).

11 For Corinth see G. R. Davidson 1937, 'The Avar invasion of Corinth', *Hesperia* 6, 227–39; G. R. Davidson 1952, *The Minor Objects* (Princeton); G. R. Davidson 1974, 'A wandering soldier's grave in Corinth', *Hesperia* 43, 512–21; Eric A. Ivison 1996, 'Burial and urbanism at Late Antique and

Early Byzantine Corinth (c. AD 400–700)', pp. 99–125 in N. Christie and S. T. Loseby (eds), *Towns in Transition: Urban Evolution in Late Antiquity and the Early Middle Ages* (Hants). For Argos see P. Aupert 1980, 'Céramique slave à Argos (585 ap. J.-C.)', pp. 373–94 in *Etudes Argiennes* (Athens).

12 J. Werner 1986, *Der Schatzfund von Vrap in Albanien: Beiträge zur Archäologie der Awarenzeit im Mittleren Donauraum* (Vienna).

13 The sixth ecumenical Council of 680–1 in Constantinople was attended by bishops of Thessalonica, Corinth, Argos and Lacedaemona (and the metropolitans of Corinth and Athens and the bishops of Nikopolis (in Epirus) were at the Council of Nicaea in 787).

14 D. M. Metcalf 1962, 'The Aegean coastlands under threat', *Annual of British School at Athens* 57, 14–23; C. Foss 1977, 'Archaeology and the twenty cities of Byzantine Asia', *American Journal of Archaeology* 81, 469–86. On the Avar tribute see Kozub, 'The chronology of the inflow of Byzantine coins'.

15 A. Toynbee 1973, *Constantine Porphyrogenitus and His World* (London), pp. 619–51.

16 I. Čremošnik 1970, 'Die Chronologie der ältesten slawischen Funde in Bosnien und der Herzegovina', *Archaeologia Iugoslavica* 11, 99–103; I. Čremošnik 1972, 'Die ältesten Ansiedlungen und Kultur der Slawen in Bosnien und der Herzegovina im Lichte der Untersuchungen in Mušici und Batkovici', *Balcanoslavica* 1, 59–64; I. Čremošnik 1975, 'Die Untersuchungen in Mušici und Zabljak: über den ersten Fund der ältesten slawischen Siedlung in Bosnien', *Wissenschaftliche Mitteilungen des bosnisch-herzegowinischen Landesmuseums* 5, 91–176. For the redating, see Curta, *The Making of the Slavs*.

17 J. Belošević 1980, *Materialna kultura Hrvata od VII do IX stoleča* (Zagreb); D. Jelovina 1976, *Starohrvatske nekropole* (Split).

18 A detailed discussion, followed by a rejection of the line of (historical) reasoning based on *DAI*, can be found in H. M. A. Evans 1989, *The Early Medieval Archaeology of Croatia A.D. 600–900* (Oxford: BAR). This book is one of the most important recent contributions to the early medieval archaeology of the Balkans, and applies an interesting model of state formation to his analysis of the Croat cemeteries.

19 F. Dvornik 1949, *The Making of Central and Eastern Europe* (London), pp. 277ff.; G. Labuda 1988, *Studia nad Początkami Państwa Polskiego* (Poznań), pp. 193–200. See also V. Popović 1975, 'Les témoins archéologiques des invasions Avaro-Slaves dans l'Illyricum Byzantine', *Mélanges de l'Ecole Française de Rome* 87, 445–504.

20 The evidence for this suggestion is not very convincing, and one has the impression that some of its supporters are concerned mainly to show a separate origin for the Serbs and Croats in the wake of the breakup of Yugoslavia.

21 These suggestions have been seen as an attempt at Serbian territorial legitimation in the aftermath of the Bosnian war. According to the author of a book on the subject (D. Jankovic 1999, *Srpske gromile*, Belgrade), the Serbs arrived in Serbia in the fourth century at the invitation of the Roman emperor.

22 S. Anamali 1964, 'La necropole de Kruje et la civilisation du haut moyen âge en Albanie du nord', *Studia Albanica* I (Tirana); B. Babić 1996, 'Badania w zakresie archeologii słowiańskiej w Republice Macedonii od 1965 do 1995 roku', *Slavia Antiqua* 37, 73–88.

23 We should perhaps rather refer to them as Proto-Bulgars, because some Bulgarian historians point out that the Bulgarian people only came into being much later as the result of the symbiosis of these Turks with the Slav substrate. For the Bulgars on the steppes see D. Dimitrov 1987, *Prabulgarite po severnoto I zapadnoto Chernomorie* (Varna).

24 Z. Szekely 1970, 'Die frühesten slawischen Siedlungen in Siebenbürgen', *Slavia Antiqua* 17, 125–36; Z. Szekely 1972, 'Slaves anciens dans le sud-est de la Transylvanie', *Balcanoslavica* 1 (1972), 55–7.

25 S. Dolinescu-Ferche 1974, *Aşezări din secolele III şi VI e.n. în sud-vestul Munteniei: cercetările de la Dulceanca* (Bucharest); 1986, 'Contributions archéologiques sur la continuité daco-romaine: Dulceanca, deuxième habitat du VI-e siècle d.n.è.', *Dacia* 30, 121–54; 1992, 'Habitats du VI-e et VII-e siècles de notre ère à Dulceanca IV', *Dacia* 36, 125–77.

26 Someşeni: M. Macrea 1959, 'Şantierul archeo-logic Someşeni-Cluj', *Materiale şi Certetări Arheologice* (Bucharest) 6, 516–20 Nuşfalău: M. Comşa 1959, 'Kurgannyj mogil'nik s

truposozhzheniem v Nuşfalău', *Dacia* NS 3, 525–34; H. Zoll-Adamikowa 1979, *Wczesnośredniowieczne cmentarzyska ciałopalne Słowian na terenie Polski (Cz. II)* (Wrocław/Cracow), p. 102, ryc. 38).

27 Unfortunately until recently some of this material was wrongly dated; these mistakes are now being corrected by dendrochronology (see above). The dates quoted here come from the most recent indications.

28 Sukow: E. Schuldt 1963, 'Die Ausgrabungen im Gebiet der "Alten Burg" von Sukow, Kr. Teterow' and 'Die Slawische Keramik von Sukow und das Problem der Feldberger Gruppe' in *Bodendenkmalpflege in Mecklenburg* (Schwerin), 217–38 and 239–61. Golancz: W. Łosiński 1972, *Początki wczesnośredniowiecznego osadnictwa grodowego w dorzeczu dolnej Parsęty (VII–X/XI w.)* (Wrocław), pp. 32–106.

29 Racibórz-Obora: M. Parczewski 1982, *Płaskowyż Głubczycki we wczesnym średniowieczu* (Cracow), pp. 54–62, Tab. 27–9. Chodlik: A. Gardawski 1970, *Chodlik (Cz. 1). Wczesnośredniowieczny zespół osadniczy* (Wrocław).

30 W. Szymański 1967, *Szeligi pod Płockiem na początku wczesnego średniowiecza, zespół osadniczy z VI–VII w.* (Wrocław). See also W. Szymański 1987, 'Próba weryfikacji datowania zespołu osadniczego ze starszych faz wczesnego średniowiecza w Szeligach, woj. płockie', *Archeologia Polski* 32, 349–76. Zimno: V. V. Aulikh 1972, *Zimnivske gorodishche – Slavianski pamiatnik VI–VII vv. n.e. v zapadnoi Volyni* (Kiev); The Haćki site is as yet unpublished.

31 Some authors (such as Herrmann) have linked the Szeligi and Sukow pottery into a 'Sukow-Szeligi' style zone. This seems however to be an intuitive oversimplification of a potentially much more complex situation, and the Szeligi-Zimno cultural group is here treated as a separate entity.

32 H. Brachmann 1978, *Slawische Stämme an Elbe und Saale: zu ihrer Geschichte und Kultur im 6. bis 10. Jh. – auf Grund archäologischer Quellen* (Berlin); H.-J. Vogt 1968, 'Zur Kenntnis der materiellen Kultur der Sorbes im Elster-Pleisse-Gebiet', *Zeitschrift für Archäologie* 2, 1–15.

33 See Z. Klanica 1986, *Počátky slovanského osídlení našich zemí* (Prague).

34 J. Eisner 1952, *Devínska Nová Ves, Slovanske pohřebiště* (Bratislava), E. Keller and V. Bierbrauer 1965, 'Beiträge zum awarenzeitlichen Gräberfeld von Devínska Nová Ves', *Slovenská Archeológia* 8, 377–97.

35 I. Kovrig 1963, 'Das awarenzeitliche Gräberfeld von Alattyán', *Archeologica Hungarica* 40; A. Točík 1968, *Slawischawarisches Gräberfeld in Holiare* (Bratislava); Z. Čilinská 1966, *Slawisch-awarisches Gräberfeld in Nové Zámky* (Bratislava); Z. Čilinská 1973, *Frühmittelalterliches Gräberfeld in Želovce* (Bratislava).

36 P. Liptak 1983, *Avars and Ancient Hungarians* (Budapest). The metalwork is accessibly illustrated in colour by Z. Čilinská 1981, *Kov v rano-slovaskom umeni* (Bratislava).

37 See F. Curta 1996, 'Slavs in Fredegar: medieval "gens" or narrative strategy?', *Acta Historica* (Szeged) 103, 3–20.

38 There are some problems with identifying this site as a stronghold as some have done. The name is Germanic and not Slav. The suffix 'burg' need not imply a constructed stronghold, but could be a defensible hill.

39 A. Gardawski 1970, *Chodlik (Cz. 1). Wcześnośredniowieczny zespół osadniczy* (Wrocław), pp. 69–102. See also K. Wachowski 1997, *Śląsk w dobie przedpiastowskiej* (Wrocław), pp. 18–19.

40 This material is considered by T. Vida 1999, *Die awarenzeitliche Keramik I. (6.–7. Jh.)* (Berlin/Budapest).

41 N. Profantová 1992, 'Awarische Funde aus dem Gebieten nördlich der awarischen Siedlungsgrenzen', pp. 605–778 in F. Daim (ed.), *Awarenforschungen II: Studien zur Archäologie der Awaren*, vol. 4 (Vienna).

42 Zoll-Adamikowa, *Wczesnośredniowieczne cmentarzyska*, pp. 222–4, ryc. 56; R. Turek 1954–6; 'Mohyly Českých Charvatů' *Slavia Antiqua* 5, 103–57; D. Bialeková 1962, 'Nové Včasnoslovanské nálezy z juhozapádného Slovenska', *Slovenská Archeológia* 10 (i), 97–145.

43 S. Pazda 1973, 'Cmentarzysko kurhanowe pod Izbickiem, pow. Strzelce Opolskie, w świetle dotychczasowych badań wykopaliskowych', *Sprawozdanie Archeologiczne* 25, 213–33; S. Pazda 1983, 'Wczesnośredniowieczne cmentarzysko kurhanowe w Izbicku, woj. opolskie', *Studia Archeologiczne* 13 (Wrocław), 96–157.

44 See Kozub, 'The chronology of the inflow of Byzantine coins'.

45 The parallel is in fact quite an apposite one. The countries of 'the West' served as the same kind of idealized Eldorado acting as a magnet for the peoples of Communist-dominated central and eastern Europe before 1989.

46 J. Werner 1950, 'Slawische Bügelfibeln des 7. Jahrhunderts', pp. 150–72 in G. Behrens and J. Werner (eds), *Reinecke Festschrift* (Mainz); Werner, 'Neues zur Frage der slawischen Bügelfibeln'. See also L. Vagalinski 1994, 'Zur Frage der ethnischen Herkunft der späten Strahlenfibeln (Finger- oder Bügelfibeln) aus dem Donau-Karpaten-Becken (6–7. Jh.)', *Zeitschrift für Archäologie* 28, 261–305. M. Kazanski's (1999) *Les Slaves: les origines (Ier–VIIe siècles après J.-C.)* (Paris) places a lot of emphasis on this decorated metalwork, perhaps giving a false impression of the nature of Slav material culture as a whole.

47 E. Cnotliwy 1998, 'Grzebienie w kulturze wczesnosłowiańskiej na terenie południowej i środkowej Polski', pp. 366–79 in H. Kóčka-Krenz and W. Łosiński (eds), *Kraje słowiańskie w wiekach średnich: profanum i sacrum* (Poznań).

48 J. Żak and L. Maćkowiak-Kotkowska 1988, *Studia nad uzbrojeniem środkowoeuropejskim VI–X wieku* (Poznań).

49 A. A. Spitsyn 1928, 'Drevnosti Antov', pp. 492–5 in *Sbornik statej v chest akademika I. Sobolevskogo* (Leningrad).

50 L. V. Pekarskaja and D. Kidd 1994, *Der Silberschatz von Martynovka (Ukraine) aus dem 6. und 7. Jahrhundert* (Innsbruck); D. S. W. Kidd 1987, 'Südrussische und donauländische Funde aus dem British Museum, London', pp. 107–13 in *Germanen, Hunnen und Awaren: Schätze der Völkerwanderungszeit* (Nuremberg).

51 I. O. Gavritukhin and A. M. Oblomski 1990, *Gaponovski klad i ego kulturno-istoricheski kontekst* (Moscow).

52 O. Shcheglova 1990, 'O dvukh gruppakh "drevnostei Antov" v Srednem Podneprove', *Materialy i Issledovania po Arkheologii Dneprovskogo Levoberezhia* (Kursk).

53 The famous 'hoard' from Male Pereshchepino is earlier than these deposits, and seems more likely to be a grave assemblage, possibly connected with the Bulgars rather than the Slavs.

54 Contacts between the tribes in the forest steppe zone with the nomads seems to have been a constant feature of the cultural development of the area.

55 The map here distinguishes between sites which seem more likely to be seventh century in origin and a series of sites in former East Germany which were included on a map by Irena Rusanova as producing pottery of this date. This now requires further verification.

56 Szymański, *Szeligi pod Płockiem*. See also Szymański, 'Próba weryfikacji datowania'. I am grateful to Dr Marek Dulinicz and Waldemar Moszczyński for information about the carbon 14 dates.

57 M. Braichevsky 1951, 'Raboty na Pastyrskom gorodishche v 1949 g.', *Kratkie Soobshchenia Instituta Istorii Materialnoi Kultury* 36, 155–64 and refs.

58 W. Szymański 1984, 'Beiträge zum Problem der Entstehung von Burgen bei den Slawen', *Archaeologia Polona* 21/22, 89–104. See also Z. Kobyliński 1988, *Struktury osadnicze na ziemiach polskich u schyłku starożytności i w początkach wczesnego średniowiecza* (Wrocław), pp. 196–8.

Chapter 4

1 L. Leciejewicz 1989, *Słowianie Zachodni: z dziejów tworzenia się średniowiecznej Europy* (Wrocław), pp. 65–6, fig. 8. See also S. Kurnatowski 1971, 'Rozwój zaludnienia Wielkopolski zachodniej we wczesnym średniowieczu i jego aspekty gospodarcze', *Archeologia Polski* 16, 465–82; S. Kurnatowski 1975, 'Wczesnośredniowieczny przełom gospodarczy w Wielkopolsce oraz jego aspekty gospodarcze', *Archeologia Polski* 20, 145–60. It should be noted that these figures were based on the older field surveys and may undergo modification when the results of recent work are synthesized.

2 See D. Obolensky 1950, 'Russia's Byzantine heritage', *Oxford Slavonic Papers* I, 37–63.

3 Popin-type material: Zh. Vazharova 1965, *Slavianske i slavianobulgarski selishche v bulgarskite zemi ot kraya na VI–XI vek* (Sofia). Garvan: Zh. Vazharova 1986, *Srednovekovnogo selishche s. Garvan, Silistrenski okrig VI–XI v.* (Sofia).

4 Slav settlement on Crete and Aegean islands as well as in Asia Minor is probably the result of resettlement of prisoners from these Byzantine wars.

5 There is a considerable literature on the Bulgarian state and its relation to the Byzantine Empire. See for example D. Obolensky 1966, 'The Empire and its northern neighbours 565–1018', *Cambridge Medieval History*, vol. IV.1 (Cambridge), pp. 475–518; D. Obolensky 1994, *Byzantium and the Slavs* (New York); S. Runciman 1930, *A History of the First Bulgarian Empire* (London); R. Browning 1975, *Byzantium and Bulgaria: A Comparative Study across the Early Medieval Frontier* (London); J. V. A. Fine 1983, *The Early Medieval Balkans: A Critical Survey from the Late Sixth to the Late Twelfth Century* (Ann Arbor); J. Shepard 1995, 'Slavs and Bulgars', *New Cambridge Medieval History*, vol. II (edited by Rosamond McKitterick) (Cambridge), pp. 228–48; D. Angelov 1980, *Die Entstehung des Bulgarischen Volkes* (Berlin).

6 The identification of this population with the 'Koman-Kruj' Culture has become one of the most controversial issues of the archaeology of the Balkans in recent years (some scholars wanting to link it with certain Slav groups).

7 Also known as Privina, he was apparently prince of Nitra. Driven out of his territory by the expansion of Mojmir of the Moravians in 833, he fled to the Frankish ruler, who had him christened and in 840 settled him in the east.

8 The nature and precise extent of the territories ruled by Pribina and Kocelj are unclear.

9 A start has been made on this problem in an interesting book: M. Parczewski 1991, *Początki kształtowania się polsko-ruskiej rubieży etnicznej w Karpatach: u źródeł rozpadu Słowiańszczyzny na odłam wschodni i zachodni* (Cracow).

10 I am grateful to Igor Gavritukhin for information on recent work on this question, some of which is included in the monograph on the Gaponovo hoard which contains much more than its title suggests (I. O. Gavritukhin and A. M. Oblomski 1996, *Gaponvski klad i ego kulturno-istoricheski kontekst* (Moscow), pp. 136–9). For the Luka Raikovetska Culture see V. K. Goncharov 1963 'Luka Raikovetska', *Materialy i Issledovania po Arkheologii SSSR* 108, 283–316; V. V. Sedov 1982, *Vostochnye slaviane v VI–XIII vv.* (Moscow, *Arkheologia SSSR* 14), pp. 90–3, tab 23.1–7; *Arkheologia Ukrainskoi SSR* II (1986), 174–91.

11 Information from Mieczysław Bienia and Wojciech Wróblewski.

12 This Sakhanovka-type material is also discussed in the monograph on the Gaponovo hoard (note 10).

13 P. P. Tolochko 1983, *Drevni Kiev* (Kiev), p. 28 (though we have seen above that some scholars have suggested an even earlier origin for this site).

14 V. K. Goncharov 1950, *Raikovetskoe gorodishche* (Kiev); Yu. V. Kukharenko 1961, *Srednevekovye pamiatniki Polesia* (Moscow); Yu. V. Kukharenko 1957, 'Razkopki na gorodishche i selishche Khotomel', *Kratkie Soobshchenia Instituta Istorii Materialnoi Kultury* 68, 90–7; Sedov, *Vostochnye slaviane*, pp. 10–87.

15 For the Volyntsevo culture see M. Gimbutas 1971, *The Slavs* (London), pp. 90–1 and refs; I. I. Liapushkin 1961, *Dneprovskoe lesostepnoe Levoberezhie v epokhu zheleza* (Moscow, *Materialy i Issledovania po Arkheologii SSSR* 104); D. T. Berezovets 1969, 'Nove razkopki v s. Volyntsevo', *Arkheologicheske Issledovannia na Ukraine v 1965–1966* (Kiev), pp. 166–9; Sedov, *Vostochnye slaviane*, pp. 135–8, tab 35; *Arkheologia Ukrainskoi SSR* II (1986), 191–201.

16 I am indebted to Igor Gavritukhin for guiding me to some of the recent literature on this. The question is also discussed in the monograph on the Gaponovo hoard (Gavritukhin and Oblomski, *Gaponvski klad i ego kulturno-istoricheski kontekst*, pp. 130–6).

17 For Romny-type sites see Gimbutas, *The Slavs*, pp. 91–2 and refs; Liapushkin, *Dneprovskoe lesostepnoe Levoberezhie*; Sedov, *Vostochnye slaviane*, pp. 135–8 and 140–2, tab 32–3; *Arkheologia Ukrainskoi SSR* II, (1986), pp. 201–12).

18 P. P. Efimenko and P. N. Tretiakov 1948, *Drevnerusskie poseleniia na Donu* (Moscow, *Materialy i Issledovania po Arkheologii SSSR* 8), pp. 14–91.

19 I. I. Liapushkin 1958, *Gorodishche Novotroitskoe. O kulture vostochnykh slavian v period slozhenia Kievskogo gosudarstva* (Moscow, *Materialy i Issledovania po Arkheologii SSSR* 74).

20 The Khazars have attracted a considerable literature. See D. M. Dunlop 1954, *The History of the Jewish Khazars* (Princeton); S. A. Pletneva 1987, *Die Chaseren: mittelalter-*

liches Reich an Don und Wolga (Leipzig);
S. A. Pletneva 1981, *Stepi Evrazii v epokhu
srednevekovia* (Moscow, Arkheologia SSSR
18). For the interrelationships between
Khazars and Slavs see also S. Franklin and
J. Shepard 1996, *The Emergence of Rus:
750–1200* (London and New York), pp. 79ff.,
and S. A. Pletneva 1989, *Na slaviano-khaz-
arskom pograniche: dmitrievski arkheo-
ligicheski kompleks* (Moscow). See also
A. P. Novoseltsev 1990, *Khazarskoe
gosudarstvo i ego rol v istorii Vostochnoi
Evropy i Kavkaza* (Moscow).

21 G. Labuda 1988, 'Polska, Czechy, Ruś i kraj
Lędzian w drugiej połowie X wieku',
pp. 167–211 in his *Studia nad Początkami
Państwa Polskiego*, vol. II (Poznań).

22 The question of the oral traditions in the *PVL*
is covered in the excellent essay (1996) by
E. A. Melnikova, 'Oral tradition in the
Primary Chronicle', pp. 93–112 in her *The
Eastern World of the Vikings* (Gothenburg).

23 Franklin and Shepard, *The Emergence of Rus*,
p. 95.

24 M. Karger 1958, *Drevni Kiev*
(Moscow/Leningrad); E. Mühle 1987, 'Die
Anfänge Kievs (bis ca. 980) in archäologischer
Sicht: ein Forschungsbericht', *Jahrbücher für
Geschichte Osteuropas* 35, 80–101;
O. M. Ioannisyan 1990, 'Archaeological
evidence for the development and urbanization
of Kiev from the 8th to the 14th centuries',
pp. 285–311 in D. Austin and L. Alcock (eds),
*From the Baltic to the Black Sea: Studies in
Early Medieval Archaeology* (London).

25 Franklin and Shepard, *The Emergence of Rus*,
p. 96.

26 D. I. Blifeld 1977, *Davnoruski pamiatky
Shestovytsi* (Kiev).

27 The material of these cultures is published in a
number of scattered publications. For
Kolochin see E. A. Simonovich 1963,
'Gorodishche Kolochin I', *Materialy i
Issledovania po Arkheologii SSSR* 108,
97–137; A. G. Mitrofanov 1978, *Zhelazny
viek Srednie Belorussii (VII–VI vv do n.e.–VIII v.
n.e.)* (Minsk); L. D. Pobol 1971, *Slavianskie
drevnosti Belorussii* (Minsk); Sedov,
Vostochnye slaviane, pp. 29–34; *Arkheologia
Ukrainskoi SSR* II (1986), 167–74. See also
M. Kazanski 1999, *Les Slaves: les origines
(Ier–VIIe siècles après J.-C.)* (Paris), pp. 33–7
and 120–9. These cultures are also briefly
summarized by P. Dolukhanov 1996, *The

Early Slavs* (London), pp. 167–70.

28 V. V. Sedov 1987, 'Origine de la branche du
Nord des Slaves orientaux', pp. 161–5 in
G. Labuda and S. Tabaczyński (eds), *Studia
nad etnogenezą Słowian*, vol. I (Warsaw).

29 For these cultures see P. N. Tretiakov and
E. A, Shmidt 1963, *Drevnie gorodishcha
Smolenshchiny* (Moscow/Leningrad);
P. N. Tretiakov 1966, *Finno-Ugri, Balty i
Slaviane na Dnepre i Volge* (Moscow/
Leningrad), pp. 113–89; V. V. Sedov 1970,
Slaviane Verkhnego Podneprovia i Podvinia
(Moscow), pp. 8–62; Pobol, *Slavianskie
drevnosti Belorussii*; Sedov, *Vostochnye
slaviane*, pp. 34–45; *Arkheologia Ukrainskoi
SSR* II (1986), 167–74; Kazanski, *Les Slaves*,
pp. 125–9.

30 V. V. Sedov 1970, *Novgorodski sopki*
(Moscow); V. V. Sedov 1974, *Dlinnye kurgany
Krivichei* (Moscow); Sedov, 'Origine'. These
sites are also discussed in English in
Dolukhanov, *The Early Slavs*, pp 168–9; see
also Kazanski, *Les Slaves*, pp. 129–35.

31 C. Goehrke 1992, *Frühzeit des Ostslaventums*
(Darmstadt, Erträge der Forschung 277).

32 This question is discussed with references by
Franklin and Shepard, *The Emergence of Rus*,
pp. 3–70.

33 See Franklin and Shepard, *The Emergence of
Rus*, pp. 50–4.

34 T. Wasilewski 1976, 'Dulebowie – Lędzianie –
Chorwaci: z zagadnień osadnictwa
plemiennego i stosunków politycznych nad
Bugiem, Sanem i Wisłą w X wieku', *Przegląd
Historyczny* 67, 181–94.

35 Labuda, 'Polska, Czechy, Ruś'.

36 Another group which has been located in this
area by certain historians (e.g., H. Łowmiański)
is the Croats, but there is good reason to locate
those mentioned in the *PVL* much further to the
east.

37 E. Schuldt 1956, *Der Slawische Keramik in
Mecklenburg* (Berlin); H. Brachmann 1978,
Slawische Stämme an Elbe und Saale (Berlin);
P. Donat 1987, 'Zur zeitlichen und regionalen
Gliederung der altslawischen Keramik
zwischen Oder und Elbe/Saale', pp. 239–54 in
Labuda and Tabaczyński (eds), *Studia nad
Etnogenezą Słowian*, vol. I.

38 M. Dulinicz 1994, 'Problem datowania
grodzisk typu Tornow i grupy Tornow-
Klenica', *Archeologia Polski* 39, 31–49.

39 Tornow: J. Herrmann 1973, *Die germanischen
und slawischen Siedlungen und das mittelalter-*

liche Dorf von Tornow, Kr. Calau (Berlin).
Klenica: E. Petersen 1937, 'Der Burgwall von
Kleinitz, Kr. Grunberg', *Altschlesien* 7 (i),
59–75.

40 S. Brather 1994, 'Feldberger Keramik und
frühe Slawen ...', *Ethnographisch-
Archäologische Zeitschrift* 35, 613–29;
S. Brather 1995, 'Nordwestslawische
Siedlungskeramik der Karolingerzeit –
Fränkische Waren als Vorbild?', *Germania*
73 (2), 403–20; S. Brather 1996, *Feldberger
Keramik und frühe Slawen: Studien zur
norwestslawischen Keramik der Karolingerzeit*
(Bonn).

41 H. Rempel 1966, *Reihengräberfriedhöfe des 8.
bis 11. Jahrhundertes aus Sachsenanhalt,
Sachsen und Thüringen* (Berlin). The proposed
redating is based on recent work on the
typology of the silver ornaments.

42 See W. Łosiński 1982, *Osadnictwo plemienne
Pomorza (VI–X wiek)* (Wrocław).

43 Brather, *Feldberger Keramik und frühe
Slawen*, pp. 187–96.

44 This traveller's account survives in the ninth-
century translation of Orosius' *History* done
by none less than the English King Alfred the
Great.

45 K. Langenheim 1937, 'Ein wichtiger frühslawischer Siedlungsfund vom "Schmiederberg"
bei Gustau Kr. Glogau', *Altschlesien* 7, 76–93;
K. Langenheim 1939, 'Der frühslawische
Burgwall von Gustau Kr. Glogau', *Altschlesien*
8, 104–27; P. Rzeźnik (in print), 'Wznowienie
badań wykopaliskowych na wczesnośredniowiecznym grodzisku w Gostyniu, gm.
Gaworzyce', *Śląskie Sprawozdania
Archeologiczne*.

46 L. Leciejewicz 1985, 'Das Karolingische Reich
und die Westslawen: zur Entfaltung einer
Kulturgrenzzone im 8.–9. Jahrhundert',
pp. 147–55 in H. Friesinger and F. Daim (eds),
Die Bayern und ihre Nachbarn (Vienna).

47 J. Henning and A. Ruttkay (eds) 1998,
*Frühmittelalterlicher Burgenbau in Mittel- und
Osteuropa* (Bonn).

48 The information is conveniently presented by
J. Herrmann 1968, *Siedlung, Wirtschaft und
gesellschaftliche Verhältnisse der slawischen
Stämme zwischen Oder/Neisse und Elbe:
Studien auf der Grundlage archäologischen
Materials* (Berlin), Abb. 24.

49 K. Wachowski 1992, *Kultura karolińska a
Słowiałńszczyzna zachodnia* (Wrocław).

50 J. Poulík 1948, *Staroslovanská Morava*
(Brno); J. Poulík 1950, *Jižní Morava, zeme
dáwnych Slovanu* (Brno).

51 The collapse of Avar power did not lead to a
break in the cultural development of the
area south of the Danube, and many of the
cemeteries of the area continued in use.
North of the Danube at the end of the Avar
period appear a series of smaller cemeteries
containing mainly armed burials. These seem
to relate to strategically placed settlements
inhabited by garrisons of warriors (e.g.
Komarno in Slovakia).

52 See J. Sláma 1986, 'Střední Čechy v raném
středověku II. Hradiště: přispěvky k jejich
dějinám a významu', *Praehistorica* 11 (Prague);
M. Gojda 1991, *The Ancient Slavs* (Edinburgh),
pp. 44–57.

53 The tribe inhabited the area of the upper
Vistula, possibly around Cracow. It is
mentioned in a ninth-century edition of
geography of Europe (the introduction to
Alfred the Great's translation of Orosius) and
in the document known as the *Bavarian
Geographer*.

54 The problem is interesting in the light of the
presence of the silver jewellery itself,
presumably made locally from melting down
silver coin.

55 The Moravian material is presented conve-
niently in English by Z. Váňa 1983, *The World
of the Ancient Slavs* (London/Detroit); also
S. Beeby, D. Buckton and Z. Klanica 1982,
*Great Moravia: The Archaeology of Ninth
Century Czechoslovakia* (London, British
Museum); another useful source in English is
J. Poulík 1975, 'Mikulčice: capital of the lords
of Great Moravia', pp. 1–31 in R. Bruce-
Mitford (ed.), *Recent Archaeological
Excavations in Europe* (London); see also
J. Dekan 1980, *Velká Morava* (Prague);
J. Dekan 1980, *Moravia Magna: Grossmähren
– Epoche und Kunst* (Bratislava); J. Poulík and
B. Chropovský 1986, *Grossmähren und die
Anfänge der tschechoslowakischen
Staatlichkeit* (Prague); L. E. Havlík 1989,
'Great Moravia, between the Franconians,
Byzantium and Rome', pp. 227–37 in *Centre
and Periphery: Comparative Studies in
Archaeology* (London); but also M. Eggers
1995, *Das Grossmährische Reich: Realität
oder Fiktion?* (Stuttgart, *Monographien zur
Geschichte des Mittelalters* 40). Two important
studies in Polish – K. Polek 1994, *Państwo
wielkomorawskie i jego sąsiedzi* (Cracow), and

K. Polek 1994 *Podstawy gospodarcze państwa wielkomorawskiego* (Cracow) – deserve to be better known.

56 The Magyars (ancestors of the Hungarians) were a Finno-Ugrian-speaking tribe with a nomadic lifestyle from the north of the Sea of Azov. They had previously been settled in a homeland which they called Etelkoz on the steppe north of the Sea of Azov.

57 The ethnic situation in the area was complex: the Carpathian basin was on the fringes of the area controlled by the Bulgars (who themselves had penetrated the area after the collapse of the Avars), and we have seen that some kind of proto-state organization had been forming here around Zalavar. There were also no doubt remnants of an 'Avar' population.

58 M. Schulze 1984, 'Das Ungarische Kriegergrab von Apres-les-Corps: Untersuchungen zu den Ungareinfälle nach Mittel-, West- und Südeuropa (899–955 n. Chr.) mit Excurs zur Münzchronologie altungarischer Gräber', *Jahrbuch des Römisch–Germanischen Zentral-museums Mainz* 31, 473–514.

59 Poulík and Chropovský, *Grossmähren und die Anfänge der tschechoslowakischen Staatlichkeit.*

60. M. Šolle 1966, *Stará Kouřim a projevy velko-moravské hmotné kultury v Čechách* (Prague).

Chapter 5

1 In writing much of this chapter I was greatly helped by consulting the volumious and fascinating fourth revised edition (1987) of Witold Hensel's *Słowiańszczyzna wczesnośredniowieczna, zarys kultury materialnej* (Warsaw). This book is richly illustrated. The shorter third edition was also issued in a German version: W. Hensel 1965, *Die Slawen im frühen Mittelalter: ihre materielle Kultur* (Berlin).

2 The account has been based on an overview of the bone reports of a number of Czech, Slovak and Polish cemeteries dating from the ninth to the eleventh century. It must be emphasized that we can expect no 'racial unity' of Slav populations, and the details of regional and temporal variations may be revealed by further work.

3 This reference illustrates the complexities of using the written sources. It is referring to a

specific situation (the dress adopted before entering a strenuous fight) and a specific geographical region. The word used by Procopius seems to be Persian in origin and would refer to a type of trousers known to the Greeks as the dress of barbarians (Persians, Scythians etc.) and ridiculed by writers from Herodotus to Plutarch.

4 Even today in rural communities (for example in northeastern Poland) married women often put on a headscarf before leaving the house.

5 T. Lewicki 1951/2, 'Ze studiów nad źródłami arabskimi', *Slavia Antiqua* III, 136–78 (the custom was observed by Abu Hamid al-Andalusi and is discussed on page 143).

6 This is however medieval (post-tenth-century), and is published in *Silesia Antiqua* (1979), 158.

7 For a brief discussion of the *zadruga* in the context of Slav social organization see M. Gimbutas 1971, *The Slavs* (London), pp. 133–41. See also J. W. Richards 1986, 'The Slavic zadruga and other archaic Indo-European elements in traditional Slavic society', *The Mankind Quarterly* 26, 321–37.

8 For example Mariusz Baumann 1982, 'From problems of the origin and collapse of the Yugoslavian zadruga', *Ethnologia Polona* 8, 131–41.

9 The most accessible English translation is to be found in M. Magnusson 1976, *Hammer of the North*, pp. 98–101.

10 This evidence is discussed by H. Zoll-Adamikowa 1979, *Wczesnośredniowieczne cmentarzyska ciałopalne Słowian na terenie Polski* (Wrocław), vol. II, pp. 133–41. The evidence is however not conclusive; the remains of the different individuals could have been deposited in the same burial at different times.

11 It is interesting that both the engagement ritual known as the *oczepiny* and *postrzyżyny* have a connection with the hair.

12 P. Donat 1980, *Haus, Hof und Dorf in Mitteleuropa vom 7. bis 12. Jahrhundert* (Berlin).

13 For the usual reconstruction see I. Pleinerová 1986, 'Březno: experiments with building Old Slavic houses and living in them', *Památky Archeologicke* 77, 104–76. The 'two-storey' idea is presented by J. Herrmann 1986, 'Wegbereiter einer neuen Welt – der Welt der Staaten und Völker des europäischen Mittelalters', pp. 41–56 in J. Herrmann (ed.)

1986, *Welt der Slawen: Geschichte, Gesellschaft, Kultur* (Leipzig/Jena/Berlin), figure on p. 45 based on evidence from Krvina in Bulgaria.

14 Slav material culture is admirably dealt with by Hensel, *Słowiańszczyzna wczesnośredniowieczna* and also finely illustrated in B. Kolchin, V. Yanin and S. Yamshchikov (eds) 1985, *Drevni Novgorod* (Moscow).

15 The evidence from the West Slav areas is presented by J. Herrmann (ed.) 1985, *Die Slawen in Deutschland* (Berlin), pp. 83–92; A. Gręzak and B. Kurach 1996, 'Konsumpcja mięsa w średniowieczu oraz w czasach nowożytnych na terenie obecnych ziem Polski w świetle danych archeologicznych', *Archeologia Polski* 41, 139–67. The evidence from Moravia and Slovakia has been summarized by K. Polek 1994, *Podstawy gospodarcze państwa wielkomorawskiego* (Cracow), pp. 61–4. The evidence from the South Slav regions is discussed by J. Henning 1987, *Südosteuropa zwischen Antike und Mittelalter* (Berlin), pp. 102–5, from which our figure is taken.

16 Dessau: B. Krüger 1967, *Dessau-Mosigkau: ein frühslawischer Siedlungsplatz im mittleren Elbegebiet* (Berlin). Březno: I. Pleinerová 1975, *Březno: vesnice prvních Slovanů v severozápadních Čechách* (Prague). Żukowice: M. Parczewski 1989, *Żukowice pod Głogowem w zaraniu średniowiecza* (Głogów, Głogowskie Zeszyty Naukowe, vol. 2). Korchak: I. P. Rusanova 1963, 'Poselenie u s. Korchaka na r. Tetereve', *Materialy i Issledovania po Arkheologii SSSR* 108, 39–50. Kodyn: I. P. Rusanova and B. A. Timoshchuk 1984, *Kodyn – slavianskie poselena V–VIII vv na r. Prut* (Moscow).

Chapter 6

1 Although the term 'tribe' has been attacked in certain schools of ethnological thought, it will be used here as it is easily understood.

2 W. Hensel 1960, *Polska przed tysiącem lat* (Wrocław), pp. 98–100.

3 See for example J. Ostoja-Zagórski 1978, 'The problem of the organisation of prehistoric communities', *Folia Praehistorica Posnaniensis* III, 209–20; D. Třeštík 1971, 'K sociální struktuře přemyslovských Čech', *Československý Časopis Historický* 21, 537–67; M. Kučera 1978, 'Probleme der Entstehung und Entwicklung des Feudalismus in der Slovakei', *Studia Historica Slovaca* 10, 11–42; also J. Gąssowski 1992, 'Problematyka wczesnej państwowości w świetle danych archeologicznych', pp. 9–25 in M. Tymowski and M. Ziółkowski (eds), *Geneza i funkcjonowanie wczesnych form państwowości na tle porównawczym* (Warsaw).

4 For an overview of the 'Marxist' archaeology of the Soviet Union see B. Trigger 1989, *A History of Archaeological Thought* (Cambridge), pp. 148–206.

5 The literature is vast. See for example E. Service 1971, *Primitive Social Organisations: An Evolutionary Approach* (New York); M. Sahlins 1968, *Tribesmen* (Englewood Cliffs); T. K. Earle 1991, *Chiefdoms: Power, Economy and Ideology* (Cambridge); C. Redman 1978, *The Rise of Civilisation* (San Francisco). For an introduction from the archaeologist's point of view see C. Renfrew and P. Bahn 1991, *Archaeology, Theories, Methods and Practice* (London), pp. 153–94.

6 F. Curta 1999, 'Feasting with kings in an ancient democracy: on the Slavic society of the Early Middle Ages (sixth to seventh centuries AD)', *Essays in Medieval Studies* 15, 19–34.

7 J. Haldon 1993, *The State and the Tributary Mode of Production* (London/New York).

8 Likewise we hear also of Slav warriors among the bodyguards of some Islamic caliphs.

9 These graves have been studied in the former Soviet Union (see below) but more recently in Great Poland: see M. Kara 1991, 'Z badań nad wczesnośredniowiecznymi grobami z uzbrojeniem z terenu Wielkopolski', pp. 118–20 in L. Leciejewicz (ed.) 1991, *Od plemienia do państwa: Śląsk na tle wczesnośredniowiecznej Słowiańszczyzny zachodniej* (Wrocław/Warsaw).

10 The example is drawn from P. Kottack 1991 (5th ed.), *Anthropology: The Exploration of Human Diversity* (New York), pp. 209–11.

11 This is a statement that archaeologists from the various People's 'Democratic' Republics of the Soviet bloc were particularly fond of quoting. Now after the fall of Communism and the rediscovery of a different democracy it is becoming popular again.

12 See for example J. Herrmann (ed.) 1985, *Die Slawen in Deutschland* (Berlin), p. 252 and refs.

13 There is only the dubious exception of the incomplete copy of a document known as *Dagome Iudex* referring to Poland (see Chapter 12). This abstract of a document (if authentic and if associated with Mieszko) would seem to suggest personal ownership of a huge area of territory by the person making the grant to the see of St Peter.

14 Z. Kurnatowska 1997, 'Territorial structures in west Poland prior to the founding of the state organisation of Mieszko I', pp. 125–35 in P. Urbańczyk (ed.), *Origins of Central Europe* (Warsaw); Z. Kurnatowska 1965, 'Małe plemiona wczesnego średniowiecza i archeologiczne sposoby ich badania', *Slavia Antiqua* 12, 83–126; Leciejewicz (ed.), *Od plemienia do państwa.*

15 The figures quoted refer to West Slav units such as in Poland and Bohemia. In the East Slav areas the tribal unions incorporated into the Kievan state appear to have had areas of the order of 40,000 to 65,000 sq km in the case of the forest steppe tribal unions (Volynians, Derevlane, Tyvercy, Severiane, Uliche and the Dregovichi, and Radimichi). The northern tribal unions covered a wider but probably sparsely populated area reaching about 145,000 sq km in the case of the Viatichi and about 126,000 sq km in the case of the Novgorod Slovienie.

16 Of the enormous literature one may select only a few publications: P. Grimm 1958, *Die vor- und frühgeschichtlichen Burgwälle der Bezirke Halle und Magdeburg* (Berlin) is still a useful overview of some of the German sites, to which may be added Herrmann (ed.), *Die Slawen in Deutschland*, pp. 186–261, and H. Brachmann 1993, *Der Frühmittelalterliche Befestigungsbau in Mitteleuropa* (Berlin, *Schriften zur Ur- und Frühgeschichte* 45); the synthesis of M. Šolle 1983, *Staroslovanské hradisko* (Prague) is based around the Bohemian material. There is much evidence from the former Soviet Union: see B. A. Kolchin (ed.) 1985, *Drevniaia Rus': gorod, zamok, selo* (Moscow, *Arkheologia SSSR* 15); P. Rappoport 1969, 'Russian military architecture', *Gladius* 8, 39–62.

17 My estimate (unpublished) is that the construction of a smallish stronghold 30 m across would take about fifty to sixty people about five weeks' stakhanite work to build (not including cutting and hauling the wood or the construction of internal buildings).

18 B. Dostál 1975, *Breclav-Pohansko IV: Velkomoravský velomožský dvorec* (Brno).

19 E. Dąbrowska 1978, 'Etapy kształtowania się osadnictwa grodowego i formowania organizacji grodowych u Słowian zachodnich we wczesnym średniowieczu', *Archeologia Polski* 23, 425–44 (though some of the dating of these changes requires modification).

20 This type of settlement enclosure is not however restricted to the Slavs; it is also the primary type of settlement known in the forest zone among the Finno-Ugrian tribes and East Balts beyond the area of Slav settlement.

21 It should be noted though in contrast that the written sources concerning the Slav invasions of Greece hint that it was part of the native Greek population which retreated to defensible hilltop and island sites.

22 R. L. Carniero 1970, 'A theory on the origin of the state', *Science* 169, 733–8; D. Light, S. Keller and C. Calhoun 1989, *Sociology* (5th ed.) (New York); J. W. Vanden Zander 1988, *The Social Experience: An Introduction to Sociology* (New York), p. 463.

23 F. Engels 1884, *Die Ursprung der Familie, des Privateigentums und des Staates* (Zurich); J. V. Stalin 1938, 'Dialectical and historical materialism' (reprinted in J. V. Stalin 1953, *Problems of Leninism* (Moscow), pp. 713–45).

24 M. H. Fried 1967, *The Evolution of Political Society: An Essay in Political Anthropology* (New York), p. 157. For the rise of the state see H. J. M. Claessons and P. Skalnik (eds) 1978, *The Early State* (The Hague/Paris/New York).

25 It is notable that such interpretations have become more popular in central European states since the collapse of Communism and the rise of a new enterprising elite. It is difficult to escape the conclusion that this is history written anew for the new Yuppie class.

26 The role of military force, of war and conquest played a considerable role in Engels's view of the origin of the state. The conquest theory (*Überlagerungstheorie*) of the origin of the state of the German sociologist F. Oppenheimer has broad resemblances to Engels's.

27 The notions of 'core' and 'periphery' have yet to be applied to central European historiography in a satisfactory manner, and current political trends towards linking central Europe to the European Union have led in some of these countries to interpretations of the nature

of East–West relationships coloured more by
fond wishes than by historical accuracy.

28 Poland: recent work by Zofia Kurnatowska
(see for example Z. Kurnatowska 1996, 'The
organisation of the Polish state – possible
interpretations of archaeological sources',
Questiones Medii Aevi Novae 1 (Warsaw),
5–24; Kurnatowska, 'Territorial structures'.
Bohemia: J. Sláma 1988, *Střední Čechy v
raném středověku III: archeologie o počátkích
přemyslovského státu* (Prague, *Praehistorica*
14).

29 A. Buko 1992, 'Origins of towns in southern
Poland: the example of medieval Sandomierz',
Archaeologia Polona 32, 171–84; A. Buko
1998; *Początki Sandomierza* (Warsaw).

30 Č. Staňa 1998, 'Polské prvky v raně
středověké keramice na Moravě', pp. 273–87
in H. Kóčka-Krenz and W. Łosiński (eds)
1998, *Kraje słowiańskie w wiekach średnich:
profanum i sacrum* (Poznań).

Chapter 7

1 There does not seem to be much synthetic
literature devoted to Slav warfare. Several of
the discussions of the Eastern Roman and
Byzantine sources (*Strategikon*, Procopius
and Theophilactus Simokattes) touch on the
written sources for Slav attacks on the frontier.
For Poland there is A. Nadolski (ed.) 1994,
Polska technika wojskowa do 1500 roku
(Warsaw), while a number of synthetic works
deal with weapons and strongholds. For
Moravia see A. Ruttkay 1982, 'The organization of troops, warfare and arms in the period
of the Great Moravian state', *Slovenská
Acheologia* 30, 165–98.

2 W. Pohl 1991, 'Conceptions of ethnicity in
early medieval studies', *Archaeologia Polona*
29, 39–50.

3 W. Timpel 1967, 'Zwei neue
frühmittelalterliche Sporengräber aus
Thüringen', *Ausgrabungen und Funde* 12,
273–7.

4 There has been much discussion about the
nature of these breeches. As we have seen, the
word used by Procopius refers to a type of
trousers known to be the dress of the eastern
barbarians.

5 The absence of metal stirrups from many sites
is not conclusive evidence against such a
hypothesis, since most of the oriental prototypes were of organic materials.

6 In the twelfth century Herbord tells us that in
Pomerania the number of horses was equal to
the number of warriors, suggesting that
here, by this period, fighting was primarily
conducted from horseback.

7 Ruttkay, 'The organization of troops'.

8 For the Ukrainian ramparts see below. The
Polish ramparts are discussed at length by
E. Kowalczyk 1987, *Systemy obronne wałów
podłużnych we wczesnym średniowieczu na
ziemiach polskich* (Wrocław); the ramparts in
Saxony and Thuringia are discussed by
P. Grimm 1958, *Die vor- und frühgeschicht-
lichen Burgwälle der Bezirke Halle und
Magdeburg* (Berlin), pp. 172–8, and his paper
(1968), 'Zu den Landwehren des oberen
Eichsfeldes', pp. 180–7 in M. Claus,
W. Haarnagel and K. Raddatz (eds), *Studien
zur europäischen Vor- und Frühgeschichte*
(Neumünster).

9 J. Sláma 1988, *Střední Čechy v raném
středověku III: archeologie o počátkích
premyslovského státu* (Prague, *Praehistorica*
14). The Polish evidence has yet to be fully
published: A. Buko 1997, 'Polska we
wspólnocie narodów Europy: początki,
perspektywy badawcze', *Zeszyty
Sandomierskie* IV (6), 3–8.

10 This is one possible explanation of what the
PVL means when it says that the 'Radimichi
and Viatichi came from the Lachy' (see above).
It is probable that this is a trace of a tradition
that the population of these areas at the time
of writing had formed from the relatively late
movements of populations from the southwest, the frontier zone of Volynia and the Bug
valley.

Chapter 8

1 An interesting and early attempt was the
seminal book by Henryk Łowmiański (1953)
on the economic basis of the formation of states
among the Slavs: *Podstawy gospodarcze
formowania się państw słowiańskich* (Warsaw),
which was based primarily on the historical
evidence but contains some sensible model-
making. A lot of information on production
and technology is scattered in various syntheses,
and there is also a great deal based on the study
of the numismatic material: R. Kiersnowski
1960, *Pieniądz kruszcowy w Polsce
wczesnośredniowiecznej* (Warsaw), is a classic
synthesis. Recent synthetic work includes

K. Polek 1994, *Podstawy gospodarcze państwa wielkomorawskiego* (Cracow). The seminal study by R. Hodges 1982, *Dark Age Economics: The Origins of Towns and Trade* (London) concentrates on western Europe and to a lesser extent Scandinavia, virtually ignoring the adjacent southeast sector of the Baltic zone, which affects the general validity of the conclusions he draws.

2 A significant difference between most parts of Slavdom and the eastern parts of the contemporary Frankish realms is the absence of scales for measuring hacksilver in the sixth to eighth centuries.

3 See several papers in H. Jankuhn *et al.* (eds) 1985, 1987, 1989, *Untersuchungen zu Handel und Verkehr der vor- und frühgeschichtlichen Zeit in Mittel- und Nord-Europa*, 6 vols (Göttingen). The subject is also covered by Hodges, *Dark Age Economics*; see also P. Charvát, 1998 *Dálkový obchod v raně středověké Evropì (7.–10. stoleti)* (Brno).

4 For farming among the Early Slavs see M. Beranová 1980, *Zemědělstvi starých Slovanů* (Prague); M. Beranová 1966, 'The raising of domestic animals among the Slavs in Early Middle Ages according to archaeological sources', *Vzník a Počatký Slovanů* (Prague) 6, 153–96; M. Beranová 1984, 'Types of Slavic agricultural production in the 6th–12th centuries', *Ethnologia Slavica* 16, 7–48; also Polek, *Podstawy gospodarcze państwa wielkomorawskiego*. For Polabia see J. Herrmann (ed.) 1985, *Die Slawen in Deutschland* (Berlin), pp. 68–92. For Russia see B. A. Kolchin (ed.) 1985, *Drevniaia Rus': gorod, zamok, selo* (Moscow, *Arkheologia SSSR* 15), ch. 5, pp. 219–42; V. P. Levasheva 1994, 'Agriculture in Rus (tenth to thirteenth centuries)', pp. 39–44 in D. H. Kaiser and G. Marker (eds) 1994, *Reinterpreting Russian History: Readings 860s to 1860s* (New York/Oxford). For an overall summary see W. Hensel 1987, *Słowiańszczyzna wczesnośredniowieczna, zarys kultury materialnej* (Warsaw), esp. pp. 15–128.

5 The exception here would be the Mediterranean zone where to some degree they would have adopted local patterns, but our evidence of farming regimes in these areas is limited.

6 F. Curta 1997, 'Blacksmiths, warriors, and tournaments of value: dating and interpreting Early Medieval hoards of iron implements in eastern Europe', *Ephemeris Napocensis* 7, 211–68.

7 See Łowmiański, *Podstawy gospodarcze formowania się państw słowiańskich*, for an attempt.

8 J. Henning 1987, *Südosteuropa zwischen Antike und Mittelalter* (Berlin).

9 Querns: see R. S. Minasian 1978, 'Klassifikatsia ruchnogo zhernovogo postava (po materialam Vostochnoi Evropy I tysiacheletia n.e.)', *Sovetskaia Arkheologia* 3, 101–12. Wooden remains of oil-presses: Herrmann (ed.), *Die Slawen in Deutschland*, pp. 79–80, Abb. 24–6.

10 The farmyard was also inhabited by dogs and cats, the bones of which are sometimes found.

11 Most of these analyses have progressed little further than a count of fragment numbers. Archaeozoology is however a fast-developing area in central and eastern Europe and we may expect the results of more sophisticated analyses to provide important new information in the near future.

12 A. Gręzak and B. Kurach 1996, 'Konsumpcja mięsa w średniowieczu oraz w czasach nowożytnych na terenie obecnych ziem Polski w świetle danych archeologicznych', *Archeologia Polski* 41, 139–67; Herrmann (ed.), *Die Slawen in Deutschland*, pp. 83–92.

13 There were important mines at Wieliczka near Cracow and near Ocna Mures in central Transylvania. This latter centre had been known since Roman times and the Salinae here produced huge quantities of salt for both Dacia and Pannonia.

14 Gręzak and Kurach, 'Konsumpcja mięsa'; Herrmann, *Die Slawen in Deutschland*, Abb. 26.

15 For craft production see H. Jankuhn, W. Jansen, R. Schmidt-Wiegard and H. Tiefenbach (eds) 1981 and 1983, *Das Handwerk in vor- und frühgeschichtlicher Zeit* (Göttingen).

16 W. Hołubowicz 1950, *Garncarstwo wiejskie zachodnich terenów Białorusi* (Toruń); see also A. Buko 1992, 'Ceramology and medieval pottery research in Poland', *Archaeologia Polona* 30, 5–25.

17 Information from I. Gavritukhin (1997).

18 The Czech writer Radomír Pleiner was especially prolific and wrote many articles and books, such as the usefully illustrated *Staré*

evropské kovářství (Prague), published in 1962.

19 J. Henning 1987, *Südosteuropa zwischen Antike und Mittelalter* (Berlin); H. Mamzer 1988, *Studia nad metalurgią żelaza na terenie północno-wschodniej Bułgarii we wczesnym średniowieczu* (Wrocław).

20 Though nails have not been accorded much attention in the literature, it may be suspected that in southern areas they may have been more common at an earlier date.

21 A. Bartošková 1986, *Slovanské depoty železných předmětů v Československu* (Brno/Prague); F. Curta 1997, 'Blacksmiths, warriors, and tournaments of value'.

22 J. Eisner 1941, 'Ein Hortfund der älteren Burgwallzeit aus der Slovakei', *Altböhmen und Altmähren* 1, 153–71.

23 Z. Kobyliński and Z. Hensel 1993, 'Imports or local products? Trace element analysis of copper-alloy artefacts from Haćki, Białystok province, Poland', *Archaeologia Polona* 31, 129–40.

24 B. Svoboda 1953, 'Poklad byzantského kovotepce v Zemianskom Vrbovku', *Památky Archeologické* 44, 33–93.

25 The first synthetic study of the West Slav silver hoards and one still retaining a certain value is that by Roman Jakimowicz 1933, 'O pochodzeniu ozdób srebrnych znajdowanych w skarbach wczesnohistorycznych', *Wiadomości Archeologiczne* 12, 103–36). For a useful recent study with many distribution maps see H. Kóčka-Krenz 1993, *Biżuteria północno-zachodnio-słowianska we wczesnym średniowieczu* (Poznań). The hoards from the former Soviet Union have been discussed in G. F. Korzukhina 1954, *Russkie klady IX–XIII v.'* (Moscow/Leningrad). The work of N. P. Kondakov 1896, *Russkie klady: issledovanie drevnostei velikokniazheskogo perioda* (St Petersburg), also remains a useful source.

26 Relationships between the Scandinavian and Slav metalwork are considered by W. Duczko 1985, *Birka V: The Filigree and Granulation Work of the Viking Period* (Stockholm). See also H. Kóčka-Krenz 1983, *Złotnictwo skandynawskie IX–XI w.* (Poznań).

27 K. Wachowski 1992, *Kultura karolińska a Słowiańszczyzna Zachodnia* (Wrocław); K. Wachowski 1989, 'Problematyka blatnicka – próba systematyki pojęć', *Przegląd Archeologiczny* 36, 209–20.

28 E. Schuldt 1988, *Der Holzbau bei den nord-westslawischen Stämme vom 8. bis 12. Jahrhundert* (Berlin, *Beiträge zum Ur- und Frühgeschichte der Bezirke Rostock, Schwerin und Neubrandenburg* 21).

29 J. Martin 1986, *Treasure from the Land of Darkness: The Fur Trade and its Significance for Medieval Russia* (Cambridge and New York).

30 J. Maik 1988, *Wyroby włókiennicze na Pomorzu z okresu rzymskiego i średniowiecza* (Wrocław).

31 E. Cnotliwy 1998, 'Grzebienie w kulturze wczesnosłowiańskiej na terenie południowej i środkowej Polski', pp. 366–79 in H. Kóčka-Krenz and W. Łosiński (eds), *Kraje Słowiańskie w wiekach średnich: profanum i sacrum* (Poznań).

32 K. Ambrosiani 1981, *Viking Age Combs, Comb Making and Comb Makers in the Light of Finds from Birka and Ribe* (Stockholm, *Studies in Archaeology* 2); E. Cnotliwy 1973, *Rzemiosło rogownicze na Pomorzu wczesnośredniowiecznym* (Wrocław).

33 J. Callmer 1977, *Trade Beads and Bead Trade in Scandinavia ca. 800–1000 A.D.* (Lund); J. Callmer 1987, 'Pragmatic notes on the early medieval beadmaterial in Scandinavia and the Baltic region ca. A.D. 600–1000', pp. 217–26 in G. Labuda and S. Tabaczyński (eds), *Studia nad etnogenezą Słowian i kulturą Europy wczesnośredniowieczej*, vol. I (Wrocław); J. Callmer 1991, 'Beads as a criterion of shifting trade- and exchange conditions', *Studien zur Sachsenforschung* 7 (Hildesheim), 25–38.

34 Callmer, *Trade Beads*; 'Pragmatic notes', 225.

35 See C. Verlinden 1955, *L'esclavage dans l'Europe médiévale I* (Bruges).

36 For shackles see J. Henning 1992, 'Gefangenenfessel im slawischen Siedlungsraum und der europäische Sklavenhandel im 6. bis 12. Jahrhundert', *Germania* 70 (2), 403–26. These objects cluster, as Henning's map shows (Abb. 8), in the Lower Danubian and Pontic region.

37 The somewhat provocative derivation of the word 'Slav' from the word 'slave' proposed by some scholars has been strenuously criticized by a number of linguists. See C. Verlinden 1937 'L'origine de "sciauus": esclave', *Bulletin de Cange* 17, 97–128.

38 It is noticeable that many of these finds come from the territory of the Veleti,

forming an important political grouping on the north-eastern edge of the Carolingian Empire. It was here that a number of 'emporia' closely connected with the development of economic systems in the Baltic were formed.

39 These excavations have been published only in interim form, with fragmentary evidence about some of the finds. The main source of information at the time of writing is M. Jagodziński 1988, *Wczesnośredniowieczna osada rzemieślniczo-handlowa w Janowie Pomorskim nad jeziorem Drużno – poszukiwane Truso? Przewodnik po wystawie* (Elbląg).

40 W. Neugebauer 1968, 'Truso und Elbing: ein Beitrag zur Frühgeschichte des Weichselmündungsgebietes', pp. 213–34 in M. Claus, W. Haarnagel and K. Raddatz (eds), *Studien zur europäischen Frühgeschichte (H. Jankuhn Festschrift)* (Neumünster).

41 W. Filipowiak 1974, 'Die Entwicklung der Stadt Wolin' in H. Jankuhn *et al.* (eds), *Vor- und Frühformen der europäischen Stadt im Mittelalter*, vol. 2. (Göttingen); W. Filipowiak and H. Gundlach 1992, *Wolin Vineta: die tatsächliche Legende vom Untergang und Aufstieg der Stadt* (Rostock); I. Lange and P. W. Lange 1988, *Vineta: Atlantis des Nordens* (Leipzig).

42 In a divided Europe, the presence of Scandinavians on the south shore of the Baltic was a politically improper concept and rarely voiced loudly, it had connotations with the Normanist theory of state origins beloved of Nazi propagandists. For a recent and somewhat more objective review of the evidence see W. Duczko 1997, 'Scandinavians in the southern Baltic between the 5th and 10th centuries A.D.', pp. 191–211 in P. Urbańczyk (ed.), *Origins of Central Europe* (Warsaw).

43 U. Schoknecht 1977, *Menzlin: ein frühgeschichtlicher Handelsplatz an der Peene* (Berlin).

44 The Ralswiek boat is well illustrated in J. Herrmann (ed.) 1985, *Die Slawen in Deutschland*, Abb. 60 and Taf. 34; the Szczecin boat is discussed by M. Rulewicz 1996, 'Wrak szczecińskiej łodzi z IX wieku', and the dendrochronological dates are cited by W. Filipowiak 1996, 'Żywot statku wczesnośredniowiecznego', both in Z. Kurnatowska (ed.) 1996, *Słowiańszczyzna w Europie*, vol. 2 (Poznań), pp. 79–96.

Excavated soil stains at Truso have been interpreted as the remains of boats.

45 V. V. Sedov (ed.) 1985, *Srednevekovaia Ladoga: nowye arkheologicheskie otkrytia i issledovania* (Leningrad). See also S. Franklin and J. Shepard 1996, *The Emergence of Rus 750–1200* (London and New York), pp. 12–21. The eastern coast of the Baltic also had a number of coastal trading sites, three in Estonia, one on the island of Saaremaa, Daugmale (Latvia), near Jelgava, Grobin, Lepaja, Klajpeda, near Zielonogradsk, Truso (Janów Pomorski near Elbląg). The latter was destroyed by Scandinavian raiders in the middle of the ninth century and never reoccupied.

46 A. N. Kirpichnikov, G. S. Lebedev, V. A. Bulkin, I. V. Dubov and V. A. Nazarenko 1980, 'Russko-skandinavskie sviazi epokhi obrazovania Kievskogo gosudarstva na sovremennom etape arkheologicheskogo izuchenia', *Kratkie Soobshchenia Instituta Arkheologii* (Moscow) 160, 24–38 (similar paper by the same authors in 1978, *Scando-Slavica* 24, 63–89); W. Łosiński 1988, 'Chronologia napływu najstarszej monety arabskiej na terytorium Europy', *Slavia Antiqua* 31, 93–181. See also Franklin and Shepard, *The Emergence of Rus 750–1200*, pp. 22–5.

47 Further to the south another important complex occurs at Gniozdovo on the Dniepr near Smolensk at the watershed between the Dniepr and Dvina waterways. Most of the spectacular development of this site (evidenced by its cemeteries) dates to the tenth century, but there was a settlement established here some time in the second half of the ninth century which it would not be unreasonable to see as another emporium. For the recent reassessment see W. Łosiński 1992, 'Miejsce Gniozdowa w rozwoju kontaktów Skandynawii z Rusią Kijowską', *Przegląd Archeologiczny* 39, 139–52.

48 One of them may be represented by the stronghold at Sarskoe Gorodishche in Merian territory, dated to the early ninth century, around which are a series of large settlements (such as those at Ugodichi and Timervo) which seem to have been involved in exchange, to judge from the large silver hoards found in some of them. For these sites see Franklin and Shepard, *The Emergence of Rus*, pp. 22–3, 36–7, 66–9.

49 One may expect that each local settlement cell was served by a more or less radial road

system connecting the centre with the periphery by the most direct routes. The direct connection of two points several hundred kilometres distant from each other would be necessary or feasible only in the case when this would have had some strategic significance or considerable traffic was expected to pass along them.

50 The Anglophone reader may use the translation by R. H. J. Jenkins 1967, published in Washington. I used the Polish translation: A. Brzostowska and W. Swoboda (eds) 1989, *Testimonia najdawniejszych dziejów Słowian* (Wrocław), pp. 301–3.

51 Another group of travellers started from the other end of the route: the Jews (or Syrians) began their trading activities in this period, but were to become of importance in central Europe only in the twelfth century (and further east only later).

52 The first mention in a written source is in the *Annales Bertiniani*, where under the year 839 is an account of a diplomatic mission from Emperor Theophilus of Byzantium to Emperor Louis the Pious in Ingelheim; with the Greeks were apparently some men of the 'Rhos' whose ruler was called a 'chachanus'. Louis found out however that they were Swedes. *Monumenta Germaniae Historica, Scriptores* I, 434.

53 Quoted after B. A. Rybakov 1989, *Kievan Rus* (Moscow), pp. 46–7.

54 Kiev: P. P. Tolochko, S. A. Vysotski and Y. E. Borovski 1981, *Novoe v arkheologii Kieva* (Kiev), p. 307. Ralswiek: Herrmann, *Die Slawen in Deutschland*, p. 292, Abb. 140g, Taf. 25b. For camels at Bolshoe Borshevo and Titchikha and a carving at Mayatskoe see Franklin and Shepard, *The Emergence of Rus*, p. 83.

55 *Monumenta Germaniae Historica Legum* sectio II, vol. I (Hanover, 1883), p. 123, §7.

56 J. Bubeník 1972, 'K problematice železných misky tzv. Slezkého typu', *Archeologické Rozhledy* 24, 542–67.

57 Hoards at Sonnenwalde in Lusatia and Lagiszowo Male near Glogau, and Maurzyce near Łowicz (R. Jakimowicz 1947, 'Chusteczki-płacidła Ibrahima ibn Jakuba w świetle wykopalisk', *Sprawozdania Polskiej Akademii Umiejętności* XLVIII (3), 109–10).

58 Detailed discussion of these issues lies outside the scope of the present work. Two concepts of the nature of these hoards have been proposed.

R. Kiersnowski (1956, 'Główne momenty rozwoju środków wymiany na Pomorzu wczesnofeudalnym', *Wiadomości Archeologiczne* 23, 229–51, and *Pieniądz kruszcowy,* 426ff.) suggested that the appearance of these hoards represents the formation of a monetary system of local exchange. S. Tabaczyński 1957, 'Z zagadnień wartości poznawczych skarbów wczesnośredniowiecznych', *Archeologia Polski* 1, 82–102, links the latter only with the period of the disappearance of these hoards.

59 These hoards occur to the north of a line running through the south of Polabia and Poland to the upper Dniestr and lower Dniepr beyond which there are no finds of oriental silver in the ninth century (and hardly any in the tenth).

60 There are over 2500 hacksilver hoards in the Baltic zone. Many are found on Gotland, they occur in Jutland, and the Danish islands, through Sweden (including Lapland), Aland Islands, Finland, the Baltic countries and northern Russia (as far east as the Upper Volga and Dniepr). These hoards contain foreign coins and hacksilver not found so regularly elsewhere in Europe. Hacksilver is not found so regularly in western European hoards of this date, except in deposits of loot.

61 Of the copious literature on these coin finds, we may select the synthetic article by K. Godłowski 1981, 'Okres wędrówek ludów na Pomorzu', *Pomerania Antiqua* 10, 65–129; see also W. Knapke 1941, 'Aurei- and Solidi- vorkommen an der Südküste der Ostsee', *Acta Archaeologica* 12, 79–118. The link between the end of the flow of these coins through Poland and the arrival here of the Slavs is postulated by K. Godłowski in his 1979 *Z badań nad zagadnieniem rozprzestrzenienia się Słowian w V–VII w. n.e.* (Cracow), pp. 40–1 ryc. 1 and 2.

62 A few coins of Justin and Justinian occur north of the Danube, for example several finds in Germany, and coins from Zimno and Kiev. The circulation of Byzantine coins in Avar territories is summarized by M. Kozub 1997, 'The chronology of the inflow of Byzantine coins into the Avar khaganate', pp. 241–6 in P. Urbańczyk (ed.), *Origins of Central Europe* (Warsaw). For hoards in the Danube region see F. Curta 1996; 'Invasion or inflation? Sixth- to seventh-century Byzantine coin hoards in eastern and southeastern Europe',

Annali dell' Istituto Italiano di Numismatica
43, 65–224.

63 This is predictable since this coinage was produced mainly for international trade purposes (according to some translations the word used by Ibn Jaqub to refer to these coins in central Europe can be rendered as 'market weights').

64 There is an extensive literature on this topic. The study of the flow of Islamic coins into central and eastern Europe has recently been much advanced by the work of Władysław Łosiński 1988, 'Chronologia napływu najstarszej monety arabskiej na terytorium Europy', *Slavia Antiqua* 31, 93–181; 1993 'Chronologia, skala i drogi napływu monet arabskich do krajów europejskich u schyłku IX i w X w.', *Slavia Antiqua* 34, 1–41. The circulation of Islamic coins in central Europe is summarized by A. Bartczak 1997, 'Finds of dirhems in central Europe prior to the beginning of the 10th century A.D.', pp. 227–39 in P. Urbańczyk (ed.), *Origins of Central Europe*. The Russian hoards are discussed in a number of papers by T. S. Noonan including his 1981, 'Ninth century dirhem hoards from European Russia: a preliminary analysis', pp. 47–118 in M. A. S. Blackburn and D. M. Metcalf (eds), *Viking Age Coinage in the Northern Lands* (Oxford, B.A.R. Supplementary series 122). See also T. S. Noonan 1994, 'The Vikings in the East: coins and commerce', pp. 215–36 in B. Ambrosiani and H. Clarke (eds), *Birka Studies* 3 (Stockholm).

65 It is worthy of note that these coins themselves were probably minted from bullion derived from dirhems.

66 These, like the coins of Ethelred and Canute, were to influence local coin design.

67 They do not date, as had been thought until recently, to the reign of Bolesław's father and predecessor Mieszko I, c. 960–92. See S. Suchodolski 1998, 'Spór o początki mennictwa w Czechach i w Polsce', *Wiadomości Numizmatyczne* 42, 5–20. Rather embarrassingly, this coin is pictured on the current Polish 10 złoty note together with a 'portrait' of Mieszko I.

68 Three gold disks in Paris and the British Museum which surfaced before the nineteenth century, possibly meant as coins or seals, were thought to be coins of the stratilata Sermon, the last Bulgar ruler of Sirmium, dating to 1017–18, an ephemeral gold issued coined as a political gesture against Byzantium. The authenticity of these old finds however has been questioned.

69 See for example W. Hensel 1967, *Anfänge der Städte bei den Ost- und Westslawen* (Bautzen); W. Hensel 1977, 'The origin of western and eastern European Slav towns', pp. 373–90 in M. Barley (ed.), *European Towns: Their Archaeology and Early History* (London).

70 A. V. Kuza 1989, *Malye goroda Drevnei Rusi* (Moscow); P. P. Tolochko 1989, *Drevnerusski feodalinyi gorod* (Kiev); E. N. Nosov 1994, 'The emergence and development of Russian towns: some outline ideas', *Archaeologia Polona* 32, 185–96; E. N. Nosov 1993, 'The problem of the emergence of early urban centres in northern Russia', pp. 236–56 in J. Chapman and P. Dolukhanov (eds) 1993, *Cultural Transformations and Interactions in Eastern Europe* (Aldershot/Avebury). For the rise of towns in Russia see also P. Dolukhanov 1996, *The Early Slavs* (London), pp. 177–81.

71 M. N. Tikhomirov 1959, *The Towns of Ancient Rus* (Moscow); A. Y. Dvornichenko 1988, *Goroda-gosudarstva Drevnei Rusi* (Leningrad); P. P. Tolochko 1989, *Drevnerusski feodalinyi gorod* (Kiev); Franklin and Shepard, *The Emergence of Rus*, pp. 278–319.

72 E. Nosov 1990, *Novgorodskoe (Rurikovo) gorodishche* (Leningrad).

73 M. Thompson 1967, *Novgorod the Great: Excavations in the Medieval City Directed by A. V. Artsikhovsky and B. A. Kolchin* (London); for some superb colour photographs of the artefacts see B. A. Kolchin, V. L. Yanin and S. V. Yamshchikov (eds) 1985, *Drevni Novgorod: prikladnoe iskusstvo i arkheologia* (Moscow); see also M. Brisbane (ed.) 1992, *Archaeology of Novgorod, Russia* (Lincoln, Society of Medieval Archaeology, monograph 13).

Chapter 9

1 There are many works on this subject, among which the most useful are: A. Brückner 1918, *Mitologia słowiańska* (Cracow); L. Niederle 1916, *Slovanské starožitnosti, Dil 2: Život starých Slovanů, svazek 1: Víra a náboženstwi* (Prague) (esp. pp. 182–263); K. Moszyński 1934, *Kultura ludowa Słowian t. 2 cz. 1: Kultura duchowa* (Warsaw, 2nd ed.); E.

Wienecke 1940, *Untersuchungen zur Religion der Westslawen* (Leipzig); H. Łowmiański 1979, *Religia Słowian i jej upadek (VI–XII w.),* (Warsaw); B. A. Rybakov 1987, *Yazychestvo Drevnei Rusi* (Moscow); B. A. Rybakov 1989, *Kievan Rus* (Moscow), esp. pp. 158–64. See also L. P. Słupecki 1994, *Slavonic Pagan Sanctuaries* (Warsaw). In addition to these, the 1986 book by Aleksander Gieysztor, *Mitologia Słowian* (Warsaw) and Jerzy Strzelczyk's 1998 *Mity, podania i wierzenia dawnych Słowian* (Poznań) were most useful in compiling this chapter.

2 Sources include Thietmar (bishop of Merseberg), Adam of Bremen, Saxo Grammaticus, and the Lives of St Otto of Bamberg (written by Ebo, Herbord, and Monachus Preiflingensis).

3 The picture presented below is to a large extent a composite and perhaps idealized model, based on the more detailed evidence presented in the works cited above and the considerable literature which they draw on. Owing to the complexity of the various layers of arguments used to construct this model, it would be difficult to provide full notes for each individual point. The reader who wishes to go into the subject in more detail is invited to consult the works cited in note 1.

4 J. Frazer 1922, *The Golden Bough* (London).

5 N. N. Vieletska 1978, *Yazycheskaia simvolika slavianskikh arkhaicheskikh ritualov* (Moscow).

6 The reference to a paramount god suggests again the sort of effects of the creation of a large pantribal association, but one wonders whether the reference to the god of thunder is not in some way merely a Christian reference to the pagan god Jupiter/Zeus rather than a real reference to a Slav god. Nevertheless a god of thunder is perhaps what one would expect from a militaristic society which was at the same time an agricultural one.

7 The iconography of the Zbrucz idol may owe something to the *Kammennye baby* ('stone women') of the steppes, isolated outliers of which occur in the upper Dniepr, in the Dniestr and as far north as Mazuria in Poland. They date from the latter half of the first millennium BC and possibly the first centuries AD and seem to be cult figures as well as in some cases grave-markers of the Iranian-speaking Sarmatian nomad tribes. They often have conical helmets and military attributes

such as sabres. Some of them hold horns in their hands.

8 This important discovery was first presented by B. A. Timoshchuk and I. P. Rusanova in *Sovetskaia Arkheologia* 4 (1986), 90–100; the discovery is placed in wider context by Rybakov, *Yazychestvo Drevnei Rusi*, pp. 236–51, and by the authors of the discovery, I. P. Rusanova and B. A. Timoshchuk 1993, *Yazycheskie sviatilishcha drevnikh slavian* (Moscow) (though see review by W. Szymański, 1997, *Archeologia Polski* 42, 286–301). Recently however doubts have been cast even on the connection between this famous statue and the Slavs: Professor Szymański in a recent thought-provoking article has suggested that it may be Thracian.

9 On Slav temples and cult places in general, a particularly useful book is Słupecki, *Slavonic Pagan Sanctuaries*. The Zbrucz temple is discussed here on p. 182, figs 73–4.

10 The excavations and their results are discussed and illustrated by Słupecki, *Slavonic Pagan Sanctuaries*, pp. 144–50.

11 Łysa Góra [bald Mountain] : E. Gąssowska and J. Gąssowski 1970, *'Łysa Góra we wczesnym średniowieczu* (Wrocław). Ślęża: see Słupecki, *Slavonic Pagan Sanctuaries*, pp. 172–97 and refs. Several authors have questioned whether Łysa Góra really was a sanctuary, and, although the evidence on which the suggestion was initially made is less secure than originally thought, the hypothesis may still be accepted.

12 Słupecki, *Slavonic Pagan Sanctuaries*, pp. 24–110.

13 Ibn Fadlan also gives fairly extensive details of the boat burial of a Rus chief which is frequently quoted in various contexts (an easily accessible translation can be found in M. Magnusson 1976, *Hammer of the North*, pp. 98–101). This burial is more reminiscent however of a largely Scandinavian rite.

14 The archaeological evidence of pagan Slav burial rites has been collected by Helena Zoll-Adamikowa in her seminal work (1975, 1979), *Wczesnośredniowieczne cmentarzyska ciałopalne Słowian na terenie Polski*, vols I and II (Wrocław), which summarizes the data from a wider area than the title suggests. The East Slav burial rites are summarized in *Arkheologia Ukrainskoi SSR* III, and V. V. Sedov 1982, *Vostochnye Slaviane v VI–XII vv.* (Moscow, Arkheologia SSSR 14). See also

H. Zoll-Adamikowa 1972, 'Zu den Brandbestattungsbräuchen der Slawen im 6. bis 10. Jahrhundert in Polen', *Ethnographisch-Archäologische Zeitschrift* 13, 497–542.

15 The report of Wulfstan in Alfred's translation of Orosius tells us that the Ests (a West Baltic tribe neighbouring with the Slavs) kept the body unburied for a long time in its house, and then burnt it 'and if after the cremation they find a portion of the body unburnt it is regarded as a great misfortune'. He also tells us that the dead man's goods were laid out on a route and claimed by men who raced horses for them.

16 This would explain the late (eleventh- and twelfth-century) occurrence of inhumation burials with grave goods in Mazovia and Podlasie, part of a state which had been nominally Christian for more than a century and a half and where cremation continued among the rural population for a considerable period after the conversion (see L. Rauhut 1973, 'Wczesnośredniowieczne cmentarzyska szkieletowe w obudowie kamiennej na Mazowszu Podlasiu', *Materiały Starożytne i Wczesnośredniowieczne* 1, 435–656.

17 For example at Haćki in northeast Poland, human bones were scattered on a prominent hilltop with broken metalwork and pottery (unpublished excavations of the Institute of Archaeology and Ethnology, Polish Academy of Sciences, Warsaw).

18 In *Materiale si Cercetari Arheologice* and excavations reports in *Studii si Cercetari de Istorie*; see also the discussion in U. Fiedler 1992, *Studien zu Gräberfelder des 6. bis 9. Jahrhunderts an der Unteren Donau*, 2 vols (Bonn).

19 The Alt-Käbelich graves are discussed by W. Łosiński 1993, 'Groby typu Alt-Käbelich w świetle badań przeprowadzonych na cmentarzysku wczesnośredniowiecznym w Świelubiu pod Kołobrzegiem', *Przegląd Archeologiczny* 41, 17–34. See also V. Schmidt 1981, 'Die urnenlose Brandbestattung in Flächgrabung aus dem Bezirk Neubranden-burg', *Zeitschrift für Archäologie* 15, 333–54. A recent find (G. Wetzel 1996, 'Ein slawischer Bestattungsplatz bei Tornow-Lichtenau, heute Kittlitz, Landkreis Dahme-Spreewald', pp. 237–41 in Z. Kurnatowska (ed.), *Słowiańszczyzna w Europie*, vol. 1, Wrocław) suggests that these burials may occur over a much wider area, at least in Polabia.

20 Long barrows of the northern forests have been discussed above, though it may be doubted that there was any connection between them and the Slavs.

21 These maps are based on those by Zoll-Adamikowa, *Wczesnośredniowieczne cmentarzyska ciałopalne*. Owing to changes suggested by later studies, the phasing and lettering of the zones used here does not coincide with those suggested in that seminal work. The data are used together with those of *Arkheologia Ukrainskoi SSR*. Unfortunately the northern part of Russia and much of the Balkans are as yet comparatively poorly mapped.

22 H. Zoll-Adamikowa, *Wczesnośredniowieczne cmentarzyska ciałopalne* vol. II, pp. 141–58.

23 *Arkheologia Ukrainskoi SSR* III, karta 3.

24 Avar burial rites are discussed by D. Csalány 1961, *Archäologische Denkmäler der Awarenzeit in Mitteleuropa* (Budapest); A. Avarenius, 1974, *Die Awaren in Europa* (Amsterdam/ Bratislava).

25 J. Eisner 1952, *Devínska Nová Ves: slovanské pohrebište* (Bratislava).

26 Fiedler, *Studien zu Gräberfelder*.

27 W. Duczko 1997, 'Scandinavians in the southern Baltic between the 5th and the 10th centuries A.D.', pp. 202–11 in P. Urbańczyk (ed.), *Origins of Central Europe* (Warsaw).

28 *Arkheologia Ukrainskoi SSR* III, karta 4.

29 Sedov, *Vostochnye slaviane*.

30 The primary sources are a series of late nineteenth- and early twentieth-century works printed in Moscow and Kiev which are so inaccessible that there seems little point in citing them here. See Sedov, *Vostochnye slaviane*, pp. 248–56.

31 See for example the studies of J. Assmann 1992, *Das kulturelle Gedächtnis: Schrift, Erinnerung und politische Identität in frühen Hochkulturen* (Munich); J. Vansina 1985, *Oral Tradition as History* (London).

32 Gallus Anonymous, *Kronika Polska* I.3. Perhaps the reticence of this foreign writer in discussing pagan history was a figure of speech hiding a real lack of information. Wincenty Kadłubek, bishop of Cracow, writing a century later, did not have such scruples and his chronicle contains much invented material.

Chapter 10

1 See F. Dvornik 1926, *Les Slavs, Byzance et Rome au IX siècle* (Paris); A. P. Vlasto 1970, *The Entry of the Slavs into Christendom* (Cambridge and New Brunswick, N.J.); F. Dvornik 1970, *Byzantine Missions among the Slavs* (New Brunswick, N.J.); Lutz E. von Padberg 1998, *Die Christianisierung Europas im Mittelalter* (Stuttgart); P. Urbańczyk (ed.) 1997, *Early Christianity in Central and East Europe* (Warsaw). See also J. Poulík 1978, 'The origins of Christianity in Slavonic countries north of the middle Danube basin', *World Archaeology* 10 (2), 158–71. The reader is also referred to the article by Jerzy Strzelczyk 2000, 'Towards a Christian Europe', in P. Urbańczyk (ed.), *Europe around the Year 1000* (Warsaw), which the present author translated while the present chapter was being compiled. In the process a number of facts and perhaps a few catchier phrases taken from that translation may be found here.

2 The study of Christianity in early medieval eastern Europe is fraught with problems of interpretation, quite apart from the potential effects of a scholar's own religious beliefs (or lack of them) on perception of some aspects of the problem. In several countries where in past decades the 'official' standpoint on the Church was the result of this institution being frowned upon by Communist regimes, the expression of alternative views could be an expression of political opposition. Such views, presented as objective interpretations, have become quite common since 1989–90. One wonders though whether this continued dialogue with Stalinist anti-Church demagogy is not perhaps obscuring some wider issues.

3 This is also the context of the attempts of the Bolsheviks to curb the activities of the Russian Church in the period after 1917; the Church acted as a focus for the revisionists. Communist action against the Church initially focused mainly on attempting to nationalize Church property and then on combating the resistance to the Soviets which this engendered.

4 According to the *Second Life of St Wojciech*, by Bruno of Querfurt (ch. 25), in an analogous situation the Prussians (West Balts) chased the missionaries off their lands declaring that 'because of such people our soil will not give a harvest, trees will not bear fruit, new animals will not be born and the old ones die'.

5 The *Kyrie Eleison* was however translated into Slavic by Boso, bishop of Merseberg in the 960s, for the use of the Polabian Slavs.

6 F. Oswald, L. Schaeffer and H. R. Sennhauser 1966–71, *Vorromanische Kirchenbauten: Katalogue der Denkmäler bis zum Ausgang der Ottonen*, 3 vols (Munich).

7 R. Krautheimer 1979, *Early Christian and Byzantine Architecture* (London, 3rd ed.); J. A. Hamilton 1956, *Byzantine Architecture and Decoration* (London).

8 See the monograph of C. Nolte 1995, *Conversio und Christianitas: Frauen in der Christianisierung vom 5. bis 8. Jahrhundert* (Stuttgart, *Monographien zur Geschichte des Mittelalters* 41).

9 His comments on language in the presence of emissaries from Moravia are interesting: 'do you hear that philosopher? . . . take many gifts and your brother Igumena Methodius and go there. You are both Solunians [Thessalonians] and all Solunians speak fluently in Slav.' This suggests that (at least in the understanding of the Emperor and his advisers) Early Slav dialects may not have differed much even at this period (the Moravian dialect had South Slav affinities).

10 The later Cyrillic alphabet used today by the Russians, Ukrainians, Belarussians, Serbs and Bulgarians, though named after Cyril, seems not to have been invented by him.

11 Cyril took to Rome the body of St Clement, which he had 'miraculously found' at Cherson on his Khazar mission. This was apparently an important factor in gaining Roman approval of the use of a liturgy in the Slav tongue. Rome took a liberal view for a while and authorized the use of a Slavic service-book.

12 The story in J. M. Neale's (1818–66) popular English Christmas carol 'Good King Wenceslas' in H. W. Baker's *Hymns Ancient and Modern* (1861) is imaginary.

13 In an attempt to legitimize their rule in the eyes of their Christian neighbours, the Hungarian rulers since the 940s had been allowing western and Byzantine missionaries to teach in their territories.

14 This was the last outpost of paganism in the whole of Slavdom, but the neighbouring Prussians and other Finno-Ugrian and Baltic-speaking peoples on the southeast and east coasts of the Baltic Sea remained pagan until

the Crusades of the Teutonic Knights in the thirteenth century.

15 The document may be compared with the similar answers to questions sent by Augustine from Kent as reported by Bede.

16 R. Sullivan 1966, 'Khan Boris and the conversion of Bulgaria: a case study of the impact of Christianity on a barbarian society', *Studies in Medieval and Renaissance History* 3, 55–139; see also L. Heiser 1979, *Die Responsa ad consulta Bulgorum des Papstes Nikolaus I* (Trier). The text of the Responses can be found in *MGH Epistolae* VI (Berlin) 1925, 568–600. There is apparently no published English translation of this document, but see the Internet Medieval Sourcebook (http://www.fordham.edu/halsall/basis/866nicholas-bulgar.html).

17 S. Franklin and J. Shepard 1996, *The Emergence of Rus 750–1200* (London and New York), p. 54.

18 The Bulgarian rulers had also previously considered Islam as a possible state religion before choosing Christianity. At the end of the eighth or beginning of the ninth century, after a flirtation with Islam and Christianity, the Khazar elite had accepted Judaism.

19 On Vladimir's decision see Franklin and Shepard, *The Emergence of Rus*, pp. 158–65. See also A. Poppe 1982, *The Rise of Christian Russia* (London).

20 This is an interesting early parallel to the later ability to practise such parallel performances (public and private) in the face of the restrictions placed on life under a totalitarian Communist regime in many parts of central and eastern Europe.

21 This was before for example the rigid order and regularization which was introduced into the western Church in the eleventh century by the efforts of such ardent 'centralizers' as Pope Gregory VII (1073–85).

22 This equation is not invariable. Some inhumations were not Christian (for example in cemeteries of the Avars), and this raises the possibility that in some areas inhumation may have been adopted independently of the introduction of Christianity. In other cemeteries in northeast Poland cremations occur alongside inhumations, and we even find there inhumations where the body was apparently set alight in the grave.

23 Attempts have been made by Teresa Rysiewska of Warsaw to determine social structure from grave characteristics in Polish non-churchyard cemeteries. The idea is interesting, but I feel yet to be proved (see above). For grave-field cemeteries in Germany see G. Fehring 1991, *The Archaeology of Medieval Germany: An introduction* (London), pp. 57–70.

24 The rite of inhumation burials in Poland was studied in an important paper by Maria Miśkiewicz 1968, 'Wczesnośredniowieczny obrządek pogrzebowy na płaskich cmentarzyskach szkieletowych w Polsce', *Materiały Wczesnośredniowieczne* 6, 241–93.

25 In Poland for example the parish system was not completed until the thirteenth century.

26 This heresy was influenced by Byzantine models which recognized the equality of good and evil; it involved a social programme which encompassed the monastic orders and minor clergy, opposed the differentiation of wealth and supported an 'antifeudal' egalitarianism. This movement spread outside Bulgaria and became the Catharism and Albigensianism of western Europe, against which the Church was still fighting in the fourteenth century. It had important influence on the 'pauperes Christi' and the Waldenses.

Chapter 11

1 The literature includes S. Runciman 1930, *A History of the First Bulgarian Empire* (London); R. Browning 1975, *Byzantium and Bulgaria* (Berkeley); D. Angelov 1980, *Die Entstehung des Bulgarischen Volkes* (Berlin); J. V. A. Fine 1983, *The Early Medieval Balkans: A Critical Survey from the Sixth to the late Twelfth Centuries* (Ann Arbor); S. Stančev 1966, *Veliki Preslav* (Sofia); J. Shepard 1995, 'Slavs and Bulgars', *New Cambridge Medieval History* II (Cambridge), pp. 228–48; P. Stephenson 2000, *Byzantium's Balkans Frontier: A Political Study of the Northern Balkans, 900–1204* (Cambridge).

2 Fine, *The Early Medieval Balkans.*

3 See M. Schulze 1984, 'Das Ungarischen Kriegergrab von Apres-les-Corps: Untersuchungen zu den Ungarn-einfällen nach Mittel-, West- und Südeuropas (899–955 n. Chr.) mit Excurs zur Münzchronologie altungarischer Gräber', *Jahrbuch des Römisch–Germanischen Zentral-museums Mainz* 31, 473–514.

4 The origin of the Romanians and the nature of the population of Transylvania before the

Hungarian conquest is still hotly disputed. Some scholars have claimed that – despite the area being penetrated by a variety of other groups in the early medieval period (including, as we have seen, Slavs) – there is evidence of a continuity of occupation of these areas by a Romance-speaking (Daco-Romanian) population, descendants of the inhabitants of the Roman province of Dacia (roughly modern Romania) after its abandonment in 270–3. This was the view increasingly favoured by the nationalisms of the Ceauşescu period. Other historians have suggested that these peoples moved into the area from Vlach communities south of the Danube only in the thirteenth and beginning of the fourteenth century (i.e., long after Hungarian occupation of Transylvania).

5   These problems make one uncomfortable with the way in which the study of the subject in the former Soviet Union tended to rely more on the written evidence (particularly the various versions of the *PVL*), to which one has the impression that to some degree the archaeological evidence has on occasion been 'fitted' (this applies for example to the question of dating of the stronghold-towns). Certain preconceptions (coupled with an authoritarian academic structure) have also had their effect on establishing the (former) 'official' views of the process of formation of the Russian state and nation, views which are now coming under increasingly critical examination.

6   The literature on the subject is immense. Good discussions may be found in G. Vernadsky 1951–2, *A History of Russia*, vol. 1, *Ancient Russia*, vol. 2, *Kievan Russia* (New Haven); R. Milner-Gulland 1997, *The Russians* (Oxford). Somewhat dated is the book by A. L. Mongait 1961, *Archaeology in the U.S.S.R.* (London, an abridgement of a book under the same title published in Moscow in 1959). For one version of the orthodox Soviet view see B. A. Rybakov 1965, *The Early Centuries of Russian History* (Moscow); B. A. Rybakov 1989, *Kievan Rus* (Moscow). A brief discussion may be found in P. Dolukhanov 1996, *The Early Slavs* (London), pp. 181–91, but the key work in English on this subject must at the time of writing be the book by S. Franklin and J. Shepard 1996 *The Emergence of Rus, 750–1200* (London and New York).

7   G. S. Lebedev 1985, *Epokha vikingov v Severnoi Evrope* (Leningrad).

8   E. A. Melnikova and V. Ya. Petrukhin 1989,

'Nazvanie "Rus" v rannei etnokulturnoi istorii Russkogo gosudarstva', pp. 42–53 in I. I. Peiros (ed.), *Lingvisticheskaia rekonstruktsia i drevneishaia istoria Vostoka* (Moscow); E. A. Melnikova and V. Ya. Petrukhin 1990–1, 'The origin and evolution of the name "Rus"', *Tor* 23 (Uppsala), 203–34.

9   K. R. Schmidt (ed.) 1970, *Varangian Problems* (Copenhagen/Munksgaard, *Scando-Slavica Supplementum* 1). An extremely valuable article by I. Jansson 1997, 'Warfare, trade or colonisation? Some general remarks on the eastern expansion of the Scandinavians in the Viking period', is published in *The Rural Viking in Russia and Sweden, Conference 19–20 October 1996 in the Manor of Karlslund, Orebro* (Orebro), pp. 9–64. The essays by E. A. Melnikova 1996, *The Eastern World of the Vikings* (Gothenburg), are also an important source of information. Franklin and Shepard, *The Emergence of Rus*, take a 'pro-Varangian' viewpoint, though applying the requisite criticism to the historical records.

10 A. Stalsberg 1982, 'Scandinavian relations with northwestern Russia during the Viking Age: the archaeological evidence', *Journal of Baltic Studies* 13, 267–95.

11 The main evidence comes from the typical Scandinavian fibulae used for fastening women's dress of characteristic style: V. V. Sedov 1982, *Vostochnye slaviane v VI–XIII vv.* (Moscow, *Arkheologia SSSR* 14), tab. 166. These seem more useful than weapons for detecting the presence of people wearing Scandinavian-type dress (though one cannot disregard other explanations).

12 This is interesting in regard to its relationship to the foundation legend of the Russian state. *PVL* (s.a. 882) tells of the expansion of Scandinavian power to Smolensk in Krivichi territory under a leader named Igor who was reputedly the son of Rurik (though this seems an artificial link between two foundation stories). It is more difficult to accept the story that the Scandinavians also annexed Kiev in the same year.

13 E. Mühle 1987, 'Die Anfänge Kievs (bis ca. 980) in archäologischer Sicht: ein Forschungsbericht', *Jahrbücher für Geschichte Osteuropas* 35, 80–101; O. M. Ioannisyan 1990, 'Archaeological evidence for the development and urbanization of Kiev from the 8th to the 14th centuries', pp. 285–311 in D. Austin and L. Alcock (eds), *From the Baltic*

to the *Black Sea: Studies in Early Medieval Archaeology* (London). See also Dolukhanov, *The Early Slavs*, pp. 191–3.

14 The Khazars played an important role in the political and economic situation in Europe owing to their geographical position between the trade routes of Europe and central Asia and the links between the latter and the land routes to the Near and Far East, developing close relations with Byzantium in the 730s to 780s and good relations with central Asian states such as Chorezm. In the ninth century (c. 860) the Khazar supremacy of the Volga–Don trade routes was broken by a Pecheneg invasion of the steppes. In the struggle for the possession of southern Russia between the nomad Turks and the Kievan principality, the Khazars played an increasingly unimportant role. From the middle of the tenth century the Khazars began to yield to Rus and Turkish pressure.

15 The case of Pereiaslavl however prompts caution in relying on the information of the *PVL* too closely. It is noted in the *PVL* as having been included in the 912 treaty with Byzantium, while the same source tells us of the circumstances surrounding its founding in 992.

16 Melnikova, *The Eastern World of the Vikings*, pp. 93–112.

17 Oleg ruled perhaps 871/9–902/912; there is an inconsistency in the correlation of the year lists of Byzantine and Russian history in the *PVL*. According to one version he died in 902, and ruled thirty-one years, in another version he died in 912 and elsewhere his reign is given as thirty-three years.

18 The word used for the coin which the Radimichi paid is *shchiliag*, which would seem to be a Germanic rather than a Slav term.

19 There is some circumstantial evidence however, in particular from the fluctuations in the flow of Islamic silver through this area, that the sequence and timing of events reported in the *PVL* might in fact bear some resemblance to real events.

20 It remains unclear why these documents were cited *in extenso* in the *PVL*: surely these were not the only Byzantine documents available for copying and they cannot have been included just as historical curiosities. Their inclusion obviously had some real significance at the time of the writing of the *PVL*. For a brief discussion and summary of these two documents see Franklin and Shepard *The Emergence of Rus*, pp. 103–4.

21 I. V. Dubov 1994, 'The ethnic history of northwest Rus in the ninth to thirteenth centuries', pp. 14–20 in D. H. Kaiser and G. Marker (eds), *Reinterpreting Russian History: Readings, 860s–1860s* (New York/ Oxford).

22 According to the *PVL*, the tribal content of the Russian army involved in the attack on Byzantium in 907 is explicitly noted as containing 'Varangians and Slavs, Chuds, Slovienie, Krivichi, Meria and Derevlane, Radimichi, Poliane and Severiane, Viatichi, Croats, Dulebi, and Tyvercy'. It seems to me unlikely that this passage can be used to define the extent of the Kievan state in 907. It is probably an interpolation, especially since it contains the names of several stronghold cities ('Kiev, Chernigov, Pereiaslavl, Liubech, Polotsk, Rostov and the other towns') which seem unlikely to be this early. The dating of these and similar sites has until recently tended to be based in Russian archaeology on the first mentions in the *PVL*, but in the near future one may hope that dendrochronology may be used to supply independent dating.

23 The modern frontiers of these countries apparently run very close to the edge of the political, social and ethnic boundary established in the early medieval period. These frontiers were drawn at Versailles on the basis of ethnic boundaries (established before the fourteenth-century expansion of ·Lithuania and the expansion of East Prussia and Russia in the late eighteenth century).

24 C. Goehrke 1992, *Frühzeit des Ostslaventums* (Darmstadt, *Erträge der Forschung* 277); see also S. A. Pivavarchik and G. M. Semianchuk 1997, *Arkheologia Belarussii, II: Epokha Syaredniavechcha* (Grodno).

25 V. V. Sedov 1996, 'Die Entstehung von Pskov', pp. 61–6 in Z. Kurnatowska (ed.), *Słowiańszczyzna w Europie*, vol. 2 (Wrocław). See also S. A. Tarakanova 1950, 'Novye materialy po arkheologii Pskova', *Kratkie Soobshchenia Instituta Istorii Materialnoi Kultury* 33, 61.

26 Though the chronicler finds comparable traits among the Derevlane and Krivichi. It is notable that the distant Slovienie are omitted from this criticism.

27 V. V. Sedov 1987, 'Origine de la branche du Nord des Slaves orientaux', pp. 161–5 in G. Labuda and S. Tabaczyński (eds), *Studia nad etnogenezą Słowian*, vol. I (Wrocław).

28 The chronicler states that Igor was the son of Rurik. This is chronologically unlikely and perhaps this literary device hides a period when the right to succession was contested.

29 W. Łosiński, 1992, 'Miejsce Gniozdowa w rozwoju kontaktów Skandynawii z Rusią Kijowską', *Przegląd Archeologiczny* 39, 139–52 (esp. pp. 148–9).

30 D. A. Avdusin and T. A. Pushkin 1988, 'Three chamber graves at Gniozdovo', *Fornvannen* 83, 20–33; D. I. Blifeld 1954, 'K istoricheskoi otsenke druzhinnykh pogrebenii v srubnykh grobnitsakh Srednego Podneprovia IX–X vv.', *Sovetskaia Arkheologia* 20, 148–62.

31 This date derived from the *PVL* is questionable since it is clearly linked with the 'early' chronology of the beginning of Igor's rule. The same chronicle would suggest that their (eldest) son Sviatoslav was born about 940.

32 For a brief discussion and summary of this document see Franklin and Shepard, *The Emergence of Rus*, pp. 117–19, but again we do not know why it was included in the *PVL*.

33 According to Leo the Deacon, in order to meet with the Byzantines in 971 he wore a plain white tunic, a bejewelled gold ring in one ear, while his scalp was shaved except for a long strand of hair displaying the nobility of his kin (Franklin and Shepard, *The Emergence of Rus*, p. 143). One might reflect on whether Sviatoslav should be pictured as Viking adventurer, Slav leader or nomad warrior.

34 These sites are discussed along with other types of Russian fortifications in the monograph by P. A. Rappoport 1956, *Ocherki po istorii russkogo voennogo zodchestva X–XIII vv.* (Moscow/Leningrad); and P. A. Rappoport 1967, *Voennoe zodchestvo zapadnorusskikh zemel X–XIV vv.* (Moscow/Leningrad). See also B. A. Kolchin (ed.) 1985, *Drevniaia Rus: gorod, zamok, selo* (Moscow, *Arkheologia SSSR* 15); P. A. Rappoport 1969, 'Russian military architecture', *Gladius* 8, 39–62.

35 M. P. Kucher 1987, *Zmievy valy sredniego Podneprovia* (Kiev). At the end of the eleventh and the early twelfth century a new system of strongholds was constructed 8–10 km apart and behind the line of the outer earthwork, and extending its line 120 km to the west. (The system was again enlarged in the twelfth and thirteenth centuries, possibly as a reaction to the threat of Mongol attack.) Pereiaslavl was defended on the east by a planned grid of strongholds built at the end of the eleventh and the beginning of the twelfth century.

36 J. G. Zverugo 1989, *Verkhnee Ponemanie v IX–XIII vv.* (Minsk).

37 This is in itself probably derived, as Władysław Duczko has observed, from a 'tamga' sign adopted from the Khazars.

38 For Byzantine architecture in the Kievan state see P. A. Rappoport 1982, *Russkaia arkhitektura X–XIII vv.: katalog pamiatnikov* (Leningrad). The architecture and decoration of the St Sophia church in Kiev is considered in a number of guidebooks, some richly illustrated with English summaries.

Chapter 12

1 Colonization of former Slav territory in the eastern Alps (and especially along the upper Danube after the defeat of the Magyars in 955) was to affect the ethnic make-up of the area and lead to the creation of modern Austria (H. Friesinger and B. Vacha 1987, *Die vielen Väter Österreichs: Römer-Germanen-Slawen, eine Spurensuche*, Vienna). The colonization of Bohemia (which for long periods was formerly a part of the German Empire) was mainly later and restricted to the western mountains (Sudeten, Erzgebirge).

2 The early history of the Bohemian state is discussed by a number of authors. The reader is referred to R. Nový 1968, *Anfänge des Böhmischen Staates*, vol. 1 (Prague); definitely to be recommended is the richly illustrated double-language text edited by J. Opat 1996, *Ilustrované české dějiny/Illustrated Czech History* (Prague), vol. 1 (authors J. Slamá and V. Vavřínek) and vol. 2 (author R. Nový). See also D. Třeštik 1986, 'Bořivoj und Svatopluk: die Entstehung des Böhmischen Staates und Grossmähren', pp. 311–44 in J. Poulík and B. Chropovský (eds) 1986, *Grossmähren und die Anfänge der Tschechoslowakischen Staatlichkeit* (Prague). For recent archaeological work see J. Fridrich (ed.) 1994, *25 Years of Archaeological Research in Bohemia* (Prague, *Památky Archeologické – Supplementum* 1).

3 Bavaria and East Frankia formed a strip of German-held territory along the Danube valley from above Regensberg to Linz and bordering on the Bohemian forest mountain range. This territory was settled by Germans in the early sixth century, and formed the ethnic back-

ground to the formation of modern Bavaria and Austria. The area had previously seen some Slav settlement too.

4 In Moravia the Middle Hillfort period dates to 800/820–906, after which the sites are abandoned.

5 See J. Slámá 1983, 'Přínos archeologie k poznání počátků přemyslovského státu', *Acta Musei Nationalis Pragae* 37 (2–3), 159–69; J. Slámá 1988, *Střední Čechy v raném středověku III: archeologie o počátcich přemyslovského státu* (Prague, *Praehistorica* 14).

6 The chronology of the ruling family has been the subject of debate for several decades. These problems seem to have been resolved for most scholars by the work of D. Třeštík (1984, 'O novém výkladu chronologie nejstarších Přemyslovců', *Československý Časopis Historický* 32, 416–21; D. Třeštík 1997, *Počátky Přemyslovců: vstup Čechu do dějin [530–935]*, Prague). The only problem is that anthropological investigation of skeletal remains thought to be of the first Přemyslids done in the 1980s by the physical anthropologist E. Vlcek has produced conflicting data on the age of death of some of them.

7 E. Dąbrowska 1973, *Wielkie grody dorzecza górnej Wisły* (Wrocław). The excellent small book by K. Wachowski 1997, *Śląsk w dobie przedpiastowskiej* (Wrocław), dealing with Silesia, is a good example of recent factographic trends (including the question of Czech influence) in Polish early medieval archaeology.

8 The first bishop of Prague, dependent on German ones, was a certain Thietmar, a monk from Magdeburg who had a good knowledge of the Slav language.

9 First noted by J. Slámá 1988, *Střední Čechy v raném středověku III: archeologie o počátcich přemyslovského státu* (Prague, *Praehistorica* 14).

10 The rise of the state in the area is discussed by J. Herrmann (ed.) 1985, *Die Slawen in Deutschland* (Berlin), esp. pp. 262–77. See also P. Heather 1997, 'Frankish imperialism and Slavic society', pp. 171–90 in P. Urbańczyk (ed.), *Origins of Central Europe* (Warsaw); H.-J. Brachmann 1983, 'Research into the early history of the Slav populations in the territory of the German Democratic Republic', *Medieval Archaeology* 27, 89–106.

11 It is less likely that this area came under Czech

rule in the 930s to 970s (see above) since by this time the area had become part of the Ottonian Empire.

12 See for example the maps in the books by J. Herrmann 1968, *Siedlung, Wirtschaft und gesellschaftliche Verhältnisse der slawische Stämmen zwischen Oder/Neisse und Elbe* (Berlin), and Herrmann (ed.), *Die Slawen in Deutschland*.

13 Again this is well demonstrated in the maps in Herrmann, *Siedlung*, and J. Herrmann (ed.), *Die Slawen in Deutschland*.

14 Brenna in particular was ideally placed as a trade centre (reflected by the concentration around it of silver hoards of 970–1100).

15 Post-1945 excavations carried out by Polish archaeologists dated the beginnings of this town to the aftermath of the Polish conquest, but the dating evidence uncovered at the time (or subsequently) does not allow such precision.

16 Pomerania was annexed by the Poles again in 1119–23, and reconverted to Christianity by missionaries such as Otto of Bamberg (a bishopric was founded at Wolin in 1140).

17 The formation of the Polish state has been considered in a number of works: see W. Hensel 1960, *The Beginnings of the Polish State* (Warsaw); W. Hensel 1964, *Polska przed tysiącem lat* (Wrocław); A. Gieysztor, S. Kieniewicz, E. Rostworowski, J. Tazbir and H. Wereszycki (eds) 1968, *History of Poland* (Warsaw); J. Topolski 1986, *An Outline History of Poland* (Warsaw); L. Leciejewicz 1976, 'Medieval archaeology in Poland – current problems and research methods', *Medieval Archaeology* 20, 1–15. Any list of the major works on the beginnings of the Polish state must include H. Łowmiański's six-volume opus (1963–73), *Początki Polski: z dziejów Słowian w I tysiącleciu n.e.* (Warsaw).

18 This new evidence comes from the work of Dr M. Krąpiec of Cracow, to whom I am grateful for supplying this information (pers. comm.). See also T. Sawicki 1998, 'Gnieźnieński zespół grodowy w świetle najnowszych badań', pp. 207–16 in A. Buko (ed.), *Studia z dziejów cywilizacji* (Warsaw). The Polish evidence is presented by M. Krąpiec 1998, 'Dendrochronological dating of Early Medieval fortified settlements in Poland', pp. 257–66 in J. Henning and A. T. Ruttkay (eds), *Frühmittelalterlicher Burgenbau in Mittel- und Osteuropa* (Bonn).

19 If coins are meant, this would be problematic, since, as we have seen above, we now know that all the coins formerly assigned by numismatists to Mieszko I were in fact issued by Mieszko II (S. Suchodolski 1998, 'Spór o początki mennictwa w Czechach i w Polsce', *Wiadomości Numizmatyczne* 42, 5–20).

20 Interdynastic marriages were an important factor in international politics of the time, well illustrated by the connections of Mieszko's family. His daughter Świętosława became the wife of the Swedish King Erik, and after his death (c. 998) of the Danish king Sven Forkbeard, by whom she bore Canute, future king of Denmark, Norway and England. She died in 1014 and the sagas refer to her as Sygurd Storráda.

21 The authority was received at the hands of the emperor, for the papal legate apparently played no part in these proceedings. Attempts to obtain a crown from the Pope in 1000 came to nothing, owing to the changing and unfavourable political situation in the relations between Rome and the Empire. Later tradition has it that a crown was prepared but it was given to Stephen of Hungary.

22 The original is now in the Hofburg Schatzkammer. What purports to be the original Polish copy given by Otto to Bolesław is in the Treasury of the cathedral in Cracow; a second copy given to the Hungarian rulers is now lost. There are some doubts about the authenticity of the Polish spear: it has odd stylistic features and may even be a later copy to replace a lost original.

23 Another missionary failure of this period was the expedition of Bruno of Querfurt to the Prussians (1009) which ended in his death. Bruno (Boniface) would have known what he was facing as he was the author of the *Life of St Wojciech* and the *Lives of the Five Martyred Brethren*. He had already worked among the Polabians and Rus, and in Hungary.

24 W. Hensel 1977, 'The origin of western and eastern European Slav towns', pp. 373–90 in M. Barley (ed.), *European Towns: Their Archaeology and Early History* (London).

25 This took place by the second half of the eleventh century, when we observe coinage from Polish mints appearing about 1070 in the reign of Bolesław the Bold (king 1058–79 – not to be confused with Bolesław the Brave) and being used on an increasing scale as an element in the formation of local markets.

26 The fact that a separate Kashubian language survived in parts of Pomerania was exploited by the Nazis. The situation in Silesia was more complex, and we noted above that it is in the records of the Cistercian monastery of Henryków in Silesia that we find the first sentence written in Polish.

Chapter 13

1 In any event Bolesław was not crowned until twenty-five years later.

2 Turkish rule in Europe was to last until the Balkan wars of the 1870s, when Bosnia and Herzegovina were occupied by the Austro-Hungarians. Serbia had become an independent principality in 1817.

3 It is from this period that we first meet the expression *Ukraina* ('at the edge'), a name for a frontier zone, which clearly indicates that the centre of the state had shifted from the middle Dniepr to the tributaries of the upper Volga.

4 It is interesting to note that similar stereotyping is reflected in American historiography, which has an even narrower view of what constitutes western European history, tending to pay less attention to Spain and Portugal and the Mediterranean countries than to the countries of the northwest.

5 For the early history of central European archaeology summarized in English see K. Sklenař 1983, *Archaeology in Central Europe: The First 500 Years* (Leicester/New York). See also J. Lech 1996, 'A short history of Polish archaeology', *World Archaeological Bulletin* 8, 177–95; and J. Lech 1997/8, 'Between captivity to freedom: Polish archaeology in the 20th century', *Archaeologia Polona* 35/36, 25–222.

6 The use of the past in creation of national identities and the relationship between scholarship and its public patronage has been examined in western historiography and especially archaeology in recent years. See P. Kohl and C. Fawcett (eds) 1995, *Nationalism, Politics and the Practice of Archaeology* (Cambridge); also M. Diaz-Andreu and T. Champion (eds) 1996, *Nationalism and Archaeology in Europe* (Boulder/San Francisco). Some of these issues may be more difficult to appreciate in the English-speaking world where the modern states of Great Britain (at least England) and

the United States accept, and in general are even proud of, the mixed ethnicity of the various contributions to the formation of their nationhood. This is not necessarily the case when such ethnic mixing or external influence is for several reasons perceived as causing a threat to the further existence of a culture, as with the states discussed here.

7 Jakob Fallmerayer 1830, *Geschichte der Halbinsel Morea während des Mittelalters* (Stuttgart).

8 Later published in *Zeitschrift des Vereins für Volkskunde* 6 (1896), 1–14.

9 M. Djilas, *Conversations with Stalin*: I used the Polish edition of 1991.

10 It is interesting to note that German *Ostforschung* took on a new role soon after the War and also served the needs of revisionist politics, while in Poland officially sanctioned study of the so-called *Kresy* really developed only after 1989.

11 The book by Ernst Petersen 1939, *Der ostelbische Raum als germanisches Kraftfeld im Lichte der Bodenfund des 6.–8. Jahrhunderts* (Leipzig), was especially strongly criticized.

12 K. Musianowicz 1960, 'Granica mazowiecko-drehowicka na Podlasiu we wczesnym średniowieczu', *Materiały Wczesnośredniowieczne* 5, 187–230.

13 K. Godłowski 1979, *Z badań nad zagadnieniem rozprzestrzenienia się Słowian w V–VII w. n.e.* (Cracow).

14 One may wonder whether the Dacian model of Romanian origins and glorification of the Magyars in Hungary, when both nations did have a Slav past which has been largely ignored, may not derive from similar needs.

15 See also J. Zeman 1979, 'K problematice časně slovanské kultury ve střední Europě', *Památky Archeologické* 70, 113–30.

16 A good example is J. Poulík, B. Chropovský *et al.* 1986, *Grossmähren und die Anfänge der tschechoslowakischen Staatlichkeit* (Prague).

17 The situation in Poland is summarized for example by P. Barford 1995, 'Marksizm w archeologii polskiej w latach 1945–1975', *Archeologia Polski* 40, 7–78.

18 This may not be so bad if one considers the very poor material base on which one can work. It seems that a decade or so of careful source-criticism and increasing the database would not go amiss. Unfortunately the financial resources of these states are not at present in a position to achieve this aim.

19 See the thought-provoking article by F. Curta 1994, 'The changing image of the Early Slavs in the Rumanian historiography and archaeological literature: a critical survey', *Sudost-Forschungen* 53, 225–310.

20 A good example is S. A. Pivavarchik and G. M. Semianchuk 1997, *Arkheologia Belarussii* II: *epokha Syaredniavechcha* (Grodno). In the Balkans a new generation of scholars is trying to create a history for each of the areas split off from the former Yugoslavia.

21 One wonders whether in some of these cases the authors have not been too enthusiastic in their desire to disprove old dogma.

22 Thus the cover of a catalogue of the State Archaeological Museum exhibition, *The Slavs in Early Medieval Europe* (M. Miskiewicze (ed.) 1998) depicts in lurid colours the Cross rising above a symbolic representation of pagan idols (and there is no text inside dedicated to the pagan religion of the Slavs).

Select Bibliography

The following bibliography is intended to reinforce and supplement that provided by the notes. First listed are the primary sources. Of the many thousands of books and articles available I have attempted to select those from which a general overview of the subject can be obtained, concentrating on relatively recent works which are either in western languages or well illustrated. One or two works not falling into either category are of interest as they reflect stages in the recent development of the subject.

Primary Sources

Adam of Bremen: Magistri Adam Bremensis gesta Hammaburgensis ecclesia pontificum, ed. Bernhard Schmeidler 1917 (Monumenta Germaniae Historica (MGH) Scriptores, Hanover and Leipzig); trans. F. J. Tschan 1959, *Adam of Bremen: History of the Archbishops of Hamburg-Bremen* (New York).

Annales Bertiniani: ed. G. H. Pertz 1844 (MGH Scriptores vol. 5, Hanover); trans. J. L. Nelson 1991, *The Annals of St-Bertin* (Manchester).

Anonymous called Gallus: Galli Anonymi Chronicae et Gesta ducum sive principium Polonorum, ed. K. Maleczyński 1952 (Monumenta Poloniae Historica (MPH) NS vol. 2, Cracow).

Bavarian Geographer: Descriptio civitatum et regionum ad septentrionalem plagam Danubii, ed. A. Bielowski (MPH vol. 1, pp. 10–11, Cracow).

Bertholdi Annales Capitularia regum Francorum: ed. A. Boretius 1883 (MGH LL, sectio ii, Hanover); trans. T. Reuter 1992 (Medieval Sources series 1992, Manchester).

DAI – Constantine Porphyrogenitus: De administrando imperio ed. and trans. G. Moravcsik and R. J. H. Jenkins (Dumbarton Oaks Texts 1: Corpus Fontium Historine Byzantinae (CFHB) 1, Washington, D.C. 1967).

Einhard: Vita Karoli Magni, 6th ed. O. Holder-Egger 1911 (MGH Scriptores Rerum Germanicarum, Hanover); trans. Lewis Thorpe 1969, *Einhard and Notker the Stammerer: Two Lives of Charlemagne* (London).

Fredegar: The Fourth Book of the Chronicle of Fredegar, ed. and trans. J. M. Wallace-Hadrill 1960 (London).

Helmold: Helmoldi presbyteri Bozoviensis Chronica Slavorum, ed. and trans. H. Stoob 1963 (Berlin).

Herbord: Herbordi Dialogus de Vita S. Ottonis episcopi Babenburgensis, ed. J. Wikarjak and K. Liman 1974 (MPH NS vol. 7, part 3, Warsaw).

Ibn Fadlan: Kitab, ed. and trans. A. Kmietowicz 1985 (Wrocław).

Ibrahim ibn Jaqub: Relacja Ibrahima ibn Jakuba z podróży do krajów słowiańskich w przekazie al-Bekriego, ed. and trans. T. Kowalski 1946 (MPH NS vol. 1, Cracow).

Ibn Rusteh: Kitab al'laq an-nafisa, ed. and trans. T. Lewicki 1977 (Źródła arabskie do dziejów Słowiańszczyzny vol. II.2, Wrocław).

John Skylitzes: Synopsis Historiarum, ed. I. Thurn 1973 (CFHB 5, New York/Berlin).

Jordanes: Getica, ed. Th. Mommsen 1882 (MGH AA 5 Berlin); trans. C. C. Mierow 1912 (New York). Also trans. E. Zwolski 1984, *Kasjodor I Jordanes, Historia Gocka, czyli scytyjska Europa* (Lublin).

Kosmas: Cosmae Pragensis Chronica Boemorum 1923 (MGH NS vol. 2, Berlin).

Liber Henrykow: Liber fundationis claustri Sanctae Marie Virginis in Heinrichow, ed. and trans. R. Grodecki 1949 (Poznań/Wrocław).

Menander Protector: History, in A. Brzóstkowska and W. Swoboda (eds) 1989, *Testimonia najdawniejszych dziejów Słowian: Seria Grecka, Zeszyt 2, pisarze z V–X wieku* (Wrocław).

Miracles of St Demetrius: in A. Brzóstkowska and W. Swoboda (eds) 1989, *Testimonia najdawniejszych dziejów Słowian: Seria Grecka, Zeszyt 2, pisarze z V–X wieku* (Wrocław).

Pseudo-Maurice: Strategicon, trans. G. T. Dennis 1984 (Philadelphia). Also in A. Brzóstkowska and W. Swoboda (eds) 1989, *Testimonia naj-dawniejszych dziejów Słowian: Seria Grecka, Zeszyt 2, pisarze z V–X wieku* (Wrocław).

Procopius of Caesarea: Wars in A. Brzóstkowska and W. Swoboda (eds) 1989, *Testimonia najdawniejszych dziejów Słowian: Seria Grecka, Zeszyt 2, pisarze z V–X wieku* (Wrocław).

Procopius of Caesarea: Anekdota in A. Brzóstkowska and W. Swoboda (eds) 1989, *Testimonia najdawniejszych dziejów Słowian: Seria Grecka, Zeszyt 2, pisarze z V–X wieku* (Wrocław).

Procopius of Caesarea: Buildings, trans. H. B. Dewing, Loeb, 7 vols 1914–40 (London). Also in A. Brzóstkowska and W. Swoboda (eds) 1989, *Testimonia najdawniejszych dziejów Słowian: Seria Grecka, Zeszyt 2, pisarze z V–X wieku* (Wrocław).

PVL – Lavrentskaja letopis (Povest Vremennych let): ed. and trans. S. H. Cross and O. P. Sherbovitz-Wetzor 1953, *The Russian Primary Chronicle, Laurentian Text* (Cambridge, Mass.).

Royal Frankish Annals: Annales Regni Francorum, ed. F. Kurze 1895 (MGH SRG, Hanover); trans. B. Scholz 1972, *Carolingian Chronicles* (Michigan).

Theophractus Simokattes: in A. Brzóstkowska and W. Swoboda (eds) 1989, *Testimonia najdawniejszych dziejów Słowian: Seria Grecka, Zeszyt 2, pisarze z V–X wieku* (Wrocław).

Thietmar of Merseberg: Thietmari Merseburgensis Episcopi Chronicon, ed. and trans. R. Holzmann 1955, *Die Chronik des Bischofs Thietmar . . .* (MGH SS NS IX, 2nd ed., Berlin); ed. and trans. M. Z. Jedlicki 1952, *Kronika Thietmara* (Poznań).

Vita of St Methodius: Pamyat i zhite sv. ottsa nashego i uchitela Metodiya 1961 (MPH vol. 1, 93–113, Warsaw); trans. into Polish T. Lehr-Spławiński 1988, *Apostołowie Słowian. Żywoty Konstantyna i Metodego* (Warsaw).

Further Reading

Angelov, D. 1980, *Die Entstehung des bulgarischen Volkes* (Berlin).

Arkheologia Ukrainskoi SSR III, 1986 (edited by V. D. Baran *et al.*) (Kiev).

Avarenius, A. 1974, *Die Awaren in Europa* (Amsterdam/Bratislava).

Baran, V. D. (ed.) 1987, *Problemy etnogeneza Slavian* (Kiev).

Baran, V. D., O. M. Prikhodniuk, R. V. Terpilovskii (*et al.*) 1985, *Etnokulturnaia karta territorii Ukrainskoi SSR v I tys. n.e.* (Kiev).

Beeby, S., D. Buckton and Z. Klanica 1982, *Great Moravia: The Archaeology of Ninth Century Czechoslovakia* (London, British Museum).

Beloševic, J. 1980, *Materialna kultura Hrvata od VII do IX stoleća* (Zagreb).

Bosl, K., A. Gieysztor, F. Graus, M. M. Postan and F. Seibt (eds) 1970, *Eastern and Western Europe in the Middle Ages* (London).

Brachmann, H.-J. 1983, *Slawische Stamme an Elbe und Saale: zu ihrer Geschichte und Kultur im 6. bis 10. Jahrhundert – auf Grund archäologischer Quellen* (Berlin).

Brachmann, H.-J. 1983, 'Research into the early history of the Slav populations in the territory of the German Democratic Republic', *Medieval Archaeology* 27, 89–106.

Brachmann, H. 1993, *Der frühmittelalterliche Befestigungsbau in Mitteleuropa* (Berlin, Schriften zur Ur- und Frühgeschichte 45).

Brachmann, H.-J. (ed.) 1995, *Burg – Burgstadt – Stadt: zur Genese mittelalterlicher nichta-grarischer Zentren in Ostmitteleuropa* (Berlin).

Comşa, M. 1960, 'La pénétration des Slavs dans le territoire de la Roumanie entre Vieme et IXeme siècle à la lumière des recherches archéologiques', *Slavia Antiqua* 7, 175–88.

Comşa, M. 1973, 'Die Slawen im karpatisch-donauländischen Raum im 6.–7. Jahrhundert', *Zeitschrift für Archäologie* 7, 197–228.

Dekan, J. 1980, *Moravia Magna: Grossmähren – Epoche und Kunst* (Bratislava).

Dolukhanov, P. 1996, *The Early Slavs* (London).

Donat, P. 1980, *Haus, Hof und Dorf in Mitteleuropa vom 7. bis 12. Jahrhundert* (Berlin).

Donnert, E. 1983, *Das Kiewer Russland: Kultur und Geistesleben vom 9. bis zum Beginnen den 13. Jh.* (Leipzig).

Dvornik, F. 1949, *The Making of Central and Eastern Europe* (London).

Dvornik, F. 1956, *The Slavs: Their Early History and Civilization* (Boston/London).

Fehring, G. 1991, *The Archaeology of Medieval Germany: An Introduction* (London).

Franklin, S. and J. Shepard 1996, *The Emergence of Rus 750–1200* (London/New York).

Fusek, G. 1994, *Slovensko vo včasnoslovanskom obdobi* (Nitra).

Gąssowski, J. 1964, *Dzieje i kultura dawnych Słowian* (Warsaw).

Gimbutas, M. 1971, *The Slavs* (London).

Godłowski, K. 1979, *Z badań nad zagadnieniem rozprzestrzenienia się Słowian w V–VII w. n.e.* (Cracow).

Godłowski, K. 1983, 'Zur Frage der Slawensitze vor der grossen Slawenwanderung im 6. Jahrhundert', pp. 257–84 in *Settimane di Studio del Centro Italiano di Studi sull'Alto Medioevo* 30 (Spoleto).

Gojda, M. 1991, *The Ancient Slavs: Settlement and Society* (Edinburgh).

Hensel, W. 1960, *The Beginnings of the Polish State* (Warsaw).

Hensel, W. 1965, *Die Slawen im Frühmittelalter: ihre materielle Kultur* (Berlin).

Hensel, W. 1967, *Anfänge der Städte bei den Ost- und Westslawen* (Bautzen).

Hensel, W. 1977, 'The origin of western and eastern European Slav towns', pp. 373–90 in M. Barley (ed.), *European Towns: Their Archaeology and Early History* (London).

Hensel, W. 1987, *Słowiańszczyzna wczesnośred-niowieczna, zarys kultury materialnej* (4th ed.) (Warsaw)

Herrmann, J. 1965, *Kultur und Kunst der Slawen in Deutschland vom 7. bis 13. Jahrhundert* (Berlin).

Herrmann, J. 1971, *Zwischen Hradschin und Vineta: frühe Kulturen der Westslawen* (Leipzig/Jena/Berlin).

Herrmann, J. (ed.) 1982, *Wikinger und Slawen: zur Frühgeschichte der Ostseevölker* (Berlin).

Herrmann, J. (ed.) 1985, *Die Slawen in Deutschland: ein Handbuch. Geschichte und Kultur der slawischen Stämme westlich von Oder und Neisse vom 6. bis 12. Jahrhundert. Neubearbeitung* (Berlin).

Herrmann, J. (ed.) 1986, *Welt der Slawen: Geschichte, Gesellschaft, Kultur* (Leipzig/Jena/Berlin).

Hilczerówna, Z. 1967, *Dorzecza górnej i środkowej Obry od VI do początków XI w.* (Wrocław/Warsaw).

Jażdżewski, K. 1984, *Urgeschichte Mitteleuropas* (Wrocław).

Kazanski, M. 1999, *Les Slavs: Les origines Ier–VIIe siècle après J.-C.* (Paris).

Kolchin, B. A., V. L. Yanin and S. V. Yamshchikov (eds) 1985, *Drevni Novgorod: prikladnoe iskusstvo i arkheologia* (Moscow).

Krüger, B. 1967, *Dessau-Mosigkau: ein frühslawischer Siedlungsplatz in mittleren Elbegebiet* (Berlin).

Leciejewicz, L. 1976, 'Medieval archaeology in Poland – current problems and research methods', *Medieval Archaeology* 20, 1–15.

Leciejewicz, L. 1980, 'Medieval archaeology and its problems', pp. 191–211 in R. Schild (ed.), *Unconventional Archaeology: New Approaches and Goals in Polish Archaeology* (Wrocław).

Leciejewicz, L. 1989, *Słowianie zachodni: z dziejów tworzenia się średniowiecznej Europy* (Wrocław).

Leciejewicz, L. 1993, 'Medieval archaeology in eastern Europe', pp. 75–83 in H. Andersson and J. Wienberg (eds), *The Study of Medieval Archaeology* (Stockholm).

Mączyńska, M. 1993, *Die Völkerwanderung: Geschichte einer ruhelosen Epoche im 4. und 5. Jahrhundert* (Zurich).

Melnikova, E. 1996, *The Eastern World of the Vikings* (Gothenburg).

Obolensky, D. 1994, *Byzantium and the Slavs* (New York).

Parczewski, M. 1991, 'Origins of Early Slav culture in Poland', *Antiquity* 65 (248), 676–83.

Parczewski, M. 1993, *Die Anfänge der frühslawischen Kultur in Polen* (Vienna, Veröffentlichungen der Österreichischen Gesellschaft für Ur- und Frühgeschichte 17).

Parczewski, M. 1997, 'Beginnings of the Slavs' culture', pp. 79–90 in P. Urbańczyk (ed.), *Origins of Central Europe* (Warsaw).

Pleinerová, I. 1975, *Březno: vesnice prvních Slovanů v severozápadních Čechách* (Prague).

Pohl, W. 1988, *Die Awaren: ein Steppenvolk in Mitteleuropa 567–822 n.Chr.* (Munich).

Pohl, W. 1991, 'Conceptions of ethnicity in early medieval studies', *Archaeologia Polona* 29, 39–49.

Pohl, W. 1997, 'The role of the steppe peoples in eastern and central Europe in the first millennium A.D.', pp. 65–78 in P. Urbańczyk (ed.), *Origins of Central Europe* (Warsaw).

Poulík, J. 1978, 'The origins of Christianity in Slavonic countries north of the middle Danube Basin', *World Archaeology* 10 (2), 158–71.

Poulík, J. and B. Chropovský (eds) 1986, *Grossmähren und die Anfänge der Tschechoslowakischen Staatlichkeit* (Prague).

Rafalovich, I. A. 1972, *Slaviane VI–IX vekov v Moldavii* (Kishinev).

Rusanova, I. P. 1976, *Slavianskie drevnosti VI–VII vv: kultura prazhskogo tipa* (Moscow).

Rybakov, B. A. 1965, *The Early Centuries of Russian History* (Moscow).

Rybakov, B. A. 1984, (1989), *Kievan Rus* (Moscow).

Sedov, V. V. 1982, *Vostochniye slaviane v VI–XIII vv.* (Moscow), *Arkheologia SSR* 14.

Sedov, V. V. 1994, *Slaviane v drevnosti* (Moscow).

Slavianie Yugo-vostochnoi Europi v predgosudarstvennyi period, 1990 (ed. V. D. Baran et al.), (Kiev)

Słupecki, L. P. 1994, *Slavonic Pagan Sanctuaries* (Warsaw).

Słownik Starożytności Słowiańskich, vols I–VIII (1961–96) (Wrocław).

Stančev, S. 1966, *Veliki Preslav* (Sofia).

Strzelczyk, J. 1988, 'Slavic and Germanic peoples in Antiquity and the early Middle Ages', *Polish Western Affairs* 2, 163–82.

Šolle, M. 1983, *Staroslovanské hradisko, charakteristika, funkce, vývoj a význam* (Prague).

Urbańczyk, P. (ed.) 1997, *Origins of Central Europe* (Warsaw).

Váňa, Z. 1970, *Einführung in die Frühgeschichte der Slawen* (Neumünster).

Váňa, Z. 1983, *The World of the Ancient Slavs* (London/Detroit).

Wieczorek, A. and H.-M. Hinz (eds) 2000, *Europas Mitte um 1000, Beiträge zur Geschichte, Kunst und Archäologie*, 3 vols (Stuttgart).

Wolfram, H. 1987, *Die Geburt Mitteleuropas* (Vienna).

Wolfram, H. and F. Daim 1980, *Die Völker an der mittleren und unteren Donau im fünften und sechsten Jahrhundert* (Vienna).

Figures

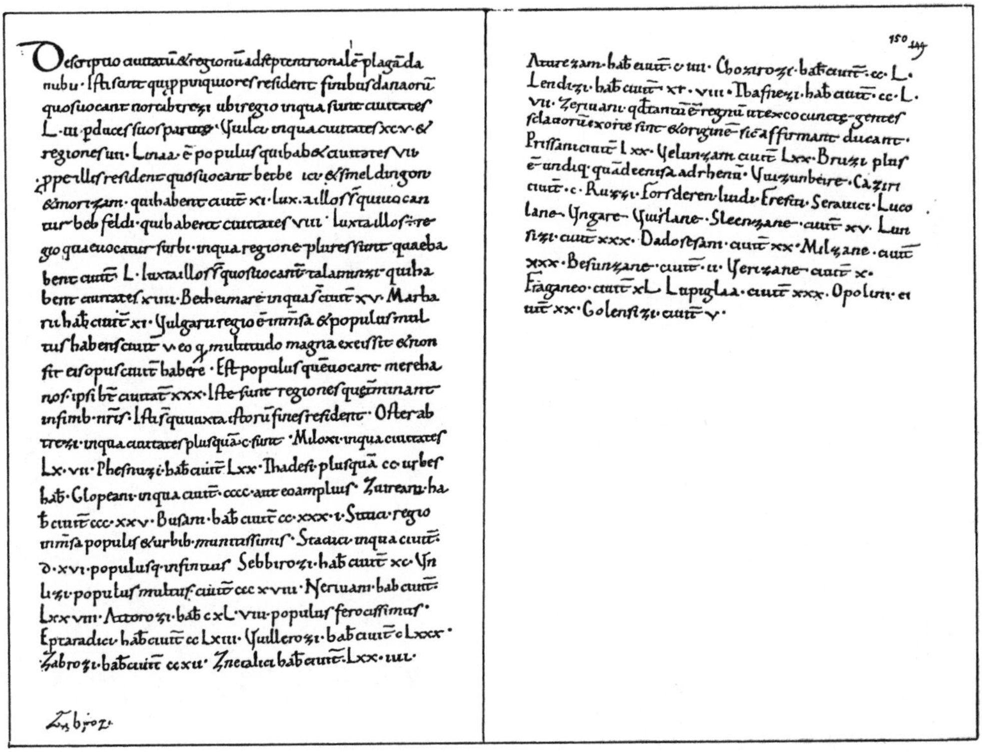
Descriptio ciuitatum et regionum ad septentrionalem plagam Da
nubii. Isti sunt qui propinquiores resident finibus Danaorum
quos uocant Nortabtrezi ubi regio in qua sunt ciuitates
LIII per duces suos partitae. Vuilci in qua ciuitates XCV et
regiones IIII. Linaa est populus qui habet ciuitates VII.
Prope illis resident quos uocant Bethenici et Smeldingon
et Morizani qui habent ciuitates XI. Iuxta illos sunt qui uocan
tur Hehfeldi qui habent ciuitates VIII. Iuxta illos est re
gio quae uocatur Surbi in qua regione plures sunt quae ha
bent ciuitates L. Iuxta illos sunt quos uocant Talaminzi qui ha
bent ciuitates XIIII. Beheimare in qua sunt ciuitates XV. Marha
rii habent ciuitates XI. Vulgarii regio est inmensa et populus mul
tus habens ciuitates V, eo quod multitudo magna ex eis sit et non
sit eis opus ciuitates habere. Est populus quem uocant Mereha
nos ipsi habent ciuitates XXX. Istae sunt regiones quae terminant
in finibus nostris. Isti sunt qui iuxta istorum fines resident. Osterab
trezi in qua ciuitates plus quam C sunt. Miloxi in qua ciuitates
LXVII. Phesnuzi habent ciuitates LXX. Thadesi plus quam CC urbes
habent. Glopeani in qua ciuitates CCCC aut eo amplius. Zuireani ha
bent ciuitates CCCXXV. Busani habent ciuitates CCXXXI. Sittici regio
inmensa populis et urbibus munitissimis. Stadici in qua ciuitates
DXVI populusque infinitus. Sebbirozi habent ciuitates XC. Un
lizi populus multus, ciuitates CCCXVIII. Neriuani habent ciuitates
LXXVIII. Attorozi habent CXLVIII populus ferocissimus.
Eptaradici habent ciuitates CCLXIII. Vuillerozi habent ciuitates CLXXX.
Zabrozi habent ciuitates CCXII. Znetalici habent ciuitates LXXIIII.

Zabrozi

150 149

Aturezani habent ciuitates CIIII. Chozirozi habent ciuitates CCL.
Lendizi habent ciuitates XCVIII. Thafnezi habent ciuitates CCL
VII. Zeriuani, quod tantum est regnum ut ex eo cunctae gentes
Sclauorum exortae sint et originem, sicut affirmant, ducant.
Prissani ciuitates LXX. Velunzani ciuitates LXX. Bruzi plus
est undique quam de Enisa ad Rhenum. Vuizunbeire. Caziri
ciuitates C. Ruzzi. Forsderen liudi. Fresiti. Seraueci. Luco
lane. Ungare. Vuislane. Sleenzane ciuitates XV. Lun
sizi ciuitates XXX. Dadosesani ciuitates XX. Milzane ciuitates
XXX. Besunzane ciuitates II. Verizane ciuitates X.
Fraganeo ciuitates XL. Lupiglaa ciuitates XXX. Opolini ci
uitates XX. Golensizi ciuitates V.

Fig. 1. The document known as the *Bavarian Geographer*, dating to about the middle of the ninth century and containing a list of the peoples to the east of the Carolingian frontier

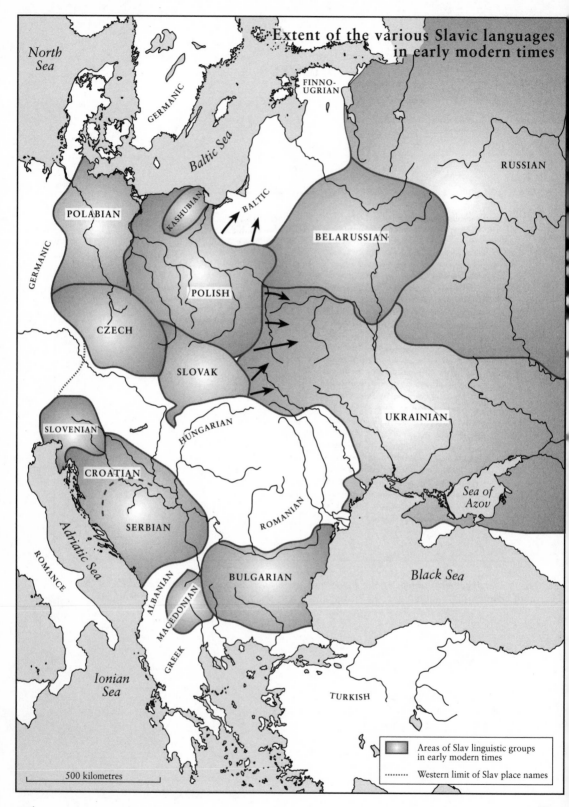

Extent of the various Slavic languages
in early modern times

North
Sea

GERMANIC

Baltic Sea

FINNO-
UGRIAN

RUSSIAN

POLABIAN

KASHUBIAN

BALTIC

BELARUSSIAN

GERMANIC

POLISH

CZECH

SLOVAK

UKRAINIAN

SLOVENIAN

HUNGARIAN

CROATIAN

Sea of
Azov

Adriatic Sea

SERBIAN

ROMANIAN

ROMANCE

Black Sea

ALBANIAN

BULGARIAN

MACEDONIAN

GREEK

Ionian
Sea

TURKISH

500 kilometres

Areas of Slav linguistic groups
in early modern times

Western limit of Slav place names

Fig. 2

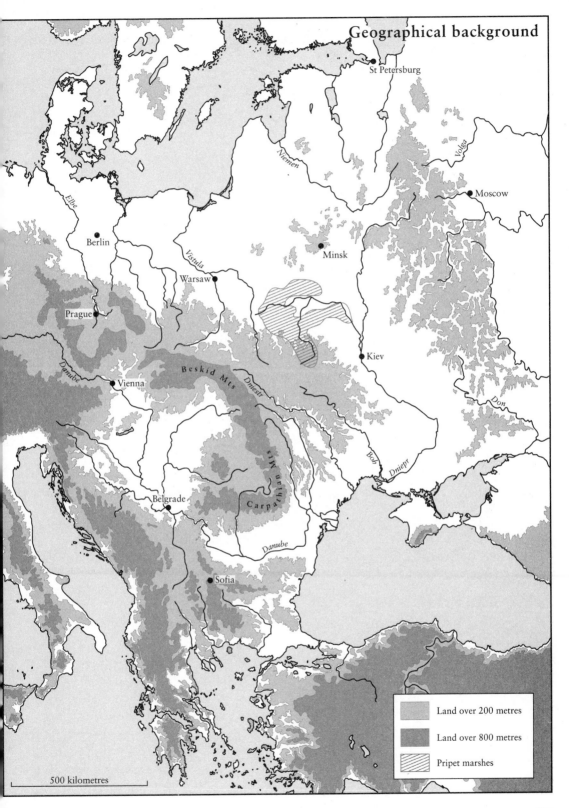

Geographical background

Land over 200 metres

Land over 800 metres

Pripet marshes

500 kilometres

Fig. 3

327

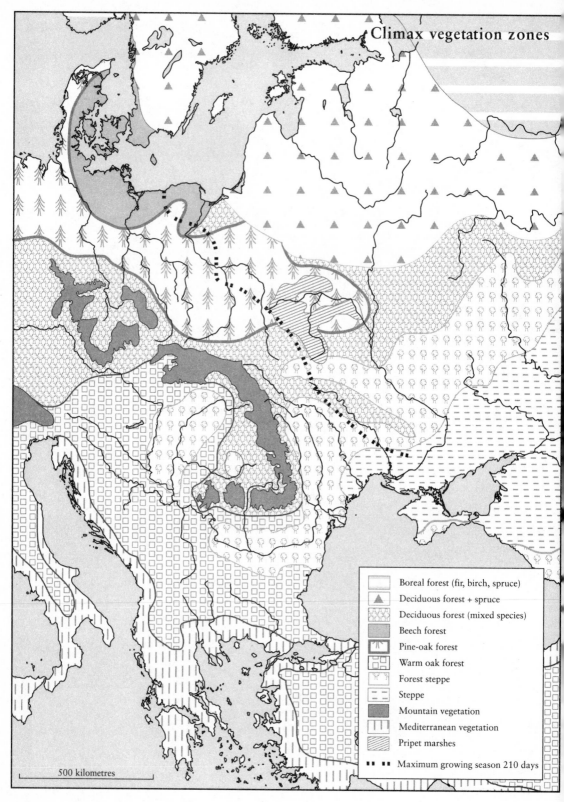

Climax vegetation zones

Boreal forest (fir, birch, spruce)
Deciduous forest + spruce
Deciduous forest (mixed species)
Beech forest
Pine-oak forest
Warm oak forest
Forest steppe
Steppe
Mountain vegetation
Mediterranean vegetation
Pripet marshes
Maximum growing season 210 days

500 kilometres

Fig. 4

Fig. 5. Typical appearance of the forest steppe zone. Photos courtesy Natalia Shishlina and Michail Gonyany

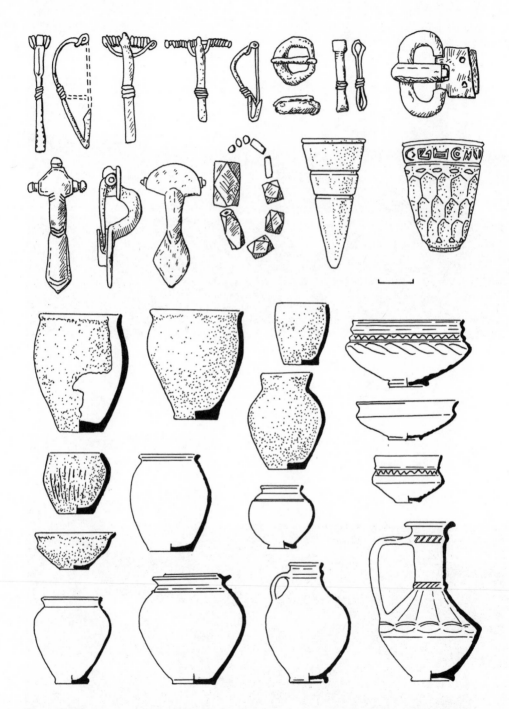

Fig. 6. Artefact types typical of the Cherniakhovo Culture at the end of antiquity: bronze fibulae, personal ornaments and toilet implements, buckles (scale about 1:2), glass vessels (1:4), handmade and wheel-thrown pottery (scale indicates 10 cm). After V. D. Baran, R. V. Terpilovski, B. V. Magomedov

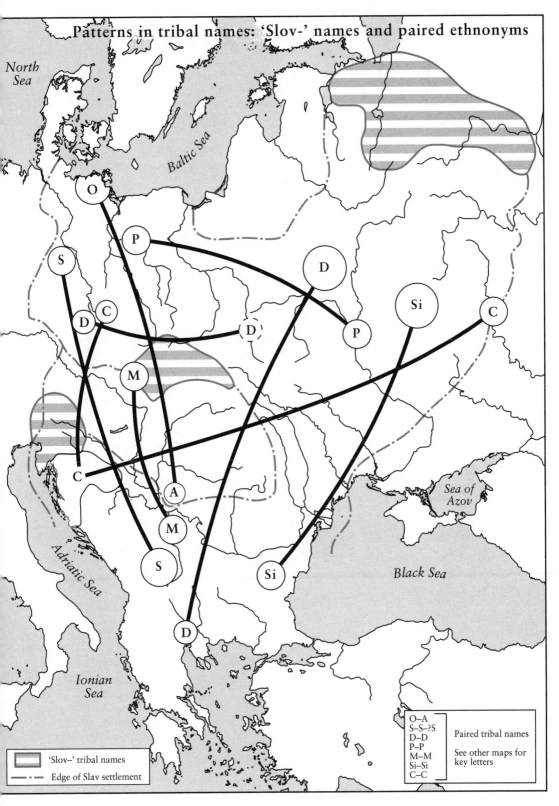

Patterns in tribal names: 'Slov-' names and paired ethnonyms

North
Sea

Baltic Sea

O

P

S

D

C

D

M

C

A

M

S

D

Si

D

P

D

Si

C

Adriatic
Sea

Ionian
Sea

Sea of
Azov

Black Sea

| O–A |
| S–S–?S |
| D–D |
| P–P |
| M–M |
| Si–Si |
| C–C |

Paired tribal names

See other maps for
key letters

'Slov–' tribal names

Edge of Slav settlement

Fig. 7

331

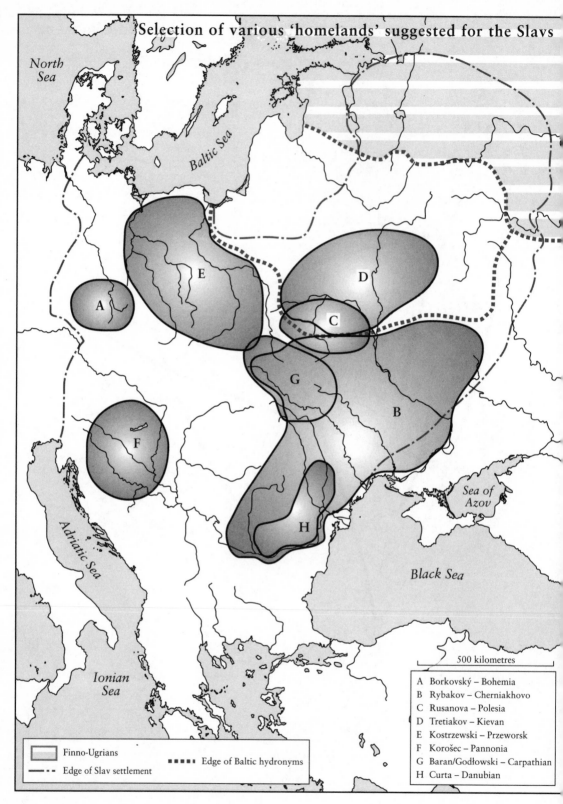

Selection of various 'homelands' suggested for the Slavs

North
Sea

Baltic Sea

A

E

D

C

G

B

F

H

Adriatic Sea

Sea of
Azov

Black Sea

Ionian
Sea

500 kilometres

Finno-Ugrians

Edge of Baltic hydronyms

Edge of Slav settlement

A Borkovský – Bohemia
B Rybakov – Cherniakhovo
C Rusanova – Polesia
D Tretiakov – Kievan
E Kostrzewski – Przeworsk
F Korošec – Pannonia
G Baran/Godłowski – Carpathian
H Curta – Danubian

Fig.

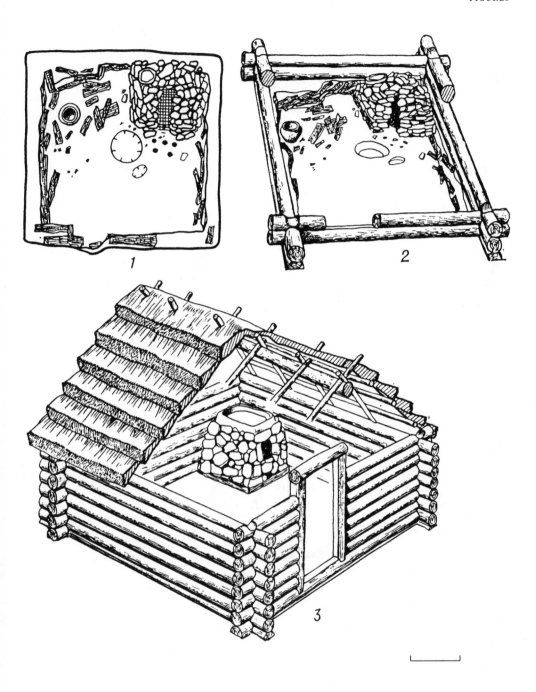

Fig. 9. Early Slav sunken-floored hut: (1) outline of pit and internal stone oven; (2) excavated remains in pit; (3) reconstruction (scale indicates 50 cm). After *Arkheologia Ukrainskoi SSR*, fig. 83

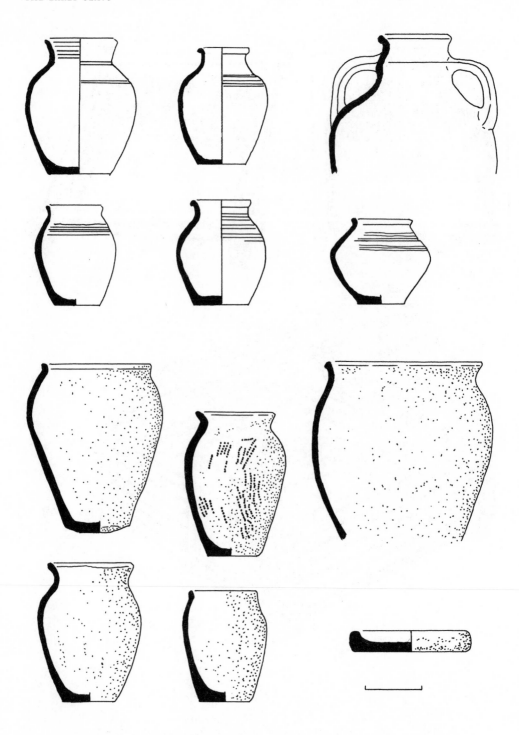

Fig. 10. Wheel-made and handmade vessels from Ipoteşti-Cîndeşti-Ciurel assemblages (scale indicates 10 cm). After M. Comşa and Z. Kurnatowska

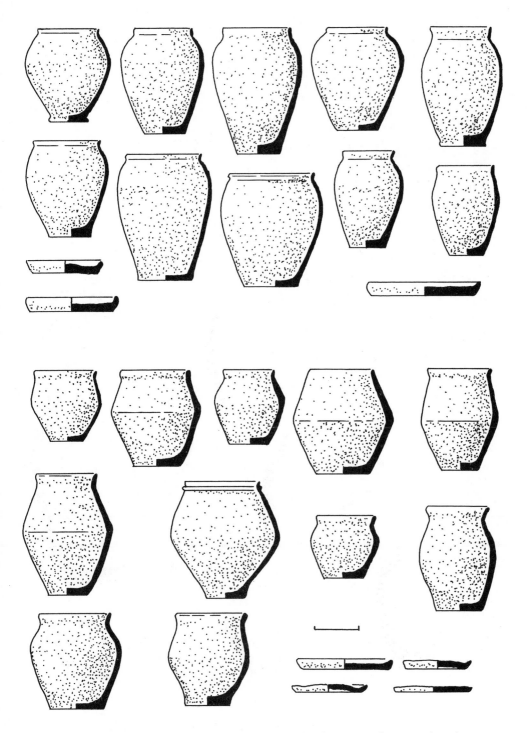

Fig. 11. Pottery of the Korchak (top) and Penkovka (bottom) Cultures (scale indicates 10 cm). After V. D. Baran and O. M. Prikhodniuk

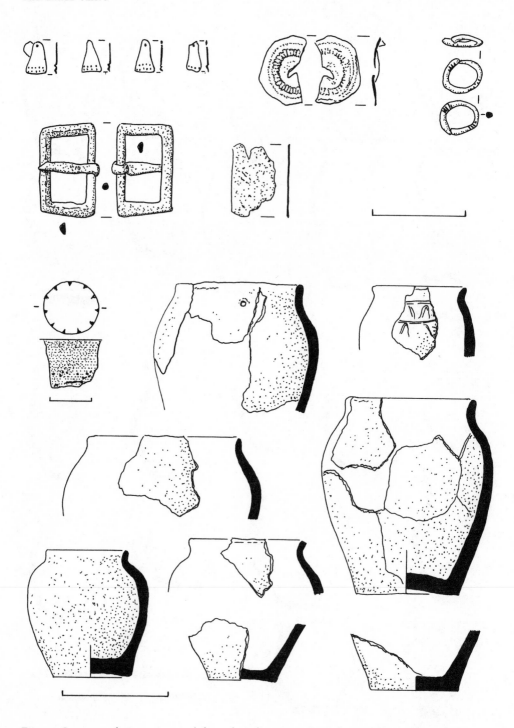

Fig. 12. Contents of pit 45 (centre left; scale indicates 1 m) on Cracow-Nowa Huta site 62, metalwork assemblage (top; scale indicates 5 cm) and pottery (bottom left; scale indicates 10 cm). After M. Parczewski, E. Dąbrowska and R. Hachulska-Ledwos

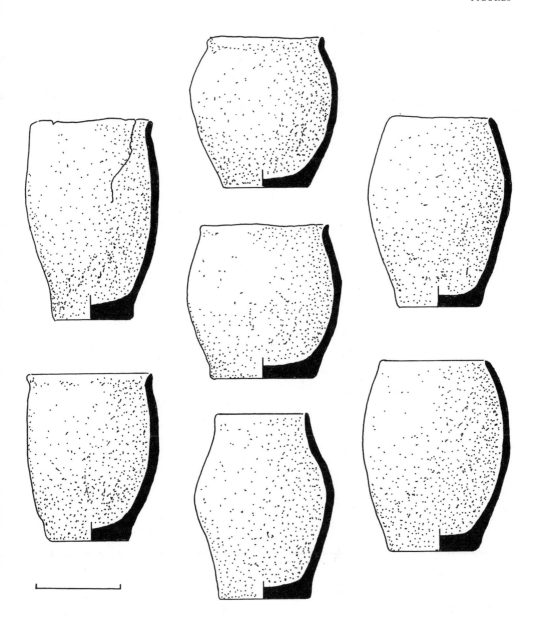

Fig. 13. Pottery vessels of the Suceava-Şipot Culture (scale indicates 10 cm).
After D. Teodor and Z. Kurnatowska

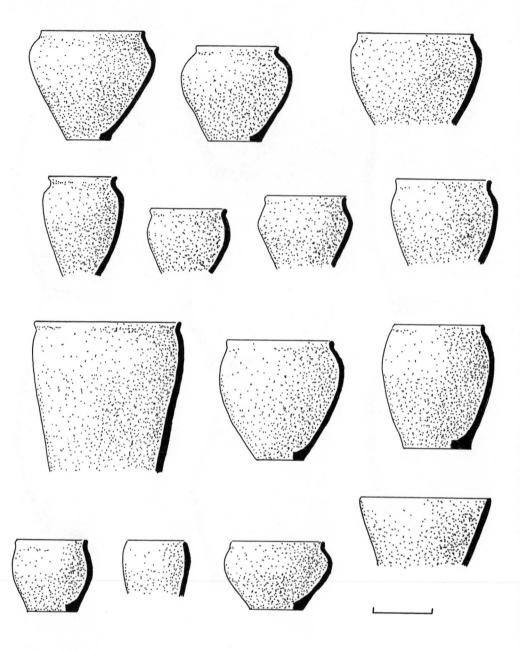

Fig. 14. Pottery vessels from the site at Dziedzice, Pomerania (scale indicates 10 cm).
After A. Porzeziński, with additions

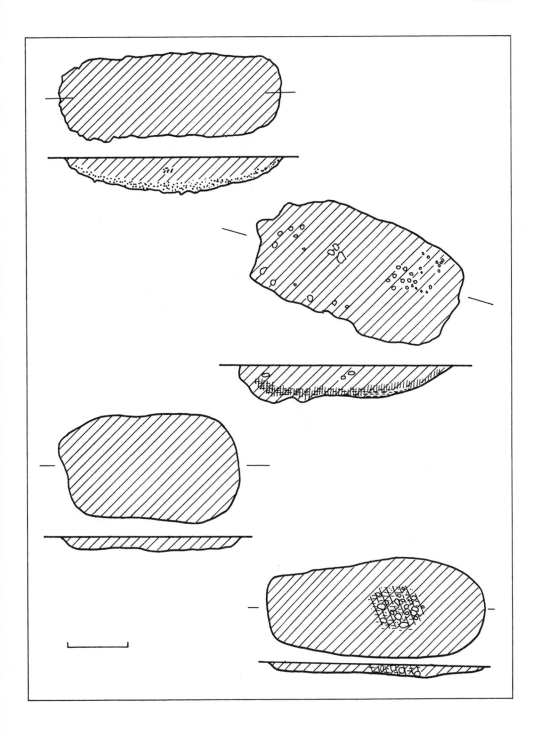

Fig. 15. So-called 'bath-shaped features' of the Sukow-Dziedzice Culture, dark earth fills with ashes and a few finds (top is north; scale indicates 1 m). After Z. Kobyliński, with amendments

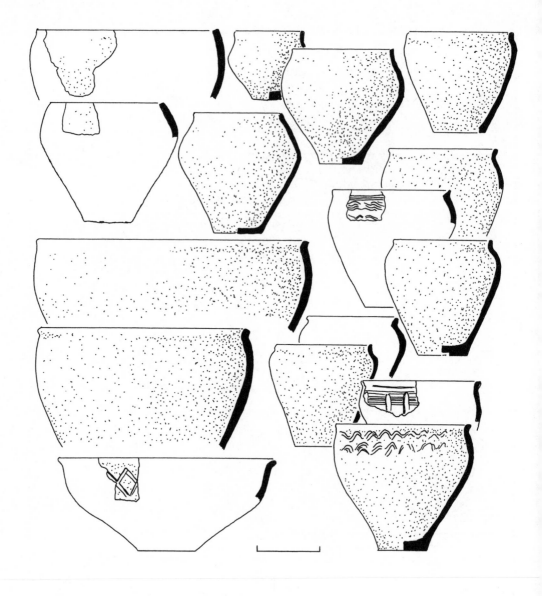

Fig. 16. Pottery vessels of the Sukow-Gołańcz type (scale indicates 10 cm). After W. Łosiński

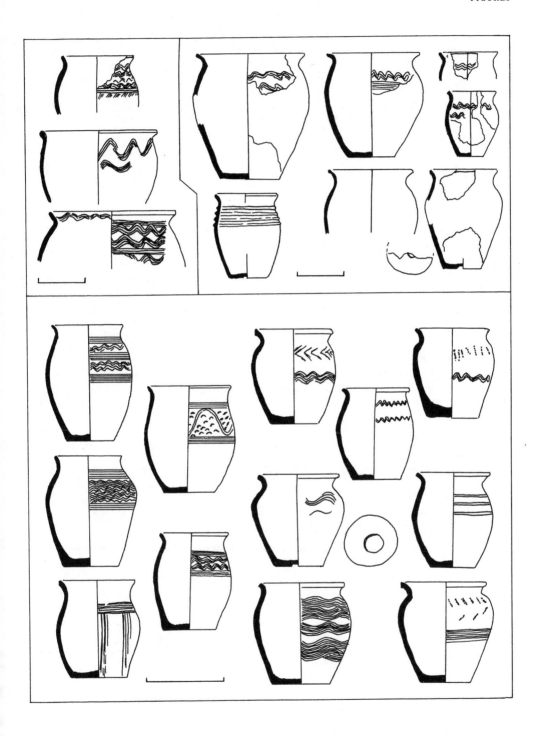

Fig. 17. Pottery of the Rüssen (top left), Racibórz-Chodlik (top right) and Devínská-Nová Ves traditions (all scales indicate 10 cm). Various sources

341

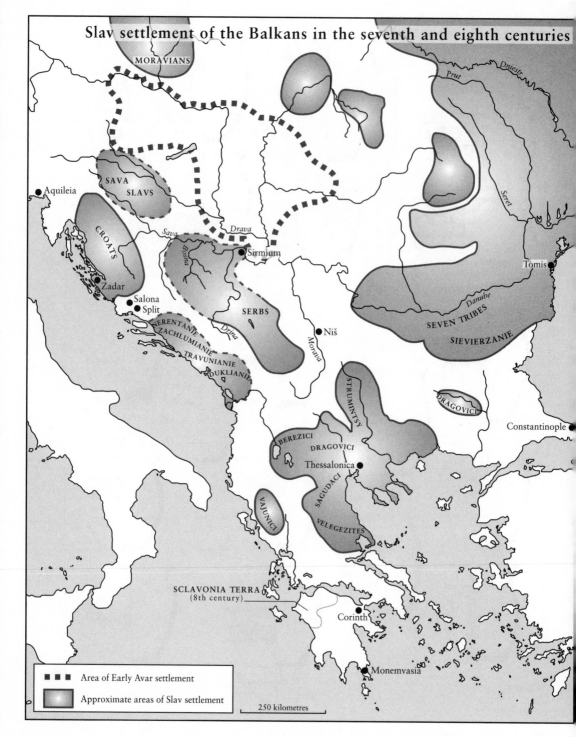

Slav settlement of the Balkans in the seventh and eighth centuries

MORAVIANS

SAVA SLAVS

Aquileia

CROATS

Zadar

Salona
Split

Sava

Bosna

Drava

Sirmium

NERENTANIE
ZACHLUMIANIE

TRAVUNIANIE

DUKLIANIE

Drina

SERBS

Morava

Niš

Prut

Dniestr

Seret

Tomis

Danube

SEVEN TRIBES

SIEVIERZANIE

STRUMINTSY

DRAGOVICI

Constantinople

BEREZICI

DRAGOVICI

Thessalonica

SAGUDACI

VAJUNICI

VELEGEZITES

SCLAVONIA TERRA
(8th century)

Corinth

Monemvasia

▪▪▪ Area of Early Avar settlement

Approximate areas of Slav settlement

250 kilometres

Fig. 18

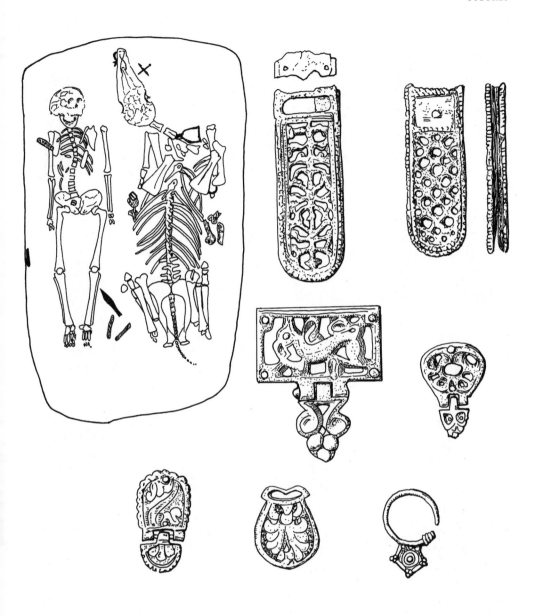

Fig. 19. Burial of Avar type with horse and harness – note the stirrups (Márfa Kom. Baranya, Hungary), belt mounts from various sites, also star-shaped temple-ring. Various sources

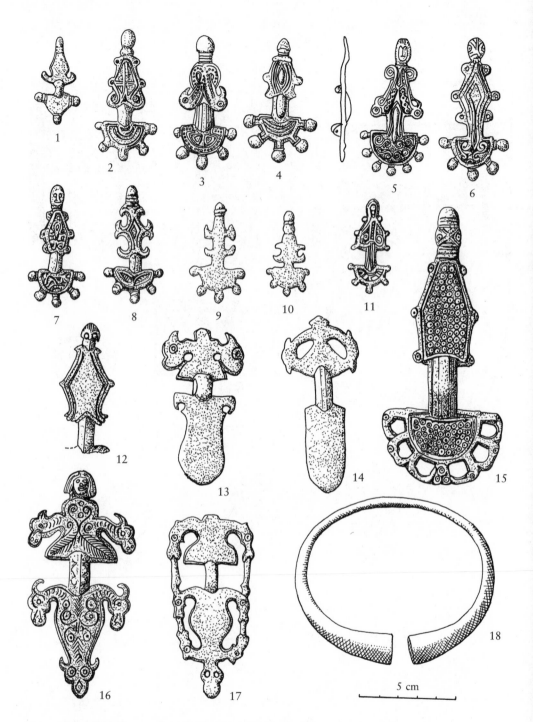

Fig. 20. (1–11) Small cast plate fibulae from the lower Danube area (seventh century, various sites); (12–17) Dniepr fibulae (Penkovka Culture, various sites); (18) bracelet with expanded terminals. After M. Kazanski

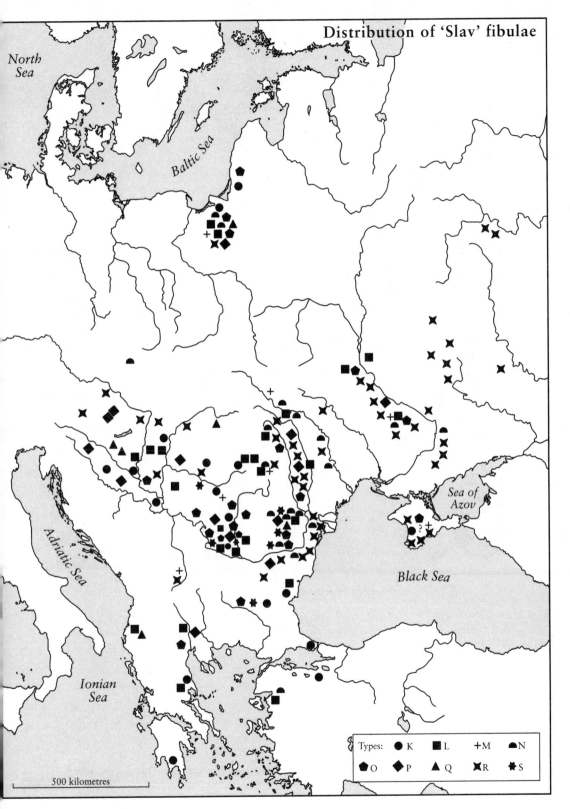

Distribution of 'Slav' fibulae

North Sea

Baltic Sea

Sea of Azov

Black Sea

Adriatic Sea

Ionian Sea

Types: ● K ■ L + M ◖ N
◆ O ◆ P ▲ Q ✳ R ✳ S

500 kilometres

Fig. 21. After L. Vagalinski

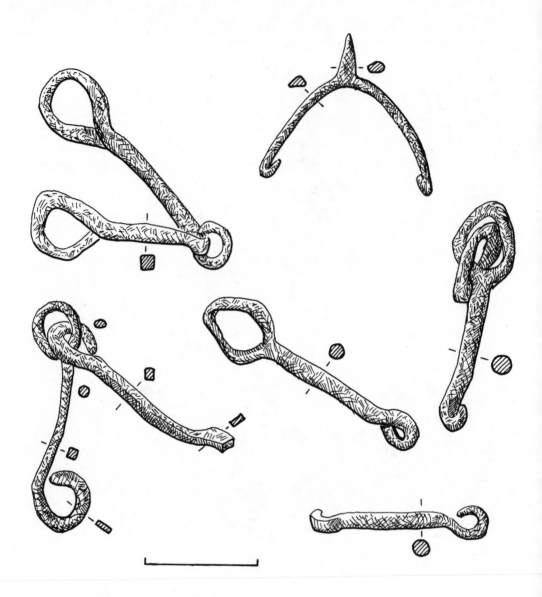

Fig. 22. Internally hooked spur, Mikulčice; bridle bits from Early Slav sites at Moschenka Smolyan and Velemichi (scale indicates 5 cm). After M. Kazanski

(*Opposite page*) Fig. 23. Items from the Martynovka hoard: zoomorphic plaquettes, belt fittings, fibula and wire ornaments. After Sedov, *Arkheologiya SSSR* 14

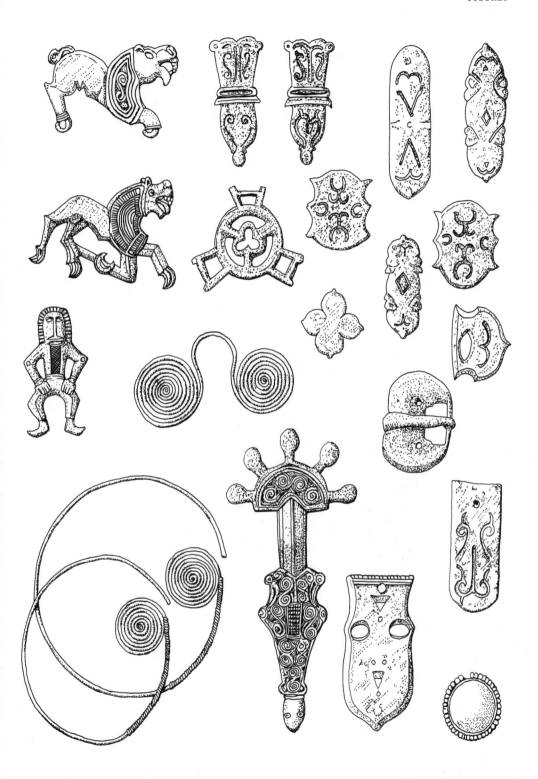

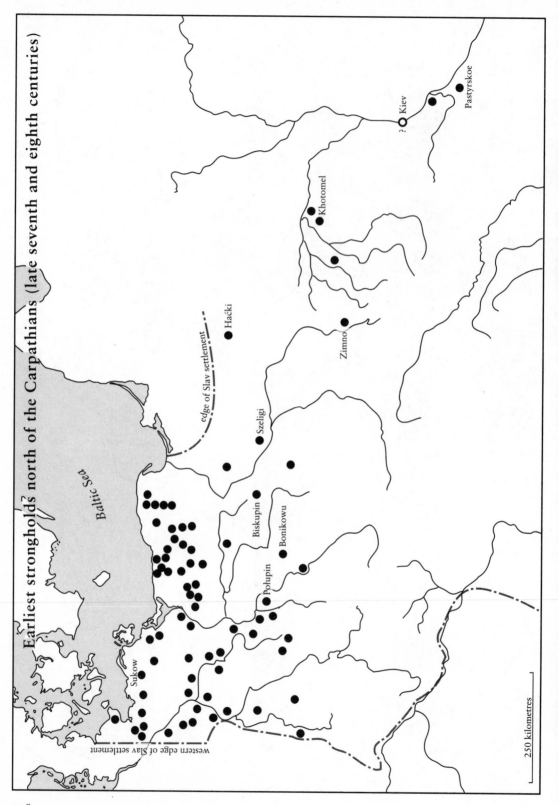

Earliest strongholds north of the Carpathians (late seventh and eighth centuries)

Baltic Sea

edge of Slav settlement

Haćki

Khotomel

Zimno

Szeligi

Biskupin

Bonikowu

Potupin

Sukow

western edge of Slav settlement

? Kiev

Pastyrskoe

250 kilometres

Fig. 24

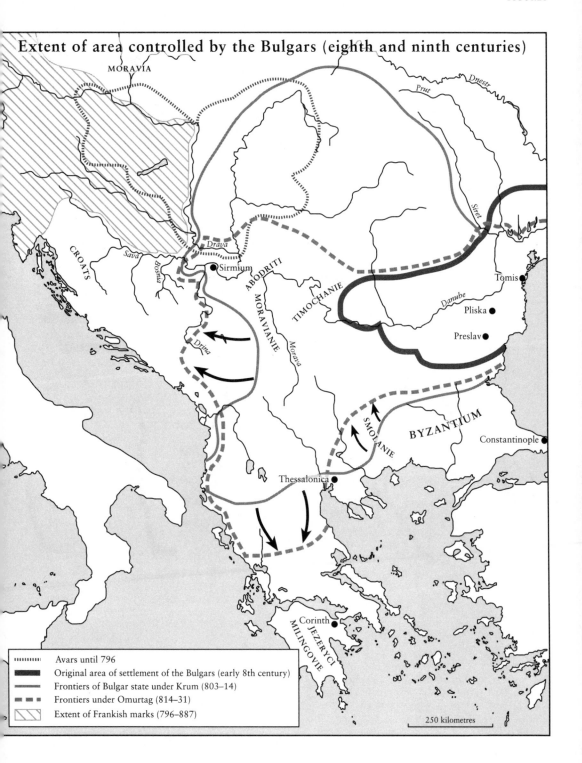

Extent of area controlled by the Bulgars (eighth and ninth centuries)

MORAVIA

Dnestr

Prut

Siret

CROATS

Sava

Bosnia

Drava

Sirmium

ABODRITI

MORAVIANIE

TIMOCHANIE

Moravia

Drina

Danube

Tomis

Pliska

Preslav

SMOLANIE

BYZANTIUM

Constantinople

Thessalonica

Corinth

JEZERYCI
MILINGOVIE

⋯⋯⋯⋯⋯	Avars until 796
▬▬▬	Original area of settlement of the Bulgars (early 8th century)
———	Frontiers of Bulgar state under Krum (803–14)
– – –	Frontiers under Omurtag (814–31)
⧄⧄⧄	Extent of Frankish marks (796–887)

250 kilometres

Fig. 25

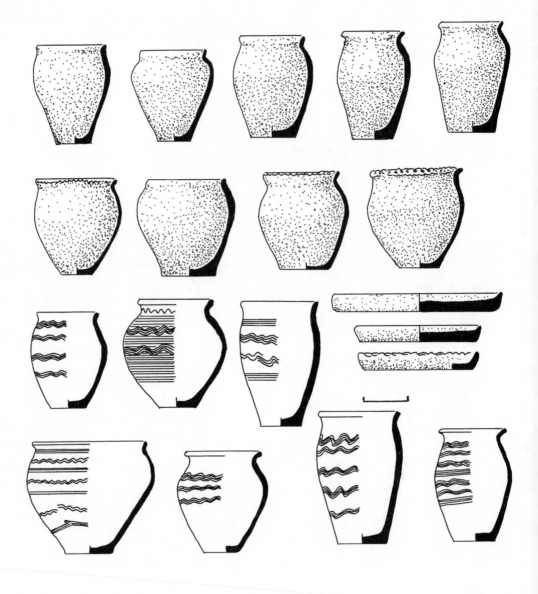

Fig. 26. Handmade (top) and wheel-thrown (bottom) pottery of the Luka Raikovetska
Culture (scale indicates 5 cm). After A. T. Smilenko and S. P. Yurenko, *Slavianie*

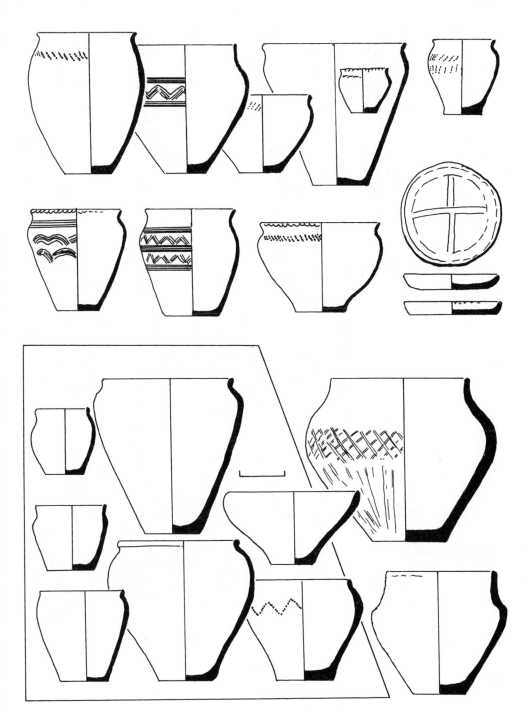

Fig. 27. Pottery of Romny/Volyntsevo type (top and right) and (bottom left) from Borshevo sites (scale indicates 10 cm). After Sedov, *Arkheologiya SSSR* 14, and O. V. Sukhobokov, *Arkheologia Ukrainskoi SSR*

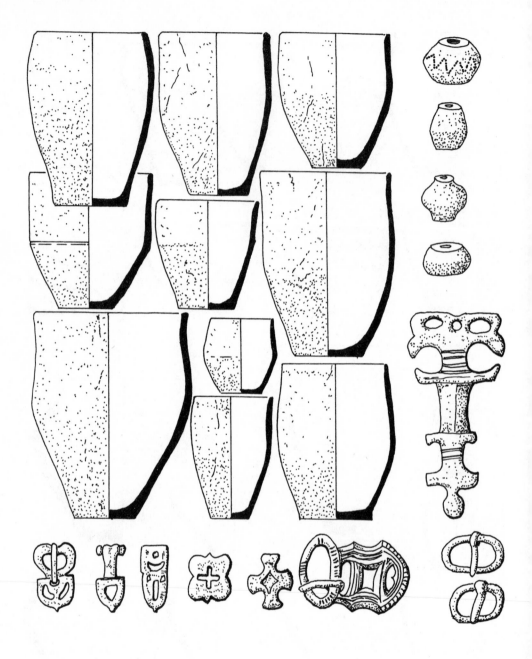

Fig. 28. Pottery, clay spindlewhorls and metal objects of the Kolochin Culture.
After Sedov, *Arkheologiya SSSR* 14

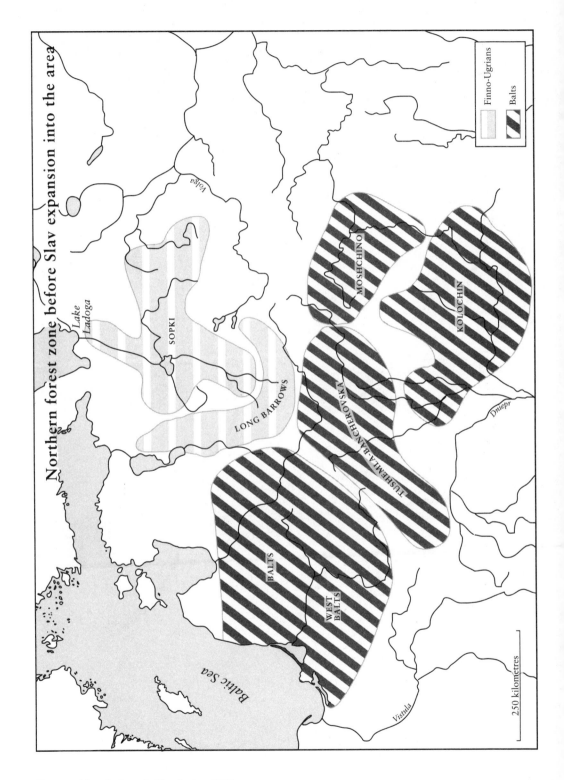

Northern forest zone before Slav expansion into the area

Finno-Ugrians

Balts

Volga

Lake Ladoga

SOPKI

MOSHCHINO

KOLOCHIN

LONG BARROWS

TUSHEMLIA-BANCHEROVSKA

Dniepr

BALTS

WEST BALTS

Baltic Sea

Vistula

250 kilometres

Fig. 29. After Sedov, *Arkheologiya SSSR* 14

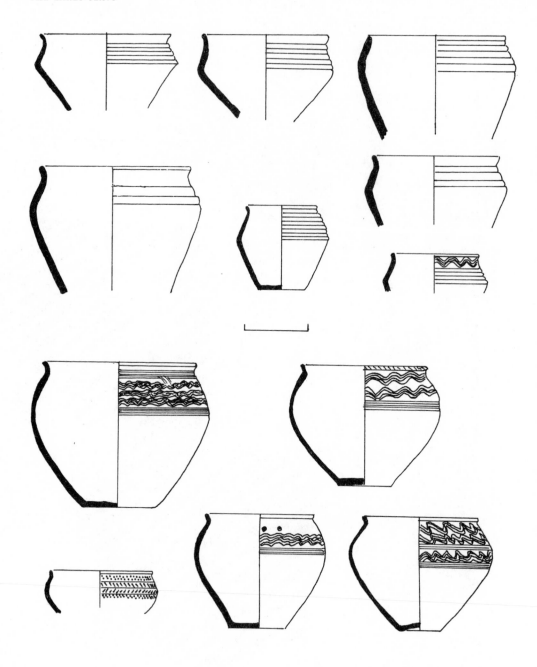

Fig. 30. Pottery of the Tornow (top) and (below) Feldberg types (scale indicates 10 cm).
After M. Dulinicz, J. Herrmann

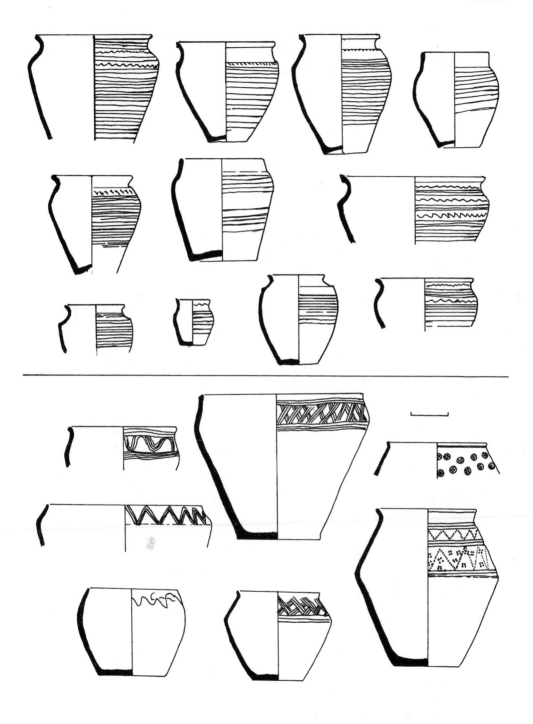

Fig. 31. Pottery of Great Polish type (top); vessels (bottom) of Menkendorf type (scale indicates 10 cm). After J. Herrmann

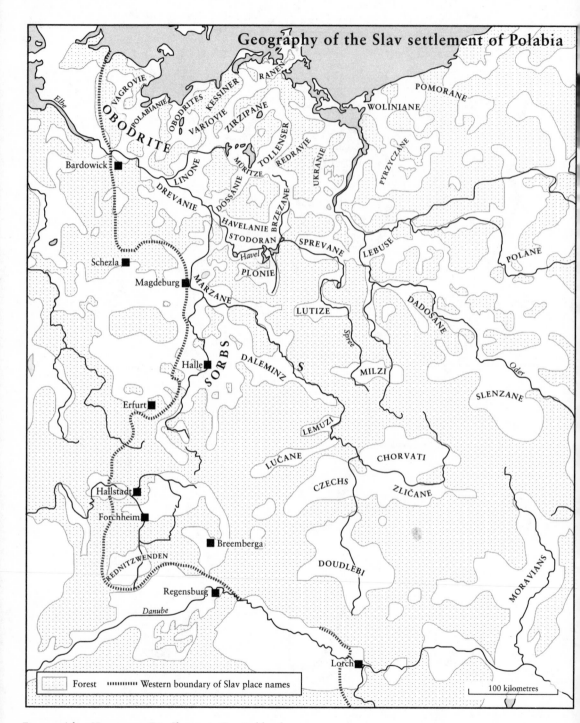

Fig. 32. After Herrmann, *Die Slawen in Deutschland*

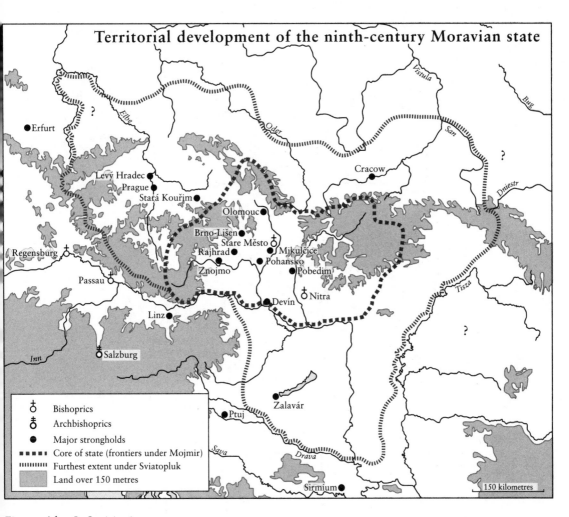

Fig. 33. After L. Leciejewicz

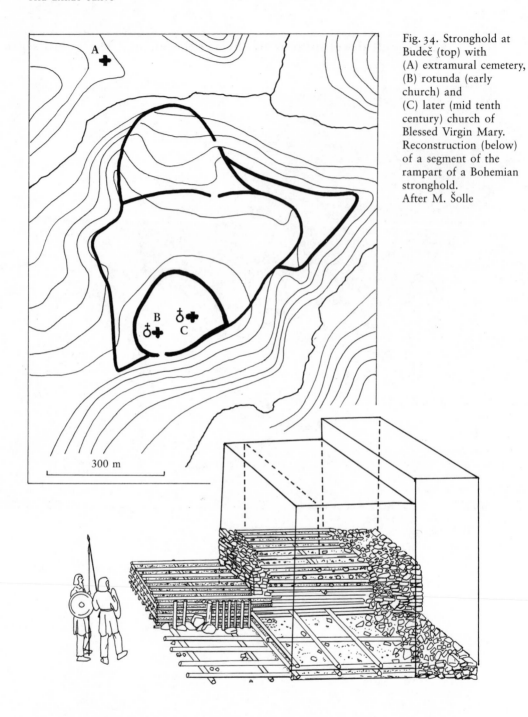

Fig. 34. Stronghold at Budeč (top) with (A) extramural cemetery, (B) rotunda (early church) and (C) later (mid tenth century) church of Blessed Virgin Mary. Reconstruction (below) of a segment of the rampart of a Bohemian stronghold. After M. Šolle

300 m

(*Opposite page*) Fig. 35. Moravian globular buttons (diameter about 30 mm) and their ornament 'unrolled'. After J. Sláma and V. Hruby, reproduced from *Ilustrované České Dějiny*, vol. 1, 1996, p. 90

Fig. 36. Types of female headdress characteristic of different local groups of the East Slavs (scale indicates 200 km). After Sedov, *Welt der Slawen*, with alterations

(*Opposite page*) Fig. 37. Antler composite comb of the type most common from the seventh century onwards (Żukowice, Poland); four silver temple-rings (bottom left), still attached to a fragment of leather strap preserved by corrosion products from an inhumation cemetery in Mazovia, Poland; Pomeranian hollow temple-ring (centre); example of the many types of silver ornament found in Polabian silver hoards (bottom right). Various sources

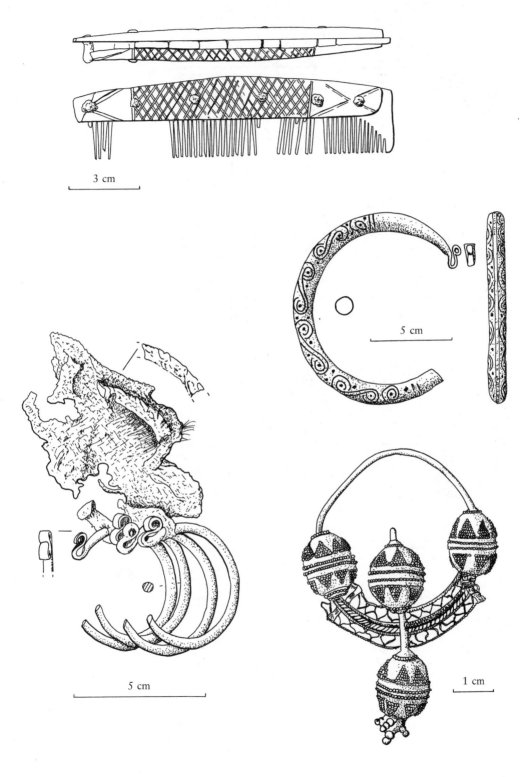

3 cm

5 cm

5 cm

1 cm

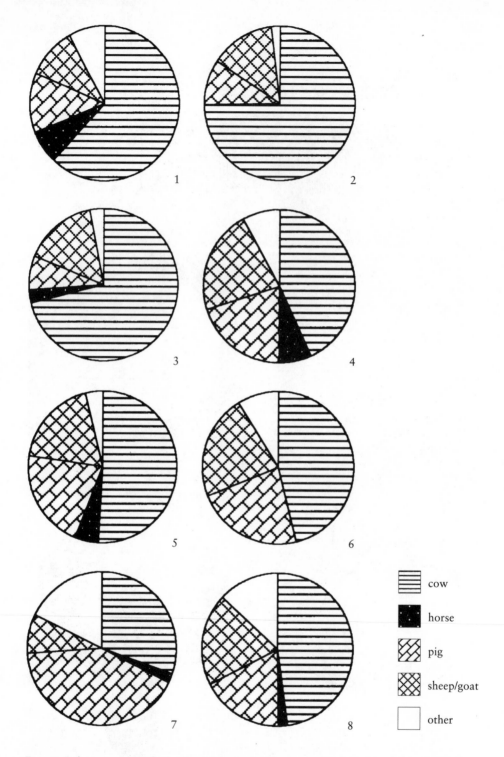

Fig. 38. Relative quantities of animal bones of different species found in eight excavated settlements in the Balkans: (1) Popina-Kaleto; (2) Garvan; (3) Koprinka; (4) Popina-Džedžovi lozja; (5) Bucov; (6) Stărmen; (7) Zalavár; (8) Dridu. After J. Henning

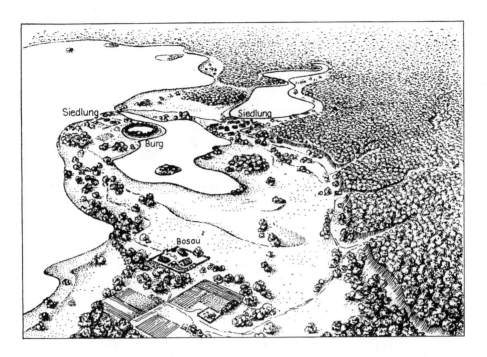

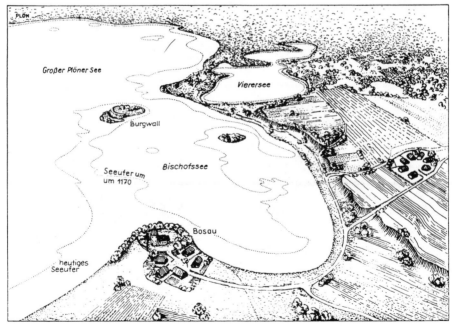

Fig. 39. Reconstruction of the landscape around the stronghold and settlements at Bosau (Ostholstein) in the ninth century and in 1170, showing alterations in the form of utilization of the land, but also later environmental change. After *Die Slawen in Deutschland*, Abb. 63

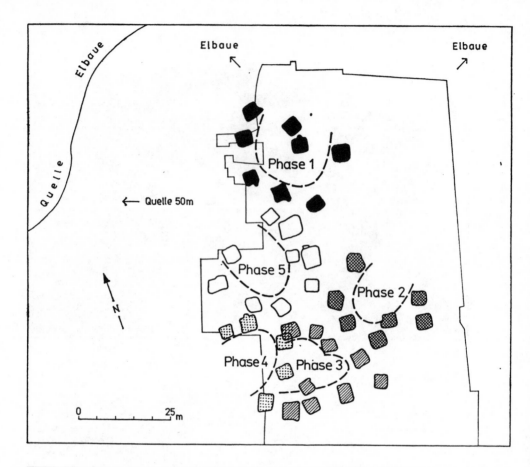

Fig. 40. Early Slav settlement at Dessau-Mosigkau in Polabia. This plan and reconstruction shows the shifting nucleus of the settlement. After *Die Slawen in Deutschland*, Abb. 65–6

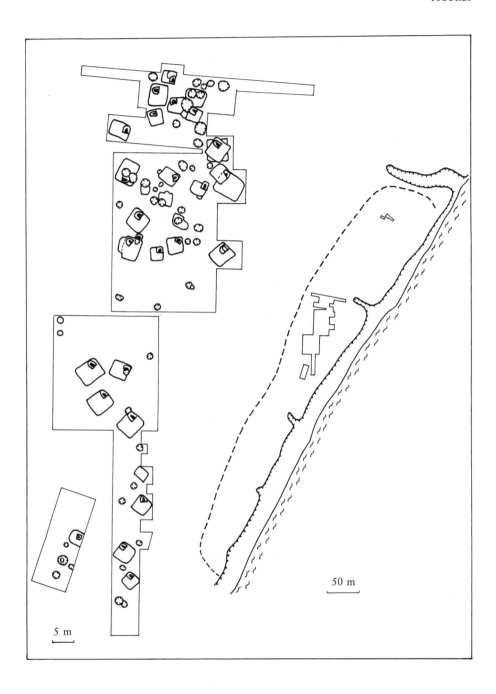

5 m

50 m

Fig. 41. Early Slav settlement at Teremtsi (western Ukraine), showing extent of site and excavated areas. After L. V. Vakulenko, O. M. Prikhodniuk and V. D. Baran

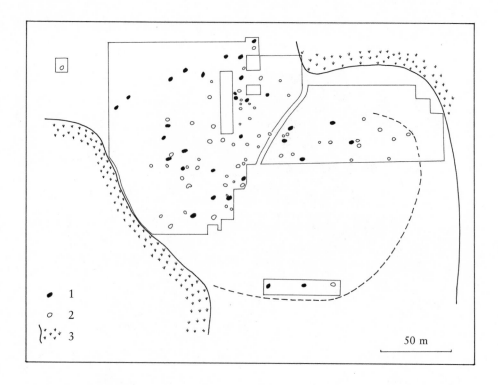

1

2

3

50 m

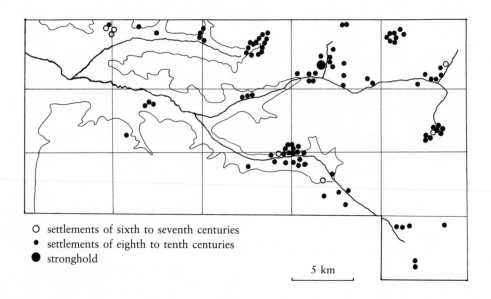

O settlements of sixth to seventh centuries
• settlements of eighth to tenth centuries
● stronghold

5 km

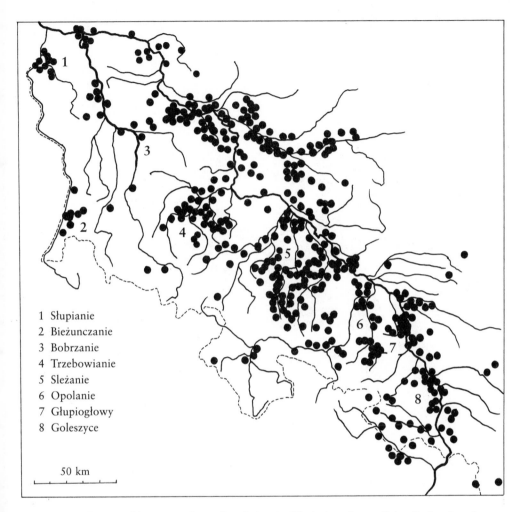

1 Słupianie
2 Bieżunczanie
3 Bobrzanie
4 Trzebowianie
5 Sleżanie
6 Opolanie
7 Głupiogłowy
8 Goleszyce

50 km

Fig. 44. Distribution of known early medieval sites in Silesia (southwest Poland) showing clusters which may be related to 'small tribes' known from written sources. After S. Moździoch

(*Opposite page, top*) Fig. 42. Early Slav settlement at Dziedzice (Pomerania, Poland), showing extent of site and excavated areas in relation to edge of water meadows: (1) 'bath-shaped features' (remains of dwellings); (2) other features; (3) wetland. After A. Porzeziński

(*Opposite page, bottom*) Fig. 43. Settlement clusters (seventh to tenth centuries) in the Wyżnica valley east of Lublin, southeast Poland, based on the results of the so-called AZP field-walking project (contour indicates 200 m). Adapted from S. Hoczyk-Siwkowa, based on fieldwork by P. Selegrat

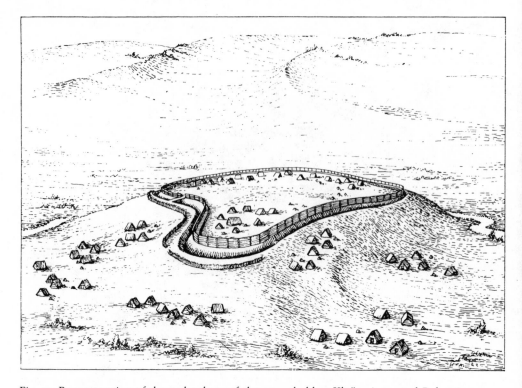

Fig. 45. Reconstruction of the early phase of the stronghold at Klučov in central Bohemia, a typical example of an extensive site. After *Die Slawen in Deutschland*, Abb. 87

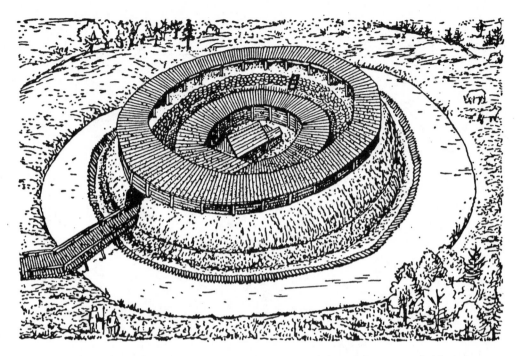

Fig. 46. Reconstruction of the early phase (ninth century) of the Polabian stronghold at Tornow, Kr. Calau. After K. Jażdżewski, *Pradzieje Europy środkowej*, ryc. 190

Fig. 47. Graffito representing Bulgar horseman from Pliska (ninth/tenth century); note the large shield, possible helmet and lance, and also the decorative elements of the harness. After photograph

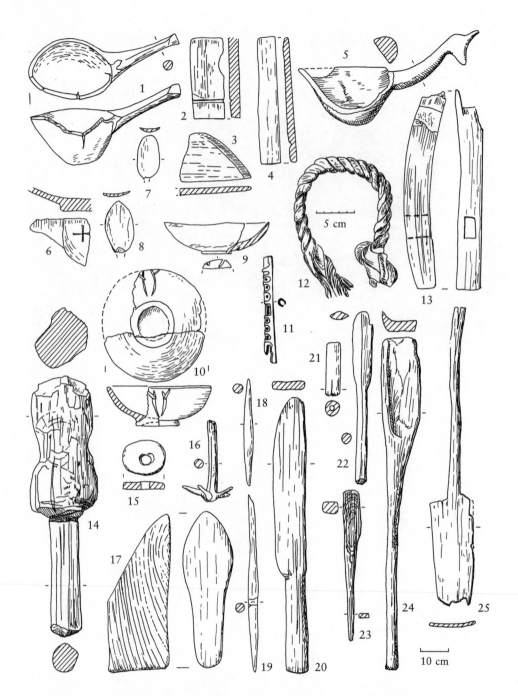

Fig. 48. Wooden objects from ninth- and tenth-century levels of the stronghold/town at Opole, southern Poland: (1–10) bowls and scoops, stave-built vessel fragments, spoons; (11) flute; (12) wicker rope; (13) wheel rim; (14) maul; (15) bark net-float; (16) pot-stirrer; (17) cobbler's last; (18–20) weaving tools; (25) wooden spade (different scale). After B. Gediga

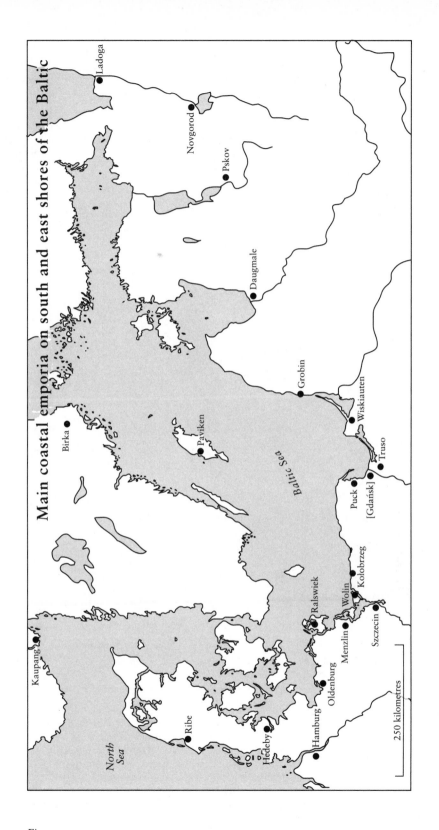

Main coastal emporia on south and east shores of the Baltic

Ladoga

Novgorod

Pskov

Daugmale

Grobin

Wiskiauten

Birka

Paviken

Truso

Baltic Sea

Puck

[Gdańsk]

Kołobrzeg

Ralswiek

Wolin

Kaupang

Szczecin

Menzlin

Oldenburg

Ribe

North
Sea

Hedeby

Hamburg

250 kilometres

Fig. 49

371

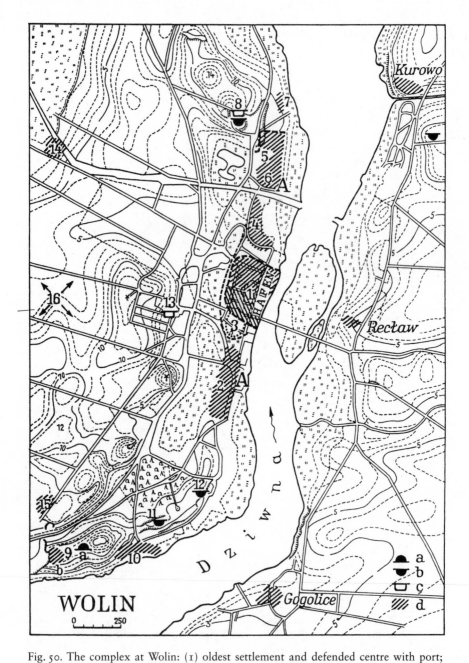

Fig. 50. The complex at Wolin: (1) oldest settlement and defended centre with port;
(2) settlement of fishermen (A: hard for beaching vessels); (3) area of pagan temple;
(4) settlement; (5) twelfth-century market; (6) 'Silberberg' craftsmen's settlement
(A: hard for beaching vessels); (7) settlement; (8) 'Młynówka' cemetery;
(9) settlement, barrow cemetery and site of 'lighthouse' (Galgenburg);
(10) settlement; (11–12) cremation graves; (13) twelfth-century Christian
inhumation cemetery; (14–15) settlements; (16) fields. Key: (a) barrow graves,
(b) cremations, (c) flat inhumation graves, (d) settlements. After W. Filipowiak

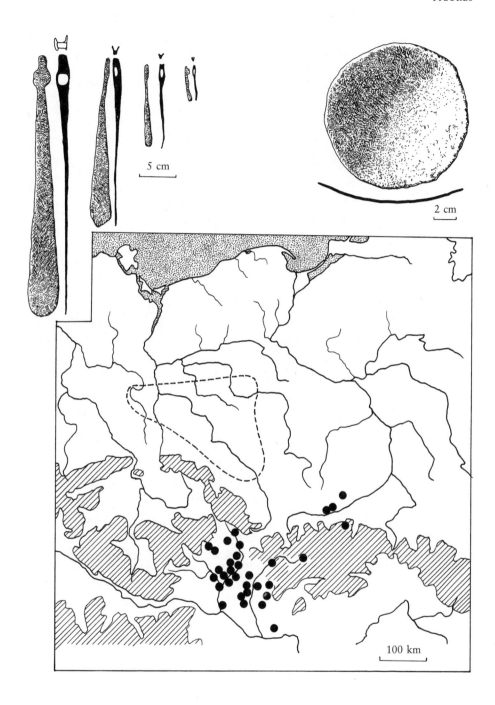

Fig. 51. Axe-shaped *grzywna* (top left), Cracow (after R. Pleiner);
Silesian iron plate (top right), Tornow (after J. Herrmann);
distribution of known finds (after K. Wachowski)

Fig. 52. Slav pot bases from tenth- and early eleventh-century levels at Kruszwica (Wielkopolska). The bases of some Slav pots, especially from West Slav territory after the tenth century, bear symbolic marks made by signs incised into the centre of the potter's wheel or turntable on which they were formed. Their function is a matter of debate. After W. Dzieduszycki

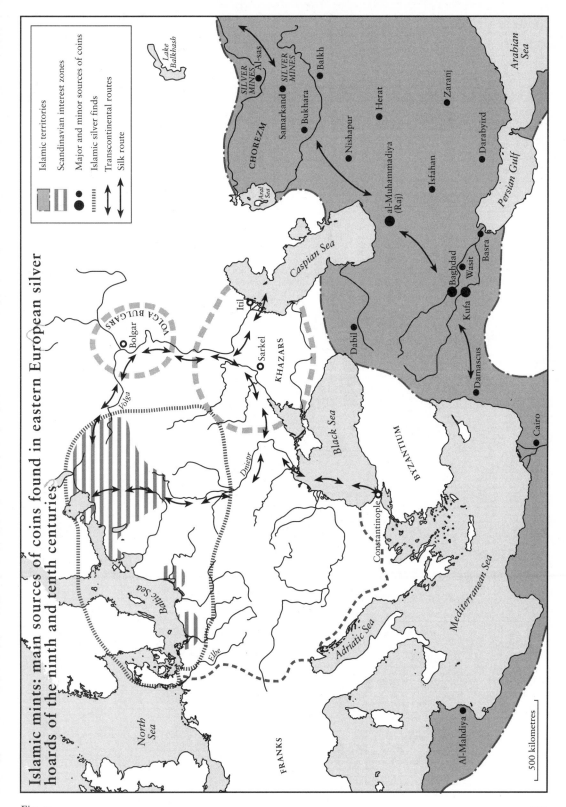

Islamic mints: main sources of coins found in eastern European silver hoards of the ninth and tenth centuries

Legend:
- Islamic territories
- Scandinavian interest zones
- Major and minor sources of coins
- Islamic silver finds
- Transcontinental routes
- Silk route

Lake Balkhash

SILVER MINES — Al-sas
SILVER MINES
Samarkand • Bukhara • Balkh
CHOREZM
Aral Sea
• Nishapur • Herat • Zaranj
al-Muhammadiya (Raj) • Isfahan • Darabyird
Arabian Sea
Persian Gulf
Basra
Baghdad • Wasit
Kufa
Dabil •
Damascus

Caspian Sea

Itil
VOLGA BULGARS
Bolgar •
Volga
Sarkel •
KHAZARS

Dniepr

Black Sea
BYZANTIUM

Constantinople

North Sea
Baltic Sea
Elbe
FRANKS

Adriatic Sea
Mediterranean Sea

Cairo •

Al-Mahdiya •

500 kilometres

Fig. 53

375

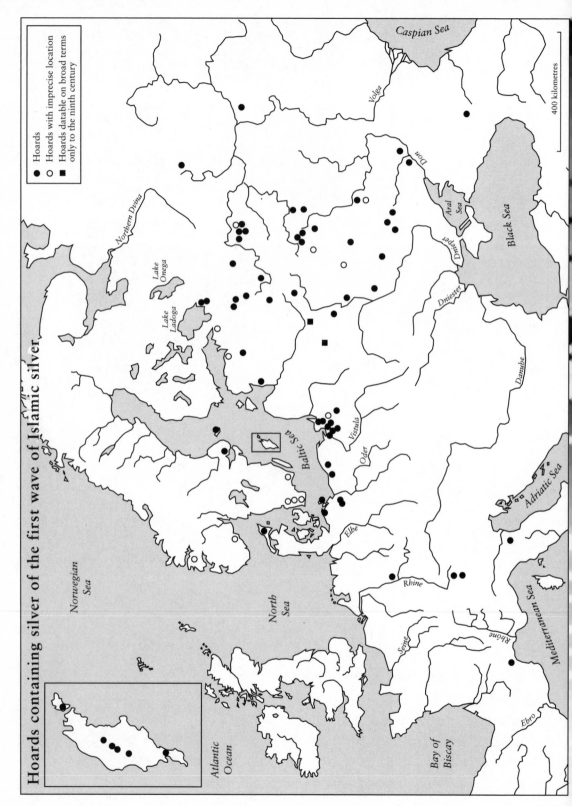

Hoards containing silver of the first wave of Islamic silver

Legend:
- ● Hoards
- ○ Hoards with imprecise location
- ■ Hoards datable on broad terms only to the ninth century

400 kilometres

Fig. 54. After W. Łosiński

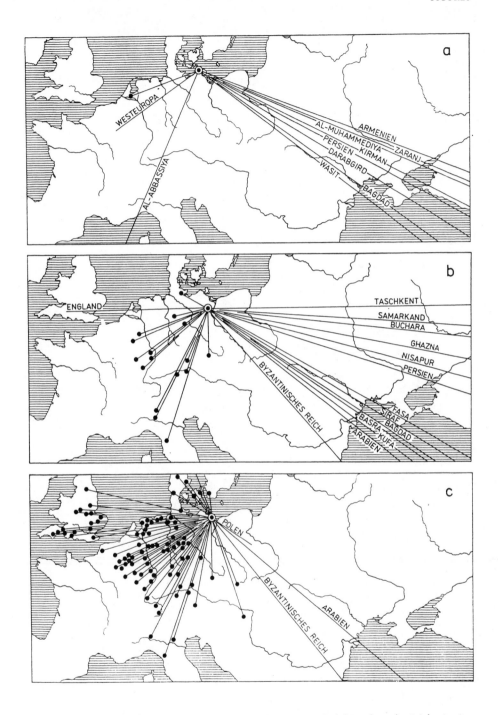

Fig. 55. The derivation of the coins in three representative Polabian hoards: (a) beginning of the ninth century, Prerow, Kr. Ribnitz-Damgarten; (b) tenth century, Prenzlau-Aleksanderhof; (c) eleventh century, Usedom-Vossberg, Kr. Wolgast. After *Die Slawen in Deutschland*, Abb. 50

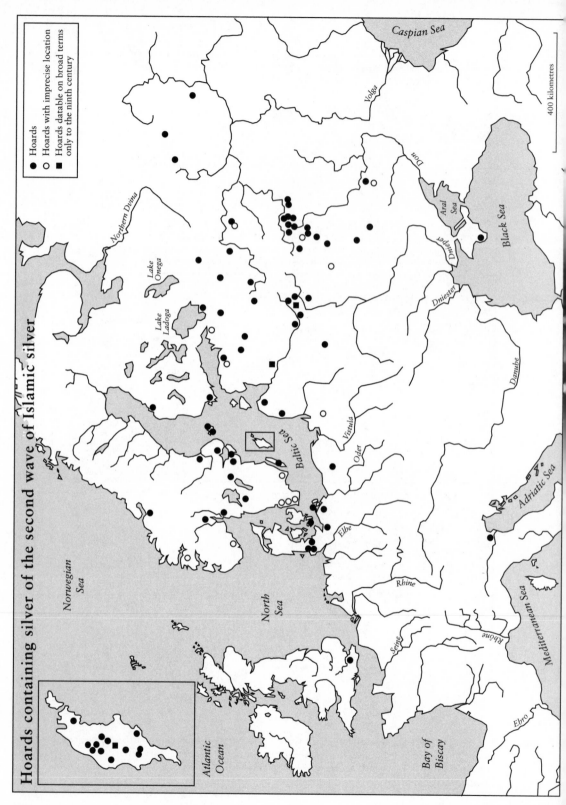

Hoards containing silver of the second wave of Islamic silver

- ● Hoards
- ○ Hoards with imprecise location
- ■ Hoards datable on broad terms only to the ninth century

400 kilometres

Fig. 56. After W. Łosiński

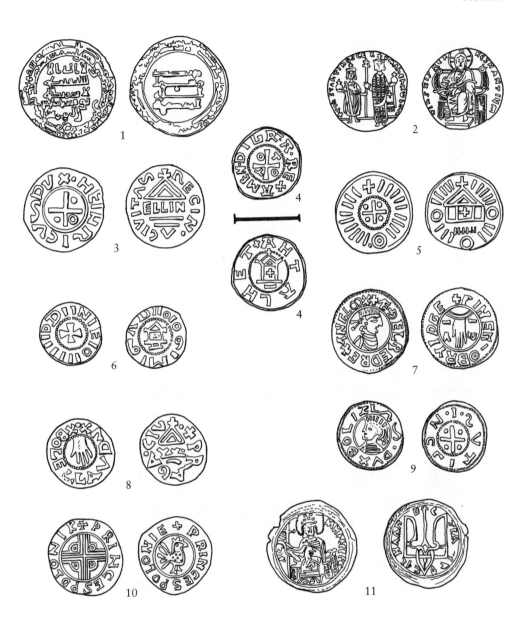

Fig. 57. Coin types used in Slav territories (scale about natural size): (1) Islamic, Abbasid dirhem of al-Muktadir (908–32); (2) Byzantine solidus of Constantine VII (913–59); (3) denar of Henry I of Bavaria (985–95); (4) Saxon 'Otto and Adeleide' denar (>951); (5) Type I *Sachsenpfennig* (c. 980?); (6) Type II *Sachsenpfennig* (c. 990?); (7) small hand penny of Ethelred II the Unready of England (978–1016); (8) coin of Boleslav I of Bohemia (c. 973); (9 and 10) Bolesław I of Poland, 'Dux inclitus' and 'Princes Poloniae' types (c. 1000–1010); (11) 'Srebnik' of Vladimir the Great of Kiev (978–1015). Various sources

Fig. 58. Stone cult statue found in the River Zbrucz near Liczkowiec, western Ukraine, in 1848 (height 2.27 m): views of the four faces. After A. Gieysztor, *Mitologia Słowian*

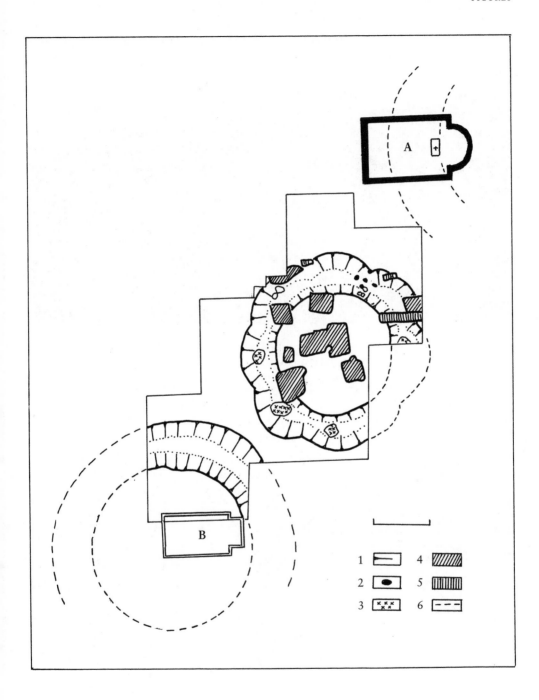

Fig. 59. The remains of the sanctuary of Perun in Novgorod, excavated in 1948–52:
(1) edge of ditches; (2) pit for cult statue; (3) hearths; (4) sunken-floored huts of the twelfth to
fourteenth centuries; (5) later disturbances; (6) excavated portions of ditches; (A) stone church;
(B) wooden church (St Nicholas?)

Fig. 60. Eleventh- to twelfth-century barrow cemetery in the Ukraine, typical of many barrow cemeteries of the area. After *Arkheologia Ukrainskoi SSR*

Fig. 61. Crucifix and crucifix-reliquary (*encolpion*) (Zlaté Moravce, and Velká Mača, Slovakia) and reverse side of silver belt-end depicting a priest (Mikulčice). After B. Chropovský and J. Poulík

GLAGOLITIC (ROUNDED)	GLAGOLITIC (ANGULAR)	CYRILLIC	APPROXIMATE TRANSLITERATION
ⴀ	ⴀ	Ⰰ	a
ⴁ	ⴁ	Ⰱ	b
ⴂ	ⴂ	Ⰲ	v
ⴃ	ⴃ	Ⰳ	g
ⴄ	ⴄ	Ⰴ	d
ⴅ	ⴅ	Ⰵ	e
ⴆ	ⴆ	Ⰶ	ž, zh
ⴇ	ⴇ	Ⰷ	dz
ⴈ	ⴈ	Ⰸ	z
ⴉ	ⴉ	Ⰻ	i, ij, ili, j
ⴊ	ⴊ	Ⰺ	i, ji, ili, j
ⴋ	ⴋ	—	j, ǧ, ġ
ⴍ	ⴍ	Ⰽ	k
ⴌ	ⴌ	Ⰾ	l
ⴎ	ⴎ	Ⰿ	m
ⴏ	ⴏ	Ⱀ	n
ⴐ	ⴐ	Ⱁ	o
ⴑ	ⴑ	Ⱂ	p
ⴓ	ⴓ	Ⱃ	r
ⴒ	ⴒ	Ⱄ	s
ⴔ	ⴔ	Ⱅ	t
ⴖ	ⴖ	Ⱆ	u
ⴕ	ⴕ	Ⱇ	f
ⴗ	ⴗ	Ⱈ	h, kh
ⴙ	ⴙ	Ⱉ	o
ⴘ	ⴘ	Ⱋ	št, šć
ⴚ	ⴚ	Ⱌ	c, ts
ⴛ	ⴛ	Ⱍ	č
ⴜ	ⴜ	Ⱎ	š
ⴝ	ⴝ	Ⱋ	šč
ⴞ	ⴞ	Ⱏ	(hard)
ⴟ ⴠ	—	Ⱏ	i
ⴡ	—	Ⱐ	'
ⴢ	ⴢ	Ⱑ	ye, ya
—	—	Ⱖ Ⱔ Ⱗ	ya, ye
ⱓ	ⱓ	Ⱓ	io
ⱔ	—	Ⱔ	ę (nasal)
ⱘ	—	Ⱘ	ǫ (nasal)
ⱙ	—	Ⱗ	yę
ⴠ	ⴠ	Ⱚ	th
ⱛ	ⱛ	Ⱛ	ps

Fig. 62. The alphabets used to represent the phonetics of Slav words in several areas of central and eastern Europe (Glagolitic and Cyrillic) with their transliteration and pronunciation

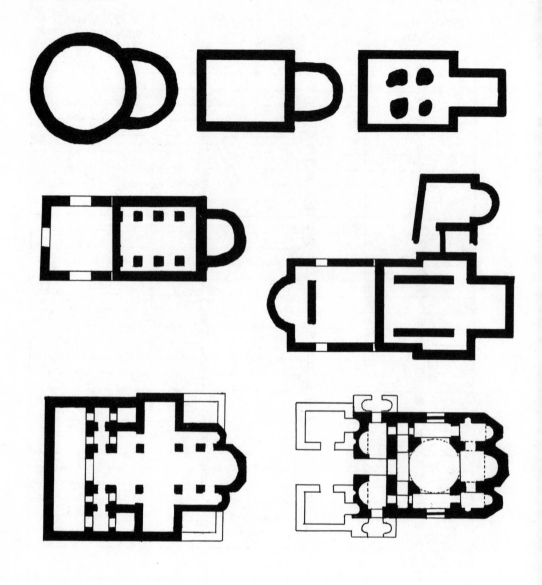

Fig. 63. Church plans: (top) five Moravian churches, vicinity of Staré Město in Uh. Hradiste; (below) two churches of eastern rite, all in Preslav. Various sources

Fig. 64. Simplified plan of inhumation cemetery at Dziekanowice, near Poznań, showing the pattern of graves and the edges of the cemetery (scale indicates 10 m). The large feature on the west is a horse grave. Excavations of A. and J. Wrzecinski

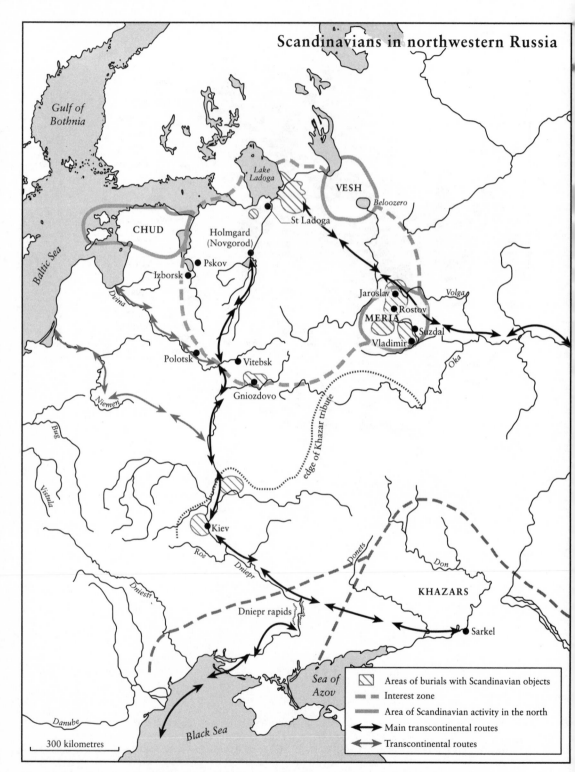

Fig. 65. Scandinavians in northwestern Russia, showing the main area of their interest in the forests of northern Russia and Belarus around the centre at Holmgard (Novgorod) and the main transit routes

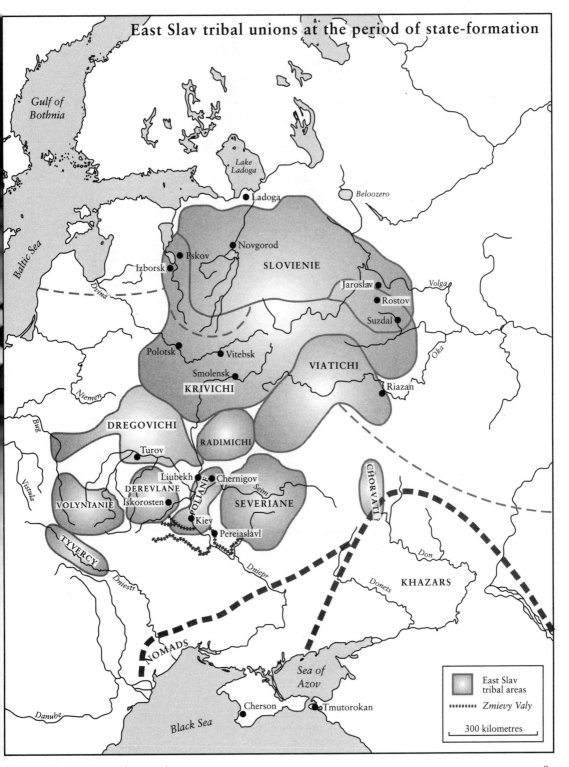

East Slav tribal unions at the period of state-formation

Gulf of Bothnia

Lake Ladoga

Baltic Sea

Beloozero

● Ladoga

● Novgorod

● Pskov

● Izborsk

SLOVIENIE

Jaroslav ●

● Rostov

Volga

Suzdal ●

● Polotsk

● Vitebsk

Dvina

Niemen

Smolensk ●

KRIVICHI

VIATICHI

Riazan ●

Oka

DREGOVICHI

Bug

RADIMICHI

● Turov

Vistula

DEREVLANE

Liubekh ●

● Chernigov

POLIANE

Seim

CHORVATI

VOLYNIANIE

Iskorosten ●

● Kiev

SEVERIANE

Don

● Pereiaslavl

TYVERCY

Dniestr

Dniepr

Donets

KHAZARS

NOMADS

Sea of Azov

Cherson ●

● Tmutorokan

Danube

Black Sea

☐ East Slav tribal areas

▬ ▬ *Zmievy Valy*

300 kilometres

Fig. 66. After Sedov, with amendments

387

Fig. 67. Reconstruction of the earth and timber constructions of the stronghold at Belgorod showing caisson construction. Below is the plan of the site with the *detinets* and the attached enclosures. After *Arkheologia Ukrainskoi SSR*, fig. 76

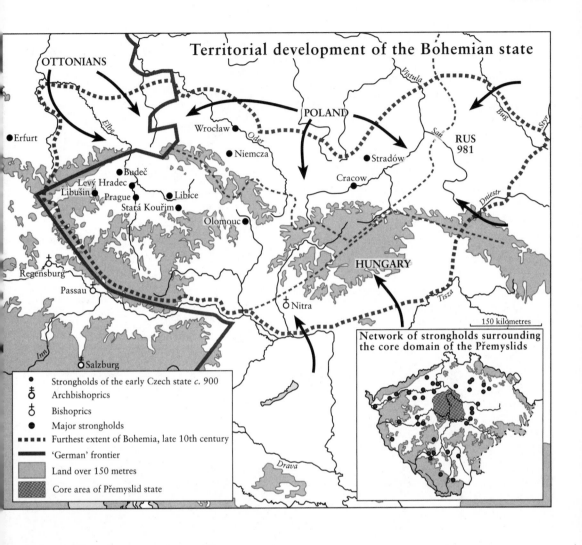

Fig. 68. Territorial development of the Bohemian state, and (inset) network of strongholds surrounding the core domain of the Přemyslids. Various sources

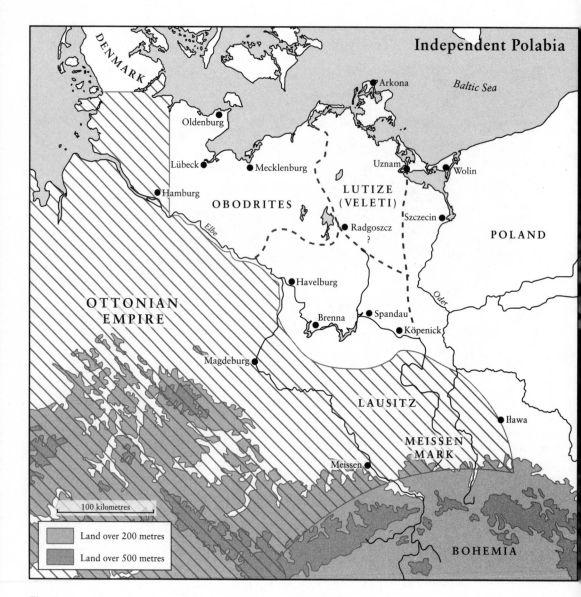

Fig. 69

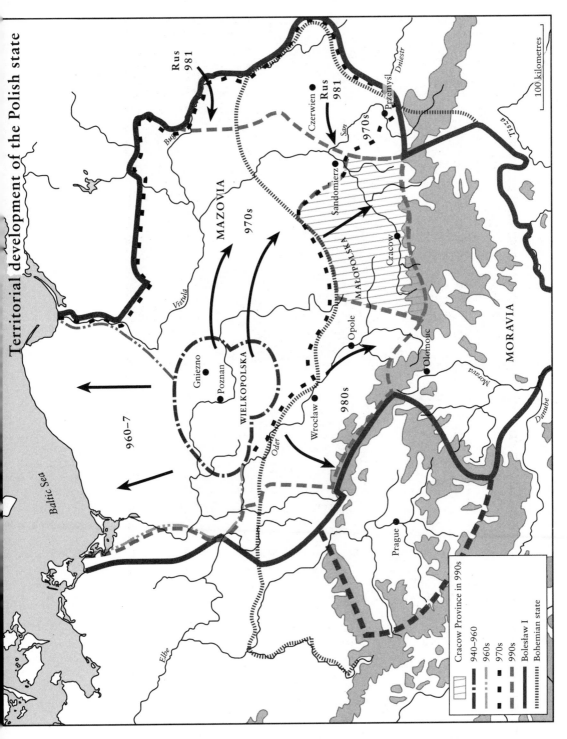

Territorial development of the Polish state

Fig. 70

Legend:
- Cracow Province in 990s
- 940–960
- 960s
- 970s
- 990s
- Bolesław I
- Bohemian state

Map labels:
Rus 981 · Czerwien · Rus 981 · Przemyśl · Dniestr · Tisza · San · 970s · Sandomierz · Bug · MAZOVIA · 970s · MAŁOPOLSKA · Cracow · Vistula · MORAVIA · Gniezno · Poznan · Opole · Olomouc · Morava · WIELKOPOLSKA · Wroclaw · 980s · Oder · Danube · 960–7 · Baltic Sea · Prague · Elbe · 100 kilometres

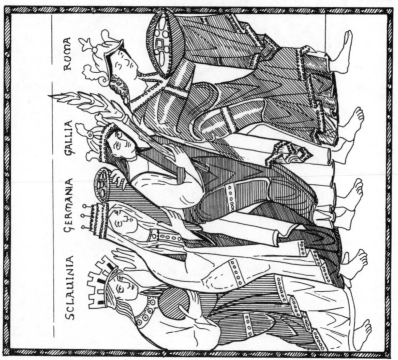

SCLAVINIA GERMANIA GALLIA ROMA

Fig. 71. The nations pay homage to Otto III. After the Gospel Book of Otto III

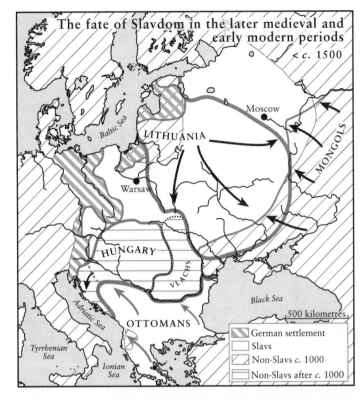

The fate of Slavdom in the later medieval and early modern periods

< c. 1500

Baltic Sea

LITHUANIA

Moscow

MONGOLS

Warsaw

HUNGARY

VLACHS

Black Sea

500 kilometres

Adriatic Sea

OTTOMANS

Tyrrhenian Sea

Ionian Sea

German settlement
Slavs
Non-Slavs c. 1000
Non-Slavs after c. 1000

c. 1800

Baltic Sea

RUSSIAN EMPIRE

Moscow

GERMAN STATES

Warsaw

AUSTRO-HUNGARIAN EMPIRE

OTTOMAN

Black Sea

EMPIRE

Adriatic Sea

Tyrrhenian Sea

Ionian Sea

500 kilometres

Fig. 72

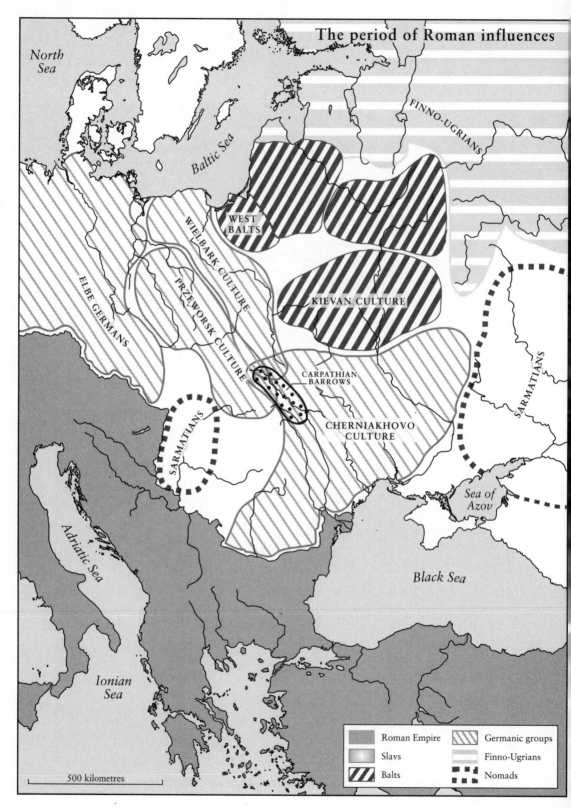

Map I

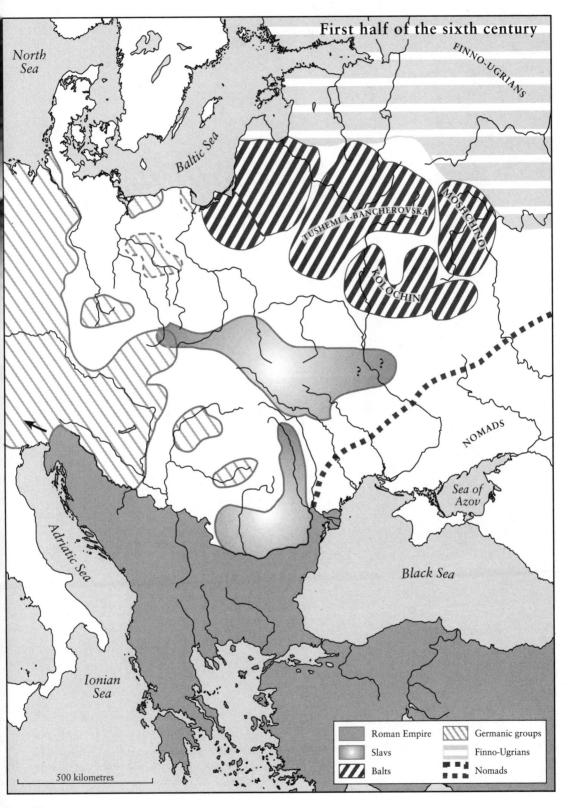

First half of the sixth century

North Sea

FINNO-UGRIANS

Baltic Sea

TUSHEMLA-BANCHEROVSKA

MOSHCHINO

KOLOCHIN

NOMADS

Sea of Azov

Adriatic Sea

Black Sea

Ionian Sea

	Roman Empire		Germanic groups
	Slavs		Finno-Ugrians
	Balts		Nomads

500 kilometres

Map II

395

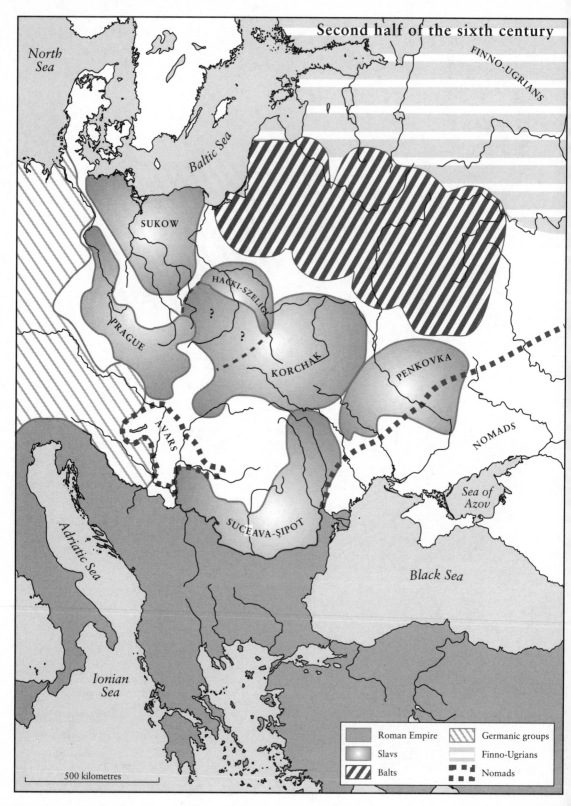

Second half of the sixth century

North Sea

FINNO-UGRIANS

Baltic Sea

SUKOW

HACKI-SZELIGI

?

PRAGUE

?

KORCHAK

PENKOVKA

AVARS

NOMADS

Sea of Azov

SUCEAVA-ŞIPOT

Adriatic Sea

Black Sea

Ionian Sea

	Roman Empire		Germanic groups
	Slavs		Finno-Ugrians
	Balts		Nomads

500 kilometres

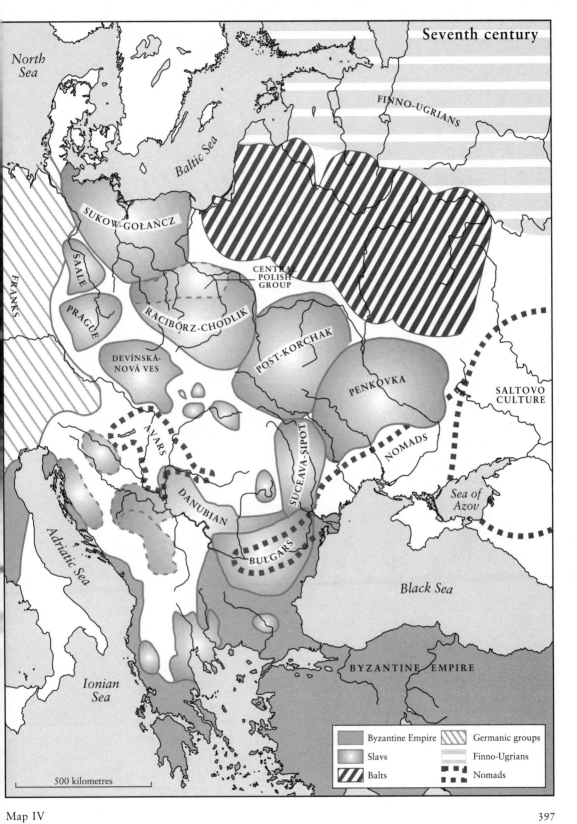

Seventh century

North
Sea

FINNO-UGRIANS

Baltic Sea

SUKOW-GOŁAŃCZ

SAALE

PRAGUE

CENTRAL
POLISH
GROUP

RACIBÓRZ-CHODLIK

DEVÍNSKÁ-
NOVÁ VES

POST-KORCHAK

FRANKS

PENKOVKA

SALTOVO
CULTURE

AVARS

NOMADS

SUCEAVA-SIPOT

DANUBIAN

Sea of
Azov

Adriatic
Sea

BULGARS

Black Sea

Ionian
Sea

BYZANTINE EMPIRE

	Byzantine Empire		Germanic groups
	Slavs		Finno-Ugrians
	Balts		Nomads

500 kilometres

Map IV

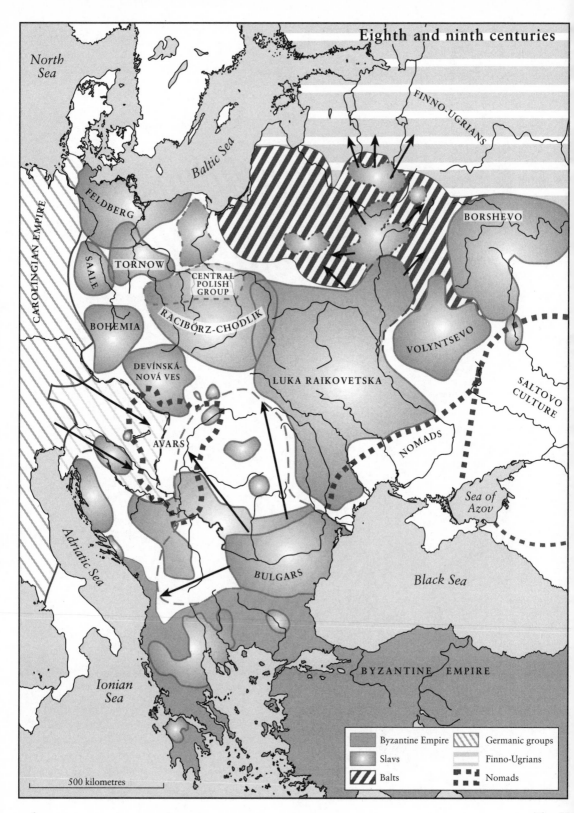

Eighth and ninth centuries

North Sea

Baltic Sea

FINNO-UGRIANS

FELDBERG

BORSHEVO

SAALE

TORNOW

CENTRAL POLISH GROUP

RACIBÓRZ-CHODLIK

BOHEMIA

VOLYNTSEVO

DEVÍNSKÁ-NOVÁ VES

SALTOVO CULTURE

LUKA RAIKOVETSKA

AVARS

NOMADS

Sea of Azov

Adriatic Sea

BULGARS

Black Sea

Ionian Sea

BYZANTINE EMPIRE

	Byzantine Empire		Germanic groups
	Slavs		Finno-Ugrians
	Balts		Nomads

500 kilometres

Map V

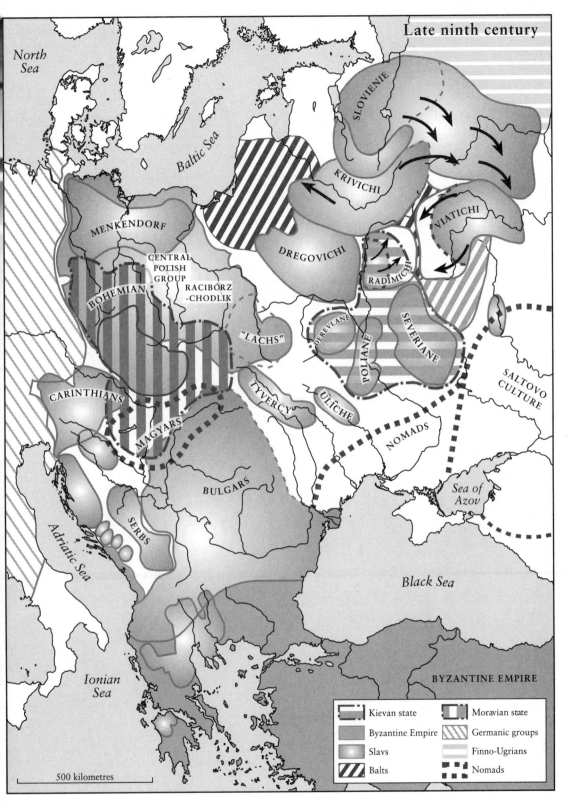

Late ninth century

North
Sea

Baltic Sea

SLOVIENIE

KRIVICHI

VIATICHI

MENKENDORF

DREGOVICHI

CENTRAL
POLISH
GROUP

RADIMICHI

BOHEMIAN

RACIBÓRZ
-CHODLIK

"LACHS"

DEREVLANE

SEVERIANE

POLIANE

SALTOVO
CULTURE

CARINTHIANS

TYVERCY

ULICHE

MAGYARS

NOMADS

Sea of
Azov

BULGARS

Adriatic Sea

SERBS

Black Sea

Ionian
Sea

BYZANTINE EMPIRE

	Kievan state		Moravian state
	Byzantine Empire		Germanic groups
	Slavs		Finno-Ugrians
	Balts		Nomads

500 kilometres

Map VI

399

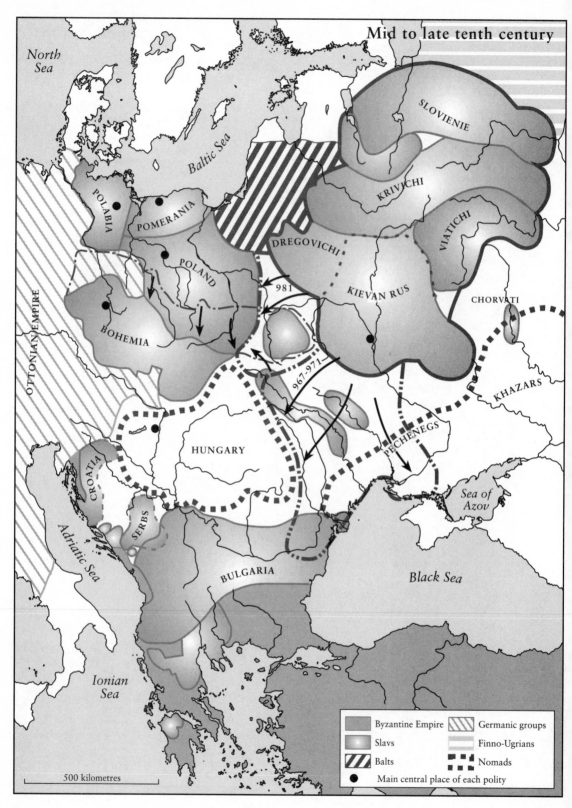

North
Sea

Baltic Sea

SLOVIENIE

KRIVICHI

POLABIA

POMERANIA

DREGOVICHI

VIATICHI

POLAND

981

KIEVAN RUS

CHORVATI

OTTONIAN EMPIRE

BOHEMIA

967-971

KHAZARS

HUNGARY

PECHENEGS

CROATIA

Sea of
Azov

Adriatic Sea

SERBS

BULGARIA

Black Sea

Ionian
Sea

	Byzantine Empire		Germanic groups
	Slavs		Finno-Ugrians
	Balts		Nomads
●	Main central place of each polity		

500 kilometres

Map VII

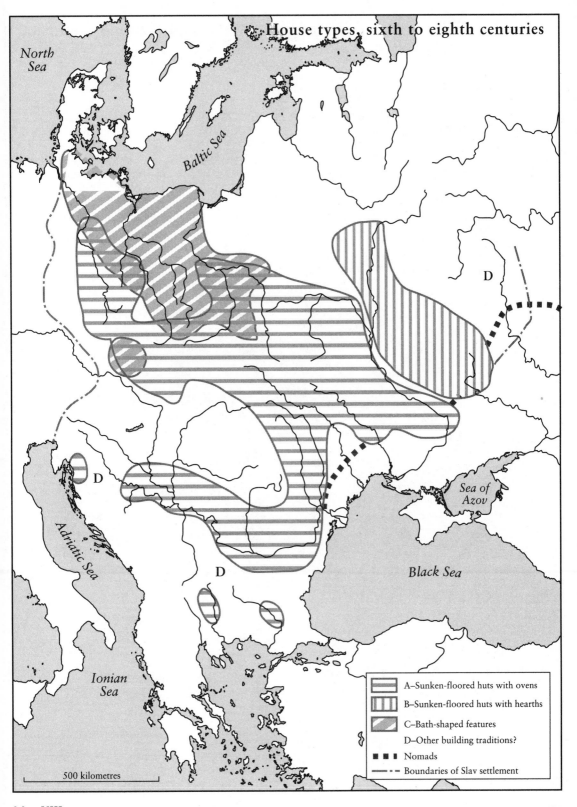

House types, sixth to eighth centuries

North Sea

Baltic Sea

D

Adriatic Sea

D

Sea of Azov

D

Black Sea

Ionian Sea

	A–Sunken-floored huts with ovens
	B–Sunken-floored huts with hearths
	C–Bath-shaped features
	D–Other building traditions?
▪▪▪	Nomads
–·–·–	Boundaries of Slav settlement

500 kilometres

Map VIII

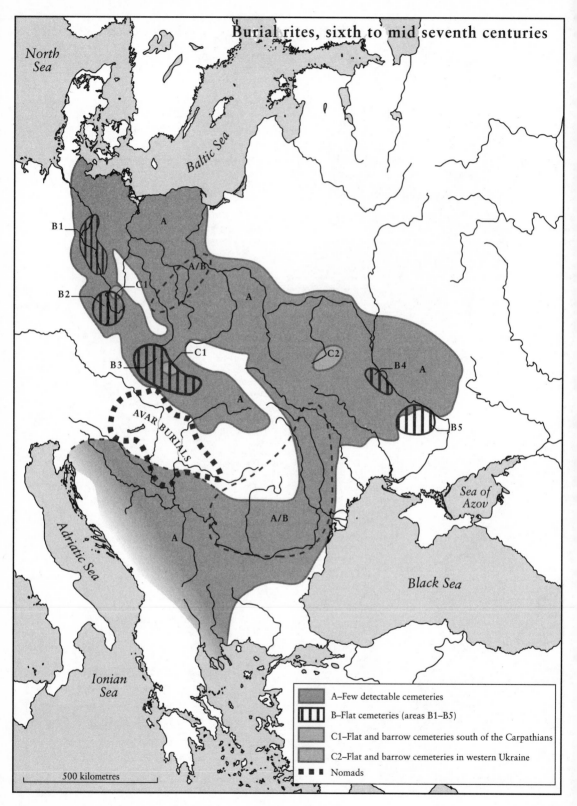

Burial rites, sixth to mid seventh centuries

North Sea

Baltic Sea

B1

A

A/B

C1

B2

A

C1

B3

C2

A

AVAR BURIALS

B4

A

C1

A

B5

Sea of Azov

A/B

Adriatic Sea

A

Black Sea

Ionian Sea

	A–Few detectable cemeteries
	B–Flat cemeteries (areas B1–B5)
	C1–Flat and barrow cemeteries south of the Carpathians
	C2–Flat and barrow cemeteries in western Ukraine
	Nomads

500 kilometres

Map IX

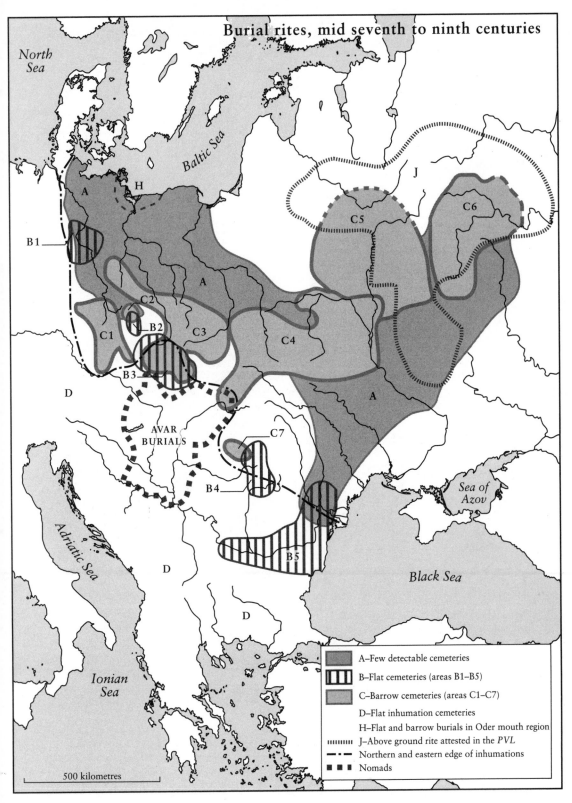

Burial rites, mid seventh to ninth centuries

North
Sea

Baltic Sea

A

H

B1

C2

B2

C1

C3

B3

D

AVAR
BURIALS

C4

A

J

C5

C6

C7

B4

Sea of
Azov

Adriatic Sea

D

B5

Black Sea

D

Ionian
Sea

A–Few detectable cemeteries

B–Flat cemeteries (areas B1–B5)

C–Barrow cemeteries (areas C1–C7)

D–Flat inhumation cemeteries

H–Flat and barrow burials in Oder mouth region

J–Above ground rite attested in the *PVL*

Northern and eastern edge of inhumations

Nomads

500 kilometres

Map X

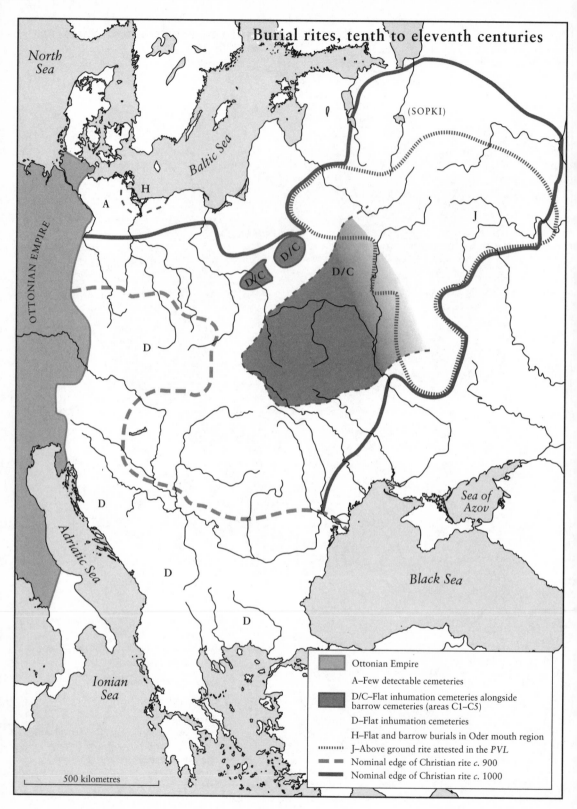

Burial rites, tenth to eleventh centuries

North
Sea

Baltic Sea

(SOPKI)

OTTONIAN EMPIRE

H

A

D/C

D/C

D/C

D/C

J

D

D

Adriatic Sea

D

Sea of
Azov

D

Black Sea

Ionian
Sea

500 kilometres

	Ottonian Empire
	A–Few detectable cemeteries
	D/C–Flat inhumation cemeteries alongside barrow cemeteries (areas C1–C5)
	D–Flat inhumation cemeteries
	H–Flat and barrow burials in Oder mouth region
....	J–Above ground rite attested in the *PVL*
– – –	Nominal edge of Christian rite *c.* 900
———	Nominal edge of Christian rite *c.* 1000

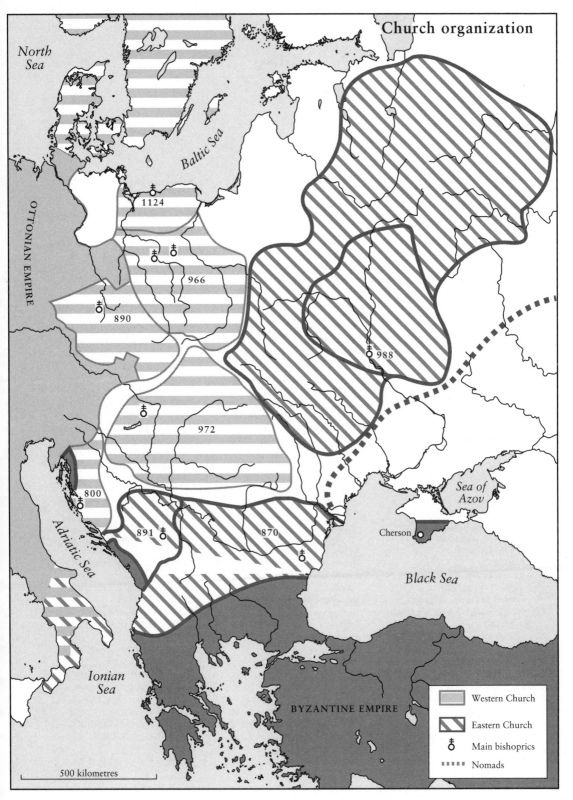

Church organization

North
Sea

OTTONIAN EMPIRE

Baltic Sea

1124

966

890

972

800

891

870

Adriatic Sea

Ionian
Sea

Cherson

Sea of
Azov

Black Sea

BYZANTINE EMPIRE

	Western Church
	Eastern Church
⚲	Main bishoprics
┅┅	Nomads

500 kilometres

Map XII

405

Index

Aachen 109, 217
Abbasids 8, 178
Abd Allah al-Ma'mun, Caliph
 178
Abodrites (see Obodrites)
Adalbert, Ottonian bishop 217,
 244
Adalbert, St (see also
 Vojtech/Wojciech, St) 255
Adalbert of Magdeburg 217, 244,
 255
Adam of Bremen, chronicler 7, 29,
 195
Adriatic Sea 57, 62, 72, 75, 230
adultery 226
Aegean Sea 57, 58, 72
agriculture 9, 13, 68–70, 98,
 125–6, 136, 150–1, 153–6, 158,
 186, 261; agricultural surplus
 125–6, 136, 151, 156, 261;
 agricultural tools 9, 13, 98, 153,
 154–5, 158, 186 (see also arable
 farming)
Aito, Carolingian official 174
al-Bekri, Islamic author 8
al-Mas'udi, Islamic author of
 Golden Meadows 8, 104, 256
al-Muhammadiya (town) 178
al-Muqtadir, Abbasid caliph 8
al-Qazvin, Islamic author 116
al-Sas (Tashkent) 178
Alans 24, 33, 75, 80, 85
Albania, Albanians 24, 61, 72, 75,
 95, 273, 276, 284
alcohol 121, 173, 198, 191
Alfred the Great, king of England
 75, 169
alphabet 110, 182–3, 215, 230,
 248
Alps, mountains 20, 57, 63, 73
Alt-Käbelich cemetery 202
amber 83, 85, 117, 165, 169, 261
Americans, native (see Plains
 Indians)
amulets 194
Anastasius, eastern emperor
 (491–518) 52
Anatolia (Asia Minor) 70, 73

animals, domestic 9, 169, 186
animals, wild 14, 21, 122, 158
animal produce (fur, wax) 10,
 21–2, 98–9, 103, 116, 122, 151,
 156, 164, 173, 175, 229, 255
Anna, Porphyrogenita, princess
 222, 248
Annals of St Bertin (see Bertinian
 Annals)
Anonymous Relation (Islamic
 source) 119, 156
Antes 35–6, 40, 50–1, 55–6, 63,
 68–9, 85, 140–1, 193, 209
Antes, treasures/antiquities of 40,
 84
antler 83, 164–5, 170, 261
arable farming 22; fallow system
 153, 156; fields 122–3, 153, 186,
 223; manuring 154, 156, 169,
 186; plough 154; slash-and-burn
 123, 154
Arabs, arab and Muslim, traders
 and writers (see Islam)
'archaeological culture' 12
Ardagastus, Slav leader 128
Arkona (temple) 198, 221
armament 59, 61, 72, 127, 140–4,
 161, 174, 208, 234, 245
Arnulf, king of Eastern Franks 111,
 158, 251
Arpad, Magyar leader 111, 231
arrows, poisoned 142
Askold, Kievan ruler 100, 208,
 236–8
Asparuch (see Isperich)
ataxis (disorder) 49
Athens 94, 177
Atlantic Ocean 60
Attila 25, 33, 43
Audulf, Carolingian official 174
Austria 56, 230, 258, 271, 275
Avars 17, 34, 50, 54, 57, 59–62,
 67–70, 72, 74–8, 79–81, 83–5,
 92, 95, 104, 108–9, 117, 128,
 141, 143–4, 156, 160, 162–3,
 174, 177, 201, 204, 206, 250
Avar-type belt fittings 72, 79, 81,
 83–4, 117, 162

Baba Yaga, female forest demon
 191
Babka, stronghold 97
Bachorz, settlement 53
Baghdad 8, 178
baking-plates 41–2, 63, 101, 121
Balkans 8, 16–7, 20–4, 30, 38, 47,
 50–2, 56, 58, 60–2, 68–75, 82–3,
 85, 91, 93–5, 104, 106, 139, 148,
 151, 154, 166, 171, 183, 190,
 204–5, 213, 217, 231, 269–70,
 272–4, 281
Balts, people, Baltic languages 14,
 19, 25, 35, 53, 63, 77, 83, 101–3,
 149, 168–70, 180, 220, 240,
 245–6, 263, 268, 270
Baltic river names 41, 101, 149
Baltic Sea (Baltic coast) 8, 20, 26,
 53, 59–60, 83, 104–6, 118,
 164–5, 168–72, 176–7, 179–181,
 240–1, 243, 247, 249, 257–61,
 263, 266, 270, 283
Baltic states (Kaliningrad Oblast
 of Russia, Lithuania, Latvia,
 Estonia) 179, 240, 270, 275,
 278
Barbaricum, barbarians 6, 23, 26,
 44, 47, 49–50, 56, 62
Basil II (the Bulgar-slayer),
 Byzantine emperor 222, 229–30
Basra 178
'bath-shaped' features 65
Bavaria, Bavarians 18, 74, 79, 94,
 176, 181–2, 214, 217, 219,
 250–4, 266, 269
Bavarian Geographer (Carolingian
 document) 7, 36, 90, 104, 107,
 109, 237, 239, 257
beads (glass, stone, metal) 9, 79,
 85, 97, 117, 166, 170
Belarussia (Belarus) 15–6, 19, 40,
 66, 87, 102, 132, 149, 190, 193,
 195, 197, 199, 205, 270–1,
 275–7, 281–2
Belgorod 186, 218, 246, 248
Beloozero lake (Belozersk) 235
Berlin 260
Bertinian Annals 29, 233–4